The Ultimate Public Campground Project

Volume 5

Utah

Table of Contents

Copyright Notice

Published by:

Roundabout Publications
P.O. Box 569
LaCygne, KS 66040

Phone: 800-455-2207
Internet: www.RoundaboutPublications.com

Agencies

This directory includes campgrounds managed and operated by a variety of agencies including federal, state, local, and others. Below is a list of the abbreviations used when identifying the various agencies.

Abbreviation	Description
AT	Appalachian Trail
BLM	Bureau of Land Management
BR	US Bureau of Reclamation
COE	Corps of Engineers
CP	County/Regional Park
FWS	US Fish & Wildlife Service
IND	Indian Reservation
MISC	Miscellaneous
MU	Municipal
NP	National Park Service
PCT	Pacific Crest Trail
PRIV	Non-profit, such as museums or conservation groups
ST	State
TVA	Tennessee Valley Authority
USFS	US Forest Service
UT	Utility Company

Abbreviations

Below is a list of abbreviations used throughout this directory.

Abbreviation	Description
AF	US Air Force
AFB	Air Force Base
ALA	Allagash National River
AMC	Appalachian Mountain Club
AR	US Army
AR GFC	Arkansas Game & Fish Commission
ARB	Air Reserve Base
ASTL	Arizona State Trust Lands
AT	Appalachian Trail
BBMWD	Big Bear Municipal Water District
BBRCD	Big Blue River Conservancy District
BCDA	Bear Creek Dev Auth
BCFS	British Columbia Forest Service
BLM	Bureau of Land Management
BMU	Basin Management Unit
BMWSD	Bistone Municipal Water Supply District
BR	Bureau of Reclamation
BRA	Brazos River Authority
CA	Conservation Area (Canada)
CDW	Colorado Division of Wildlife
CG	Campground
CG	US Coast Guard
CGC	Colorado River - Grand Canyon
CID	Carlsbad Irrigation District
Cntr	Center
Co	County
COE	US Armp Corps of Engineers
COL	Colorado River
Cons	Conservation
CP	County Park
CPWD	Chickasha Public Works Division
CRMWD	Colorado River Municipal Water District
CTC	Cumberland Trail Conference
CUA	Concentrated Use Area
DEC	Department of Conservation
DEL	Delaware River
DEP	Department of Environmental Protection
DES	Deschutes River
DFWR	Department of Fish & Wildlife Resource

Abbreviation	Description
DGF	Department of Game and Fish
DNR	Department of Natural Resources
DNRC	Department of Natural Resources & Conservation
DOW	Divison of Wildlife
DPR	Department of Parks and Recreation
DPRA	Don Pedro Recreation Agency
DSF	Demonstration State Forest
DWC	Department of Wildlife Conservation
DWR	Division of Wildlife Resources
EB	East-Bound
EBMUD	East Bay Municipal Utility District
ECWSD	Eastland County Water Supply District
EID	El Dorado Irrigation District
FAS	Fishing Access Site
FCWD	Franklin County Water District
FFS	Florida Forest Service
FG	Fish and Game
FHU	Full hookups (E/W/S)
FLT	Florida Trail
FM	Farm to Market Road
FN	First Nation/Native American
FPT	Florida Paddle Trail
FWC	Fish and Wildlife Conservation
FWS	US Fish & Wildlife Service
GBRA	Guadalupe-Blanco River Authority
GFD	Game & Fish Department
GMIWA	Greenbelt Municipal & Industrial Water Authority
GPC	Game & Parks Commission
GPL	Georgia Power Lakes
GPUD	Grant Public Utility District
GRE	Green River
GRR	Grande Ronde River
GSM	Great Smokey Mountains
HMU	Habitat Management Unit
HP	Historical Park
HSP	Historical State Park
IFG	Idaho Fish & Game
IF&W	Department of Inland Fisheries and Wildlife
IOOF	International Order of Odd Fellows

Abbreviation	Description
IP	Idaho Power
JB	Joint Base
JDR	John Day River
KDWP	Kansas Department of Wildlife, Parks and Tourism
KRMB	Kickapoo Reserve Management Board
LBNRD	Little Blue Natural Resources District
LBTL	Land Between the Lakes
LCRA	Lower Colorado River Authority
LCDUP	Lewis County Public Utility District
LECA	Lake Eau Claire Association
LENRD	Lower Elkhorn Natural Resources District
LKRWCD	Little Kentucky River Watershed Conservancy District
LNRA	Lavaca-Navidad River Authority
LPD	Loup Power District
LPN NRD	Lower Platte North Natural Resource District
LSR	Lower Salmon River
LTVA	Long Term Visitors Area
LUA	Lakeside Use Area
MC	US Marine Corps
MCAS	Marine Corps Air Station
MCB	Marine Corps Base
MDC	Missouri Department of Conservation
MDWFP	Mississippi Department of Wildlife, Fisheries & Parks
MFS	Middle Fork Salmon River
MID	Merced Irrigation District
MMWA	MacKenzie Municipal Water Authority
MRA	Motorized Recreational Area
MRCA	Mountains Recreation and Conservation Authority
MROSD	Midpeninsula Regional Open Space District
MU	Municipal
MU	Management Unit
MUA	Multiple Use Area
MVIC	Malad Valley Irrigation Co
MWCD	Muskingum Watershed Conservancy District
NA	US Navy
NAS	Naval Air Station
NCA	National Conservation Area
NCBC	Naval Construction Battalion Center
NCTMWA	North Central Texas Municipal Water Authority
NDOW	Neveada Dept of Wildlife
NEED	Northeast Educational Development Foundation
NG	National Guard
NG	National Grassland

Abbreviation	Description
NHP	National Historic Park
NID	Nevada Irrigation District
NM	National Monument
NMCWD	North Marin County Water District
NMGF	New Mexico Department of Game & Fish
NMSLO	New Mexico State Land Office
NMW	North Main Woods
NNL	National Natural Location
NNRD	Nemaha Natural Resources District
NP	National Park
NPS	National Park Service
NR	National River
NRA	National Recreation Area
NRD	Natural Resources District
NRRA	National River & Recreation Area
NRT	National Recreation Trail
NS	Naval Station
NASA	National Aeronautics and Space Administration
NSA	Naval Support Activity
NU	Northern Unit
NWFP	Northwest Forest Permit
NWR	National Wild River
NWR	National Wildlife Refuge
NWS	Naval Weapons Station
OHV	Off-Highway Vehicle
OHVA	Off-Highway Vehicle Area
ORA	Outdoor Recreation Area
OSU	Oklahoma State University
PCFWD	Panola County Fresh Water District
PCT	Pacific Crest Trail
PDRA	Palo Duro River Authority
PFA	Public Fishing Access
PG	Proving Ground
PGE	Pacific Gas & Electric
PHWD	Pat Harrison Waterway District
PP	Pacific Power
PP	Provincial Park
PPL	Pittsburgh Power & Light
PRBDD	Pearl River Basin Development District
NP	Non-Profit
PRVWSD	Pearl River Valley Water Supply District
PRL	Public Reserved Lands
PUF	Public Use Facility

Abbreviation	Description
PWD	Pawnee Watershed District
RA	Recreation Area
RBWCD	Rio Blanco Water Conservancy District
Reg	Regional
Res	Reservation
RMC	Randolph Mountain Club
RLCSD	Ruth Lake Community Services District
ROG	Rogue River
RP	Regional Park (Canada)
RRWC	Red River Waterway Commission
SAL	Salmon River
SB	State Beach
SCE	Southern California Edison
SCR	St Croix River
SEL	Selway River
SEP	Southeast Paddle Trail
SF	State Forest
SFA	State Fishing Area
SFC	State Forest Campground
SFWA	State Fish and Wildlife Area
SGMA	State Game Management Area
SGR	State Game Refuge
SHP	State Historic Park
SHS	State Historic Site
SISCRA	Southwestern Idaho Senior Citizen Recreation Association
SJR	San Juan River
SMI	Smith River
SMUD	Sacramento Municipal Utility District
SNA	State Natural Area
SNA	Snake River
SP	State Park
SPP	Sierra Pacific Power
SRA	State Recreation Area
SRP	State Resort Park
SRS	State Recreation Site
SRSP	Scenic River State Park
ST	State Trail
SU	Southern Unit
SVRA	State Vehicular Recreation Area
SWA	State Wildlife Area
SWFA	State Wildlife and Fishing Area
SWRA	State Wildlife Recreation Area
TAT	Three Affiliated Tribes

Abbreviation	Description
TC	Trail Camp
TCFSD	Titus County Freshwater Supply District
TH	Trail Head
TMA	Travel Management Area
TMPA	Texas Municipal Power Agency
TP	Territorial Park (Canada)
TPU	Tacoma Public Utilities
TRA	Trinity River Authority
TRDA	Tellico Reservoir Development Agency
TVA	Tennessee Valley Authority
TWRA	Tennessee Wildlife Resources Agency
UFN	Until Further Notice
Unk	Unknown
UPPCO	Upper Peninsula Power Company
USBR	US Bureau of Reclamation
USCG	US Coast Guard
USFS	US Forest Service
WA	Wildlife Area
WB	West-Bound
WCA	Wildlife Conservation Area
WCFPD	Winnebago County Forest Preserve District
WCTMWD	West Central Texas Municipal Water District
WDFW	Washington Department of Fish & Wildlife
WEA	Wildlife and Environmental Area
WEPCO	Wisconsin Electric Power Company
WGF	Wyoming Game & Fish
WHMA	Wildlife Habitat Management Area
WMA	Wildlife Management Area
WRD	Wildlife Resource Division
WRWA	White River Water Authority
WSA	Wilderness Study Area
Y-G	Yampa-Green Rivers
YP	Yellow Post (USFS term for dispersed sites)

Introduction

About The Ultimate Public Campground Project

The Ultimate Public Campground Project was conceived in 2008 to provide a consolidated and comprehensive source for public campgrounds of all types. It all began with a simple POI (Point of Interest) list of GPS coordinates and names, nothing more, totaling perhaps 5,000 locations. As the list grew in size and information provided, a website was designed to display the data on a map. Next came mobile apps, first iOS and Mac apps and more recently Android versions.

Ultimate Campgrounds is NOT the product of some large company with deep pockets. We are a team of three, all working on this as a part-time avocation: Ted is the founder of Ultimate Campgrounds and its Data Meister, Bill is our iOS and Mac developer and Geoff is our Android guy. Both Ted and Bill have been camping for many years and Ultimate Campgrounds reflects their interest in accurate and useful campground information.

Please note that despite our best efforts, there will always be errors to be found in the data. With over 43,000 records in our database, it is impossible to ensure that each one is always up-to-date. Ted tries to work his way through the data at least once a year to pick up things like increased fees and URL's that always seem to be changing. On an annual basis, it requires reviewing over 115 locations each and every day of the year – that's a pretty tall order.

Thus we always appreciate input from users who have found errors...or would like to submit a new location. Our goal is accuracy and we will gratefully accept any and all input.

We decided some years ago to focus on just one thing, publicly-owned camping locations, and try to be the best at it.

You can find a lot more information about Ultimate Campgrounds on our website: www.ultimatecampgrounds.com.

Feel free to address any questions or comments to us at info@ultimatecampgounds.com.

Happy Camping!

State Maps

A state map is provided to aid you in locating camping areas. Lines of latitude and longitude degrees are shown on each map, which is used when cross-referencing with the Location Chart.

Location Charts

Following the state map is a Location Chart. The chart lists every camping area by it's primary latitude and longitude, which is used to help identify locations on the map. It also indicates the availability of sites with electric hookups and free camping areas. The managing agency and name of a nearby city or town is also provided.

Campground Details

Campground details include various information about the public camping areas within the state. Preceding each camping area's name is an Entry ID number. This is used when cross-referencing with the charts. Details of each camping area generally include the following:

- Total number of sites or dispersed camping
- Number of RV sites
- Sites with electric hookups
- Full hookup sites, if available
- Water (central location or spigots at site)
- Showers
- RV dump station
- Toilets (flush, pit/vault, or none)
- Laundry facilities
- Camp store
- Maximum RV size limits (if any)
- Reservation information (accepted, not accepted, recommended or required)
- Generator use and hours (if limited)
- Operating season
- Camping fees charged
- Miscellaneous notes
- Length of stay limit
- Elevation in feet and meters
- Telephone number
- Nearby city or town
- Managing agency
- GPS coordinates

UTAH

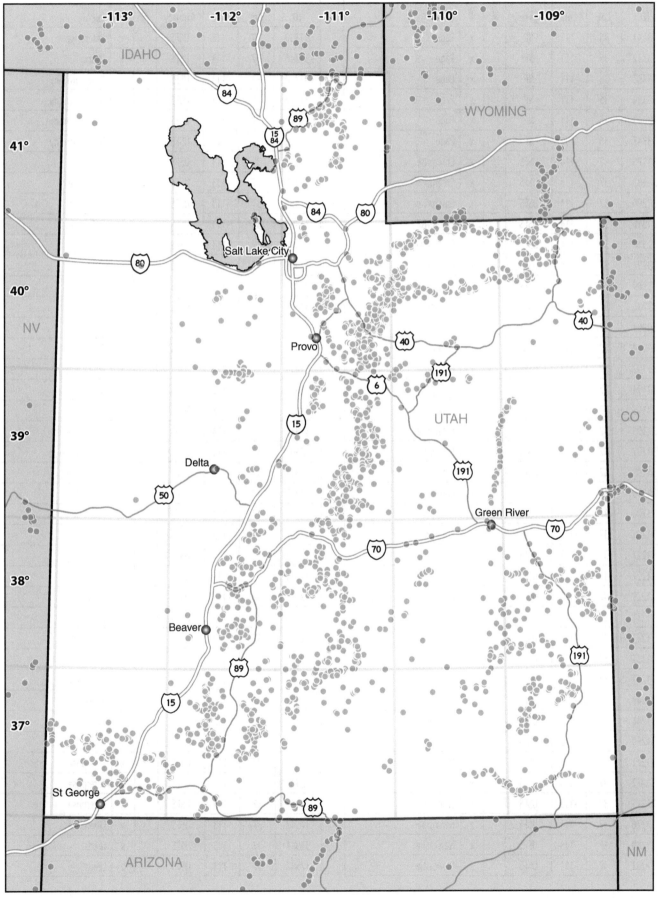

ID	Lat	Lon	Agency	Electric	Free	Locale
33331	36	-111	NP		x	Page
33332	36	-111	NP		x	Page
33333	36	-111	NP		x	Page
33334	36	-111	NP		x	Page
33343	36	-111	NP		x	Page
33347	36	-111	NP		x	Page
31175	37	-114	USFS		x	Enterprise
31182	37	-114	USFS		x	Enterprise
31290	37	-114	USFS		x	Enterprise
31818	37	-114	USFS		x	Enterprise
32510	37	-114	USFS		x	Enterprise
33297	37	-114	USFS		x	Enterprise
33309	37	-114	USFS		x	Enterprise
33726	37	-114	USFS		x	Enterprise
30903	37	-113	BLM			St George
31044	37	-113	BLM		x	Rockville
31192	37	-113	USFS		x	Enterprise
31194	37	-113	USFS		x	Enterprise
31195	37	-113	USFS		x	Enterprise
31196	37	-113	USFS		x	Enterprise
31197	37	-113	USFS		x	Enterprise
31198	37	-113	USFS		x	Enterprise
31199	37	-113	USFS		x	Enterprise
31200	37	-113	USFS		x	Enterprise
31201	37	-113	USFS		x	Enterprise
31217	37	-113	USFS		x	Veyo
31227	37	-113	USFS		x	Enterprise
31229	37	-113	USFS		x	Enterprise
31231	37	-113	USFS		x	Enterprise
31233	37	-113	USFS		x	Enterprise
31235	37	-113	USFS		x	Enterprise
31237	37	-113	USFS		x	Enterprise
31243	37	-113	USFS		x	Enterprise
31246	37	-113	USFS		x	Enterprise
31250	37	-113	USFS		x	Enterprise
31271	37	-113	USFS		x	Newcastle
31272	37	-113	USFS		x	Newcastle
31275	37	-113	USFS		x	Enterprise
31276	37	-113	USFS		x	Enterprise
31280	37	-113	USFS		x	Newcastle
31282	37	-113	USFS		x	Newcastle
31339	37	-113	USFS		x	Enterprise
31346	37	-113	USFS		x	Central
31370	37	-113	USFS		x	New Harmony
31372	37	-113	USFS		x	New Harmony
31373	37	-113	USFS		x	New Harmony
31374	37	-113	USFS		x	New Harmony
31390	37	-113	USFS		x	Leeds
31391	37	-113	USFS		x	St George
31394	37	-113	USFS		x	St George
31395	37	-113	USFS		x	St George
31396	37	-113	USFS		x	St George
31405	37	-113	USFS		x	Leeds
31406	37	-113	USFS		x	Leeds
31407	37	-113	USFS		x	Leeds
31408	37	-113	USFS		x	Leeds
31412	37	-113	USFS		x	St George
31414	37	-113	USFS		x	Pine Valley
31820	37	-113	USFS		x	Newcastle
31832	37	-113	USFS		x	Central
31833	37	-113	USFS		x	Pine Valley
32301	37	-113	USFS		x	Kanarraville
32411	37	-113	USFS		x	Pine Valley
32412	37	-113	USFS		x	Pine Valley
32415	37	-113	USFS		x	Pine Valley
32442	37	-113	USFS		x	Enterprise
32494	37	-113	USFS		x	Pine Valley
32511	37	-113	USFS		x	St George
32512	37	-113	USFS		x	Leeds
32516	37	-113	USFS		x	Enterprise
32517	37	-113	USFS		x	Newcastle
32518	37	-113	USFS		x	Pine Valley
32519	37	-113	USFS		x	Newcastle
32521	37	-113	USFS		x	Pine Valley
32523	37	-113	USFS		x	Newcastle
32525	37	-113	USFS		x	Enterprise
32532	37	-113	USFS		x	Enterprise
32533	37	-113	USFS		x	Enterprise
32541	37	-113	USFS		x	Enterprise
32542	37	-113	USFS		x	Enterprise
32584	37	-113	USFS		x	Leeds
32587	37	-113	USFS		x	Leeds

ID	Lat	Lon	Agency	Electric	Free	Locale
32589	37	-113	USFS		x	St George
32590	37	-113	USFS		x	St George
32591	37	-113	USFS		x	St George
32592	37	-113	USFS		x	St George
32594	37	-113	USFS		x	Enterprise
33137	37	-113	USFS		x	Enterprise
33138	37	-113	USFS		x	Enterprise
33141	37	-113	USFS		x	Pine Valley
33276	37	-113	USFS		x	Enterprise
33277	37	-113	USFS		x	Enterprise
33278	37	-113	USFS		x	Enterprise
33279	37	-113	USFS		x	Enterprise
33280	37	-113	USFS		x	Enterprise
33290	37	-113	USFS		x	Pine Valley
33291	37	-113	USFS		x	Pine Valley
33292	37	-113	USFS		x	Pine Valley
33293	37	-113	USFS		x	Central
33295	37	-113	USFS		x	Enterprise
33296	37	-113	USFS		x	Veyo
33298	37	-113	USFS		x	Enterprise
33304	37	-113	USFS		x	St George
33305	37	-113	USFS		x	St George
33330	37	-113	BLM		x	Virgin
33356	37	-113	BLM		x	Apple Valley
33464	37	-113	ST			St George
33488	37	-113	USFS			Enterprise
33491	37	-113	BLM		x	Dammeron Valley
33492	37	-113	BLM		x	Dammeron Valley
33493	37	-113	BLM		x	Dammeron Valley
33494	37	-113	BLM		x	Dammeron Valley
33495	37	-113	BLM		x	Dammeron Valley
33503	37	-113	BLM		x	Hurricane
33504	37	-113	BLM		x	Hurricane
33505	37	-113	BLM		x	Hurricane
33506	37	-113	BLM		x	Hurricane
33507	37	-113	BLM		x	Hurricane
33552	37	-113	BLM		x	Virgin
33553	37	-113	CP		x	Cedar City
33554	37	-113	CP		x	Cedar City
33555	37	-113	CP		x	Cedar City
33597	37	-113	BLM		x	St George

ID	Lat	Lon	Agency	Electric	Free	Locale
33619	37	-113	BLM		x	Dammeron
33676	37	-113	ST		x	Newcastle
33697	37	-113	USFS			Leeds
33729	37	-113	USFS			Pine Valley
33730	37	-113	USFS			Pine Valley
33731	37	-113	USFS			Pine Valley
33732	37	-113	USFS			Central
33733	37	-113	USFS			Pine Valley
33734	37	-113	USFS			Pine Valley
33735	37	-113	USFS			Pine Valley
33751	37	-113	ST			Hurricane
33758	37	-113	BLM			Leeds
33759	37	-113	BLM		x	Hurricane
33767	37	-113	BLM		x	Diamond Valley
33891	37	-113	ST	x		Hurricane
33892	37	-113	ST	x		Hurricane
33910	37	-113	BLM		x	Rockville
33911	37	-113	ST	x		Ivins
33971	37	-113	BLM		x	Toquerville
34010	37	-113	BLM		x	La Verkin
34011	37	-113	BLM		x	La Verkin
34012	37	-113	BLM		x	La Verkin
34013	37	-113	BLM		x	La Verkin
34061	37	-113	NP			Rockville
34063	37	-113	NP			Rockville
34073	37	-113	NP			Rockville
34074	37	-113	NP			Rockville
34075	37	-113	NP			Rockville
34076	37	-113	NP			Rockville
34077	37	-113	NP			Rockville
34079	37	-113	NP			Rockville
34080	37	-113	NP			Rockville
34081	37	-113	NP			Rockville
34083	37	-113	NP			Rockville
34085	37	-113	NP			Rockville
34086	37	-113	NP			Rockville
34087	37	-113	NP			Rockville
34088	37	-113	NP			Rockville
34090	37	-113	NP		x	Springdale
34091	37	-113	NP			Rockville
34092	37	-113	NP			Rockville

ID	Lat	Lon	Agency	Electric	Free	Locale
34095	37	-113	NP			Rockville
34097	37	-113	NP			Rockville
34098	37	-113	NP			Rockville
34102	37	-113	NP			Rockville
34105	37	-113	NP			Rockville
34106	37	-113	BLM		x	Virgin
30879	37	-112	USFS			Parowan
30920	37	-112	PRIV	x		Kanab
30955	37	-112	NP			Bryce
30956	37	-112	NP			Bryce
30957	37	-112	NP			Bryce
30958	37	-112	NP			Bryce Canyon
30959	37	-112	NP			Bryce
30960	37	-112	NP			Bryce
30961	37	-112	NP			Bryce Canyon
30962	37	-112	NP			Bryce
30963	37	-112	NP			Bryce
30964	37	-112	NP			Bryce Canyon
30965	37	-112	NP			Bryce Canyon
30966	37	-112	NP			Bryce Canyon
30967	37	-112	NP			Bryce
30968	37	-112	NP			Bryce
30969	37	-112	NP			Bryce
30973	37	-112	BLM		x	Page AZ
31025	37	-112	USFS		x	Panguitch
31027	37	-112	NP			Cedar City
31028	37	-112	USFS			Cedar City
31075	37	-112	BLM		x	Kanab
31076	37	-112	BLM			Kanab
31077	37	-112	BLM		x	Kanab
31078	37	-112	BLM		x	Kanab
31079	37	-112	ST	x		Kanab
31080	37	-112	ST			Kanab
31088	37	-112	USFS			Panguitch
31107	37	-112	USFS			Cedar City
31129	37	-112	USFS			Cedar City
31496	37	-112	USFS		x	Duck Creek
31497	37	-112	USFS		x	Parowan
31498	37	-112	USFS		x	Parowan
31521	37	-112	USFS		x	Cedar City
31522	37	-112	USFS		x	Cedar City

ID	Lat	Lon	Agency	Electric	Free	Locale
31524	37	-112	USFS		x	Cedar City
31589	37	-112	USFS		x	Duck Creek
31590	37	-112	USFS		x	Duck Creek
31594	37	-112	USFS		x	Duck Creek Village
31595	37	-112	USFS		x	Duck Creek
31596	37	-112	USFS		x	Duck Creek
31599	37	-112	USFS		x	Alton
31600	37	-112	USFS		x	Alton
31604	37	-112	USFS		x	Duck Creek
31605	37	-112	USFS		x	Duck Creek
31606	37	-112	USFS		x	Duck Creek
31607	37	-112	USFS		x	Duck Creek
31608	37	-112	USFS		x	Duck Creek
31609	37	-112	USFS		x	Duck Creek
31614	37	-112	USFS		x	Duck Creek
31615	37	-112	USFS		x	Cedar City
31627	37	-112	USFS		x	Cedar City
31628	37	-112	USFS		x	Cedar City
31633	37	-112	USFS		x	Hatch
31634	37	-112	USFS		x	Hatch
31638	37	-112	USFS		x	Hatch
31642	37	-112	USFS		x	Hatch
31657	37	-112	USFS		x	Paragonah
31658	37	-112	USFS		x	Paragonah
31659	37	-112	USFS		x	Paragonah
31660	37	-112	USFS		x	Paragonah
31661	37	-112	USFS		x	Paragonah
31662	37	-112	USFS		x	Paragonah
31663	37	-112	USFS		x	Panguitch
31666	37	-112	USFS		x	Paragonah
31667	37	-112	USFS		x	Paragonah
31668	37	-112	USFS		x	Paragonah
31669	37	-112	USFS		x	Paragonah
31670	37	-112	USFS		x	Paragonah
31671	37	-112	USFS		x	Paragonah
31689	37	-112	USFS		x	Panguitch
31710	37	-112	USFS		x	Panguitch
31742	37	-112	USFS		x	Paragonah
31743	37	-112	USFS		x	Paragonah
31744	37	-112	USFS		x	Paragonah
31745	37	-112	USFS		x	Hatch

ID	Lat	Lon	Agency	Electric	Free	Locale
31746	37	-112	USFS		x	Hatch
31747	37	-112	USFS		x	Alton
31748	37	-112	USFS		x	Alton
31750	37	-112	USFS		x	Bryce
31751	37	-112	USFS		x	Bryce
31752	37	-112	USFS		x	Bryce
31771	37	-112	USFS		x	Hatch
31773	37	-112	USFS		x	Hatch
31781	37	-112	USFS		x	Hatch
31797	37	-112	USFS		x	Cedar City
31808	37	-112	USFS		x	Hatch
31841	37	-112	USFS		x	Panguitch
31842	37	-112	USFS		x	Panguitch
31843	37	-112	USFS		x	Panguitch
31851	37	-112	USFS		x	Alton
31868	37	-112	USFS		x	Hatch
31871	37	-112	USFS		x	Panguitch
31875	37	-112	USFS		x	Hatch
31876	37	-112	USFS		x	Hatch
31877	37	-112	USFS		x	Hatch
31886	37	-112	USFS		x	Panguitch
31899	37	-112	USFS		x	Hatch
31900	37	-112	USFS		x	Hatch
31913	37	-112	USFS		x	Panguitch
31915	37	-112	USFS		x	Bryce
31927	37	-112	USFS		x	Panguitch
31928	37	-112	USFS		x	Panguitch
31929	37	-112	USFS		x	Panguitch
31930	37	-112	USFS		x	Panguitch
31931	37	-112	USFS		x	Panguitch
31936	37	-112	USFS		x	Bryce
31937	37	-112	USFS		x	Bryce
31938	37	-112	USFS		x	Bryce
31939	37	-112	USFS		x	Bryce
31942	37	-112	USFS		x	Alton
31949	37	-112	USFS		x	Alton
31956	37	-112	USFS		x	Bryce
31957	37	-112	USFS		x	Panguitch
31958	37	-112	USFS		x	Panguitch
31959	37	-112	USFS		x	Panguitch
31960	37	-112	USFS		x	Panguitch
31976	37	-112	USFS		x	Panguitch
31980	37	-112	USFS		x	Panguitch
31981	37	-112	USFS		x	Panguitch
31987	37	-112	USFS		x	Alton
32135	37	-112	USFS		x	Hatch
32136	37	-112	USFS		x	Hatch
32152	37	-112	USFS		x	Duck Creek
32155	37	-112	USFS		x	Duck Creek
32176	37	-112	USFS		x	Cedar City
32182	37	-112	USFS		x	Cedar City
32192	37	-112	USFS		x	Alton
32193	37	-112	USFS		x	Alton
32197	37	-112	USFS		x	Duck Creek
32213	37	-112	USFS		x	Duck Creek
32216	37	-112	USFS		x	Duck Creek
32218	37	-112	USFS		x	Duck Creek
32220	37	-112	USFS		x	Duck Creek
32241	37	-112	USFS		x	Bryce
32244	37	-112	USFS		x	Panguitch
32245	37	-112	USFS		x	Duck Creek
32248	37	-112	USFS		x	Panguitch
32249	37	-112	USFS		x	Panguitch
32254	37	-112	USFS		x	Hatch
32260	37	-112	USFS		x	Cedar City
32261	37	-112	USFS		x	Cedar City
32272	37	-112	USFS		x	Duck Creek
32273	37	-112	USFS		x	Alton
32274	37	-112	USFS		x	Alton
32277	37	-112	USFS		x	Hatch
32290	37	-112	USFS		x	Alton
32296	37	-112	USFS		x	Alton
32297	37	-112	USFS		x	Panguitch
32337	37	-112	USFS		x	Duck Creek
32338	37	-112	USFS		x	Duck Creek
32348	37	-112	USFS		x	Hatch
32356	37	-112	USFS		x	Cedar City
32362	37	-112	USFS		x	Duck Creek
32364	37	-112	USFS		x	Cedar City
32365	37	-112	USFS		x	Duck Creek
32366	37	-112	USFS		x	Duck Creek
32367	37	-112	USFS		x	Duck Creek

ID	Lat	Lon	Agency	Electric	Free	Locale
32368	37	-112	USFS		x	Duck Creek
32369	37	-112	USFS		x	Cedar City
32370	37	-112	USFS		x	Cedar City
32371	37	-112	USFS		x	Cedar City
32372	37	-112	USFS		x	Cedar City
32373	37	-112	USFS		x	Cedar City
32374	37	-112	USFS		x	Cedar City
32375	37	-112	USFS		x	Duck Creek
32376	37	-112	USFS		x	Duck Creek
32377	37	-112	USFS		x	Hatch
32378	37	-112	USFS		x	Alton
32408	37	-112	USFS		x	Duck Creek
32436	37	-112	USFS		x	Panguitch
32449	37	-112	USFS		x	Duck Creek
32450	37	-112	USFS		x	Duck Creek
32451	37	-112	USFS		x	Duck Creek
32456	37	-112	USFS		x	Paragonah
32458	37	-112	USFS		x	Parowan
32459	37	-112	USFS		x	Parowan
32460	37	-112	USFS		x	Parowan
32469	37	-112	USFS		x	Panguitch
32470	37	-112	USFS		x	Panguitch
32472	37	-112	USFS		x	Hatch
32485	37	-112	USFS		x	Alton
32487	37	-112	USFS		x	Duck Creek
32528	37	-112	USFS		x	Duck Creek
32529	37	-112	USFS		x	Panguitch
32530	37	-112	USFS		x	Hatch
32531	37	-112	USFS		x	Hatch
32537	37	-112	USFS		x	Paragonah
32538	37	-112	USFS		x	Paragonah
32547	37	-112	USFS		x	Cedar City
32549	37	-112	USFS		x	Cedar City
32551	37	-112	USFS		x	Panguitch
32552	37	-112	USFS		x	Hatch
32554	37	-112	USFS		x	Hatch
32555	37	-112	USFS		x	Hatch
32556	37	-112	USFS		x	Hatch
32557	37	-112	USFS		x	Duck Creek
32558	37	-112	USFS		x	Duck Creek
32559	37	-112	USFS		x	Duck Creek

ID	Lat	Lon	Agency	Electric	Free	Locale
32593	37	-112	USFS		x	Cedar City
32602	37	-112	USFS		x	Alton
32641	37	-112	USFS		x	Duck Creek
33162	37	-112	USFS		x	Alton
33168	37	-112	USFS		x	Duck Creek
33169	37	-112	USFS		x	Duck Creek
33170	37	-112	USFS		x	Duck Creek
33171	37	-112	USFS		x	Duck Creek
33185	37	-112	USFS		x	Duck Creek
33186	37	-112	USFS		x	Duck Creek
33187	37	-112	USFS		x	Duck Creek
33203	37	-112	USFS		x	Panguitch
33205	37	-112	USFS		x	Panguitch
33225	37	-112	USFS		x	Cedar City
33226	37	-112	USFS		x	Cedar City
33229	37	-112	USFS		x	Duck Creek
33294	37	-112	USFS		x	Hatch
33328	37	-112	USFS		x	Cedar City
33369	37	-112	BLM		x	Kanab
33373	37	-112	BLM		x	Kanab
33480	37	-112	USFS		x	Panguitch
33537	37	-112	USFS			Panguitch
33562	37	-112	USFS		x	Duck Creek
33599	37	-112	USFS		x	Panguitch
33600	37	-112	USFS		x	Panguitch
33618	37	-112	USFS		x	Duck Creek
33665	37	-112	BLM		x	Kanab
33666	37	-112	BLM		x	Mt Carmel
33673	37	-112	USFS			Cedar City
33713	37	-112	USFS			Panguitch
33714	37	-112	USFS			Panguitch
33716	37	-112	ST		x	Paragonah
33719	37	-112	BLM		x	Parowan
33721	37	-112	BLM		x	Kanab
33756	37	-112	USFS			Panguitch
33935	37	-112	USFS			Cedar City
33937	37	-112	BLM		x	Kanab
33945	37	-112	USFS		x	Duck Creek
33957	37	-112	USFS			Cedar City
33959	37	-112	BLM		x	Kanab
33960	37	-112	BLM		x	Kanab

ID	Lat	Lon	Agency	Electric	Free	Locale
33961	37	-112	BLM		x	Kanab
33975	37	-112	BLM		x	Mt Carmel Jct
33980	37	-112	USFS		x	Duck Creek
34025	37	-112	USFS			Panguitch
34045	37	-112	BLM			Glen Canyon
34051	37	-112	USFS			Cedar City
34054	37	-112	BLM		x	Kanab
34055	37	-112	BLM		x	Kanab
34062	37	-112	NP			Rockville
34064	37	-112	NP			Rockville
34065	37	-112	NP			Rockville
34066	37	-112	NP			Rockville
34067	37	-112	NP			Rockville
34068	37	-112	NP			Rockville
34069	37	-112	NP			Rockville
34070	37	-112	NP			Rockville
34071	37	-112	NP			Rockville
34072	37	-112	NP			Rockville
34078	37	-112	NP			Rockville
34082	37	-112	NP			Rockville
34084	37	-112	NP			Rockville
34089	37	-112	NP			Rockville
34093	37	-112	NP			Rockville
34094	37	-112	NP			Rockville
34096	37	-112	NP			Rockville
34099	37	-112	NP			Rockville
34100	37	-112	NP			Springdale
34101	37	-112	NP			Rockville
34103	37	-112	NP			Rockville
34104	37	-112	NP	x		Springdale
30905	37	-111	USFS			Escalante
30906	37	-111	USFS			Escalante
30907	37	-111	USFS			Escalante
30937	37	-111	USFS			Escalante
31046	37	-111	BLM		x	Kanab
31083	37	-111	BLM		x	Paria
31084	37	-111	BLM		x	Kanab
31085	37	-111	BLM		x	Kanab
31140	37	-111	NP		x	Boulder
31141	37	-111	ST	x		Escalante
31142	37	-111	ST			Escalante

ID	Lat	Lon	Agency	Electric	Free	Locale
32007	37	-111	USFS		x	Escalante
32008	37	-111	USFS		x	Escalante
32009	37	-111	USFS		x	Escalante
32010	37	-111	USFS		x	Escalante
32011	37	-111	USFS		x	Escalante
32013	37	-111	USFS		x	Escalante
32024	37	-111	USFS		x	Escalante
32039	37	-111	USFS		x	Antimony
32054	37	-111	USFS		x	Escalante
32055	37	-111	USFS		x	Escalante
32071	37	-111	USFS		x	Escalante
32072	37	-111	USFS		x	Escalante
32086	37	-111	USFS		x	Escalante
32094	37	-111	USFS		x	Boulder
32109	37	-111	USFS		x	Escalante
32110	37	-111	USFS		x	Escalante
32125	37	-111	USFS		x	Escalante
32126	37	-111	USFS		x	Escalante
32131	37	-111	USFS		x	Escalante
32132	37	-111	USFS		x	Boulder
32133	37	-111	USFS		x	Boulder
32134	37	-111	USFS		x	Boulder
32137	37	-111	USFS		x	Antimony
32138	37	-111	USFS		x	Escalante
32139	37	-111	USFS		x	Antimony
32172	37	-111	USFS		x	Teasdale
32173	37	-111	USFS		x	Teasdale
32174	37	-111	USFS		x	Teasdale
32175	37	-111	USFS		x	Teasdale
32189	37	-111	USFS		x	Escalante
32349	37	-111	USFS		x	Antimony
32350	37	-111	USFS		x	Antimony
32437	37	-111	USFS		x	Escalante
32438	37	-111	USFS		x	Escalante
32439	37	-111	USFS		x	Escalante
32570	37	-111	USFS		x	Escalante
32576	37	-111	USFS		x	Escalante
32578	37	-111	USFS		x	Antimony
32581	37	-111	USFS		x	Escalante
32617	37	-111	USFS		x	Antimony
32618	37	-111	USFS		x	Antimony

ID	Lat	Lon	Agency	Electric	Free	Locale
32619	37	-111	USFS		x	Antimony
32656	37	-111	USFS		x	Teasdale
33011	37	-111	USFS		x	Teasdale
33142	37	-111	USFS		x	Boulder
33236	37	-111	USFS		x	Boulder
33335	37	-111	NP		x	Big Water
33346	37	-111	NP			Kanab
33360	37	-111	BLM			Escalante
33361	37	-111	BLM		x	Escalante
33362	37	-111	BLM			Boulder
33363	37	-111	BLM		x	Boulder
33364	37	-111	BLM		x	Escalante
33365	37	-111	BLM		x	Henrieville
33366	37	-111	BLM		x	Henrieville
33367	37	-111	BLM		x	Henrieville
33368	37	-111	BLM		x	Escalante
33370	37	-111	BLM		x	Boulder
33371	37	-111	BLM		x	Kanab
33372	37	-111	BLM		x	Henrieville
33374	37	-111	BLM		x	Escalante
33375	37	-111	BLM		x	Escalante
33376	37	-111	BLM		x	Boulder
33377	37	-111	BLM		x	Boulder
33378	37	-111	BLM		x	Escalante
33379	37	-111	BLM			Page AZ
33542	37	-111	ST			Cannonville
33543	37	-111	ST	x		Cannonville
33544	37	-111	ST			Cannonville
33717	37	-111	BLM		x	Kanab
33718	37	-111	BLM		x	Kanab
33725	37	-111	USFS			Bryce Canyon
33745	37	-111	USFS			Escalante
30936	37	-110	BLM		x	Bluff
31039	37	-110	BLM		x	Irish Green
31052	37	-110	NP			Moab
31057	37	-110	NP			Moab
31065	37	-110	NP			Moab
31066	37	-110	NP			Moab
31067	37	-110	NP			Moab
31068	37	-110	NP			Moab
31069	37	-110	NP			Moab
33336	37	-110	NP		x	Hite
33337	37	-110	NP	x		Bullfrog
33338	37	-110	NP			Bullfrog
33339	37	-110	NP			Hite
33340	37	-110	NP			Hite
33341	37	-110	NP			Hite
33342	37	-110	NP			Hite
33344	37	-110	NP	x		Halls Crossing
33345	37	-110	NP			Hite
33348	37	-110	NP			Bullfrog
33349	37	-110	NP		x	Hite
33468	37	-110	BLM		x	Ticaboo
33520	37	-110	BLM		x	Fry Canyon
33815	37	-110	BLM		x	Mexican Hat
33816	37	-110	BLM		x	Mexican Hat
33817	37	-110	BLM		x	Mexican Hat
33818	37	-110	BLM		x	Mexican Hat
33819	37	-110	BLM		x	Mexican Hat
33820	37	-110	BLM		x	Mexican Hat
33821	37	-110	BLM		x	Mexican Hat
33822	37	-110	BLM		x	Mexican Hat
33823	37	-110	BLM		x	Mexican Hat
33824	37	-110	BLM		x	Mexican Hat
33825	37	-110	BLM		x	Mexican Hat
33826	37	-110	BLM		x	Mexican Hat
33827	37	-110	BLM		x	Mexican Hat
33828	37	-110	BLM		x	Mexican Hat
33829	37	-110	BLM		x	Mexican Hat
33831	37	-110	BLM		x	Mexican Hat
33841	37	-110	BLM		x	Mexican Hat
33843	37	-110	BLM		x	Mexican Hat
33845	37	-110	BLM		x	Mexican Hat
33846	37	-110	BLM		x	Irish Green
33849	37	-110	BLM		x	Mexican Hat
33856	37	-110	BLM		x	Mexican Hat
33863	37	-110	BLM		x	Irish Green
33869	37	-110	BLM		x	Mexican Hat
33871	37	-110	BLM		x	Irish Green
33872	37	-110	BLM		x	Irish Green
33873	37	-110	BLM		x	Irish Green
33874	37	-110	BLM		x	Irish Green

ID	Lat	Lon	Agency	Electric	Free	Locale
33878	37	-110	BLM		x	Irish Green
33936	37	-110	BLM			Hanksville
33947	37	-110	BLM		x	Hite
30893	37	-109	BLM		x	Blanding
30902	37	-109	BLM		x	Blanding
30935	37	-109	USFS		x	Monticello
30971	37	-109	USFS			Monticello
31099	37	-109	USFS			Monticello
31111	37	-109	USFS			Blanding
31155	37	-109	USFS		x	Monticello
32835	37	-109	USFS		x	Blanding
32836	37	-109	USFS		x	Blanding
32837	37	-109	USFS		x	Blanding
32838	37	-109	USFS		x	Blanding
32839	37	-109	USFS		x	Monticello
32840	37	-109	USFS		x	Monticello
32841	37	-109	USFS		x	Monticello
32842	37	-109	USFS		x	Monticello
32843	37	-109	USFS		x	Blanding
32844	37	-109	USFS		x	Monticello
32845	37	-109	USFS		x	Monticello
32846	37	-109	USFS		x	Monticello
32847	37	-109	USFS		x	Monticello
32848	37	-109	USFS		x	Monticello
32849	37	-109	USFS		x	Monticello
32850	37	-109	USFS		x	Monticello
32851	37	-109	USFS		x	Blanding
32852	37	-109	USFS		x	Blanding
32853	37	-109	USFS		x	Monticello
32854	37	-109	USFS		x	Monticello
32855	37	-109	USFS		x	Monticello
32856	37	-109	USFS		x	Monticello
32857	37	-109	USFS		x	Monticello
32858	37	-109	USFS		x	Monticello
32859	37	-109	USFS		x	Blanding
32860	37	-109	USFS		x	Blanding
32861	37	-109	USFS		x	Monticello
32862	37	-109	USFS		x	Monticello
32863	37	-109	USFS		x	Blanding
32864	37	-109	USFS		x	Blanding
32865	37	-109	USFS		x	Blanding
32866	37	-109	USFS		x	Blanding
32867	37	-109	USFS		x	Blanding
32868	37	-109	USFS		x	Monticello
32869	37	-109	USFS		x	Monticello
32870	37	-109	USFS		x	Monticello
32871	37	-109	USFS		x	Monticello
32872	37	-109	USFS		x	Monticello
32874	37	-109	USFS		x	Monticello
32875	37	-109	USFS		x	Blanding
32876	37	-109	USFS		x	Blanding
32947	37	-109	USFS		x	Monticello
32948	37	-109	USFS		x	Monticello
32949	37	-109	USFS		x	Monticello
32950	37	-109	USFS		x	Monticello
32951	37	-109	USFS		x	Monticello
32952	37	-109	USFS		x	Blanding
32953	37	-109	USFS		x	Blanding
32954	37	-109	USFS		x	Blanding
32955	37	-109	USFS		x	Blanding
32956	37	-109	USFS		x	Monticello
32989	37	-109	USFS		x	Monticello
32990	37	-109	USFS		x	Monticello
32992	37	-109	USFS		x	Monticello
33000	37	-109	USFS		x	Monticello
33072	37	-109	USFS		x	Blanding
33073	37	-109	USFS		x	Monticello
33074	37	-109	USFS		x	Monticello
33075	37	-109	USFS		x	Monticello
33076	37	-109	USFS		x	Monticello
33103	37	-109	USFS		x	Monticello
33104	37	-109	USFS		x	Monticello
33105	37	-109	USFS		x	Blanding
33106	37	-109	USFS		x	Blanding
33107	37	-109	USFS		x	Blanding
33108	37	-109	USFS		x	Monticello
33109	37	-109	USFS		x	Monticello
33110	37	-109	USFS		x	Monticello
33111	37	-109	USFS		x	Monticello
33112	37	-109	USFS		x	Blanding
33113	37	-109	USFS		x	Blanding
33114	37	-109	USFS		x	Blanding

ID	Lat	Lon	Agency	Electric	Free	Locale
33115	37	-109	USFS		x	Blanding
33116	37	-109	USFS		x	Blanding
33117	37	-109	USFS		x	Blanding
33118	37	-109	USFS		x	Blanding
33121	37	-109	USFS		x	Blanding
33122	37	-109	USFS		x	Blanding
33123	37	-109	USFS		x	Blanding
33124	37	-109	USFS		x	Blanding
33125	37	-109	USFS		x	Blanding
33126	37	-109	USFS		x	Blanding
33128	37	-109	USFS		x	Blanding
33129	37	-109	USFS		x	Blanding
33130	37	-109	USFS		x	Blanding
33358	37	-109	ST			Blanding
33359	37	-109	BLM		x	Blanding
33498	37	-109	NP			Blanding
33523	37	-109	BLM		x	Blanding
33586	37	-109	BLM		x	Monticello
33638	37	-109	BLM		x	Mexican Hat
33656	37	-109	USFS		x	Monticello
33668	37	-109	BLM		x	Mexican Hat
33672	37	-109	NP			Blanding
33679	37	-109	USFS			Blanding
33753	37	-109	BLM		x	Blanding
33754	37	-109	BLM		x	Blanding
33783	37	-109	BLM		x	Bluff
33784	37	-109	BLM		x	Bluff
33785	37	-109	BLM		x	Bluff
33786	37	-109	BLM		x	Bluff
33787	37	-109	BLM		x	Bluff
33788	37	-109	BLM		x	Bluff
33789	37	-109	BLM		x	Bluff
33790	37	-109	BLM		x	Bluff
33791	37	-109	BLM		x	Bluff
33792	37	-109	BLM		x	Bluff
33793	37	-109	BLM		x	Bluff
33794	37	-109	BLM		x	Mexican Hat
33795	37	-109	BLM		x	Mexican Hat
33796	37	-109	BLM		x	Mexican Hat
33797	37	-109	BLM		x	Mexican Hat
33798	37	-109	BLM		x	Bluff

ID	Lat	Lon	Agency	Electric	Free	Locale
33799	37	-109	BLM		x	Mexican Hat
33800	37	-109	BLM		x	Mexican Hat
33801	37	-109	BLM		x	Mexican Hat
33802	37	-109	BLM		x	Mexican Hat
33803	37	-109	BLM		x	Bluff
33804	37	-109	BLM		x	Mexican Hat
33805	37	-109	BLM		x	Mexican Hat
33806	37	-109	BLM		x	Mexican Hat
33807	37	-109	BLM		x	Mexican Hat
33808	37	-109	BLM		x	Mexican Hat
33809	37	-109	BLM		x	Mexican Hat
33810	37	-109	BLM		x	Mexican Hat
33811	37	-109	BLM		x	Mexican Hat
33812	37	-109	BLM		x	Mexican Hat
33813	37	-109	BLM		x	Mexican Hat
33814	37	-109	BLM		x	Mexican Hat
33830	37	-109	BLM		x	Mexican Hat
33832	37	-109	BLM		x	Mexican Hat
33833	37	-109	BLM		x	Mexican Hat
33834	37	-109	BLM		x	Bluff
33835	37	-109	BLM		x	Mexican Hat
33836	37	-109	BLM		x	Bluff
33837	37	-109	BLM		x	Bluff
33838	37	-109	BLM		x	Bluff
33839	37	-109	BLM		x	Bluff
33840	37	-109	BLM		x	Mexican Hat
33842	37	-109	BLM		x	Mexican Hat
33844	37	-109	BLM		x	Bluff
33847	37	-109	BLM		x	Mexican Hat
33848	37	-109	BLM		x	Mexican Hat
33850	37	-109	BLM		x	Mexican Hat
33851	37	-109	BLM		x	Mexican Hat
33852	37	-109	BLM		x	Mexican Hat
33853	37	-109	BLM		x	Mexican Hat
33854	37	-109	BLM		x	Mexican Hat
33855	37	-109	BLM		x	Mexican Hat
33857	37	-109	BLM		x	Mexican Hat
33858	37	-109	BLM		x	Mexican Hat
33859	37	-109	BLM		x	Mexican Hat
33860	37	-109	BLM		x	Mexican Hat
33861	37	-109	BLM		x	Mexican Hat

ID	Lat	Lon	Agency	Electric	Free	Locale
33862	37	-109	BLM		x	Mexican Hat
33864	37	-109	BLM		x	Mexican Hat
33865	37	-109	BLM		x	Mexican Hat
33866	37	-109	BLM		x	Mexican Hat
33867	37	-109	BLM		x	Bluff
33868	37	-109	BLM		x	Mexican Hat
33870	37	-109	BLM			Bluff
33875	37	-109	BLM		x	Bluff
33876	37	-109	BLM		x	Bluff
33877	37	-109	BLM		x	Mexican Hat
33879	37	-109	BLM		x	Mexican Hat
33880	37	-109	BLM		x	Mexican Hat
33881	37	-109	BLM		x	Mexican Hat
33919	37	-109	USFS		x	Monticello
34008	37	-109	BLM		x	Bluff
33573	38	-113	MU			Milford
30880	38	-112	USFS			Kanosh
30887	38	-112	USFS			Beaver
30923	38	-112	USFS		x	Beaver
30924	38	-112	USFS		x	Beaver
30928	38	-112	USFS			Circleville
31038	38	-112	USFS			Beaver
31093	38	-112	USFS		x	Kanosh
31162	38	-112	ST			Joseph
31163	38	-112	ST	x		Joseph
31265	38	-112	USFS		x	Beaver
31617	38	-112	USFS		x	Greenwich
31631	38	-112	USFS		x	Greenwich
31632	38	-112	USFS		x	Kingston
31639	38	-112	USFS		x	Greenwich
31673	38	-112	USFS		x	Monroe
31674	38	-112	USFS		x	Koosharem
31675	38	-112	USFS		x	Koosharem
31690	38	-112	USFS		x	Greenwich
31701	38	-112	USFS		x	Greenwich
31702	38	-112	USFS		x	Greenwich
31798	38	-112	USFS		x	Richfield
31799	38	-112	USFS		x	Richfield
31800	38	-112	USFS		x	Richfield
31811	38	-112	USFS		x	Fillmore
31812	38	-112	USFS		x	Fillmore

ID	Lat	Lon	Agency	Electric	Free	Locale
31813	38	-112	USFS		x	Fillmore
31814	38	-112	USFS		x	Fillmore
31815	38	-112	USFS		x	Fillmore
31816	38	-112	USFS		x	Fillmore
31819	38	-112	USFS		x	Beaver
31821	38	-112	USFS		x	Salina
31822	38	-112	USFS		x	Salina
31823	38	-112	USFS		x	Salina
31824	38	-112	USFS		x	Fillmore
31825	38	-112	USFS		x	Fillmore
31826	38	-112	USFS		x	Fillmore
31827	38	-112	USFS		x	Fillmore
31831	38	-112	USFS		x	Fillmore
31834	38	-112	USFS		x	Fillmore
31849	38	-112	USFS		x	Elsinore
31850	38	-112	USFS		x	Elsinore
31852	38	-112	USFS		x	Marysvale
31855	38	-112	USFS		x	Kanosh
31858	38	-112	USFS		x	Beaver
31859	38	-112	USFS		x	Beaver
31860	38	-112	USFS		x	Beaver
31861	38	-112	USFS		x	Kanosh
31862	38	-112	USFS		x	Kanosh
31863	38	-112	USFS		x	Beaver
31864	38	-112	USFS		x	Kanosh
31865	38	-112	USFS		x	Joseph
31872	38	-112	USFS		x	Kanosh
31887	38	-112	USFS		x	Joseph
31888	38	-112	USFS		x	Joseph
31889	38	-112	USFS		x	Joseph
31890	38	-112	USFS		x	Marysvale
31891	38	-112	USFS		x	Marysvale
31892	38	-112	USFS		x	Marysvale
31893	38	-112	USFS		x	Sevier
31894	38	-112	USFS		x	Sevier
31897	38	-112	USFS		x	Elsinore
31898	38	-112	USFS		x	Joseph
31901	38	-112	USFS		x	Kanosh
31902	38	-112	USFS		x	Joseph
31905	38	-112	USFS		x	Marysvale
31906	38	-112	USFS		x	Marysvale

ID	Lat	Lon	Agency	Electric	Free	Locale
31908	38	-112	USFS		x	Marysvale
31909	38	-112	USFS		x	Marysvale
31910	38	-112	USFS		x	Marysvale
31911	38	-112	USFS		x	Marysvale
31912	38	-112	USFS		x	Marysvale
31914	38	-112	USFS		x	Marysvale
31916	38	-112	USFS		x	Marysvale
31919	38	-112	USFS		x	Cove Fort
31943	38	-112	USFS		x	Beaver
31944	38	-112	USFS		x	Beaver
31945	38	-112	USFS		x	Beaver
31946	38	-112	USFS		x	Beaver
31955	38	-112	USFS		x	Beaver
31961	38	-112	USFS		x	Glenwood
31963	38	-112	USFS		x	Beaver
31971	38	-112	USFS		x	Antimony
31973	38	-112	USFS		x	Junction
31974	38	-112	USFS		x	Greenwich
31977	38	-112	USFS		x	Beaver
32022	38	-112	USFS		x	Beaver
32029	38	-112	USFS		x	Beaver
32040	38	-112	USFS		x	Marysvale
32044	38	-112	USFS		x	Beaver
32046	38	-112	USFS		x	Beaver
32047	38	-112	USFS		x	Beaver
32048	38	-112	USFS		x	Beaver
32056	38	-112	USFS		x	Beaver
32068	38	-112	USFS		x	Beaver
32148	38	-112	USFS		x	Greenwich
32149	38	-112	USFS		x	Greenwich
32153	38	-112	USFS		x	Greenwich
32160	38	-112	USFS		x	Monroe
32181	38	-112	USFS		x	Joseph
32233	38	-112	USFS		x	Fillmore
32234	38	-112	USFS		x	Beaver
32235	38	-112	USFS		x	Beaver
32253	38	-112	USFS		x	Greenwich
32307	38	-112	USFS		x	Monroe
32326	38	-112	USFS		x	Kanosh
32327	38	-112	USFS		x	Kanosh
32331	38	-112	USFS		x	Elsinore
32332	38	-112	USFS		x	Elsinore
32333	38	-112	USFS		x	Elsinore
32334	38	-112	USFS		x	Elsinore
32336	38	-112	USFS		x	Kanosh
32342	38	-112	USFS		x	Sevier
32353	38	-112	USFS		x	Junction
32354	38	-112	USFS		x	Junction
32357	38	-112	USFS		x	Junction
32363	38	-112	USFS		x	Circleville
32428	38	-112	USFS		x	Fillmore
32550	38	-112	USFS		x	Circleville
32560	38	-112	USFS		x	Antimony
32567	38	-112	USFS		x	Beaver
32582	38	-112	USFS		x	Fillmore
32596	38	-112	USFS		x	Fillmore
32638	38	-112	USFS		x	Marysvale
32642	38	-112	USFS		x	Beaver
32644	38	-112	USFS		x	Joseph
32645	38	-112	USFS		x	Joseph
32648	38	-112	USFS		x	Kanosh
32649	38	-112	USFS		x	Kanosh
32652	38	-112	USFS		x	Kanosh
32873	38	-112	USFS		x	Fillmore
32996	38	-112	USFS		x	Richfield
33146	38	-112	USFS		x	Junction
33147	38	-112	USFS		x	Junction
33148	38	-112	USFS		x	Joseph
33149	38	-112	USFS		x	Joseph
33155	38	-112	USFS		x	Beaver
33156	38	-112	USFS		x	Beaver
33213	38	-112	USFS		x	Beaver
33237	38	-112	USFS		x	Richfield
33306	38	-112	USFS		x	Beaver
33316	38	-112	USFS		x	Elsinore
33324	38	-112	USFS		x	Beaver
33325	38	-112	USFS		x	Beaver
33512	38	-112	USFS		x	Manderfield
33536	38	-112	USFS			Beaver
33561	38	-112	USFS		x	Junction
33563	38	-112	USFS			Beaver
33575	38	-112	USFS			Beaver

ID	Lat	Lon	Agency	Electric	Free	Locale
33579	38	-112	USFS			Beaver
33616	38	-112	USFS			Beaver
33620	38	-112	USFS		x	Greenwich
33621	38	-112	ST		x	Greenwich
33622	38	-112	ST		x	Greenwich
33652	38	-112	ST		x	Minersville
33653	38	-112	CP	x		Minersville
33705	38	-112	BLM		x	Antimony
33706	38	-112	ST			Antimony
33707	38	-112	ST			Antimony
33738	38	-112	ST			Antimony
33769	38	-112	BLM		x	Milford
33904	38	-112	USFS		x	Cove Fort
33916	38	-112	USFS		x	Beaver
33967	38	-112	USFS		x	Junction
33973	38	-112	USFS			Beaver
33984	38	-112	USFS		x	Greenwich
33992	38	-112	USFS		x	Beaver
33993	38	-112	USFS		x	Beaver
33994	38	-112	USFS		x	Beaver
33995	38	-112	USFS		x	Beaver
33996	38	-112	USFS		x	Beaver
33997	38	-112	USFS		x	Beaver
30882	38	-111	CP		x	Loa
30892	38	-111	USFS		x	Salina
30908	38	-111	BLM		x	Torrey
30925	38	-111	USFS		x	Glenwood
30930	38	-111	ST		x	Antimony
30932	38	-111	USFS		x	Fremont
30942	38	-111	USFS			Loa
30953	38	-111	USFS		x	Salina
30975	38	-111	BLM		x	Hanksville
31020	38	-111	NP		x	Torrey
31021	38	-111	NP		x	Torrey
31022	38	-111	NP			Torrey
31047	38	-111	USFS		x	Salina
31089	38	-111	USFS		x	Teasdale
31090	38	-111	USFS		x	Grover
31120	38	-111	USFS			Loa
31139	38	-111	USFS			Loa
31153	38	-111	USFS		x	Fremont

ID	Lat	Lon	Agency	Electric	Free	Locale
31164	38	-111	BLM		x	Hanksville
31165	38	-111	USFS		x	Lyman
31166	38	-111	USFS		x	Lyman
31167	38	-111	USFS		x	Lyman
31168	38	-111	USFS		x	Lyman
31169	38	-111	USFS		x	Lyman
31170	38	-111	USFS		x	Lyman
31173	38	-111	USFS			Loa
31185	38	-111	USFS		x	Redmond
31186	38	-111	USFS		x	Redmond
31193	38	-111	USFS		x	Salina
31202	38	-111	USFS		x	Redmond
31203	38	-111	USFS		x	Redmond
31204	38	-111	USFS		x	Redmond
31263	38	-111	USFS		x	Salina
31264	38	-111	USFS		x	Salina
31270	38	-111	USFS		x	Salina
31273	38	-111	USFS		x	Redmond
31285	38	-111	USFS		x	Salina
31304	38	-111	USFS		x	Fremont
31306	38	-111	USFS		x	Fremont
31308	38	-111	USFS		x	Fremont
31310	38	-111	USFS		x	Fremont
31312	38	-111	USFS		x	Fremont
31314	38	-111	USFS		x	Loa
31319	38	-111	USFS		x	Fremont
31329	38	-111	USFS		x	Fremont
31337	38	-111	USFS		x	Fremont
31338	38	-111	USFS		x	Lyman
31340	38	-111	USFS		x	Lyman
31341	38	-111	USFS		x	Lyman
31344	38	-111	USFS		x	Lyman
31345	38	-111	USFS		x	Fremont
31347	38	-111	USFS		x	Lyman
31348	38	-111	USFS		x	Lyman
31349	38	-111	USFS		x	Lyman
31350	38	-111	USFS		x	Lyman
31357	38	-111	USFS		x	Salina
31404	38	-111	USFS		x	Salina
31409	38	-111	USFS		x	Salina
31410	38	-111	USFS		x	Salina

ID	Lat	Lon	Agency	Electric	Free	Locale
31411	38	-111	USFS		x	Salina
31429	38	-111	USFS		x	Lyman
31442	38	-111	USFS		x	Salina
31443	38	-111	USFS		x	Salina
31448	38	-111	USFS		x	Salina
31449	38	-111	USFS		x	Salina
31459	38	-111	USFS		x	Koosharem
31464	38	-111	USFS		x	Koosharem
31478	38	-111	USFS		x	Koosharem
31479	38	-111	USFS		x	Koosharem
31539	38	-111	USFS		x	Glenwood
31540	38	-111	USFS		x	Glenwood
31541	38	-111	USFS		x	Glenwood
31542	38	-111	USFS		x	Glenwood
31554	38	-111	USFS		x	Koosharem
31555	38	-111	USFS		x	Koosharem
31556	38	-111	USFS		x	Koosharem
31567	38	-111	USFS		x	Glenwood
31582	38	-111	USFS		x	Koosharem
31625	38	-111	USFS		x	Glenwood
31626	38	-111	USFS		x	Glenwood
31629	38	-111	USFS		x	Koosharem
31630	38	-111	USFS		x	Glenwood
31655	38	-111	USFS		x	Koosharem
31656	38	-111	USFS		x	Koosharem
31664	38	-111	USFS		x	Koosharem
31817	38	-111	USFS		x	Grover
31918	38	-111	USFS		x	Glenwood
31926	38	-111	USFS		x	Koosharem
31978	38	-111	USFS		x	Salina
31979	38	-111	USFS		x	Glenwood
31984	38	-111	USFS		x	Teasdale
31986	38	-111	USFS		x	Grover
31990	38	-111	USFS		x	Teasdale
32020	38	-111	USFS		x	Grover
32021	38	-111	USFS		x	Grover
32025	38	-111	USFS		x	Grover
32027	38	-111	USFS		x	Antimony
32035	38	-111	USFS		x	Antimony
32057	38	-111	USFS		x	Antimony
32058	38	-111	USFS		x	Antimony

ID	Lat	Lon	Agency	Electric	Free	Locale
32059	38	-111	USFS		x	Antimony
32060	38	-111	USFS		x	Antimony
32061	38	-111	USFS		x	Antimony
32062	38	-111	USFS		x	Antimony
32063	38	-111	USFS		x	Antimony
32064	38	-111	USFS		x	Antimony
32065	38	-111	USFS		x	Antimony
32066	38	-111	USFS		x	Antimony
32067	38	-111	USFS		x	Antimony
32070	38	-111	USFS		x	Antimony
32073	38	-111	USFS		x	Salina
32074	38	-111	USFS		x	Teasdale
32075	38	-111	USFS		x	Salina
32076	38	-111	USFS		x	Salina
32077	38	-111	USFS		x	Salina
32123	38	-111	USFS		x	Loa
32128	38	-111	USFS		x	Fremont
32140	38	-111	USFS		x	Antimony
32141	38	-111	USFS		x	Antimony
32142	38	-111	USFS		x	Antimony
32143	38	-111	USFS		x	Antimony
32157	38	-111	USFS		x	Teasdale
32158	38	-111	USFS		x	Teasdale
32159	38	-111	USFS		x	Teasdale
32168	38	-111	USFS		x	Teasdale
32169	38	-111	USFS		x	Teasdale
32170	38	-111	USFS		x	Teasdale
32180	38	-111	USFS		x	Grover
32186	38	-111	USFS		x	Grover
32187	38	-111	USFS		x	Grover
32188	38	-111	USFS		x	Grover
32217	38	-111	USFS		x	Teasdale
32221	38	-111	USFS		x	Grover
32222	38	-111	USFS		x	Grover
32223	38	-111	USFS		x	Grover
32224	38	-111	USFS		x	Grover
32225	38	-111	USFS		x	Grover
32267	38	-111	USFS		x	Glenwood
32271	38	-111	USFS		x	Salina
32275	38	-111	USFS		x	Lyman
32279	38	-111	USFS		x	Lyman

ID	Lat	Lon	Agency	Electric	Free	Locale
32280	38	-111	USFS		x	Lyman
32281	38	-111	USFS		x	Lyman
32282	38	-111	USFS		x	Lyman
32283	38	-111	USFS		x	Lyman
32284	38	-111	USFS		x	Lyman
32285	38	-111	USFS		x	Lyman
32286	38	-111	USFS		x	Lyman
32287	38	-111	USFS		x	Lyman
32288	38	-111	USFS		x	Torrey
32291	38	-111	USFS		x	Lyman
32292	38	-111	USFS		x	Lyman
32293	38	-111	USFS		x	Lyman
32294	38	-111	USFS		x	Lyman
32298	38	-111	USFS		x	Lyman
32300	38	-111	USFS		x	Salina
32304	38	-111	USFS		x	Glenwood
32309	38	-111	USFS		x	Fremont
32310	38	-111	USFS		x	Koosharem
32313	38	-111	USFS		x	Koosharem
32323	38	-111	USFS		x	Salina
32399	38	-111	USFS		x	Grover
32400	38	-111	USFS		x	Grover
32402	38	-111	USFS		x	Lyman
32403	38	-111	USFS		x	Salina
32404	38	-111	USFS		x	Salina
32414	38	-111	USFS		x	Fremont
32416	38	-111	USFS		x	Koosharem
32417	38	-111	USFS		x	Koosharem
32420	38	-111	USFS		x	Teasdale
32424	38	-111	USFS		x	Salina
32425	38	-111	USFS		x	Salina
32427	38	-111	USFS		x	Redmond
32432	38	-111	USFS		x	Glenwood
32440	38	-111	USFS		x	Teasdale
32441	38	-111	USFS		x	Teasdale
32495	38	-111	USFS		x	Koosharem
32504	38	-111	USFS		x	Teasdale
32505	38	-111	USFS		x	Grover
32506	38	-111	USFS		x	Grover
32507	38	-111	USFS		x	Grover
32509	38	-111	USFS		x	Teasdale
32534	38	-111	USFS		x	Salina
32536	38	-111	USFS		x	Koosharem
32539	38	-111	USFS		x	Koosharem
32569	38	-111	USFS		x	Antimony
32577	38	-111	USFS		x	Antimony
32580	38	-111	USFS		x	Grover
32635	38	-111	USFS		x	Teasdale
32646	38	-111	USFS		x	Loa
32651	38	-111	USFS		x	Redmond
32720	38	-111	USFS		x	Mayfield
33012	38	-111	USFS		x	Teasdale
33013	38	-111	USFS		x	Teasdale
33014	38	-111	USFS		x	Teasdale
33017	38	-111	USFS		x	Grover
33024	38	-111	USFS		x	Teasdale
33025	38	-111	USFS		x	Teasdale
33026	38	-111	USFS		x	Teasdale
33027	38	-111	USFS		x	Teasdale
33028	38	-111	USFS		x	Teasdale
33029	38	-111	USFS		x	Teasdale
33048	38	-111	USFS		x	Teasdale
33088	38	-111	USFS		x	Teasdale
33119	38	-111	USFS		x	Grover
33120	38	-111	USFS		x	Grover
33143	38	-111	USFS		x	Grover
33144	38	-111	USFS		x	Grover
33197	38	-111	USFS		x	Salina
33198	38	-111	USFS		x	Koosharem
33300	38	-111	USFS		x	Loa
33329	38	-111	USFS		x	Salina
33353	38	-111	USFS			Salina
33355	38	-111	USFS		x	Salina
33477	38	-111	USFS		x	Salina
33508	38	-111	BLM		x	Torrey
33556	38	-111	USFS		x	Koosharem
33557	38	-111	BLM		x	Koosharem
33602	38	-111	USFS			Torrey
33603	38	-111	USFS		x	Greenwich
33605	38	-111	USFS		x	Salina
33614	38	-111	USFS			Loa
33617	38	-111	USFS			Richfield

ID	Lat	Lon	Agency	Electric	Free	Locale
33649	38	-111	USFS		x	Greenwich
33661	38	-111	USFS		x	Lyman
33662	38	-111	USFS		x	Lyman
33678	38	-111	USFS		x	Salina
33692	38	-111	BLM		x	Hanksville
33694	38	-111	USFS			Teasdale
33698	38	-111	USFS		x	Salina
33737	38	-111	USFS			Loa
33740	38	-111	USFS			Torrey
33764	38	-111	USFS		x	Salina
33778	38	-111	USFS			Grover
33779	38	-111	USFS		x	Lyman
33780	38	-111	USFS		x	Lyman
33781	38	-111	USFS		x	Salina
33782	38	-111	USFS		x	Salina
33906	38	-111	USFS			Torrey
33912	38	-111	USFS		x	Lyman
33948	38	-111	USFS			Bicknell
33954	38	-111	USFS			Loa
33963	38	-111	BLM		x	Hanksville
33978	38	-111	USFS		x	Salina
30931	38	-110	BLM		x	Green River
30984	38	-110	NP		x	Moab
30987	38	-110	NP		x	Hite
30988	38	-110	NP		x	Hite
30990	38	-110	NP		x	Hite
30991	38	-110	NP		x	Monticello
30992	38	-110	NP		x	Hanksville
30996	38	-110	NP		x	Monticello
30997	38	-110	NP		x	Monticello
31000	38	-110	NP		x	Hite
31001	38	-110	NP		x	Moab
31003	38	-110	NP		x	Monticello
31009	38	-110	NP		x	Hite
31011	38	-110	NP		x	Hite
31013	38	-110	NP		x	Hite
31015	38	-110	NP		x	Monticello
31016	38	-110	NP		x	Monticello
31036	38	-110	BLM		x	Green River
31043	38	-110	BLM		x	Hanksville
31049	38	-110	NP			Moab

ID	Lat	Lon	Agency	Electric	Free	Locale
31053	38	-110	NP			Moab
31054	38	-110	NP			Moab
31055	38	-110	NP			Moab
31061	38	-110	NP			Moab
31094	38	-110	BLM		x	Green River
31097	38	-110	BLM		x	Green River
31143	38	-110	BLM		x	Hanksville
31144	38	-110	BLM		x	Hanksville
33350	38	-110	ST			Hanksville
33386	38	-110	BLM			Moab
33415	38	-110	BLM			Moab
33453	38	-110	BLM			Green River
33457	38	-110	ST	x		Green River
33496	38	-110	BLM		x	Hanksville
33531	38	-110	BLM		x	Green River
33585	38	-110	BLM		x	Green River
33592	38	-110	BLM		x	Green River
33593	38	-110	BLM			Hanksville
33612	38	-110	BLM		x	Green River
33636	38	-110	BLM			Hanksville
33884	38	-110	BLM		x	Green River
33893	38	-110	BLM		x	Hanksville
33921	38	-110	BLM		x	Hanksville
33955	38	-110	BLM		x	Green River
33958	38	-110	BLM		x	Green River
33965	38	-110	BLM		x	Green River
33976	38	-110	BLM		x	Green River
34027	38	-110	BLM		x	Moab
34030	38	-110	BLM		x	Green River
34046	38	-110	BLM		x	Hanksville
30895	38	-109	NP			Moab
30921	38	-109	BLM			Moab
30922	38	-109	BLM		x	Moab
30945	38	-109	BLM		x	Moab
30950	38	-109	BLM		x	Monticello
30979	38	-109	NP		x	Monticello
30980	38	-109	NP		x	Monticello
30981	38	-109	NP		x	Monticello
30982	38	-109	NP		x	Monticello
30983	38	-109	NP		x	Monticello
30985	38	-109	NP		x	Monticello

ID	Lat	Lon	Agency	Electric	Free	Locale
30986	38	-109	NP		x	Moab
30989	38	-109	NP		x	Monticello
30993	38	-109	NP		x	Hite
30994	38	-109	NP			Monticello
30995	38	-109	NP		x	Monticello
30998	38	-109	NP		x	Monticello
30999	38	-109	NP		x	Moab
31002	38	-109	NP		x	Monticello
31004	38	-109	NP		x	Monticello
31005	38	-109	NP		x	Monticello
31006	38	-109	NP		x	Monticello
31007	38	-109	NP			Monticello
31008	38	-109	NP		x	Monticello
31010	38	-109	NP		x	Monticello
31012	38	-109	NP		x	Monticello
31014	38	-109	NP			Monticello
31017	38	-109	NP		x	Monticello
31018	38	-109	NP		x	Monticello
31019	38	-109	NP			Monticello
31024	38	-109	PRIV		x	Moab
31037	38	-109	BLM		x	Cisco
31048	38	-109	BLM			Cisco
31050	38	-109	BLM			Cisco
31051	38	-109	BLM			Cisco
31072	38	-109	NP			Moab
31073	38	-109	NP			Moab
31074	38	-109	BLM		x	Moab
31086	38	-109	BLM			Moab
31087	38	-109	BLM			Moab
31096	38	-109	BLM			Monticello
31100	38	-109	BLM		x	Moab
31101	38	-109	BLM		x	Moab
31102	38	-109	ST	x		Moab
31103	38	-109	ST	x		Moab
31112	38	-109	BLM			Moab
31121	38	-109	BLM			Moab
31122	38	-109	BLM		x	Moab
31125	38	-109	BLM		x	Moab
31126	38	-109	BLM		x	Moab
31150	38	-109	BLM			Moab
32637	38	-109	USFS		x	Moab

ID	Lat	Lon	Agency	Electric	Free	Locale
32722	38	-109	USFS		x	Moab
32723	38	-109	USFS		x	Moab
32724	38	-109	USFS		x	Moab
32800	38	-109	USFS		x	Moab
32801	38	-109	USFS		x	Moab
32802	38	-109	USFS		x	Moab
32803	38	-109	USFS		x	Moab
32804	38	-109	USFS		x	Moab
32805	38	-109	USFS		x	Moab
32806	38	-109	USFS		x	Moab
32807	38	-109	USFS		x	Moab
32813	38	-109	USFS		x	Moab
32814	38	-109	USFS		x	Moab
32815	38	-109	USFS		x	Moab
32816	38	-109	USFS		x	Moab
32817	38	-109	USFS		x	Moab
32818	38	-109	USFS		x	Moab
32819	38	-109	USFS		x	Moab
32820	38	-109	USFS		x	Moab
32821	38	-109	USFS		x	Moab
32822	38	-109	USFS		x	Moab
32823	38	-109	USFS		x	Paradox
32824	38	-109	USFS		x	Moab
32825	38	-109	USFS		x	Moab
32826	38	-109	USFS		x	Moab
32827	38	-109	USFS		x	La Sal
32828	38	-109	USFS		x	Moab
32829	38	-109	USFS		x	Moab
32830	38	-109	USFS		x	Moab
32831	38	-109	USFS		x	Moab
32832	38	-109	USFS		x	Moab
32833	38	-109	USFS		x	Moab
32834	38	-109	USFS		x	Moab
32886	38	-109	USFS		x	Moab
32887	38	-109	USFS		x	Moab
32888	38	-109	USFS		x	Moab
32894	38	-109	USFS		x	Moab
32895	38	-109	USFS		x	Moab
32896	38	-109	USFS		x	Moab
32960	38	-109	USFS		x	Moab
32961	38	-109	USFS		x	Moab

ID	Lat	Lon	Agency	Electric	Free	Locale
32965	38	-109	USFS		x	Moab
32966	38	-109	USFS		x	Moab
33086	38	-109	USFS		x	Moab
33087	38	-109	USFS		x	Moab
33089	38	-109	USFS		x	Moab
33090	38	-109	USFS		x	Moab
33091	38	-109	USFS		x	Moab
33092	38	-109	USFS		x	Moab
33093	38	-109	USFS		x	Moab
33094	38	-109	USFS		x	Moab
33095	38	-109	USFS		x	Moab
33096	38	-109	USFS		x	Moab
33099	38	-109	USFS		x	Moab
33100	38	-109	USFS		x	La Sal
33101	38	-109	USFS		x	Moab
33102	38	-109	USFS		x	Moab
33351	38	-109	BLM			Moab
33352	38	-109	BLM			Moab
33380	38	-109	BLM			Moab
33444	38	-109	BLM			Hite
33467	38	-109	BLM			Moab
33469	38	-109	BLM			Moab
33470	38	-109	BLM		x	Monticello
33471	38	-109	BLM		x	Monticello
33472	38	-109	BLM		x	Monticello
33473	38	-109	BLM		x	Monticello
33474	38	-109	BLM		x	Monticello
33475	38	-109	BLM		x	Monticello
33476	38	-109	BLM		x	Monticello
33479	38	-109	BLM			Moab
33486	38	-109	BLM			Moab
33497	38	-109	BLM			Moab
33499	38	-109	BLM			Moab
33513	38	-109	BLM			Monticello
33522	38	-109	BLM			Moab
33533	38	-109	BLM			Moab
33535	38	-109	BLM			Moab
33539	38	-109	BLM			Moab
33540	38	-109	BLM		x	Moab
33546	38	-109	BLM			Moab
33547	38	-109	BLM			Moab

ID	Lat	Lon	Agency	Electric	Free	Locale
33548	38	-109	BLM			Moab
33549	38	-109	USFS		x	Castle Valley
33550	38	-109	BLM			Moab
33564	38	-109	BLM			Moab
33565	38	-109	BLM			Moab
33566	38	-109	BLM			Moab
33567	38	-109	BLM			Moab
33568	38	-109	BLM			Moab
33587	38	-109	BLM		x	Moab
33591	38	-109	BLM			Moab
33594	38	-109	BLM		x	Moab
33609	38	-109	BLM			Moab
33632	38	-109	USFS			Moab
33645	38	-109	BLM		x	Moab
33650	38	-109	BLM		x	Moab
33659	38	-109	BLM			Moab
33680	38	-109	USFS		x	Moab
33681	38	-109	USFS		x	Moab
33696	38	-109	BLM			Moab
33703	38	-109	USFS			Moab
33708	38	-109	USFS		x	Spanish Valley
33724	38	-109	BLM		x	Moab
33750	38	-109	BLM		x	Moab
33885	38	-109	BLM			Moab
33886	38	-109	BLM			Moab
33887	38	-109	BLM			Moab
33888	38	-109	BLM			Moab
33889	38	-109	BLM			Moab
33890	38	-109	BLM			Moab
33927	38	-109	BLM		x	Moab
33928	38	-109	BLM		x	Moab
33929	38	-109	BLM		x	Moab
33930	38	-109	BLM		x	Moab
33931	38	-109	BLM		x	Moab
33933	38	-109	BLM			Moab
33950	38	-109	BLM			Monticello
33983	38	-109	BLM			Moab
33988	38	-109	BLM			Moab
34016	38	-109	USFS			Moab
34035	38	-109	BLM			Moab
34038	38	-109	BLM		x	Moab

ID	Lat	Lon	Agency	Electric	Free	Locale
34039	38	-109	BLM		x	Moab
34042	38	-109	BLM			Moab
30885	39	-113	BLM		x	Delta
31109	39	-112	MU	x		Delta
31205	39	-112	USFS		x	Vernon
31208	39	-112	USFS		x	Vernon
31211	39	-112	USFS		x	Vernon
31213	39	-112	USFS		x	Vernon
31214	39	-112	USFS		x	Vernon
31215	39	-112	USFS		x	Vernon
31216	39	-112	USFS		x	Vernon
31218	39	-112	USFS		x	Vernon
31219	39	-112	USFS		x	Vernon
31228	39	-112	USFS		x	Vernon
31230	39	-112	USFS		x	Vernon
31232	39	-112	USFS		x	Vernon
31234	39	-112	USFS		x	Vernon
31236	39	-112	USFS		x	Vernon
31238	39	-112	USFS		x	Vernon
31239	39	-112	USFS		x	Vernon
31241	39	-112	USFS		x	Vernon
31440	39	-112	USFS		x	Vernon
31444	39	-112	USFS		x	Vernon
31445	39	-112	USFS		x	Vernon
31446	39	-112	USFS		x	Vernon
31447	39	-112	USFS		x	Vernon
31760	39	-112	USFS		x	Oak City
31761	39	-112	USFS		x	Vernon
31762	39	-112	USFS		x	Vernon
31763	39	-112	USFS		x	Vernon
31764	39	-112	USFS		x	Vernon
31765	39	-112	USFS		x	Vernon
31766	39	-112	USFS		x	Delta
31782	39	-112	USFS		x	Scipio
31783	39	-112	USFS		x	Scipio
31806	39	-112	USFS		x	Holden
31807	39	-112	USFS		x	Holden
31809	39	-112	USFS		x	Holden
31810	39	-112	USFS		x	Holden
32171	39	-112	USFS		x	Oak City
32198	39	-112	USFS		x	Delta
32325	39	-112	USFS		x	Salina
32608	39	-112	USFS		x	Oak City
32609	39	-112	USFS		x	Oak City
32627	39	-112	USFS		x	Scipio
33131	39	-112	USFS		x	Vernon
33133	39	-112	USFS		x	Vernon
33134	39	-112	USFS		x	Vernon
33135	39	-112	USFS		x	Vernon
33157	39	-112	USFS		x	Vernon
33160	39	-112	USFS		x	Vernon
33161	39	-112	USFS		x	Vernon
33163	39	-112	USFS		x	Vernon
33164	39	-112	USFS		x	Vernon
33180	39	-112	USFS		x	Vernon
33181	39	-112	USFS		x	Vernon
33232	39	-112	USFS		x	Vernon
33238	39	-112	USFS		x	Leamington
33299	39	-112	USFS		x	Salina
33581	39	-112	BLM		x	Nephi
33582	39	-112	BLM		x	Nephi
33583	39	-112	BLM		x	Nephi
33584	39	-112	BLM		x	Nephi
33627	39	-112	USFS			Scipio
33628	39	-112	USFS		x	Holden
33695	39	-112	USFS			Oak City
33739	39	-112	USFS		x	Oak City
34009	39	-112	USFS		x	Vernon
34058	39	-112	ST			Levan
34059	39	-112	ST	x		Levan
30909	39	-111	USFS			Payson
30910	39	-111	CP			Huntington City
30918	39	-111	USFS		x	Huntington
30926	39	-111	USFS			Huntington
30933	39	-111	USFS			Payson
30934	39	-111	USFS			Payson
30952	39	-111	USFS			Huntington
31032	39	-111	USFS		x	Levan
31040	39	-111	USFS		x	Fairview
31081	39	-111	USFS		x	Nephi
31091	39	-111	USFS		x	Ephraim
31092	39	-111	USFS		x	Ephraim

ID	Lat	Lon	Agency	Electric	Free	Locale
31130	39	-111	ST		x	Ferron
31131	39	-111	BLM		x	Ferron
31145	39	-111	USFS			Ferron
31146	39	-111	USFS			Ferron
31147	39	-111	USFS			Ferron
31149	39	-111	USFS			Scofield
31151	39	-111	USFS			Fairview
31152	39	-111	USFS			Huntington
31183	39	-111	USFS		x	Redmond
31184	39	-111	USFS		x	Redmond
31187	39	-111	USFS		x	Redmond
31190	39	-111	USFS		x	Redmond
31191	39	-111	USFS		x	Redmond
31274	39	-111	USFS		x	Redmond
31279	39	-111	USFS		x	Levan
31284	39	-111	USFS			Huntington
31291	39	-111	USFS		x	Santaquin
31292	39	-111	USFS		x	Mona
31295	39	-111	USFS		x	Mona
31297	39	-111	USFS		x	Mona
31298	39	-111	USFS		x	Nephi
31300	39	-111	USFS		x	Nephi
31301	39	-111	USFS		x	Nephi
31302	39	-111	USFS		x	Nephi
31303	39	-111	USFS		x	Santaquin
31305	39	-111	USFS		x	Santaquin
31307	39	-111	USFS		x	Santaquin
31309	39	-111	USFS		x	Mona
31311	39	-111	USFS		x	Mona
31313	39	-111	USFS		x	Mona
31315	39	-111	USFS		x	Mona
31318	39	-111	USFS		x	Mona
31320	39	-111	USFS		x	Nephi
31323	39	-111	USFS		x	Nephi
31324	39	-111	USFS		x	Nephi
31325	39	-111	USFS		x	Nephi
31326	39	-111	USFS		x	Nephi
31327	39	-111	USFS		x	Nephi
31328	39	-111	USFS		x	Nephi
31682	39	-111	USFS		x	Spanish Fork
32096	39	-111	USFS		x	Spanish Fork

ID	Lat	Lon	Agency	Electric	Free	Locale
32162	39	-111	USFS		x	Nephi
32184	39	-111	USFS		x	Nephi
32191	39	-111	USFS		x	Santaquin
32476	39	-111	USFS		x	Payson
32477	39	-111	USFS		x	Santaquin
32478	39	-111	USFS		x	Santaquin
32479	39	-111	USFS		x	Santaquin
32480	39	-111	USFS		x	Santaquin
32481	39	-111	USFS		x	Santaquin
32482	39	-111	USFS		x	Santaquin
32483	39	-111	USFS		x	Santaquin
32630	39	-111	USFS		x	Nephi
32631	39	-111	USFS		x	Nephi
32632	39	-111	USFS		x	Nephi
32658	39	-111	USFS		x	Manti
32659	39	-111	USFS		x	Manti
32660	39	-111	USFS		x	Manti
32661	39	-111	USFS		x	Manti
32662	39	-111	USFS		x	Manti
32663	39	-111	USFS		x	Manti
32664	39	-111	USFS		x	Manti
32665	39	-111	USFS		x	Manti
32666	39	-111	USFS		x	Manti
32667	39	-111	USFS		x	Manti
32668	39	-111	USFS		x	Spanish Fork
32669	39	-111	USFS		x	Spanish Fork
32670	39	-111	USFS		x	Spanish Fork
32671	39	-111	USFS		x	Spanish Fork
32672	39	-111	USFS		x	Spanish Fork
32673	39	-111	USFS		x	Spanish Fork
32674	39	-111	USFS		x	Mayfield
32675	39	-111	USFS		x	Huntington
32676	39	-111	USFS		x	Mount Pleasant
32677	39	-111	USFS		x	Mount Pleasant
32678	39	-111	USFS		x	Mount Pleasant
32679	39	-111	USFS		x	Huntington
32680	39	-111	USFS		x	Huntington
32681	39	-111	USFS		x	Huntington
32682	39	-111	USFS		x	Huntington
32683	39	-111	USFS		x	Huntington
32684	39	-111	USFS		x	Huntington

ID	Lat	Lon	Agency	Electric	Free	Locale
32685	39	-111	USFS		x	Huntington
32686	39	-111	USFS		x	Huntington
32687	39	-111	USFS		x	Huntington
32688	39	-111	USFS		x	Huntington
32689	39	-111	USFS		x	Huntington
32690	39	-111	USFS		x	Huntington
32691	39	-111	USFS		x	Huntington
32692	39	-111	USFS		x	Huntington
32693	39	-111	USFS		x	Fairview
32694	39	-111	USFS		x	Fairview
32695	39	-111	USFS		x	Fairview
32696	39	-111	USFS		x	Fairview
32697	39	-111	USFS		x	Huntington
32698	39	-111	USFS		x	Huntington
32699	39	-111	USFS		x	Ferron
32700	39	-111	USFS		x	Ferron
32701	39	-111	USFS		x	Mayfield
32702	39	-111	USFS		x	Mayfield
32703	39	-111	USFS		x	Mayfield
32704	39	-111	USFS		x	Mayfield
32705	39	-111	USFS		x	Mayfield
32706	39	-111	USFS		x	Mayfield
32707	39	-111	USFS		x	Mayfield
32708	39	-111	USFS		x	Mayfield
32709	39	-111	USFS		x	Mayfield
32710	39	-111	USFS		x	Ferron
32711	39	-111	USFS		x	Mayfield
32712	39	-111	USFS		x	Mayfield
32713	39	-111	USFS		x	Ferron
32714	39	-111	USFS		x	Ferron
32715	39	-111	USFS		x	Ferron
32716	39	-111	USFS		x	Ferron
32717	39	-111	USFS		x	Ferron
32718	39	-111	USFS		x	Ferron
32719	39	-111	USFS		x	Ferron
32721	39	-111	USFS		x	Ferron
32725	39	-111	USFS		x	Huntington
32726	39	-111	USFS		x	Huntington
32727	39	-111	USFS		x	Huntington
32728	39	-111	USFS		x	Huntington
32729	39	-111	USFS		x	Huntington

ID	Lat	Lon	Agency	Electric	Free	Locale
32730	39	-111	USFS		x	Mount Pleasant
32731	39	-111	USFS		x	Mount Pleasant
32732	39	-111	USFS		x	Huntington
32733	39	-111	USFS		x	Huntington
32734	39	-111	USFS		x	Huntington
32735	39	-111	USFS		x	Huntington
32736	39	-111	USFS		x	Huntington
32737	39	-111	USFS		x	Huntington
32738	39	-111	USFS		x	Huntington
32739	39	-111	USFS		x	Huntington
32740	39	-111	USFS		x	Ephraim
32741	39	-111	USFS		x	Huntington
32742	39	-111	USFS		x	Huntington
32743	39	-111	USFS		x	Huntington
32744	39	-111	USFS		x	Huntington
32745	39	-111	USFS		x	Ferron
32746	39	-111	USFS		x	Ferron
32747	39	-111	USFS		x	Ferron
32748	39	-111	USFS		x	Ferron
32749	39	-111	USFS		x	Ferron
32750	39	-111	USFS		x	Ferron
32751	39	-111	USFS		x	Ferron
32752	39	-111	USFS		x	Mayfield
32753	39	-111	USFS		x	Mayfield
32754	39	-111	USFS		x	Mayfield
32755	39	-111	USFS		x	Mayfield
32756	39	-111	USFS		x	Mayfield
32757	39	-111	USFS		x	Mayfield
32758	39	-111	USFS		x	Mayfield
32759	39	-111	USFS		x	Manti
32760	39	-111	USFS		x	Manti
32761	39	-111	USFS		x	Manti
32762	39	-111	USFS		x	Manti
32763	39	-111	USFS		x	Manti
32764	39	-111	USFS		x	Manti
32765	39	-111	USFS		x	Manti
32766	39	-111	USFS		x	Manti
32767	39	-111	USFS		x	Manti
32768	39	-111	USFS		x	Manti
32769	39	-111	USFS		x	Manti
32770	39	-111	USFS		x	Manti

ID	Lat	Lon	Agency	Electric	Free	Locale
32771	39	-111	USFS		x	Manti
32772	39	-111	USFS		x	Manti
32773	39	-111	USFS		x	Mayfield
32774	39	-111	USFS		x	Mayfield
32775	39	-111	USFS		x	Mayfield
32776	39	-111	USFS		x	Mayfield
32777	39	-111	USFS		x	Mayfield
32778	39	-111	USFS		x	Ferron
32779	39	-111	USFS		x	Ferron
32780	39	-111	USFS		x	Ferron
32781	39	-111	USFS		x	Ferron
32782	39	-111	USFS		x	Ferron
32783	39	-111	USFS		x	Ferron
32784	39	-111	USFS		x	Ephraim
32785	39	-111	USFS		x	Ephraim
32786	39	-111	USFS		x	Ephraim
32787	39	-111	USFS		x	Ephraim
32788	39	-111	USFS		x	Ephraim
32789	39	-111	USFS		x	Ephraim
32790	39	-111	USFS		x	Ephraim
32791	39	-111	USFS		x	Ephraim
32792	39	-111	USFS		x	Ephraim
32793	39	-111	USFS		x	Ephraim
32794	39	-111	USFS		x	Ephraim
32795	39	-111	USFS		x	Ephraim
32796	39	-111	USFS		x	Ephraim
32797	39	-111	USFS		x	Fairview
32798	39	-111	USFS		x	Fairview
32799	39	-111	USFS		x	Fairview
32808	39	-111	USFS		x	Spanish Fork
32809	39	-111	USFS		x	Spanish Fork
32810	39	-111	USFS		x	Spanish Fork
32811	39	-111	USFS		x	Spanish Fork
32812	39	-111	USFS		x	Spanish Fork
32877	39	-111	USFS		x	Huntington
32878	39	-111	USFS		x	Huntington
32879	39	-111	USFS		x	Ephraim
32880	39	-111	USFS		x	Ephraim
32881	39	-111	USFS		x	Ephraim
32882	39	-111	USFS		x	Spanish Fork
32883	39	-111	USFS		x	Spanish Fork
32884	39	-111	USFS		x	Fairview
32885	39	-111	USFS		x	Spanish Fork
32889	39	-111	USFS		x	Manti
32890	39	-111	USFS		x	Manti
32891	39	-111	USFS		x	Mayfield
32892	39	-111	USFS		x	Mayfield
32893	39	-111	USFS		x	Fairview
32897	39	-111	USFS		x	Huntington
32898	39	-111	USFS		x	Mayfield
32899	39	-111	USFS		x	Ephraim
32900	39	-111	USFS		x	Ephraim
32901	39	-111	USFS		x	Ephraim
32902	39	-111	USFS		x	Ephraim
32903	39	-111	USFS		x	Ephraim
32904	39	-111	USFS		x	Ephraim
32905	39	-111	USFS		x	Ephraim
32906	39	-111	USFS		x	Ephraim
32907	39	-111	USFS		x	Huntington
32908	39	-111	USFS		x	Huntington
32909	39	-111	USFS		x	Mayfield
32910	39	-111	USFS		x	Huntington
32911	39	-111	USFS		x	Huntington
32912	39	-111	USFS		x	Huntington
32913	39	-111	USFS		x	Huntington
32914	39	-111	USFS		x	Huntington
32915	39	-111	USFS		x	Huntington
32916	39	-111	USFS		x	Mount Pleasant
32917	39	-111	USFS		x	Mount Pleasant
32918	39	-111	USFS		x	Mount Pleasant
32919	39	-111	USFS		x	Mount Pleasant
32920	39	-111	USFS		x	Mayfield
32921	39	-111	USFS		x	Mount Pleasant
32922	39	-111	USFS		x	Mount Pleasant
32923	39	-111	USFS		x	Fairview
32924	39	-111	USFS		x	Fairview
32925	39	-111	USFS		x	Fairview
32926	39	-111	USFS		x	Fairview
32927	39	-111	USFS		x	Fairview
32928	39	-111	USFS		x	Fairview
32929	39	-111	USFS		x	Fairview
32930	39	-111	USFS		x	Fairview

ID	Lat	Lon	Agency	Electric	Free	Locale
32931	39	-111	USFS		x	Mayfield
32932	39	-111	USFS		x	Fairview
32933	39	-111	USFS		x	Spanish Fork
32934	39	-111	USFS		x	Spanish Fork
32935	39	-111	USFS		x	Spanish Fork
32936	39	-111	USFS		x	Spanish Fork
32937	39	-111	USFS		x	Spanish Fork
32938	39	-111	USFS		x	Mayfield
32939	39	-111	USFS		x	Mayfield
32940	39	-111	USFS		x	Mayfield
32941	39	-111	USFS		x	Ephraim
32942	39	-111	USFS		x	Ephraim
32943	39	-111	USFS		x	Mayfield
32944	39	-111	USFS		x	Mayfield
32945	39	-111	USFS		x	Mayfield
32946	39	-111	USFS		x	Fairview
32957	39	-111	USFS		x	Manti
32958	39	-111	USFS		x	Manti
32962	39	-111	USFS		x	Fairview
32963	39	-111	USFS		x	Fairview
32964	39	-111	USFS		x	Fairview
32967	39	-111	USFS		x	Huntington
32968	39	-111	USFS		x	Huntington
32969	39	-111	USFS		x	Huntington
32970	39	-111	USFS		x	Huntington
32971	39	-111	USFS		x	Huntington
32972	39	-111	USFS		x	Mount Pleasant
32973	39	-111	USFS		x	Mount Pleasant
32974	39	-111	USFS		x	Huntington
32975	39	-111	USFS		x	Mount Pleasant
32976	39	-111	USFS		x	Huntington
32977	39	-111	USFS		x	Huntington
32978	39	-111	USFS		x	Huntington
32979	39	-111	USFS		x	Huntington
32980	39	-111	USFS		x	Ephraim
32981	39	-111	USFS		x	Ephraim
32982	39	-111	USFS		x	Mayfield
32987	39	-111	USFS		x	Ferron
32988	39	-111	USFS		x	Mount Pleasant
32991	39	-111	USFS		x	Ephraim
33001	39	-111	USFS		x	Fairview

ID	Lat	Lon	Agency	Electric	Free	Locale
33002	39	-111	USFS		x	Mount Pleasant
33003	39	-111	USFS		x	Manti
33004	39	-111	USFS		x	Manti
33005	39	-111	USFS		x	Mayfield
33006	39	-111	USFS		x	Fairview
33007	39	-111	USFS		x	Manti
33008	39	-111	USFS		x	Mayfield
33009	39	-111	USFS		x	Manti
33010	39	-111	USFS		x	Manti
33018	39	-111	USFS		x	Mayfield
33019	39	-111	USFS		x	Ferron
33020	39	-111	USFS		x	Ferron
33021	39	-111	USFS		x	Ferron
33022	39	-111	USFS		x	Ferron
33023	39	-111	USFS		x	Ferron
33030	39	-111	USFS		x	Orangeville
33031	39	-111	USFS		x	Ephraim
33032	39	-111	USFS		x	Ephraim
33034	39	-111	USFS		x	Huntington
33035	39	-111	USFS		x	Huntington
33036	39	-111	USFS		x	Manti
33037	39	-111	USFS		x	Manti
33038	39	-111	USFS		x	Manti
33039	39	-111	USFS		x	Manti
33040	39	-111	USFS		x	Manti
33041	39	-111	USFS		x	Manti
33043	39	-111	USFS		x	Ferron
33044	39	-111	USFS		x	Ferron
33045	39	-111	USFS		x	Mayfield
33046	39	-111	USFS		x	Mayfield
33047	39	-111	USFS		x	Huntington
33050	39	-111	USFS		x	Huntington
33051	39	-111	USFS		x	Mount Pleasant
33052	39	-111	USFS		x	Mount Pleasant
33053	39	-111	USFS		x	Mount Pleasant
33054	39	-111	USFS		x	Mount Pleasant
33056	39	-111	USFS		x	Fairview
33057	39	-111	USFS		x	Huntington
33058	39	-111	USFS		x	Mount Pleasant
33059	39	-111	USFS		x	Mount Pleasant
33060	39	-111	USFS		x	Mount Pleasant

ID	Lat	Lon	Agency	Electric	Free	Locale
33061	39	-111	USFS		x	Mount Pleasant
33062	39	-111	USFS		x	Mount Pleasant
33063	39	-111	USFS		x	Mount Pleasant
33064	39	-111	USFS		x	Mount Pleasant
33065	39	-111	USFS		x	Mount Pleasant
33066	39	-111	USFS		x	Mount Pleasant
33067	39	-111	USFS		x	Mount Pleasant
33068	39	-111	USFS		x	Mount Pleasant
33069	39	-111	USFS		x	Fairview
33070	39	-111	USFS		x	Mount Pleasant
33071	39	-111	USFS		x	Fairview
33269	39	-111	USFS		x	Santaquin
33270	39	-111	USFS		x	Santaquin
33271	39	-111	USFS		x	Santaquin
33354	39	-111	USFS			Fairview
33357	39	-111	USFS			Fairview
33500	39	-111	USFS		x	Fairview
33501	39	-111	USFS		x	Fairview
33509	39	-111	USFS		x	Fairview
33510	39	-111	USFS		x	Fairview
33514	39	-111	USFS			Huntington
33524	39	-111	USFS			Orangeville
33558	39	-111	USFS			Fairview
33560	39	-111	USFS			Ephraim
33570	39	-111	MU			Levan
33574	39	-111	USFS			Huntington
33580	39	-111	USFS			Huntington
33606	39	-111	USFS			Huntington
33624	39	-111	USFS			Manti
33625	39	-111	USFS			Payson
33626	39	-111	USFS			Moroni
33629	39	-111	USFS			Payson
33648	39	-111	ST	x		Ferron
33674	39	-111	USFS			Nephi
33691	39	-111	USFS		x	Fairview
33701	39	-111	USFS			Huntington
33709	39	-111	ST	x		Sterling
33710	39	-111	ST			Sterling
33711	39	-111	ST	x		Sterling
33712	39	-111	ST	x		Sterling
33720	39	-111	USFS			Payson
33743	39	-111	USFS			Nephi
33746	39	-111	USFS			Huntington
33747	39	-111	USFS			Huntington
33765	39	-111	USFS			Huntington
33895	39	-111	ST	x		Huntington
33896	39	-111	ST			Huntington
33900	39	-111	USFS		x	Thistle
33920	39	-111	USFS		x	Standardville
33962	39	-111	USFS			Huntington
33969	39	-111	USFS			Santaquin
33974	39	-111	USFS			Mayfield
33977	39	-111	USFS			Mayfield
33985	39	-111	USFS		x	Huntington
33990	39	-111	USFS		x	Sterling
34036	39	-111	USFS			Ferron
34057	39	-111	ST			Levan
34060	39	-111	ST	x		Levan
30901	39	-110	USFS			Duchesne
30972	39	-110	BLM			Lawrence
31029	39	-110	BLM		x	Green River
31413	39	-110	USFS		x	Spanish Fork
31637	39	-110	USFS		x	Spanish Fork
31774	39	-110	USFS		x	Spanish Fork
32107	39	-110	USFS		x	Spanish Fork
32127	39	-110	USFS		x	Duchesne
32144	39	-110	USFS		x	Duchesne
32185	39	-110	USFS		x	Spanish Fork
32457	39	-110	USFS		x	Duchesne
32461	39	-110	USFS		x	Duchesne
32491	39	-110	USFS		x	Spanish Fork
32499	39	-110	USFS		x	Spanish Fork
32502	39	-110	USFS		x	Duchesne
32508	39	-110	USFS		x	Duchesne
32513	39	-110	USFS		x	Duchesne
32514	39	-110	USFS		x	Duchesne
33259	39	-110	USFS		x	Spanish Fork
33390	39	-110	BLM			Sunnyside
33392	39	-110	BLM			East Carbon
33393	39	-110	BLM			Green River
33399	39	-110	BLM			Sunnyside
33400	39	-110	BLM			Sunnyside

ID	Lat	Lon	Agency	Electric	Free	Locale
33401	39	-110	BLM			Sunnyside
33402	39	-110	BLM			East Carbon
33403	39	-110	BLM			Green River
33405	39	-110	BLM			East Carbon
33406	39	-110	BLM			East Carbon
33408	39	-110	BLM			Green River
33411	39	-110	BLM			Sunnyside
33414	39	-110	BLM			Sunnyside
33420	39	-110	BLM			East Carbon
33421	39	-110	BLM			East Carbon
33423	39	-110	BLM			Sunnyside
33426	39	-110	BLM			East Carbon
33427	39	-110	BLM			East Carbon
33428	39	-110	BLM			East Carbon
33429	39	-110	BLM			East Carbon
33430	39	-110	BLM			Sunnyside
33432	39	-110	BLM			Green River
33434	39	-110	BLM			Green River
33435	39	-110	BLM			Green River
33437	39	-110	BLM			East Carbon
33440	39	-110	BLM			Green River
33441	39	-110	BLM			Green River
33443	39	-110	BLM			East Carbon
33445	39	-110	BLM			Sunnyside
33448	39	-110	BLM			East Carbon
33449	39	-110	BLM			Green River
33450	39	-110	BLM			East Carbon
33455	39	-110	BLM			East Carbon
33478	39	-110	BLM		x	Green River
33502	39	-110	ST	x		Huntington
33667	39	-110	BLM		x	Wellington
33675	39	-110	BLM		x	Green River
33749	39	-110	BLM			Price
33882	39	-110	BLM			Cleveland
33883	39	-110	BLM		x	Green River
33951	39	-110	BLM			Green River
33964	39	-110	BLM		x	Green River
30898	39	-109	BLM		x	Bonanza
30899	39	-109	BLM		x	Bonanza
30939	39	-109	BLM		x	Mack CO
30970	39	-109	BLM		x	Cisco
31056	39	-109	BLM			Cisco
31058	39	-109	BLM		x	Fruita CO
31059	39	-109	BLM			Cisco
31060	39	-109	BLM		x	Fruita CO
31062	39	-109	BLM			Cisco
31063	39	-109	BLM			Cisco
31064	39	-109	BLM			Cisco
31070	39	-109	BLM		x	Fruita CO
31071	39	-109	BLM			Cisco
31114	39	-109	BLM		x	Thompson
31119	39	-109	BLM		x	Thompson
33394	39	-109	BLM			Sunnyside
33395	39	-109	BLM			Sunnyside
33396	39	-109	BLM			Sunnyside
33397	39	-109	BLM			Sunnyside
33398	39	-109	BLM			Sunnyside
33412	39	-109	BLM			Sunnyside
33413	39	-109	BLM			Sunnyside
33418	39	-109	BLM			Sunnyside
33422	39	-109	BLM			Sunnyside
33424	39	-109	BLM			Sunnyside
33425	39	-109	BLM			Sunnyside
33431	39	-109	BLM			Sunnyside
33438	39	-109	BLM			Sunnyside
33442	39	-109	BLM			Sunnyside
33454	39	-109	BLM			Sunnyside
33545	39	-109	BLM			Mack CO
33551	39	-109	BLM			Fruita CO
33634	39	-109	BLM		x	Thompson
33635	39	-109	BLM		x	Thompson
33897	39	-109	BLM		x	Mack CO
34044	39	-109	BLM		x	Mack CO
30938	40	-113	BLM		x	Wendover
33541	40	-113	BLM			Wendover
30929	40	-112	BLM		x	Eureka
30944	40	-112	USFS			Salt Lake City
31042	40	-112	BLM			Tooele
31082	40	-112	USFS			Salt Lake City
31110	40	-112	CP	x		Tooele
31176	40	-112	USFS		x	Grantsville
31221	40	-112	USFS		x	Vernon

ID	Lat	Lon	Agency	Electric	Free	Locale
31438	40	-112	USFS		x	Vernon
31439	40	-112	USFS		x	Vernon
31729	40	-112	USFS		x	Vernon
33173	40	-112	USFS		x	Vernon
33179	40	-112	USFS		x	Vernon
33182	40	-112	USFS		x	Vernon
33220	40	-112	USFS		x	Vernon
33221	40	-112	USFS		x	Vernon
33222	40	-112	USFS		x	Vernon
33223	40	-112	USFS		x	Vernon
33228	40	-112	USFS		x	Vernon
33382	40	-112	CP			Grantsville
33383	40	-112	ST	x		Salt Lake City
33517	40	-112	USFS			Salt Lake City
33598	40	-112	USFS			Salt Lake City
33608	40	-112	USFS			Stockton
33639	40	-112	CP			Tooele
33640	40	-112	CP			Tooele
33641	40	-112	CP			Tooele
33642	40	-112	CP			Tooele
33643	40	-112	CP			Tooele
33644	40	-112	CP			Tooele
33704	40	-112	CP			Tooele
33898	40	-112	CP	x		Tooele
33905	40	-112	BLM			Lehi
33987	40	-112	USFS			Salt Lake City
34026	40	-112	BLM		x	Tooele
30881	40	-111	USFS			Alta
30884	40	-111	USFS			Orem
30897	40	-111	USFS	x		Hanna
30904	40	-111	USFS			Springville
30941	40	-111	USFS			Farmington
30978	40	-111	MU	x		Spanish Fork
31031	40	-111	USFS			Springville
31098	40	-111	USFS			Heber City
31105	40	-111	ST	x		Midway
31106	40	-111	ST			Midway
31113	40	-111	USFS			Thistle
31124	40	-111	USFS		x	Spanish Fork
31132	40	-111	USFS		x	Alta
31133	40	-111	ST			Morgan

ID	Lat	Lon	Agency	Electric	Free	Locale
31134	40	-111	ST	x		Morgan
31138	40	-111	ST			Coalville
31174	40	-111	USFS		x	Cedar Hills
31245	40	-111	USFS		x	Midway
31248	40	-111	USFS		x	Midway
31251	40	-111	USFS		x	Midway
31253	40	-111	USFS		x	Midway
31256	40	-111	USFS		x	Midway
31259	40	-111	USFS		x	Midway
31266	40	-111	USFS		x	Farmington
31268	40	-111	USFS		x	Cedar Hills
31269	40	-111	USFS		x	Farmington
31351	40	-111	USFS		x	Heber City
31352	40	-111	USFS		x	Heber City
31353	40	-111	USFS		x	Heber City
31354	40	-111	USFS		x	Heber City
31358	40	-111	USFS		x	Orem
31359	40	-111	USFS		x	Orem
31362	40	-111	USFS		x	Orem
31363	40	-111	USFS		x	Orem
31364	40	-111	USFS		x	Orem
31365	40	-111	USFS		x	Orem
31366	40	-111	USFS		x	Orem
31367	40	-111	USFS		x	Orem
31368	40	-111	USFS		x	Orem
31369	40	-111	USFS		x	Orem
31371	40	-111	USFS		x	Springville
31375	40	-111	USFS		x	Springville
31376	40	-111	USFS		x	Springville
31377	40	-111	USFS		x	Springville
31378	40	-111	USFS		x	Springville
31379	40	-111	USFS		x	Springville
31380	40	-111	USFS		x	Oakley
31382	40	-111	USFS		x	Oakley
31383	40	-111	USFS		x	Oakley
31392	40	-111	USFS		x	Thistle
31393	40	-111	USFS		x	Thistle
31397	40	-111	USFS		x	Oakley
31398	40	-111	USFS		x	Thistle
31399	40	-111	USFS		x	Thistle
31400	40	-111	USFS		x	Thistle

ID	Lat	Lon	Agency	Electric	Free	Locale
31401	40	-111	USFS		x	Thistle
31415	40	-111	USFS		x	Samak
31416	40	-111	USFS		x	Samak
31417	40	-111	USFS		x	Samak
31418	40	-111	USFS		x	Samak
31419	40	-111	USFS		x	Kamas
31420	40	-111	USFS		x	Kamas
31421	40	-111	USFS		x	Kamas
31422	40	-111	USFS		x	Kamas
31423	40	-111	USFS		x	Kamas
31424	40	-111	USFS		x	Kamas
31425	40	-111	USFS		x	Kamas
31426	40	-111	USFS		x	Kamas
31427	40	-111	USFS		x	Kamas
31428	40	-111	USFS		x	Kamas
31430	40	-111	USFS		x	Woodland
31431	40	-111	USFS		x	Woodland
31432	40	-111	USFS		x	Woodland
31433	40	-111	USFS		x	Woodland
31434	40	-111	USFS		x	Woodland
31435	40	-111	USFS		x	Woodland
31436	40	-111	USFS		x	Woodland
31437	40	-111	USFS		x	Woodland
31457	40	-111	USFS		x	Spanish Fork
31458	40	-111	USFS		x	Spanish Fork
31463	40	-111	USFS		x	Heber City
31465	40	-111	USFS		x	Heber City
31466	40	-111	USFS		x	Heber City
31467	40	-111	USFS		x	Heber City
31468	40	-111	USFS		x	Heber City
31470	40	-111	USFS		x	Heber City
31471	40	-111	USFS		x	Heber City
31472	40	-111	USFS		x	Heber City
31473	40	-111	USFS		x	Heber City
31474	40	-111	USFS		x	Heber City
31475	40	-111	USFS		x	Heber City
31476	40	-111	USFS		x	Heber City
31477	40	-111	USFS		x	Heber City
31486	40	-111	USFS		x	Kamas
31487	40	-111	USFS		x	Heber City
31489	40	-111	USFS		x	Heber City
31490	40	-111	USFS		x	Heber City
31491	40	-111	USFS		x	Heber City
31495	40	-111	USFS		x	Heber City
31499	40	-111	USFS		x	Heber City
31500	40	-111	USFS		x	Heber City
31501	40	-111	USFS		x	Heber City
31502	40	-111	USFS		x	Heber City
31503	40	-111	USFS		x	Heber City
31504	40	-111	USFS		x	Heber City
31505	40	-111	USFS		x	Heber City
31506	40	-111	USFS		x	Heber City
31507	40	-111	USFS		x	Thistle
31508	40	-111	USFS		x	Spanish Fork
31509	40	-111	USFS		x	Spanish Fork
31510	40	-111	USFS		x	Spanish Fork
31511	40	-111	USFS		x	Spanish Fork
31512	40	-111	USFS		x	Springville
31513	40	-111	USFS		x	Springville
31515	40	-111	USFS		x	Woodland
31516	40	-111	USFS		x	Woodland
31517	40	-111	USFS		x	Woodland
31518	40	-111	USFS		x	Woodland
31519	40	-111	USFS		x	Woodland
31525	40	-111	USFS		x	Kamas
31526	40	-111	USFS		x	Woodland
31527	40	-111	USFS		x	Heber City
31528	40	-111	USFS		x	Heber City
31529	40	-111	USFS		x	Heber City
31535	40	-111	USFS		x	Oakley
31536	40	-111	USFS		x	Oakley
31537	40	-111	USFS		x	Heber City
31546	40	-111	USFS		x	Cedar HIlls
31547	40	-111	USFS		x	Cedar HIlls
31548	40	-111	USFS		x	Pleasant Grove
31549	40	-111	USFS		x	Pleasant Grove
31550	40	-111	USFS		x	Pleasant Grove
31557	40	-111	USFS		x	Springville
31558	40	-111	USFS		x	Springville
31559	40	-111	USFS		x	Springville
31568	40	-111	USFS		x	Springville
31569	40	-111	USFS		x	Springville

ID	Lat	Lon	Agency	Electric	Free	Locale
31570	40	-111	USFS		x	Springville
31571	40	-111	USFS		x	Springville
31572	40	-111	USFS		x	Springville
31573	40	-111	USFS		x	Springville
31574	40	-111	USFS		x	Springville
31575	40	-111	USFS		x	Springville
31635	40	-111	USFS		x	Spanish Fork
31636	40	-111	USFS		x	Spanish Fork
31665	40	-111	USFS		x	Springville
31676	40	-111	USFS		x	Heber City
31677	40	-111	USFS		x	Heber City
31678	40	-111	USFS		x	Heber City
31683	40	-111	USFS		x	Heber City
31684	40	-111	USFS		x	Heber City
31685	40	-111	USFS		x	Heber City
31686	40	-111	USFS		x	Heber City
31692	40	-111	USFS		x	Heber City
31693	40	-111	USFS		x	Heber City
31694	40	-111	USFS		x	Heber City
31695	40	-111	USFS		x	Heber City
31696	40	-111	USFS		x	Heber City
31697	40	-111	USFS		x	Heber City
31698	40	-111	USFS		x	Heber City
31699	40	-111	USFS		x	Heber City
31700	40	-111	USFS		x	Heber City
31704	40	-111	USFS		x	Farmington
31711	40	-111	USFS		x	Heber City
31712	40	-111	USFS		x	Heber City
31713	40	-111	USFS		x	Heber City
31714	40	-111	USFS		x	Heber City
31715	40	-111	USFS		x	Farmington
31716	40	-111	USFS		x	Heber City
31717	40	-111	USFS		x	Heber City
31718	40	-111	USFS		x	Heber City
31726	40	-111	USFS		x	Cedar Hills
31727	40	-111	USFS		x	Midway
31728	40	-111	USFS		x	Cedar Hills
31730	40	-111	USFS		x	Midway
31731	40	-111	USFS		x	Midway
31732	40	-111	USFS		x	Midway
31733	40	-111	USFS		x	Midway

ID	Lat	Lon	Agency	Electric	Free	Locale
31734	40	-111	USFS		x	Midway
31735	40	-111	USFS		x	Midway
31736	40	-111	USFS		x	Midway
31737	40	-111	USFS		x	Midway
31738	40	-111	USFS		x	Midway
31753	40	-111	USFS		x	Samak
31754	40	-111	USFS		x	Springville
31755	40	-111	USFS		x	Woodland
31756	40	-111	USFS		x	Woodland
31757	40	-111	USFS		x	Woodland
31768	40	-111	USFS		x	Spanish Fork
31769	40	-111	USFS		x	Spanish Fork
31770	40	-111	USFS		x	Heber City
31772	40	-111	USFS		x	Heber City
31775	40	-111	USFS		x	Heber City
31776	40	-111	USFS		x	Heber City
31777	40	-111	USFS		x	Heber City
31778	40	-111	USFS		x	Heber City
31779	40	-111	USFS		x	Heber City
31780	40	-111	USFS		x	Heber City
31784	40	-111	USFS		x	Heber City
31785	40	-111	USFS		x	Heber City
31786	40	-111	USFS		x	Heber City
31787	40	-111	USFS		x	Heber City
31788	40	-111	USFS		x	Heber City
31789	40	-111	USFS		x	Heber City
31790	40	-111	USFS		x	Heber City
31792	40	-111	USFS		x	Heber City
31793	40	-111	USFS		x	Heber City
31794	40	-111	USFS		x	Heber City
31795	40	-111	USFS		x	Heber City
31802	40	-111	USFS		x	Heber City
31803	40	-111	USFS		x	Heber City
31804	40	-111	USFS		x	Heber City
31805	40	-111	USFS		x	Heber City
31828	40	-111	USFS		x	Woodland
31829	40	-111	USFS		x	Woodland
31830	40	-111	USFS		x	Woodland
31857	40	-111	USFS		x	Heber City
31878	40	-111	USFS		x	Spanish Fork
31879	40	-111	USFS		x	Spanish Fork

ID	Lat	Lon	Agency	Electric	Free	Locale
31880	40	-111	USFS		x	Spanish Fork
31881	40	-111	USFS		x	Spanish Fork
31882	40	-111	USFS		x	Spanish Fork
31896	40	-111	USFS		x	Midway
31917	40	-111	USFS		x	Charleston
31922	40	-111	USFS		x	Springville
31923	40	-111	USFS		x	Springville
31924	40	-111	USFS		x	Springville
31953	40	-111	USFS		x	Orem
31954	40	-111	USFS		x	Orem
31967	40	-111	USFS		x	Woodland
31968	40	-111	USFS		x	Woodland
31969	40	-111	USFS		x	Woodland
31970	40	-111	USFS		x	Woodland
31975	40	-111	USFS		x	Heber City
31994	40	-111	USFS		x	Spanish Fork
31995	40	-111	USFS		x	Spanish Fork
31996	40	-111	USFS		x	Spanish Fork
31998	40	-111	USFS		x	Spanish Fork
31999	40	-111	USFS		x	Spanish Fork
32000	40	-111	USFS		x	Springville
32001	40	-111	USFS		x	Springville
32002	40	-111	USFS		x	Springville
32003	40	-111	USFS		x	Springville
32004	40	-111	USFS		x	Springville
32012	40	-111	USFS		x	Springville
32014	40	-111	USFS		x	Springville
32015	40	-111	USFS		x	Springville
32016	40	-111	USFS		x	Springville
32017	40	-111	USFS		x	Springville
32018	40	-111	USFS		x	Springville
32019	40	-111	USFS		x	Springville
32030	40	-111	USFS		x	Springville
32031	40	-111	USFS		x	Springville
32032	40	-111	USFS		x	Springville
32033	40	-111	USFS		x	Springville
32034	40	-111	USFS		x	Springville
32041	40	-111	USFS		x	Springville
32042	40	-111	USFS		x	Springville
32049	40	-111	USFS		x	Heber City
32050	40	-111	USFS		x	Heber City

ID	Lat	Lon	Agency	Electric	Free	Locale
32087	40	-111	USFS		x	Heber City
32088	40	-111	USFS		x	Heber City
32089	40	-111	USFS		x	Heber City
32090	40	-111	USFS		x	Heber City
32101	40	-111	USFS		x	Heber City
32106	40	-111	USFS		x	Spanish Fork
32114	40	-111	USFS		x	Springville
32115	40	-111	USFS		x	Springville
32116	40	-111	USFS		x	Springville
32117	40	-111	USFS		x	Springville
32118	40	-111	USFS		x	Springville
32119	40	-111	USFS		x	Springville
32120	40	-111	USFS		x	Springville
32121	40	-111	USFS		x	Springville
32122	40	-111	USFS		x	Springville
32201	40	-111	USFS		x	Heber City
32202	40	-111	USFS		x	Heber City
32203	40	-111	USFS		x	Heber City
32204	40	-111	USFS		x	Heber City
32219	40	-111	USFS		x	Farmington
32226	40	-111	USFS		x	Charleston
32227	40	-111	USFS		x	Charleston
32228	40	-111	USFS		x	Charleston
32229	40	-111	USFS		x	Charleston
32230	40	-111	USFS		x	Charleston
32231	40	-111	USFS		x	Charleston
32237	40	-111	USFS		x	Woodland
32238	40	-111	USFS		x	Midway
32240	40	-111	USFS		x	Midway
32242	40	-111	USFS		x	Midway
32255	40	-111	USFS		x	Midway
32256	40	-111	USFS		x	Midway
32258	40	-111	USFS		x	Woodland
32262	40	-111	USFS		x	Midway
32264	40	-111	USFS		x	Midway
32265	40	-111	USFS		x	Midway
32266	40	-111	USFS		x	Midway
32269	40	-111	USFS		x	Woodland
32270	40	-111	USFS		x	Woodland
32299	40	-111	USFS		x	Charleston
32305	40	-111	USFS		x	Charleston

ID	Lat	Lon	Agency	Electric	Free	Locale
32306	40	-111	USFS		x	Springville
32312	40	-111	USFS		x	Charleston
32316	40	-111	USFS		x	Springville
32317	40	-111	USFS		x	Charleston
32355	40	-111	USFS		x	Heber City
32379	40	-111	USFS		x	Heber City
32381	40	-111	USFS		x	Heber City
32382	40	-111	USFS		x	Woodland
32397	40	-111	USFS		x	Heber City
32398	40	-111	USFS		x	Heber City
32401	40	-111	USFS		x	Heber City
32405	40	-111	USFS		x	Heber City
32421	40	-111	USFS		x	Heber City
32422	40	-111	USFS		x	Heber City
32423	40	-111	USFS		x	Heber City
32426	40	-111	USFS		x	Heber City
32429	40	-111	USFS		x	Heber City
32430	40	-111	USFS		x	Heber City
32431	40	-111	USFS		x	Heber City
32443	40	-111	USFS		x	Heber City
32452	40	-111	USFS		x	Springville
32462	40	-111	USFS		x	Woodland
32463	40	-111	USFS		x	Woodland
32468	40	-111	USFS		x	Springville
32489	40	-111	USFS		x	Midway
32490	40	-111	USFS		x	Midway
32492	40	-111	USFS		x	Pleasant Grove
32493	40	-111	USFS		x	Orem
32496	40	-111	USFS		x	Heber City
32497	40	-111	USFS		x	Heber City
32500	40	-111	USFS		x	Heber City
32501	40	-111	USFS		x	Heber City
32503	40	-111	USFS		x	Heber City
32563	40	-111	USFS		x	Heber City
32571	40	-111	USFS		x	Heber City
32573	40	-111	USFS		x	Heber City
32574	40	-111	USFS		x	Heber City
32585	40	-111	USFS		x	Woodland
32586	40	-111	USFS		x	Woodland
32595	40	-111	USFS		x	Oakley
32604	40	-111	USFS		x	Woodland
32605	40	-111	USFS		x	Woodland
32610	40	-111	USFS		x	Pleasant Grove
32612	40	-111	USFS		x	Midway
32613	40	-111	USFS		x	Midway
32614	40	-111	USFS		x	Kamas
32615	40	-111	USFS		x	Heber City
32616	40	-111	USFS		x	Woodland
32620	40	-111	USFS		x	Heber City
32625	40	-111	USFS		x	Spanish Fork
32626	40	-111	USFS		x	Spanish Fork
32633	40	-111	USFS		x	Springville
32634	40	-111	USFS		x	Heber City
32636	40	-111	USFS		x	Woodland
32639	40	-111	USFS		x	Charleston
32640	40	-111	USFS		x	Charleston
32643	40	-111	USFS		x	Oakley
32647	40	-111	USFS		x	Heber City
32653	40	-111	USFS		x	Heber City
32657	40	-111	USFS		x	Springville
32959	40	-111	USFS		x	Heber City
32983	40	-111	USFS		x	Heber City
32984	40	-111	USFS		x	Heber City
32985	40	-111	USFS		x	Heber City
32986	40	-111	USFS		x	Heber City
32995	40	-111	USFS		x	Heber City
32997	40	-111	USFS		x	Springville
32999	40	-111	USFS		x	Heber City
33015	40	-111	USFS		x	Spanish Fork
33016	40	-111	USFS		x	Spanish Fork
33077	40	-111	USFS		x	Woodland
33132	40	-111	USFS		x	Woodland
33145	40	-111	USFS		x	Heber City
33150	40	-111	USFS		x	Cedar Hills
33151	40	-111	USFS		x	Cedar Hills
33166	40	-111	USFS		x	Woodland
33175	40	-111	USFS		x	Orem
33176	40	-111	USFS		x	Springville
33177	40	-111	USFS		x	Springville
33184	40	-111	USFS		x	Heber City
33192	40	-111	USFS		x	Springville
33195	40	-111	USFS		x	Springville

ID	Lat	Lon	Agency	Electric	Free	Locale
33207	40	-111	USFS		x	Springville
33208	40	-111	USFS		x	Springville
33209	40	-111	USFS		x	Springville
33210	40	-111	USFS		x	Springville
33211	40	-111	USFS		x	Springville
33214	40	-111	USFS		x	Springville
33224	40	-111	USFS		x	Springville
33230	40	-111	USFS		x	Spanish Fork
33233	40	-111	USFS		x	Spanish Fork
33242	40	-111	USFS		x	Springville
33243	40	-111	USFS		x	Springville
33244	40	-111	USFS		x	Springville
33245	40	-111	USFS		x	Springville
33246	40	-111	USFS		x	Springville
33247	40	-111	USFS		x	Springville
33248	40	-111	USFS		x	Springville
33249	40	-111	USFS		x	Charleston
33256	40	-111	USFS		x	Heber City
33257	40	-111	USFS		x	Heber City
33258	40	-111	USFS		x	Heber City
33261	40	-111	USFS		x	Heber City
33267	40	-111	USFS		x	Orem
33268	40	-111	USFS		x	Orem
33284	40	-111	USFS		x	Farmington
33285	40	-111	USFS		x	Farmington
33286	40	-111	USFS		x	Farmington
33287	40	-111	USFS		x	Farmington
33289	40	-111	USFS		x	Woodland
33301	40	-111	USFS		x	Heber City
33302	40	-111	USFS		x	Heber City
33303	40	-111	USFS		x	Oakley
33311	40	-111	USFS		x	Woodland
33381	40	-111	USFS			Cedar Hills
33490	40	-111	USFS			Orem
33525	40	-111	USFS			Wasatch
33526	40	-111	ST	x		Heber City
33527	40	-111	ST			Heber City
33528	40	-111	ST			Heber City
33529	40	-111	ST			Heber City
33569	40	-111	USFS			Oakley
33578	40	-111	USFS			American Forks
33589	40	-111	USFS			Heber City
33604	40	-111	USFS		x	Kamas
33610	40	-111	USFS			Kamas
33647	40	-111	USFS			Woodland
33663	40	-111	USFS			Orem
33693	40	-111	CP			Orem
33727	40	-111	USFS		x	Kamas
33728	40	-111	USFS			Kamas
33744	40	-111	USFS			Kamas
33761	40	-111	USFS			Murray
33762	40	-111	USFS			Heber City
33768	40	-111	USFS			Heber City
33771	40	-111	ST			Peoa
33772	40	-111	ST			Peoa
33773	40	-111	ST			Peoa
33774	40	-111	ST	x		Peoa
33775	40	-111	ST			Peoa
33776	40	-111	ST			Peoa
33777	40	-111	ST			Peoa
33894	40	-111	USFS		x	Mapleton
33899	40	-111	USFS			Kamas
33903	40	-111	USFS			Kamas
33908	40	-111	USFS			Oakley
33913	40	-111	USFS			Kamas
33914	40	-111	USFS			Heber City
33915	40	-111	USFS		x	Charleston
33922	40	-111	CP			Spanish Fork
33923	40	-111	MU			Spanish Fork
33934	40	-111	USFS			Salt Lake City
33941	40	-111	USFS			Provo
33942	40	-111	USFS			Provo
33943	40	-111	USFS	x		Provo
33944	40	-111	USFS			Provo
33953	40	-111	USFS			Sandy
33956	40	-111	USFS			Kamas
33966	40	-111	USFS			Orem
33968	40	-111	USFS			American Forks
33982	40	-111	USFS		x	Thistle
34007	40	-111	ST	x		Provo
34017	40	-111	ST	x		Midway
34018	40	-111	ST			Midway

ID	Lat	Lon	Agency	Electric	Free	Locale
34019	40	-111	ST	x		Midway
34020	40	-111	ST	x		Midway
34029	40	-111	USFS			Mapleton
34037	40	-111	CP			Lehi
34047	40	-111	USFS			Heber City
34053	40	-111	USFS			Kamas
30896	40	-110	USFS			Hanna
30917	40	-110	USFS			Evanston
30919	40	-110	USFS			Evanston
30946	40	-110	USFS			Altamont
30951	40	-110	USFS			Mountain View
30974	40	-110	USFS			Kamas
31033	40	-110	USFS			Mountain View
31034	40	-110	USFS			Mountain View
31035	40	-110	USFS			Evanston
31045	40	-110	USFS			Kamas
31127	40	-110	CP		x	Duchesne
31128	40	-110	USFS			Kamas
31135	40	-110	USFS			Evanston
31136	40	-110	USFS		x	Mountain View
31156	40	-110	ST			Duchesne
31157	40	-110	ST			Duchesne
31158	40	-110	ST			Duchesne
31159	40	-110	ST	x		Duchesne
31160	40	-110	ST			Duchesne
31161	40	-110	ST			Duchesne
31316	40	-110	USFS		x	Manila
31322	40	-110	USFS		x	Mountain View WY
31330	40	-110	USFS		x	Mountain View WY
31402	40	-110	USFS		x	Oakley
31403	40	-110	USFS		x	Oakley
31450	40	-110	USFS		x	Oakley
31451	40	-110	USFS		x	Oakley
31452	40	-110	USFS		x	Oakley
31453	40	-110	USFS		x	Oakley
31454	40	-110	USFS		x	Oakley
31455	40	-110	USFS		x	Oakley
31456	40	-110	USFS		x	Oakley
31469	40	-110	USFS		x	Mountain View WY
31494	40	-110	USFS		x	Heber City
31551	40	-110	USFS		x	Oakley

ID	Lat	Lon	Agency	Electric	Free	Locale
31560	40	-110	USFS		x	Oakley
31561	40	-110	USFS		x	Oakley
31562	40	-110	USFS		x	Oakley
31563	40	-110	USFS		x	Oakley
31564	40	-110	USFS		x	Oakley
31580	40	-110	USFS		x	Oakley
31581	40	-110	USFS		x	Oakley
31591	40	-110	USFS		x	Oakley
31592	40	-110	USFS		x	Oakley
31593	40	-110	USFS		x	Oakley
31598	40	-110	USFS		x	Oakley
31601	40	-110	USFS		x	Oakley
31602	40	-110	USFS		x	Oakley
31603	40	-110	USFS		x	Oakley
31613	40	-110	USFS		x	Oakley
31641	40	-110	USFS		x	Oakley
31647	40	-110	USFS		x	Mountain View WY
31648	40	-110	USFS		x	Mountain View WY
31649	40	-110	USFS		x	Mountain View WY
31650	40	-110	USFS		x	Mountain View WY
31653	40	-110	USFS		x	Oakley
31654	40	-110	USFS		x	Mountain View WY
31672	40	-110	USFS		x	Mountain View WY
31687	40	-110	USFS		x	Mountain View WY
31688	40	-110	USFS		x	Mountain View WY
31719	40	-110	USFS		x	Oakley
31741	40	-110	USFS		x	Oakley
31749	40	-110	USFS		x	Mountain View WY
31758	40	-110	USFS		x	Woodland
31759	40	-110	USFS		x	Woodland
31767	40	-110	USFS		x	Oakley
31853	40	-110	USFS		x	Oakley
31866	40	-110	USFS		x	Oakley
31867	40	-110	USFS		x	Oakley
31869	40	-110	USFS		x	Oakley
31870	40	-110	USFS		x	Oakley
31873	40	-110	USFS		x	Oakley
31874	40	-110	USFS		x	Oakley
31883	40	-110	USFS		x	Oakley
31884	40	-110	USFS		x	Oakley
31885	40	-110	USFS		x	Oakley

ID	Lat	Lon	Agency	Electric	Free	Locale
31895	40	-110	USFS		x	Oakley
31903	40	-110	USFS		x	Oakley
31920	40	-110	USFS		x	Whiterocks
31921	40	-110	USFS		x	Oakley
31925	40	-110	USFS		x	Oakley
31932	40	-110	USFS		x	Whiterocks
31933	40	-110	USFS		x	Whiterocks
31935	40	-110	USFS		x	Whiterocks
31940	40	-110	USFS		x	Whiterocks
31941	40	-110	USFS		x	Whiterocks
31947	40	-110	USFS		x	Altamont
31948	40	-110	USFS		x	Oakley
31950	40	-110	USFS		x	Oakley
31951	40	-110	USFS		x	Oakley
31952	40	-110	USFS		x	Oakley
31962	40	-110	USFS		x	Mountain View WY
31964	40	-110	USFS		x	Altamont
31965	40	-110	USFS		x	Altamont
31966	40	-110	USFS		x	Oakley
31972	40	-110	USFS		x	Altamont
31982	40	-110	USFS		x	Mountain View WY
31983	40	-110	USFS		x	Mountain View WY
31985	40	-110	USFS		x	Mountain View WY
31988	40	-110	USFS		x	Mountain View WY
31989	40	-110	USFS		x	Oakley
31991	40	-110	USFS		x	Altamont
31992	40	-110	USFS		x	Mountain View WY
31993	40	-110	USFS		x	Altamont
31997	40	-110	USFS		x	Oakley
32023	40	-110	USFS		x	Hanna
32026	40	-110	USFS		x	Duchesne
32028	40	-110	USFS		x	Duchesne
32036	40	-110	USFS		x	Mountain Home
32037	40	-110	USFS		x	Mountain Home
32038	40	-110	USFS		x	Oakley
32043	40	-110	USFS		x	Oakley
32045	40	-110	USFS		x	Oakley
32051	40	-110	USFS		x	Oakley
32052	40	-110	USFS		x	Oakley
32053	40	-110	USFS		x	Oakley
32069	40	-110	USFS		x	Hanna

ID	Lat	Lon	Agency	Electric	Free	Locale
32078	40	-110	USFS		x	Oakley
32091	40	-110	USFS		x	Mountain Home
32092	40	-110	USFS		x	Mountain Home
32093	40	-110	USFS		x	Oakley
32097	40	-110	USFS		x	Hanna
32104	40	-110	USFS		x	Oakley
32111	40	-110	USFS		x	Duchesne
32112	40	-110	USFS		x	Duchesne
32113	40	-110	USFS		x	Oakley
32124	40	-110	USFS		x	Woodland
32145	40	-110	USFS		x	Mountain View WY
32146	40	-110	USFS		x	Oakley
32147	40	-110	USFS		x	Oakley
32150	40	-110	USFS		x	Oakley
32154	40	-110	USFS		x	Oakley
32163	40	-110	USFS		x	Oakley
32164	40	-110	USFS		x	Mountain View WY
32165	40	-110	USFS		x	Mountain View WY
32166	40	-110	USFS		x	Mountain View WY
32167	40	-110	USFS		x	Mountain View WY
32179	40	-110	USFS		x	Duchesne
32200	40	-110	USFS		x	Hanna
32205	40	-110	USFS		x	Hanna
32206	40	-110	USFS		x	Heber City
32207	40	-110	USFS		x	Heber City
32208	40	-110	USFS		x	Heber City
32209	40	-110	USFS		x	Heber City
32210	40	-110	USFS		x	Heber City
32211	40	-110	USFS		x	Heber City
32212	40	-110	USFS		x	Heber City
32232	40	-110	USFS		x	Hanna
32243	40	-110	USFS		x	Altamont
32247	40	-110	USFS		x	Mountain View WY
32259	40	-110	USFS		x	Altamont
32263	40	-110	USFS		x	Hanna
32303	40	-110	USFS		x	Whiterocks
32311	40	-110	USFS		x	Hanna
32315	40	-110	USFS		x	Mountain View WY
32322	40	-110	USFS		x	Manila
32328	40	-110	USFS		x	Altamont
32329	40	-110	USFS		x	Altamont

ID	Lat	Lon	Agency	Electric	Free	Locale
32330	40	-110	USFS		x	Altamont
32343	40	-110	USFS		x	Altamont
32344	40	-110	USFS		x	Altamont
32345	40	-110	USFS		x	Altamont
32346	40	-110	USFS		x	Altamont
32347	40	-110	USFS		x	Altamont
32380	40	-110	USFS		x	Duchesne
32419	40	-110	USFS		x	Woodland
32435	40	-110	USFS		x	Altamont
32447	40	-110	USFS		x	Whiterocks
32448	40	-110	USFS		x	Whiterocks
32453	40	-110	USFS		x	Whiterocks
32464	40	-110	USFS		x	Woodland
32465	40	-110	USFS		x	Woodland
32466	40	-110	USFS		x	Whiterocks
32467	40	-110	USFS		x	Oakley
32473	40	-110	USFS		x	Oakley
32474	40	-110	USFS		x	Oakley
32475	40	-110	USFS		x	Oakley
32484	40	-110	USFS		x	Oakley
32486	40	-110	USFS		x	Hanna
32498	40	-110	USFS		x	Oakley
32515	40	-110	USFS		x	Oakley
32524	40	-110	USFS		x	Oakley
32526	40	-110	USFS		x	Whiterocks
32527	40	-110	USFS		x	Oakley
32535	40	-110	USFS		x	Whiterocks
32540	40	-110	USFS		x	Whiterocks
32543	40	-110	USFS		x	Whiterocks
32544	40	-110	USFS		x	Whiterocks
32545	40	-110	USFS		x	Duchesne
32546	40	-110	USFS		x	Whiterocks
32548	40	-110	USFS		x	Whiterocks
32553	40	-110	USFS		x	Altamont
32561	40	-110	USFS		x	Oakley
32562	40	-110	USFS		x	Oakley
32564	40	-110	USFS		x	Oakley
32565	40	-110	USFS		x	Oakley
32566	40	-110	USFS		x	Evanston
32568	40	-110	USFS		x	Oakley
32572	40	-110	USFS		x	Oakley
32575	40	-110	USFS		x	Oakley
32579	40	-110	USFS		x	Mountain View WY
32583	40	-110	USFS		x	Altamont
32588	40	-110	USFS		x	Altamont
32597	40	-110	USFS		x	Mountain View WY
32598	40	-110	USFS		x	Oakley
32599	40	-110	USFS		x	Mountain View WY
32600	40	-110	USFS		x	Mountain View WY
32601	40	-110	USFS		x	Hanna
32603	40	-110	USFS		x	Woodland
32606	40	-110	USFS		x	Woodland
32607	40	-110	USFS		x	Woodland
32611	40	-110	USFS		x	Oakley
32624	40	-110	USFS		x	Whiterocks
32628	40	-110	USFS		x	Hanna
32629	40	-110	USFS		x	Hanna
32650	40	-110	USFS		x	Mountain Home
33033	40	-110	USFS		x	Oakley
33055	40	-110	USFS		x	Oakley
33136	40	-110	USFS		x	Woodland
33139	40	-110	USFS		x	Woodland
33140	40	-110	USFS		x	Woodland
33152	40	-110	USFS		x	Mountain View WY
33165	40	-110	USFS		x	Mountain View WY
33167	40	-110	USFS		x	Mountain View WY
33191	40	-110	USFS		x	Oakley
33193	40	-110	USFS		x	Oakley
33199	40	-110	USFS		x	Oakley
33202	40	-110	USFS		x	Oakley
33204	40	-110	USFS		x	Oakley
33206	40	-110	USFS		x	Mountain Home
33212	40	-110	USFS		x	Oakley
33215	40	-110	USFS		x	Oakley
33216	40	-110	USFS		x	Oakley
33217	40	-110	USFS		x	Oakley
33218	40	-110	USFS		x	Oakley
33219	40	-110	USFS		x	Oakley
33227	40	-110	USFS		x	Oakley
33231	40	-110	USFS		x	Altamont
33235	40	-110	USFS		x	Altamont
33253	40	-110	USFS		x	Mountain View WY

ID	Lat	Lon	Agency	Electric	Free	Locale
33262	40	-110	USFS		x	Evanston
33266	40	-110	USFS		x	Woodland
33281	40	-110	USFS		x	Mountain View WY
33282	40	-110	USFS		x	Oakley
33312	40	-110	USFS		x	Oakley
33313	40	-110	USFS		x	Oakley
33314	40	-110	USFS		x	Oakley
33315	40	-110	USFS		x	Oakley
33317	40	-110	USFS		x	Oakley
33318	40	-110	USFS		x	Oakley
33319	40	-110	USFS		x	Oakley
33320	40	-110	USFS		x	Oakley
33321	40	-110	USFS		x	Oakley
33322	40	-110	USFS		x	Oakley
33323	40	-110	USFS		x	Oakley
33326	40	-110	USFS		x	Oakley
33327	40	-110	USFS		x	Woodland
33466	40	-110	USFS			Hanna
33481	40	-110	USFS			Evanston
33482	40	-110	USFS		x	Mountain View WY
33483	40	-110	USFS		x	Mountain View WY
33489	40	-110	USFS			Mountain View WY
33518	40	-110	USFS			Hanna
33519	40	-110	USFS		x	Fruitland
33559	40	-110	ST		x	Duchesne
33572	40	-110	USFS			Kamas
33577	40	-110	USFS			Mountain View WY
33601	40	-110	USFS			Kamas
33613	40	-110	USFS		x	Mountain View
33631	40	-110	USFS			Mountain View
33646	40	-110	USFS		x	Hanna
33651	40	-110	USFS			Duchesne
33654	40	-110	USFS			Kamas
33657	40	-110	USFS			Duchesne
33658	40	-110	USFS			Duchesne
33660	40	-110	USFS			Kamas
33669	40	-110	USFS		x	Kamas
33670	40	-110	USFS		x	Oakley
33741	40	-110	USFS		x	Whiterocks
33742	40	-110	USFS			Whiterocks
33763	40	-110	USFS			Roosevelt

ID	Lat	Lon	Agency	Electric	Free	Locale
33766	40	-110	USFS			Altonah
33770	40	-110	USFS			Duchesne
33924	40	-110	USFS			Manila
33925	40	-110	USFS		x	Hanna
33938	40	-110	USFS			Mountain View
33940	40	-110	USFS			Evanston
33946	40	-110	USFS			Evanston WY
33952	40	-110	USFS			Altamont
33972	40	-110	USFS			Kamas
33979	40	-110	USFS			Roosevelt
33981	40	-110	USFS			Roosevelt
33989	40	-110	USFS		x	Defas Park
33991	40	-110	USFS			Mountain Home
34014	40	-110	USFS			Roosevelt
34021	40	-110	USFS			Kamas
34022	40	-110	USFS			Oakley
34024	40	-110	USFS			Mountain View
34048	40	-110	USFS			Peoa
34049	40	-110	USFS		x	Evanston
34052	40	-110	USFS			Mountain Home
34056	40	-110	USFS			Mountain Home
30883	40	-109	USFS		x	Vernal
30888	40	-109	USFS			Dutch John
30894	40	-109	USFS			Vernal
30900	40	-109	USFS		x	Manila
30947	40	-109	BLM			Vernal
30948	40	-109	BLM		x	Vernal
30954	40	-109	USFS			Flaming Gorge
30976	40	-109	ST		x	Vernal
30977	40	-109	USFS			Dutch John
31023	40	-109	USFS			Manila
31026	40	-109	USFS			Dutch John
31030	40	-109	USFS			Dutch John
31041	40	-109	BLM		x	Vernal
31104	40	-109	USFS			Manila
31108	40	-109	USFS			Dutch John
31115	40	-109	NP		x	Naples
31116	40	-109	NP			Jensen
31117	40	-109	NP			Jensen
31118	40	-109	NP			Jensen
31123	40	-109	USFS			Dutch John

ID	Lat	Lon	Agency	Electric	Free	Locale
31137	40	-109	USFS			Vernal
31148	40	-109	USFS			Dutch John
31177	40	-109	USFS		x	Manila
31178	40	-109	USFS		x	Manila
31179	40	-109	USFS		x	Manila
31180	40	-109	USFS		x	Manila
31181	40	-109	USFS		x	Manila
31188	40	-109	USFS		x	Manila
31189	40	-109	USFS		x	Manila
31207	40	-109	USFS		x	Manila
31210	40	-109	USFS		x	Manila
31254	40	-109	USFS		x	Manila
31257	40	-109	USFS		x	Manila
31277	40	-109	USFS		x	Manila
31278	40	-109	USFS		x	Manila
31286	40	-109	USFS		x	Manila
31293	40	-109	USFS		x	Manila
31294	40	-109	USFS		x	Manila
31296	40	-109	USFS		x	Manila
31299	40	-109	USFS		x	Manila
31317	40	-109	USFS		x	Manila
31331	40	-109	USFS		x	Vernal
31332	40	-109	USFS		x	Vernal
31333	40	-109	USFS		x	Vernal
31334	40	-109	USFS		x	Vernal
31335	40	-109	USFS		x	Vernal
31336	40	-109	USFS		x	Vernal
31342	40	-109	USFS		x	Dutch John
31343	40	-109	USFS		x	Dutch John
31355	40	-109	USFS		x	Vernal
31356	40	-109	USFS		x	Vernal
31360	40	-109	USFS		x	Vernal
31361	40	-109	USFS		x	Vernal
31381	40	-109	USFS		x	Vernal
31384	40	-109	USFS		x	Vernal
31385	40	-109	USFS		x	Vernal
31386	40	-109	USFS		x	Vernal
31387	40	-109	USFS		x	Vernal
31388	40	-109	USFS		x	Vernal
31389	40	-109	USFS		x	Vernal
31441	40	-109	USFS		x	Vernal
31460	40	-109	USFS		x	Vernal
31461	40	-109	USFS		x	Vernal
31462	40	-109	USFS		x	Vernal
31492	40	-109	USFS		x	Dutch John
31493	40	-109	USFS		x	Dutch John
31565	40	-109	USFS		x	Manila
31566	40	-109	USFS		x	Vernal
31583	40	-109	USFS		x	Vernal
31584	40	-109	USFS		x	Vernal
31597	40	-109	USFS		x	Red Canyon
31624	40	-109	USFS		x	Vernal
31791	40	-109	USFS		x	Manila
31801	40	-109	USFS		x	Manila
31835	40	-109	USFS		x	Vernal
31836	40	-109	USFS		x	Vernal
31837	40	-109	USFS		x	Vernal
31838	40	-109	USFS		x	Vernal
31839	40	-109	USFS		x	Vernal
31840	40	-109	USFS		x	Vernal
31934	40	-109	USFS		x	Whiterocks
32239	40	-109	USFS		x	Manila
32289	40	-109	USFS		x	Manila
32295	40	-109	USFS		x	Manila
32314	40	-109	USFS		x	Manila
32319	40	-109	USFS		x	Manila
32320	40	-109	USFS		x	Manila
32321	40	-109	USFS		x	Manila
32335	40	-109	USFS		x	Manila
32351	40	-109	USFS		x	Vernal
32352	40	-109	USFS		x	Vernal
32413	40	-109	USFS		x	Dutch John
32454	40	-109	USFS		x	Vernal
32455	40	-109	USFS		x	Vernal
32471	40	-109	USFS		x	Dutch John
32488	40	-109	USFS		x	Manila
32522	40	-109	USFS		x	Manila
32621	40	-109	USFS		x	Vernal
32622	40	-109	USFS		x	Vernal
32623	40	-109	USFS		x	Vernal
32654	40	-109	USFS		x	Vernal
32655	40	-109	USFS		x	Vernal

ID	Lat	Lon	Agency	Electric	Free	Locale
32993	40	-109	USFS		x	Manila
32994	40	-109	USFS		x	Manila
32998	40	-109	USFS		x	Vernal
33042	40	-109	USFS		x	Manila
33049	40	-109	USFS		x	Manila
33078	40	-109	USFS		x	Manila
33079	40	-109	USFS		x	Manila
33080	40	-109	USFS		x	Manila
33081	40	-109	USFS		x	Manila
33082	40	-109	USFS		x	Manila
33083	40	-109	USFS		x	Manila
33084	40	-109	USFS		x	Manila
33085	40	-109	USFS		x	Manila
33097	40	-109	USFS		x	Dutch John
33098	40	-109	USFS		x	Dutch John
33127	40	-109	USFS		x	Manila
33153	40	-109	USFS		x	Manila
33154	40	-109	USFS		x	Manila
33158	40	-109	USFS		x	Manila
33159	40	-109	USFS		x	Manila
33172	40	-109	USFS		x	Manila
33174	40	-109	USFS		x	Manila
33178	40	-109	USFS		x	Manila
33183	40	-109	USFS		x	Manila
33188	40	-109	USFS		x	Manila
33189	40	-109	USFS		x	Manila
33190	40	-109	USFS		x	Manila
33194	40	-109	USFS		x	Manila
33196	40	-109	USFS		x	Manila
33200	40	-109	USFS		x	Manila
33201	40	-109	USFS		x	Manila
33234	40	-109	USFS		x	Manila
33254	40	-109	USFS		x	Vernal
33263	40	-109	USFS		x	Vernal
33264	40	-109	USFS		x	Vernal
33265	40	-109	USFS		x	Vernal
33272	40	-109	USFS		x	Vernal
33273	40	-109	USFS		x	Vernal
33274	40	-109	USFS		x	Dutch John
33275	40	-109	USFS		x	Vernal
33283	40	-109	USFS		x	Manila
33288	40	-109	USFS		x	Manila
33307	40	-109	USFS		x	Manila
33308	40	-109	USFS		x	Manila
33310	40	-109	USFS		x	Red Canyon
33384	40	-109	USFS		x	Dinosaur CO
33385	40	-109	USFS		x	Naples
33387	40	-109	USFS			Dutch John
33388	40	-109	BLM			Jensen
33389	40	-109	USFS			Dutch John
33391	40	-109	USFS			Dutch John
33404	40	-109	USFS			Dutch John
33407	40	-109	USFS			Dutch John
33409	40	-109	BLM			Dinosaur CO
33410	40	-109	USFS			Dutch John
33416	40	-109	USFS			Dutch John
33417	40	-109	BLM			Jensen
33419	40	-109	USFS			Dutch John
33433	40	-109	USFS			Dutch John
33436	40	-109	USFS			Dutch John
33439	40	-109	USFS			Dutch John
33446	40	-109	USFS			Dutch John
33447	40	-109	BLM			Jensen
33451	40	-109	USFS			Dutch John
33452	40	-109	USFS			Dutch John
33456	40	-109	BLM		x	Vernal
33458	40	-109	USFS			Dutch John
33459	40	-109	USFS			Dutch John
33460	40	-109	USFS			Dutch John
33461	40	-109	USFS		x	Dutch John
33465	40	-109	USFS		x	Vernal
33484	40	-109	USFS			Manila
33515	40	-109	BLM			Vernal
33521	40	-109	USFS			Dutch John
33530	40	-109	USFS		x	Vernal
33532	40	-109	USFS		x	Vernal
33534	40	-109	USFS		x	Vernal
33538	40	-109	USFS			Manila
33590	40	-109	USFS			Dutch John
33595	40	-109	USFS		x	Vernal
33596	40	-109	USFS		x	Manila
33611	40	-109	USFS	x		Manila

ID	Lat	Lon	Agency	Electric	Free	Locale
33623	40	-109	USFS			Manila
33633	40	-109	USFS		x	Vernal
33671	40	-109	USFS			Dutch John
33689	40	-109	USFS		x	Vernal
33690	40	-109	USFS			Vernal
33699	40	-109	USFS		x	Vernal
33702	40	-109	USFS		x	Vernal
33715	40	-109	USFS			Lapoint
33722	40	-109	BLM		x	Vernal
33752	40	-109	USFS		x	Vernal
33757	40	-109	USFS			Dutch John
33760	40	-109	ST	x		Vernal
33901	40	-109	USFS			Manila
33902	40	-109	USFS		x	Flaming Gorge
33907	40	-109	USFS			Dutch John
33918	40	-109	USFS		x	Mountain Home
33939	40	-109	ST	x		Vernal
33998	40	-109	USFS		x	Manila
33999	40	-109	USFS		x	Manila
34000	40	-109	USFS		x	Manila
34001	40	-109	USFS		x	Manila
34028	40	-109	USFS			Whiterocks
34041	40	-109	USFS			Manila
34043	40	-109	USFS		x	Vernal
33462	41	-113	MU			Grouse Creek
33516	41	-113	BLM		x	Grouse Creek
30889	41	-112	ST			Ogden
30890	41	-112	ST			Ogden
30891	41	-112	ST			Ogden
31740	41	-112	USFS		x	Mendon
34032	41	-112	ST	x		Willard
34033	41	-112	ST	x		Willard
34034	41	-112	ST			Willard
30886	41	-111	USFS			Ogden
30911	41	-111	ST	x		Garden City
30912	41	-111	ST			Garden City
30913	41	-111	ST			Garden City
30915	41	-111	ST			Garden City
30916	41	-111	ST			Garden City
30927	41	-111	BLM		x	Woodruff
30940	41	-111	USFS			Ogden

ID	Lat	Lon	Agency	Electric	Free	Locale
30943	41	-111	USFS			Brigham City
30949	41	-111	USFS			Logan
31095	41	-111	BLM		x	Randolph
31154	41	-111	CP			Ogden
31171	41	-111	USFS			Logan
31172	41	-111	USFS		x	Garden City
31206	41	-111	USFS		x	Garden City
31209	41	-111	USFS		x	Garden City
31212	41	-111	USFS		x	Garden City
31220	41	-111	USFS		x	Garden City
31222	41	-111	USFS		x	Garden City
31223	41	-111	USFS		x	Garden City
31224	41	-111	USFS		x	Garden City
31225	41	-111	USFS		x	Garden City
31226	41	-111	USFS		x	Garden City
31240	41	-111	USFS		x	Garden City
31242	41	-111	USFS		x	Garden City
31244	41	-111	USFS		x	Logan
31247	41	-111	USFS		x	Logan
31249	41	-111	USFS		x	Logan
31252	41	-111	USFS		x	Logan
31255	41	-111	USFS		x	Logan
31258	41	-111	USFS		x	Logan
31260	41	-111	USFS		x	Logan
31261	41	-111	USFS		x	Logan
31262	41	-111	USFS		x	Logan
31267	41	-111	USFS		x	Logan
31281	41	-111	USFS		x	Garden City
31283	41	-111	USFS		x	Garden City
31287	41	-111	USFS		x	Garden City
31288	41	-111	USFS		x	Garden City
31289	41	-111	USFS		x	Garden City
31321	41	-111	USFS		x	Woodruff
31480	41	-111	USFS		x	Logan
31481	41	-111	USFS		x	Logan
31482	41	-111	USFS		x	Logan
31483	41	-111	USFS		x	Richmond
31484	41	-111	USFS		x	Richmond
31485	41	-111	USFS		x	Richmond
31488	41	-111	USFS		x	Smithfield
31514	41	-111	USFS		x	Logan

ID	Lat	Lon	Agency	Electric	Free	Locale
31520	41	-111	USFS		x	Logan
31523	41	-111	USFS		x	Logan
31530	41	-111	USFS		x	Garden City
31531	41	-111	USFS		x	Garden City
31532	41	-111	USFS		x	Garden City
31533	41	-111	USFS		x	Garden City
31534	41	-111	USFS		x	Garden City
31538	41	-111	USFS		x	Logan
31543	41	-111	USFS		x	Logan
31544	41	-111	USFS		x	Logan
31545	41	-111	USFS		x	Logan
31552	41	-111	USFS		x	Woodruff
31553	41	-111	USFS		x	Woodruff
31576	41	-111	USFS		x	Randolph
31577	41	-111	USFS		x	Woodruff
31578	41	-111	USFS		x	Woodruff
31579	41	-111	USFS		x	Woodruff
31585	41	-111	USFS		x	Randolph
31586	41	-111	USFS		x	Randolph
31587	41	-111	USFS		x	Randolph
31588	41	-111	USFS		x	Randolph
31610	41	-111	USFS		x	Woodruff
31611	41	-111	USFS		x	Woodruff
31612	41	-111	USFS		x	Woodruff
31616	41	-111	USFS		x	Woodruff
31618	41	-111	USFS		x	Woodruff
31619	41	-111	USFS		x	Woodruff
31620	41	-111	USFS		x	Woodruff
31621	41	-111	USFS		x	Woodruff
31622	41	-111	USFS		x	Woodruff
31623	41	-111	USFS		x	Woodruff
31640	41	-111	USFS		x	Woodruff
31643	41	-111	USFS		x	Woodruff
31644	41	-111	USFS		x	Woodruff
31645	41	-111	USFS		x	Woodruff
31646	41	-111	USFS		x	Woodruff
31651	41	-111	USFS		x	Woodruff
31652	41	-111	USFS		x	Woodruff
31679	41	-111	USFS		x	Logan
31680	41	-111	USFS		x	Logan
31681	41	-111	USFS		x	Logan

ID	Lat	Lon	Agency	Electric	Free	Locale
31691	41	-111	USFS		x	Logan
31703	41	-111	USFS		x	Woodruff
31705	41	-111	USFS		x	Woodruff
31706	41	-111	USFS		x	Woodruff
31707	41	-111	USFS		x	Woodruff
31708	41	-111	USFS		x	Woodruff
31709	41	-111	USFS		x	Woodruff
31720	41	-111	USFS		x	Woodruff
31721	41	-111	USFS		x	Woodruff
31722	41	-111	USFS		x	Woodruff
31723	41	-111	USFS		x	Woodruff
31724	41	-111	USFS		x	Woodruff
31725	41	-111	USFS		x	Woodruff
31739	41	-111	USFS		x	Mendon
31796	41	-111	USFS		x	Garden City
31844	41	-111	USFS		x	Logan
31845	41	-111	USFS		x	Logan
31846	41	-111	USFS		x	Logan
31847	41	-111	USFS		x	Hyrum
31848	41	-111	USFS		x	Hyrum
31854	41	-111	USFS		x	Garden City
31856	41	-111	USFS		x	Garden City
31904	41	-111	USFS		x	Woodruff
31907	41	-111	USFS		x	Woodruff
32005	41	-111	USFS		x	Woodruff
32006	41	-111	USFS		x	Woodruff
32079	41	-111	USFS		x	Logan
32080	41	-111	USFS		x	Logan
32081	41	-111	USFS		x	Logan
32082	41	-111	USFS		x	Logan
32083	41	-111	USFS		x	Logan
32084	41	-111	USFS		x	Logan
32085	41	-111	USFS		x	Logan
32095	41	-111	USFS		x	Randolph
32098	41	-111	USFS		x	Hyrum
32099	41	-111	USFS		x	Hyrum
32100	41	-111	USFS		x	Hyrum
32102	41	-111	USFS		x	Logan
32103	41	-111	USFS		x	Logan
32105	41	-111	USFS		x	Logan
32108	41	-111	USFS		x	Hyrum

ID	Lat	Lon	Agency	Electric	Free	Locale
32129	41	-111	USFS		x	Logan
32130	41	-111	USFS		x	Logan
32151	41	-111	USFS		x	Logan
32156	41	-111	USFS		x	Randolph
32161	41	-111	USFS		x	Garden City
32177	41	-111	USFS		x	Logan
32178	41	-111	USFS		x	Millville
32183	41	-111	USFS		x	Logan
32190	41	-111	USFS		x	Logan
32194	41	-111	USFS		x	Garden City
32195	41	-111	USFS		x	Garden City
32196	41	-111	USFS		x	Garden City
32199	41	-111	USFS		x	Garden City
32214	41	-111	USFS		x	Garden City
32215	41	-111	USFS		x	Garden City
32236	41	-111	USFS		x	Logan
32246	41	-111	USFS		x	Woodruff
32250	41	-111	USFS		x	Randolph
32251	41	-111	USFS		x	Randolph
32252	41	-111	USFS		x	Randolph
32257	41	-111	USFS		x	Woodruff
32268	41	-111	USFS		x	Woodruff
32276	41	-111	USFS		x	Randolph
32278	41	-111	USFS		x	Woodruff
32302	41	-111	USFS		x	Randolph
32308	41	-111	USFS		x	Randolph
32318	41	-111	USFS		x	Randolph
32324	41	-111	USFS		x	Woodruff
32339	41	-111	USFS		x	Hyrum
32340	41	-111	USFS		x	Hyrum
32341	41	-111	USFS		x	Hyrum
32358	41	-111	USFS		x	Garden City
32359	41	-111	USFS		x	Garden City
32360	41	-111	USFS		x	Garden City
32361	41	-111	USFS		x	Garden City
32383	41	-111	USFS		x	Hyrum
32384	41	-111	USFS		x	Hyrum
32385	41	-111	USFS		x	Hyrum
32386	41	-111	USFS		x	Hyrum
32387	41	-111	USFS		x	Hyrum
32388	41	-111	USFS		x	Hyrum

ID	Lat	Lon	Agency	Electric	Free	Locale
32389	41	-111	USFS		x	Hyrum
32390	41	-111	USFS		x	Hyrum
32391	41	-111	USFS		x	Hyrum
32392	41	-111	USFS		x	Hyrum
32393	41	-111	USFS		x	Hyrum
32394	41	-111	USFS		x	Hyrum
32395	41	-111	USFS		x	Hyrum
32396	41	-111	USFS		x	Hyrum
32406	41	-111	USFS		x	Garden City
32407	41	-111	USFS		x	Garden City
32409	41	-111	USFS		x	Garden City
32410	41	-111	USFS		x	Garden City
32418	41	-111	USFS		x	Farmington
32433	41	-111	USFS		x	Garden City
32434	41	-111	USFS		x	Garden City
32444	41	-111	USFS		x	Garden City
32445	41	-111	USFS		x	Garden City
32446	41	-111	USFS		x	Garden City
32520	41	-111	USFS		x	Garden City
33239	41	-111	USFS		x	Woodruff
33240	41	-111	USFS		x	Randolph
33241	41	-111	USFS		x	Randolph
33250	41	-111	USFS		x	Woodruff
33251	41	-111	USFS		x	Woodruff
33252	41	-111	USFS		x	Woodruff
33255	41	-111	USFS		x	Woodruff
33260	41	-111	USFS		x	Woodruff
33463	41	-111	USFS			Logan
33485	41	-111	USFS		x	Logan
33487	41	-111	USFS		x	Huntsville
33511	41	-111	ST	x		Hyrum
33571	41	-111	USFS			Garden City
33576	41	-111	BLM			Randolph
33588	41	-111	USFS			Logan
33607	41	-111	USFS			Ogden
33615	41	-111	USFS			Ogden
33630	41	-111	USFS		x	Ogden
33655	41	-111	USFS			Woodruff
33664	41	-111	ST		x	Hyrum
33677	41	-111	BR		x	Newton
33682	41	-111	CP			Eden

ID	Lat	Lon	Agency	Electric	Free	Locale
33683	41	-111	CP			Eden
33684	41	-111	CP			Eden
33685	41	-111	CP			Eden
33686	41	-111	CP			Eden
33687	41	-111	CP			Eden
33688	41	-111	CP			Eden
33700	41	-111	CP		x	Eden
33723	41	-111	USFS			Ogden
33736	41	-111	USFS			Hyrum
33748	41	-111	USFS			Logan
33755	41	-111	USFS			Garden City
33909	41	-111	USFS			Heber City
33917	41	-111	USFS			Huntsville
33926	41	-111	USFS			Logan
33932	41	-111	USFS			Logan
33949	41	-111	USFS			Garden City
33970	41	-111	USFS			Logan
33986	41	-111	USFS			Ogden
34002	41	-111	USFS		x	Hyrum
34003	41	-111	USFS		x	Hyrum
34004	41	-111	USFS		x	Hyrum
34005	41	-111	USFS		x	Hyrum
34006	41	-111	USFS		x	Hyrum
34015	41	-111	ST		x	Hyrum
34023	41	-111	CP			Huntsville
34031	41	-111	USFS		x	Woodruff
34040	41	-111	USFS			Ogden
34050	41	-111	USFS			Logan
33637	41	-110	USFS			Mountain View
30914	42	-111	ST			Garden City

30879 • 2nd Left Hand Canyon - USFS
Dispersed sites, No water, Vault toilets, Tent & RV camping: Fee unk, CG closed through 2021 - fire damage, Elev: 6818ft/2078m, Nearest town: Parowan, Agency: USFS, GPS: 37.788273, -112.809117

30880 • Adelaide - USFS
Total sites: 10, RV sites: 10, Elec sites: 0, Central water, No RV dump, No showers, Flush toilets, Reservations not accepted, Open May-Sep, Tent & RV camping: $12, Reservable group site: $50, Elev: 5591ft/1704m, Tel: 435-743-5721, Nearest town: Kanosh, Agency: USFS, GPS: 38.753946, -112.364498

30881 • Albion Basin - USFS
Total sites: 19, RV sites: 19, Elec sites: 0, No water, No RV dump, No showers, Vault toilets, Reservations accepted, Open Jul-Sep, Tent & RV camping: $25, Stay limit: 7 days, Elev: 9442ft/2878m, Tel: 801-733-2660, Nearest town: Alta , Agency: USFS, GPS: 40.577881, -111.613525

30882 • Allred Point CP
Dispersed sites, Central water, No toilets, Tent & RV camping: Free, Elev: 7108ft/2167m, Nearest town: Loa, Agency: CP, GPS: 38.433086, -111.631621

30883 • Alma Taylor Lake Dispersed - USFS
Dispersed sites, No water, No toilets, Reservations not accepted, Open all year, Tent & RV camping: Free, Elev: 9008ft/2746m, Tel: 435-789-1181, Nearest town: Vernal, Agency: USFS, GPS: 40.642688, -109.704284

30884 • Altamont Group - USFS
Total sites: 1, Elec sites: 0, Central water, No RV dump, No showers, No toilets, Max length: 30ft, Reservations accepted, Open Jun-Sep, Group site: $255, Stay limit: 7 days, Elev: 7290ft/2222m, Tel: 801-785-3563, Nearest town: Orem, Agency: USFS, GPS: 40.434551, -111.634855

30885 • Amasa ATV Area - BLM
Dispersed sites, No water, Vault toilets, Tent & RV camping: Free, Elev: 6027ft/1837m, Tel: 435-743-3123, Nearest town: Delta, Agency: BLM, GPS: 39.141673, -113.307273

30886 • Anderson Cove - USFS
Total sites: 67, RV sites: 67, Elec sites: 0, Central water, RV dump, No showers, Vault toilets, Generator hours: 0600-2200, Reservations accepted, Open May-Oct, Tent & RV camping: $28, Group site: $255, Stay limit: 7 days, Elev: 4931ft/1503m, Tel: 801-745-3215, Nearest town: Ogden, Agency: USFS, GPS: 41.250184, -111.787519

30887 • Anderson Meadow - USFS
Total sites: 10, RV sites: 10, Elec sites: 0, Central water, No RV dump, No showers, Vault toilets, Reservations accepted, Open Jun-Sep, Tent & RV camping: $14, Elev: 9593ft/2924m, Tel: 435-438-2436, Nearest town: Beaver, Agency: USFS, GPS: 38.210649, -112.431714

30888 • Antelope Flat - USFS
Total sites: 46, RV sites: 46, Elec sites: 0, Potable water, RV dump, No showers, No toilets, Max length: 45ft, Reservations accepted, Open May-Sep, Tent & RV camping: $18, Group sites: $105-$120, Elev: 6083ft/1854m, Tel: 435-889-3000, Nearest town: Dutch John, Agency: USFS, GPS: 40.965164, -109.550618

30889 • Antelope Island SP - Bridger Bay
Total sites: 25, RV sites: 25, Elec sites: 0, Central water, RV dump, Showers, Flush toilets, Max length: 90ft, Reservations accepted, Open all year, Tent & RV camping: $20, Elev: 4239ft/1292m, Tel: 801-773-2941, Nearest town: Ogden, Agency: ST, GPS: 41.040103, -112.259208

30890 • Antelope Island SP - Ladyfinger
Total sites: 5, RV sites: 0, Elec sites: 0, Reservations accepted, Open all year, Tents only: $20, Elev: 4271ft/1302m, Tel: 801-773-2941, Nearest town: Ogden, Agency: ST, GPS: 41.058239, -112.249395

30891 • Antelope Island SP - White Rock Bay Group
Total sites: 20, RV sites: 20, Elec sites: 0, Reservations accepted, Open all year, Group site: $40, Elev: 4286ft/1306m, Tel: 801-773-2941, Nearest town: Ogden, Agency: ST, GPS: 41.023845, -112.239717

30892 • Anthony Flat TH - USFS
Dispersed sites, No water, Vault toilets, Tent & RV camping: Free, Elev: 7806ft/2379m, Tel: 435-896-9233, Nearest town: Salina, Agency: USFS, GPS: 38.991471, -111.636383

30893 • Arch Canyon/Comb Wash - BLM
Dispersed sites, No water, Vault toilets, Reservations not accepted, Open all year, Tent & RV camping: Free, Elev: 4845ft/1477m, Tel: 435-587-1500, Nearest town: Blanding, Agency: BLM, GPS: 37.507801, -109.655044

30894 • Arch Dam Group - USFS
Total sites: 3, Elec sites: 0, Central water, No RV dump, No showers, Vault toilets, Open May-Sep, Group site: $100, Elev: 6243ft/1903m, Tel: 435-889-3000, Nearest town: Vernal, Agency: USFS, GPS: 40.911831, -109.410075

30895 • Arches NP - Devils Garden CG
Total sites: 50, RV sites: 50, Elec sites: 0, Central water, No RV dump, No showers, Flush toilets, Max length: 30ft, Generator hours: 0800-1000/1600-2000, Reservations accepted, Open all year, Tent & RV camping: $25, Several group sites - $75-$250, Elev: 5243ft/1598m, Tel: 518-885-3639, Nearest town: Moab, Agency: NP, GPS: 38.775843, -109.588551

30896 • Aspen - USFS
Total sites: 29, RV sites: 29, Elec sites: 0, Central water, No RV dump, No showers, Vault toilets, Reservations accepted, Open May-Sep, Tent & RV camping: $10, Elev: 7169ft/2185m, Tel: 435-738-2482, Nearest town: Hanna, Agency: USFS, GPS: 40.49707, -110.846436

30897 • Aspen Grove - USFS
Total sites: 53, RV sites: 53, Elec sites: 1, Central water, No RV dump, No showers, Flush toilets, Reservations accepted, Open Jun-Oct, Tents: $23/RV's: $23-36, 1 FHU: $36, Stay limit: 7 days, Elev: 7779ft/2371m, Tel: 801-226-3564, Nearest town: Hanna, Agency: USFS, GPS: 40.120767, -111.036691

30898 • Atchee Ridge 1 - BLM
Dispersed sites, No water, No toilets, Tent & RV camping: Free, Elev: 7748ft/2362m, Nearest town: Bonanza, Agency: BLM, GPS: 39.660605, -109.096294

30899 • Atchee Ridge 2 - BLM
Dispersed sites, No water, No toilets, Tent & RV camping: Free, Elev: 7243ft/2208m, Nearest town: Bonanza, Agency: BLM, GPS: 39.706875, -109.143266

30900 • ATV Trail 166 Dispersed - USFS
Dispersed sites, No water, No toilets, Reservations not accepted, Open all year, Tents only: Free, Walk-to sites, Elev: 8491ft/2588m, Tel: 435-789-1181, Nearest town: Manila, Agency: USFS, GPS: 40.883845, -109.794428

30901 • Avintaquin - USFS
Total sites: 17, RV sites: 17, Elec sites: 0, No water, Vault toilets, Reservations accepted, Open Jun-Sep, Tent & RV camping: $5, Group site $20, Elev: 8983ft/2738m, Tel: 435-738-2482, Nearest town: Duchesne, Agency: USFS, GPS: 39.884033, -110.775879

30902 • Bailey S Lower Rd - BLM
Dispersed sites, No water, No toilets, Tent & RV camping: Free, Elev: 6099ft/1859m, Nearest town: Blanding, Agency: BLM, GPS: 37.522409, -109.748447

30903 • Baker Dam - BLM
Total sites: 16, RV sites: 16, Elec sites: 0, No water, Vault toilets, Max length: 25ft, Reservations not accepted, Open all year, Tent & RV camping: $6, Elev: 4954ft/1510m, Tel: 435-688-3200, Nearest town: St George, Agency: BLM, GPS: 37.378038, -113.643368

30904 • Balsam - USFS
Total sites: 25, RV sites: 12, Elec sites: 0, Central water, No RV dump, No showers, Vault toilets, Reservations accepted, Open May-Sep, Tent & RV camping: $23, Group site: $65-$220, Stay limit: 16 days, Elev: 6020ft/1835m, Tel: 801-226-3564, Nearest town: Springville, Agency: USFS, GPS: 40.198486, -111.4021

30905 • Barker Reservoir - USFS
Total sites: 13, RV sites: 13, Elec sites: 0, Central water, No RV dump, No showers, Vault toilets, Reservations accepted, Open May-Sep, Tent & RV camping: $11, FSR 149 is steep single-lane with switchbacks and turnouts, Elev: 9305ft/2836m, Tel: 435-826-5499, Nearest town: Escalante, Agency: USFS, GPS: 37.920443, -111.816583

30906 • Barker Reservoir Group G01 - USFS
Total sites: 1, RV sites: 1, Elec sites: 0, Central water, No RV dump, No showers, Vault toilets, Reservations accepted, Open May-Sep, Group site $50-$95, FSR 149 is steep single-lane with switchbacks and turnouts, Elev: 9375ft/2858m, Tel: 435-826-5499, Nearest town: Escalante, Agency: USFS, GPS: 37.919838, -111.819374

30907 • Barker Reservoir Group P01 - USFS
Total sites: 1, RV sites: 1, Elec sites: 0, Central water, No RV dump, No showers, Vault toilets, Reservations accepted, Open May-Sep, Group site $50-$95, FSR 149 is steep single-lane with switchbacks and turnouts, Elev: 9489ft/2892m, Tel: 435-826-5499, Nearest town: Escalante, Agency: USFS, GPS: 37.921992, -111.822646

30908 • Bea's Lewis Flat - BLM
Dispersed sites, No water, No toilets, Open all year, Tent & RV camping: Free, Elev: 6744ft/2056m, Nearest town: Torrey, Agency: BLM, GPS: 38.297556, -111.388149

30909 • Bear Canyon - USFS
Total sites: 6, RV sites: 6, Elec sites: 0, Central water, Flush toilets, Reservations not accepted, Open May-Oct, Tent & RV camping: $21, Reservable group sites: $75-$105, Non-potable water, Stay limit: 16 days, Elev: 6700ft/2042m, Tel: 801-798-3571, Nearest town: Payson, Agency: USFS, GPS: 39.787699, -111.731098

30910 • Bear Creek
Total sites: 29, RV sites: 29, Elec sites: 0, Water at site, No RV dump, No showers, No toilets, Reservations accepted, Open May-Sep, Tent & RV camping: $10, Elev: 6640ft/2024m, Tel: 435-381-3505, Nearest town: Huntington City, Agency: CP, GPS: 39.393206, -111.09901

30911 • Bear Lake SP - Birch (Rendezvouz Beach)
Total sites: 143, RV sites: 106, Elec sites: 106, Water at site, RV dump, Showers, Flush toilets, Max length: 80ft, Reservations accepted, Open May-Oct, Tents: $17-20/RV's: $25-28, FHU sites, Elev: 5928ft/1807m, Tel: 435-946-3343, Nearest town: Garden City, Agency: ST, GPS: 41.844879, -111.338744

30912 • Bear Lake SP - Cisco Beach
Dispersed sites, No water, Vault toilets, Reservations not accepted, Open all year, Tent & RV camping: $12-20, Elev: 5974ft/1821m, Tel: 435-946-3343, Nearest town: Garden City, Agency: ST, GPS: 41.946434, -111.278322

30913 • Bear Lake SP - First Point
Dispersed sites, No water, Vault toilets, Reservations not accepted, Open all year, Tent & RV camping: $12-20, Elev: 5942ft/1811m, Tel: 435-946-3343, Nearest town: Garden City, Agency: ST, GPS: 41.876175, -111.295911

30914 • Bear Lake SP - North Eden
Total sites: 6, RV sites: 6, Elec sites: 0, No water, Vault toilets, Reservations not accepted, Open May-Oct, Tent & RV camping: $15-20, Elev: 5942ft/1811m, Tel: 435-946-3343, Nearest town: Garden City, Agency: ST, GPS: 42.000698, -111.261428

30915 • Bear Lake SP - Rainbow Cove
Dispersed sites, No water, Vault toilets, Reservations not accepted, Open all year, Tent & RV camping: $12-20, 4 sites in winter: $12, Elev: 5968ft/1819m, Tel: 435-946-3343, Nearest town: Garden City, Agency: ST, GPS: 41.968397, -111.271806

30916 • Bear Lake SP - South Eden

Total sites: 23, RV sites: 23, Elec sites: 0, Water at site, No RV dump, No showers, Vault toilets, Max length: 35ft, Reservations accepted, Open May-Oct, Tent & RV camping: $18-25, Group sites: $100-$140, Elev: 5945ft/1812m, Tel: 435-946-3343, Nearest town: Garden City, Agency: ST, GPS: 41.930994, -111.283398

30917 • Bear River - USFS

Total sites: 4, RV sites: 4, Elec sites: 0, Central water, No RV dump, No showers, Vault toilets, Reservations not accepted, Open all year, Tent & RV camping: $18, No water in winter, Stay limit: 14 days, Elev: 8360ft/2548m, Tel: 307-789-3194, Nearest town: Evanston, Agency: USFS, GPS: 40.910239, -110.830246

30918 • Beaver Dam - USFS

Dispersed sites, No water, No toilets, Reservations not accepted, Tent & RV camping: Free, Elev: 7880ft/2402m, Nearest town: Huntington, Agency: USFS, GPS: 39.521369, -111.154072

30919 • Beaver View - USFS

Total sites: 17, RV sites: 17, Elec sites: 0, Central water, No RV dump, No showers, Vault toilets, Reservations not accepted, Tent & RV camping: $21, Elev: 8990ft/2740m, Tel: 307-789-3194, Nearest town: Evanston, Agency: USFS, GPS: 40.823828, -110.863135

30920 • Best Friends Animal Sanctuary

Total sites: 2, RV sites: 2, Elec sites: 2, Water at site, Reservations accepted, Open Mar-Oct, No tents/RV's: $30-50, 2 FHU, Elev: 5185ft/1580m, Tel: 435-644-2001, Nearest town: Kanab, Agency: PRIV, GPS: 37.113717, -112.546691

30921 • Big Bend - BLM

Total sites: 23, RV sites: 23, Elec sites: 0, No water, Vault toilets, Max length: 40ft, Reservations not accepted, Open all year, Tent & RV camping: $20, 3 group sites - $75, Stay limit: 14 days, Elev: 4014ft/1223m, Tel: 435-259-2100, Nearest town: Moab, Agency: BLM, GPS: 38.648707, -109.479982

30922 • Big Bend Creek - BLM

Dispersed sites, No water, Vault toilets, Reservations not accepted, Tents only: Free, Elev: 4078ft/1243m, Nearest town: Moab, Agency: BLM, GPS: 38.651913, -109.477491

30923 • Big Flat - USFS

Dispersed sites, No water, Vault toilets, Reservations not accepted, Tent & RV camping: Free, Drinking water is available at Big Flat Guard Station, Elev: 10223ft/3116m, Tel: 435-896-9233, Nearest town: Beaver, Agency: USFS, GPS: 38.284011, -112.353258

30924 • Big John Flat - USFS

Dispersed sites, No water, No toilets, Tent & RV camping: Free, Elev: 9965ft/3037m, Tel: 435-438-2436, Nearest town: Beaver, Agency: USFS, GPS: 38.343984, -112.400723

30925 • Big Lake - USFS

Dispersed sites, No water, No toilets, Tent & RV camping: Free, Elev: 9366ft/2855m, Tel: 435-896-9233, Nearest town: Glenwood, Agency: USFS, GPS: 38.651634, -111.964774

30926 • Big Rock Group - USFS

Dispersed sites, No water, Group site: $50, Elev: 7785ft/2373m, Tel: 435-637-2817, Nearest town: Huntington, Agency: USFS, GPS: 39.512574, -111.155524

30927 • Birch Creek - BLM

Dispersed sites, No water, Vault toilets, Reservations not accepted, Open May-Oct, Tent & RV camping: Free, Elev: 6929ft/2112m, Tel: 801-977-4300, Nearest town: Woodruff, Agency: BLM, GPS: 41.505868, -111.317264

30928 • Birch Creek - USFS

Total sites: 1, RV sites: 0, Elec sites: 0, No water, Vault toilets, Group site, Elev: 7868ft/2398m, Tel: 435-438-2436, Nearest town: Circleville, Agency: USFS, GPS: 38.174646, -112.362015

30929 • Bismarck Peak Dispersed - BLM

Dispersed sites, No water, No toilets, Reservations not accepted, Tent & RV camping: Free, Elev: 5744ft/1751m, Nearest town: Eureka, Agency: BLM, GPS: 40.051927, -112.120545

30930 • Black Canyon Pull-out #4 Dispersed - DWR

Dispersed sites, No water, No toilets, Reservations not accepted, Tents only: Free, Elev: 6887ft/2099m, Tel: 801-538-4700, Nearest town: Antimony, Agency: ST, GPS: 38.011581, -111.968604

30931 • Black Dragon Canyon Dispersed - BLM

Dispersed sites, No water, No toilets, Tent & RV camping: Free, Elev: 4323ft/1318m, Nearest town: Green River, Agency: BLM, GPS: 38.937449, -110.419039

30932 • Black Flat - USFS

Dispersed sites, No water, Vault toilets, Tent & RV camping: Free, Elev: 9409ft/2868m, Tel: 435-836-2800, Nearest town: Fremont, Agency: USFS, GPS: 38.678504, -111.596261

30933 • Blackhawk Group - USFS

Total sites: 20, Elec sites: 0, Central water, RV dump, No showers, Flush toilets, Reservation required, Open May-Sep, Group sites: $115-$220, Elev: 7979ft/2432m, Tel: 801-798-3571, Nearest town: Payson, Agency: USFS, GPS: 39.893133, -111.627899

30934 • Blackhawk Horse Camp - USFS

Total sites: 15, RV sites: 15, Elec sites: 0, Central water, RV dump, No showers, Flush toilets, Reservation required, Open May-Sep, Tent & RV camping: $23, Elev: 7864ft/2397m, Tel: 801-798-3571, Nearest town: Payson, Agency: USFS, GPS: 39.889477, -111.625858

30935 • Blue Mt - USFS

Dispersed sites, No water, No toilets, Tent & RV camping: Free, Elev: 8851ft/2698m, Nearest town: Monticello, Agency: USFS, GPS: 37.862258, -109.433294

30936 • Blue Notch Road - BLM

Dispersed sites, No water, No toilets, Tent & RV camping: Free, Elev: 4831ft/1472m, Nearest town: Bluff, Agency: BLM, GPS: 37.763527, -110.293623

30937 • Blue Spruce - USFS
Total sites: 6, RV sites: 4, Elec sites: 0, Central water, No RV dump, No showers, Vault toilets, Reservations not accepted, Open all year, Tent & RV camping: $9, Stay limit: 14 days, Elev: 7979ft/2432m, Tel: 435-826-5499, Nearest town: Escalante, Agency: USFS, GPS: 37.972745, -111.651841

30938 • Bonneville Salt Flats - BLM
Dispersed sites, No water, No toilets, Tent & RV camping: Free, Elev: 4285ft/1306m, Nearest town: Wendover, Agency: BLM, GPS: 40.771949, -113.981459

30939 • Book Cliffs Ridge - BLM
Dispersed sites, No water, No toilets, Tent & RV camping: Free, Numerous dispersed sites along road, Elev: 8417ft/2566m, Nearest town: Mack CO, Agency: BLM, GPS: 39.451047, -109.180469

30940 • Botts - USFS
Total sites: 8, RV sites: 8, Elec sites: 0, Central water, No RV dump, No showers, Vault toilets, Generator hours: 0800-2200, Reservations not accepted, Open May-Dec, Tent & RV camping: $23, Elev: 5282ft/1610m, Tel: 801-226-3564, Nearest town: Ogden, Agency: USFS, GPS: 41.278549, -111.657137

30941 • Bountiful Peak - USFS
Total sites: 43, RV sites: 43, Elec sites: 0, Potable water, No RV dump, No showers, Vault toilets, Max length: 24ft, Reservations not accepted, Tent & RV camping: $16, Stay limit: 7 days, Elev: 7526ft/2294m, Tel: 801-733-2660, Nearest town: Farmington, Agency: USFS, GPS: 40.979801, -111.804612

30942 • Bowery Creek - USFS
Total sites: 44, RV sites: 44, Elec sites: 0, Central water, RV dump, No showers, Flush toilets, Generator hours: 0600-2200, Reservations accepted, Open May-Sep, Tent & RV camping: $15, Group sites: $45, Stay limit: 10 days, Elev: 8924ft/2720m, Tel: 435-638-1069, Nearest town: Loa, Agency: USFS, GPS: 38.560547, -111.709961

30943 • Box Elder - USFS
Total sites: 25, RV sites: 20, Elec sites: 0, Central water, No RV dump, No showers, Flush toilets, Reservations accepted, Open May-Oct, Tent & RV camping: $22, 4 group sites $70-$180, Stay limit: 7 days, Elev: 5158ft/1572m, Tel: 435-755-3620, Nearest town: Brigham City, Agency: USFS, GPS: 41.494325, -111.950222

30944 • Boy Scout - USFS
Total sites: 8, RV sites: 8, Elec sites: 0, No water, No toilets, Reservations not accepted, Open May-Oct, Tent & RV camping: $14, 1 group site: $45, Stay limit: 7 days, Elev: 6532ft/1991m, Tel: 801-733-2660, Nearest town: Salt Lake City, Agency: USFS, GPS: 40.494091, -112.578581

30945 • Bride Canyon - BLM
Total sites: 6, RV sites: 6, Elec sites: 0, No water, No toilets, Reservations not accepted, Tent & RV camping: Free, Elev: 4874ft/1486m, Tel: 435-259-2100, Nearest town: Moab, Agency: BLM, GPS: 38.612017, -109.666318

30946 • Bridge - USFS
Total sites: 5, RV sites: 5, Elec sites: 0, Potable water, No RV dump, No showers, Vault toilets, Max length: 15ft, Open May-Sep, Tent & RV camping: $8, Elev: 7680ft/2341m, Nearest town: Altamont, Agency: USFS, GPS: 40.545594, -110.334169

30947 • Bridge Hollow - BLM
Total sites: 13, RV sites: 13, Elec sites: 0, Vault toilets, Reservations not accepted, Open all year, Tent & RV camping: $5, 1 group site, Elev: 5408ft/1648m, Tel: 435-781-4400, Nearest town: Vernal, Agency: BLM, GPS: 40.898667, -109.170169

30948 • Bridgeport - BLM
Dispersed sites, No water, No toilets, Max length: 18ft, Reservations not accepted, Tent & RV camping: Free, Elev: 5433ft/1656m, Tel: 435-781-4400, Nearest town: Vernal, Agency: BLM, GPS: 40.879303, -109.135604

30949 • Bridger - USFS
Total sites: 10, RV sites: 10, Elec sites: 0, Potable water, No RV dump, No showers, No toilets, Reservations not accepted, Open May-Sep, Tent & RV camping: $20, Stay limit: 7 days, Elev: 5158ft/1572m, Tel: 435-755-3620, Nearest town: Logan, Agency: USFS, GPS: 41.748047, -111.735352

30950 • Bridger Jack Mesa - BLM
Dispersed sites, No water, No toilets, Reservations not accepted, Open all year, Tent & RV camping: Free, Elev: 5287ft/1611m, Tel: 435-587-1500, Nearest town: Monticello, Agency: BLM, GPS: 38.086116, -109.594379

30951 • Bridger Lake - USFS
Total sites: 30, RV sites: 30, Elec sites: 0, No water, Vault toilets, Reservations accepted, Open Jun-Oct, Tent & RV camping: $21, Stay limit: 14 days, Elev: 9403ft/2866m, Tel: 307-789-3194, Nearest town: Mountain View, Agency: USFS, GPS: 40.964701, -110.387964

30952 • Bridges - USFS
Total sites: 4, RV sites: 4, Elec sites: 0, No water, Vault toilets, Open Jun-Sep, Tent & RV camping: $5, 2 group sites: $40-$50, Elev: 8251ft/2515m, Tel: 435-637-2817, Nearest town: Huntington, Agency: USFS, GPS: 39.561755, -111.174854

30953 • Brown's Hole TH - USFS
Dispersed sites, No water, Vault toilets, Reservations not accepted, Tent & RV camping: Free, Elev: 8871ft/2704m, Tel: 435-896-9233, Nearest town: Salina, Agency: USFS, GPS: 38.803083, -111.644773

30954 • Browne Lake - USFS
Total sites: 20, RV sites: 20, Elec sites: 0, No water, Vault toilets, Reservations not accepted, Open May-Sep, Tent & RV camping: $14, Reservable group site: $60, Elev: 8363ft/2549m, Tel: 435-784-3483, Nearest town: Flaming Gorge, Agency: USFS, GPS: 40.861164, -109.816312

30955 • Bryce Canyon NP - Corral Hollow

Dispersed sites, No water, No toilets, Reservations accepted, Tents only: $5, Hike-in, No open fires, Permit required, Elev: 7932ft/2418m, Tel: 435-834-5322, Nearest town: Bryce, Agency: NP, GPS: 37.465098, -112.234073

30956 • Bryce Canyon NP - Iron Spring

Dispersed sites, No water, No toilets, Reservations accepted, Tents only: $5, Hike-in, No open fires, Permit required, Elev: 7890ft/2405m, Tel: 435-834-5322, Nearest town: Bryce, Agency: NP, GPS: 37.490628, -112.243951

30957 • Bryce Canyon NP - Natural Bridge

Dispersed sites, No water, No toilets, Reservations accepted, Tents only: $5, Hike-in, No open fires, Permit required, Elev: 7549ft/2301m, Tel: 435-834-5322, Nearest town: Bryce, Agency: NP, GPS: 37.526791, -112.241177

30958 • Bryce Canyon NP - North CG

Total sites: 99, RV sites: 99, Elec sites: 0, Central water, RV dump, Pay showers, Flush toilets, Laundry, Generator hours: 0800-2000, Reservations not accepted, Open all year, Tents: $20/RV's: $30, $5 dump fee, Elev: 7976ft/2431m, Tel: 435-834-5322, Nearest town: Bryce Canyon, Agency: NP, GPS: 37.636153, -112.166055

30959 • Bryce Canyon NP - Riggs Spring

Dispersed sites, No water, No toilets, Reservations accepted, Tents only: $5, Hike-in, No open fires, Permit required, Elev: 7471ft/2277m, Tel: 435-834-5322, Nearest town: Bryce, Agency: NP, GPS: 37.450294, -112.240644

30960 • Bryce Canyon NP - Riggs Spring Group Site

Dispersed sites, No water, No toilets, Reservations accepted, Tents only: $5, Hike-in, No open fires, Permit required, Elev: 7429ft/2264m, Tel: 435-834-5322, Nearest town: Bryce, Agency: NP, GPS: 37.449407, -112.238225

30961 • Bryce Canyon NP - Right Fork Swamp Canyon

Dispersed sites, No water, No toilets, Reservations accepted, Tents only: $5, Hike-in, No open fires, Permit required, Elev: 7473ft/2278m, Tel: 435-834-5322, Nearest town: Bryce Canyon, Agency: NP, GPS: 37.576843, -112.212651

30962 • Bryce Canyon NP - Right Fork Yellow Creek

Dispersed sites, No water, No toilets, Reservations accepted, Tents only: $5, Hike-in, No open fires, Permit required, Elev: 7005ft/2135m, Tel: 435-834-5322, Nearest town: Bryce, Agency: NP, GPS: 37.588063, -112.147517

30963 • Bryce Canyon NP - Sheep Creek

Dispersed sites, No water, No toilets, Reservations accepted, Tents only: $5, Hike-in, No open fires, Permit required, Elev: 7256ft/2212m, Tel: 435-834-5322, Nearest town: Bryce, Agency: NP, GPS: 37.571928, -112.199575

30964 • Bryce Canyon NP - Sunset CG - Loop A

Total sites: 52, RV sites: 52, Elec sites: 0, Central water, No RV dump, No showers, Flush toilets, Max length: 45ft, Generator hours: 0800-2000, Reservations not accepted, Open Apr-Oct, No tents/RV's: $30, Elev: 8015ft/2443m, Tel: 435-834-5322, Nearest town: Bryce Canyon, Agency: NP, GPS: 37.622924, -112.173958

30965 • Bryce Canyon NP - Sunset CG - Loops B and C

Total sites: 52, Elec sites: 0, Central water, No RV dump, No showers, No toilets, Generators prohibited, Reservations accepted, Open Apr-Oct, Tents only: $20, Elev: 8045ft/2452m, Tel: 435-834-5322, Nearest town: Bryce Canyon, Agency: NP, GPS: 37.621403, -112.176138

30966 • Bryce Canyon NP - Swamp Canyon

Dispersed sites, No water, No toilets, Reservations accepted, Tents only: $5, Hike-in, No open fires, Permit required, Elev: 8214ft/2504m, Tel: 435-834-5322, Nearest town: Bryce Canyon, Agency: NP, GPS: 37.561203, -112.230075

30967 • Bryce Canyon NP - Yellow Creek

Dispersed sites, No water, No toilets, Reservations accepted, Tents only: $5, Hike-in, No open fires, Permit required, Elev: 7135ft/2175m, Tel: 435-834-5322, Nearest town: Bryce, Agency: NP, GPS: 37.584857, -112.162338

30968 • Bryce Canyon NP - Yellow Creek Group Site

Dispersed sites, No water, No toilets, Reservations accepted, Tents only: $5, Hike-in, No open fires, Permit required, Elev: 6822ft/2079m, Tel: 435-834-5322, Nearest town: Bryce, Agency: NP, GPS: 37.575349, -112.147475

30969 • Bryce Canyon NP - Yovimpa Pass

Dispersed sites, No water, No toilets, Reservations accepted, Tents only: $5, Hike-in, No open fires, Permit required, Elev: 8355ft/2547m, Tel: 435-834-5322, Nearest town: Bryce, Agency: NP, GPS: 37.462982, -112.257902

30970 • Bryson Canyon Dispersed - BLM

Dispersed sites, No water, No toilets, Reservations not accepted, No tents/RV's: Free, Elev: 5042ft/1537m, Nearest town: Cisco, Agency: BLM, GPS: 39.237879, -109.202382

30971 • Buckboard - USFS

Total sites: 8, RV sites: 8, Elec sites: 0, Central water, No RV dump, No showers, Vault toilets, Reservations accepted, Open May-Sep, Tent & RV camping: $10, Group site: $50, Elev: 8724ft/2659m, Tel: 435-637-2817, Nearest town: Monticello, Agency: USFS, GPS: 37.880649, -109.449293

30972 • Buckhorn Wash - BLM

Dispersed sites, No water, No toilets, Reservations not accepted, Tent & RV camping: Fee unk, Elev: 5568ft/1697m, Tel: 435-636-3600, Nearest town: Lawrence, Agency: BLM, GPS: 39.166901, -110.737517

30973 • Buckskin Gulch Trailhead - BLM

Dispersed sites, No water, No toilets, Tent & RV camping: Free, Nearby BLM ranger station has maps and information on other camping areas, Elev: 4836ft/1474m, Tel: 435-688-3200, Nearest town: Page,AZ, Agency: BLM, GPS: 37.067008, -112.000579

30974 • Butterfly Lake - USFS

Total sites: 20, RV sites: 20, Elec sites: 0, Potable water, No RV dump, No showers, Vault toilets, Reservations not accepted, Open Jul-Sep, Tent & RV camping: $21, Stay limit: 7 days, Elev: 10354ft/3156m, Tel: 435-654-0470, Nearest town: Kamas, Agency: USFS, GPS: 40.721436, -110.869141

30975 • Cainville Wash Road Dispersed - BLM

Dispersed sites, No water, No toilets, Tents only: Free, 4x4 recommended, Elev: 5050ft/1539m, Nearest town: Hanksville, Agency: BLM, GPS: 38.391212, -111.026977

30976 • Calder Reservoir FA - DWR

Dispersed sites, No water, Vault toilets, Reservations not accepted, Tent & RV camping: Free, Elev: 7282ft/2220m, Tel: 801-538-4700, Nearest town: Vernal, Agency: ST, GPS: 40.728167, -109.205032

30977 • Canyon Rim - USFS

Total sites: 15, RV sites: 7, Elec sites: 0, Potable water, No RV dump, No showers, Vault toilets, Max length: 45ft, Open May-Sep, Tent & RV camping: $20, 7 sites open for pack-in until snow closes, Elev: 7431ft/2265m, Tel: 435-784-3445, Nearest town: Dutch John, Agency: USFS, GPS: 40.884521, -109.546875

30978 • Canyon View RV Park

Total sites: 24, RV sites: 24, Elec sites: 24, Water at site, RV dump, Generator hours: 0700-2200, Open Apr-Oct, Tent & RV camping: $20, Stay limit: 14 days, Elev: 4718ft/1438m, Tel: 801-798-5000, Nearest town: Spanish Fork, Agency: MU, GPS: 40.081737, -111.60142

30979 • Canyonlands NP - Airport Tower

Total sites: 4, RV sites: 0, Elec sites: 0, No water, No toilets, Reservations accepted, Tents only: Free, Back-country, 4x4 needed, Elev: 4505ft/1373m, Tel: 435-719-2100, Nearest town: Monticello, Agency: NP, GPS: 38.391624, -109.793687

30980 • Canyonlands NP - Bobby Jo

Total sites: 2, Elec sites: 0, No water, Vault toilets, Reservations accepted, Tents only: Free, Back-country, 4x4 needed, Elev: 5535ft/1687m, Tel: 435-719-2100, Nearest town: Monticello, Agency: NP, GPS: 38.093458, -109.88168

30981 • Canyonlands NP - Butler Flat

Dispersed sites, No water, No toilets, Reservations accepted, Tents only: Free, Back-country, 4x4 needed, Elev: 5436ft/1657m, Tel: 435-719-2100, Nearest town: Monticello, Agency: NP, GPS: 38.096811, -109.877703

30982 • Canyonlands NP - Candlestick

Total sites: 1, RV sites: 0, Elec sites: 0, No water, No toilets, Reservations accepted, Tents only: Free, Back-country, 4x4 needed, Elev: 4373ft/1333m, Tel: 435-719-2100, Nearest town: Monticello, Agency: NP, GPS: 38.374158, -109.965309

30983 • Canyonlands NP - Chimney Rock

Total sites: 1, Elec sites: 0, No water, No toilets, Reservations accepted, Tents only: Free, Back-country, 4x4 needed, Elev: 5456ft/1663m, Tel: 435-719-2100, Nearest town: Monticello, Agency: NP, GPS: 38.185807, -109.975055

30984 • Canyonlands NP - Cleopatra's Chair

Total sites: 1, Elec: Unk, No water, No toilets, Tents only: Free, Back-country, 4x4 needed, Elev: 6220ft/1896m, Tel: 435-719-2100, Nearest town: Moab, Agency: NP, GPS: 38.302284, -110.078577

30985 • Canyonlands NP - Devils Kitchen

Total sites: 4, Elec sites: 0, No water, Vault toilets, Reservations accepted, Tents only: Free, Back-country, 4x4 needed, Elev: 5387ft/1642m, Tel: 435-719-2100, Nearest town: Monticello, Agency: NP, GPS: 38.136033, -109.859974

30986 • Canyonlands NP - Ekker Butte

Total sites: 1, Elec: Unk, No water, No toilets, Tents only: Free, Back-country, 4x4 needed, Elev: 4911ft/1497m, Tel: 435-719-2100, Nearest town: Moab, Agency: NP, GPS: 38.283244, -109.968305

30987 • Canyonlands NP - Flint Sheep

Total sites: 1, Elec: Unk, No water, No toilets, Tents only: Free, Back-country, 4x4 needed, Elev: 6810ft/2076m, Tel: 435-719-2100, Nearest town: Hite, Agency: NP, GPS: 38.130688, -110.134838

30988 • Canyonlands NP - Golden Stairs

Total sites: 1, Elec: Unk, No water, No toilets, Tents only: Free, Back-country, 4x4 needed, Elev: 6064ft/1848m, Tel: 435-719-2100, Nearest town: Hite, Agency: NP, GPS: 38.141893, -110.086956

30989 • Canyonlands NP - Gooseberry

Dispersed sites, No water, No toilets, Reservations accepted, Tent & RV camping: Free, Back-country, 4x4 needed, Elev: 4754ft/1449m, Tel: 435-719-2100, Nearest town: Monticello, Agency: NP, GPS: 38.330883, -109.827365

30990 • Canyonlands NP - Happy Canyon

Total sites: 1, Elec: Unk, No water, No toilets, Tents only: Free, Back-country, 4x4 needed, Elev: 6870ft/2094m, Tel: 435-719-2100, Nearest town: Hite, Agency: NP, GPS: 38.108406, -110.136742

30991 • Canyonlands NP - Hardscrabble Bottom

Total sites: 2, RV sites: 2, Elec sites: 0, No water, No toilets, Reservations accepted, Tent & RV camping: Free, Back-country, 4x4 needed, Elev: 3966ft/1209m, Tel: 435-719-2100, Nearest town: Monticello, Agency: NP, GPS: 38.448394, -110.010298

30992 • Canyonlands NP - High Spur

Total sites: 1, Elec: Unk, No water, No toilets, Tents only: Free, Back-country, 4x4 needed, Elev: 6162ft/1878m, Tel: 435-719-2100, Nearest town: Hanksville, Agency: NP, GPS: 38.378964, -110.127159

30993 • Canyonlands NP - Horsehoof

Total sites: 1, Elec: Unk, No water, No toilets, Tents only: Free, Back-country, 4x4 needed, Elev: 5560ft/1695m, Tel: 435-719-2100, Nearest town: Hite, Agency: NP, GPS: 38.098421, -109.880214

30994 • Canyonlands NP - Island in the Sky (Willow Flat)
Total sites: 12, RV sites: 12, Elec sites: 0, No water, Vault toilets, Max length: 28ft, Generator hours: 0800-1000/1600-1800, Reservations not accepted, Open all year, Tent & RV camping: $15, Elev: 6079ft/1853m, Tel: 435-719-2100, Nearest town: Monticello, Agency: NP, GPS: 38.383182, -109.887874

30995 • Canyonlands NP - Labyrinth
Total sites: 2, RV sites: 2, Elec sites: 0, No water, No toilets, Reservations accepted, Tent & RV camping: Free, Back-country, 4x4 needed, Elev: 4003ft/1220m, Tel: 435-719-2100, Nearest town: Monticello, Agency: NP, GPS: 38.474984, -109.999666

30996 • Canyonlands NP - Maze Overlook
Total sites: 2, Elec sites: 0, No water, No toilets, Reservations accepted, Tents only: Free, Back-country, 4x4 needed, Elev: 5171ft/1576m, Tel: 435-719-2100, Nearest town: Monticello, Agency: NP, GPS: 38.232845, -110.002958

30997 • Canyonlands NP - Millard Canyon
Total sites: 1, Elec: Unk, No water, No toilets, Reservations accepted, Tents only: Free, Back-country, 4x4 needed, Elev: 3934ft/1199m, Tel: 435-719-2100, Nearest town: Monticello, Agency: NP, GPS: 38.38921, -110.03439

30998 • Canyonlands NP - Murphy Hogback
Dispersed sites, No water, No toilets, Reservations accepted, Tents only: Free, Back-country, 4x4 needed, Elev: 5279ft/1609m, Tel: 435-719-2100, Nearest town: Monticello, Agency: NP, GPS: 38.321721, -109.906248

30999 • Canyonlands NP - New Bates Wilson
Total sites: 1, Elec: Unk, No water, No toilets, Reservations accepted, Tents only: Free, Back-country, 4x4 needed, Elev: 5128ft/1563m, Tel: 435-719-2100, Nearest town: Moab, Agency: NP, GPS: 38.159576, -109.860513

31000 • Canyonlands NP - North Point
Total sites: 1, Elec: Unk, No water, No toilets, Tents only: Free, Back-country, 4x4 needed, Elev: 6543ft/1994m, Tel: 435-719-2100, Nearest town: Hite, Agency: NP, GPS: 38.236415, -110.147373

31001 • Canyonlands NP - Panorama Point
Total sites: 1, Elec: Unk, No water, No toilets, Tents only: Free, Back-country, 4x4 needed, Elev: 6268ft/1910m, Tel: 435-719-2100, Nearest town: Moab, Agency: NP, GPS: 38.272203, -110.040375

31002 • Canyonlands NP - Peekaboo Spring
Total sites: 2, Elec sites: 0, No water, Vault toilets, Reservations accepted, Tents only: Free, Back-country, 4x4 needed, Elev: 5066ft/1544m, Tel: 435-719-2100, Nearest town: Monticello, Agency: NP, GPS: 38.112238, -109.753435

31003 • Canyonlands NP - Potato Bottom
Total sites: 3, RV sites: 0, Elec sites: 0, No water, No toilets, Reservations accepted, Tents only: Free, 4x4 needed, Elev: 3970ft/1210m, Tel: 435-719-2100, Nearest town: Monticello, Agency: NP, GPS: 38.431564, -110.010736

31004 • Canyonlands NP - Rivers Overlook
Dispersed sites, No water, No toilets, Reservations accepted, Tents only: Free, Back-country, 4x4 needed, Elev: 5226ft/1593m, Tel: 435-719-2100, Nearest town: Monticello, Agency: NP, GPS: 38.160279, -109.947727

31005 • Canyonlands NP - Shafer Canyon
Total sites: 1, RV sites: 1, Elec sites: 0, No water, No toilets, Reservations accepted, Tent & RV camping: Free, Back-country, 4x4 needed, Elev: 4308ft/1313m, Tel: 435-719-2100, Nearest town: Monticello, Agency: NP, GPS: 38.466123, -109.781405

31006 • Canyonlands NP - Spanish Bottom
Dispersed sites, No water, No toilets, Reservations accepted, Tents only: Free, Back-country, 4x4 needed, Elev: 3901ft/1189m, Tel: 435-719-2100, Nearest town: Monticello, Agency: NP, GPS: 38.157889, -109.934395

31007 • Canyonlands NP - Split Top Group
Total sites: 1, RV sites: 0, Elec sites: 0, Vault toilets, Max length: 25ft, Reservations accepted, Open Mar-Nov, Group site, Elev: 4931ft/1503m, Tel: 435-719-2100, Nearest town: Monticello, Agency: NP, GPS: 38.155457, -109.755058

31008 • Canyonlands NP - Standing Rock
Total sites: 1, Elec sites: 0, No water, No toilets, Reservations accepted, Tents only: Free, Back-country, 4x4 needed, Elev: 5515ft/1681m, Tel: 435-719-2100, Nearest town: Monticello, Agency: NP, GPS: 38.176109, -109.991118

31009 • Canyonlands NP - Sunset Pass
Total sites: 1, Elec: Unk, No water, No toilets, Tents only: Free, Back-country, 4x4 needed, Elev: 5629ft/1716m, Tel: 435-719-2100, Nearest town: Hite, Agency: NP, GPS: 38.061249, -110.147873

31010 • Canyonlands NP - Taylor Canyon
Total sites: 1, RV sites: 1, Elec sites: 0, No water, No toilets, Reservations accepted, Tent & RV camping: Free, Back-country, 4x4 needed, Elev: 4380ft/1335m, Tel: 435-719-2100, Nearest town: Monticello, Agency: NP, GPS: 38.476372, -109.922979

31011 • Canyonlands NP - Teapot Rock
Total sites: 1, Elec: Unk, No water, No toilets, Tents only: Free, Back-country, 4x4 needed, Elev: 5607ft/1709m, Tel: 435-719-2100, Nearest town: Hite, Agency: NP, GPS: 38.078496, -110.108916

31012 • Canyonlands NP - The Doll House
Dispersed sites, No water, No toilets, Reservations accepted, Tents only: Free, Back-country, 4x4 needed, Elev: 5112ft/1558m, Tel: 435-719-2100, Nearest town: Monticello, Agency: NP, GPS: 38.150597, -109.95213

31013 • Canyonlands NP - The Neck
Total sites: 1, Elec: Unk, No water, No toilets, Tents only: Free, Back-country, 4x4 needed, Elev: 6923ft/2110m, Tel: 435-719-2100, Nearest town: Hite, Agency: NP, GPS: 38.087451, -110.144362

31014 • Canyonlands NP - The Needles (Squaw Flat)
Total sites: 26, RV sites: 26, Elec sites: 0, Central water, No RV dump, No showers, Flush toilets, Max length: 28ft, Generator hours: 0800-1000/1600-1800, Reservations accepted, Open all year, Tent & RV camping: $20, Group site available, Elev: 5096ft/1553m, Tel: 435-719-2100, Nearest town: Monticello, Agency: NP, GPS: 38.149066, -109.796375

31015 • Canyonlands NP - The Wall
Total sites: 1, Elec sites: 0, No water, No toilets, Reservations accepted, Tents only: Free, Back-country, 4x4 needed, Elev: 5450ft/1661m, Tel: 435-719-2100, Nearest town: Monticello, Agency: NP, GPS: 38.170763, -110.019203

31016 • Canyonlands NP - Upheaval Bottom
Dispersed sites, No water, No toilets, Reservations accepted, Tents only: Free, Back-country, 4x4 needed, Elev: 4012ft/1223m, Tel: 435-719-2100, Nearest town: Monticello, Agency: NP, GPS: 38.474531, -110.000768

31017 • Canyonlands NP - Upheaval Canyon
Dispersed sites, No water, No toilets, Reservations accepted, Tents only: Free, Back-country, 4x4 needed, Elev: 3960ft/1207m, Tel: 435-719-2100, Nearest town: Monticello, Agency: NP, GPS: 38.468208, -109.998715

31018 • Canyonlands NP - White Crack
Total sites: 1, RV sites: 1, Elec sites: 0, No water, No toilets, Reservations accepted, Tent & RV camping: Free, Back-country, 4x4 needed, Elev: 5171ft/1576m, Tel: 435-719-2100, Nearest town: Monticello, Agency: NP, GPS: 38.257035, -109.865459

31019 • Canyonlands NP - Wooden Shoe Group
Total sites: 1, RV sites: 0, Elec sites: 0, Vault toilets, Max length: 25ft, Reservations accepted, Open Mar-Nov, Group site, Elev: 5046ft/1538m, Tel: 435-719-2100, Nearest town: Monticello, Agency: NP, GPS: 38.147711, -109.784506

31020 • Capitol Reef NP - Cathedral Valley
Total sites: 6, RV sites: 6, Elec sites: 0, No water, Vault toilets, Reservations not accepted, Open all year, Tent & RV camping: Free, Elev: 6939ft/2115m, Tel: 435-425-3791, Nearest town: Torrey, Agency: NP, GPS: 38.474731, -111.367641

31021 • Capitol Reef NP - Cedar Mesa
Total sites: 5, RV sites: 5, Elec sites: 0, No water, Vault toilets, Reservations not accepted, Open all year, Tent & RV camping: Free, Elev: 5610ft/1710m, Tel: 435-425-3791, Nearest town: Torrey, Agency: NP, GPS: 38.007, -111.085

31022 • Capitol Reef NP - Fruita CG
Total sites: 71, RV sites: 64, Elec sites: 0, Central water, RV dump, No showers, Flush toilets, Generator hours: 0800-1000/1800-2000, Reservation required, Open all year, Tent & RV camping: $20, First-come/first-served available only Nov-Feb, Elev: 5463ft/1665m, Tel: 435-425-3791, Nearest town: Torrey, Agency: NP, GPS: 38.2822, -111.24671

31023 • Carmel - USFS
Total sites: 15, RV sites: 15, Elec sites: 0, No water, Vault toilets, Max length: 25ft, Reservations not accepted, Open May-Sep, Tent & RV camping: $12, Elev: 6293ft/1918m, Nearest town: Manila, Agency: USFS, GPS: 40.931043, -109.731705

31024 • Castleton Tower - SITLA
Total sites: 2, RV sites: 0, Elec sites: 0, No water, Vault toilets, Open all year, Tents only: Free, Popular climbers' campsite, Elev: 4920ft/1500m, Nearest town: Moab, Agency: PRIV, GPS: 38.642332, -109.376791

31025 • Casto Canyon - USFS
Total sites: 5, RV sites: 5, Elec sites: 0, No water, No toilets, Max length: 35ft, Tent & RV camping: Free, Elev: 7028ft/2142m, Tel: 435-676-2676, Nearest town: Panguitch, Agency: USFS, GPS: 37.785266, -112.339231

31026 • Cats Paw River Camp - USFS
Dispersed sites, No water, No toilets, Reservations accepted, Tents only: $13, Hike-in/boat-in, Elev: 5530ft/1686m, Nearest town: Dutch John, Agency: USFS, GPS: 40.908615, -109.306552

31027 • Cedar Breaks NM - Point Supreme
Total sites: 28, RV sites: 20, Elec sites: 0, Central water, No RV dump, Showers, Flush toilets, Max length: 24ft, Generator hours: 0600-2200, Reservations accepted, Open Jun-Sep, Tent & RV camping: $24, Only credit/debit cards accepted - no cash or checks, Elev: 10282ft/3134m, Tel: 435-586-9451, Nearest town: Cedar City, Agency: NP, GPS: 37.61036, -112.83038

31028 • Cedar Canyon - USFS
Total sites: 18, RV sites: 18, Elec sites: 0, Central water, No RV dump, No showers, Flush toilets, Reservations accepted, Open May-Sep, Tent & RV camping: $17, Group site: $55, Elev: 8547ft/2605m, Tel: 435-865-3200, Nearest town: Cedar City, Agency: USFS, GPS: 37.591355, -112.903665

31029 • Cedar Mt Overlook Dispersed - BLM
Dispersed sites, No water, No toilets, Tents only: Free, Elev: 7556ft/2303m, Nearest town: Green River, Agency: BLM, GPS: 39.176759, -110.630995

31030 • Cedar Springs - USFS
Total sites: 21, RV sites: 21, Elec sites: 0, Central water, RV dump, No showers, Vault toilets, Max length: 45ft, Reservations accepted, Open Apr-Sep, Tent & RV camping: $25, Elev: 6129ft/1868m, Tel: 435-889-3000, Nearest town: Dutch John, Agency: USFS, GPS: 40.908936, -109.450439

31031 • Cherry - USFS
Total sites: 28, RV sites: 28, Elec sites: 0, Central water, No RV dump, No showers, Vault toilets, Reservations accepted, Open May-Sep, Tent & RV camping: $23, 4 group sites: $115-$155, Elev: 5282ft/1610m, Tel: 801-226-3564, Nearest town: Springville, Agency: USFS, GPS: 40.168705, -111.476704

31032 • Chicken Creek - USFS
Total sites: 7, RV sites: 7, Elec sites: 0, No water, Vault toilets, Reservations not accepted, Open May-Nov, Tent & RV camping: Free, Elev: 6125ft/1867m, Nearest town: Levan, Agency: USFS, GPS: 39.53, -111.774

31033 • China Meadows - USFS
Total sites: 9, RV sites: 9, Elec sites: 0, No water, Vault toilets, Reservations not accepted, Open Jun-Oct, Tent & RV camping: $16, Stay limit: 14 days, Elev: 9406ft/2867m, Tel: 307-782-6555, Nearest town: Mountain View, Agency: USFS, GPS: 40.931114, -110.403468

31034 • China Meadows TH - USFS
Total sites: 11, RV sites: 11, Elec: Unk, No water, Vault toilets, Reservations not accepted, Tent & RV camping: $14, Elev: 9484ft/2891m, Tel: 307-782-6555, Nearest town: Mountain View, Agency: USFS, GPS: 40.924208, -110.405997

31035 • Christmas Meadows - USFS
Total sites: 11, RV sites: 11, Elec sites: 0, Central water, No RV dump, No showers, Vault toilets, Reservations accepted, Open Jun-Oct, Tent & RV camping: $21, Stay limit: 14 days, Elev: 8839ft/2694m, Tel: 307-789-3194, Nearest town: Evanston, Agency: USFS, GPS: 40.824396, -110.802154

31036 • Chute Canyon TH Dispersed - BLM
Dispersed sites, No water, No toilets, Tents only: Free, Elev: 5177ft/1578m, Nearest town: Green River, Agency: BLM, GPS: 38.629154, -110.763255

31037 • Cisco Boat Ramp - BLM
Dispersed sites, No water, No toilets, Reservations not accepted, Tent & RV camping: Free, Elev: 4163ft/1269m, Nearest town: Cisco, Agency: BLM, GPS: 38.969865, -109.251941

31038 • City Creek - USFS
Total sites: 5, RV sites: 5, Elec sites: 0, Potable water, No RV dump, No showers, Vault toilets, Max length: 24ft, Reservations accepted, Open May-Sep, Tent & RV camping: Fee unk, Group sites, Elev: 7540ft/2298m, Tel: 435-896-9233, Nearest town: Beaver, Agency: USFS, GPS: 38.269726, -112.311266

31039 • Clay Hills - BLM
Dispersed sites, No water, Tent & RV camping: Free, Elev: 3721ft/1134m, Nearest town: Irish Green, Agency: BLM, GPS: 37.294118, -110.397711

31040 • Cleveland Reservoir Dispersed - USFS
Dispersed sites, No water, Vault toilets, Reservations not accepted, Tent & RV camping: Free, Elev: 8876ft/2705m, Nearest town: Fairview, Agency: USFS, GPS: 39.588416, -111.243919

31041 • Cliff Ridge - BLM
Dispersed sites, No water, No toilets, Tent & RV camping: Free, Hang-gliding area, Elev: 8123ft/2476m, Tel: 435-781-4400, Nearest town: Vernal, Agency: BLM, GPS: 40.367685, -109.119664

31042 • Clover Springs - BLM
Total sites: 10, RV sites: 10, Elec sites: 0, No water, Vault toilets, Max length: 30ft, Reservations not accepted, Open May-Oct, Tent & RV camping: $12, Group site: $45, Elev: 6063ft/1848m, Tel: 801-977-4300, Nearest town: Tooele, Agency: BLM, GPS: 40.347131, -112.550598

31043 • Coal Mine Wash - BLM
Dispersed sites, No water, Vault toilets, Tent & RV camping: Free, Elev: 4662ft/1421m, Nearest town: Hanksville, Agency: BLM, GPS: 38.378011, -110.899811

31044 • Coal Pits Wash Dispersed - BLM
Dispersed sites, No water, No toilets, Tents only: Free, Elev: 3677ft/1121m, Nearest town: Rockville, Agency: BLM, GPS: 37.170951, -113.081676

31045 • Cobblerest - USFS
Total sites: 18, RV sites: 18, Elec sites: 0, Potable water, No RV dump, No showers, Vault toilets, Reservations not accepted, Open Jun-Sep, Tent & RV camping: $21, Stay limit: 7 days, Elev: 8333ft/2540m, Tel: 435-783-4338, Nearest town: Kamas, Agency: USFS, GPS: 40.594482, -110.975342

31046 • Cockscomb Dispersed - BLM
Dispersed sites, No water, No toilets, Reservations not accepted, Open all year, Tent & RV camping: Free, Elev: 4504ft/1373m, Nearest town: Kanab, Agency: BLM, GPS: 37.126449, -111.954795

31047 • Cold Springs - USFS
Total sites: 9, RV sites: 9, Elec: Unk, No water, Vault toilets, Reservations not accepted, Tent & RV camping: Free, Elev: 9152ft/2790m, Tel: 435-896-9233, Nearest town: Salina, Agency: USFS, GPS: 38.782456, -111.643283

31048 • Colorado River - Bald Eagle - BLM
Dispersed sites, No water, No toilets, Tents only: Fee unk, Boat-in, Elev: 4166ft/1270m, Nearest town: Cisco, Agency: BLM, GPS: 38.960199, -109.210152

31049 • Colorado River - Big Drop Beach - NPS
Dispersed sites, No water, No toilets, Tents only: Fee unk, Boat-in, Elev: 3748ft/1142m, Nearest town: Moab, Agency: NP, GPS: 38.081694, -110.038296

31050 • Colorado River - Big Hole - BLM
Dispersed sites, No water, No toilets, Tents only: Fee unk, Boat-in, Elev: 4178ft/1273m, Nearest town: Cisco, Agency: BLM, GPS: 38.981929, -109.177498

31051 • Colorado River - Big Horn - BLM
Dispersed sites, No water, No toilets, Tents only: Fee unk, Boat-in, Elev: 4168ft/1270m, Nearest town: Cisco, Agency: BLM, GPS: 38.964602, -109.193306

31052 • Colorado River - Bowdie Canyon - NPS

Dispersed sites, No water, No toilets, Tents only: Fee unk, Boat-in, Elev: 3708ft/1130m, Nearest town: Moab, Agency: NP, GPS: 37.98468, -110.15597

31053 • Colorado River - Camp A - NPS

Dispersed sites, No water, No toilets, Tents only: Fee unk, Boat-in, Elev: 3728ft/1136m, Nearest town: Moab, Agency: NP, GPS: 38.065089, -110.044681

31054 • Colorado River - Camp B - NPS

Dispersed sites, No water, No toilets, Tents only: Fee unk, Boat-in, Elev: 3710ft/1131m, Nearest town: Moab, Agency: NP, GPS: 38.054432, -110.043146

31055 • Colorado River - Clearwater Canyon - NPS

Dispersed sites, No water, No toilets, Tents only: Fee unk, Boat-in, Elev: 3708ft/1130m, Nearest town: Moab, Agency: NP, GPS: 38.003403, -110.137244

31056 • Colorado River - Cougar Bar - BLM

Dispersed sites, No water, No toilets, Tents only: Fee unk, Boat-in, Elev: 4267ft/1301m, Nearest town: Cisco, Agency: BLM, GPS: 39.025467, -109.130296

31057 • Colorado River - Dark Canyon - NPS

Dispersed sites, No water, No toilets, Tents only: Fee unk, Boat-in, Elev: 3708ft/1130m, Nearest town: Moab, Agency: NP, GPS: 37.895383, -110.204916

31058 • Colorado River - Grand Camp - BLM

Dispersed sites, No water, Tents only: Free, Also boat-in sites, No open fires, Elev: 4333ft/1321m, Nearest town: Fruita, CO, Agency: BLM, GPS: 39.121814, -109.065428

31059 • Colorado River - Hades Bar - BLM

Dispersed sites, No water, No toilets, Tents only: Fee unk, Boat-in, Elev: 4251ft/1296m, Nearest town: Cisco, Agency: BLM, GPS: 39.012523, -109.14697

31060 • Colorado River - Halliday - BLM

Dispersed sites, No water, Tents only: Free, Boat-in, No open fires,, Elev: 4331ft/1320m, Nearest town: Fruita, CO, Agency: BLM, GPS: 39.118422, -109.077977

31061 • Colorado River - Imperial Canyon - NPS

Dispersed sites, No water, No toilets, Tents only: Fee unk, Boat-in, Elev: 3708ft/1130m, Nearest town: Moab, Agency: NP, GPS: 38.048189, -110.050126

31062 • Colorado River - Little Dolores - BLM

Dispersed sites, No water, No toilets, Tents only: Fee unk, Boat-in, Elev: 4254ft/1297m, Nearest town: Cisco, Agency: BLM, GPS: 39.015621, -109.144884

31063 • Colorado River - Little Hole - BLM

Dispersed sites, No water, No toilets, Tents only: Fee unk, Boat-in, Elev: 4258ft/1298m, Nearest town: Cisco, Agency: BLM, GPS: 39.019652, -109.144403

31064 • Colorado River - Miners Cabin - BLM

Dispersed sites, No water, No toilets, Tents only: Fee unk, Boat-in, Elev: 4289ft/1307m, Nearest town: Cisco, Agency: BLM, GPS: 39.051535, -109.131877

31065 • Colorado River - Piano Leg - NPS

Dispersed sites, No water, No toilets, Tents only: Fee unk, Boat-in, Elev: 3708ft/1130m, Nearest town: Moab, Agency: NP, GPS: 37.884987, -110.277942

31066 • Colorado River - Rock Fall Left - NPS

Dispersed sites, No water, No toilets, Tents only: Fee unk, Boat-in, Elev: 3708ft/1130m, Nearest town: Moab, Agency: NP, GPS: 37.912186, -110.198888

31067 • Colorado River - Rock Fall Right - NPS

Dispersed sites, No water, No toilets, Tents only: Fee unk, Boat-in, Elev: 3708ft/1130m, Nearest town: Moab, Agency: NP, GPS: 37.908775, -110.203803

31068 • Colorado River - Sheep Canyon - NPS

Dispersed sites, No water, No toilets, Tents only: Fee unk, Boat-in, Elev: 3707ft/1130m, Nearest town: Moab, Agency: NP, GPS: 37.870099, -110.276639

31069 • Colorado River - Slab Camp - NPS

Dispersed sites, No water, No toilets, Tents only: Fee unk, Boat-in, Elev: 3708ft/1130m, Nearest town: Moab, Agency: NP, GPS: 37.976071, -110.164116

31070 • Colorado River - Stateline - BLM

Dispersed sites, No water, Tents only: Free, Also boat-in sites, No open fires, Elev: 4333ft/1321m, Nearest town: Fruita, CO, Agency: BLM, GPS: 39.118068, -109.051685

31071 • Colorado River - Upper Cougar Bar - BLM

Dispersed sites, No water, No toilets, Tents only: Fee unk, Boat-in, Elev: 4267ft/1301m, Nearest town: Cisco, Agency: BLM, GPS: 39.029176, -109.126088

31072 • Colorado River - X-Y Left - NPS

Dispersed sites, No water, No toilets, Tents only: Fee unk, Boat-in, Elev: 3839ft/1170m, Nearest town: Moab, Agency: NP, GPS: 38.112243, -109.966511

31073 • Colorado River - X-Y Right - NPS

Dispersed sites, No water, No toilets, Tents only: Fee unk, Boat-in, Elev: 3839ft/1170m, Nearest town: Moab, Agency: NP, GPS: 38.112639, -109.969696

31074 • Copper Ridge Dinosaur Tracksite - BLM

Dispersed sites, No water, Vault toilets, Reservations not accepted, Open all year, Tent & RV camping: Free, Many sites along road, Avoid No Camping spots and No Vehicle signs, No shade, Verizon/ATT both OK, Stay limit: 14 days, Elev: 4695ft/1431m, Nearest town: Moab, Agency: BLM, GPS: 38.829819, -109.765039

31075 • Coral Pink Sand Dunes - Meadows - BLM

Dispersed sites, No water, No toilets, Reservations not accepted, Tent & RV camping: Free, Elev: 6151ft/1875m, Tel: 435-644-

1200, Nearest town: Kanab, Agency: BLM, GPS: 37.067627, -112.703822

31076 • Coral Pink Sand Dunes - Ponderosa Grove - BLM
Total sites: 9, RV sites: 9, Elec sites: 0, No water, Vault toilets, Max length: 24ft, Reservations not accepted, Tent & RV camping: $5, Elev: 6306ft/1922m, Tel: 435-644-1200, Nearest town: Kanab, Agency: BLM, GPS: 37.088816, -112.672346

31077 • Coral Pink Sand Dunes - Sand Spring - BLM
Dispersed sites, No water, No toilets, Reservations not accepted, Tent & RV camping: Free, Elev: 6185ft/1885m, Tel: 435-644-1200, Nearest town: Kanab, Agency: BLM, GPS: 37.077798, -112.661815

31078 • Coral Pink Sand Dunes Dispersed - BLM
Dispersed sites, No water, No toilets, Reservations not accepted, Tent & RV camping: Free, Elev: 5870ft/1789m, Tel: 435-644-1200, Nearest town: Kanab, Agency: BLM, GPS: 37.033381, -112.747553

31079 • Coral Pink Sand Dunes SP - New CG
Total sites: 9, RV sites: 9, Elec sites: 9, Water at site, RV dump, Showers, Flush toilets, Max length: 40ft, Reservations accepted, Open all year, Tent & RV camping: $30, Group site: $120, Elev: 5951ft/1814m, Tel: 435-648-2800, Nearest town: Kanab, Agency: ST, GPS: 37.037246, -112.730331

31080 • Coral Pink Sand Dunes SP - Old CG
Total sites: 22, RV sites: 22, Elec sites: 0, RV dump, Showers, Flush toilets, Max length: 40ft, Reservations accepted, Open all year, Tent & RV camping: $20, Elev: 5928ft/1807m, Tel: 435-648-2800, Nearest town: Kanab, Agency: ST, GPS: 37.034315, -112.734305

31081 • Cottonwood (SFRD) - USFS
Total sites: 18, RV sites: 18, Elec sites: 0, No water, Vault toilets, Reservations not accepted, Open Apr-Oct, Tent & RV camping: Free, Stay limit: 7 days, Elev: 6594ft/2010m, Tel: 801-798-3571, Nearest town: Nephi, Agency: USFS, GPS: 39.780366, -111.723377

31082 • Cottonwood (SLRD) - USFS
Total sites: 3, RV sites: 3, Elec sites: 0, No toilets, Reservations not accepted, Tent & RV camping: $14, Stay limit: 7 days, Elev: 6119ft/1865m, Tel: 801-733-2660, Nearest town: Salt Lake City, Agency: USFS, GPS: 40.501555, -112.559697

31083 • Cottonwood Canyon Dispersed - BLM
Dispersed sites, No water, No toilets, Tent & RV camping: Free, Elev: 4721ft/1439m, Nearest town: Paria, Agency: BLM, GPS: 37.240713, -111.920923

31084 • Cottonwood Canyon Dispersed - BLM
Dispersed sites, No water, No toilets, Reservations not accepted, Open all year, Tent & RV camping: Free, 2nd site .25 mi west at end of road, Elev: 4784ft/1458m, Nearest town: Kanab, Agency: BLM, GPS: 37.117754, -111.853156

31085 • Cottonwood Canyon Dispersed - BLM
Dispersed sites, No water, No toilets, Reservations not accepted, Open all year, Tent & RV camping: Free, 2 sites, Elev: 4867ft/1483m, Nearest town: Kanab, Agency: BLM, GPS: 37.119354, -111.849618

31086 • Courthouse Rock - BLM
Total sites: 20, RV sites: 20, Elec sites: 0, No water, No RV dump, No showers, Vault toilets, Generator hours: 0800-2000, Reservations not accepted, Tent & RV camping: $20, Stay limit: 14 days, Elev: 4531ft/1381m, Tel: 435-259-2100, Nearest town: Moab, Agency: BLM, GPS: 38.720285, -109.734087

31087 • Cowboy Camp - BLM
Total sites: 7, Elec sites: 0, No water, Vault toilets, Reservations not accepted, Tents only: $20, Stay limit: 14 days, Elev: 6146ft/1873m, Tel: 435-259-2100, Nearest town: Moab, Agency: BLM, GPS: 38.561861, -109.796468

31088 • Coyote Hollow Horse Camp - USFS
Total sites: 4, RV sites: 4, Elec sites: 0, No water, Vault toilets, Reservations not accepted, Open all year, Tent & RV camping: $10, Elev: 7864ft/2397m, Tel: 435-676-2676, Nearest town: Panguitch, Agency: USFS, GPS: 37.713993, -112.270952

31089 • CR 12 Dispersed - USFS
Dispersed sites, No water, No toilets, Reservations not accepted, Open all year, Tent & RV camping: Free, Elev: 9475ft/2888m, Nearest town: Teasdale, Agency: USFS, GPS: 38.013628, -111.356285

31090 • CR 12 Dispersed - USFS
Dispersed sites, No water, No toilets, Reservations not accepted, Open all year, Tent & RV camping: Free, Road not maintained for passenger cars, Elev: 9432ft/2875m, Tel: 435-836-2800, Nearest town: Grover, Agency: USFS, GPS: 38.047784, -111.325583

31091 • CR 29 Dispersed - USFS
Dispersed sites, No water, No toilets, Reservations not accepted, Open all year, Tent & RV camping: Free, Elev: 9024ft/2751m, Tel: 435-637-2817, Nearest town: Ephraim, Agency: USFS, GPS: 39.322457, -111.469311

31092 • CR 29 Dispersed - USFS
Dispersed sites, No water, No toilets, Reservations not accepted, Open all year, Tent & RV camping: Free, Elev: 10020ft/3054m, Tel: 435-637-2817, Nearest town: Ephraim, Agency: USFS, GPS: 39.328287, -111.441073

31093 • CR 4580 Dispersed - USFS
Dispersed sites, No water, No toilets, Reservations not accepted, Open all year, Tent & RV camping: Free, Road not maintained for passenger cars, Elev: 5372ft/1637m, Tel: 435-743-5721, Nearest town: Kanosh, Agency: USFS, GPS: 38.739534, -112.533139

31094 • Crack Canyon TH Dispersed - BLM
Dispersed sites, No water, No toilets, Tents only: Free, Elev: 5541ft/1689m, Nearest town: Green River, Agency: BLM, GPS: 38.643072, -110.745229

31095 • Crawford Dispersed - BLM
Dispersed sites, No water, No toilets, Tent & RV camping: Free, Elev: 7608ft/2319m, Nearest town: Randolph, Agency: BLM, GPS: 41.660204, -111.095804

31096 • Creek Pasture - BLM
Total sites: 32, RV sites: 32, Elec sites: 0, No water, Vault toilets, Reservations not accepted, Open all year, Tent & RV camping: $15, Group fee: $65, Elev: 4867ft/1483m, Tel: 435-587-1500, Nearest town: Monticello, Agency: BLM, GPS: 38.166514, -109.631814

31097 • Crystal Geyser Dispersed - BLM
Dispersed sites, No water, No toilets, Tent & RV camping: Free, Elev: 4058ft/1237m, Nearest town: Green River, Agency: BLM, GPS: 38.937007, -110.134721

31098 • Currant Creek - USFS
Total sites: 98, RV sites: 98, Elec sites: 0, Central water, RV dump, No showers, Flush toilets, Max length: 32ft, Reservations accepted, Open Jun-Sep, Tent & RV camping: $23, 4 group sites $90-$120, Stay limit: 7 days, Elev: 7848ft/2392m, Tel: 435-654-0470, Nearest town: Heber City, Agency: USFS, GPS: 40.331399, -111.066636

31099 • Dalton Springs - USFS
Total sites: 16, RV sites: 16, Elec sites: 0, Central water, No RV dump, No showers, Vault toilets, Max length: 30ft, Reservations not accepted, Open May-Sep, Tent & RV camping: $10, Elev: 8386ft/2556m, Tel: 435-637-2817, Nearest town: Monticello, Agency: USFS, GPS: 37.873914, -109.432817

31100 • Dalton Well Road Dispersed - BLM
Dispersed sites, No water, No toilets, Tent & RV camping: Free, Elev: 4403ft/1342m, Nearest town: Moab, Agency: BLM, GPS: 38.716143, -109.691953

31101 • Dalton Well Road Dispersed - BLM
Dispersed sites, No water, No toilets, Reservations not accepted, Open all year, Tent & RV camping: Free, Elev: 4414ft/1345m, Nearest town: Moab, Agency: BLM, GPS: 38.722837, -109.690397

31102 • Dead Horse Point SP - Kayenta
Total sites: 21, RV sites: 21, Elec sites: 21, Central water, RV dump, No showers, Flush toilets, Max length: 65ft, Reservations accepted, Open all year, Tent & RV camping: $40, RV's must fill water tank before arriving at park, Elev: 5968ft/1819m, Tel: 435-259-2614, Nearest town: Moab, Agency: ST, GPS: 38.486609, -109.740352

31103 • Dead Horse Point SP - Wingate
Total sites: 31, RV sites: 20, Elec sites: 20, Central water, RV dump, No showers, Flush toilets, Max length: 56ft, Reservations accepted, Open all year, Tents: $35/RV's: $40, Also walk-to sites, RV's must fill water tank before arriving at park, Elev: 5997ft/1828m, Tel: 435-259-2614, Nearest town: Moab, Agency: ST, GPS: 38.480895, -109.740079

31104 • Deep Creek - USFS
Total sites: 17, RV sites: 17, Elec sites: 0, No water, Vault toilets, Max length: 30ft, Reservations not accepted, Open May-Sep, Tent & RV camping: $12, Elev: 7730ft/2356m, Nearest town: Manila, Agency: USFS, GPS: 40.855824, -109.729974

31105 • Deer Creek SP - Choke Cherry
Total sites: 40, RV sites: 34, Elec sites: 34, Water at site, RV dump, Showers, Flush toilets, Max length: 73ft, Reservations accepted, Open all year, Tents: $15/RV's: $20-30, FHU, No water in winter, Elev: 5482ft/1671m, Tel: 435-654-0171, Nearest town: Midway, Agency: ST, GPS: 40.411352, -111.502517

31106 • Deer Creek SP - Great Horned Owl
Total sites: 23, RV sites: 23, Elec sites: 0, Central water, No RV dump, Showers, Flush toilets, Reservations accepted, Open all year, Tent & RV camping: $20, Elev: 5450ft/1661m, Tel: 435-654-0171, Nearest town: Midway, Agency: ST, GPS: 40.413888, -111.504671

31107 • Deer Haven - USFS
Total sites: 10, RV sites: 10, Elec sites: 0, Central water, No RV dump, No showers, Flush toilets, Generator hours: 0600-2200, Reservations not accepted, Open May-Sep, Tent & RV camping: $17, Reservable group site $65-$205, Elev: 9176ft/2797m, Tel: 435-865-3200, Nearest town: Cedar City, Agency: USFS, GPS: 37.574116, -112.910502

31108 • Deer Run - USFS
Total sites: 13, RV sites: 13, Elec sites: 0, Central water, RV dump, Showers, Flush toilets, Max length: 25ft, Reservations accepted, Open Apr-Oct, Tent & RV camping: $25, Elev: 6207ft/1892m, Tel: 435-889-3000, Nearest town: Dutch John, Agency: USFS, GPS: 40.905701, -109.444214

31109 • Delta City RV Parking
Total sites: 1, RV sites: 1, Elec sites: 1, No water, No toilets, No tents/RV's: Fee unk, Unconfirmed, 2-day limit, Elev: 4644ft/1415m, Nearest town: Delta, Agency: MU, GPS: 39.353889, -112.578959

31110 • Deseret Peak Complex
Total sites: 26, RV sites: 26, Elec sites: 26, Water at site, RV dump, Reservations accepted, Open all year, Tents: $10/RV's: $15-25, 6 FHU, Elev: 4474ft/1364m, Tel: 435-843-4003, Nearest town: Tooele, Agency: CP, GPS: 40.572064, -112.370238

31111 • Devils Canyon - USFS
Total sites: 42, RV sites: 42, Elec sites: 0, Central water, No RV dump, No showers, Vault toilets, Max length: 35ft, Reservations accepted, Open all year, Tent & RV camping: $10, Elev: 7093ft/2162m, Tel: 435-587-2041, Nearest town: Blanding, Agency: USFS, GPS: 37.738858, -109.406363

31112 • Dewey Bridge - BLM
Total sites: 7, RV sites: 7, Elec sites: 0, No water, Vault toilets, Max length: 25ft, Reservations not accepted, Open all year, Tent & RV camping: $20, 2 group sites $75, Stay limit: 14 days, Elev: 4114ft/1254m, Tel: 435-259-2100, Nearest town: Moab, Agency: BLM, GPS: 38.810694, -109.307838

31113 • Diamond - USFS

Total sites: 50, RV sites: 50, Elec sites: 0, Central water, No RV dump, No showers, Vault toilets, Max length: 32ft, Reservations accepted, Open May-Oct, Tent & RV camping: $24, 7 group sites: $50-$190, Elev: 5236ft/1596m, Tel: 801-226-3564, Nearest town: Thistle, Agency: USFS, GPS: 40.072122, -111.428203

31114 • Dick Canyon - BLM

Dispersed sites, No water, No toilets, Tent & RV camping: Free, Elev: 8217ft/2505m, Nearest town: Thompson, Agency: BLM, GPS: 39.483769, -109.090487

31115 • Dinosaur NM - Ely Creek TC - NPS

Total sites: 2, RV sites: 0, No water, No toilets, Tents only: Free, Hike-in, Permit required, Elev: 5304ft/1617m, Tel: 435-636-3600, Nearest town: Naples, Agency: NP, GPS: 40.565268, -109.057093

31116 • Dinosaur NM - Green River

Total sites: 80, RV sites: 80, Elec sites: 0, Central water, No RV dump, No showers, Flush toilets, Reservations accepted, Open Apr-Oct, Tent & RV camping: $18, Elev: 4793ft/1461m, Tel: 435-781-7700, Nearest town: Jensen, Agency: NP, GPS: 40.421143, -109.243408

31117 • Dinosaur NM - Rainbow Park

Total sites: 4, RV sites: 0, Elec sites: 0, No water, Vault toilets, Reservations not accepted, Open all year, Tents only: $6, Walk-to sites, Road unpassable when wet, Elev: 4957ft/1511m, Tel: 435-781-7700, Nearest town: Jensen, Agency: NP, GPS: 40.499494, -109.170507

31118 • Dinosaur NM - Split Mountain Group

Total sites: 4, RV sites: 4, Elec sites: 0, Central water, No RV dump, No showers, Flush toilets, Reservations accepted, Open all year, For groups-only when Green River CG is open, No water in winter - $6, Elev: 4862ft/1482m, Tel: 435-781-7700, Nearest town: Jensen, Agency: NP, GPS: 40.443784, -109.252894

31119 • Divide Ridge - BLM

Dispersed sites, No water, No toilets, Tent & RV camping: Free, Elev: 8240ft/2512m, Nearest town: Thompson, Agency: BLM, GPS: 39.416928, -109.332891

31120 • Doctor Creek - USFS

Total sites: 30, RV sites: 30, Elec sites: 0, Central water, RV dump, No showers, Flush toilets, Max length: 22ft, Reservations accepted, Open May-Sep, Tent & RV camping: $15, 2 reservable group sites: $100, Elev: 8924ft/2720m, Tel: 435-638-1069, Nearest town: Loa, Agency: USFS, GPS: 38.527965, -111.743433

31121 • Drinks Canyon - BLM

Total sites: 17, RV sites: 13, Elec sites: 0, No water, Vault toilets, Max length: 18ft, Reservations not accepted, Open all year, Tent & RV camping: $20, Stay limit: 14 days, Elev: 3986ft/1215m, Tel: 435-259-2100, Nearest town: Moab, Agency: BLM, GPS: 38.633007, -109.486419

31122 • Dripping Spring - BLM

Dispersed sites, No water, No toilets, Tents only: Free, Elev: 4355ft/1327m, Tel: 435-259-2100, Nearest town: Moab, Agency: BLM, GPS: 38.746016, -109.966119

31123 • Dripping Springs - USFS

Total sites: 23, RV sites: 23, Elec sites: 0, Central water, No RV dump, No showers, Flush toilets, Max length: 45ft, Reservations accepted, Open all year, Tent & RV camping: $18, 4 group sites: $95-$115, No water in winter - $5, Elev: 6145ft/1873m, Tel: 435-889-3000, Nearest town: Dutch John, Agency: USFS, GPS: 40.923558, -109.360253

31124 • Dry Canyon (Diamond Fork) - USFS

Dispersed sites, Vault toilets, Tent & RV camping: Free, Elev: 5518ft/1682m, Nearest town: Spanish Fork, Agency: USFS, GPS: 40.080159, -111.363755

31125 • Dubinky Well Road #1 - BLM

Dispersed sites, No water, No toilets, Tent & RV camping: Free, Elev: 5298ft/1615m, Tel: 435-259-2100, Nearest town: Moab, Agency: BLM, GPS: 38.643814, -109.819371

31126 • Dubinky Well Road #2 - BLM

Dispersed sites, No water, No toilets, Tent & RV camping: Free, Elev: 5187ft/1581m, Tel: 435-259-2100, Nearest town: Moab, Agency: BLM, GPS: 38.656348, -109.827185

31127 • Duchesne County Fairground

Total sites: 40, RV sites: 30, Elec sites: 0, No toilets, No tents/RV's: Free, Elev: 5515ft/1681m, Tel: 435-454-3211, Nearest town: Duchesne, Agency: CP, GPS: 40.158235, -110.399277

31128 • Duchesne Tunnel - USFS

Dispersed sites, No water, No toilets, Open May-Oct, Group site, Elev: 8169ft/2490m, Nearest town: Kamas, Agency: USFS, GPS: 40.593131, -110.998402

31129 • Duck Creek - USFS

Total sites: 54, RV sites: 54, Elec sites: 0, Potable water, RV dump, No showers, Flush toilets, Max length: 32ft, Reservations accepted, Open May-Sep, Tent & RV camping: $17, Group site $115, Elev: 8638ft/2633m, Tel: 435-865-3200, Nearest town: Cedar City, Agency: USFS, GPS: 37.520621, -112.698352

31130 • Duck Fort Reservoir FA - DWR

Dispersed sites, No water, Vault toilets, Reservations not accepted, Tent & RV camping: Free, Nothing larger than P/U camper, Elev: 9309ft/2837m, Tel: 801-538-4700, Nearest town: Ferron, Agency: ST, GPS: 39.172104, -111.449873

31131 • Dutch Flat Dispersed - BLM

Dispersed sites, No water, No toilets, Tent & RV camping: Free, Elev: 6079ft/1853m, Nearest town: Ferron, Agency: BLM, GPS: 39.058163, -111.040176

31132 • Dutchman Flat Dispersed - USFS
Dispersed sites, No water, No toilets, Tent & RV camping: Free, Elev: 7586ft/2312m, Nearest town: Alta, Agency: USFS, GPS: 40.528183, -111.600517

31133 • East Canyon SP - Big Rock
Total sites: 21, RV sites: 21, Elec sites: 0, No water, No RV dump, No showers, No toilets, Max length: 40ft, Open all year, Tent & RV camping: $25, Elev: 5778ft/1761m, Tel: 801-829-6866, Nearest town: Morgan, Agency: ST, GPS: 40.881007, -111.580292

31134 • East Canyon SP - Dixie Creek
Total sites: 33, RV sites: 33, Elec sites: 33, Water at site, RV dump, Showers, Flush toilets, Max length: 42ft, Open all year, Tent & RV camping: $35-40, Some FHU, Elev: 5787ft/1764m, Tel: 801-829-6866, Nearest town: Morgan, Agency: ST, GPS: 40.925119, -111.587241

31135 • East Fork Bear River - USFS
Total sites: 7, RV sites: 7, Elec sites: 0, No water, Reservations not accepted, Tent & RV camping: $18, Stay limit: 14 days, Elev: 8309ft/2533m, Tel: 307-789-3194, Nearest town: Evanston, Agency: USFS, GPS: 40.912889, -110.829167

31136 • East Fork Blacks Fork TH - USFS
Total sites: 8, RV sites: 8, Elec: Unk, No water, Vault toilets, Reservations not accepted, Tent & RV camping: Free, Elev: 9351ft/2850m, Nearest town: Mountain View, Agency: USFS, GPS: 40.884487, -110.538462

31137 • East Park - USFS
Total sites: 21, RV sites: 21, Elec sites: 0, Central water, No RV dump, No showers, Vault toilets, Max length: 25ft, Reservations not accepted, Open Jun-Sep, Tent & RV camping: $12, Elev: 9052ft/2759m, Tel: 435-789-1181, Nearest town: Vernal, Agency: USFS, GPS: 40.783019, -109.553264

31138 • Echo SP - Dry Hollow
Total sites: 14, RV sites: 14, Elec sites: 0, Central water, Flush toilets, Reservations accepted, Open all year, Tent & RV camping: $20, CG closed til spring 2020, Elev: 5580ft/1701m, Nearest town: Coalville, Agency: ST, GPS: 40.961058, -111.411109

31139 • Elk Horn - USFS
Total sites: 6, RV sites: 6, Elec sites: 0, Central water, No RV dump, No showers, Vault toilets, Reservations not accepted, Open Jun-Sep, Tent & RV camping: $8, Group site: $35, Elev: 9820ft/2993m, Tel: 435-836-2811, Nearest town: Loa, Agency: USFS, GPS: 38.463768, -111.456071

31140 • Escalante NM - Burr Trail Rd
Dispersed sites, No water, No toilets, Tent & RV camping: Free, Free permit required, Elev: 5844ft/1781m, Nearest town: Boulder, Agency: NP, GPS: 37.848684, -111.370475

31141 • Escalante Petrified Forest SP - Lakeview
Total sites: 17, RV sites: 17, Elec sites: 3, Water at site, RV dump, Showers, Flush toilets, Max length: 40ft, Reservations accepted, Open all year, Tents: $20/RV's: $28, Group site: $75, Showers closed mid-Nov to mid-Mar, Elev: 5955ft/1815m, Tel: 435-826-4466, Nearest town: Escalante, Agency: ST, GPS: 37.788354, -111.632004

31142 • Escalante Petrified Forest SP - Wide Hollow
Total sites: 16, RV sites: 16, Elec sites: 0, Central water, No RV dump, Showers, Flush toilets, Max length: 40ft, Reservations accepted, Open all year, Tent & RV camping: $20, Showers closed mid-Nov to mid-Mar, Elev: 5953ft/1814m, Tel: 435-826-4466, Nearest town: Escalante, Agency: ST, GPS: 37.787747, -111.631017

31143 • Factory Butte - Swing Arm City OHV Area - BLM
Dispersed sites, No water, No toilets, Reservations not accepted, Tent & RV camping: Free, Elev: 4504ft/1373m, Tel: 435-896-1500, Nearest town: Hanksville, Agency: BLM, GPS: 38.365783, -110.912165

31144 • Factory Butte Dispersed - BLM
Dispersed sites, No water, No toilets, Reservations not accepted, Tent & RV camping: Free, Elev: 4786ft/1459m, Nearest town: Hanksville, Agency: BLM, GPS: 38.460529, -110.888207

31145 • Ferron Reservoir Northeast - USFS
Total sites: 6, RV sites: 6, Elec sites: 0, Central water, No RV dump, No showers, Vault toilets, Max length: 22ft, Reservations not accepted, Open May-Oct, Tent & RV camping: $10, Elev: 9498ft/2895m, Tel: 435-384-2372, Nearest town: Ferron, Agency: USFS, GPS: 39.145866, -111.449602

31146 • Ferron Reservoir South - USFS
Total sites: 7, RV sites: 7, Elec sites: 0, Central water, No RV dump, No showers, Vault toilets, Max length: 22ft, Reservations not accepted, Open May-Oct, Tent & RV camping: $10, Elev: 9489ft/2892m, Tel: 435-384-2372, Nearest town: Ferron, Agency: USFS, GPS: 39.138425, -111.453058

31147 • Ferron Reservoir West - USFS
Total sites: 14, RV sites: 14, Elec sites: 0, Central water, No RV dump, No showers, Vault toilets, Max length: 22ft, Reservations accepted, Open May-Oct, Tent & RV camping: $10, Group site: $40, Elev: 9495ft/2894m, Tel: 435-384-2372, Nearest town: Ferron, Agency: USFS, GPS: 39.14273, -111.455298

31148 • Firefighter's Memorial - USFS
Total sites: 94, RV sites: 94, Elec sites: 0, Central water, RV dump, No showers, Flush toilets, Max length: 45ft, Reservations accepted, Open May-Sep, Tent & RV camping: $22, Elev: 6864ft/2092m, Tel: 435-789-1181, Nearest town: Dutch John, Agency: USFS, GPS: 40.892653, -109.454951

31149 • Fish Creek - USFS
Total sites: 7, RV sites: 7, Elec sites: 0, No water, Vault toilets, Reservations not accepted, Open May-Sep, Tent & RV camping: $7, Elev: 7697ft/2346m, Tel: 435-637-2817, Nearest town: Scofield, Agency: USFS, GPS: 39.774, -111.203

31150 • Fisher Towers - BLM

Total sites: 5, RV sites: 0, Elec sites: 0, No water, Vault toilets, Max length: 18ft, Reservations not accepted, Open all year, Tents only: $20, Stay limit: 14 days, Elev: 4711ft/1436m, Tel: 435-259-2100, Nearest town: Moab, Agency: BLM, GPS: 38.725313, -109.309127

31151 • Flat Canyon - USFS

Total sites: 12, RV sites: 12, Elec sites: 0, Central water, No RV dump, No showers, Vault toilets, Reservations accepted, Open Jun-Sep, Tent & RV camping: $10, Group site: $50, Elev: 8884ft/2708m, Tel: 435-384-2372, Nearest town: Fairview, Agency: USFS, GPS: 39.646201, -111.259767

31152 • Forks of Huntington - USFS

Total sites: 5, RV sites: 5, Elec sites: 0, Central water, No RV dump, No showers, Vault toilets, Reservations not accepted, Open May-Sep, Tent & RV camping: $10, Reservable group site: $40, Elev: 7700ft/2347m, Tel: 435-384-2372, Nearest town: Huntington, Agency: USFS, GPS: 39.500731, -111.160091

31153 • Forsyth Reservoir Dispersed - USFS

Dispersed sites, No water, Vault toilets, Tent & RV camping: Free, Several sites in this area, Elev: 8018ft/2444m, Nearest town: Fremont, Agency: USFS, GPS: 38.521206, -111.527499

31154 • Fort Buenaventura

Total sites: 15, RV sites: 15, Central water, No RV dump, No showers, Vault toilets, Reservations not accepted, Open Jun-Sep, Tent & RV camping: $20, Reservable group sites, Beside RR yard, Elev: 4331ft/1320m, Tel: 801-399-8491, Nearest town: Ogden, Agency: CP, GPS: 41.215928, -111.988539

31155 • Foy Lake - USFS

Dispersed sites, No water, Vault toilets, Reservations not accepted, Tent & RV camping: Free, Elev: 8328ft/2538m, Tel: 435-587-2041, Nearest town: Monticello, Agency: USFS, GPS: 37.903473, -109.510954

31156 • Fred Hays SP - Indian Bay

Dispersed sites, No water, Vault toilets, Open all year, Tent & RV camping: $15, Many sites, Elev: 5736ft/1748m, Tel: 435-738-2326, Nearest town: Duchesne, Agency: ST, GPS: 40.178072, -110.463359

31157 • Fred Hays SP - Juniper Point

Dispersed sites, No water, Vault toilets, Open all year, Tent & RV camping: $12, Elev: 5725ft/1745m, Tel: 435-738-2326, Nearest town: Duchesne, Agency: ST, GPS: 40.196517, -110.435033

31158 • Fred Hays SP - Knight Hollow

Dispersed sites, No water, Vault toilets, Open all year, Tent & RV camping: $12, Elev: 5771ft/1759m, Tel: 435-738-2326, Nearest town: Duchesne, Agency: ST, GPS: 40.217351, -110.423074

31159 • Fred Hays SP - Lower Beach

Total sites: 33, RV sites: 33, Elec sites: 24, Water at site, RV dump, Showers, Flush toilets, Max length: 40ft, Open all year, Tent & RV camping: $28, Elev: 5712ft/1741m, Tel: 435-738-2326, Nearest town: Duchesne, Agency: ST, GPS: 40.191644, -110.458744

31160 • Fred Hays SP - Mountain View

Total sites: 30, RV sites: 30, Elec sites: 0, Central water, No RV dump, Showers, Flush toilets, Max length: 25ft, Open all year, Tent & RV camping: $25-28, Elev: 5728ft/1746m, Tel: 435-738-2326, Nearest town: Duchesne, Agency: ST, GPS: 40.190651, -110.452751

31161 • Fred Hays SP - Rabbit Gulch

Dispersed sites, No water, Vault toilets, Open all year, Tent & RV camping: $12, Many sites, Elev: 5730ft/1747m, Tel: 435-738-2326, Nearest town: Duchesne, Agency: ST, GPS: 40.180697, -110.495573

31162 • Fremont Indian SP - Castle Rock

Total sites: 31, RV sites: 31, Elec sites: 0, Potable water, No RV dump, No showers, No toilets, Max length: 45ft, Reservations accepted, Open Apr-Sep, Tent & RV camping: $15, Elev: 6230ft/1899m, Tel: 435-527-4631, Nearest town: Joseph, Agency: ST, GPS: 38.553891, -112.355393

31163 • Fremont Indian SP - Sam Stowe

Total sites: 7, RV sites: 7, Elec sites: 7, Water at site, RV dump, Pay showers, Reservations accepted, Open Apr-Sep, Tent & RV camping: $25, Group site: $150 w/ RV hookups, Elev: 5835ft/1779m, Tel: 435-527-4631, Nearest town: Joseph, Agency: ST, GPS: 38.580743, -112.321024

31164 • Fremont River - BLM

Dispersed sites, No water, No toilets, Tent & RV camping: Free, Elev: 4827ft/1471m, Nearest town: Hanksville, Agency: BLM, GPS: 38.275295, -111.081531

31165 • Fremont River Dispersed 1 - USFS

Dispersed sites, No water, No toilets, Tent & RV camping: Free, Elev: 7942ft/2421m, Tel: 435-836-2800, Nearest town: Lyman, Agency: USFS, GPS: 38.553318, -111.587879

31166 • Fremont River Dispersed 2 - USFS

Dispersed sites, No water, Vault toilets, Tent & RV camping: Free, Elev: 7857ft/2395m, Tel: 435-836-2800, Nearest town: Lyman, Agency: USFS, GPS: 38.542232, -111.582667

31167 • Fremont River Dispersed 3 - USFS

Dispersed sites, No water, Vault toilets, Tent & RV camping: Free, Elev: 7708ft/2349m, Tel: 435-836-2800, Nearest town: Lyman, Agency: USFS, GPS: 38.520177, -111.570552

31168 • Fremont River Dispersed 4 - USFS

Dispersed sites, No water, No toilets, Tent & RV camping: Free, Elev: 7693ft/2345m, Tel: 435-836-2800, Nearest town: Lyman, Agency: USFS, GPS: 38.517332, -111.566491

31169 • Fremont River Dispersed 5 - USFS

Dispersed sites, No water, No toilets, Tent & RV camping: Free, Elev: 7718ft/2352m, Tel: 435-836-2800, Nearest town: Lyman, Agency: USFS, GPS: 38.512722, -111.563397

31170 • Fremont River Dispersed 6 - USFS
Dispersed sites, No water, Vault toilets, Tent & RV camping: Free, Elev: 7721ft/2353m, Tel: 435-836-2800, Nearest town: Lyman, Agency: USFS, GPS: 38.504548, -111.564943

31171 • Friendship - USFS
Total sites: 5, RV sites: 5, Elec sites: 0, No water, No RV dump, No showers, Vault toilets, Reservations accepted, Open May-Sep, Tent & RV camping: $12, Group site: $50, Stay limit: 7 days, Elev: 5459ft/1664m, Tel: 435-755-3620, Nearest town: Logan, Agency: USFS, GPS: 41.660749, -111.665259

31172 • FRS 006 Dispersed - USFS
Dispersed sites, No water, No toilets, Reservations not accepted, Tent & RV camping: Free, Elev: 6694ft/2040m, Tel: 435-755-3620, Nearest town: Garden City, Agency: USFS, GPS: 41.932997, -111.566217

31173 • Frying Pan - USFS
Total sites: 11, RV sites: 11, Elec sites: 0, Central water, No RV dump, No showers, Flush toilets, Reservations accepted, Open May-Sep, Tent & RV camping: $15, 1 group site $70, Elev: 9078ft/2767m, Tel: 435-638-1069, Nearest town: Loa, Agency: USFS, GPS: 38.608887, -111.679688

31174 • FS Trail 039 Dispersed - USFS
Dispersed sites, No water, No toilets, Tents only: Free, Hike-in, Elev: 6871ft/2094m, Nearest town: Cedar Hills, Agency: USFS, GPS: 40.494173, -111.634848

31175 • FSR 001 Dispersed 1 - USFS
Dispersed sites, No water, No toilets, Reservations not accepted, Open all year, Tent & RV camping: Free, Elev: 6124ft/1867m, Tel: 435-789-1181, Nearest town: Enterprise, Agency: USFS, GPS: 37.543665, -114.017633

31176 • FSR 001 Dispersed 1 - USFS
Dispersed sites, No water, No toilets, Reservations not accepted, Open all year, Tent & RV camping: Free, Numerous sites along 1 mile of road, Elev: 6154ft/1876m, Tel: 801-723-2660, Nearest town: Grantsville, Agency: USFS, GPS: 40.530621, -112.582443

31177 • FSR 001 Dispersed 10 - USFS
Dispersed sites, No water, No toilets, Reservations not accepted, Open all year, Tent & RV camping: Free, Elev: 9461ft/2884m, Tel: 435-789-1181, Nearest town: Manila, Agency: USFS, GPS: 40.879004, -109.963756

31178 • FSR 001 Dispersed 11 - USFS
Dispersed sites, No water, No toilets, Reservations not accepted, Open all year, Tent & RV camping: Free, Both sides of road, Elev: 9655ft/2943m, Tel: 435-789-1181, Nearest town: Manila, Agency: USFS, GPS: 40.869198, -109.976874

31179 • FSR 001 Dispersed 12 - USFS
Dispersed sites, No water, No toilets, Reservations not accepted, Open all year, Tent & RV camping: Free, Elev: 9669ft/2947m, Tel: 435-789-1181, Nearest town: Manila, Agency: USFS, GPS: 40.867794, -109.978803

31180 • FSR 001 Dispersed 13 - USFS
Dispersed sites, No water, No toilets, Reservations not accepted, Open all year, Tent & RV camping: Free, Elev: 10085ft/3074m, Tel: 435-789-1181, Nearest town: Manila, Agency: USFS, GPS: 40.849714, -109.998888

31181 • FSR 001 Dispersed 14 - USFS
Dispersed sites, No water, No toilets, Reservations not accepted, Open all year, Tent & RV camping: Free, Elev: 10194ft/3107m, Tel: 435-789-1181, Nearest town: Manila, Agency: USFS, GPS: 40.844319, -109.997676

31182 • FSR 001 Dispersed 2 - USFS
Dispersed sites, No water, No toilets, Reservations not accepted, Open all year, Tent & RV camping: Free, Elev: 6125ft/1867m, Tel: 435-789-1181, Nearest town: Enterprise, Agency: USFS, GPS: 37.535624, -114.025379

31183 • FSR 001 Dispersed 3 - USFS
Dispersed sites, No water, No toilets, Reservations not accepted, Open all year, Tent & RV camping: Free, Elev: 6533ft/1991m, Tel: 435-896-9233, Nearest town: Redmond, Agency: USFS, GPS: 39.009775, -111.683455

31184 • FSR 001 Dispersed 4 - USFS
Dispersed sites, No water, No toilets, Reservations not accepted, Open all year, Tent & RV camping: Free, Elev: 6721ft/2049m, Tel: 435-896-9233, Nearest town: Redmond, Agency: USFS, GPS: 39.006594, -111.669008

31185 • FSR 001 Dispersed 5 - USFS
Dispersed sites, No water, No toilets, Reservations not accepted, Open all year, Tent & RV camping: Free, Numerous sites in this area, Elev: 7708ft/2349m, Tel: 435-896-9233, Nearest town: Redmond, Agency: USFS, GPS: 38.993649, -111.638537

31186 • FSR 001 Dispersed 6 - USFS
Dispersed sites, No water, No toilets, Reservations not accepted, Open all year, Tent & RV camping: Free, Elev: 7925ft/2416m, Tel: 435-896-9233, Nearest town: Redmond, Agency: USFS, GPS: 38.999966, -111.633476

31187 • FSR 001 Dispersed 7 - USFS
Dispersed sites, No water, No toilets, Reservations not accepted, Open all year, Tent & RV camping: Free, Elev: 8926ft/2721m, Tel: 435-896-9233, Nearest town: Redmond, Agency: USFS, GPS: 39.013897, -111.593242

31188 • FSR 001 Dispersed 8 - USFS
Dispersed sites, No water, No toilets, Reservations not accepted, Open all year, Tent & RV camping: Free, Elev: 9168ft/2794m, Tel: 435-789-1181, Nearest town: Manila, Agency: USFS, GPS: 40.891073, -109.953295

31189 • FSR 001 Dispersed 9 - USFS
Dispersed sites, No water, No toilets, Reservations not accepted, Open all year, Tent & RV camping: Free, Elev: 9183ft/2799m, Tel: 435-789-1181, Nearest town: Manila, Agency: USFS, GPS: 40.891529, -109.955679

31190 • FSR 001G/H Dispersed 1 - USFS

Dispersed sites, No water, No toilets, Reservations not accepted, Open all year, Tent & RV camping: Free, Both sides of road, Elev: 8003ft/2439m, Tel: 435-896-9233, Nearest town: Redmond, Agency: USFS, GPS: 39.001173, -111.617602

31191 • FSR 001K Dispersed 2 - USFS

Dispersed sites, No water, No toilets, Reservations not accepted, Open all year, Tent & RV camping: Free, Elev: 7998ft/2438m, Tel: 435-896-9233, Nearest town: Redmond, Agency: USFS, GPS: 39.000798, -111.615043

31192 • FSR 002 Dispersed 1 - USFS

Dispersed sites, No water, No toilets, Reservations not accepted, Open all year, Tent & RV camping: Free, Road not maintained for passenger cars, Elev: 5831ft/1777m, Tel: 435-789-1181, Nearest town: Enterprise, Agency: USFS, GPS: 37.601709, -113.923555

31193 • FSR 002 Dispersed 2 - USFS

Dispersed sites, No water, No toilets, Reservations not accepted, Open all year, Tent & RV camping: Free, Road not maintained for passenger cars, Elev: 7286ft/2221m, Tel: 435-896-9233, Nearest town: Salina, Agency: USFS, GPS: 38.981608, -111.733005

31194 • FSR 003 Dispersed - USFS

Dispersed sites, No water, No toilets, Reservations not accepted, Open all year, Tents only: Free, Road not maintained for passenger cars, Elev: 5801ft/1768m, Tel: 435-789-1181, Nearest town: Enterprise, Agency: USFS, GPS: 37.503088, -113.866108

31195 • FSR 003 Dispersed 1 - USFS

Dispersed sites, No water, No toilets, Reservations not accepted, Open all year, Tent & RV camping: Free, Road not maintained for passenger cars, Elev: 5850ft/1783m, Tel: 435-789-1181, Nearest town: Enterprise, Agency: USFS, GPS: 37.498801, -113.872015

31196 • FSR 003 Dispersed 2 - USFS

Dispersed sites, No water, No toilets, Reservations not accepted, Open all year, Tent & RV camping: Free, Road not maintained for passenger cars, Elev: 5902ft/1799m, Tel: 435-789-1181, Nearest town: Enterprise, Agency: USFS, GPS: 37.494834, -113.875214

31197 • FSR 003 Dispersed 3 - USFS

Dispersed sites, No water, No toilets, Reservations not accepted, Open all year, Tent & RV camping: Free, Road not maintained for passenger cars, Elev: 5887ft/1794m, Tel: 435-789-1181, Nearest town: Enterprise, Agency: USFS, GPS: 37.495508, -113.877007

31198 • FSR 003 Dispersed 4 - USFS

Dispersed sites, No water, No toilets, Reservations not accepted, Open all year, Tent & RV camping: Free, Road not maintained for passenger cars, Elev: 6076ft/1852m, Tel: 435-789-1181, Nearest town: Enterprise, Agency: USFS, GPS: 37.499869, -113.891236

31199 • FSR 003 Dispersed 5 - USFS

Dispersed sites, No water, No toilets, Reservations not accepted, Open all year, Tent & RV camping: Free, Road not maintained for passenger cars, Elev: 6212ft/1893m, Tel: 435-789-1181, Nearest town: Enterprise, Agency: USFS, GPS: 37.505304, -113.914279

31200 • FSR 003 Dispersed 6 - USFS

Dispersed sites, No water, No toilets, Reservations not accepted, Open all year, Tent & RV camping: Free, Road not maintained for passenger cars, Elev: 6658ft/2029m, Tel: 435-789-1181, Nearest town: Enterprise, Agency: USFS, GPS: 37.502015, -113.922554

31201 • FSR 003 Dispersed 7 - USFS

Dispersed sites, No water, No toilets, Reservations not accepted, Open all year, Tent & RV camping: Free, Road not maintained for passenger cars, Elev: 6623ft/2019m, Tel: 435-789-1181, Nearest town: Enterprise, Agency: USFS, GPS: 37.495797, -113.929165

31202 • FSR 004B Dispersed 1 - USFS

Dispersed sites, No water, No toilets, Reservations not accepted, Open all year, Tent & RV camping: Free, Road not maintained for passenger cars, Elev: 8214ft/2504m, Tel: 435-896-9233, Nearest town: Redmond, Agency: USFS, GPS: 38.985561, -111.645941

31203 • FSR 004D Dispersed 1 - USFS

Dispersed sites, No water, No toilets, Reservations not accepted, Open all year, Tent & RV camping: Free, Road not maintained for passenger cars, Elev: 8405ft/2562m, Tel: 435-896-9233, Nearest town: Redmond, Agency: USFS, GPS: 38.976774, -111.645482

31204 • FSR 004F Dispersed 1 - USFS

Dispersed sites, No water, No toilets, Reservations not accepted, Open all year, Tent & RV camping: Free, Road not maintained for passenger cars, Elev: 8128ft/2477m, Tel: 435-896-9233, Nearest town: Redmond, Agency: USFS, GPS: 38.939426, -111.638334

31205 • FSR 005 Dispersed 1 - USFS

Dispersed sites, No water, No toilets, Reservations not accepted, Open all year, Tent & RV camping: Free, Road not maintained for passenger cars, Elev: 6344ft/1934m, Tel: 801-798-3571, Nearest town: Vernon, Agency: USFS, GPS: 39.966438, -112.373313

31206 • FSR 005 Dispersed 1 - USFS

Dispersed sites, No water, No toilets, Reservations not accepted, Open all year, Tent & RV camping: Free, Road not maintained for passenger cars, Elev: 7153ft/2180m, Tel: 435-755-3620, Nearest town: Garden City, Agency: USFS, GPS: 41.873935, -111.604488

31207 • FSR 005 Dispersed 1 - USFS

Dispersed sites, No water, No toilets, Reservations not accepted, Open all year, Tent & RV camping: Free, Elev: 8543ft/2604m, Tel: 435-789-1181, Nearest town: Manila, Agency: USFS, GPS: 40.872542, -109.784407

31208 • FSR 005 Dispersed 2 - USFS

Dispersed sites, No water, No toilets, Reservations not accepted, Open all year, Tent & RV camping: Free, Road not maintained for passenger cars, Elev: 6406ft/1953m, Tel: 801-798-3571, Nearest town: Vernon, Agency: USFS, GPS: 39.960531, -112.369516

31209 • FSR 005 Dispersed 2 - USFS

Dispersed sites, No water, No toilets, Reservations not accepted, Open all year, Tent & RV camping: Free, Road not maintained for passenger cars, Elev: 7582ft/2311m, Tel: 435-755-3620, Nearest town: Garden City, Agency: USFS, GPS: 41.869264, -111.611914

31210 • FSR 005 Dispersed 2 - USFS

Dispersed sites, No water, No toilets, Reservations not accepted, Open all year, Tent & RV camping: Free, Elev: 8580ft/2615m, Tel: 435-789-1181, Nearest town: Manila, Agency: USFS, GPS: 40.869394, -109.786839

31211 • FSR 005 Dispersed 3 - USFS

Dispersed sites, No water, No toilets, Reservations not accepted, Open all year, Tent & RV camping: Free, Road not maintained for passenger cars, Elev: 6439ft/1963m, Tel: 801-798-3571, Nearest town: Vernon, Agency: USFS, GPS: 39.956665, -112.367953

31212 • FSR 005 Dispersed 3 - USFS

Dispersed sites, No water, No toilets, Reservations not accepted, Open all year, Tent & RV camping: Free, Road not maintained for passenger cars, Elev: 7718ft/2352m, Tel: 435-755-3620, Nearest town: Garden City, Agency: USFS, GPS: 41.870211, -111.615906

31213 • FSR 005 Dispersed 4 - USFS

Dispersed sites, No water, No toilets, Reservations not accepted, Open all year, Tent & RV camping: Free, Road not maintained for passenger cars, Elev: 6460ft/1969m, Tel: 801-798-3571, Nearest town: Vernon, Agency: USFS, GPS: 39.955322, -112.366983

31214 • FSR 005 Dispersed 5 - USFS

Dispersed sites, No water, No toilets, Reservations not accepted, Open all year, Tent & RV camping: Free, Road not maintained for passenger cars, Elev: 6540ft/1993m, Tel: 801-798-3571, Nearest town: Vernon, Agency: USFS, GPS: 39.947772, -112.35782

31215 • FSR 005 Dispersed 6 - USFS

Dispersed sites, No water, No toilets, Reservations not accepted, Open all year, Tent & RV camping: Free, Road not maintained for passenger cars, Elev: 6558ft/1999m, Tel: 801-798-3571, Nearest town: Vernon, Agency: USFS, GPS: 39.946966, -112.355401

31216 • FSR 005 Dispersed 7 - USFS

Dispersed sites, No water, No toilets, Reservations not accepted, Open all year, Tent & RV camping: Free, Road not maintained for passenger cars, Elev: 6594ft/2010m, Tel: 801-798-3571, Nearest town: Vernon, Agency: USFS, GPS: 39.944399, -112.353365

31217 • FSR 006 Dispersed 1 - USFS

Dispersed sites, No water, No toilets, Reservations not accepted, Open all year, Tent & RV camping: Free, Road not maintained for passenger cars, Elev: 4947ft/1508m, Tel: 435-789-1181, Nearest town: Veyo, Agency: USFS, GPS: 37.387971, -113.749834

31218 • FSR 006 Dispersed 1 - USFS

Dispersed sites, No water, No toilets, Reservations not accepted, Open all year, Tent & RV camping: Free, Road not maintained for passenger cars, Elev: 6359ft/1938m, Tel: 801-798-3571, Nearest town: Vernon, Agency: USFS, GPS: 39.963885, -112.372931

31219 • FSR 006 Dispersed 10 - USFS

Dispersed sites, No water, No toilets, Reservations not accepted, Open all year, Tent & RV camping: Free, Road not maintained for passenger cars, Elev: 6123ft/1866m, Tel: 801-798-3571, Nearest town: Vernon, Agency: USFS, GPS: 39.999749, -112.428025

31220 • FSR 006 Dispersed 10 - USFS

Dispersed sites, No water, No toilets, Reservations not accepted, Tent & RV camping: Free, Elev: 6896ft/2102m, Tel: 435-755-3620, Nearest town: Garden City, Agency: USFS, GPS: 41.946166, -111.580152

31221 • FSR 006 Dispersed 11 - USFS

Dispersed sites, No water, No toilets, Reservations not accepted, Open all year, Tent & RV camping: Free, Road not maintained for passenger cars, Elev: 6102ft/1860m, Tel: 801-798-3571, Nearest town: Vernon, Agency: USFS, GPS: 40.001344, -112.427433

31222 • FSR 006 Dispersed 11 - USFS

Dispersed sites, No water, No toilets, Reservations not accepted, Tent & RV camping: Free, Elev: 6952ft/2119m, Tel: 435-755-3620, Nearest town: Garden City, Agency: USFS, GPS: 41.951238, -111.583817

31223 • FSR 006 Dispersed 12 - USFS

Dispersed sites, No water, No toilets, Reservations not accepted, Tent & RV camping: Free, Elev: 7113ft/2168m, Tel: 435-755-3620, Nearest town: Garden City, Agency: USFS, GPS: 41.960264, -111.591114

31224 • FSR 006 Dispersed 13 - USFS

Dispersed sites, No water, No toilets, Reservations not accepted, Tent & RV camping: Free, Both sides of road, Elev: 7184ft/2190m, Tel: 435-755-3620, Nearest town: Garden City, Agency: USFS, GPS: 41.964508, -111.593246

31225 • FSR 006 Dispersed 14 - USFS

Dispersed sites, No water, No toilets, Reservations not accepted, Open all year, Tent & RV camping: Free, Elev: 7272ft/2217m, Tel: 435-755-3620, Nearest town: Garden City, Agency: USFS, GPS: 41.968234, -111.595114

31226 • FSR 006 Dispersed 15 - USFS

Dispersed sites, No water, No toilets, Reservations not accepted, Tent & RV camping: Free, Elev: 7300ft/2225m, Tel: 435-755-3620, Nearest town: Garden City, Agency: USFS, GPS: 41.967807, -111.597032

31227 • FSR 006 Dispersed 2 - USFS

Dispersed sites, No water, No toilets, Reservations not accepted, Open all year, Tents only: Free, Road not maintained for passenger cars, Elev: 5719ft/1743m, Tel: 435-789-1181, Nearest town: Enterprise, Agency: USFS, GPS: 37.442708, -113.830884

31228 • FSR 006 Dispersed 2 - USFS

Dispersed sites, No water, No toilets, Reservations not accepted, Open all year, Tent & RV camping: Free, Road not maintained for passenger cars, Elev: 6440ft/1963m, Tel: 801-798-3571, Nearest town: Vernon, Agency: USFS, GPS: 39.960131, -112.378443

31229 • FSR 006 Dispersed 3 - USFS

Dispersed sites, No water, No toilets, Reservations not accepted, Open all year, Tent & RV camping: Free, Road not maintained for passenger cars, Elev: 5569ft/1697m, Tel: 435-789-1181, Nearest town: Enterprise, Agency: USFS, GPS: 37.459273, -113.828533

31230 • FSR 006 Dispersed 3 - USFS

Dispersed sites, No water, No toilets, Reservations not accepted, Open all year, Tent & RV camping: Free, Road not maintained for passenger cars, Elev: 6542ft/1994m, Tel: 801-798-3571, Nearest town: Vernon, Agency: USFS, GPS: 39.959527, -112.386055

31231 • FSR 006 Dispersed 4 - USFS

Dispersed sites, No water, No toilets, Reservations not accepted, Open all year, Tents only: Free, Road not maintained for passenger cars, Elev: 5648ft/1722m, Tel: 435-789-1181, Nearest town: Enterprise, Agency: USFS, GPS: 37.468323, -113.828928

31232 • FSR 006 Dispersed 4 - USFS

Dispersed sites, No water, No toilets, Reservations not accepted, Open all year, Tent & RV camping: Free, Road not maintained for passenger cars, Elev: 6585ft/2007m, Tel: 801-798-3571, Nearest town: Vernon, Agency: USFS, GPS: 39.959623, -112.387855

31233 • FSR 006 Dispersed 5 - USFS

Dispersed sites, No water, No toilets, Reservations not accepted, Open all year, Tent & RV camping: Free, Road not maintained for passenger cars, Elev: 6159ft/1877m, Tel: 435-789-1181, Nearest town: Enterprise, Agency: USFS, GPS: 37.478402, -113.839108

31234 • FSR 006 Dispersed 5 - USFS

Dispersed sites, No water, No toilets, Reservations not accepted, Open all year, Tent & RV camping: Free, Road not maintained for passenger cars, Elev: 6290ft/1917m, Tel: 801-798-3571, Nearest town: Vernon, Agency: USFS, GPS: 39.987517, -112.430501

31235 • FSR 006 Dispersed 6 - USFS

Dispersed sites, No water, No toilets, Reservations not accepted, Open all year, Tent & RV camping: Free, Road not maintained for passenger cars, Elev: 6088ft/1856m, Tel: 435-789-1181, Nearest town: Enterprise, Agency: USFS, GPS: 37.479661, -113.842463

31236 • FSR 006 Dispersed 6 - USFS

Dispersed sites, No water, No toilets, Reservations not accepted, Open all year, Tent & RV camping: Free, Road not maintained for passenger cars, Elev: 6264ft/1909m, Tel: 801-798-3571, Nearest town: Vernon, Agency: USFS, GPS: 39.989672, -112.428726

31237 • FSR 006 Dispersed 7 - USFS

Dispersed sites, No water, No toilets, Reservations not accepted, Open all year, Tent & RV camping: Free, Elev: 5715ft/1742m, Tel: 435-789-1181, Nearest town: Enterprise, Agency: USFS, GPS: 37.544511, -113.845297

31238 • FSR 006 Dispersed 7 - USFS

Dispersed sites, No water, No toilets, Reservations not accepted, Open all year, Tent & RV camping: Free, Road not maintained for passenger cars, Elev: 6217ft/1895m, Tel: 801-798-3571, Nearest town: Vernon, Agency: USFS, GPS: 39.992524, -112.427802

31239 • FSR 006 Dispersed 8 - USFS

Dispersed sites, No water, No toilets, Reservations not accepted, Open all year, Tent & RV camping: Free, Road not maintained for passenger cars, Elev: 6184ft/1885m, Tel: 801-798-3571, Nearest town: Vernon, Agency: USFS, GPS: 39.994496, -112.428338

31240 • FSR 006 Dispersed 8 - USFS

Dispersed sites, No water, No toilets, Reservations not accepted, Tent & RV camping: Free, Elev: 6762ft/2061m, Tel: 435-755-3620, Nearest town: Garden City, Agency: USFS, GPS: 41.938159, -111.570505

31241 • FSR 006 Dispersed 9 - USFS

Dispersed sites, No water, No toilets, Reservations not accepted, Open all year, Tent & RV camping: Free, Road not maintained for passenger cars, Elev: 6143ft/1872m, Tel: 801-798-3571, Nearest town: Vernon, Agency: USFS, GPS: 39.997659, -112.426831

31242 • FSR 006 Dispersed 9 - USFS

Dispersed sites, No water, No toilets, Reservations not accepted, Open all year, Tent & RV camping: Free, Elev: 6814ft/2077m, Tel: 435-755-3620, Nearest town: Garden City, Agency: USFS, GPS: 41.943598, -111.574236

31243 • FSR 007 Dispersed 1 - USFS

Dispersed sites, No water, No toilets, Reservations not accepted, Open all year, Tent & RV camping: Free, Road not maintained for passenger cars, Elev: 5490ft/1673m, Tel: 435-789-1181, Nearest town: Enterprise, Agency: USFS, GPS: 37.545434, -113.718697

31244 • FSR 007 Dispersed 1 - USFS

Dispersed sites, No water, No toilets, Reservations not accepted, Open Jun-Nov, Tent & RV camping: Free, Elev: 6300ft/1920m, Tel: 435-755-3620, Nearest town: Logan, Agency: USFS, GPS: 41.814578, -111.570437

31245 • FSR 007 Dispersed 1 - USFS

Dispersed sites, No water, No toilets, Reservations not accepted, Open Apr-Nov, Tent & RV camping: Free, Road not maintained for passenger cars, Elev: 7885ft/2403m, Tel: 801-785-3563, Nearest town: Midway, Agency: USFS, GPS: 40.547364, -111.598616

31246 • FSR 007 Dispersed 2 - USFS

Dispersed sites, No water, No toilets, Reservations not accepted, Open all year, Tent & RV camping: Free, Elev: 5636ft/1718m, Tel: 435-789-1181, Nearest town: Enterprise, Agency: USFS, GPS: 37.520486, -113.710071

31247 • FSR 007 Dispersed 2 - USFS

Dispersed sites, No water, No toilets, Reservations not accepted, Open Jun-Nov, Tent & RV camping: Free, Several sites in this area, Elev: 6366ft/1940m, Tel: 435-755-3620, Nearest town: Logan, Agency: USFS, GPS: 41.817456, -111.574716

31248 • FSR 007 Dispersed 2 - USFS

Dispersed sites, No water, No toilets, Reservations not accepted, Open Apr-Nov, Tent & RV camping: Free, Road not maintained for passenger cars, Elev: 7815ft/2382m, Tel: 801-785-3563, Nearest town: Midway, Agency: USFS, GPS: 40.544843, -111.595315

31249 • FSR 007 Dispersed 3 - USFS

Dispersed sites, No water, No toilets, Reservations not accepted, Open Jun-Nov, Tent & RV camping: Free, Elev: 5910ft/1801m, Tel: 435-755-3620, Nearest town: Logan, Agency: USFS, GPS: 41.829553, -111.579008

31250 • FSR 007 Dispersed 3 - USFS

Dispersed sites, No water, No toilets, Reservations not accepted, Open all year, Tent & RV camping: Free, Road not maintained for passenger cars, Elev: 6237ft/1901m, Tel: 435-789-1181, Nearest town: Enterprise, Agency: USFS, GPS: 37.496703, -113.727632

31251 • FSR 007 Dispersed 3 - USFS

Dispersed sites, No water, No toilets, Reservations not accepted, Open Apr-Nov, Tent & RV camping: Free, Road not maintained for passenger cars, Elev: 7804ft/2379m, Tel: 801-785-3563, Nearest town: Midway, Agency: USFS, GPS: 40.543315, -111.594878

31252 • FSR 007 Dispersed 4 - USFS

Dispersed sites, No water, No toilets, Reservations not accepted, Open Jun-Nov, Tent & RV camping: Free, Road not maintained for passenger cars, Elev: 6514ft/1985m, Tel: 435-755-3620, Nearest town: Logan, Agency: USFS, GPS: 41.794742, -111.566352

31253 • FSR 007 Dispersed 4 - USFS

Dispersed sites, No water, No toilets, Reservations not accepted, Open Apr-Nov, Tent & RV camping: Free, Road not maintained for passenger cars, Elev: 7735ft/2358m, Tel: 801-785-3563, Nearest town: Midway, Agency: USFS, GPS: 40.538685, -111.593274

31254 • FSR 007 Dispersed 4 - USFS

Dispersed sites, No water, No toilets, Reservations not accepted, Open all year, Tent & RV camping: Free, Road not maintained for passenger cars, Elev: 8168ft/2490m, Tel: 435-789-1181, Nearest town: Manila, Agency: USFS, GPS: 40.866531, -109.755484

31255 • FSR 007 Dispersed 5 - USFS

Dispersed sites, No water, No toilets, Reservations not accepted, Open Jun-Nov, Tent & RV camping: Free, Elev: 6554ft/1998m, Tel: 435-755-3620, Nearest town: Logan, Agency: USFS, GPS: 41.792886, -111.566334

31256 • FSR 007 Dispersed 5 - USFS

Dispersed sites, No water, No toilets, Reservations not accepted, Open Apr-Nov, Tent & RV camping: Free, Road not maintained for passenger cars, Elev: 7707ft/2349m, Tel: 801-785-3563, Nearest town: Midway, Agency: USFS, GPS: 40.536867, -111.593575

31257 • FSR 007 Dispersed 5 - USFS

Dispersed sites, No water, No toilets, Reservations not accepted, Open all year, Tent & RV camping: Free, Road not maintained for passenger cars, Elev: 8186ft/2495m, Tel: 435-789-1181, Nearest town: Manila, Agency: USFS, GPS: 40.865917, -109.758102

31258 • FSR 007 Dispersed 6 - USFS

Dispersed sites, No water, No toilets, Reservations not accepted, Open Jun-Nov, Tent & RV camping: Free, Elev: 7495ft/2284m, Tel: 435-755-3620, Nearest town: Logan, Agency: USFS, GPS: 41.793776, -111.543641

31259 • FSR 007 Dispersed 6 - USFS

Dispersed sites, No water, No toilets, Reservations not accepted, Open Apr-Nov, Tent & RV camping: Free, Road not maintained for passenger cars, Elev: 7691ft/2344m, Tel: 801-785-3563, Nearest town: Midway, Agency: USFS, GPS: 40.535283, -111.594139

31260 • FSR 007 Dispersed 7 - USFS

Dispersed sites, No water, No toilets, Reservations not accepted, Open Jun-Nov, Tent & RV camping: Free, Elev: 7423ft/2263m, Tel: 435-755-3620, Nearest town: Logan, Agency: USFS, GPS: 41.792966, -111.541163

31261 • FSR 007 Dispersed 8 - USFS

Dispersed sites, No water, No toilets, Reservations not accepted, Open Jun-Nov, Tent & RV camping: Free, Elev: 7603ft/2317m, Tel: 435-755-3620, Nearest town: Logan, Agency: USFS, GPS: 41.790679, -111.527841

31262 • FSR 007 Dispersed 9 - USFS

Dispersed sites, No water, No toilets, Reservations not accepted, Open Jun-Nov, Tent & RV camping: Free, Elev: 7572ft/2308m, Tel: 435-755-3620, Nearest town: Logan, Agency: USFS, GPS: 41.804779, -111.482295

31263 • FSR 007A Dispersed 1 - USFS

Dispersed sites, No water, No toilets, Reservations not accepted, Open all year, Tent & RV camping: Free, Nothing larger than truck camper/van - no trailers, Road not maintained for passenger cars, Elev: 8232ft/2509m, Tel: 435-896-9233, Nearest town: Salina, Agency: USFS, GPS: 38.920185, -111.445447

31264 • FSR 007C Dispersed 1 - USFS

Dispersed sites, No water, No toilets, Reservations not accepted, Open all year, Tent & RV camping: Free, Road not maintained for passenger cars, Elev: 8309ft/2533m, Tel: 435-896-9233, Nearest town: Salina, Agency: USFS, GPS: 38.970334, -111.394352

31265 • FSR 008 Dispersed 1 - USFS

Dispersed sites, No water, No toilets, Reservations not accepted, Open all year, Tent & RV camping: Free, Road not maintained for passenger cars, Elev: 7367ft/2245m, Tel: 435-438-2427, Nearest town: Beaver, Agency: USFS, GPS: 38.176942, -112.508833

31266 • FSR 008 Dispersed 1 - USFS

Dispersed sites, No water, No toilets, Reservations not accepted, Open all year, Tent & RV camping: Free, Elev: 7539ft/2298m, Tel: 801-723-2660, Nearest town: Farmington, Agency: USFS, GPS: 40.982987, -111.807914

31267 • FSR 008 Dispersed 1 - USFS

Dispersed sites, No water, No toilets, Reservations not accepted, Open all year, Tent & RV camping: Free, Numerous sites in area, Elev: 7545ft/2300m, Tel: 435-755-3620, Nearest town: Logan, Agency: USFS, GPS: 41.808472, -111.458706

31268 • FSR 008 Dispersed 1 - USFS

Dispersed sites, No water, No toilets, Reservations not accepted, Open Apr-Nov, Tent & RV camping: Free, Road not maintained for passenger cars, Elev: 7729ft/2356m, Tel: 801-785-3563, Nearest town: Cedar Hills, Agency: USFS, GPS: 40.511836, -111.655977

31269 • FSR 008 Dispersed 2 - USFS

Dispersed sites, No water, No toilets, Reservations not accepted, Open all year, Tent & RV camping: Free, Elev: 8230ft/2509m, Tel:

801-723-2660, Nearest town: Farmington, Agency: USFS, GPS: 40.972394, -111.814254

31270 • FSR 009 (Lazy Mtn) Dispersed 1 - USFS
Total sites: 13, RV sites: 13, Elec: Unk, No water, No toilets, Reservations not accepted, Open all year, Tent & RV camping: Free, Elev: 7093ft/2162m, Tel: 435-896-9233, Nearest town: Salina, Agency: USFS, GPS: 38.915623, -111.530678

31271 • FSR 009 Dispersed 1 - USFS
Dispersed sites, No water, No toilets, Reservations not accepted, Open all year, Tent & RV camping: Free, Road not maintained for passenger cars, Elev: 6582ft/2006m, Tel: 435-789-1181, Nearest town: Newcastle, Agency: USFS, GPS: 37.597249, -113.376123

31272 • FSR 009 Dispersed 2 - USFS
Dispersed sites, No water, No toilets, Reservations not accepted, Open all year, Tent & RV camping: Free, Road not maintained for passenger cars, Elev: 6296ft/1919m, Tel: 435-789-1181, Nearest town: Newcastle, Agency: USFS, GPS: 37.560351, -113.451235

31273 • FSR 009 Dispersed 3 - USFS
Dispersed sites, No water, No toilets, Reservations not accepted, Open all year, Tent & RV camping: Free, Elev: 8513ft/2595m, Tel: 435-896-9233, Nearest town: Redmond, Agency: USFS, GPS: 38.965334, -111.568933

31274 • FSR 009F Dispersed 1 - USFS
Dispersed sites, No water, No toilets, Reservations not accepted, Open all year, Tent & RV camping: Free, Elev: 8922ft/2719m, Tel: 435-896-9233, Nearest town: Redmond, Agency: USFS, GPS: 39.006275, -111.587799

31275 • FSR 010 Dispersed 1 - USFS
Dispersed sites, No water, No toilets, Reservations not accepted, Open all year, Tent & RV camping: Free, Road not maintained for passenger cars, Elev: 5588ft/1703m, Tel: 435-789-1181, Nearest town: Enterprise, Agency: USFS, GPS: 37.561014, -113.616062

31276 • FSR 010 Dispersed 2 - USFS
Dispersed sites, No water, No toilets, Reservations not accepted, Open all year, Tent & RV camping: Free, Road not maintained for passenger cars, Elev: 5906ft/1800m, Tel: 435-789-1181, Nearest town: Enterprise, Agency: USFS, GPS: 37.545658, -113.606101

31277 • FSR 010 Dispersed 3 - USFS
Dispersed sites, No water, No toilets, Reservations not accepted, Open all year, Tent & RV camping: Free, Elev: 8623ft/2628m, Tel: 435-789-1181, Nearest town: Manila, Agency: USFS, GPS: 40.875482, -109.861172

31278 • FSR 010 Dispersed 4 - USFS
Dispersed sites, No water, No toilets, Reservations not accepted, Open all year, Tent & RV camping: Free, Elev: 8620ft/2627m, Tel: 435-789-1181, Nearest town: Manila, Agency: USFS, GPS: 40.874514, -109.865243

31279 • FSR 0101 Dispersed 1 - USFS
Dispersed sites, No water, No toilets, Tent & RV camping: Free, Elev: 6011ft/1832m, Nearest town: Levan, Agency: USFS, GPS: 39.536701, -111.778149

31280 • FSR 011 Dispersed 1 - USFS
Dispersed sites, No water, No toilets, Reservations not accepted, Open all year, Tent & RV camping: Free, Elev: 5716ft/1742m, Tel: 435-789-1181, Nearest town: Newcastle, Agency: USFS, GPS: 37.593159, -113.521343

31281 • FSR 011 Dispersed 1 - USFS
Dispersed sites, No water, No toilets, Reservations not accepted, Open all year, Tent & RV camping: Free, Elev: 7316ft/2230m, Tel: 435-755-3620, Nearest town: Garden City, Agency: USFS, GPS: 41.988779, -111.525323

31282 • FSR 011 Dispersed 2 - USFS
Dispersed sites, No water, No toilets, Reservations not accepted, Open all year, Tent & RV camping: Free, Elev: 6265ft/1910m, Tel: 435-789-1181, Nearest town: Newcastle, Agency: USFS, GPS: 37.506646, -113.500417

31283 • FSR 011 Dispersed 2 - USFS
Dispersed sites, No water, No toilets, Reservations not accepted, Open all year, Tent & RV camping: Free, Elev: 7514ft/2290m, Tel: 435-755-3620, Nearest town: Garden City, Agency: USFS, GPS: 41.996109, -111.521879

31284 • FSR 0110 Dispersed 1 - USFS
Total sites: 3, RV sites: 3, Elec sites: 0, No water, Vault toilets, Reservations not accepted, Open May-Sep, Tent & RV camping: $3, Elev: 8212ft/2503m, Tel: 435-636-3500, Nearest town: Huntington, Agency: USFS, GPS: 39.534858, -111.140891

31285 • FSR 011A Dispersed 1 - USFS
Dispersed sites, No water, No toilets, Reservations not accepted, Open all year, Tent & RV camping: Free, Road not maintained for passenger cars, Elev: 8285ft/2525m, Tel: 435-896-9233, Nearest town: Salina, Agency: USFS, GPS: 38.845931, -111.452452

31286 • FSR 012 Dispersed 1 - USFS
Dispersed sites, No water, No toilets, Reservations not accepted, Open all year, Tent & RV camping: Free, Road not maintained for passenger cars, Elev: 6616ft/2017m, Tel: 435-789-1181, Nearest town: Manila, Agency: USFS, GPS: 40.959978, -109.466622

31287 • FSR 014 Dispersed 1 - USFS
Dispersed sites, No water, No toilets, Reservations not accepted, Open all year, Tent & RV camping: Free, Several sites in this area, Elev: 8346ft/2544m, Tel: 435-755-3620, Nearest town: Garden City, Agency: USFS, GPS: 41.991132, -111.486287

31288 • FSR 014 Dispersed 2 - USFS
Dispersed sites, No water, No toilets, Reservations not accepted, Open all year, Tent & RV camping: Free, Elev: 8385ft/2556m, Tel: 435-755-3620, Nearest town: Garden City, Agency: USFS, GPS: 41.976129, -111.487783

31289 • FSR 014 Dispersed 3 - USFS

Dispersed sites, No water, No toilets, Reservations not accepted, Open all year, Tent & RV camping: Free, Elev: 7681ft/2341m, Tel: 435-755-3620, Nearest town: Garden City, Agency: USFS, GPS: 41.957747, -111.488971

31290 • FSR 015 Dispersed 1 - USFS

Dispersed sites, No water, No toilets, Reservations not accepted, Open all year, Tent & RV camping: Free, Road not maintained for passenger cars, Elev: 5992ft/1826m, Tel: 435-789-1181, Nearest town: Enterprise, Agency: USFS, GPS: 37.562664, -114.022781

31291 • FSR 015 Dispersed 1 - USFS

Dispersed sites, No water, No toilets, Reservations not accepted, Open Mar-Dec, Tent & RV camping: Free, Elev: 8075ft/2461m, Tel: 801-798-3571, Nearest town: Santaquin, Agency: USFS, GPS: 39.924129, -111.630978

31292 • FSR 015 Dispersed 10 - USFS

Dispersed sites, No water, No toilets, Reservations not accepted, Open Mar-Dec, Tent & RV camping: Free, Elev: 8737ft/2663m, Tel: 801-798-3571, Nearest town: Mona, Agency: USFS, GPS: 39.883415, -111.688122

31293 • FSR 015 Dispersed 10 - USFS

Dispersed sites, No water, No toilets, Reservations not accepted, Open all year, Tent & RV camping: Free, Road not maintained for passenger cars, Elev: 8874ft/2705m, Tel: 435-789-1181, Nearest town: Manila, Agency: USFS, GPS: 40.921289, -109.914704

31294 • FSR 015 Dispersed 11 - USFS

Dispersed sites, No water, No toilets, Reservations not accepted, Open all year, Tent & RV camping: Free, Road not maintained for passenger cars, Elev: 8736ft/2663m, Tel: 435-789-1181, Nearest town: Manila, Agency: USFS, GPS: 40.906864, -109.905028

31295 • FSR 015 Dispersed 11 - USFS

Dispersed sites, No water, No toilets, Reservations not accepted, Open Mar-Dec, Tent & RV camping: Free, Elev: 8897ft/2712m, Tel: 801-798-3571, Nearest town: Mona, Agency: USFS, GPS: 39.866311, -111.686118

31296 • FSR 015 Dispersed 12 - USFS

Dispersed sites, No water, No toilets, Reservations not accepted, Open all year, Tent & RV camping: Free, Road not maintained for passenger cars, Elev: 8732ft/2662m, Tel: 435-789-1181, Nearest town: Manila, Agency: USFS, GPS: 40.904961, -109.896935

31297 • FSR 015 Dispersed 12 - USFS

Dispersed sites, No water, Vault toilets, Reservations not accepted, Open Mar-Dec, Tent & RV camping: Free, Vault toilet across road, Elev: 9278ft/2828m, Tel: 801-798-3571, Nearest town: Mona, Agency: USFS, GPS: 39.842482, -111.719266

31298 • FSR 015 Dispersed 13 - USFS

Dispersed sites, No water, No toilets, Reservations not accepted, Open Mar-Dec, Tent & RV camping: Free, Elev: 8359ft/2548m, Tel: 801-798-3571, Nearest town: Nephi, Agency: USFS, GPS: 39.807803, -111.696028

31299 • FSR 015 Dispersed 13 - USFS

Dispersed sites, No water, No toilets, Reservations not accepted, Open all year, Tent & RV camping: Free, Road not maintained for passenger cars, Elev: 8730ft/2661m, Tel: 435-789-1181, Nearest town: Manila, Agency: USFS, GPS: 40.904127, -109.891505

31300 • FSR 015 Dispersed 14 - USFS

Dispersed sites, No water, No toilets, Reservations not accepted, Open Mar-Dec, Tent & RV camping: Free, Elev: 7983ft/2433m, Tel: 801-798-3571, Nearest town: Nephi, Agency: USFS, GPS: 39.790689, -111.678568

31301 • FSR 015 Dispersed 15 - USFS

Dispersed sites, No water, No toilets, Reservations not accepted, Open Mar-Dec, Tent & RV camping: Free, Numerous sites, Elev: 6194ft/1888m, Tel: 801-798-3571, Nearest town: Nephi, Agency: USFS, GPS: 39.760555, -111.710301

31302 • FSR 015 Dispersed 16 - USFS

Dispersed sites, No water, No toilets, Reservations not accepted, Open Mar-Dec, Tent & RV camping: Free, Elev: 6151ft/1875m, Tel: 801-798-3571, Nearest town: Nephi, Agency: USFS, GPS: 39.757725, -111.709781

31303 • FSR 015 Dispersed 2 - USFS

Dispersed sites, No water, No toilets, Reservations not accepted, Open Mar-Dec, Tent & RV camping: Free, Elev: 8137ft/2480m, Tel: 801-798-3571, Nearest town: Santaquin, Agency: USFS, GPS: 39.920305, -111.633369

31304 • FSR 015 Dispersed 2 - USFS

Dispersed sites, No water, No toilets, Reservations not accepted, Open all year, Tent & RV camping: Free, Elev: 8595ft/2620m, Tel: 435-836-2800, Nearest town: Fremont, Agency: USFS, GPS: 38.652158, -111.477508

31305 • FSR 015 Dispersed 3 - USFS

Dispersed sites, No water, No toilets, Reservations not accepted, Open Mar-Dec, Tent & RV camping: Free, Several sites, Elev: 8201ft/2500m, Tel: 801-798-3571, Nearest town: Santaquin, Agency: USFS, GPS: 39.916353, -111.634712

31306 • FSR 015 Dispersed 3 - USFS

Dispersed sites, No water, No toilets, Reservations not accepted, Open all year, Tent & RV camping: Free, Several sites, Road not maintained for passenger cars, Elev: 9591ft/2923m, Tel: 435-836-2800, Nearest town: Fremont, Agency: USFS, GPS: 38.676781, -111.506238

31307 • FSR 015 Dispersed 4 - USFS

Dispersed sites, No water, No toilets, Reservations not accepted, Open Mar-Dec, Tent & RV camping: Free, Several sites, Elev: 8380ft/2554m, Tel: 801-798-3571, Nearest town: Santaquin, Agency: USFS, GPS: 39.910801, -111.642155

31308 • FSR 015 Dispersed 4 - USFS

Dispersed sites, No water, No toilets, Reservations not accepted, Open all year, Tent & RV camping: Free, Road not maintained for

passenger cars, Elev: 9613ft/2930m, Tel: 435-836-2800, Nearest town: Fremont, Agency: USFS, GPS: 38.679055, -111.508241

31309 • FSR 015 Dispersed 5 - USFS
Dispersed sites, No water, No toilets, Reservations not accepted, Open Mar-Dec, Tent & RV camping: Free, Elev: 8429ft/2569m, Tel: 801-798-3571, Nearest town: Mona, Agency: USFS, GPS: 39.906319, -111.649217

31310 • FSR 015 Dispersed 5 - USFS
Dispersed sites, No water, No toilets, Reservations not accepted, Open all year, Tent & RV camping: Free, Road not maintained for passenger cars, Elev: 9496ft/2894m, Tel: 435-836-2800, Nearest town: Fremont, Agency: USFS, GPS: 38.685896, -111.517003

31311 • FSR 015 Dispersed 6 - USFS
Dispersed sites, No water, No toilets, Reservations not accepted, Open Mar-Dec, Tent & RV camping: Free, Elev: 8469ft/2581m, Tel: 801-798-3571, Nearest town: Mona, Agency: USFS, GPS: 39.897957, -111.656152

31312 • FSR 015 Dispersed 6 - USFS
Dispersed sites, No water, No toilets, Reservations not accepted, Open all year, Tent & RV camping: Free, Numerous sites in this area, Elev: 9042ft/2756m, Tel: 435-836-2800, Nearest town: Fremont, Agency: USFS, GPS: 38.648722, -111.595279

31313 • FSR 015 Dispersed 7 - USFS
Dispersed sites, No water, No toilets, Reservations not accepted, Open Mar-Dec, Tent & RV camping: Free, Elev: 8513ft/2595m, Tel: 801-798-3571, Nearest town: Mona, Agency: USFS, GPS: 39.898409, -111.659875

31314 • FSR 015 Dispersed 7 - USFS
Dispersed sites, No water, No toilets, Tent & RV camping: Free, Several sites in this area, Elev: 9081ft/2768m, Tel: 435-836-2800, Nearest town: Loa, Agency: USFS, GPS: 38.614628, -111.614046

31315 • FSR 015 Dispersed 8 - USFS
Dispersed sites, No water, No toilets, Reservations not accepted, Open Mar-Dec, Tent & RV camping: Free, Elev: 8517ft/2596m, Tel: 801-798-3571, Nearest town: Mona, Agency: USFS, GPS: 39.902354, -111.673054

31316 • FSR 015 Dispersed 8 - USFS
Dispersed sites, No water, No toilets, Reservations not accepted, Open all year, Tent & RV camping: Free, Road not maintained for passenger cars, Elev: 8702ft/2652m, Tel: 435-789-1181, Nearest town: Manila, Agency: USFS, GPS: 40.929574, -110.002324

31317 • FSR 015 Dispersed 9 - USFS
Dispersed sites, No water, No toilets, Reservations not accepted, Open all year, Tents only: Free, Road not maintained for passenger cars, Elev: 9013ft/2747m, Tel: 435-789-1181, Nearest town: Manila, Agency: USFS, GPS: 40.927084, -109.935987

31318 • FSR 015 Dispersed 9 - USFS
Dispersed sites, No water, No toilets, Reservations not accepted, Open Mar-Dec, Tent & RV camping: Free, Elev: 8428ft/2569m,

Tel: 801-798-3571, Nearest town: Mona, Agency: USFS, GPS: 39.902243, -111.678161

31319 • FSR 015D Dispersed 1 - USFS
Dispersed sites, No water, No toilets, Reservations not accepted, Open all year, Tent & RV camping: Free, Road not maintained for passenger cars, Elev: 9411ft/2868m, Tel: 435-836-2800, Nearest town: Fremont, Agency: USFS, GPS: 38.690875, -111.517854

31320 • FSR 016 Dispersed 1 - USFS
Dispersed sites, No water, No toilets, Reservations not accepted, Open Mar-Dec, Tent & RV camping: Free, Several sites in area, Elev: 6022ft/1836m, Tel: 801-798-3571, Nearest town: Nephi, Agency: USFS, GPS: 39.743744, -111.711472

31321 • FSR 016 Dispersed 1 - USFS
Dispersed sites, No water, No toilets, Reservations not accepted, Open all year, Tent & RV camping: Free, Numerous sites in area, Elev: 8347ft/2544m, Tel: 801-625-5112, Nearest town: Woodruff, Agency: USFS, GPS: 41.414114, -111.536722

31322 • FSR 016 Dispersed 1 - USFS
Dispersed sites, No water, No toilets, Reservations not accepted, Open all year, Tent & RV camping: Free, Road not maintained for passenger cars, Elev: 9234ft/2815m, Tel: 307-782-6555, Nearest town: Mountain View (WY), Agency: USFS, GPS: 40.977383, -110.483629

31323 • FSR 016 Dispersed 2 - USFS
Dispersed sites, No water, No toilets, Reservations not accepted, Open Mar-Dec, Tent & RV camping: Free, Road not maintained for passenger cars, Elev: 6588ft/2008m, Tel: 801-798-3571, Nearest town: Nephi, Agency: USFS, GPS: 39.767182, -111.682165

31324 • FSR 016 Dispersed 3 - USFS
Dispersed sites, No water, No toilets, Reservations not accepted, Open Mar-Dec, Tent & RV camping: Free, Road not maintained for passenger cars, Elev: 6670ft/2033m, Tel: 801-798-3571, Nearest town: Nephi, Agency: USFS, GPS: 39.769524, -111.675348

31325 • FSR 016 Dispersed 4 - USFS
Dispersed sites, No water, No toilets, Reservations not accepted, Open Mar-Dec, Tent & RV camping: Free, Road not maintained for passenger cars, Elev: 6891ft/2100m, Tel: 801-798-3571, Nearest town: Nephi, Agency: USFS, GPS: 39.770918, -111.661319

31326 • FSR 016 Dispersed 5 - USFS
Dispersed sites, No water, No toilets, Reservations not accepted, Open Mar-Dec, Tent & RV camping: Free, Road not maintained for passenger cars, Elev: 6944ft/2117m, Tel: 801-798-3571, Nearest town: Nephi, Agency: USFS, GPS: 39.769285, -111.659013

31327 • FSR 016 Dispersed 6 - USFS
Dispersed sites, No water, No toilets, Reservations not accepted, Open Mar-Dec, Tent & RV camping: Free, Road not maintained for passenger cars, Elev: 7064ft/2153m, Tel: 801-798-3571, Nearest town: Nephi, Agency: USFS, GPS: 39.769794, -111.652209

31328 • FSR 016 Dispersed 7 - USFS

Dispersed sites, No water, No toilets, Reservations not accepted, Open Mar-Dec, Tent & RV camping: Free, At end of road, Road not maintained for passenger cars, Elev: 7491ft/2283m, Tel: 801-798-3571, Nearest town: Nephi, Agency: USFS, GPS: 39.774251, -111.630331

31329 • FSR 017 Dispersed 1 - USFS

Dispersed sites, No water, No toilets, Reservations not accepted, Open Apr-Dec, Tents only: Free, Road not maintained for passenger cars, Elev: 9105ft/2775m, Tel: 435-836-2800, Nearest town: Fremont, Agency: USFS, GPS: 38.602975, -111.518343

31330 • FSR 017 Dispersed 2 - USFS

Dispersed sites, No water, No toilets, Reservations not accepted, Open all year, Tent & RV camping: Free, Elev: 9386ft/2861m, Tel: 307-782-6555, Nearest town: Mountain View (WY), Agency: USFS, GPS: 40.979445, -110.342986

31331 • FSR 018 Dispersed 1 - USFS

Dispersed sites, No water, No toilets, Reservations not accepted, Open all year, Tent & RV camping: Free, Elev: 9229ft/2813m, Tel: 435-789-1181, Nearest town: Vernal, Agency: USFS, GPS: 40.743929, -109.639908

31332 • FSR 018 Dispersed 2 - USFS

Dispersed sites, No water, No toilets, Reservations not accepted, Open all year, Tent & RV camping: Free, Elev: 9316ft/2840m, Tel: 435-789-1181, Nearest town: Vernal, Agency: USFS, GPS: 40.746476, -109.676299

31333 • FSR 018 Dispersed 3 - USFS

Dispersed sites, No water, No toilets, Reservations not accepted, Open all year, Tent & RV camping: Free, Elev: 9349ft/2850m, Tel: 435-789-1181, Nearest town: Vernal, Agency: USFS, GPS: 40.743468, -109.687241

31334 • FSR 018 Dispersed 4 - USFS

Dispersed sites, No water, No toilets, Reservations not accepted, Open all year, Tent & RV camping: Free, Elev: 9447ft/2879m, Tel: 435-789-1181, Nearest town: Vernal, Agency: USFS, GPS: 40.741724, -109.709247

31335 • FSR 018 Dispersed 5 - USFS

Dispersed sites, No water, No toilets, Reservations not accepted, Open all year, Tent & RV camping: Free, Elev: 9793ft/2985m, Tel: 435-789-1181, Nearest town: Vernal, Agency: USFS, GPS: 40.701448, -109.749296

31336 • FSR 018 Dispersed 6 - USFS

Dispersed sites, No water, No toilets, Reservations not accepted, Open all year, Tent & RV camping: Free, Elev: 9422ft/2872m, Tel: 435-789-1181, Nearest town: Vernal, Agency: USFS, GPS: 40.668354, -109.741818

31337 • FSR 018D Dispersed 1 - USFS

Dispersed sites, No water, No toilets, Reservations not accepted, Open Apr-Dec, Tent & RV camping: Free, Road not maintained for passenger cars, Elev: 8996ft/2742m, Tel: 435-836-2800, Nearest town: Fremont, Agency: USFS, GPS: 38.593631, -111.549614

31338 • FSR 019 (Meeks Lake) Dispersed 3 - USFS

Dispersed sites, No water, No toilets, Reservations not accepted, Open all year, Tent & RV camping: Free, Road not maintained for passenger cars, Elev: 8417ft/2566m, Tel: 435-836-2800, Nearest town: Lyman, Agency: USFS, GPS: 38.537263, -111.453128

31339 • FSR 019 Dispersed 1 - USFS

Dispersed sites, No water, No toilets, Reservations not accepted, Open all year, Tent & RV camping: Free, Road not maintained for passenger cars, Elev: 6075ft/1852m, Tel: 435-789-1181, Nearest town: Enterprise, Agency: USFS, GPS: 37.633616, -113.990892

31340 • FSR 019 Dispersed 2 - USFS

Dispersed sites, No water, No toilets, Reservations not accepted, Open all year, Tent & RV camping: Free, Road not maintained for passenger cars, Elev: 7907ft/2410m, Tel: 435-836-2800, Nearest town: Lyman, Agency: USFS, GPS: 38.544629, -111.430175

31341 • FSR 019A (Meeks Lake) Dispersed - USFS

Dispersed sites, No water, No toilets, Reservations not accepted, Open all year, Tent & RV camping: Free, Road not maintained for passenger cars, Elev: 8425ft/2568m, Tel: 435-836-2800, Nearest town: Lyman, Agency: USFS, GPS: 38.538232, -111.452372

31342 • FSR 020 Dispersed 1 - USFS

Dispersed sites, No water, No toilets, Reservations not accepted, Open all year, Tent & RV camping: Free, Elev: 9395ft/2864m, Tel: 435-789-1181, Nearest town: Dutch John, Agency: USFS, GPS: 40.796655, -109.572296

31343 • FSR 020 Dispersed 2 - USFS

Dispersed sites, No water, No toilets, Reservations not accepted, Open all year, Tent & RV camping: Free, Elev: 9351ft/2850m, Tel: 435-789-1181, Nearest town: Dutch John, Agency: USFS, GPS: 40.796654, -109.586179

31344 • FSR 020E Dispersed 1 - USFS

Dispersed sites, No water, No toilets, Reservations not accepted, Open all year, Tent & RV camping: Free, Road not maintained for passenger cars, Elev: 8265ft/2519m, Tel: 435-836-2800, Nearest town: Lyman, Agency: USFS, GPS: 38.524698, -111.433558

31345 • FSR 021A Dispersed 1 - USFS

Dispersed sites, No water, No toilets, Reservations not accepted, Open all year, Tent & RV camping: Free, Elev: 8944ft/2726m, Tel: 435-836-2800, Nearest town: Fremont, Agency: USFS, GPS: 38.582459, -111.480489

31346 • FSR 022 Dispersed 1 - USFS

Dispersed sites, No water, No toilets, Reservations not accepted, Open all year, Tent & RV camping: Free, Road not maintained for passenger cars, Elev: 5908ft/1801m, Tel: 435-789-1181, Nearest town: Central, Agency: USFS, GPS: 37.416157, -113.571911

31347 • FSR 022 Dispersed 2 - USFS

Dispersed sites, No water, No toilets, Reservations not accepted, Open all year, Tent & RV camping: Free, Road not maintained for passenger cars, Elev: 7771ft/2369m, Tel: 435-836-2800, Nearest town: Lyman, Agency: USFS, GPS: 38.471959, -111.400112

31348 • FSR 022 Dispersed 3 - USFS

Dispersed sites, No water, No toilets, Reservations not accepted, Open all year, Tent & RV camping: Free, Road not maintained for passenger cars, Elev: 9043ft/2756m, Tel: 435-836-2800, Nearest town: Lyman, Agency: USFS, GPS: 38.486454, -111.443512

31349 • FSR 022A Dispersed 1 - USFS

Dispersed sites, No water, No toilets, Reservations not accepted, Open all year, Tent & RV camping: Free, Elev: 9445ft/2879m, Tel: 435-836-2800, Nearest town: Lyman, Agency: USFS, GPS: 38.497182, -111.457346

31350 • FSR 022D Dispersed 1 - USFS

Dispersed sites, No water, No toilets, Reservations not accepted, Open all year, Tent & RV camping: Free, Elev: 9382ft/2860m, Tel: 435-836-2800, Nearest town: Lyman, Agency: USFS, GPS: 38.490905, -111.454612

31351 • FSR 023 Dispersed 1 - USFS

Dispersed sites, No water, No toilets, Reservations not accepted, Open all year, Tent & RV camping: Free, Road not maintained for passenger cars, Elev: 9385ft/2861m, Tel: 435-783-4338, Nearest town: Heber City, Agency: USFS, GPS: 40.449107, -111.153116

31352 • FSR 026 Dispersed 1 - USFS

Dispersed sites, No water, No toilets, Reservations not accepted, Open all year, Tent & RV camping: Free, Road not maintained for passenger cars, Elev: 9431ft/2875m, Tel: 435-783-4338, Nearest town: Heber City, Agency: USFS, GPS: 40.428056, -111.160873

31353 • FSR 026 Dispersed 2 - USFS

Dispersed sites, No water, No toilets, Reservations not accepted, Open all year, Tent & RV camping: Free, Road not maintained for passenger cars, Elev: 9391ft/2862m, Tel: 435-783-4338, Nearest town: Heber City, Agency: USFS, GPS: 40.429875, -111.159607

31354 • FSR 026 Dispersed 3 - USFS

Dispersed sites, No water, No toilets, Reservations not accepted, Open all year, Tent & RV camping: Free, Road not maintained for passenger cars, Elev: 9236ft/2815m, Tel: 435-783-4338, Nearest town: Heber City, Agency: USFS, GPS: 40.431311, -111.142824

31355 • FSR 026 Dispersed 4 - USFS

Dispersed sites, No water, No toilets, Reservations not accepted, Open all year, Tent & RV camping: Free, Elev: 9932ft/3027m, Tel: 435-789-1181, Nearest town: Vernal, Agency: USFS, GPS: 40.775088, -109.752684

31356 • FSR 026 Dispersed 5 - USFS

Dispersed sites, No water, No toilets, Reservations not accepted, Open all year, Tent & RV camping: Free, Elev: 9891ft/3015m, Tel: 435-789-1181, Nearest town: Vernal, Agency: USFS, GPS: 40.791331, -109.759243

31357 • FSR 0269 (Skutumpah Reservoir) Dispersed 1 - USFS

Dispersed sites, No water, No toilets, Reservations not accepted, Open all year, Tent & RV camping: Free, Road not maintained for passenger cars, Elev: 7907ft/2410m, Tel: 435-896-9233, Nearest town: Salina, Agency: USFS, GPS: 38.938638, -111.490295

31358 • FSR 027 Dispersed 1 - USFS

Dispersed sites, No water, No toilets, Reservations not accepted, Open May-Nov, Tents only: Free, Walk-to sites, Elev: 6064ft/1848m, Tel: 801-785-3563, Nearest town: Orem, Agency: USFS, GPS: 40.309963, -111.629705

31359 • FSR 027 Dispersed 10 - USFS

Dispersed sites, No water, No toilets, Reservations not accepted, Open May-Nov, Tents only: Free, Walk-to sites, Road not maintained for passenger cars, Elev: 7126ft/2172m, Tel: 801-798-3571, Nearest town: Orem, Agency: USFS, GPS: 40.191356, -111.546583

31360 • FSR 027 Dispersed 11 - USFS

Dispersed sites, No water, No toilets, Reservations not accepted, Open all year, Tent & RV camping: Free, Elev: 9880ft/3011m, Tel: 435-789-1181, Nearest town: Vernal, Agency: USFS, GPS: 40.702489, -109.762217

31361 • FSR 027 Dispersed 12 - USFS

Dispersed sites, No water, No toilets, Reservations not accepted, Open all year, Tent & RV camping: Free, Elev: 10404ft/3171m, Tel: 435-789-1181, Nearest town: Vernal, Agency: USFS, GPS: 40.710927, -109.788346

31362 • FSR 027 Dispersed 2 - USFS

Dispersed sites, No toilets, Reservations not accepted, Open May-Nov, Tent & RV camping: Free, Several sites, Elev: 7372ft/2247m, Tel: 801-785-3563, Nearest town: Orem, Agency: USFS, GPS: 40.291204, -111.608285

31363 • FSR 027 Dispersed 3 - USFS

Dispersed sites, No water, No toilets, Reservations not accepted, Open May-Nov, Tents only: Free, Walk-to sites, Elev: 7587ft/2313m, Tel: 801-785-3563, Nearest town: Orem, Agency: USFS, GPS: 40.288169, -111.603712

31364 • FSR 027 Dispersed 4 - USFS

Dispersed sites, No water, No toilets, Reservations not accepted, Open May-Nov, Tents only: Free, Walk-to sites, Elev: 7659ft/2334m, Tel: 801-785-3563, Nearest town: Orem, Agency: USFS, GPS: 40.285167, -111.603366

31365 • FSR 027 Dispersed 5 - USFS

Dispersed sites, No water, No toilets, Reservations not accepted, Open May-Nov, Tents only: Free, Walk-to sites, Elev: 7387ft/2252m, Tel: 801-785-3563, Nearest town: Orem, Agency: USFS, GPS: 40.276528, -111.598431

31366 • FSR 027 Dispersed 6 - USFS

Dispersed sites, No water, No toilets, Reservations not accepted, Open May-Nov, Tents only: Free, Walk-to sites, Road not maintained for passenger cars, Elev: 8015ft/2443m, Tel: 801-785-3563, Nearest town: Orem, Agency: USFS, GPS: 40.250847, -111.575872

31367 • FSR 027 Dispersed 7 - USFS
Dispersed sites, No water, No toilets, Reservations not accepted, Open May-Nov, Tents only: Free, Walk-to sites, Road not maintained for passenger cars, Elev: 8076ft/2462m, Tel: 801-785-3563, Nearest town: Orem, Agency: USFS, GPS: 40.247989, -111.577926

31368 • FSR 027 Dispersed 8 - USFS
Dispersed sites, No water, No toilets, Reservations not accepted, Open May-Nov, Tents only: Free, Walk-to sites, Road not maintained for passenger cars, Elev: 8353ft/2546m, Tel: 801-785-3563, Nearest town: Orem, Agency: USFS, GPS: 40.233484, -111.574479

31369 • FSR 027 Dispersed 9 - USFS
Dispersed sites, No water, No toilets, Reservations not accepted, Open May-Nov, Tents only: Free, Walk-to sites, Road not maintained for passenger cars, Elev: 8555ft/2608m, Tel: 801-785-3563, Nearest town: Orem, Agency: USFS, GPS: 40.212149, -111.571643

31370 • FSR 029 Dispersed 1 - USFS
Dispersed sites, No water, No toilets, Reservations not accepted, Open all year, Tent & RV camping: Free, Elev: 5848ft/1782m, Tel: 435-789-1181, Nearest town: New Harmony, Agency: USFS, GPS: 37.523757, -113.328868

31371 • FSR 029 Dispersed 10 - USFS
Dispersed sites, No water, No toilets, Reservations not accepted, Open Jun-Oct, Tent & RV camping: Free, Elev: 6265ft/1910m, Tel: 435-783-4338, Nearest town: Springville, Agency: USFS, GPS: 40.152828, -111.332773

31372 • FSR 029 Dispersed 2 - USFS
Dispersed sites, No water, No toilets, Reservations not accepted, Open all year, Tent & RV camping: Free, Elev: 6458ft/1968m, Tel: 435-789-1181, Nearest town: New Harmony, Agency: USFS, GPS: 37.547293, -113.348316

31373 • FSR 029 Dispersed 3 - USFS
Dispersed sites, No water, No toilets, Reservations not accepted, Open all year, Tent & RV camping: Free, Elev: 6864ft/2092m, Tel: 435-789-1181, Nearest town: New Harmony, Agency: USFS, GPS: 37.548107, -113.362826

31374 • FSR 029 Dispersed 4 - USFS
Dispersed sites, No water, No toilets, Reservations not accepted, Open all year, Tent & RV camping: Free, Elev: 6633ft/2022m, Tel: 435-789-1181, Nearest town: New Harmony, Agency: USFS, GPS: 37.539858, -113.372117

31375 • FSR 029 Dispersed 5 - USFS
Dispersed sites, No water, No toilets, Reservations not accepted, Open Jun-Oct, Tent & RV camping: Free, Elev: 6064ft/1848m,

Tel: 435-783-4338, Nearest town: Springville, Agency: USFS, GPS: 40.127356, -111.337973

31376 • FSR 029 Dispersed 6 - USFS
Dispersed sites, No water, No toilets, Reservations not accepted, Open Jun-Oct, Tent & RV camping: Free, Elev: 6076ft/1852m, Tel: 435-783-4338, Nearest town: Springville, Agency: USFS, GPS: 40.129499, -111.338679

31377 • FSR 029 Dispersed 7 - USFS
Dispersed sites, No water, No toilets, Reservations not accepted, Open Jun-Oct, Tent & RV camping: Free, Elev: 6099ft/1859m, Tel: 435-783-4338, Nearest town: Springville, Agency: USFS, GPS: 40.132226, -111.338856

31378 • FSR 029 Dispersed 8 - USFS
Dispersed sites, No water, No toilets, Reservations not accepted, Open Jun-Oct, Tent & RV camping: Free, Elev: 6165ft/1879m, Tel: 435-783-4338, Nearest town: Springville, Agency: USFS, GPS: 40.138566, -111.340093

31379 • FSR 029 Dispersed 9 - USFS
Dispersed sites, No water, No toilets, Reservations not accepted, Open Jun-Oct, Tent & RV camping: Free, Elev: 6264ft/1909m, Tel: 435-783-4338, Nearest town: Springville, Agency: USFS, GPS: 40.148517, -111.337396

31380 • FSR 030 Dispersed 1 - USFS
Dispersed sites, No water, No toilets, Reservations not accepted, Open all year, Tent & RV camping: Free, Road not maintained for passenger cars, Elev: 7979ft/2432m, Tel: 435-783-4338, Nearest town: Oakley, Agency: USFS, GPS: 40.735232, -111.106166

31381 • FSR 030 Dispersed 10 - USFS
Dispersed sites, No water, No toilets, Reservations not accepted, Open all year, Tent & RV camping: Free, Elev: 9066ft/2763m, Tel: 435-789-1181, Nearest town: Vernal, Agency: USFS, GPS: 40.644621, -109.712427

31382 • FSR 030 Dispersed 2 - USFS
Dispersed sites, No water, No toilets, Reservations not accepted, Open all year, Tent & RV camping: Free, Road not maintained for passenger cars, Elev: 8009ft/2441m, Tel: 435-783-4338, Nearest town: Oakley, Agency: USFS, GPS: 40.732453, -111.109274

31383 • FSR 030 Dispersed 3 - USFS
Dispersed sites, No water, No toilets, Reservations not accepted, Open all year, Tent & RV camping: Free, Road not maintained for passenger cars, Elev: 9326ft/2843m, Tel: 435-783-4338, Nearest town: Oakley, Agency: USFS, GPS: 40.730991, -111.128436

31384 • FSR 030 Dispersed 4 - USFS
Dispersed sites, No water, No toilets, Reservations not accepted, Open all year, Tent & RV camping: Free, Road not maintained for passenger cars, Elev: 8902ft/2713m, Tel: 435-789-1181, Nearest town: Vernal, Agency: USFS, GPS: 40.605041, -109.689288

31385 • FSR 030 Dispersed 5 - USFS

Dispersed sites, No water, No toilets, Reservations not accepted, Open all year, Tent & RV camping: Free, Road not maintained for passenger cars, Elev: 8905ft/2714m, Tel: 435-789-1181, Nearest town: Vernal, Agency: USFS, GPS: 40.606545, -109.689559

31386 • FSR 030 Dispersed 6 - USFS

Dispersed sites, No water, No toilets, Reservations not accepted, Open all year, Tent & RV camping: Free, Road not maintained for passenger cars, Elev: 8984ft/2738m, Tel: 435-789-1181, Nearest town: Vernal, Agency: USFS, GPS: 40.609175, -109.688265

31387 • FSR 030 Dispersed 7 - USFS

Dispersed sites, No water, No toilets, Reservations not accepted, Open all year, Tent & RV camping: Free, Road not maintained for passenger cars, Elev: 9033ft/2753m, Tel: 435-789-1181, Nearest town: Vernal, Agency: USFS, GPS: 40.623825, -109.696474

31388 • FSR 030 Dispersed 8 - USFS

Dispersed sites, No water, No toilets, Reservations not accepted, Open all year, Tent & RV camping: Free, Road not maintained for passenger cars, Elev: 9050ft/2758m, Tel: 435-789-1181, Nearest town: Vernal, Agency: USFS, GPS: 40.625896, -109.696779

31389 • FSR 030 Dispersed 9 - USFS

Dispersed sites, No water, No toilets, Reservations not accepted, Open all year, Tent & RV camping: Free, Road not maintained for passenger cars, Elev: 9083ft/2768m, Tel: 435-789-1181, Nearest town: Vernal, Agency: USFS, GPS: 40.630549, -109.698797

31390 • FSR 031 Dispersed - USFS

Dispersed sites, No water, No toilets, Reservations not accepted, Open all year, Tent & RV camping: Free, Elev: 4242ft/1293m, Tel: 435-789-1181, Nearest town: Leeds, Agency: USFS, GPS: 37.264666, -113.414268

31391 • FSR 031 Dispersed 1 - USFS

Dispersed sites, No water, No toilets, Reservations not accepted, Open all year, Tent & RV camping: Free, Road not maintained for passenger cars, Elev: 4991ft/1521m, Tel: 435-789-1181, Nearest town: St George, Agency: USFS, GPS: 37.233014, -113.560767

31392 • FSR 031 Dispersed 10 - USFS

Dispersed sites, No water, No toilets, Reservations not accepted, Open May-Nov, Tent & RV camping: Free, Elev: 5648ft/1722m, Tel: 801-798-3571, Nearest town: Thistle, Agency: USFS, GPS: 40.113152, -111.436104

31393 • FSR 031 Dispersed 11 - USFS

Dispersed sites, No water, No toilets, Reservations not accepted, Open May-Nov, Tent & RV camping: Free, Elev: 5953ft/1814m, Tel: 801-798-3571, Nearest town: Thistle, Agency: USFS, GPS: 40.127456, -111.422185

31394 • FSR 031 Dispersed 2 - USFS

Dispersed sites, No water, No toilets, Reservations not accepted, Open all year, Tent & RV camping: Free, Road not maintained for passenger cars, Elev: 5144ft/1568m, Tel: 435-789-1181, Nearest town: St George, Agency: USFS, GPS: 37.243525, -113.539865

31395 • FSR 031 Dispersed 3 - USFS

Dispersed sites, No water, No toilets, Reservations not accepted, Open all year, Tent & RV camping: Free, Road not maintained for passenger cars, Elev: 5050ft/1539m, Tel: 435-789-1181, Nearest town: St George, Agency: USFS, GPS: 37.244801, -113.519164

31396 • FSR 031 Dispersed 4 - USFS

Dispersed sites, No water, No toilets, Reservations not accepted, Open all year, Tent & RV camping: Free, Road not maintained for passenger cars, Elev: 4340ft/1323m, Tel: 435-789-1181, Nearest town: St George, Agency: USFS, GPS: 37.235989, -113.454014

31397 • FSR 031 Dispersed 5 - USFS

Dispersed sites, No water, No toilets, Reservations not accepted, Open all year, Tent & RV camping: Free, Road not maintained for passenger cars, Elev: 7216ft/2199m, Tel: 435-783-4338, Nearest town: Oakley, Agency: USFS, GPS: 40.742697, -111.181736

31398 • FSR 031 Dispersed 6 - USFS

Dispersed sites, No water, No toilets, Reservations not accepted, Open May-Nov, Tent & RV camping: Free, Elev: 5385ft/1641m, Tel: 801-798-3571, Nearest town: Thistle, Agency: USFS, GPS: 40.088173, -111.433899

31399 • FSR 031 Dispersed 7 - USFS

Dispersed sites, No water, No toilets, Reservations not accepted, Open May-Nov, Tent & RV camping: Free, Elev: 5431ft/1655m, Tel: 801-798-3571, Nearest town: Thistle, Agency: USFS, GPS: 40.093469, -111.436405

31400 • FSR 031 Dispersed 8 - USFS

Dispersed sites, No water, No toilets, Reservations not accepted, Open May-Nov, Tent & RV camping: Free, Elev: 5456ft/1663m, Tel: 801-798-3571, Nearest town: Thistle, Agency: USFS, GPS: 40.096001, -111.435843

31401 • FSR 031 Dispersed 9 - USFS

Dispersed sites, No water, No toilets, Reservations not accepted, Open May-Nov, Tent & RV camping: Free, Elev: 5574ft/1699m, Tel: 801-798-3571, Nearest town: Thistle, Agency: USFS, GPS: 40.107548, -111.436294

31402 • FSR 032 (Whitney Reservoir) Dispersed 1 - USFS

Dispersed sites, No water, No toilets, Reservations not accepted, Open May-Dec, Tent & RV camping: Free, Numerous sites in this area, Elev: 9274ft/2827m, Tel: 307-789-3194, Nearest town: Oakley, Agency: USFS, GPS: 40.843695, -110.930052

31403 • FSR 032 Dispersed 2 - USFS

Dispersed sites, No water, No toilets, Reservations not accepted, Open May-Dec, Tent & RV camping: Free, Elev: 9169ft/2795m, Tel: 307-789-3194, Nearest town: Oakley, Agency: USFS, GPS: 40.853049, -110.867949

31404 • FSR 032 Dispersed 3 - USFS

Dispersed sites, No water, No toilets, Reservations not accepted, Open all year, Tent & RV camping: Free, Road not maintained for passenger cars, Elev: 8330ft/2539m, Tel: 435-896-9233, Nearest town: Salina, Agency: USFS, GPS: 38.807119, -111.670801

31405 • FSR 032 Dispersed 4 - USFS

Dispersed sites, No water, No toilets, Reservations not accepted, Tent & RV camping: Free, Elev: 4126ft/1258m, Tel: 435-652-3100, Nearest town: Leeds, Agency: USFS, GPS: 37.268688, -113.373191

31406 • FSR 032 Dispersed 5 - USFS

Dispersed sites, No water, No toilets, Tent & RV camping: Free, Elev: 4378ft/1334m, Nearest town: Leeds, Agency: USFS, GPS: 37.272896, -113.388598

31407 • FSR 032 Dispersed 6 - USFS

Dispersed sites, No water, No toilets, Reservations not accepted, Tent & RV camping: Free, Elev: 5090ft/1551m, Tel: 435-652-3100, Nearest town: Leeds, Agency: USFS, GPS: 37.291977, -113.412744

31408 • FSR 032 Dispersed 7 - USFS

Dispersed sites, No water, No toilets, Max length: 18ft, Reservations not accepted, Open May-Oct, Tent & RV camping: Free, Elev: 5894ft/1796m, Tel: 435-789-1181, Nearest town: Leeds, Agency: USFS, GPS: 37.310553, -113.433932

31409 • FSR 032B Dispersed 1 - USFS

Dispersed sites, No water, No toilets, Reservations not accepted, Open all year, Tent & RV camping: Free, Road not maintained for passenger cars, Elev: 8399ft/2560m, Tel: 435-896-9233, Nearest town: Salina, Agency: USFS, GPS: 38.808227, -111.669162

31410 • FSR 032D Dispersed 1 - USFS

Dispersed sites, No water, No toilets, Reservations not accepted, Open all year, Tent & RV camping: Free, Road not maintained for passenger cars, Elev: 8473ft/2583m, Tel: 435-896-9233, Nearest town: Salina, Agency: USFS, GPS: 38.810859, -111.668856

31411 • FSR 032E Dispersed 1 - USFS

Dispersed sites, No water, No toilets, Reservations not accepted, Open all year, Tent & RV camping: Free, Road not maintained for passenger cars, Elev: 8872ft/2704m, Tel: 435-896-9233, Nearest town: Salina, Agency: USFS, GPS: 38.820868, -111.665946

31412 • FSR 033 Dispersed 1 - USFS

Dispersed sites, No water, No toilets, Reservations not accepted, Open all year, Tent & RV camping: Free, Road not maintained for passenger cars, Elev: 5394ft/1644m, Tel: 435-789-1181, Nearest town: St George, Agency: USFS, GPS: 37.251529, -113.526973

31413 • FSR 033 Dispersed 2 - USFS

Dispersed sites, No water, No toilets, Reservations not accepted, Open all year, Tent & RV camping: Free, High-clearance vehicle required, Elev: 9050ft/2758m, Tel: 435-738-2482, Nearest town: Spanish Fork, Agency: USFS, GPS: 39.995644, -110.985633

31414 • FSR 034 Dispersed 1 - USFS

Dispersed sites, No water, No toilets, Reservations not accepted, Open all year, Tent & RV camping: Free, Road not maintained for passenger cars, Elev: 7057ft/2151m, Tel: 435-789-1181, Nearest town: Pine Valley, Agency: USFS, GPS: 37.339841, -113.557723

31415 • FSR 034 Dispersed 2 - USFS

Dispersed sites, No water, No toilets, Reservations not accepted, Open all year, Tent & RV camping: Free, Elev: 7801ft/2378m, Tel: 435-783-4338, Nearest town: Samak, Agency: USFS, GPS: 40.623476, -111.138507

31416 • FSR 034 Dispersed 3 - USFS

Dispersed sites, No water, No toilets, Reservations not accepted, Open all year, Tent & RV camping: Free, Elev: 7773ft/2369m, Tel: 435-783-4338, Nearest town: Samak, Agency: USFS, GPS: 40.628473, -111.148491

31417 • FSR 034 Dispersed 4 - USFS

Dispersed sites, No water, No toilets, Reservations not accepted, Open all year, Tent & RV camping: Free, Elev: 8389ft/2557m, Tel: 435-783-4338, Nearest town: Samak, Agency: USFS, GPS: 40.635688, -111.144784

31418 • FSR 034 Dispersed 5 - USFS

Dispersed sites, No water, No toilets, Reservations not accepted, Open all year, Tent & RV camping: Free, Road not maintained for passenger cars, Elev: 8879ft/2706m, Tel: 435-783-4338, Nearest town: Samak, Agency: USFS, GPS: 40.644264, -111.129949

31419 • FSR 035 Dispersed 1 - USFS

Dispersed sites, No water, No toilets, Reservations not accepted, Tent & RV camping: Free, Elev: 7779ft/2371m, Tel: 435-783-4338, Nearest town: Kamas, Agency: USFS, GPS: 40.604108, -111.103639

31420 • FSR 035 Dispersed 10 - USFS

Dispersed sites, No water, No toilets, Reservations not accepted, Tent & RV camping: Free, Elev: 8971ft/2734m, Tel: 435-783-4338, Nearest town: Kamas, Agency: USFS, GPS: 40.629451, -111.077214

31421 • FSR 035 Dispersed 2 - USFS

Dispersed sites, No water, No toilets, Reservations not accepted, Tent & RV camping: Free, Elev: 7830ft/2387m, Tel: 435-783-4338, Nearest town: Kamas, Agency: USFS, GPS: 40.603651, -111.100599

31422 • FSR 035 Dispersed 3 - USFS

Dispersed sites, No water, No toilets, Reservations not accepted, Tent & RV camping: Free, Elev: 7917ft/2413m, Tel: 435-783-4338, Nearest town: Kamas, Agency: USFS, GPS: 40.605135, -111.098624

31423 • FSR 035 Dispersed 4 - USFS

Dispersed sites, No water, No toilets, Reservations not accepted, Tent & RV camping: Free, Elev: 7979ft/2432m, Tel: 435-783-4338, Nearest town: Kamas, Agency: USFS, GPS: 40.606421, -111.099781

31424 • FSR 035 Dispersed 5 - USFS

Dispersed sites, No water, No toilets, Reservations not accepted, Tent & RV camping: Free, Elev: 8158ft/2487m, Tel: 435-783-4338, Nearest town: Kamas, Agency: USFS, GPS: 40.609231, -111.099569

31425 • FSR 035 Dispersed 6 - USFS

Dispersed sites, No water, No toilets, Reservations not accepted, Tents only: Free, Elev: 8210ft/2502m, Tel: 435-783-4338, Nearest town: Kamas, Agency: USFS, GPS: 40.610809, -111.099874

31426 • FSR 035 Dispersed 7 - USFS

Dispersed sites, No water, No toilets, Reservations not accepted, Tent & RV camping: Free, Elev: 8325ft/2537m, Tel: 435-783-4338, Nearest town: Kamas, Agency: USFS, GPS: 40.614545, -111.094608

31427 • FSR 035 Dispersed 8 - USFS

Dispersed sites, No water, No toilets, Reservations not accepted, Tent & RV camping: Free, Elev: 8506ft/2593m, Tel: 435-783-4338, Nearest town: Kamas, Agency: USFS, GPS: 40.616268, -111.085093

31428 • FSR 035 Dispersed 9 - USFS

Dispersed sites, No water, No toilets, Reservations not accepted, Tent & RV camping: Free, Elev: 8534ft/2601m, Tel: 435-783-4338, Nearest town: Kamas, Agency: USFS, GPS: 40.617638, -111.084734

31429 • FSR 036B Dispersed 1 - USFS

Dispersed sites, No water, No toilets, Reservations not accepted, Open all year, Tent & RV camping: Free, Road not maintained for passenger cars, Elev: 7687ft/2343m, Tel: 435-836-2800, Nearest town: Lyman, Agency: USFS, GPS: 38.503249, -111.558407

31430 • FSR 037 Dispersed 1 - USFS

Dispersed sites, No water, No toilets, Reservations not accepted, Open all year, Tent & RV camping: Free, Elev: 8157ft/2486m, Tel: 435-783-4338, Nearest town: Woodland, Agency: USFS, GPS: 40.569608, -111.041538

31431 • FSR 037 Dispersed 2 - USFS

Dispersed sites, No water, No toilets, Reservations not accepted, Open all year, Tent & RV camping: Free, Elev: 8596ft/2620m, Tel: 435-783-4338, Nearest town: Woodland, Agency: USFS, GPS: 40.560648, -111.033836

31432 • FSR 037 Dispersed 3 - USFS

Dispersed sites, No water, No toilets, Reservations not accepted, Open all year, Tent & RV camping: Free, Numerous sites, Elev: 8590ft/2618m, Tel: 435-783-4338, Nearest town: Woodland, Agency: USFS, GPS: 40.555039, -111.031219

31433 • FSR 037 Dispersed 4 - USFS

Dispersed sites, No water, No toilets, Reservations not accepted, Open all year, Tent & RV camping: Free, Numerous sites, Elev: 8591ft/2619m, Tel: 435-783-4338, Nearest town: Woodland, Agency: USFS, GPS: 40.548256, -111.033488

31434 • FSR 037 Dispersed 5 - USFS

Dispersed sites, No water, No toilets, Reservations not accepted, Open all year, Tent & RV camping: Free, Several sites in this area, Elev: 8889ft/2709m, Tel: 435-783-4338, Nearest town: Woodland, Agency: USFS, GPS: 40.539605, -111.039188

31435 • FSR 037 Dispersed 6 - USFS

Dispersed sites, No water, No toilets, Reservations not accepted, Open all year, Tent & RV camping: Free, Several sites in this area, Elev: 9101ft/2774m, Tel: 435-783-4338, Nearest town: Woodland, Agency: USFS, GPS: 40.531693, -111.031229

31436 • FSR 037 Dispersed 7 - USFS

Dispersed sites, No water, No toilets, Reservations not accepted, Open all year, Tent & RV camping: Free, Elev: 8636ft/2632m, Tel: 435-783-4338, Nearest town: Woodland, Agency: USFS, GPS: 40.518941, -111.038739

31437 • FSR 037 Dispersed 8 - USFS

Dispersed sites, No water, No toilets, Reservations not accepted, Open all year, Tent & RV camping: Free, Elev: 8405ft/2562m, Tel: 435-783-4338, Nearest town: Woodland, Agency: USFS, GPS: 40.518716, -111.044415

31438 • FSR 038 Dispersed 1 - USFS

Dispersed sites, No water, No toilets, Reservations not accepted, Open all year, Tent & RV camping: Free, Road not maintained for passenger cars, Elev: 6079ft/1853m, Tel: 801-798-3571, Nearest town: Vernon, Agency: USFS, GPS: 40.009753, -112.350462

31439 • FSR 038 Dispersed 2 - USFS

Dispersed sites, No water, No toilets, Reservations not accepted, Open all year, Tent & RV camping: Free, Road not maintained for passenger cars, Elev: 6221ft/1896m, Tel: 801-798-3571, Nearest town: Vernon, Agency: USFS, GPS: 40.000645, -112.370309

31440 • FSR 038 Dispersed 3 - USFS

Dispersed sites, No water, No toilets, Reservations not accepted, Open all year, Tent & RV camping: Free, Road not maintained for passenger cars, Elev: 6229ft/1899m, Tel: 801-798-3571, Nearest town: Vernon, Agency: USFS, GPS: 39.997922, -112.377662

31441 • FSR 038 Dispersed 4 - USFS

Dispersed sites, No water, No toilets, Reservations not accepted, Open all year, Tent & RV camping: Free, Road not maintained for passenger cars, Elev: 9557ft/2913m, Tel: 435-789-1181, Nearest town: Vernal, Agency: USFS, GPS: 40.764899, -109.708977

31442 • FSR 038 Dispersed 5 - USFS

Dispersed sites, No water, No toilets, Reservations not accepted, Open all year, Tent & RV camping: Free, Road not maintained for passenger cars, Elev: 8447ft/2575m, Tel: 435-896-9233, Nearest town: Salina, Agency: USFS, GPS: 38.816384, -111.634464

31443 • FSR 038 Dispersed 6 - USFS

Dispersed sites, No water, No toilets, Reservations not accepted, Open all year, Tent & RV camping: Free, Road not maintained for passenger cars, Elev: 8705ft/2653m, Tel: 435-896-9233, Nearest town: Salina, Agency: USFS, GPS: 38.809969, -111.638575

31444 • FSR 040 Dispersed 1 - USFS

Dispersed sites, No water, No toilets, Reservations not accepted, Open all year, Tent & RV camping: Free, Road not maintained for passenger cars, Elev: 7321ft/2231m, Tel: 801-798-3571, Nearest town: Vernon, Agency: USFS, GPS: 39.976087, -112.498184

31445 • FSR 040 Dispersed 2 - USFS

Dispersed sites, No water, No toilets, Reservations not accepted, Open all year, Tent & RV camping: Free, Road not maintained for passenger cars, Elev: 6919ft/2109m, Tel: 801-798-3571, Nearest town: Vernon, Agency: USFS, GPS: 39.977898, -112.486906

31446 • FSR 040 Dispersed 3 - USFS

Dispersed sites, No water, No toilets, Reservations not accepted, Open all year, Tent & RV camping: Free, Road not maintained for passenger cars, Elev: 6832ft/2082m, Tel: 801-798-3571, Nearest town: Vernon, Agency: USFS, GPS: 39.979234, -112.480914

31447 • FSR 040 Dispersed 4 - USFS

Dispersed sites, No water, No toilets, Reservations not accepted, Open all year, Tent & RV camping: Free, Road not maintained for passenger cars, Elev: 6237ft/1901m, Tel: 801-798-3571, Nearest town: Vernon, Agency: USFS, GPS: 39.998769, -112.465972

31448 • FSR 040 Dispersed 5 - USFS

Dispersed sites, No water, No toilets, Reservations not accepted, Open all year, Tent & RV camping: Free, Numerous sites in this area, Road not maintained for passenger cars, Elev: 10400ft/3170m, Tel: 435-836-2800, Nearest town: Salina, Agency: USFS, GPS: 38.752188, -111.675825

31449 • FSR 040E Dispersed 1 - USFS

Dispersed sites, No water, No toilets, Reservations not accepted, Open all year, Tent & RV camping: Free, Road not maintained for passenger cars, Elev: 10282ft/3134m, Tel: 435-836-2800, Nearest town: Salina, Agency: USFS, GPS: 38.758068, -111.681714

31450 • FSR 041 Dispersed 1 - USFS

Dispersed sites, No water, No toilets, Reservations not accepted, Open all year, Tent & RV camping: Free, Elev: 8791ft/2679m, Tel: 435-783-4338, Nearest town: Oakley, Agency: USFS, GPS: 40.601847, -110.999688

31451 • FSR 041 Dispersed 2 - USFS

Dispersed sites, No water, No toilets, Reservations not accepted, Open all year, Tent & RV camping: Free, Road not maintained for passenger cars, Elev: 9572ft/2918m, Tel: 435-783-4338, Nearest town: Oakley, Agency: USFS, GPS: 40.617899, -110.975619

31452 • FSR 041 Dispersed 3 - USFS

Dispersed sites, No water, No toilets, Reservations not accepted, Open all year, Tent & RV camping: Free, Road not maintained for passenger cars, Elev: 9585ft/2922m, Tel: 435-783-4338, Nearest town: Oakley, Agency: USFS, GPS: 40.617988, -110.973115

31453 • FSR 041 Dispersed 4 - USFS

Dispersed sites, No water, No toilets, Reservations not accepted, Open all year, Tent & RV camping: Free, Road not maintained for passenger cars, Elev: 9747ft/2971m, Tel: 435-783-4338, Nearest town: Oakley, Agency: USFS, GPS: 40.633456, -110.975479

31454 • FSR 041 Dispersed 5 - USFS

Dispersed sites, No water, No toilets, Reservations not accepted, Open all year, Tent & RV camping: Free, Road not maintained for passenger cars, Elev: 9798ft/2986m, Tel: 435-783-4338, Nearest town: Oakley, Agency: USFS, GPS: 40.638932, -110.967841

31455 • FSR 041 Dispersed 6 - USFS

Dispersed sites, No water, No toilets, Reservations not accepted, Open all year, Tent & RV camping: Free, Road not maintained for passenger cars, Elev: 9892ft/3015m, Tel: 435-783-4338, Nearest town: Oakley, Agency: USFS, GPS: 40.654651, -110.961234

31456 • FSR 041 Dispersed 7 - USFS

Dispersed sites, No water, No toilets, Reservations not accepted, Open all year, Tent & RV camping: Free, Road not maintained for passenger cars, Elev: 9800ft/2987m, Tel: 435-783-4338, Nearest town: Oakley, Agency: USFS, GPS: 40.659151, -110.962202

31457 • FSR 042 Dispersed 1 - USFS

Dispersed sites, No water, No toilets, Reservations not accepted, Open all year, Tent & RV camping: Free, Elev: 7703ft/2348m, Tel: 435-783-4338, Nearest town: Spanish Fork, Agency: USFS, GPS: 40.033067, -111.268651

31458 • FSR 042 Dispersed 2 - USFS

Dispersed sites, No water, No toilets, Reservations not accepted, Open all year, Tent & RV camping: Free, Elev: 8617ft/2626m, Tel: 435-783-4338, Nearest town: Spanish Fork, Agency: USFS, GPS: 40.041888, -111.214812

31459 • FSR 042A Dispersed 1 - USFS

Dispersed sites, No water, No toilets, Reservations not accepted, Open all year, Tent & RV camping: Free, Road not maintained for passenger cars, Elev: 9630ft/2935m, Tel: 435-836-2800, Nearest town: Koosharem, Agency: USFS, GPS: 38.674598, -111.662473

31460 • FSR 043 Dispersed 1 - USFS

Dispersed sites, No water, No toilets, Reservations not accepted, Open all year, Tent & RV camping: Free, Elev: 9527ft/2904m, Tel: 435-789-1181, Nearest town: Vernal, Agency: USFS, GPS: 40.763949, -109.715174

31461 • FSR 043 Dispersed 2 - USFS

Dispersed sites, No water, No toilets, Reservations not accepted, Open all year, Tent & RV camping: Free, Elev: 9590ft/2923m, Tel: 435-789-1181, Nearest town: Vernal, Agency: USFS, GPS: 40.766127, -109.724406

31462 • FSR 043 Dispersed 3 - USFS

Dispersed sites, No water, No toilets, Reservations not accepted, Open all year, Tent & RV camping: Free, Elev: 10923ft/3329m, Tel: 435-789-1181, Nearest town: Vernal, Agency: USFS, GPS: 40.777234, -109.814834

31463 • FSR 044 Dispersed 1 - USFS

Dispersed sites, No water, No toilets, Reservations not accepted, Open Apr-Nov, Tent & RV camping: Free, Road not maintained for passenger cars, Elev: 8774ft/2674m, Tel: 435-783-4338, Nearest town: Heber City, Agency: USFS, GPS: 40.342263, -111.313291

31464 • FSR 045E Dispersed 1 - USFS

Dispersed sites, No water, No toilets, Reservations not accepted, Open all year, Tent & RV camping: Free, Road not maintained for passenger cars, Elev: 9584ft/2921m, Tel: 435-836-2800, Nearest town: Koosharem, Agency: USFS, GPS: 38.555726, -111.679007

31465 • FSR 046 Dispersed 1 - USFS

Dispersed sites, No water, No toilets, Reservations not accepted, Open all year, Tent & RV camping: Free, Road not maintained for passenger cars, Elev: 6496ft/1980m, Tel: 435-783-4338, Nearest town: Heber City, Agency: USFS, GPS: 40.331556, -111.373357

31466 • FSR 046 Dispersed 10 - USFS

Dispersed sites, No water, No toilets, Reservations not accepted, Open all year, Tent & RV camping: Free, Elev: 8152ft/2485m, Tel: 435-783-4338, Nearest town: Heber City, Agency: USFS, GPS: 40.298557, -111.262578

31467 • FSR 046 Dispersed 11 - USFS

Dispersed sites, No water, No toilets, Reservations not accepted, Open all year, Tent & RV camping: Free, Elev: 8099ft/2469m, Tel: 435-783-4338, Nearest town: Heber City, Agency: USFS, GPS: 40.298479, -111.259445

31468 • FSR 046 Dispersed 12 - USFS

Dispersed sites, No water, No toilets, Reservations not accepted, Open all year, Tent & RV camping: Free, Numerous sites in this area, Elev: 8037ft/2450m, Tel: 435-783-4338, Nearest town: Heber City, Agency: USFS, GPS: 40.298585, -111.256449

31469 • FSR 046 Dispersed 13- USFS

Dispersed sites, No water, No toilets, Reservations not accepted, Open all year, Tent & RV camping: Free, Road not maintained for passenger cars, Elev: 8984ft/2738m, Tel: 307-782-6555, Nearest town: Mountain View (WY), Agency: USFS, GPS: 40.968216, -110.259441

31470 • FSR 046 Dispersed 2 - USFS

Dispersed sites, No water, No toilets, Reservations not accepted, Open all year, Tent & RV camping: Free, Road not maintained for passenger cars, Elev: 7255ft/2211m, Tel: 435-783-4338, Nearest town: Heber City, Agency: USFS, GPS: 40.314562, -111.344748

31471 • FSR 046 Dispersed 3 - USFS

Dispersed sites, No water, No toilets, Reservations not accepted, Open all year, Tent & RV camping: Free, Road not maintained for passenger cars, Elev: 8027ft/2447m, Tel: 435-783-4338, Nearest town: Heber City, Agency: USFS, GPS: 40.326951, -111.321526

31472 • FSR 046 Dispersed 4 - USFS

Dispersed sites, No water, No toilets, Reservations not accepted, Open all year, Tent & RV camping: Free, Numerous sites in area, Elev: 8709ft/2655m, Tel: 435-783-4338, Nearest town: Heber City, Agency: USFS, GPS: 40.341287, -111.309698

31473 • FSR 046 Dispersed 5 - USFS

Dispersed sites, No water, No toilets, Reservations not accepted, Open all year, Tent & RV camping: Free, Elev: 8839ft/2694m, Tel: 435-783-4338, Nearest town: Heber City, Agency: USFS, GPS: 40.339376, -111.305188

31474 • FSR 046 Dispersed 6 - USFS

Dispersed sites, No water, No toilets, Reservations not accepted, Open all year, Tent & RV camping: Free, Elev: 8942ft/2726m, Tel: 435-783-4338, Nearest town: Heber City, Agency: USFS, GPS: 40.326277, -111.289409

31475 • FSR 046 Dispersed 7 - USFS

Dispersed sites, No water, No toilets, Reservations not accepted, Open all year, Tent & RV camping: Free, Elev: 8734ft/2662m, Tel: 435-783-4338, Nearest town: Heber City, Agency: USFS, GPS: 40.317649, -111.283701

31476 • FSR 046 Dispersed 8 - USFS

Dispersed sites, No water, No toilets, Reservations not accepted, Open all year, Tent & RV camping: Free, Elev: 8565ft/2611m, Tel: 435-783-4338, Nearest town: Heber City, Agency: USFS, GPS: 40.303368, -111.277297

31477 • FSR 046 Dispersed 9 - USFS

Dispersed sites, No water, No toilets, Reservations not accepted, Open all year, Tent & RV camping: Free, Elev: 8294ft/2528m, Tel: 435-783-4338, Nearest town: Heber City, Agency: USFS, GPS: 40.299425, -111.268085

31478 • FSR 046A Dispersed 1 - USFS

Dispersed sites, No water, No toilets, Reservations not accepted, Open all year, Tent & RV camping: Free, Road not maintained for passenger cars, Elev: 8796ft/2681m, Tel: 435-836-2800, Nearest town: Koosharem, Agency: USFS, GPS: 38.505076, -111.767116

31479 • FSR 046H Dispersed 1 - USFS

Dispersed sites, No water, No toilets, Reservations not accepted, Open all year, Tent & RV camping: Free, Road not maintained for passenger cars, Elev: 9718ft/2962m, Tel: 435-836-2800, Nearest town: Koosharem, Agency: USFS, GPS: 38.504668, -111.728327

31480 • FSR 047 Dispersed - USFS

Dispersed sites, No water, No toilets, Reservations not accepted, Open all year, Tent & RV camping: Free, Elev: 5733ft/1747m, Tel: 435-755-3620, Nearest town: Logan, Agency: USFS, GPS: 41.767955, -111.619995

31481 • FSR 047 Dispersed 2 - USFS

Dispersed sites, No water, No toilets, Reservations not accepted, Open Jun-Nov, Tent & RV camping: Free, Elev: 6530ft/1990m, Tel: 435-755-3620, Nearest town: Logan, Agency: USFS, GPS: 41.734274, -111.617001

31482 • FSR 047 Dispersed 3 - USFS

Dispersed sites, No water, No toilets, Reservations not accepted, Open Jun-Nov, Tent & RV camping: Free, Elev: 6663ft/2031m, Tel: 435-755-3620, Nearest town: Logan, Agency: USFS, GPS: 41.728804, -111.615932

31483 • FSR 048 Dispersed 1 - USFS

Dispersed sites, No water, No toilets, Reservations not accepted, Open Jun-Nov, Tent & RV camping: Free, Elev: 5247ft/1599m, Tel: 435-755-3620, Nearest town: Richmond, Agency: USFS, GPS: 41.977872, -111.753932

31484 • FSR 048 Dispersed 2 - USFS

Dispersed sites, No water, No toilets, Reservations not accepted, Open Jun-Nov, Tent & RV camping: Free, Several sites in this area, Elev: 5396ft/1645m, Tel: 435-755-3620, Nearest town: Richmond, Agency: USFS, GPS: 41.978387, -111.743899

31485 • FSR 048 Dispersed 3 - USFS

Dispersed sites, No water, No toilets, Reservations not accepted, Open Jun-Nov, Tent & RV camping: Free, Elev: 5701ft/1738m, Tel: 435-755-3620, Nearest town: Richmond, Agency: USFS, GPS: 41.974703, -111.726386

31486 • FSR 048 Dispersed 4 - USFS

Dispersed sites, No water, No toilets, Reservations not accepted, Tent & RV camping: Free, Elev: 7594ft/2315m, Tel: 435-783-4338, Nearest town: Kamas, Agency: USFS, GPS: 40.607939, -111.124671

31487 • FSR 049 (Mill B Cow Camp) Dispersed 2 - USFS

Dispersed sites, No water, No toilets, Reservations not accepted, Open all year, Tent & RV camping: Free, Numerous sites in this area, Elev: 8289ft/2526m, Tel: 435-783-4338, Nearest town: Heber City, Agency: USFS, GPS: 40.362393, -111.225182

31488 • FSR 049 Dispersed 1 - USFS

Dispersed sites, No water, No toilets, Reservations not accepted, Open Apr-Nov, Tent & RV camping: Free, Road not maintained for passenger cars, Elev: 5944ft/1812m, Tel: 435-755-3620, Nearest town: Smithfield, Agency: USFS, GPS: 41.881905, -111.725371

31489 • FSR 049 Dispersed 3 - USFS

Dispersed sites, No water, No toilets, Reservations not accepted, Open all year, Tent & RV camping: Free, Several single sites in this area, Elev: 8228ft/2508m, Tel: 435-783-4338, Nearest town: Heber City, Agency: USFS, GPS: 40.329984, -111.228449

31490 • FSR 049 Dispersed 4 - USFS

Dispersed sites, No water, No toilets, Reservations not accepted, Open all year, Tent & RV camping: Free, Elev: 7909ft/2411m, Tel: 435-783-4338, Nearest town: Heber City, Agency: USFS, GPS: 40.312535, -111.225075

31491 • FSR 049 Dispersed 5 - USFS

Dispersed sites, No water, Vault toilets, Reservations not accepted, Open all year, Tent & RV camping: Free, Parking lot, Elev: 7756ft/2364m, Tel: 435-783-4338, Nearest town: Heber City, Agency: USFS, GPS: 40.280226, -111.218979

31492 • FSR 049 Dispersed 6 - USFS

Dispersed sites, No water, No toilets, Reservations not accepted, Open all year, Tent & RV camping: Free, Road not maintained for passenger cars, Several sites in this area, Elev: 8194ft/2498m, Tel: 435-789-1181, Nearest town: Dutch John, Agency: USFS, GPS: 40.797037, -109.462181

31493 • FSR 049 Dispersed 7 - USFS

Dispersed sites, No water, No toilets, Reservations not accepted, Open all year, Tent & RV camping: Free, Road not maintained for passenger cars, Numerous sites in this area, Elev: 8109ft/2472m, Tel: 435-789-1181, Nearest town: Dutch John, Agency: USFS, GPS: 40.803105, -109.455517

31494 • FSR 050 Dispersed 1 - USFS

Dispersed sites, No water, No toilets, Reservations not accepted, Open all year, Tent & RV camping: Free, Elev: 7668ft/2337m, Tel: 435-783-4338, Nearest town: Heber City, Agency: USFS, GPS: 40.450037, -110.978583

31495 • FSR 050 Dispersed 10 - USFS

Dispersed sites, No water, No toilets, Reservations not accepted, Open all year, Tent & RV camping: Free, Road not maintained for passenger cars, Elev: 9050ft/2758m, Tel: 435-783-4338, Nearest town: Heber City, Agency: USFS, GPS: 40.439598, -111.149853

31496 • FSR 050 Dispersed 11 - USFS

Dispersed sites, No water, No toilets, Reservations not accepted, Open all year, Tent & RV camping: Free, Road not maintained for passenger cars, Elev: 8089ft/2466m, Tel: 435-789-1181, Nearest town: Duck Creek, Agency: USFS, GPS: 37.598733, -112.623018

31497 • FSR 050 Dispersed 12 - USFS

Dispersed sites, No water, No toilets, Reservations not accepted, Open all year, Tent & RV camping: Free, Road not maintained for passenger cars, Elev: 8632ft/2631m, Tel: 435-789-1181, Nearest town: Parowan, Agency: USFS, GPS: 37.732438, -112.700179

31498 • FSR 050 Dispersed 13 - USFS

Dispersed sites, No water, No toilets, Reservations not accepted, Open all year, Tent & RV camping: Free, Road not maintained for passenger cars, Elev: 9954ft/3034m, Tel: 435-789-1181, Nearest town: Parowan, Agency: USFS, GPS: 37.748335, -112.744422

31499 • FSR 050 Dispersed 2 - USFS

Dispersed sites, No water, No toilets, Reservations not accepted, Open all year, Tent & RV camping: Free, Elev: 7939ft/2420m, Tel: 435-783-4338, Nearest town: Heber City, Agency: USFS, GPS: 40.447174, -111.023199

31500 • FSR 050 Dispersed 3 - USFS

Dispersed sites, No water, No toilets, Reservations not accepted, Open all year, Tent & RV camping: Free, Road not maintained for passenger cars, Elev: 7990ft/2435m, Tel: 435-783-4338, Nearest town: Heber City, Agency: USFS, GPS: 40.447186, -111.034492

31501 • FSR 050 Dispersed 4 - USFS

Dispersed sites, No water, No toilets, Reservations not accepted, Open all year, Tent & RV camping: Free, Road not maintained for passenger cars, Elev: 8164ft/2488m, Tel: 435-783-4338, Nearest town: Heber City, Agency: USFS, GPS: 40.450064, -111.055935

31502 • FSR 050 Dispersed 5 - USFS

Dispersed sites, No water, No toilets, Reservations not accepted, Open all year, Tent & RV camping: Free, Road not maintained for passenger cars, Elev: 8357ft/2547m, Tel: 435-783-4338, Nearest town: Heber City, Agency: USFS, GPS: 40.444444, -111.084031

31503 • FSR 050 Dispersed 6 - USFS

Dispersed sites, No water, No toilets, Reservations not accepted, Open all year, Tents only: Free, Road not maintained for passenger cars, Elev: 8353ft/2546m, Tel: 435-783-4338, Nearest town: Heber City, Agency: USFS, GPS: 40.441956, -111.087163

31504 • FSR 050 Dispersed 7 - USFS

Dispersed sites, No water, No toilets, Reservations not accepted, Open all year, Tent & RV camping: Free, Road not maintained for passenger cars, Elev: 8612ft/2625m, Tel: 435-783-4338, Nearest town: Heber City, Agency: USFS, GPS: 40.444795, -111.102314

31505 • FSR 050 Dispersed 8 - USFS

Dispersed sites, No water, No toilets, Reservations not accepted, Open all year, Tent & RV camping: Free, Road not maintained for passenger cars, Elev: 8742ft/2665m, Tel: 435-783-4338, Nearest town: Heber City, Agency: USFS, GPS: 40.446515, -111.121966

31506 • FSR 050 Dispersed 9 - USFS

Dispersed sites, No water, No toilets, Reservations not accepted, Open all year, Tent & RV camping: Free, Road not maintained for passenger cars, Elev: 8780ft/2676m, Tel: 435-783-4338, Nearest town: Heber City, Agency: USFS, GPS: 40.446614, -111.125874

31507 • FSR 051 Dispersed 1 - USFS

Dispersed sites, No water, No toilets, Reservations not accepted, Open Apr-Dec, Tent & RV camping: Free, Elev: 7616ft/2321m, Tel: 801-798-3571, Nearest town: Thistle, Agency: USFS, GPS: 40.034994, -111.285151

31508 • FSR 051 Dispersed 2 - USFS

Dispersed sites, No water, No toilets, Reservations not accepted, Open Jun-Oct, Tent & RV camping: Free, Elev: 7325ft/2233m, Tel: 435-783-4338, Nearest town: Spanish Fork, Agency: USFS, GPS: 40.054859, -111.279792

31509 • FSR 051 Dispersed 3 - USFS

Dispersed sites, No water, No toilets, Reservations not accepted, Open Jun-Oct, Tent & RV camping: Free, Elev: 7257ft/2212m, Tel: 435-783-4338, Nearest town: Spanish Fork, Agency: USFS, GPS: 40.079292, -111.281933

31510 • FSR 051 Dispersed 4 - USFS

Dispersed sites, No water, No toilets, Reservations not accepted, Open Jun-Oct, Tent & RV camping: Free, Elev: 7237ft/2206m, Tel: 435-783-4338, Nearest town: Spanish Fork, Agency: USFS, GPS: 40.079582, -111.283946

31511 • FSR 051 Dispersed 5 - USFS

Dispersed sites, No water, No toilets, Reservations not accepted, Open Jun-Oct, Tent & RV camping: Free, Elev: 7136ft/2175m, Tel: 435-783-4338, Nearest town: Spanish Fork, Agency: USFS, GPS: 40.098952, -111.285602

31512 • FSR 051 Dispersed 6 - USFS

Dispersed sites, No water, No toilets, Reservations not accepted, Open Jun-Oct, Tent & RV camping: Free, Elev: 7028ft/2142m, Tel: 435-783-4338, Nearest town: Springville, Agency: USFS, GPS: 40.136863, -111.295032

31513 • FSR 051 Dispersed 7 - USFS

Dispersed sites, No water, No toilets, Reservations not accepted, Open Jun-Oct, Tent & RV camping: Free, Elev: 6853ft/2089m, Tel: 435-783-4338, Nearest town: Springville, Agency: USFS, GPS: 40.146155, -111.309491

31514 • FSR 052 Dispersed 6 - USFS

Dispersed sites, No water, No toilets, Reservations not accepted, Open all year, Tent & RV camping: Free, Road not maintained for passenger cars, Elev: 6901ft/2103m, Tel: 435-755-3620, Nearest town: Logan, Agency: USFS, GPS: 41.724613, -111.623081

31515 • FSR 052 Dispersed 1 - USFS

Dispersed sites, No water, No toilets, Reservations not accepted, Open all year, Tent & RV camping: Free, Road not maintained for passenger cars, Elev: 7120ft/2170m, Tel: 435-783-4338, Nearest town: Woodland, Agency: USFS, GPS: 40.547148, -111.189899

31516 • FSR 052 Dispersed 2 - USFS

Dispersed sites, No water, No toilets, Reservations not accepted, Open all year, Tent & RV camping: Free, Road not maintained for passenger cars, Elev: 7212ft/2198m, Tel: 435-783-4338, Nearest town: Woodland, Agency: USFS, GPS: 40.538739, -111.189341

31517 • FSR 052 Dispersed 3 - USFS

Dispersed sites, No water, No toilets, Reservations not accepted, Open all year, Tent & RV camping: Free, Road not maintained for passenger cars, Elev: 7321ft/2231m, Tel: 435-783-4338, Nearest town: Woodland, Agency: USFS, GPS: 40.536687, -111.188333

31518 • FSR 052 Dispersed 4 - USFS

Dispersed sites, No water, No toilets, Reservations not accepted, Open all year, Tent & RV camping: Free, Road not maintained for passenger cars, Elev: 8047ft/2453m, Tel: 435-783-4338, Nearest town: Woodland, Agency: USFS, GPS: 40.538985, -111.163584

31519 • FSR 052 Dispersed 5 - USFS

Dispersed sites, No water, No toilets, Reservations not accepted, Open all year, Tent & RV camping: Free, Road not maintained for passenger cars, Elev: 7621ft/2323m, Tel: 435-783-4338, Nearest town: Woodland, Agency: USFS, GPS: 40.513329, -111.165506

31520 • FSR 052 Dispersed 7 - USFS

Dispersed sites, No water, No toilets, Reservations not accepted, Open all year, Tent & RV camping: Free, Road not maintained for passenger cars, Elev: 7506ft/2288m, Tel: 435-755-3620, Nearest town: Logan, Agency: USFS, GPS: 41.725953, -111.637095

31521 • FSR 052 Dispersed 8 - USFS

Dispersed sites, No water, No toilets, Reservations not accepted, Open all year, Tent & RV camping: Free, Road not maintained for passenger cars, Elev: 9090ft/2771m, Tel: 435-789-1181, Nearest town: Cedar City, Agency: USFS, GPS: 37.567436, -112.902423

31522 • FSR 052 Dispersed 9 - USFS
Dispersed sites, No water, No toilets, Reservations not accepted, Open all year, Tent & RV camping: Free, Several sites on his road, Road not maintained for passenger cars, Elev: 9149ft/2789m, Tel: 435-789-1181, Nearest town: Cedar City, Agency: USFS, GPS: 37.566833, -112.907966

31523 • FSR 052A Dispersed 1 - USFS
Dispersed sites, No water, No toilets, Reservations not accepted, Open all year, Tent & RV camping: Free, Road not maintained for passenger cars, Elev: 8206ft/2501m, Tel: 435-755-3620, Nearest town: Logan, Agency: USFS, GPS: 41.708521, -111.682173

31524 • FSR 052A Dispersed 2 - USFS
Dispersed sites, No water, No toilets, Reservations not accepted, Open all year, Tent & RV camping: Free, Road not maintained for passenger cars, Elev: 9135ft/2784m, Tel: 435-789-1181, Nearest town: Cedar City, Agency: USFS, GPS: 37.570746, -112.907872

31525 • FSR 053 Dispersed 1 - USFS
Dispersed sites, No water, No toilets, Reservations not accepted, Tent & RV camping: Free, Elev: 7422ft/2262m, Tel: 435-783-4338, Nearest town: Kamas, Agency: USFS, GPS: 40.595601, -111.117955

31526 • FSR 054 Dispersed 1 - USFS
Dispersed sites, No water, No toilets, Reservations not accepted, Open all year, Tent & RV camping: Free, Elev: 8142ft/2482m, Tel: 435-783-4338, Nearest town: Woodland, Agency: USFS, GPS: 40.506549, -111.074827

31527 • FSR 054 Dispersed 2 - USFS
Dispersed sites, No water, No toilets, Reservations not accepted, Open all year, Tent & RV camping: Free, Road not maintained for passenger cars, Elev: 8987ft/2739m, Tel: 435-783-4338, Nearest town: Heber City, Agency: USFS, GPS: 40.488836, -111.112522

31528 • FSR 054 Dispersed 3 - USFS
Dispersed sites, No water, No toilets, Reservations not accepted, Open all year, Tent & RV camping: Free, Elev: 9258ft/2822m, Tel: 435-783-4338, Nearest town: Heber City, Agency: USFS, GPS: 40.479048, -111.123136

31529 • FSR 054 Dispersed 4 - USFS
Dispersed sites, No water, No toilets, Reservations not accepted, Open all year, Tent & RV camping: Free, Elev: 9367ft/2855m, Tel: 435-783-4338, Nearest town: Heber City, Agency: USFS, GPS: 40.444465, -111.163429

31530 • FSR 055 Dispersed 1 - USFS
Dispersed sites, No water, No toilets, Reservations not accepted, Open all year, Tent & RV camping: Free, Elev: 7976ft/2431m, Tel: 435-755-3620, Nearest town: Garden City, Agency: USFS, GPS: 41.889724, -111.486038

31531 • FSR 055 Dispersed 2 - USFS
Dispersed sites, No water, No toilets, Reservations not accepted, Open all year, Tent & RV camping: Free, Both sides of road, Elev: 8081ft/2463m, Tel: 435-755-3620, Nearest town: Garden City, Agency: USFS, GPS: 41.886305, -111.486253

31532 • FSR 055 Dispersed 3 - USFS
Dispersed sites, No water, No toilets, Reservations not accepted, Open all year, Tent & RV camping: Free, Elev: 8142ft/2482m, Tel: 435-755-3620, Nearest town: Garden City, Agency: USFS, GPS: 41.883996, -111.489543

31533 • FSR 055 Dispersed 4 - USFS
Dispersed sites, No water, No toilets, Reservations not accepted, Open all year, Tent & RV camping: Free, Elev: 8154ft/2485m, Tel: 435-755-3620, Nearest town: Garden City, Agency: USFS, GPS: 41.882877, -111.490513

31534 • FSR 055 Dispersed 5 - USFS
Dispersed sites, No water, No toilets, Reservations not accepted, Open all year, Tent & RV camping: Free, Elev: 8180ft/2493m, Tel: 435-755-3620, Nearest town: Garden City, Agency: USFS, GPS: 41.880868, -111.493391

31535 • FSR 055 Dispersed 6 - USFS
Dispersed sites, No water, No toilets, Reservations not accepted, Open Jun-Apr, Tent & RV camping: Free, Road not maintained for passenger cars, Elev: 8914ft/2717m, Tel: 435-783-4338, Nearest town: Oakley, Agency: USFS, GPS: 40.758997, -111.020714

31536 • FSR 055 Dispersed 7 - USFS
Dispersed sites, No water, No toilets, Reservations not accepted, Open Jun-Apr, Tent & RV camping: Free, Road not maintained for passenger cars, Elev: 8566ft/2611m, Tel: 435-783-4338, Nearest town: Oakley, Agency: USFS, GPS: 40.770079, -111.015202

31537 • FSR 055 Dispersed 8 - USFS
Dispersed sites, No water, No toilets, Reservations not accepted, Open all year, Tent & RV camping: Free, Road not maintained for passenger cars, Elev: 9933ft/3028m, Tel: 435-783-4338, Nearest town: Heber City, Agency: USFS, GPS: 40.442181, -111.182081

31538 • FSR 056 Dispersed 1 - USFS
Dispersed sites, No water, No toilets, Reservations not accepted, Open Jun-Nov, Tent & RV camping: Free, Road not maintained for passenger cars, Elev: 6527ft/1989m, Tel: 435-755-3620, Nearest town: Logan, Agency: USFS, GPS: 41.694222, -111.526888

31539 • FSR 056 Dispersed 10 - USFS
Dispersed sites, No water, No toilets, Reservations not accepted, Open all year, Tent & RV camping: Free, Both sides of road, Road not maintained for passenger cars, Elev: 8047ft/2453m, Tel: 435-836-2800, Nearest town: Glenwood, Agency: USFS, GPS: 38.735453, -111.779423

31540 • FSR 056 Dispersed 11 - USFS
Dispersed sites, No water, No toilets, Reservations not accepted, Open all year, Tent & RV camping: Free, Road not maintained for passenger cars, Elev: 8774ft/2674m, Tel: 435-836-2800, Nearest town: Glenwood, Agency: USFS, GPS: 38.734034, -111.752554

31541 • FSR 056 Dispersed 12 - USFS

Dispersed sites, No water, No toilets, Reservations not accepted, Open all year, Tent & RV camping: Free, Road not maintained for passenger cars, Elev: 8944ft/2726m, Tel: 435-836-2800, Nearest town: Glenwood, Agency: USFS, GPS: 38.730103, -111.753286

31542 • FSR 056 Dispersed 13 - USFS

Dispersed sites, No water, No toilets, Reservations not accepted, Open all year, Tent & RV camping: Free, Road not maintained for passenger cars, Elev: 9044ft/2757m, Tel: 435-836-2800, Nearest town: Glenwood, Agency: USFS, GPS: 38.726844, -111.751823

31543 • FSR 056 Dispersed 2 - USFS

Dispersed sites, No water, No toilets, Reservations not accepted, Open Jun-Nov, Tent & RV camping: Free, Road not maintained for passenger cars, Elev: 6821ft/2079m, Tel: 435-755-3620, Nearest town: Logan, Agency: USFS, GPS: 41.697054, -111.536068

31544 • FSR 056 Dispersed 3 - USFS

Dispersed sites, No water, No toilets, Reservations not accepted, Open Jun-Nov, Tent & RV camping: Free, Road not maintained for passenger cars, Elev: 7238ft/2206m, Tel: 435-755-3620, Nearest town: Logan, Agency: USFS, GPS: 41.718996, -111.546859

31545 • FSR 056 Dispersed 4 - USFS

Dispersed sites, No water, No toilets, Reservations not accepted, Open Jun-Nov, Tent & RV camping: Free, Road not maintained for passenger cars, Elev: 7321ft/2231m, Tel: 435-755-3620, Nearest town: Logan, Agency: USFS, GPS: 41.723542, -111.549116

31546 • FSR 056 Dispersed 5 - USFS

Dispersed sites, No water, No toilets, Reservations not accepted, Open May-Oct, Tent & RV camping: Free, Road not maintained for passenger cars, Elev: 8228ft/2508m, Tel: 801-785-3563, Nearest town: Cedar HIlls, Agency: USFS, GPS: 40.436952, -111.661608

31547 • FSR 056 Dispersed 6 - USFS

Dispersed sites, No water, No toilets, Reservations not accepted, Open May-Oct, Tent & RV camping: Free, Road not maintained for passenger cars, Elev: 8239ft/2511m, Tel: 801-785-3563, Nearest town: Cedar HIlls, Agency: USFS, GPS: 40.436238, -111.664328

31548 • FSR 056 Dispersed 7 - USFS

Dispersed sites, No water, No toilets, Reservations not accepted, Open May-Oct, Tent & RV camping: Free, Road not maintained for passenger cars, Elev: 8639ft/2633m, Tel: 801-785-3563, Nearest town: Pleasant Grove, Agency: USFS, GPS: 40.422526, -111.690532

31549 • FSR 056 Dispersed 8 - USFS

Dispersed sites, No water, No toilets, Reservations not accepted, Open May-Oct, Tent & RV camping: Free, Road not maintained for passenger cars, Elev: 8443ft/2573m, Tel: 801-785-3563, Nearest town: Pleasant Grove, Agency: USFS, GPS: 40.421595, -111.699763

31550 • FSR 056 Dispersed 9 - USFS

Dispersed sites, No water, No toilets, Reservations not accepted, Open May-Oct, Tent & RV camping: Free, Road not maintained for passenger cars, Elev: 8195ft/2498m, Tel: 801-785-3563, Nearest town: Pleasant Grove, Agency: USFS, GPS: 40.411611, -111.693056

31551 • FSR 057 Dispersed - USFS

Dispersed sites, No water, No toilets, Reservations not accepted, Open all year, Tent & RV camping: Free, Several sites in this area, Road not maintained for passenger cars, Elev: 8614ft/2626m, Tel: 307-789-3194, Nearest town: Oakley, Agency: USFS, GPS: 40.859698, -110.827026

31552 • FSR 057 Dispersed 1 - USFS

Dispersed sites, No water, No toilets, Reservations not accepted, Open all year, Tent & RV camping: Free, Road not maintained for passenger cars, Elev: 8388ft/2557m, Tel: 801-625-5112, Nearest town: Woodruff, Agency: USFS, GPS: 41.522849, -111.472732

31553 • FSR 057 Dispersed 2 - USFS

Dispersed sites, No water, No toilets, Reservations not accepted, Open all year, Tent & RV camping: Free, Road not maintained for passenger cars, Elev: 8437ft/2572m, Tel: 801-625-5112, Nearest town: Woodruff, Agency: USFS, GPS: 41.521646, -111.473681

31554 • FSR 057 Dispersed 3 - USFS

Dispersed sites, No water, No toilets, Reservations not accepted, Open all year, Tent & RV camping: Free, Elev: 8936ft/2724m, Tel: 435-836-2800, Nearest town: Koosharem, Agency: USFS, GPS: 38.542538, -111.795445

31555 • FSR 057G Dispersed 1 - USFS

Dispersed sites, No water, No toilets, Reservations not accepted, Open all year, Tent & RV camping: Free, Road not maintained for passenger cars, Elev: 9698ft/2956m, Tel: 435-836-2800, Nearest town: Koosharem, Agency: USFS, GPS: 38.573376, -111.782557

31556 • FSR 057G Dispersed 2 - USFS

Dispersed sites, No water, No toilets, Reservations not accepted, Open all year, Tent & RV camping: Free, Road not maintained for passenger cars, Elev: 9740ft/2969m, Tel: 435-836-2800, Nearest town: Koosharem, Agency: USFS, GPS: 38.573078, -111.784775

31557 • FSR 058 Dispersed 1 - USFS

Dispersed sites, No water, No toilets, Reservations not accepted, Open Jun-Oct, Tent & RV camping: Free, Elev: 6321ft/1927m, Tel: 435-783-4338, Nearest town: Springville, Agency: USFS, GPS: 40.191296, -111.386022

31558 • FSR 058 Dispersed 10 - USFS

Dispersed sites, No water, No toilets, Reservations not accepted, Open Jun-Oct, Tent & RV camping: Free, Elev: 6433ft/1961m, Tel: 435-783-4338, Nearest town: Springville, Agency: USFS, GPS: 40.172096, -111.330668

31559 • FSR 058 Dispersed 11 - USFS

Dispersed sites, No water, No toilets, Reservations not accepted, Open Jun-Oct, Tent & RV camping: Free, Several sites in this area, Elev: 6371ft/1942m, Tel: 435-783-4338, Nearest town: Springville, Agency: USFS, GPS: 40.165163, -111.329992

31560 • FSR 058 Dispersed 12 - USFS

Dispersed sites, No water, No toilets, Reservations not accepted, Open May-Dec, Tent & RV camping: Free, Several sites, Elev: 8408ft/2563m, Tel: 307-789-3194, Nearest town: Oakley, Agency: USFS, GPS: 40.913087, -110.823759

31561 • FSR 058 Dispersed 13 - USFS

Dispersed sites, No water, No toilets, Reservations not accepted, Open May-Dec, Tent & RV camping: Free, Elev: 8750ft/2667m, Tel: 307-789-3194, Nearest town: Oakley, Agency: USFS, GPS: 40.931213, -110.749348

31562 • FSR 058 Dispersed 14 - USFS

Dispersed sites, No water, No toilets, Reservations not accepted, Open May-Dec, Tent & RV camping: Free, Elev: 8860ft/2701m, Tel: 307-789-3194, Nearest town: Oakley, Agency: USFS, GPS: 40.958248, -110.581294

31563 • FSR 058 Dispersed 15 - USFS

Dispersed sites, No water, No toilets, Reservations not accepted, Open May-Dec, Tent & RV camping: Free, Road not maintained for passenger cars, Elev: 9038ft/2755m, Tel: 307-789-3194, Nearest town: Oakley, Agency: USFS, GPS: 40.935622, -110.595099

31564 • FSR 058 Dispersed 16 - USFS

Dispersed sites, No water, No toilets, Reservations not accepted, Open May-Dec, Tent & RV camping: Free, Both sides of road, Road not maintained for passenger cars, Elev: 9057ft/2761m, Tel: 307-789-3194, Nearest town: Oakley, Agency: USFS, GPS: 40.933948, -110.599832

31565 • FSR 058 Dispersed 17 - USFS

Dispersed sites, No water, No toilets, Reservations not accepted, Open all year, Tent & RV camping: Free, Elev: 9424ft/2872m, Tel: 435-789-1181, Nearest town: Manila, Agency: USFS, GPS: 40.907949, -109.994212

31566 • FSR 058 Dispersed 18 - USFS

Dispersed sites, No water, No toilets, Max length: 16ft, Reservations not accepted, Open all year, Tent & RV camping: Free, Elev: 7135ft/2175m, Tel: 435-789-1181, Nearest town: Vernal, Agency: USFS, GPS: 40.598925, -109.732394

31567 • FSR 058 Dispersed 19 - USFS

Dispersed sites, No water, No toilets, Reservations not accepted, Open all year, Tent & RV camping: Free, Road not maintained for passenger cars, Elev: 7136ft/2175m, Tel: 435-836-2800, Nearest town: Glenwood, Agency: USFS, GPS: 38.704634, -111.827321

31568 • FSR 058 Dispersed 2 - USFS

Dispersed sites, No water, No toilets, Reservations not accepted, Open Jun-Oct, Tent & RV camping: Free, Elev: 6362ft/1939m, Tel: 435-783-4338, Nearest town: Springville, Agency: USFS, GPS: 40.191246, -111.384297

31569 • FSR 058 Dispersed 3 - USFS

Dispersed sites, No water, No toilets, Reservations not accepted, Open Jun-Oct, Tent & RV camping: Free, Elev: 6718ft/2048m, Tel: 435-783-4338, Nearest town: Springville, Agency: USFS, GPS: 40.194094, -111.381327

31570 • FSR 058 Dispersed 4 - USFS

Dispersed sites, No water, No toilets, Reservations not accepted, Open Jun-Oct, Tent & RV camping: Free, Elev: 7310ft/2228m, Tel: 435-783-4338, Nearest town: Springville, Agency: USFS, GPS: 40.189539, -111.363026

31571 • FSR 058 Dispersed 5 - USFS

Dispersed sites, No water, No toilets, Reservations not accepted, Open Jun-Oct, Tent & RV camping: Free, Elev: 7337ft/2236m, Tel: 435-783-4338, Nearest town: Springville, Agency: USFS, GPS: 40.189922, -111.356357

31572 • FSR 058 Dispersed 6 - USFS

Dispersed sites, No water, No toilets, Reservations not accepted, Open Jun-Oct, Tent & RV camping: Free, Elev: 6925ft/2111m, Tel: 435-783-4338, Nearest town: Springville, Agency: USFS, GPS: 40.191082, -111.343766

31573 • FSR 058 Dispersed 7 - USFS

Dispersed sites, No water, No toilets, Reservations not accepted, Open Jun-Oct, Tent & RV camping: Free, Elev: 6876ft/2096m, Tel: 435-783-4338, Nearest town: Springville, Agency: USFS, GPS: 40.193691, -111.344027

31574 • FSR 058 Dispersed 8 - USFS

Dispersed sites, No water, No toilets, Reservations not accepted, Open Jun-Oct, Tent & RV camping: Free, Elev: 6510ft/1984m, Tel: 435-783-4338, Nearest town: Springville, Agency: USFS, GPS: 40.177775, -111.329796

31575 • FSR 058 Dispersed 9 - USFS

Dispersed sites, No water, No toilets, Reservations not accepted, Open Jun-Oct, Tent & RV camping: Free, Elev: 6454ft/1967m, Tel: 435-783-4338, Nearest town: Springville, Agency: USFS, GPS: 40.174828, -111.330366

31576 • FSR 059 Dispersed 1 - USFS

Dispersed sites, No water, No toilets, Reservations not accepted, Open all year, Tent & RV camping: Free, Elev: 8406ft/2562m, Tel: 801-625-5112, Nearest town: Randolph, Agency: USFS, GPS: 41.607694, -111.436482

31577 • FSR 059 Dispersed 2 - USFS

Dispersed sites, No water, No toilets, Reservations not accepted, Open all year, Tent & RV camping: Free, 2 separate sites, Elev: 8388ft/2557m, Tel: 801-625-5112, Nearest town: Woodruff, Agency: USFS, GPS: 41.519213, -111.470985

31578 • FSR 059 Dispersed 3 - USFS

Dispersed sites, No water, No toilets, Reservations not accepted, Open all year, Tent & RV camping: Free, Elev: 8479ft/2584m, Tel: 801-625-5112, Nearest town: Woodruff, Agency: USFS, GPS: 41.514051, -111.468813

31579 • FSR 059 Dispersed 4 - USFS

Dispersed sites, No water, No toilets, Reservations not accepted, Open all year, Tent & RV camping: Free, Elev: 8582ft/2616m, Tel: 801-625-5112, Nearest town: Woodruff, Agency: USFS, GPS: 41.512925, -111.465426

31580 • FSR 059 Dispersed 5 - USFS

Dispersed sites, No water, No toilets, Reservations not accepted, Open all year, Tent & RV camping: Free, Elev: 8732ft/2662m, Tel: 307-789-3194, Nearest town: Oakley, Agency: USFS, GPS: 40.880222, -110.787658

31581 • FSR 059 Dispersed 6 - USFS

Dispersed sites, No water, No toilets, Reservations not accepted, Open all year, Tent & RV camping: Free, Numerous sites in this area, Elev: 8802ft/2683m, Tel: 307-789-3194, Nearest town: Oakley, Agency: USFS, GPS: 40.873945, -110.782492

31582 • FSR 059 Dispersed 7 - USFS

Dispersed sites, No water, No toilets, Reservations not accepted, Open all year, Tent & RV camping: Free, Road not maintained for passenger cars, Elev: 9609ft/2929m, Tel: 435-836-2800, Nearest town: Koosharem, Agency: USFS, GPS: 38.519508, -111.725962

31583 • FSR 059 Dispersed 8 - USFS

Dispersed sites, No water, No toilets, Reservations not accepted, Open all year, Tent & RV camping: Free, Road not maintained for passenger cars, Elev: 9744ft/2970m, Tel: 435-789-1181, Nearest town: Vernal, Agency: USFS, GPS: 40.774227, -109.738187

31584 • FSR 059 Dispersed 9 - USFS

Dispersed sites, No water, No toilets, Reservations not accepted, Open all year, Tent & RV camping: Free, Road not maintained for passenger cars, Elev: 9749ft/2971m, Tel: 435-789-1181, Nearest town: Vernal, Agency: USFS, GPS: 40.775528, -109.738027

31585 • FSR 060 Dispersed 1 - USFS

Dispersed sites, No water, No toilets, Reservations not accepted, Open all year, Tent & RV camping: Free, Road not maintained for passenger cars, Elev: 8117ft/2474m, Tel: 801-625-5112, Nearest town: Randolph, Agency: USFS, GPS: 41.677394, -111.424488

31586 • FSR 060 Dispersed 2 - USFS

Dispersed sites, No water, No toilets, Reservations not accepted, Open all year, Tent & RV camping: Free, Road not maintained for passenger cars, Elev: 7462ft/2274m, Tel: 801-625-5112, Nearest town: Randolph, Agency: USFS, GPS: 41.664003, -111.437035

31587 • FSR 060 Dispersed 3 - USFS

Dispersed sites, No water, No toilets, Reservations not accepted, Open all year, Tent & RV camping: Free, Road not maintained for passenger cars, Elev: 7414ft/2260m, Tel: 801-625-5112, Nearest town: Randolph, Agency: USFS, GPS: 41.660009, -111.437098

31588 • FSR 060 Dispersed 4 - USFS

Dispersed sites, No water, No toilets, Reservations not accepted, Open all year, Tent & RV camping: Free, Road not maintained for passenger cars, Elev: 8294ft/2528m, Tel: 801-625-5112, Nearest town: Randolph, Agency: USFS, GPS: 41.630059, -111.421859

31589 • FSR 060 Dispersed 5 - USFS

Dispersed sites, No water, No toilets, Reservations not accepted, Open all year, Tent & RV camping: Free, Elev: 7898ft/2407m, Tel: 435-789-1181, Nearest town: Duck Creek, Agency: USFS, GPS: 37.437808, -112.651979

31590 • FSR 060 Dispersed 6 - USFS

Dispersed sites, No water, No toilets, Reservations not accepted, Open all year, Tent & RV camping: Free, Elev: 8019ft/2444m, Tel: 435-789-1181, Nearest town: Duck Creek, Agency: USFS, GPS: 37.433699, -112.674335

31591 • FSR 061 Dispersed 1 - USFS

Dispersed sites, No water, No toilets, Reservations not accepted, Open all year, Tent & RV camping: Free, Several sites in this area, Elev: 8883ft/2708m, Tel: 307-789-3194, Nearest town: Oakley, Agency: USFS, GPS: 40.922825, -110.737002

31592 • FSR 061 Dispersed 2 - USFS

Dispersed sites, No water, No toilets, Reservations not accepted, Open all year, Tent & RV camping: Free, Elev: 9162ft/2793m, Tel: 307-789-3194, Nearest town: Oakley, Agency: USFS, GPS: 40.906089, -110.738663

31593 • FSR 061 Dispersed 3 - USFS

Dispersed sites, No water, No toilets, Reservations not accepted, Open all year, Tent & RV camping: Free, Elev: 9220ft/2810m, Tel: 307-789-3194, Nearest town: Oakley, Agency: USFS, GPS: 40.903417, -110.738803

31594 • FSR 061/062 Dispersed 1 - USFS

Dispersed sites, No water, No toilets, Reservations not accepted, Tent & RV camping: Free, Elev: 7842ft/2390m, Nearest town: Duck Creek Village, Agency: USFS, GPS: 37.490933, -112.563154

31595 • FSR 062 Dispersed 1 - USFS

Dispersed sites, No water, No toilets, Reservations not accepted, Open all year, Tent & RV camping: Free, Elev: 8074ft/2461m, Tel: 435-789-1181, Nearest town: Duck Creek, Agency: USFS, GPS: 37.470113, -112.592677

31596 • FSR 062 Dispersed 2 - USFS

Dispersed sites, No water, No toilets, Reservations not accepted, Open all year, Tent & RV camping: Free, Elev: 7973ft/2430m, Tel: 435-789-1181, Nearest town: Duck Creek, Agency: USFS, GPS: 37.433885, -112.644616

31597 • FSR 062 Dispersed 3 - USFS

Dispersed sites, No water, No toilets, Reservations not accepted, Open all year, Tent & RV camping: Free, Road not maintained for passenger cars, Several sites in this area, Elev: 8235ft/2510m, Tel: 435-789-1181, Nearest town: Red Canyon, Agency: USFS, GPS: 40.793133, -109.475221

31598 • FSR 062 Dispersed 4 - USFS

Dispersed sites, No water, No toilets, Reservations not accepted, Open all year, Tent & RV camping: Free, Road not maintained for passenger cars, Elev: 10332ft/3149m, Tel: 307-789-3194, Nearest town: Oakley, Agency: USFS, GPS: 40.940271, -110.671222

31599 • FSR 063 Dispersed 1 - USFS

Dispersed sites, No water, No toilets, Reservations not accepted, Open all year, Tent & RV camping: Free, Elev: 6917ft/2108m, Tel: 435-789-1181, Nearest town: Alton, Agency: USFS, GPS: 37.432999, -112.576399

31600 • FSR 063 Dispersed 2 - USFS

Dispersed sites, No water, No toilets, Reservations not accepted, Open all year, Tent & RV camping: Free, Elev: 6974ft/2126m, Tel: 435-789-1181, Nearest town: Alton, Agency: USFS, GPS: 37.437656, -112.574017

31601 • FSR 063 Dispersed 3 - USFS

Dispersed sites, No water, No toilets, Reservations not accepted, Open all year, Tent & RV camping: Free, Road not maintained for passenger cars, Elev: 9270ft/2825m, Tel: 307-789-3194, Nearest town: Oakley, Agency: USFS, GPS: 40.913355, -110.644168

31602 • FSR 063 Dispersed 4 - USFS

Dispersed sites, No water, No toilets, Reservations not accepted, Open all year, Tent & RV camping: Free, Road not maintained for passenger cars, Elev: 9352ft/2850m, Tel: 307-789-3194, Nearest town: Oakley, Agency: USFS, GPS: 40.883875, -110.672078

31603 • FSR 063 Dispersed 5 - USFS

Dispersed sites, No water, No toilets, Reservations not accepted, Open all year, Tent & RV camping: Free, Road not maintained for passenger cars, Elev: 9457ft/2882m, Tel: 307-789-3194, Nearest town: Oakley, Agency: USFS, GPS: 40.868345, -110.667167

31604 • FSR 064 Dispersed 1 - USFS

Dispersed sites, No water, No toilets, Reservations not accepted, Open all year, Tent & RV camping: Free, Road not maintained for passenger cars, Elev: 7877ft/2401m, Tel: 435-789-1181, Nearest town: Duck Creek, Agency: USFS, GPS: 37.534665, -112.591108

31605 • FSR 064 Dispersed 2 - USFS

Dispersed sites, No water, No toilets, Reservations not accepted, Open all year, Tent & RV camping: Free, Elev: 7882ft/2402m, Tel: 435-789-1181, Nearest town: Duck Creek, Agency: USFS, GPS: 37.529146, -112.595049

31606 • FSR 064 Dispersed 3 - USFS

Dispersed sites, No water, No toilets, Reservations not accepted, Open all year, Tent & RV camping: Free, Numerous sites along this stretch of road, Elev: 7983ft/2433m, Tel: 435-789-1181, Nearest town: Duck Creek, Agency: USFS, GPS: 37.524735, -112.599154

31607 • FSR 064 Dispersed 4 - USFS

Dispersed sites, No water, No toilets, Reservations not accepted, Open all year, Tent & RV camping: Free, Elev: 8025ft/2446m, Tel: 435-789-1181, Nearest town: Duck Creek, Agency: USFS, GPS: 37.519059, -112.605086

31608 • FSR 064 Dispersed 5 - USFS

Dispersed sites, No water, No toilets, Reservations not accepted, Open all year, Tent & RV camping: Free, Elev: 8051ft/2454m, Tel: 435-789-1181, Nearest town: Duck Creek, Agency: USFS, GPS: 37.517829, -112.608136

31609 • FSR 064 Dispersed 6 - USFS

Dispersed sites, No water, No toilets, Reservations not accepted, Open all year, Tent & RV camping: Free, Elev: 8068ft/2459m, Tel: 435-789-1181, Nearest town: Duck Creek, Agency: USFS, GPS: 37.517465, -112.609888

31610 • FSR 067 Dispersed 1 - USFS

Dispersed sites, No water, No toilets, Reservations not accepted, Open all year, Tent & RV camping: Free, Elev: 8963ft/2732m, Tel: 801-625-5112, Nearest town: Woodruff, Agency: USFS, GPS: 41.436147, -111.501639

31611 • FSR 067 Dispersed 2 - USFS

Dispersed sites, No water, No toilets, Reservations not accepted, Open all year, Tent & RV camping: Free, Elev: 8575ft/2614m, Tel: 801-625-5112, Nearest town: Woodruff, Agency: USFS, GPS: 41.435452, -111.478864

31612 • FSR 067 Dispersed 3 - USFS

Dispersed sites, No water, No toilets, Reservations not accepted, Open all year, Tent & RV camping: Free, Elev: 8506ft/2593m, Tel: 801-625-5112, Nearest town: Woodruff, Agency: USFS, GPS: 41.433454, -111.466064

31613 • FSR 067 Dispersed 4 - USFS

Dispersed sites, No water, No toilets, Reservations not accepted, Open all year, Tent & RV camping: Free, Road not maintained for passenger cars, Elev: 10279ft/3133m, Tel: 307-789-3194, Nearest town: Oakley, Agency: USFS, GPS: 40.933624, -110.666162

31614 • FSR 067 Dispersed 5 - USFS

Dispersed sites, No water, No toilets, Reservations not accepted, Open all year, Tent & RV camping: Free, Road not maintained for passenger cars, Elev: 7865ft/2397m, Tel: 435-789-1181, Nearest town: Duck Creek, Agency: USFS, GPS: 37.587146, -112.600624

31615 • FSR 068 Dispersed - USFS

Dispersed sites, No water, No toilets, Reservations not accepted, Open all year, Tent & RV camping: Free, Road not maintained for passenger cars, Elev: 8499ft/2590m, Tel: 435-789-1181, Nearest town: Cedar City, Agency: USFS, GPS: 37.646063, -112.674103

31616 • FSR 068 Dispersed 1 - USFS

Dispersed sites, No water, No toilets, Reservations not accepted, Open all year, Tent & RV camping: Free, Elev: 8491ft/2588m, Tel: 801-625-5112, Nearest town: Woodruff, Agency: USFS, GPS: 41.404551, -111.489164

31617 • FSR 068 Dispersed 10 - USFS

Dispersed sites, No water, No toilets, Reservations not accepted, Open all year, Tent & RV camping: Free, Road not maintained for passenger cars, Elev: 9012ft/2747m, Tel: 435-896-9233, Nearest town: Greenwich, Agency: USFS, GPS: 38.483962, -112.002568

31618 • FSR 068 Dispersed 2 - USFS

Dispersed sites, No water, No toilets, Reservations not accepted, Open all year, Tent & RV camping: Free, Elev: 8871ft/2704m, Tel: 801-625-5112, Nearest town: Woodruff, Agency: USFS, GPS: 41.419498, -111.510898

31619 • FSR 068 Dispersed 3 - USFS

Dispersed sites, No water, No toilets, Reservations not accepted, Open all year, Tent & RV camping: Free, Elev: 8469ft/2581m, Tel: 801-625-5112, Nearest town: Woodruff, Agency: USFS, GPS: 41.384171, -111.474679

31620 • FSR 068 Dispersed 4 - USFS

Dispersed sites, No water, No toilets, Reservations not accepted, Open all year, Tent & RV camping: Free, Elev: 8508ft/2593m, Tel: 801-625-5112, Nearest town: Woodruff, Agency: USFS, GPS: 41.381178, -111.466194

31621 • FSR 068 Dispersed 5 - USFS

Dispersed sites, No water, No toilets, Reservations not accepted, Open all year, Tent & RV camping: Free, Elev: 8512ft/2594m, Tel: 801-625-5112, Nearest town: Woodruff, Agency: USFS, GPS: 41.379776, -111.462482

31622 • FSR 068 Dispersed 6 - USFS

Dispersed sites, No water, No toilets, Reservations not accepted, Open all year, Tent & RV camping: Free, Elev: 8451ft/2576m, Tel: 801-625-5112, Nearest town: Woodruff, Agency: USFS, GPS: 41.387517, -111.477999

31623 • FSR 068 Dispersed 7 - USFS

Dispersed sites, No water, No toilets, Reservations not accepted, Open all year, Tent & RV camping: Free, Elev: 8524ft/2598m, Tel: 801-625-5112, Nearest town: Woodruff, Agency: USFS, GPS: 41.393215, -111.477306

31624 • FSR 068 Dispersed 8 - USFS

Dispersed sites, No water, No toilets, Reservations not accepted, Open all year, Tent & RV camping: Free, Elev: 9276ft/2827m, Tel: 435-789-1181, Nearest town: Vernal, Agency: USFS, GPS: 40.738168, -109.680351

31625 • FSR 068 Dispersed 9 - USFS

Dispersed sites, No water, No toilets, Reservations not accepted, Open all year, Tent & RV camping: Free, Elev: 8971ft/2734m, Tel: 435-896-9233, Nearest town: Glenwood, Agency: USFS, GPS: 38.659049, -111.943112

31626 • FSR 068AA Dispersed 1 - USFS

Dispersed sites, No water, No toilets, Reservations not accepted, Open all year, Tent & RV camping: Free, Elev: 8308ft/2532m, Tel: 435-896-9233, Nearest town: Glenwood, Agency: USFS, GPS: 38.678866, -111.947496

31627 • FSR 068C Dispersed 1 - USFS

Dispersed sites, No water, No toilets, Reservations not accepted, Open all year, Tent & RV camping: Free, Several sites in this area, Road not maintained for passenger cars, Elev: 8499ft/2590m, Tel: 435-789-1181, Nearest town: Cedar City, Agency: USFS, GPS: 37.652609, -112.673672

31628 • FSR 068C Dispersed 2 - USFS

Dispersed sites, No water, No toilets, Reservations not accepted, Open all year, Tent & RV camping: Free, Several sites in this area, Road not maintained for passenger cars, Elev: 8537ft/2602m, Tel: 435-789-1181, Nearest town: Cedar City, Agency: USFS, GPS: 37.649639, -112.679979

31629 • FSR 068E Dispersed 1 - USFS

Dispersed sites, No water, No toilets, Reservations not accepted, Open all year, Tent & RV camping: Free, Elev: 9203ft/2805m, Tel: 435-896-9233, Nearest town: Koosharem, Agency: USFS, GPS: 38.545169, -111.967916

31630 • FSR 068G Dispersed 1 - USFS

Dispersed sites, No water, No toilets, Reservations not accepted, Open all year, Tent & RV camping: Free, Elev: 8380ft/2554m, Tel: 435-896-9233, Nearest town: Glenwood, Agency: USFS, GPS: 38.677024, -111.945247

31631 • FSR 068K Dispersed 1 - USFS

Dispersed sites, No water, No toilets, Reservations not accepted, Open all year, Tent & RV camping: Free, Road not maintained for passenger cars, Elev: 9036ft/2754m, Tel: 435-896-9233, Nearest town: Greenwich, Agency: USFS, GPS: 38.473924, -112.004796

31632 • FSR 068Z Dispersed 1 - USFS

Dispersed sites, No water, No toilets, Reservations not accepted, Open all year, Tent & RV camping: Free, Road not maintained for passenger cars, Elev: 8746ft/2666m, Tel: 435-896-9233, Nearest town: Kingston, Agency: USFS, GPS: 38.291473, -112.079459

31633 • FSR 069 Dispersed 1 - USFS

Dispersed sites, No water, No toilets, Reservations not accepted, Open all year, Tent & RV camping: Free, Road not maintained for passenger cars, Elev: 8511ft/2594m, Tel: 435-789-1181, Nearest town: Hatch, Agency: USFS, GPS: 37.672513, -112.664955

31634 • FSR 069 Dispersed 2 - USFS

Dispersed sites, No water, No toilets, Reservations not accepted, Open all year, Tent & RV camping: Free, Road not maintained for passenger cars, Elev: 8545ft/2605m, Tel: 435-789-1181, Nearest town: Hatch, Agency: USFS, GPS: 37.673802, -112.660946

31635 • FSR 070 Dispersed 1 - USFS

Dispersed sites, No water, No toilets, Reservations not accepted, Open Jun-Oct, Tent & RV camping: Free, Road not maintained for passenger cars, Elev: 7371ft/2247m, Tel: 801-798-3571, Nearest town: Spanish Fork, Agency: USFS, GPS: 40.013113, -111.307704

31636 • FSR 070 Dispersed 2 - USFS

Dispersed sites, No water, No toilets, Reservations not accepted, Open Jun-Oct, Tent & RV camping: Free, Road not maintained for passenger cars, Elev: 7387ft/2252m, Tel: 435-783-4338, Nearest town: Spanish Fork, Agency: USFS, GPS: 40.011159, -111.310766

31637 • FSR 070 Dispersed 3 - USFS

Dispersed sites, No water, No toilets, Reservations not accepted, Open all year, Tent & RV camping: Free, High-clearance vehicle required, Elev: 8949ft/2728m, Tel: 435-738-2482, Nearest town: Spanish Fork, Agency: USFS, GPS: 39.957696, -110.977082

31638 • FSR 070 Dispersed 4 - USFS

Dispersed sites, No water, No toilets, Reservations not accepted, Open all year, Tent & RV camping: Free, Road not maintained for passenger cars, Elev: 7801ft/2378m, Tel: 435-789-1181, Nearest town: Hatch, Agency: USFS, GPS: 37.690129, -112.558528

31639 • FSR 070O Dispersed 1 - USFS

Dispersed sites, No water, No toilets, Reservations not accepted, Open all year, Tent & RV camping: Free, Road not maintained for passenger cars, Elev: 9515ft/2900m, Tel: 435-896-9233, Nearest town: Greenwich, Agency: USFS, GPS: 38.431028, -112.061552

31640 • FSR 071 Dispersed 1 - USFS

Dispersed sites, No water, No toilets, Reservations not accepted, Open all year, Tent & RV camping: Free, Road not maintained for passenger cars, Elev: 7776ft/2370m, Tel: 801-625-5112, Nearest town: Woodruff, Agency: USFS, GPS: 41.425084, -111.445302

31641 • FSR 071 Dispersed 2 - USFS

Dispersed sites, No water, No toilets, Reservations not accepted, Open May-Dec, Tent & RV camping: Free, Elev: 9646ft/2940m, Tel: 307-789-3194, Nearest town: Oakley, Agency: USFS, GPS: 40.850655, -110.967344

31642 • FSR 071 Dispersed 3 - USFS

Dispersed sites, No water, No toilets, Reservations not accepted, Open all year, Tent & RV camping: Free, Road not maintained for passenger cars, Elev: 8666ft/2641m, Tel: 435-789-1181, Nearest town: Hatch, Agency: USFS, GPS: 37.670158, -112.637987

31643 • FSR 071B Dispersed 1 - USFS

Dispersed sites, No water, No toilets, Reservations not accepted, Open all year, Tent & RV camping: Free, Road not maintained for passenger cars, Elev: 8493ft/2589m, Tel: 801-625-5112, Nearest town: Woodruff, Agency: USFS, GPS: 41.401992, -111.481374

31644 • FSR 072 Dispersed 1 - USFS

Dispersed sites, No water, No toilets, Reservations not accepted, Open all year, Tent & RV camping: Free, Road not maintained for passenger cars, Elev: 8407ft/2562m, Tel: 801-625-5112, Nearest town: Woodruff, Agency: USFS, GPS: 41.378977, -111.486188

31645 • FSR 072 Dispersed 2 - USFS

Dispersed sites, No water, No toilets, Reservations not accepted, Open all year, Tent & RV camping: Free, Road not maintained for passenger cars, Elev: 8395ft/2559m, Tel: 801-625-5112, Nearest town: Woodruff, Agency: USFS, GPS: 41.380803, -111.483398

31646 • FSR 072 Dispersed 3 - USFS

Dispersed sites, No water, No toilets, Reservations not accepted, Open all year, Tent & RV camping: Free, Road not maintained for passenger cars, Elev: 8439ft/2572m, Tel: 801-625-5112, Nearest town: Woodruff, Agency: USFS, GPS: 41.381774, -111.481535

31647 • FSR 072 Dispersed 4 - USFS

Dispersed sites, No water, No toilets, Reservations not accepted, Open all year, Tent & RV camping: Free, Elev: 9179ft/2798m, Tel: 307-782-6555, Nearest town: Mountain View (WY), Agency: USFS, GPS: 40.988597, -110.381677

31648 • FSR 072 Dispersed 5 - USFS

Dispersed sites, No water, No toilets, Reservations not accepted, Open all year, Tent & RV camping: Free, Elev: 9317ft/2840m, Tel: 307-782-6555, Nearest town: Mountain View (WY), Agency: USFS, GPS: 40.970026, -110.390885

31649 • FSR 072 Dispersed 6 - USFS

Dispersed sites, No water, No toilets, Reservations not accepted, Open all year, Tent & RV camping: Free, Elev: 9384ft/2860m, Tel: 307-782-6555, Nearest town: Mountain View (WY), Agency: USFS, GPS: 40.964066, -110.392236

31650 • FSR 072 Dispersed 7 - USFS

Dispersed sites, No water, No toilets, Reservations not accepted, Open all year, Tent & RV camping: Free, Elev: 9390ft/2862m, Tel: 307-782-6555, Nearest town: Mountain View (WY), Agency: USFS, GPS: 40.962835, -110.392141

31651 • FSR 073 Dispersed 1 - USFS

Dispersed sites, No water, No toilets, Reservations not accepted, Open all year, Tent & RV camping: Free, Road not maintained for passenger cars, Elev: 7972ft/2430m, Tel: 801-625-5112, Nearest town: Woodruff, Agency: USFS, GPS: 41.397498, -111.545207

31652 • FSR 073 Dispersed 2 - USFS

Dispersed sites, No water, No toilets, Reservations not accepted, Open all year, Tent & RV camping: Free, Road not maintained for passenger cars, Elev: 7776ft/2370m, Tel: 801-625-5112, Nearest town: Woodruff, Agency: USFS, GPS: 41.389119, -111.543119

31653 • FSR 073 Dispersed 3 - USFS

Dispersed sites, No water, No toilets, Reservations not accepted, Open all year, Tent & RV camping: Free, Elev: 8831ft/2692m, Tel: 307-789-3194, Nearest town: Oakley, Agency: USFS, GPS: 40.959001, -110.578347

31654 • FSR 073 Dispersed 4 - USFS

Dispersed sites, No water, No toilets, Reservations not accepted, Open all year, Tent & RV camping: Free, Road not maintained for passenger cars, Elev: 9549ft/2911m, Tel: 307-782-6555, Nearest town: Mountain View (WY), Agency: USFS, GPS: 40.948795, -110.476834

31655 • FSR 076 Dispersed 1 - USFS

Dispersed sites, No water, No toilets, Reservations not accepted, Open all year, Tent & RV camping: Free, Elev: 7404ft/2257m, Tel: 435-896-9233, Nearest town: Koosharem, Agency: USFS, GPS: 38.526793, -111.915591

31656 • FSR 076 Dispersed 2 - USFS

Dispersed sites, No water, No toilets, Reservations not accepted, Open all year, Tent & RV camping: Free, Elev: 7454ft/2272m, Tel: 435-896-9233, Nearest town: Koosharem, Agency: USFS, GPS: 38.523878, -111.916379

31657 • FSR 076 Dispersed 3 - USFS

Dispersed sites, No water, No toilets, Reservations not accepted, Open all year, Tent & RV camping: Free, Elev: 7581ft/2311m, Tel:

435-789-1181, Nearest town: Paragonah, Agency: USFS, GPS: 37.873632, -112.652592

31658 • FSR 076 Dispersed 4 - USFS

Dispersed sites, No water, No toilets, Reservations not accepted, Open all year, Tent & RV camping: Free, Road not maintained for passenger cars, Elev: 7966ft/2428m, Tel: 435-789-1181, Nearest town: Paragonah, Agency: USFS, GPS: 37.864047, -112.656261

31659 • FSR 076 Dispersed 5 - USFS

Dispersed sites, No water, No toilets, Reservations not accepted, Open all year, Tent & RV camping: Free, Elev: 8027ft/2447m, Tel: 435-789-1181, Nearest town: Paragonah, Agency: USFS, GPS: 37.864136, -112.658117

31660 • FSR 076 Dispersed 6 - USFS

Dispersed sites, No water, No toilets, Reservations not accepted, Open all year, Tent & RV camping: Free, Both sides of road, Elev: 8039ft/2450m, Tel: 435-789-1181, Nearest town: Paragonah, Agency: USFS, GPS: 37.862155, -112.658283

31661 • FSR 076 Dispersed 7 - USFS

Dispersed sites, No water, No toilets, Reservations not accepted, Open all year, Tent & RV camping: Free, Elev: 8307ft/2532m, Tel: 435-789-1181, Nearest town: Paragonah, Agency: USFS, GPS: 37.854496, -112.661233

31662 • FSR 076 Dispersed 8 - USFS

Dispersed sites, No water, No toilets, Reservations not accepted, Open all year, Tent & RV camping: Free, Elev: 8807ft/2684m, Tel: 435-789-1181, Nearest town: Paragonah, Agency: USFS, GPS: 37.833166, -112.670294

31663 • FSR 076 Dispersed 9 - USFS

Dispersed sites, No water, No toilets, Reservations not accepted, Open all year, Tent & RV camping: Free, Elev: 9458ft/2883m, Tel: 435-789-1181, Nearest town: Panguitch, Agency: USFS, GPS: 37.773601, -112.676541

31664 • FSR 076A Dispersed 1 - USFS

Dispersed sites, No water, No toilets, Reservations not accepted, Open all year, Tent & RV camping: Free, Elev: 8894ft/2711m, Tel: 435-896-9233, Nearest town: Koosharem, Agency: USFS, GPS: 38.538053, -111.956972

31665 • FSR 077 Dispersed 1 - USFS

Dispersed sites, No water, No toilets, Reservations not accepted, Open Jul-Nov, Tent & RV camping: Free, Road not maintained for passenger cars, Elev: 6914ft/2107m, Tel: 801-798-3571, Nearest town: Springville, Agency: USFS, GPS: 40.262946, -111.392958

31666 • FSR 077 Dispersed 2 - USFS

Dispersed sites, No water, No toilets, Tent & RV camping: Free, Elev: 7203ft/2195m, Nearest town: Paragonah, Agency: USFS, GPS: 37.894192, -112.677945

31667 • FSR 077 Dispersed 3 - USFS

Dispersed sites, No water, No toilets, Reservations not accepted, Open all year, Tent & RV camping: Free, Road not maintained for

passenger cars, Elev: 7316ft/2230m, Tel: 435-789-1181, Nearest town: Paragonah, Agency: USFS, GPS: 37.886743, -112.664941

31668 • FSR 077 Dispersed 4 - USFS

Dispersed sites, No water, No toilets, Reservations not accepted, Open all year, Tent & RV camping: Free, Road not maintained for passenger cars, Elev: 7938ft/2420m, Tel: 435-789-1181, Nearest town: Paragonah, Agency: USFS, GPS: 37.896521, -112.643124

31669 • FSR 077 Dispersed 5 - USFS

Dispersed sites, No water, No toilets, Reservations not accepted, Open all year, Tent & RV camping: Free, Road not maintained for passenger cars, Elev: 8108ft/2471m, Tel: 435-789-1181, Nearest town: Paragonah, Agency: USFS, GPS: 37.907978, -112.636491

31670 • FSR 077 Dispersed 6 - USFS

Dispersed sites, No water, No toilets, Reservations not accepted, Open all year, Tent & RV camping: Free, 4x4 required, Elev: 7877ft/2401m, Tel: 435-789-1181, Nearest town: Paragonah, Agency: USFS, GPS: 37.916025, -112.628889

31671 • FSR 078 Dispersed 1 - USFS

Dispersed sites, No water, No toilets, Reservations not accepted, Open all year, Tent & RV camping: Free, Elev: 8125ft/2476m, Tel: 435-789-1181, Nearest town: Paragonah, Agency: USFS, GPS: 37.854881, -112.671516

31672 • FSR 078 Dispersed 2 - USFS

Dispersed sites, No water, No toilets, Reservations not accepted, Open all year, Tent & RV camping: Free, Elev: 8614ft/2626m, Tel: 307-782-6555, Nearest town: Mountain View (WY), Agency: USFS, GPS: 40.936037, -110.152328

31673 • FSR 078 Dispersed 3 - USFS

Dispersed sites, No water, No toilets, Reservations not accepted, Open all year, Tent & RV camping: Free, Elev: 8728ft/2660m, Tel: 435-896-9233, Nearest town: Monroe, Agency: USFS, GPS: 38.561375, -112.080299

31674 • FSR 078 Dispersed 4 - USFS

Dispersed sites, No water, No toilets, Reservations not accepted, Open all year, Tent & RV camping: Free, Elev: 9624ft/2933m, Tel: 435-896-9233, Nearest town: Koosharem, Agency: USFS, GPS: 38.502276, -112.019424

31675 • FSR 078 Dispersed 5 - USFS

Dispersed sites, No water, No toilets, Reservations not accepted, Open all year, Tent & RV camping: Free, Elev: 9531ft/2905m, Tel: 435-896-9233, Nearest town: Koosharem, Agency: USFS, GPS: 38.501199, -112.015816

31676 • FSR 080 Dispersed 1 - USFS

Dispersed sites, No water, No toilets, Reservations not accepted, Open all year, Tent & RV camping: Free, Road not maintained for passenger cars, Elev: 9726ft/2964m, Tel: 435-783-4338, Nearest town: Heber City, Agency: USFS, GPS: 40.387933, -111.164304

31677 • FSR 080 Dispersed 2 - USFS

Dispersed sites, No water, No toilets, Reservations not accepted, Open all year, Tent & RV camping: Free, Road not maintained for passenger cars, Elev: 9688ft/2953m, Tel: 435-783-4338, Nearest town: Heber City, Agency: USFS, GPS: 40.389958, -111.157978

31678 • FSR 080 Dispersed 3 - USFS

Dispersed sites, No water, No toilets, Reservations not accepted, Open all year, Tent & RV camping: Free, Road not maintained for passenger cars, Elev: 9798ft/2986m, Tel: 435-783-4338, Nearest town: Heber City, Agency: USFS, GPS: 40.391998, -111.153603

31679 • FSR 081 Dispersed 1 - USFS

Dispersed sites, No water, No toilets, Reservations not accepted, Open all year, Tent & RV camping: Free, Elev: 5368ft/1636m, Tel: 435-755-3620, Nearest town: Logan, Agency: USFS, GPS: 41.780197, -111.632885

31680 • FSR 081 Dispersed 2 - USFS

Dispersed sites, No water, No toilets, Reservations not accepted, Open all year, Tent & RV camping: Free, Elev: 5401ft/1646m, Tel: 435-755-3620, Nearest town: Logan, Agency: USFS, GPS: 41.779715, -111.629863

31681 • FSR 081 Dispersed 3 - USFS

Dispersed sites, No water, No toilets, Reservations not accepted, Open all year, Tent & RV camping: Free, Elev: 5420ft/1652m, Tel: 435-755-3620, Nearest town: Logan, Agency: USFS, GPS: 41.779415, -111.627088

31682 • FSR 081 Dispersed 4 - USFS

Dispersed sites, No water, No toilets, Tent & RV camping: Free, Elev: 7626ft/2324m, Nearest town: Spanish Fork, Agency: USFS, GPS: 39.958747, -111.019569

31683 • FSR 082 Dispersed 1 - USFS

Dispersed sites, No water, No toilets, Reservations not accepted, Open all year, Tent & RV camping: Free, Elev: 7913ft/2412m, Tel: 435-783-4338, Nearest town: Heber City, Agency: USFS, GPS: 40.275948, -111.162922

31684 • FSR 082 Dispersed 2 - USFS

Dispersed sites, No water, No toilets, Reservations not accepted, Tent & RV camping: Free, Many sites in this area, Elev: 8014ft/2443m, Tel: 435-783-4338, Nearest town: Heber City, Agency: USFS, GPS: 40.282153, -111.166831

31685 • FSR 082 Dispersed 3 - USFS

Dispersed sites, No water, No toilets, Reservations not accepted, Open all year, Tent & RV camping: Free, Elev: 8037ft/2450m, Tel: 435-783-4338, Nearest town: Heber City, Agency: USFS, GPS: 40.359863, -111.097324

31686 • FSR 082 Dispersed 4 - USFS

Dispersed sites, No water, No toilets, Reservations not accepted, Open all year, Tent & RV camping: Free, Elev: 7926ft/2416m, Tel: 435-783-4338, Nearest town: Heber City, Agency: USFS, GPS: 40.357643, -111.088854

31687 • FSR 082 Dispersed 5 - USFS

Dispersed sites, No water, No toilets, Reservations not accepted, Open all year, Tent & RV camping: Free, Road not maintained for passenger cars, Elev: 8668ft/2642m, Tel: 307-782-6555, Nearest town: Mountain View (WY), Agency: USFS, GPS: 40.942883, -110.180232

31688 • FSR 082 Dispersed 6 - USFS

Dispersed sites, No water, No toilets, Reservations not accepted, Open all year, Tent & RV camping: Free, Road not maintained for passenger cars, Elev: 9025ft/2751m, Tel: 307-782-6555, Nearest town: Mountain View (WY), Agency: USFS, GPS: 40.940575, -110.230577

31689 • FSR 082 Dispersed 7 - USFS

Dispersed sites, No water, No toilets, Reservations not accepted, Open all year, Tent & RV camping: Free, Elev: 7799ft/2377m, Tel: 435-789-1181, Nearest town: Panguitch, Agency: USFS, GPS: 37.776192, -112.560659

31690 • FSR 082B Dispersed 1 - USFS

Dispersed sites, No water, No toilets, Reservations not accepted, Open all year, Tent & RV camping: Free, Road not maintained for passenger cars, Elev: 9940ft/3030m, Tel: 435-896-9233, Nearest town: Greenwich, Agency: USFS, GPS: 38.382332, -112.016513

31691 • FSR 083 Dispersed 1 - USFS

Dispersed sites, No water, No toilets, Reservations not accepted, Open all year, Tent & RV camping: Free, Road not maintained for passenger cars, Elev: 8135ft/2480m, Tel: 435-755-3620, Nearest town: Logan, Agency: USFS, GPS: 41.713446, -111.676432

31692 • FSR 083 Dispersed 10 - USFS

Dispersed sites, No water, No toilets, Reservations not accepted, Open all year, Tent & RV camping: Free, Numerous sites in this area, Road not maintained for passenger cars, Elev: 9070ft/2765m, Tel: 435-783-4338, Nearest town: Heber City, Agency: USFS, GPS: 40.440856, -111.202547

31693 • FSR 083 Dispersed 2 - USFS

Dispersed sites, No water, No toilets, Reservations not accepted, Open all year, Tent & RV camping: Free, 5 separated sites, Elev: 8925ft/2720m, Tel: 435-783-4338, Nearest town: Heber City, Agency: USFS, GPS: 40.357719, -111.140118

31694 • FSR 083 Dispersed 3 - USFS

Dispersed sites, No water, No toilets, Reservations not accepted, Open all year, Tent & RV camping: Free, Elev: 8913ft/2717m, Tel: 435-783-4338, Nearest town: Heber City, Agency: USFS, GPS: 40.359148, -111.137023

31695 • FSR 083 Dispersed 4 - USFS

Dispersed sites, No water, No toilets, Reservations not accepted, Open all year, Tent & RV camping: Free, Elev: 9129ft/2783m, Tel: 435-783-4338, Nearest town: Heber City, Agency: USFS, GPS: 40.372133, -111.134183

31696 • FSR 083 Dispersed 5 - USFS

Dispersed sites, No water, No toilets, Reservations not accepted, Open all year, Tent & RV camping: Free, Elev: 9892ft/3015m, Tel: 435-783-4338, Nearest town: Heber City, Agency: USFS, GPS: 40.389866, -111.167252

31697 • FSR 083 Dispersed 6 - USFS

Dispersed sites, No water, No toilets, Reservations not accepted, Open all year, Tent & RV camping: Free, Elev: 9677ft/2950m, Tel: 435-783-4338, Nearest town: Heber City, Agency: USFS, GPS: 40.423625, -111.182199

31698 • FSR 083 Dispersed 7 - USFS

Dispersed sites, No water, No toilets, Reservations not accepted, Open all year, Tent & RV camping: Free, Elev: 9474ft/2888m, Tel: 435-783-4338, Nearest town: Heber City, Agency: USFS, GPS: 40.426341, -111.191139

31699 • FSR 083 Dispersed 8 - USFS

Dispersed sites, No water, No toilets, Reservations not accepted, Open all year, Tent & RV camping: Free, Elev: 9313ft/2839m, Tel: 435-783-4338, Nearest town: Heber City, Agency: USFS, GPS: 40.429925, -111.196096

31700 • FSR 083 Dispersed 9 - USFS

Dispersed sites, No water, No toilets, Reservations not accepted, Open all year, Tent & RV camping: Free, 2 separated sites, Road not maintained for passenger cars, Elev: 9096ft/2772m, Tel: 435-783-4338, Nearest town: Heber City, Agency: USFS, GPS: 40.436723, -111.200457

31701 • FSR 083F Dispersed 1 - USFS

Dispersed sites, No water, No toilets, Reservations not accepted, Open all year, Tent & RV camping: Free, Road not maintained for passenger cars, Elev: 9794ft/2985m, Tel: 435-896-9233, Nearest town: Greenwich, Agency: USFS, GPS: 38.495055, -112.068969

31702 • FSR 083J Dispersed 1 - USFS

Dispersed sites, No water, No toilets, Reservations not accepted, Open all year, Tent & RV camping: Free, Road not maintained for passenger cars, Elev: 9323ft/2842m, Tel: 435-896-9233, Nearest town: Greenwich, Agency: USFS, GPS: 38.458716, -112.056092

31703 • FSR 084 (Dock Flat TH) Dispersed 4 - USFS

Dispersed sites, No water, No toilets, Reservations not accepted, Open all year, Tent & RV camping: Free, Elev: 5822ft/1775m, Tel: 801-625-5112, Nearest town: Woodruff, Agency: USFS, GPS: 41.461092, -111.943941

31704 • FSR 084 Dispersed 1 - USFS

Dispersed sites, No water, No toilets, Reservations not accepted, Open all year, Tent & RV camping: Free, Road not maintained for passenger cars, Elev: 7671ft/2338m, Tel: 801-723-2660, Nearest town: Farmington, Agency: USFS, GPS: 40.973131, -111.800803

31705 • FSR 084 Dispersed 10 - USFS

Dispersed sites, No water, No toilets, Reservations not accepted, Open all year, Tents only: Free, Road not maintained for passenger cars, Elev: 8441ft/2573m, Tel: 801-625-5112, Nearest town: Woodruff, Agency: USFS, GPS: 41.411549, -111.964397

31706 • FSR 084 Dispersed 11 - USFS

Dispersed sites, No water, No toilets, Reservations not accepted, Open all year, Tent & RV camping: Free, Road not maintained for passenger cars, Elev: 8784ft/2677m, Tel: 801-625-5112, Nearest town: Woodruff, Agency: USFS, GPS: 41.410671, -111.968604

31707 • FSR 084 Dispersed 12 - USFS

Dispersed sites, No water, No toilets, Reservations not accepted, Open Jul-Nov, Tent & RV camping: Free, Road not maintained for passenger cars, Elev: 8681ft/2646m, Tel: 801-625-5112, Nearest town: Woodruff, Agency: USFS, GPS: 41.398487, -111.971013

31708 • FSR 084 Dispersed 13 - USFS

Dispersed sites, No water, No toilets, Reservations not accepted, Open Jul-Nov, Tent & RV camping: Free, Road not maintained for passenger cars, Elev: 8867ft/2703m, Tel: 801-625-5112, Nearest town: Woodruff, Agency: USFS, GPS: 41.396722, -111.985965

31709 • FSR 084 Dispersed 14 - USFS

Dispersed sites, No water, No toilets, Reservations not accepted, Open Jul-Nov, Tent & RV camping: Free, Road not maintained for passenger cars, Elev: 9110ft/2777m, Tel: 801-625-5112, Nearest town: Woodruff, Agency: USFS, GPS: 41.394589, -111.984094

31710 • FSR 084 Dispersed 15 - USFS

Dispersed sites, No water, No toilets, Reservations not accepted, Open all year, Tent & RV camping: Free, Road not maintained for passenger cars, Elev: 8559ft/2609m, Tel: 435-789-1181, Nearest town: Panguitch, Agency: USFS, GPS: 37.776487, -112.616082

31711 • FSR 084 Dispersed 16 - USFS

Dispersed sites, No water, No toilets, Reservations not accepted, Open all year, Tent & RV camping: Free, Both sidesw of road, Road not maintained for passenger cars, Elev: 7832ft/2387m, Tel: 435-783-4338, Nearest town: Heber City, Agency: USFS, GPS: 40.238675, -111.112413

31712 • FSR 084 Dispersed 17- USFS

Dispersed sites, No water, No toilets, Reservations not accepted, Open all year, Tent & RV camping: Free, Road not maintained for passenger cars, Elev: 7906ft/2410m, Tel: 435-783-4338, Nearest town: Heber City, Agency: USFS, GPS: 40.241735, -111.108541

31713 • FSR 084 Dispersed 18 - USFS

Dispersed sites, No water, No toilets, Reservations not accepted, Open all year, Tent & RV camping: Free, Road not maintained for passenger cars, Elev: 7984ft/2434m, Tel: 435-783-4338, Nearest town: Heber City, Agency: USFS, GPS: 40.245125, -111.105815

31714 • FSR 084 Dispersed 19 - USFS

Dispersed sites, No water, No toilets, Reservations not accepted, Open all year, Tent & RV camping: Free, Several spots, Road not maintained for passenger cars, Elev: 8404ft/2562m, Tel: 435-783-4338, Nearest town: Heber City, Agency: USFS, GPS: 40.256011, -111.102996

31715 • FSR 084 Dispersed 2 - USFS

Dispersed sites, No water, No toilets, Reservations not accepted, Open all year, Tent & RV camping: Free, Road not maintained for passenger cars, Elev: 7641ft/2329m, Tel: 801-723-2660, Nearest town: Farmington, Agency: USFS, GPS: 40.968474, -111.796367

31716 • FSR 084 Dispersed 20 - USFS

Dispersed sites, No water, No toilets, Reservations not accepted, Open all year, Tent & RV camping: Free, Road not maintained for passenger cars, Elev: 8349ft/2545m, Tel: 435-783-4338, Nearest town: Heber City, Agency: USFS, GPS: 40.258199, -111.102607

31717 • FSR 084 Dispersed 21 - USFS

Dispersed sites, No water, No toilets, Reservations not accepted, Open all year, Tent & RV camping: Free, Road not maintained for passenger cars, Elev: 8550ft/2606m, Tel: 435-783-4338, Nearest town: Heber City, Agency: USFS, GPS: 40.264973, -111.104277

31718 • FSR 084 Dispersed 22 - USFS

Dispersed sites, No water, No toilets, Reservations not accepted, Open all year, Tent & RV camping: Free, Road not maintained for passenger cars, Elev: 9430ft/2874m, Tel: 435-783-4338, Nearest town: Heber City, Agency: USFS, GPS: 40.280459, -111.105844

31719 • FSR 084 Dispersed 23 - USFS

Dispersed sites, No water, No toilets, Reservations not accepted, Open all year, Tent & RV camping: Free, Road not maintained for passenger cars, Elev: 9077ft/2767m, Tel: 307-789-3194, Nearest town: Oakley, Agency: USFS, GPS: 40.935864, -110.599504

31720 • FSR 084 Dispersed 3 - USFS

Dispersed sites, No water, No toilets, Reservations not accepted, Open all year, Tent & RV camping: Free, Room for many rigs, Elev: 5762ft/1756m, Tel: 801-625-5112, Nearest town: Woodruff, Agency: USFS, GPS: 41.462665, -111.942237

31721 • FSR 084 Dispersed 5 - USFS

Dispersed sites, No water, No toilets, Reservations not accepted, Open all year, Tent & RV camping: Free, Several sites in this area, Elev: 5964ft/1818m, Tel: 801-625-5112, Nearest town: Woodruff, Agency: USFS, GPS: 41.459776, -111.940334

31722 • FSR 084 Dispersed 6 - USFS

Dispersed sites, No water, No toilets, Reservations not accepted, Open all year, Tent & RV camping: Free, Elev: 6674ft/2034m, Tel: 801-625-5112, Nearest town: Woodruff, Agency: USFS, GPS: 41.444654, -111.942669

31723 • FSR 084 Dispersed 7 - USFS

Dispersed sites, No water, No toilets, Reservations not accepted, Open all year, Tent & RV camping: Free, Elev: 6716ft/2047m, Tel: 801-625-5112, Nearest town: Woodruff, Agency: USFS, GPS: 41.445466, -111.944526

31724 • FSR 084 Dispersed 8 - USFS

Dispersed sites, No water, No toilets, Reservations not accepted, Open all year, Tent & RV camping: Free, Road not maintained for passenger cars, Elev: 7831ft/2387m, Tel: 801-625-5112, Nearest town: Woodruff, Agency: USFS, GPS: 41.424917, -111.964965

31725 • FSR 084 Dispersed 9 - USFS

Dispersed sites, No water, No toilets, Reservations not accepted, Open all year, Tent & RV camping: Free, Road not maintained for passenger cars, Elev: 8122ft/2476m, Tel: 801-625-5112, Nearest town: Woodruff, Agency: USFS, GPS: 41.417373, -111.966249

31726 • FSR 085 (Holman Flat) Dispersed 10 - USFS

Dispersed sites, No water, No toilets, Reservations not accepted, Open Apr-Nov, Tent & RV camping: Free, Road not maintained for passenger cars, Elev: 6760ft/2060m, Tel: 801-785-3563, Nearest town: Cedar Hills, Agency: USFS, GPS: 40.499195, -111.636312

31727 • FSR 085 Dispersed 1 - USFS

Dispersed sites, No water, No toilets, Reservations not accepted, Open Apr-Nov, Tent & RV camping: Free, Road not maintained for passenger cars, Elev: 8594ft/2619m, Tel: 801-785-3563, Nearest town: Midway, Agency: USFS, GPS: 40.538768, -111.548874

31728 • FSR 085 Dispersed 11 - USFS

Dispersed sites, No water, No toilets, Reservations not accepted, Open Apr-Nov, Tent & RV camping: Free, Road not maintained for passenger cars, Elev: 6442ft/1964m, Tel: 801-785-3563, Nearest town: Cedar Hills, Agency: USFS, GPS: 40.486658, -111.637934

31729 • FSR 085 Dispersed 12 - USFS

Dispersed sites, No water, No toilets, Reservations not accepted, Open all year, Tent & RV camping: Free, Road not maintained for passenger cars, Elev: 6178ft/1883m, Tel: 801-798-3571, Nearest town: Vernon, Agency: USFS, GPS: 40.003967, -112.613949

31730 • FSR 085 Dispersed 2 - USFS

Dispersed sites, No water, No toilets, Reservations not accepted, Open Apr-Nov, Tent & RV camping: Free, Road not maintained for passenger cars, Elev: 8494ft/2589m, Tel: 801-785-3563, Nearest town: Midway, Agency: USFS, GPS: 40.555623, -111.558429

31731 • FSR 085 Dispersed 3 - USFS

Dispersed sites, No water, No toilets, Reservations not accepted, Open Apr-Nov, Tent & RV camping: Free, Road not maintained for passenger cars, Elev: 7655ft/2333m, Tel: 801-785-3563, Nearest town: Midway, Agency: USFS, GPS: 40.527073, -111.597474

31732 • FSR 085 Dispersed 3 - USFS

Dispersed sites, No water, No toilets, Reservations not accepted, Open Apr-Nov, Tent & RV camping: Free, Road not maintained for passenger cars, Elev: 8155ft/2486m, Tel: 801-785-3563, Nearest town: Midway, Agency: USFS, GPS: 40.560674, -111.552731

31733 • FSR 085 Dispersed 4 - USFS

Dispersed sites, No water, No toilets, Reservations not accepted, Open Apr-Nov, Tent & RV camping: Free, Road not maintained for passenger cars, Elev: 7603ft/2317m, Tel: 801-785-3563, Nearest town: Midway, Agency: USFS, GPS: 40.528734, -111.599067

31734 • FSR 085 Dispersed 5 - USFS

Dispersed sites, No water, No toilets, Reservations not accepted, Open Apr-Nov, Tent & RV camping: Free, Road not maintained for passenger cars, Elev: 7617ft/2322m, Tel: 801-785-3563, Nearest town: Midway, Agency: USFS, GPS: 40.526925, -111.599689

31735 • FSR 085 Dispersed 6 - USFS
Dispersed sites, No water, No toilets, Reservations not accepted, Open Apr-Nov, Tent & RV camping: Free, Road not maintained for passenger cars, Elev: 7576ft/2309m, Tel: 801-785-3563, Nearest town: Midway, Agency: USFS, GPS: 40.527126, -111.601521

31736 • FSR 085 Dispersed 7 - USFS
Dispersed sites, No water, No toilets, Reservations not accepted, Open Apr-Nov, Tent & RV camping: Free, Both sides of road, Road not maintained for passenger cars, Elev: 7601ft/2317m, Tel: 801-785-3563, Nearest town: Midway, Agency: USFS, GPS: 40.527429, -111.603174

31737 • FSR 085 Dispersed 8 - USFS
Dispersed sites, No water, No toilets, Reservations not accepted, Open Apr-Nov, Tent & RV camping: Free, Road not maintained for passenger cars, Elev: 7577ft/2309m, Tel: 801-785-3563, Nearest town: Midway, Agency: USFS, GPS: 40.525386, -111.607401

31738 • FSR 085 Dispersed 9 - USFS
Dispersed sites, No water, No toilets, Reservations not accepted, Open Apr-Nov, Tents only: Free, Walk-to sites, Road not maintained for passenger cars, Elev: 7578ft/2310m, Tel: 801-785-3563, Nearest town: Midway, Agency: USFS, GPS: 40.526544, -111.605929

31739 • FSR 086 Dispersed 1 - USFS
Dispersed sites, No water, No toilets, Reservations not accepted, Open all year, Tent & RV camping: Free, Road not maintained for passenger cars, Elev: 5797ft/1767m, Tel: 435-755-3620, Nearest town: Mendon, Agency: USFS, GPS: 41.684441, -111.998318

31740 • FSR 086 Dispersed 2 - USFS
Dispersed sites, No water, No toilets, Reservations not accepted, Open all year, Tent & RV camping: Free, Road not maintained for passenger cars, Elev: 5864ft/1787m, Tel: 435-755-3620, Nearest town: Mendon, Agency: USFS, GPS: 41.682295, -112.000349

31741 • FSR 086 Dispersed 3 - USFS
Dispersed sites, No water, No toilets, Reservations not accepted, Open all year, Tent & RV camping: Free, Road not maintained for passenger cars, Elev: 8892ft/2710m, Tel: 307-789-3194, Nearest town: Oakley, Agency: USFS, GPS: 40.946637, -110.579819

31742 • FSR 086 Dispersed 4 - USFS
Dispersed sites, No water, No toilets, Reservations not accepted, Open all year, Tent & RV camping: Free, Road not maintained for passenger cars, Elev: 6665ft/2031m, Tel: 435-865-3200, Nearest town: Paragonah, Agency: USFS, GPS: 37.982443, -112.656461

31743 • FSR 086 Dispersed 5 - USFS
Dispersed sites, No water, No toilets, Reservations not accepted, Open all year, Tent & RV camping: Free, Road not maintained for passenger cars, Elev: 6796ft/2071m, Tel: 435-865-3200, Nearest town: Paragonah, Agency: USFS, GPS: 37.977167, -112.652116

31744 • FSR 086 Dispersed 6 - USFS
Dispersed sites, No water, No toilets, Reservations not accepted, Open all year, Tent & RV camping: Free, Road not maintained for passenger cars, Elev: 8114ft/2473m, Tel: 435-865-3200, Nearest town: Paragonah, Agency: USFS, GPS: 37.947081, -112.611791

31745 • FSR 087 Dispersed 1 - USFS
Dispersed sites, No water, No toilets, Reservations not accepted, Open all year, Tent & RV camping: Free, Elev: 7815ft/2382m, Tel: 435-676-9316, Nearest town: Hatch, Agency: USFS, GPS: 37.620015, -112.245538

31746 • FSR 087 Dispersed 2 - USFS
Dispersed sites, No water, No toilets, Reservations not accepted, Open all year, Tent & RV camping: Free, Elev: 7892ft/2405m, Tel: 435-676-9316, Nearest town: Hatch, Agency: USFS, GPS: 37.584515, -112.259255

31747 • FSR 087 Dispersed 3 - USFS
Dispersed sites, No water, No toilets, Reservations not accepted, Open all year, Tent & RV camping: Free, Elev: 8260ft/2518m, Tel: 435-676-9316, Nearest town: Alton, Agency: USFS, GPS: 37.449831, -112.332461

31748 • FSR 087 Dispersed 4 - USFS
Dispersed sites, No water, No toilets, Reservations not accepted, Open all year, Tent & RV camping: Free, Elev: 8274ft/2522m, Tel: 435-676-9316, Nearest town: Alton, Agency: USFS, GPS: 37.446891, -112.334196

31749 • FSR 087 Dispersed 5 - USFS
Dispersed sites, No water, No toilets, Reservations not accepted, Open all year, Tent & RV camping: Free, Road not maintained for passenger cars, Elev: 9577ft/2919m, Tel: 307-782-6555, Nearest town: Mountain View (WY), Agency: USFS, GPS: 40.973136, -110.353382

31750 • FSR 088 Dispersed 1 - USFS
Dispersed sites, No water, No toilets, Reservations not accepted, Open all year, Tent & RV camping: Free, Elev: 7971ft/2430m, Tel: 435-676-9316, Nearest town: Bryce, Agency: USFS, GPS: 37.626499, -112.228143

31751 • FSR 088 Dispersed 2 - USFS
Dispersed sites, No water, No toilets, Reservations not accepted, Open all year, Tent & RV camping: Free, Elev: 7990ft/2435m, Tel: 435-676-9316, Nearest town: Bryce, Agency: USFS, GPS: 37.637544, -112.192641

31752 • FSR 088 Dispersed 3 - USFS
Dispersed sites, No water, No toilets, Reservations not accepted, Open all year, Tent & RV camping: Free, Road not maintained for passenger cars, Elev: 7746ft/2361m, Tel: 435-676-9316, Nearest town: Bryce, Agency: USFS, GPS: 37.672661, -112.205106

31753 • FSR 088 Dispersed 4 - USFS
Dispersed sites, No water, No toilets, Reservations not accepted, Open all year, Tent & RV camping: Free, Elev: 7536ft/2297m, Tel: 435-783-4338, Nearest town: Samak, Agency: USFS, GPS: 40.625317, -111.134835

31754 • FSR 088A Dispersed 1 - USFS

Dispersed sites, No water, No toilets, Reservations not accepted, Open Jun-Oct, Tent & RV camping: Free, Road not maintained for passenger cars, Elev: 7903ft/2409m, Tel: 435-783-4338, Nearest town: Springville, Agency: USFS, GPS: 40.223419, -111.286982

31755 • FSR 089 Dispersed 1 - USFS

Dispersed sites, No water, No toilets, Reservations not accepted, Open all year, Tent & RV camping: Free, Several sites in this area, Elev: 9097ft/2773m, Tel: 435-783-4338, Nearest town: Woodland, Agency: USFS, GPS: 40.534543, -111.018422

31756 • FSR 089 Dispersed 2 - USFS

Dispersed sites, No water, No toilets, Reservations not accepted, Open all year, Tent & RV camping: Free, Road not maintained for passenger cars, Elev: 9143ft/2787m, Tel: 435-783-4338, Nearest town: Woodland, Agency: USFS, GPS: 40.538512, -111.005255

31757 • FSR 089 Dispersed 3 - USFS

Dispersed sites, No water, No toilets, Reservations not accepted, Open all year, Tent & RV camping: Free, Road not maintained for passenger cars, Elev: 9226ft/2812m, Tel: 435-783-4338, Nearest town: Woodland, Agency: USFS, GPS: 40.535954, -111.003972

31758 • FSR 089 Dispersed 4 - USFS

Dispersed sites, No water, No toilets, Reservations not accepted, Open all year, Tent & RV camping: Free, Road not maintained for passenger cars, Elev: 9270ft/2825m, Tel: 435-783-4338, Nearest town: Woodland, Agency: USFS, GPS: 40.532446, -110.998951

31759 • FSR 089 Dispersed 5 - USFS

Dispersed sites, No water, No toilets, Reservations not accepted, Open all year, Tent & RV camping: Free, Road not maintained for passenger cars, Elev: 9457ft/2882m, Tel: 435-783-4338, Nearest town: Woodland, Agency: USFS, GPS: 40.524755, -110.981587

31760 • FSR 089 Dispersed 6 - USFS

Dispersed sites, No water, No toilets, Reservations not accepted, Open all year, Tent & RV camping: Free, Elev: 6238ft/1901m, Tel: 435-743-5721, Nearest town: Oak City, Agency: USFS, GPS: 39.355339, -112.249965

31761 • FSR 090 Dispersed 1 - USFS

Dispersed sites, No water, No toilets, Reservations not accepted, Open all year, Tent & RV camping: Free, Road not maintained for passenger cars, Elev: 6753ft/2058m, Tel: 801-798-3571, Nearest town: Vernon, Agency: USFS, GPS: 39.996815, -112.506251

31762 • FSR 090 Dispersed 2 - USFS

Dispersed sites, No water, No toilets, Reservations not accepted, Open all year, Tent & RV camping: Free, Road not maintained for passenger cars, Elev: 6954ft/2120m, Tel: 801-798-3571, Nearest town: Vernon, Agency: USFS, GPS: 39.992724, -112.510214

31763 • FSR 090 Dispersed 3 - USFS

Dispersed sites, No water, No toilets, Reservations not accepted, Open all year, Tent & RV camping: Free, Road not maintained for passenger cars, Elev: 7213ft/2199m, Tel: 801-798-3571, Nearest town: Vernon, Agency: USFS, GPS: 39.986425, -112.514618

31764 • FSR 090 Dispersed 4 - USFS

Dispersed sites, No water, No toilets, Reservations not accepted, Open all year, Tent & RV camping: Free, Road not maintained for passenger cars, Elev: 7429ft/2264m, Tel: 801-798-3571, Nearest town: Vernon, Agency: USFS, GPS: 39.983045, -112.517727

31765 • FSR 090 Dispersed 5 - USFS

Dispersed sites, No water, No toilets, Reservations not accepted, Open all year, Tent & RV camping: Free, Road not maintained for passenger cars, Elev: 7709ft/2350m, Tel: 801-798-3571, Nearest town: Vernon, Agency: USFS, GPS: 39.979561, -112.521778

31766 • FSR 090 Dispersed 6 - USFS

Dispersed sites, No water, No toilets, Reservations not accepted, Open all year, Tent & RV camping: Free, Road not maintained for passenger cars, Elev: 5273ft/1607m, Tel: 435-743-5721, Nearest town: Delta, Agency: USFS, GPS: 39.299465, -112.369474

31767 • FSR 090 Dispersed 7 - USFS

Dispersed sites, No water, No toilets, Reservations not accepted, Open all year, Tent & RV camping: Free, Road not maintained for passenger cars, Elev: 8891ft/2710m, Tel: 307-789-3194, Nearest town: Oakley, Agency: USFS, GPS: 40.954345, -110.573553

31768 • FSR 090 Dispersed 8 - USFS

Dispersed sites, No water, No toilets, Reservations not accepted, Open all year, Tent & RV camping: Free, Road not maintained for passenger cars, Elev: 9414ft/2869m, Tel: 435-783-4338, Nearest town: Spanish Fork, Agency: USFS, GPS: 40.066705, -111.127442

31769 • FSR 090 Dispersed 9 - USFS

Dispersed sites, No water, No toilets, Reservations not accepted, Open all year, Tent & RV camping: Free, Road not maintained for passenger cars, Elev: 9542ft/2908m, Tel: 435-783-4338, Nearest town: Spanish Fork, Agency: USFS, GPS: 40.062798, -111.131655

31770 • FSR 091 (Yellow Lake) Dispersed 1 - USFS

Dispersed sites, No water, No toilets, Reservations not accepted, Open all year, Tent & RV camping: Free, Elev: 9790ft/2984m, Tel: 435-783-4338, Nearest town: Heber City, Agency: USFS, GPS: 40.464957, -111.090917

31771 • FSR 091 Dispersed 1 - USFS

Dispersed sites, No water, No toilets, Reservations not accepted, Open all year, Tent & RV camping: Free, Road not maintained for passenger cars, Elev: 7788ft/2374m, Tel: 435-676-9315, Nearest town: Hatch, Agency: USFS, GPS: 37.622025, -112.246541

31772 • FSR 091 Dispersed 10 - USFS

Dispersed sites, No water, No toilets, Reservations not accepted, Open all year, Tent & RV camping: Free, Elev: 9848ft/3002m, Tel: 435-783-4338, Nearest town: Heber City, Agency: USFS, GPS: 40.461931, -111.132596

31773 • FSR 091 Dispersed 2 - USFS

Dispersed sites, No water, No toilets, Reservations not accepted, Open all year, Tent & RV camping: Free, Road not maintained for

passenger cars, Elev: 7797ft/2377m, Tel: 435-676-9315, Nearest town: Hatch, Agency: USFS, GPS: 37.619365, -112.247422

31774 • FSR 091 Dispersed 3 - USFS
Dispersed sites, No water, No toilets, Reservations not accepted, Open all year, Tent & RV camping: Free, High-clearance vehicle required, Elev: 8795ft/2681m, Tel: 435-738-2482, Nearest town: Spanish Fork, Agency: USFS, GPS: 39.914031, -110.868134

31775 • FSR 091 Dispersed 4 - USFS
Dispersed sites, No water, No toilets, Reservations not accepted, Open all year, Tent & RV camping: Free, Elev: 9457ft/2882m, Tel: 435-783-4338, Nearest town: Heber City, Agency: USFS, GPS: 40.482877, -111.036025

31776 • FSR 091 Dispersed 5 - USFS
Dispersed sites, No water, No toilets, Reservations not accepted, Open all year, Tent & RV camping: Free, Elev: 9844ft/3000m, Tel: 435-783-4338, Nearest town: Heber City, Agency: USFS, GPS: 40.472632, -111.055731

31777 • FSR 091 Dispersed 6 - USFS
Dispersed sites, No water, No toilets, Reservations not accepted, Open all year, Tent & RV camping: Free, Elev: 9783ft/2982m, Tel: 435-783-4338, Nearest town: Heber City, Agency: USFS, GPS: 40.470746, -111.064309

31778 • FSR 091 Dispersed 7 - USFS
Dispersed sites, No water, No toilets, Reservations not accepted, Open all year, Tent & RV camping: Free, Elev: 9862ft/3006m, Tel: 435-783-4338, Nearest town: Heber City, Agency: USFS, GPS: 40.457468, -111.089474

31779 • FSR 091 Dispersed 8 - USFS
Dispersed sites, No water, No toilets, Reservations not accepted, Open all year, Tent & RV camping: Free, Elev: 9856ft/3004m, Tel: 435-783-4338, Nearest town: Heber City, Agency: USFS, GPS: 40.463376, -111.130126

31780 • FSR 091 Dispersed 9 - USFS
Dispersed sites, No water, No toilets, Reservations not accepted, Open all year, Tent & RV camping: Free, Elev: 9855ft/3004m, Tel: 435-783-4338, Nearest town: Heber City, Agency: USFS, GPS: 40.462586, -111.132065

31781 • FSR 091C Dispersed 1 - USFS
Dispersed sites, No water, No toilets, Reservations not accepted, Open all year, Tent & RV camping: Free, Road not maintained for passenger cars, Elev: 7881ft/2402m, Tel: 435-676-9316, Nearest town: Hatch, Agency: USFS, GPS: 37.578511, -112.266253

31782 • FSR 092 Dispersed 1 - USFS
Dispersed sites, No water, No toilets, Reservations not accepted, Open all year, Tent & RV camping: Free, Road not maintained for passenger cars, Elev: 5827ft/1776m, Tel: 435-743-5721, Nearest town: Scipio, Agency: USFS, GPS: 39.269139, -112.315992

31783 • FSR 092 Dispersed 2 - USFS
Dispersed sites, No water, No toilets, Reservations not accepted, Open all year, Tent & RV camping: Free, Road not maintained for passenger cars, Elev: 5851ft/1783m, Tel: 435-743-5721, Nearest town: Scipio, Agency: USFS, GPS: 39.270008, -112.315319

31784 • FSR 092 Dispersed 3 - USFS
Dispersed sites, No water, No toilets, Reservations not accepted, Open all year, Tent & RV camping: Free, Road not maintained for passenger cars, Elev: 8190ft/2496m, Tel: 435-783-4338, Nearest town: Heber City, Agency: USFS, GPS: 40.346532, -111.216463

31785 • FSR 092 Dispersed 4 - USFS
Dispersed sites, No water, No toilets, Reservations not accepted, Open all year, Tent & RV camping: Free, Road not maintained for passenger cars, Elev: 8256ft/2516m, Tel: 435-783-4338, Nearest town: Heber City, Agency: USFS, GPS: 40.346885, -111.207813

31786 • FSR 092 Dispersed 5 - USFS
Dispersed sites, No water, No toilets, Reservations not accepted, Open all year, Tent & RV camping: Free, Road not maintained for passenger cars, Elev: 8328ft/2538m, Tel: 435-783-4338, Nearest town: Heber City, Agency: USFS, GPS: 40.334554, -111.199911

31787 • FSR 092 Dispersed 6 - USFS
Dispersed sites, No water, No toilets, Reservations not accepted, Open all year, Tent & RV camping: Free, Road not maintained for passenger cars, Elev: 8503ft/2592m, Tel: 435-783-4338, Nearest town: Heber City, Agency: USFS, GPS: 40.342345, -111.195234

31788 • FSR 092 Dispersed 7 - USFS
Dispersed sites, No water, No toilets, Reservations not accepted, Open all year, Tent & RV camping: Free, Road not maintained for passenger cars, Elev: 8945ft/2726m, Tel: 435-783-4338, Nearest town: Heber City, Agency: USFS, GPS: 40.345906, -111.176815

31789 • FSR 092 Dispersed 8 - USFS
Dispersed sites, No water, No toilets, Reservations not accepted, Open all year, Tent & RV camping: Free, Road not maintained for passenger cars, Elev: 8971ft/2734m, Tel: 435-783-4338, Nearest town: Heber City, Agency: USFS, GPS: 40.343614, -111.177146

31790 • FSR 092 Dispersed 9 - USFS
Dispersed sites, No water, No toilets, Reservations not accepted, Open all year, Tent & RV camping: Free, Road not maintained for passenger cars, Elev: 9505ft/2897m, Tel: 435-783-4338, Nearest town: Heber City, Agency: USFS, GPS: 40.345546, -111.161781

31791 • FSR 093 Dispersed 1 - USFS
Dispersed sites, No water, No toilets, Reservations not accepted, Open all year, Tent & RV camping: Free, Elev: 8218ft/2505m, Tel: 435-789-1181, Nearest town: Manila, Agency: USFS, GPS: 40.886046, -109.761092

31792 • FSR 093 Dispersed 2 - USFS
Dispersed sites, No water, No toilets, Reservations not accepted, Open all year, Tent & RV camping: Free, Road not maintained for passenger cars, Elev: 9055ft/2760m, Tel: 435-783-4338, Nearest town: Heber City, Agency: USFS, GPS: 40.378128, -111.206951

31793 • FSR 093 Dispersed 3 - USFS

Dispersed sites, No water, No toilets, Reservations not accepted, Open all year, Tent & RV camping: Free, Road not maintained for passenger cars, Elev: 9163ft/2793m, Tel: 435-783-4338, Nearest town: Heber City, Agency: USFS, GPS: 40.382149, -111.206587

31794 • FSR 093 Dispersed 4 - USFS

Dispersed sites, No water, No toilets, Reservations not accepted, Open all year, Tent & RV camping: Free, Road not maintained for passenger cars, Elev: 9753ft/2973m, Tel: 435-783-4338, Nearest town: Heber City, Agency: USFS, GPS: 40.476759, -111.031891

31795 • FSR 093 Dispersed 5 - USFS

Dispersed sites, No water, No toilets, Reservations not accepted, Open all year, Tent & RV camping: Free, Road not maintained for passenger cars, Elev: 9870ft/3008m, Tel: 435-783-4338, Nearest town: Heber City, Agency: USFS, GPS: 40.473742, -111.048161

31796 • FSR 094 Dispersed - USFS

Dispersed sites, No water, No toilets, Reservations not accepted, Open Jun-Nov, Tent & RV camping: Free, Elev: 6206ft/1892m, Tel: 435-755-3620, Nearest town: Garden City, Agency: USFS, GPS: 41.863997, -111.573778

31797 • FSR 095 Dispersed 1 - USFS

Dispersed sites, No water, No toilets, Reservations not accepted, Open all year, Tent & RV camping: Free, Road not maintained for passenger cars, Elev: 8957ft/2730m, Tel: 435-789-1181, Nearest town: Cedar City, Agency: USFS, GPS: 37.651475, -112.698766

31798 • FSR 096 Dispersed 2 - USFS

Dispersed sites, No water, No toilets, Reservations not accepted, Open all year, Tent & RV camping: Free, Elev: 6078ft/1853m, Tel: 435-743-5721, Nearest town: Richfield, Agency: USFS, GPS: 38.777968, -112.116994

31799 • FSR 096 Dispersed 3 - USFS

Dispersed sites, No water, No toilets, Reservations not accepted, Open all year, Tent & RV camping: Free, Elev: 7833ft/2387m, Tel: 435-743-5721, Nearest town: Richfield, Agency: USFS, GPS: 38.797941, -112.216066

31800 • FSR 096 Dispersed 4 - USFS

Dispersed sites, No water, No toilets, Reservations not accepted, Open all year, Tent & RV camping: Free, Elev: 8433ft/2570m, Tel: 435-743-5721, Nearest town: Richfield, Agency: USFS, GPS: 38.821287, -112.221966

31801 • FSR 096 Dispersed 5 - USFS

Dispersed sites, No water, No toilets, Reservations not accepted, Open all year, Tent & RV camping: Free, Elev: 8439ft/2572m, Tel: 435-789-1181, Nearest town: Manila, Agency: USFS, GPS: 40.871432, -109.839493

31802 • FSR 096 Dispersed 6 - USFS

Dispersed sites, No water, No toilets, Reservations not accepted, Open all year, Tent & RV camping: Free, Road not maintained for passenger cars, Elev: 9037ft/2754m, Tel: 435-783-4338, Nearest town: Heber City, Agency: USFS, GPS: 40.449873, -111.205044

31803 • FSR 096 Dispersed 7 - USFS

Dispersed sites, No water, No toilets, Reservations not accepted, Open all year, Tent & RV camping: Free, Road not maintained for passenger cars, Elev: 9048ft/2758m, Tel: 435-783-4338, Nearest town: Heber City, Agency: USFS, GPS: 40.447089, -111.206002

31804 • FSR 096 Dispersed 8 - USFS

Dispersed sites, No water, No toilets, Reservations not accepted, Open all year, Tent & RV camping: Free, Road not maintained for passenger cars, Elev: 9779ft/2981m, Tel: 435-783-4338, Nearest town: Heber City, Agency: USFS, GPS: 40.460127, -111.150816

31805 • FSR 097 (Heart Lake) Dispersed 1 - USFS

Dispersed sites, No water, No toilets, Reservations not accepted, Open all year, Tents only: Free, Road not maintained for passenger cars, Elev: 9198ft/2804m, Tel: 435-783-4338, Nearest town: Heber City, Agency: USFS, GPS: 40.463714, -111.056724

31806 • FSR 098 Dispersed 1 - USFS

Dispersed sites, No water, No toilets, Reservations not accepted, Open all year, Tent & RV camping: Free, Elev: 6671ft/2033m, Tel: 435-743-5721, Nearest town: Holden, Agency: USFS, GPS: 39.061711, -112.185172

31807 • FSR 098 Dispersed 2 - USFS

Dispersed sites, No water, No toilets, Reservations not accepted, Open all year, Tent & RV camping: Free, Elev: 6784ft/2068m, Tel: 435-743-5721, Nearest town: Holden, Agency: USFS, GPS: 39.061942, -112.181781

31808 • FSR 098A Dispersed 1 - USFS

Dispersed sites, No water, No toilets, Reservations not accepted, Open all year, Tent & RV camping: Free, Road not maintained for passenger cars, Elev: 7936ft/2419m, Tel: 435-676-9316, Nearest town: Hatch, Agency: USFS, GPS: 37.547956, -112.275987

31809 • FSR 099 Dispersed 1 - USFS

Dispersed sites, No water, No toilets, Reservations not accepted, Open all year, Tent & RV camping: Free, Road not maintained for passenger cars, Elev: 6027ft/1837m, Tel: 435-743-5721, Nearest town: Holden, Agency: USFS, GPS: 39.036678, -112.221609

31810 • FSR 099 Dispersed 2 - USFS

Dispersed sites, No water, No toilets, Reservations not accepted, Open all year, Tent & RV camping: Free, Road not maintained for passenger cars, Elev: 6065ft/1849m, Tel: 435-743-5721, Nearest town: Holden, Agency: USFS, GPS: 39.037015, -112.219758

31811 • FSR 100 Dispersed 1 - USFS

Dispersed sites, No water, No toilets, Reservations not accepted, Open all year, Tent & RV camping: Free, Several sites in this area, Road not maintained for passenger cars, Elev: 6239ft/1902m, Tel: 435-743-5721, Nearest town: Fillmore, Agency: USFS, GPS: 38.930728, -112.264718

31812 • FSR 100 Dispersed 2 - USFS

Dispersed sites, No water, No toilets, Reservations not accepted, Open all year, Tent & RV camping: Free, Road not maintained for

passenger cars, Elev: 6639ft/2024m, Tel: 435-743-5721, Nearest town: Fillmore, Agency: USFS, GPS: 38.934384, -112.250827

31813 • FSR 100 Dispersed 3 - USFS
Dispersed sites, No water, No toilets, Reservations not accepted, Open all year, Tent & RV camping: Free, Road not maintained for passenger cars, Elev: 6535ft/1992m, Tel: 435-743-5721, Nearest town: Fillmore, Agency: USFS, GPS: 38.935293, -112.238867

31814 • FSR 100 Dispersed 4 - USFS
Dispersed sites, No water, No toilets, Reservations not accepted, Open all year, Tent & RV camping: Free, Elev: 7199ft/2194m, Tel: 435-743-5721, Nearest town: Fillmore, Agency: USFS, GPS: 38.918977, -112.206234

31815 • FSR 100 Dispersed 5 - USFS
Dispersed sites, No water, No toilets, Reservations not accepted, Open all year, Tent & RV camping: Free, Elev: 9349ft/2850m, Tel: 435-743-5721, Nearest town: Fillmore, Agency: USFS, GPS: 38.936394, -112.169713

31816 • FSR 100 Dispersed 6 - USFS
Dispersed sites, No water, No toilets, Reservations not accepted, Open all year, Tent & RV camping: Free, Elev: 9333ft/2845m, Tel: 435-743-5721, Nearest town: Fillmore, Agency: USFS, GPS: 38.929774, -112.165275

31817 • FSR 1001 (Bess Lake) Dispersed 1 - USFS
Dispersed sites, No water, No toilets, Reservations not accepted, Open all year, Tent & RV camping: Free, Road not maintained for passenger cars, Elev: 11080ft/3377m, Tel: 435-836-2800, Nearest town: Grover, Agency: USFS, GPS: 38.134685, -111.456064

31818 • FSR 1003 Dispersed 1 - USFS
Dispersed sites, No water, No toilets, Reservations not accepted, Open all year, Tent & RV camping: Free, Road not maintained for passenger cars, Elev: 6164ft/1879m, Tel: 435-789-1181, Nearest town: Enterprise, Agency: USFS, GPS: 37.652749, -114.027546

31819 • FSR 1005 Dispersed 1 - USFS
Dispersed sites, No water, No toilets, Reservations not accepted, Open Apr-Dec, Tent & RV camping: Free, Road not maintained for passenger cars, Elev: 7262ft/2213m, Tel: 435-438-2426, Nearest town: Beaver, Agency: USFS, GPS: 38.150727, -112.521598

31820 • FSR 1017 Dispersed 1 - USFS
Dispersed sites, No water, No toilets, Reservations not accepted, Open all year, Tent & RV camping: Free, Road not maintained for passenger cars, Elev: 6540ft/1993m, Tel: 435-789-1181, Nearest town: Newcastle, Agency: USFS, GPS: 37.522136, -113.562325

31821 • FSR 102 Dispersed 1 - USFS
Dispersed sites, No water, No toilets, Reservations not accepted, Open all year, Tent & RV camping: Free, Road not maintained for passenger cars, Elev: 6701ft/2042m, Tel: 435-743-5721, Nearest town: Salina, Agency: USFS, GPS: 38.987368, -112.066759

31822 • FSR 102 Dispersed 2 - USFS
Dispersed sites, No water, No toilets, Reservations not accepted, Open all year, Tent & RV camping: Free, Road not maintained for passenger cars, Elev: 8776ft/2675m, Tel: 435-743-5721, Nearest town: Salina, Agency: USFS, GPS: 38.960845, -112.091611

31823 • FSR 102 Dispersed 3 - USFS
Dispersed sites, No water, No toilets, Reservations not accepted, Open all year, Tent & RV camping: Free, Several separated sites, Road not maintained for passenger cars, Elev: 8831ft/2692m, Tel: 435-743-5721, Nearest town: Salina, Agency: USFS, GPS: 38.961602, -112.096123

31824 • FSR 103 Dispersed 2 - USFS
Dispersed sites, No water, No toilets, Reservations not accepted, Open all year, Tent & RV camping: Free, Road not maintained for passenger cars, Elev: 6512ft/1985m, Tel: 435-743-5721, Nearest town: Fillmore, Agency: USFS, GPS: 38.919541, -112.277298

31825 • FSR 103 Dispersed 3 - USFS
Dispersed sites, No water, No toilets, Reservations not accepted, Open all year, Tent & RV camping: Free, Road not maintained for passenger cars, Elev: 6823ft/2080m, Tel: 435-743-5721, Nearest town: Fillmore, Agency: USFS, GPS: 38.913274, -112.270933

31826 • FSR 103 Dispersed 4 - USFS
Dispersed sites, No water, No toilets, Reservations not accepted, Open all year, Tent & RV camping: Free, Road not maintained for passenger cars, Elev: 8375ft/2553m, Tel: 435-743-5721, Nearest town: Fillmore, Agency: USFS, GPS: 38.896703, -112.260648

31827 • FSR 103 Dispersed 5 - USFS
Dispersed sites, No water, No toilets, Reservations not accepted, Open all year, Tent & RV camping: Free, Road not maintained for passenger cars, Elev: 8825ft/2690m, Tel: 435-743-5721, Nearest town: Fillmore, Agency: USFS, GPS: 38.880972, -112.247025

31828 • FSR 103 Dispersed 6 - USFS
Dispersed sites, No water, No toilets, Reservations not accepted, Open all year, Tent & RV camping: Free, Road not maintained for passenger cars, Elev: 9090ft/2771m, Tel: 435-783-4338, Nearest town: Woodland, Agency: USFS, GPS: 40.529813, -111.034014

31829 • FSR 103 Dispersed 7 - USFS
Dispersed sites, No water, No toilets, Reservations not accepted, Open all year, Tent & RV camping: Free, Road not maintained for passenger cars, Elev: 9096ft/2772m, Tel: 435-783-4338, Nearest town: Woodland, Agency: USFS, GPS: 40.531381, -111.035135

31830 • FSR 103 Dispersed 8 - USFS
Dispersed sites, No water, No toilets, Reservations not accepted, Open all year, Tent & RV camping: Free, Road not maintained for passenger cars, Elev: 9243ft/2817m, Tel: 435-783-4338, Nearest town: Woodland, Agency: USFS, GPS: 40.531463, -111.040364

31831 • FSR 103 Dispersed1 - USFS
Dispersed sites, No water, No toilets, Reservations not accepted, Open all year, Tent & RV camping: Free, Road not maintained for

passenger cars, Elev: 6044ft/1842m, Tel: 435-743-5721, Nearest town: Fillmore, Agency: USFS, GPS: 38.919968, -112.287824

31832 • FSR 1032 Dispersed 1 - USFS
Dispersed sites, No water, No toilets, Reservations not accepted, Open all year, Tent & RV camping: Free, Road not maintained for passenger cars, Elev: 5729ft/1746m, Tel: 435-789-1181, Nearest town: Central, Agency: USFS, GPS: 37.406075, -113.585351

31833 • FSR 1032 Dispersed 2 - USFS
Dispersed sites, No water, No toilets, Reservations not accepted, Open all year, Tent & RV camping: Free, Road not maintained for passenger cars, Elev: 6579ft/2005m, Tel: 435-789-1181, Nearest town: Pine Valley, Agency: USFS, GPS: 37.404594, -113.533003

31834 • FSR 104 Dispersed 1 - USFS
Dispersed sites, No water, No toilets, Reservations not accepted, Open all year, Tent & RV camping: Free, Road not maintained for passenger cars, Elev: 6236ft/1901m, Tel: 435-743-5721, Nearest town: Fillmore, Agency: USFS, GPS: 38.882537, -112.337364

31835 • FSR 104 Dispersed 2 - USFS
Dispersed sites, No water, No toilets, Reservations not accepted, Open all year, Tent & RV camping: Free, Elev: 8160ft/2487m, Tel: 435-789-1181, Nearest town: Vernal, Agency: USFS, GPS: 40.594006, -109.834419

31836 • FSR 104 Dispersed 3 - USFS
Dispersed sites, No water, No toilets, Reservations not accepted, Open all year, Tent & RV camping: Free, Elev: 9484ft/2891m, Tel: 435-789-1181, Nearest town: Vernal, Agency: USFS, GPS: 40.608413, -109.883598

31837 • FSR 104 Dispersed 4 - USFS
Dispersed sites, No water, No toilets, Reservations not accepted, Open all year, Tent & RV camping: Free, Elev: 9972ft/3039m, Tel: 435-789-1181, Nearest town: Vernal, Agency: USFS, GPS: 40.660718, -109.916807

31838 • FSR 104 Dispersed 5 - USFS
Dispersed sites, No water, No toilets, Reservations not accepted, Open all year, Tent & RV camping: Free, Elev: 10260ft/3127m, Tel: 435-789-1181, Nearest town: Vernal, Agency: USFS, GPS: 40.674419, -109.939842

31839 • FSR 104 Dispersed 6 - USFS
Dispersed sites, No water, No toilets, Reservations not accepted, Open all year, Tent & RV camping: Free, Elev: 10296ft/3138m, Tel: 435-789-1181, Nearest town: Vernal, Agency: USFS, GPS: 40.676412, -109.942529

31840 • FSR 104 Dispersed 7 - USFS
Dispersed sites, No water, No toilets, Reservations not accepted, Open all year, Tent & RV camping: Free, Elev: 10492ft/3198m, Tel: 435-789-1181, Nearest town: Vernal, Agency: USFS, GPS: 40.679897, -109.956362

31841 • FSR 1042 Dispersed 1 - USFS
Dispersed sites, No water, No toilets, Reservations not accepted, Open all year, Tent & RV camping: Free, Road not maintained for passenger cars, Elev: 7192ft/2192m, Tel: 435-789-1181, Nearest town: Panguitch, Agency: USFS, GPS: 37.867236, -112.525867

31842 • FSR 1048 Dispersed 1 - USFS
Dispersed sites, No water, No toilets, Reservations not accepted, Open all year, Tent & RV camping: Free, Road not maintained for passenger cars, Elev: 7794ft/2376m, Tel: 435-789-1181, Nearest town: Panguitch, Agency: USFS, GPS: 37.770558, -112.533979

31843 • FSR 1049 Dispersed 1 - USFS
Dispersed sites, No water, No toilets, Reservations not accepted, Open all year, Tent & RV camping: Free, Road not maintained for passenger cars, Elev: 8022ft/2445m, Tel: 435-789-1181, Nearest town: Panguitch, Agency: USFS, GPS: 37.763914, -112.535497

31844 • FSR 105 Dispersed 1 - USFS
Dispersed sites, No water, No toilets, Reservations not accepted, Open all year, Tent & RV camping: Free, Road not maintained for passenger cars, Elev: 7251ft/2210m, Tel: 435-755-3620, Nearest town: Logan, Agency: USFS, GPS: 41.795593, -111.472882

31845 • FSR 105 Dispersed 2 - USFS
Dispersed sites, No water, No toilets, Reservations not accepted, Open all year, Tent & RV camping: Free, Road not maintained for passenger cars, Elev: 7105ft/2166m, Tel: 435-755-3620, Nearest town: Logan, Agency: USFS, GPS: 41.785415, -111.473704

31846 • FSR 105 Dispersed 3 - USFS
Dispersed sites, No water, No toilets, Reservations not accepted, Open all year, Tent & RV camping: Free, Road not maintained for passenger cars, Elev: 6879ft/2097m, Tel: 435-755-3620, Nearest town: Logan, Agency: USFS, GPS: 41.761926, -111.474267

31847 • FSR 105 Dispersed 4 - USFS
Dispersed sites, No water, No toilets, Reservations not accepted, Open all year, Tent & RV camping: Free, Road not maintained for passenger cars, Elev: 6541ft/1994m, Tel: 435-755-3620, Nearest town: Hyrum, Agency: USFS, GPS: 41.716041, -111.505124

31848 • FSR 105 Dispersed 5 - USFS
Dispersed sites, No water, No toilets, Reservations not accepted, Open all year, Tent & RV camping: Free, Road not maintained for passenger cars, Elev: 6375ft/1943m, Tel: 435-755-3620, Nearest town: Hyrum, Agency: USFS, GPS: 41.689242, -111.524428

31849 • FSR 105 Dispersed 6 - USFS
Dispersed sites, No water, No toilets, Reservations not accepted, Open all year, Tent & RV camping: Free, Elev: 7061ft/2152m, Tel: 435-743-5721, Nearest town: Elsinore, Agency: USFS, GPS: 38.713259, -112.189932

31850 • FSR 105 Dispersed 7 - USFS
Dispersed sites, No water, No toilets, Reservations not accepted, Open all year, Tent & RV camping: Free, Elev: 7004ft/2135m, Tel: 435-743-5721, Nearest town: Elsinore, Agency: USFS, GPS: 38.711458, -112.185822

31851 • FSR 105 Dispersed 8 - USFS

Dispersed sites, No water, No toilets, Reservations not accepted, Open all year, Tent & RV camping: Free, Road not maintained for passenger cars, Elev: 8943ft/2726m, Tel: 435-676-9316, Nearest town: Alton, Agency: USFS, GPS: 37.460097, -112.383733

31852 • FSR 1051 Dispersed 1 - USFS

Dispersed sites, No water, No toilets, Reservations not accepted, Open all year, Tent & RV camping: Free, Road not maintained for passenger cars, Elev: 9917ft/3023m, Tel: 435-438-2430, Nearest town: Marysvale, Agency: USFS, GPS: 38.425956, -112.390366

31853 • FSR 106 (Whitney Reservoir) Dispersed 3 - USFS

Dispersed sites, No water, No toilets, Reservations not accepted, Open May-Dec, Tent & RV camping: Free, Road not maintained for passenger cars, Elev: 9295ft/2833m, Tel: 307-789-3194, Nearest town: Oakley, Agency: USFS, GPS: 40.828503, -110.933177

31854 • FSR 106 Dispersed 1 - USFS

Dispersed sites, No water, No toilets, Reservations not accepted, Open all year, Tent & RV camping: Free, Road not maintained for passenger cars, Elev: 7587ft/2313m, Tel: 435-755-3620, Nearest town: Garden City, Agency: USFS, GPS: 41.925923, -111.463793

31855 • FSR 106 Dispersed 10 - USFS

Dispersed sites, No water, No toilets, Reservations not accepted, Open all year, Tent & RV camping: Free, Elev: 5495ft/1675m, Tel: 435-743-5721, Nearest town: Kanosh, Agency: USFS, GPS: 38.758294, -112.376746

31856 • FSR 106 Dispersed 2 - USFS

Dispersed sites, No water, No toilets, Reservations not accepted, Open all year, Tent & RV camping: Free, Road not maintained for passenger cars, Elev: 7477ft/2279m, Tel: 435-755-3620, Nearest town: Garden City, Agency: USFS, GPS: 41.929478, -111.454606

31857 • FSR 106 Dispersed 4 - USFS

Dispersed sites, No water, No toilets, Reservations not accepted, Open all year, Tent & RV camping: Free, Road not maintained for passenger cars, Elev: 8282ft/2524m, Tel: 435-783-4338, Nearest town: Heber City, Agency: USFS, GPS: 40.384278, -111.075335

31858 • FSR 106 Dispersed 5 - USFS

Dispersed sites, No water, No toilets, Reservations not accepted, Open all year, Tent & RV camping: Free, Road not maintained for passenger cars, Elev: 6835ft/2083m, Tel: 435-438-2430, Nearest town: Beaver, Agency: USFS, GPS: 38.593942, -112.467041

31859 • FSR 106 Dispersed 6 - USFS

Dispersed sites, No water, No toilets, Reservations not accepted, Open all year, Tent & RV camping: Free, Road not maintained for passenger cars, Elev: 6882ft/2098m, Tel: 435-438-2430, Nearest town: Beaver, Agency: USFS, GPS: 38.597062, -112.465985

31860 • FSR 106 Dispersed 7 - USFS

Dispersed sites, No water, No toilets, Reservations not accepted, Open all year, Tent & RV camping: Free, Road not maintained for passenger cars, Elev: 7114ft/2168m, Tel: 435-438-2430, Nearest town: Beaver, Agency: USFS, GPS: 38.608379, -112.455845

31861 • FSR 106 Dispersed 8 - USFS

Dispersed sites, No water, No toilets, Reservations not accepted, Open all year, Tent & RV camping: Free, Elev: 6629ft/2021m, Tel: 435-743-5721, Nearest town: Kanosh, Agency: USFS, GPS: 38.705333, -112.408027

31862 • FSR 106 Dispersed 9 - USFS

Dispersed sites, No water, No toilets, Reservations not accepted, Open all year, Tent & RV camping: Free, Elev: 6153ft/1875m, Tel: 435-743-5721, Nearest town: Kanosh, Agency: USFS, GPS: 38.721265, -112.360874

31863 • FSR 1064A Dispersed 1 - USFS

Dispersed sites, No water, No toilets, Reservations not accepted, Open all year, Tent & RV camping: Free, Road not maintained for passenger cars, Elev: 9456ft/2882m, Tel: 435-438-2430, Nearest town: Beaver, Agency: USFS, GPS: 38.300451, -112.478597

31864 • FSR 106C Dispersed 1 - USFS

Dispersed sites, No water, No toilets, Reservations not accepted, Open all year, Tent & RV camping: Free, Road not maintained for passenger cars, Elev: 7145ft/2178m, Tel: 435-743-5721, Nearest town: Kanosh, Agency: USFS, GPS: 38.681617, -112.423113

31865 • FSR 107 Dispersed 1 - USFS

Dispersed sites, No water, No toilets, Reservations not accepted, Open all year, Tent & RV camping: Free, Elev: 7723ft/2354m, Tel: 435-743-5721, Nearest town: Joseph, Agency: USFS, GPS: 38.698264, -112.298712

31866 • FSR 107 Dispersed 2 - USFS

Dispersed sites, No water, No toilets, Reservations not accepted, Open all year, Tent & RV camping: Free, Road not maintained for passenger cars, Elev: 9030ft/2752m, Tel: 435-783-4338, Nearest town: Oakley, Agency: USFS, GPS: 40.606776, -110.992257

31867 • FSR 107 Dispersed 3 - USFS

Dispersed sites, No water, No toilets, Reservations not accepted, Open all year, Tent & RV camping: Free, Road not maintained for passenger cars, Elev: 9519ft/2901m, Tel: 435-783-4338, Nearest town: Oakley, Agency: USFS, GPS: 40.620263, -110.994298

31868 • FSR 108 Dispersed 1 - USFS

Dispersed sites, No water, No toilets, Reservations not accepted, Open all year, Tent & RV camping: Free, Road not maintained for passenger cars, Elev: 8403ft/2561m, Tel: 435-676-9314, Nearest town: Hatch, Agency: USFS, GPS: 37.611531, -112.289684

31869 • FSR 108 Dispersed 2 - USFS

Dispersed sites, No water, No toilets, Reservations not accepted, Open all year, Tent & RV camping: Free, Elev: 9303ft/2836m, Tel: 435-783-4338, Nearest town: Oakley, Agency: USFS, GPS: 40.632408, -110.935273

31870 • FSR 108 Dispersed 3 - USFS

Dispersed sites, No water, No toilets, Reservations not accepted, Open May-Dec, Tent & RV camping: Free, Road not maintained for passenger cars, Elev: 9810ft/2990m, Tel: 307-789-3194, Nearest town: Oakley, Agency: USFS, GPS: 40.828089, -110.911452

31871 • FSR 1085 Dispersed 1 - USFS

Dispersed sites, No water, No toilets, Reservations not accepted, Open all year, Tent & RV camping: Free, Road not maintained for passenger cars, Elev: 7961ft/2427m, Tel: 435-676-9309, Nearest town: Panguitch, Agency: USFS, GPS: 37.783331, -112.171703

31872 • FSR 109 Dispersed 1 - USFS

Dispersed sites, No water, No toilets, Reservations not accepted, Open all year, Tent & RV camping: Free, Road not maintained for passenger cars, Elev: 5415ft/1650m, Tel: 435-743-5721, Nearest town: Kanosh, Agency: USFS, GPS: 38.757518, -112.466373

31873 • FSR 109 Dispersed 10 - USFS

Dispersed sites, No water, No toilets, Reservations not accepted, Open May-Dec, Tent & RV camping: Free, Road not maintained for passenger cars, Elev: 9404ft/2866m, Tel: 307-789-3194, Nearest town: Oakley, Agency: USFS, GPS: 40.811162, -110.889874

31874 • FSR 109 Dispersed 11 - USFS

Dispersed sites, No water, No toilets, Reservations not accepted, Open May-Dec, Tent & RV camping: Free, Road not maintained for passenger cars, Elev: 9476ft/2888m, Tel: 307-789-3194, Nearest town: Oakley, Agency: USFS, GPS: 40.808736, -110.894432

31875 • FSR 109 Dispersed 12 - USFS

Dispersed sites, No water, No toilets, Reservations not accepted, Open all year, Tent & RV camping: Free, Road not maintained for passenger cars, Elev: 8146ft/2483m, Tel: 435-676-9316, Nearest town: Hatch, Agency: USFS, GPS: 37.594302, -112.284648

31876 • FSR 109 Dispersed 13 - USFS

Dispersed sites, No water, No toilets, Reservations not accepted, Open all year, Tent & RV camping: Free, Road not maintained for passenger cars, Elev: 8245ft/2513m, Tel: 435-676-9316, Nearest town: Hatch, Agency: USFS, GPS: 37.594622, -112.298251

31877 • FSR 109 Dispersed 14 - USFS

Dispersed sites, No water, No toilets, Reservations not accepted, Open all year, Tent & RV camping: Free, Road not maintained for passenger cars, Elev: 8360ft/2548m, Tel: 435-676-9316, Nearest town: Hatch, Agency: USFS, GPS: 37.593379, -112.307586

31878 • FSR 109 Dispersed 2 - USFS

Dispersed sites, No water, No toilets, Reservations not accepted, Open all year, Tent & RV camping: Free, Elev: 7709ft/2350m, Tel: 435-783-4338, Nearest town: Spanish Fork, Agency: USFS, GPS: 40.099282, -111.149576

31879 • FSR 109 Dispersed 3 - USFS

Dispersed sites, No water, No toilets, Reservations not accepted, Open all year, Tent & RV camping: Free, Several sites in this area, Elev: 7945ft/2422m, Tel: 435-783-4338, Nearest town: Spanish Fork, Agency: USFS, GPS: 40.093291, -111.137896

31880 • FSR 109 Dispersed 4 - USFS

Dispersed sites, No water, No toilets, Reservations not accepted, Open all year, Tent & RV camping: Free, Elev: 7996ft/2437m, Tel: 435-783-4338, Nearest town: Spanish Fork, Agency: USFS, GPS: 40.092951, -111.135984

31881 • FSR 109 Dispersed 5 - USFS

Dispersed sites, No water, No toilets, Reservations not accepted, Open all year, Tent & RV camping: Free, Elev: 8023ft/2445m, Tel: 435-783-4338, Nearest town: Spanish Fork, Agency: USFS, GPS: 40.095091, -111.134877

31882 • FSR 109 Dispersed 6 - USFS

Dispersed sites, No water, No toilets, Reservations not accepted, Open all year, Tent & RV camping: Free, Elev: 8784ft/2677m, Tel: 435-783-4338, Nearest town: Spanish Fork, Agency: USFS, GPS: 40.089082, -111.121362

31883 • FSR 109 Dispersed 7 - USFS

Dispersed sites, No water, No toilets, Reservations not accepted, Open May-Dec, Tent & RV camping: Free, Road not maintained for passenger cars, Elev: 9242ft/2817m, Tel: 307-789-3194, Nearest town: Oakley, Agency: USFS, GPS: 40.850088, -110.869932

31884 • FSR 109 Dispersed 8 - USFS

Dispersed sites, No water, No toilets, Reservations not accepted, Open May-Dec, Tent & RV camping: Free, Road not maintained for passenger cars, Elev: 9256ft/2821m, Tel: 307-789-3194, Nearest town: Oakley, Agency: USFS, GPS: 40.840362, -110.872816

31885 • FSR 109 Dispersed 9 - USFS

Dispersed sites, No water, No toilets, Reservations not accepted, Open May-Dec, Tent & RV camping: Free, Road not maintained for passenger cars, Elev: 9327ft/2843m, Tel: 307-789-3194, Nearest town: Oakley, Agency: USFS, GPS: 40.832097, -110.875181

31886 • FSR 1091 Dispersed 1 - USFS

Dispersed sites, No water, No toilets, Reservations not accepted, Open all year, Tent & RV camping: Free, Road not maintained for passenger cars, Elev: 8729ft/2661m, Tel: 435-676-9305, Nearest town: Panguitch, Agency: USFS, GPS: 37.862434, -112.203646

31887 • FSR 110 Dispersed 1 - USFS

Dispersed sites, No water, No toilets, Reservations not accepted, Open all year, Tent & RV camping: Free, Road not maintained for passenger cars, Elev: 6971ft/2125m, Tel: 435-743-5721, Nearest town: Joseph, Agency: USFS, GPS: 38.640028, -112.271424

31888 • FSR 110 Dispersed 3 - USFS

Dispersed sites, No water, No toilets, Reservations not accepted, Open all year, Tent & RV camping: Free, Road not maintained for passenger cars, Elev: 7137ft/2175m, Tel: 435-438-2430, Nearest town: Joseph, Agency: USFS, GPS: 38.644169, -112.274263

31889 • FSR 110 Dispersed 3 - USFS

Dispersed sites, No water, No toilets, Reservations not accepted, Open all year, Tent & RV camping: Free, Road not maintained for passenger cars, Elev: 7171ft/2186m, Tel: 435-438-2430, Nearest town: Joseph, Agency: USFS, GPS: 38.646563, -112.274417

31890 • FSR 1100 Dispersed 1 - USFS

Dispersed sites, No water, No toilets, Reservations not accepted, Open all year, Tent & RV camping: Free, Road not maintained for passenger cars, Elev: 6772ft/2064m, Tel: 435-438-2430, Nearest town: Marysvale, Agency: USFS, GPS: 38.464495, -112.306322

31891 • FSR 1106 Dispersed 1 - USFS

Dispersed sites, No water, No toilets, Reservations not accepted, Open all year, Tent & RV camping: Free, Road not maintained for passenger cars, Elev: 7042ft/2146m, Tel: 435-438-2430, Nearest town: Marysvale, Agency: USFS, GPS: 38.417499, -112.297994

31892 • FSR 1106 Dispersed 2 - USFS

Dispersed sites, No water, No toilets, Reservations not accepted, Open all year, Tent & RV camping: Free, At end of road, Road not maintained for passenger cars, Elev: 7155ft/2181m, Tel: 435-438-2430, Nearest town: Marysvale, Agency: USFS, GPS: 38.414975, -112.296448

31893 • FSR 110A Dispersed 1 - USFS

Dispersed sites, No water, No toilets, Reservations not accepted, Open all year, Tent & RV camping: Free, Road not maintained for passenger cars, Elev: 8510ft/2594m, Tel: 435-743-5721, Nearest town: Sevier, Agency: USFS, GPS: 38.656096, -112.343834

31894 • FSR 110B Dispersed 1 - USFS

Dispersed sites, No water, No toilets, Reservations not accepted, Open all year, Tent & RV camping: Free, Road not maintained for passenger cars, Elev: 8496ft/2590m, Tel: 435-743-5721, Nearest town: Sevier, Agency: USFS, GPS: 38.654807, -112.345277

31895 • FSR 111 (Shoestring Lake) Dispersed 1 - USFS

Dispersed sites, No water, No toilets, Reservations not accepted, Open all year, Tent & RV camping: Free, Road not maintained for passenger cars, Elev: 9899ft/3017m, Tel: 435-783-4338, Nearest town: Oakley, Agency: USFS, GPS: 40.670018, -110.958227

31896 • FSR 111 Dispersed 1 - USFS

Dispersed sites, No water, No toilets, Reservations not accepted, Open Apr-Nov, Tent & RV camping: Free, Road not maintained for passenger cars, Elev: 7744ft/2360m, Tel: 801-785-3563, Nearest town: Midway, Agency: USFS, GPS: 40.527336, -111.614784

31897 • FSR 111 Dispersed 2 - USFS

Dispersed sites, No water, No toilets, Reservations not accepted, Open all year, Tent & RV camping: Free, Road not maintained for passenger cars, Elev: 7994ft/2437m, Tel: 435-743-5721, Nearest town: Elsinore, Agency: USFS, GPS: 38.720431, -112.237806

31898 • FSR 111 Dispersed 3 - USFS

Dispersed sites, No water, No toilets, Reservations not accepted, Open all year, Tent & RV camping: Free, Road not maintained for passenger cars, Elev: 8389ft/2557m, Tel: 435-743-5721, Nearest town: Joseph, Agency: USFS, GPS: 38.694569, -112.277179

31899 • FSR 1119 Dispersed 1 - USFS

Dispersed sites, No water, No toilets, Reservations not accepted, Open all year, Tent & RV camping: Free, Road not maintained for passenger cars, Elev: 8197ft/2498m, Tel: 435-676-9316, Nearest town: Hatch, Agency: USFS, GPS: 37.594678, -112.290146

31900 • FSR 1119 Dispersed 2 - USFS

Dispersed sites, No water, No toilets, Reservations not accepted, Open all year, Tent & RV camping: Free, Road not maintained for passenger cars, Elev: 8201ft/2500m, Tel: 435-676-9316, Nearest town: Hatch, Agency: USFS, GPS: 37.592909, -112.291372

31901 • FSR 112 Dispersed 1 - USFS

Dispersed sites, No water, No toilets, Reservations not accepted, Open all year, Tent & RV camping: Free, Road not maintained for passenger cars, Elev: 7129ft/2173m, Tel: 435-743-5721, Nearest town: Kanosh, Agency: USFS, GPS: 38.703165, -112.363634

31902 • FSR 112 Dispersed 2 - USFS

Dispersed sites, No water, No toilets, Reservations not accepted, Open all year, Tent & RV camping: Free, Road not maintained for passenger cars, Elev: 7775ft/2370m, Tel: 435-743-5721, Nearest town: Joseph, Agency: USFS, GPS: 38.694058, -112.351324

31903 • FSR 112 Dispersed 3 - USFS

Dispersed sites, No water, No toilets, Reservations not accepted, Open May-Dec, Tent & RV camping: Free, Road not maintained for passenger cars, Elev: 8817ft/2687m, Tel: 307-789-3194, Nearest town: Oakley, Agency: USFS, GPS: 40.887996, -110.816094

31904 • FSR 113 Dispersed 1 - USFS

Dispersed sites, No water, No toilets, Reservations not accepted, Open Jun-Nov, Tent & RV camping: Free, Elev: 6113ft/1863m, Tel: 801-625-5112, Nearest town: Woodruff, Agency: USFS, GPS: 41.453667, -111.856175

31905 • FSR 113 Dispersed 10 - USFS

Dispersed sites, No water, No toilets, Reservations not accepted, Open all year, Tent & RV camping: Free, Elev: 6694ft/2040m, Tel: 435-438-2430, Nearest town: Marysvale, Agency: USFS, GPS: 38.536781, -112.389385

31906 • FSR 113 Dispersed 11 - USFS

Dispersed sites, No water, No toilets, Reservations not accepted, Open all year, Tent & RV camping: Free, Right beside interstate, Elev: 6070ft/1850m, Tel: 435-438-2430, Nearest town: Marysvale, Agency: USFS, GPS: 38.562718, -112.361751

31907 • FSR 113 Dispersed 2 - USFS

Dispersed sites, No water, No toilets, Reservations not accepted, Open Jun-Nov, Tent & RV camping: Free, Elev: 6035ft/1839m, Tel: 801-625-5112, Nearest town: Woodruff, Agency: USFS, GPS: 41.453304, -111.852007

31908 • FSR 113 Dispersed 3 - USFS

Dispersed sites, No water, No toilets, Reservations not accepted, Open all year, Tent & RV camping: Free, Elev: 6572ft/2003m, Tel: 435-438-2430, Nearest town: Marysvale, Agency: USFS, GPS: 38.544371, -112.385925

31909 • FSR 113 Dispersed 4 - USFS

Dispersed sites, No water, No toilets, Reservations not accepted, Open all year, Tent & RV camping: Free, Elev: 6886ft/2099m, Tel: 435-438-2430, Nearest town: Marysvale, Agency: USFS, GPS: 38.525568, -112.393156

31910 • FSR 113 Dispersed 5 - USFS
Dispersed sites, No water, No toilets, Reservations not accepted, Open all year, Tent & RV camping: Free, Elev: 7966ft/2428m, Tel: 435-438-2430, Nearest town: Marysvale, Agency: USFS, GPS: 38.503326, -112.394934

31911 • FSR 113 Dispersed 6 - USFS
Dispersed sites, No water, No toilets, Reservations not accepted, Open all year, Tent & RV camping: Free, Elev: 8921ft/2719m, Tel: 435-438-2430, Nearest town: Marysvale, Agency: USFS, GPS: 38.470917, -112.345456

31912 • FSR 113 Dispersed 7 - USFS
Dispersed sites, No water, No toilets, Reservations not accepted, Open all year, Tent & RV camping: Free, Elev: 6665ft/2031m, Tel: 435-438-2430, Nearest town: Marysvale, Agency: USFS, GPS: 38.462255, -112.298754

31913 • FSR 113 Dispersed 8 - USFS
Dispersed sites, No water, No toilets, Reservations not accepted, Open all year, Tent & RV camping: Free, Road not maintained for passenger cars, Elev: 8071ft/2460m, Tel: 435-676-9310, Nearest town: Panguitch, Agency: USFS, GPS: 37.703335, -112.278554

31914 • FSR 113 Dispersed 9 - USFS
Dispersed sites, No water, No toilets, Reservations not accepted, Open all year, Tent & RV camping: Free, Elev: 6639ft/2024m, Tel: 435-438-2430, Nearest town: Marysvale, Agency: USFS, GPS: 38.539976, -112.387284

31915 • FSR 1134 Dispersed 1 - USFS
Dispersed sites, No water, No toilets, Reservations not accepted, Open all year, Tent & RV camping: Free, Road not maintained for passenger cars, Elev: 8577ft/2614m, Tel: 435-676-9316, Nearest town: Bryce, Agency: USFS, GPS: 37.586337, -112.237348

31916 • FSR 113C Dispersed 1 - USFS
Dispersed sites, No water, No toilets, Reservations not accepted, Open all year, Tent & RV camping: Free, Elev: 8811ft/2686m, Tel: 435-438-2430, Nearest town: Marysvale, Agency: USFS, GPS: 38.471709, -112.364203

31917 • FSR 114 Dispersed 1 - USFS
Dispersed sites, No water, No toilets, Reservations not accepted, Open all year, Tent & RV camping: Free, Elev: 7711ft/2350m, Tel: 801-785-3563, Nearest town: Charleston, Agency: USFS, GPS: 40.440979, -111.611207

31918 • FSR 1144A Dispersed 1 - USFS
Dispersed sites, No water, No toilets, Reservations not accepted, Open all year, Tent & RV camping: Free, Elev: 8483ft/2586m, Tel: 435-896-9233, Nearest town: Glenwood, Agency: USFS, GPS: 38.671284, -111.945413

31919 • FSR 114A Dispersed 1 - USFS
Dispersed sites, No water, No toilets, Reservations not accepted, Tent & RV camping: Free, Elev: 6711ft/2046m, Nearest town: Cove Fort, Agency: USFS, GPS: 38.580701, -112.463809

31920 • FSR 115 Dispersed 1 - USFS
Dispersed sites, No water, No toilets, Reservations not accepted, Open all year, Tent & RV camping: Free, Elev: 7522ft/2293m, Tel: 435-738-2482, Nearest town: Whiterocks, Agency: USFS, GPS: 40.611201, -110.128741

31921 • FSR 115 Dispersed 2 - USFS
Dispersed sites, No water, No toilets, Reservations not accepted, Open May-Dec, Tent & RV camping: Free, Road not maintained for passenger cars, Elev: 9250ft/2819m, Tel: 307-789-3194, Nearest town: Oakley, Agency: USFS, GPS: 40.858333, -110.906018

31922 • FSR 115 Dispersed 3 - USFS
Dispersed sites, No water, No toilets, Reservations not accepted, Open Jun-Oct, Tent & RV camping: Free, Road not maintained for passenger cars, Elev: 7551ft/2302m, Tel: 435-783-4338, Nearest town: Springville, Agency: USFS, GPS: 40.182552, -111.357003

31923 • FSR 115 Dispersed 4 - USFS
Dispersed sites, No water, No toilets, Reservations not accepted, Open Jun-Oct, Tent & RV camping: Free, Road not maintained for passenger cars, Elev: 7592ft/2314m, Tel: 435-783-4338, Nearest town: Springville, Agency: USFS, GPS: 40.180791, -111.355185

31924 • FSR 115 Dispersed 5 - USFS
Dispersed sites, No water, No toilets, Reservations not accepted, Open Jun-Oct, Tent & RV camping: Free, Road not maintained for passenger cars, Elev: 7821ft/2384m, Tel: 435-783-4338, Nearest town: Springville, Agency: USFS, GPS: 40.175703, -111.360988

31925 • FSR 116 Dispersed 1 - USFS
Dispersed sites, No water, No toilets, Reservations not accepted, Open May-Dec, Tent & RV camping: Free, Road not maintained for passenger cars, Elev: 9364ft/2854m, Tel: 307-789-3194, Nearest town: Oakley, Agency: USFS, GPS: 40.854416, -110.897068

31926 • FSR 1165B Dispersed 1 - USFS
Dispersed sites, No water, No toilets, Reservations not accepted, Open all year, Tent & RV camping: Free, Elev: 9315ft/2839m, Tel: 435-896-9233, Nearest town: Koosharem, Agency: USFS, GPS: 38.550714, -111.978066

31927 • FSR 117 Dispersed - Site 1 - USFS
Dispersed sites, No water, No toilets, Tent & RV camping: Free, 3 sites, Elev: 7890ft/2405m, Tel: 435-676-9300, Nearest town: Panguitch, Agency: USFS, GPS: 37.729066, -112.243029

31928 • FSR 117 Dispersed - Site 3 - USFS
Dispersed sites, No water, No toilets, Tent & RV camping: Free, Several sites along road, Elev: 7864ft/2397m, Tel: 435-676-9300, Nearest town: Panguitch, Agency: USFS, GPS: 37.722847, -112.251314

31929 • FSR 117 Dispersed - Site 4 - USFS
Dispersed sites, No water, No toilets, Tent & RV camping: Free, Several sites along road, Elev: 7874ft/2400m, Tel: 435-676-9300, Nearest town: Panguitch, Agency: USFS, GPS: 37.730856, -112.252642

31930 • FSR 117 Dispersed - Site 5 - USFS

Dispersed sites, No water, No toilets, Tent & RV camping: Free, Elev: 7866ft/2398m, Tel: 435-676-9300, Nearest town: Panguitch, Agency: USFS, GPS: 37.731989, -112.240579

31931 • FSR 117 Dispersed - Site 6 - USFS

Dispersed sites, No water, No toilets, Tent & RV camping: Free, Elev: 7882ft/2402m, Tel: 435-676-9300, Nearest town: Panguitch, Agency: USFS, GPS: 37.727272, -112.247218

31932 • FSR 117 Dispersed 10 - USFS

Dispersed sites, No water, No toilets, Reservations not accepted, Open all year, Tent & RV camping: Free, Elev: 10013ft/3052m, Tel: 435-738-2482, Nearest town: Whiterocks, Agency: USFS, GPS: 40.647593, -110.036371

31933 • FSR 117 Dispersed 7 - USFS

Dispersed sites, No water, No toilets, Reservations not accepted, Open all year, Tent & RV camping: Free, Elev: 8480ft/2585m, Tel: 435-738-2482, Nearest town: Whiterocks, Agency: USFS, GPS: 40.613504, -110.100702

31934 • FSR 117 Dispersed 8 - USFS

Dispersed sites, No water, No toilets, Reservations not accepted, Open all year, Tent & RV camping: Free, Elev: 8715ft/2656m, Tel: 435-738-2482, Nearest town: Whiterocks, Agency: USFS, GPS: 40.592126, -109.997393

31935 • FSR 117 Dispersed 9 - USFS

Dispersed sites, No water, No toilets, Reservations not accepted, Open all year, Tent & RV camping: Free, Several sites along road, High-clearance vehicle required, Elev: 10016ft/3053m, Tel: 435-738-2482, Nearest town: Whiterocks, Agency: USFS, GPS: 40.623178, -110.039419

31936 • FSR 117 Dispersed Site 2 - USFS

Dispersed sites, No water, No toilets, Tent & RV camping: Free, Elev: 7824ft/2385m, Nearest town: Bryce, Agency: USFS, GPS: 37.721509, -112.254686

31937 • FSR 1173 Dispersed 1 - USFS

Dispersed sites, No water, No toilets, Tent & RV camping: Free, Elev: 7716ft/2352m, Tel: 435-676-9300, Nearest town: Bryce, Agency: USFS, GPS: 37.662522, -112.163945

31938 • FSR 1173 Dispersed 2 - USFS

Dispersed sites, No water, No toilets, Reservations not accepted, Open all year, Tent & RV camping: Free, Road not maintained for passenger cars, Elev: 7782ft/2372m, Tel: 435-676-9316, Nearest town: Bryce, Agency: USFS, GPS: 37.666739, -112.173489

31939 • FSR 1175 Dispersed 1 - USFS

Dispersed sites, No water, No toilets, Reservations not accepted, Open all year, Tent & RV camping: Free, Elev: 7761ft/2366m, Nearest town: Bryce, Agency: USFS, GPS: 37.658117, -112.167866

31940 • FSR 118 Dispersed 1 - USFS

Dispersed sites, No water, No toilets, Reservations not accepted, Open all year, Tent & RV camping: Free, Elev: 7467ft/2276m, Tel: 435-738-2482, Nearest town: Whiterocks, Agency: USFS, GPS: 40.604697, -110.123997

31941 • FSR 118 Dispersed 2 - USFS

Dispersed sites, No water, No toilets, Reservations not accepted, Open all year, Tent & RV camping: Free, Elev: 7502ft/2287m, Tel: 435-738-2482, Nearest town: Whiterocks, Agency: USFS, GPS: 40.607394, -110.126876

31942 • FSR 1180 Dispersed 1 - USFS

Dispersed sites, No water, No toilets, Reservations not accepted, Open all year, Tents only: Free, Spectacular spot on top of 1000' bluff, Road not maintained for passenger cars, Elev: 9035ft/2754m, Tel: 435-676-9316, Nearest town: Alton, Agency: USFS, GPS: 37.432335, -112.399372

31943 • FSR 119 Dispersed 1 - USFS

Dispersed sites, No water, No toilets, Reservations not accepted, Open all year, Tent & RV camping: Free, Road not maintained for passenger cars, Elev: 7086ft/2160m, Tel: 435-438-2430, Nearest town: Beaver, Agency: USFS, GPS: 38.433735, -112.567634

31944 • FSR 119 Dispersed 2 - USFS

Dispersed sites, No water, No toilets, Reservations not accepted, Open all year, Tent & RV camping: Free, Road not maintained for passenger cars, Elev: 7641ft/2329m, Tel: 435-438-2430, Nearest town: Beaver, Agency: USFS, GPS: 38.419784, -112.507762

31945 • FSR 119 Dispersed 3 - USFS

Dispersed sites, No water, No toilets, Reservations not accepted, Open all year, Tent & RV camping: Free, Road not maintained for passenger cars, Elev: 7768ft/2368m, Tel: 435-438-2430, Nearest town: Beaver, Agency: USFS, GPS: 38.419051, -112.494533

31946 • FSR 119 Dispersed 4 - USFS

Dispersed sites, No water, No toilets, Reservations not accepted, Open all year, Tent & RV camping: Free, Road not maintained for passenger cars, Elev: 7882ft/2402m, Tel: 435-438-2430, Nearest town: Beaver, Agency: USFS, GPS: 38.422968, -112.487839

31947 • FSR 119 Dispersed 5 - USFS

Dispersed sites, No water, No toilets, Reservations not accepted, Open all year, Tent & RV camping: Free, Elev: 7896ft/2407m, Tel: 435-738-2482, Nearest town: Altamont, Agency: USFS, GPS: 40.537483, -110.234644

31948 • FSR 119 Dispersed 6 - USFS

Dispersed sites, No water, No toilets, Reservations not accepted, Open all year, Tent & RV camping: Free, Elev: 8766ft/2672m, Tel: 307-789-3194, Nearest town: Oakley, Agency: USFS, GPS: 40.841886, -110.845825

31949 • FSR 1193 Dispersed 1 - USFS

Dispersed sites, No water, No toilets, Reservations not accepted, Open all year, Tent & RV camping: Free, Road not maintained for

passenger cars, Elev: 8322ft/2537m, Tel: 435-676-9316, Nearest town: Alton, Agency: USFS, GPS: 37.490629, -112.344124

31950 • FSR 120 (Lily Lake) Dispersed 1 - USFS

Dispersed sites, No water, No toilets, Reservations not accepted, Open all year, Tent & RV camping: Free, Numerous sites, Road not maintained for passenger cars, Elev: 8926ft/2721m, Tel: 307-789-3194, Nearest town: Oakley, Agency: USFS, GPS: 40.879275, -110.809917

31951 • FSR 120 Dispersed 2 - USFS

Dispersed sites, No water, No toilets, Reservations not accepted, Open all year, Tent & RV camping: Free, Road not maintained for passenger cars, Elev: 8636ft/2632m, Tel: 307-789-3194, Nearest town: Oakley, Agency: USFS, GPS: 40.892043, -110.821109

31952 • FSR 120 Dispersed 3 - USFS

Dispersed sites, No water, No toilets, Reservations not accepted, Open all year, Tent & RV camping: Free, Road not maintained for passenger cars, Elev: 8771ft/2673m, Tel: 307-789-3194, Nearest town: Oakley, Agency: USFS, GPS: 40.888904, -110.817957

31953 • FSR 121 Dispersed 1 - USFS

Dispersed sites, No water, No toilets, Reservations not accepted, Open all year, Tent & RV camping: Free, Road not maintained for passenger cars, Elev: 6819ft/2078m, Tel: 435-783-4338, Nearest town: Orem, Agency: USFS, GPS: 40.325229, -111.416866

31954 • FSR 121 Dispersed 2 - USFS

Dispersed sites, No water, No toilets, Reservations not accepted, Open all year, Tent & RV camping: Free, Several sites, Road not maintained for passenger cars, Elev: 7037ft/2145m, Tel: 435-783-4338, Nearest town: Orem, Agency: USFS, GPS: 40.312462, -111.412207

31955 • FSR 121 Dispersed 3 - USFS

Dispersed sites, No water, No toilets, Reservations not accepted, Open all year, Tent & RV camping: Free, Elev: 7543ft/2299m, Tel: 435-438-2430, Nearest town: Beaver, Agency: USFS, GPS: 38.169021, -112.354144

31956 • FSR 121 Dispersed 4 - USFS

Dispersed sites, No water, No toilets, Tent & RV camping: Free, Elev: 7684ft/2342m, Nearest town: Bryce, Agency: USFS, GPS: 37.734464, -112.268188

31957 • FSR 121 Dispersed 5 - USFS

Dispersed sites, No water, No toilets, Reservations not accepted, Open all year, Tent & RV camping: Free, Elev: 8024ft/2446m, Tel: 435-676-9304, Nearest town: Panguitch, Agency: USFS, GPS: 37.808021, -112.254247

31958 • FSR 121 Dispersed 6 - USFS

Dispersed sites, No water, No toilets, Reservations not accepted, Open all year, Tent & RV camping: Free, Elev: 8145ft/2483m, Tel: 435-676-9304, Nearest town: Panguitch, Agency: USFS, GPS: 37.811522, -112.249514

31959 • FSR 121 Dispersed 7 - USFS

Dispersed sites, No water, No toilets, Reservations not accepted, Open all year, Tent & RV camping: Free, Elev: 7974ft/2430m, Tel: 435-676-9304, Nearest town: Panguitch, Agency: USFS, GPS: 37.839514, -112.279282

31960 • FSR 121 Dispersed 8 - USFS

Dispersed sites, No water, No toilets, Reservations not accepted, Open all year, Tent & RV camping: Free, Elev: 8511ft/2594m, Tel: 435-676-9304, Nearest town: Panguitch, Agency: USFS, GPS: 37.919069, -112.253777

31961 • FSR 1211 Dispersed 1 - USFS

Dispersed sites, No water, No toilets, Reservations not accepted, Open all year, Tent & RV camping: Free, Road not maintained for passenger cars, Elev: 9820ft/2993m, Tel: 435-896-9233, Nearest town: Glenwood, Agency: USFS, GPS: 38.660019, -112.010889

31962 • FSR 121A Dispersed 1 - USFS

Dispersed sites, No water, No toilets, Reservations not accepted, Open all year, Tent & RV camping: Free, Elev: 8922ft/2719m, Tel: 307-782-6555, Nearest town: Mountain View (WY), Agency: USFS, GPS: 40.961645, -110.308587

31963 • FSR 121C Dispersed 1 - USFS

Dispersed sites, No water, No toilets, Reservations not accepted, Open all year, Tent & RV camping: Free, Road not maintained for passenger cars, Elev: 8245ft/2513m, Tel: 435-438-2430, Nearest town: Beaver, Agency: USFS, GPS: 38.163139, -112.384132

31964 • FSR 122 Dispersed 1 - USFS

Dispersed sites, No water, No toilets, Reservations not accepted, Open all year, Tent & RV camping: Free, High-clearance vehicle required, Elev: 7887ft/2404m, Tel: 435-738-2482, Nearest town: Altamont, Agency: USFS, GPS: 40.543485, -110.222457

31965 • FSR 122 Dispersed 2 - USFS

Dispersed sites, No water, No toilets, Reservations not accepted, Open all year, Tent & RV camping: Free, High-clearance vehicle required, Elev: 8126ft/2477m, Tel: 435-738-2482, Nearest town: Altamont, Agency: USFS, GPS: 40.556753, -110.228734

31966 • FSR 122 Dispersed 3 - USFS

Dispersed sites, No water, No toilets, Reservations not accepted, Open May-Dec, Tent & RV camping: Free, Road not maintained for passenger cars, Elev: 9265ft/2824m, Tel: 307-789-3194, Nearest town: Oakley, Agency: USFS, GPS: 40.855476, -110.886569

31967 • FSR 122 Dispersed 4 - USFS

Dispersed sites, No water, No toilets, Reservations not accepted, Open all year, Tent & RV camping: Free, Road not maintained for passenger cars, Elev: 8533ft/2601m, Tel: 435-783-4338, Nearest town: Woodland, Agency: USFS, GPS: 40.497544, -111.084481

31968 • FSR 122 Dispersed 5 - USFS

Dispersed sites, No water, No toilets, Reservations not accepted, Open all year, Tent & RV camping: Free, Road not maintained for passenger cars, Elev: 8632ft/2631m, Tel: 435-783-4338, Nearest town: Woodland, Agency: USFS, GPS: 40.500149, -111.083232

31969 • FSR 122 Dispersed 6 - USFS

Dispersed sites, No water, No toilets, Reservations not accepted, Open all year, Tent & RV camping: Free, Road not maintained for passenger cars, Elev: 8705ft/2653m, Tel: 435-783-4338, Nearest town: Woodland, Agency: USFS, GPS: 40.499464, -111.086313

31970 • FSR 122 Dispersed 7 - USFS

Dispersed sites, No water, No toilets, Reservations not accepted, Open all year, Tents only: Free, Road not maintained for passenger cars, Elev: 8725ft/2659m, Tel: 435-783-4338, Nearest town: Woodland, Agency: USFS, GPS: 40.499404, -111.087797

31971 • FSR 1229 Dispersed 1 - USFS

Dispersed sites, No water, No toilets, Reservations not accepted, Open all year, Tent & RV camping: Free, Road not maintained for passenger cars, Elev: 9193ft/2802m, Tel: 435-676-9300, Nearest town: Antimony, Agency: USFS, GPS: 38.069594, -112.134575

31972 • FSR 123 Dispersed 1 - USFS

Dispersed sites, No water, No toilets, Reservations not accepted, Open all year, Tent & RV camping: Free, High-clearance vehicle required, Elev: 8651ft/2637m, Tel: 435-738-2482, Nearest town: Altamont, Agency: USFS, GPS: 40.554614, -110.310359

31973 • FSR 123 Dispersed 2 - USFS

Dispersed sites, No water, No toilets, Reservations not accepted, Open all year, Tent & RV camping: Free, Elev: 8877ft/2706m, Tel: 435-438-2430, Nearest town: Junction, Agency: USFS, GPS: 38.313226, -112.415168

31974 • FSR 1230 Dispersed 1 - USFS

Dispersed sites, No water, No toilets, Reservations not accepted, Open all year, Tent & RV camping: Free, Road not maintained for passenger cars, Elev: 9736ft/2968m, Tel: 435-896-9233, Nearest town: Greenwich, Agency: USFS, GPS: 38.434658, -112.074429

31975 • FSR 124 Dispersed 1 - USFS

Dispersed sites, No water, No toilets, Reservations not accepted, Open all year, Tent & RV camping: Free, Road not maintained for passenger cars, Elev: 7685ft/2342m, Tel: 435-783-4338, Nearest town: Heber City, Agency: USFS, GPS: 40.257633, -111.212408

31976 • FSR 124 Dispersed 2 - USFS

Dispersed sites, No water, No toilets, Reservations not accepted, Open all year, Tent & RV camping: Free, Road not maintained for passenger cars, Elev: 7744ft/2360m, Tel: 435-676-9306, Nearest town: Panguitch, Agency: USFS, GPS: 37.873433, -112.095453

31977 • FSR 124 Dispersed 3 - USFS

Dispersed sites, No water, No toilets, Reservations not accepted, Open all year, Tent & RV camping: Free, Road not maintained for passenger cars, Elev: 8498ft/2590m, Tel: 435-438-2430, Nearest town: Beaver, Agency: USFS, GPS: 38.298794, -112.442527

31978 • FSR 1242 Dispersed 1 - USFS

Dispersed sites, No water, No toilets, Reservations not accepted, Open all year, Tent & RV camping: Free, Road not maintained for passenger cars, Elev: 9673ft/2948m, Tel: 435-836-2800, Nearest town: Salina, Agency: USFS, GPS: 38.728095, -111.699027

31979 • FSR 1247 Dispersed 1 - USFS

Dispersed sites, No water, No toilets, Reservations not accepted, Open all year, Tent & RV camping: Free, 2nd site 600' north, Road not maintained for passenger cars, Elev: 7610ft/2320m, Tel: 435-836-2800, Nearest town: Glenwood, Agency: USFS, GPS: 38.731639, -111.793289

31980 • FSR 125 Dispersed 1 - USFS

Dispersed sites, No water, No toilets, Reservations not accepted, Open all year, Tent & RV camping: Free, Road not maintained for passenger cars, Elev: 8114ft/2473m, Tel: 435-676-9303, Nearest town: Panguitch, Agency: USFS, GPS: 37.944589, -112.123179

31981 • FSR 125 Dispersed 2 - USFS

Dispersed sites, No water, No toilets, Reservations not accepted, Open all year, Tent & RV camping: Free, Road not maintained for passenger cars, Elev: 8281ft/2524m, Tel: 435-676-9303, Nearest town: Panguitch, Agency: USFS, GPS: 37.940759, -112.139108

31982 • FSR 125 Dispersed 3 - USFS

Dispersed sites, No water, No toilets, Reservations not accepted, Open all year, Tent & RV camping: Free, Elev: 9434ft/2875m, Tel: 307-782-6555, Nearest town: Mountain View (WY), Agency: USFS, GPS: 40.928817, -110.404592

31983 • FSR 126 Dispersed 1 - USFS

Dispersed sites, No water, No toilets, Reservations not accepted, Open all year, Tent & RV camping: Free, Road not maintained for passenger cars, Elev: 8983ft/2738m, Tel: 307-782-6555, Nearest town: Mountain View (WY), Agency: USFS, GPS: 40.952212, -110.310605

31984 • FSR 1262 Dispersed 1 - USFS

Dispersed sites, No water, No toilets, Reservations not accepted, Open all year, Tent & RV camping: Free, Road not maintained for passenger cars, Elev: 9839ft/2999m, Tel: 435-836-2800, Nearest town: Teasdale, Agency: USFS, GPS: 38.110724, -111.689743

31985 • FSR 127 Dispersed 1 - USFS

Dispersed sites, No water, No toilets, Reservations not accepted, Open all year, Tent & RV camping: Free, Road not maintained for passenger cars, Elev: 8878ft/2706m, Tel: 307-782-6555, Nearest town: Mountain View (WY), Agency: USFS, GPS: 40.977393, -110.305312

31986 • FSR 1277 (Spectacle Lake) Dispersed 1 - USFS

Dispersed sites, No water, No toilets, Reservations not accepted, Open all year, Tent & RV camping: Free, Road not maintained for passenger cars, Elev: 10900ft/3322m, Tel: 435-836-2800, Nearest town: Grover, Agency: USFS, GPS: 38.077751, -111.508729

31987 • FSR 1281 Dispersed 1 - USFS

Dispersed sites, No water, No toilets, Reservations not accepted, Open all year, Tent & RV camping: Free, Road not maintained for passenger cars, Elev: 8819ft/2688m, Tel: 435-676-9316, Nearest town: Alton, Agency: USFS, GPS: 37.439559, -112.394023

31988 • FSR 129 Dispersed 1 - USFS

Dispersed sites, No water, No toilets, Reservations not accepted, Open all year, Tent & RV camping: Free, Elev: 9240ft/2816m, Tel: 307-782-6555, Nearest town: Mountain View (WY), Agency: USFS, GPS: 40.924853, -110.319547

31989 • FSR 130 Dispersed 1 - USFS

Dispersed sites, No water, No toilets, Reservations not accepted, Open all year, Tent & RV camping: Free, Road not maintained for passenger cars, Elev: 8721ft/2658m, Tel: 307-789-3194, Nearest town: Oakley, Agency: USFS, GPS: 40.855266, -110.822329

31990 • FSR 1308 (Flatiron Lakes) Dispersed 1 - USFS

Dispersed sites, No water, No toilets, Reservations not accepted, Open all year, Tent & RV camping: Free, Road not maintained for passenger cars, Elev: 8371ft/2551m, Tel: 435-836-2800, Nearest town: Teasdale, Agency: USFS, GPS: 38.253167, -111.490441

31991 • FSR 131 Dispersed 1 - USFS

Dispersed sites, No water, No toilets, Reservations not accepted, Open all year, Tent & RV camping: Free, Elev: 8055ft/2455m, Tel: 435-738-2482, Nearest town: Altamont, Agency: USFS, GPS: 40.558635, -110.488369

31992 • FSR 131 Dispersed 2 - USFS

Dispersed sites, No water, No toilets, Reservations not accepted, Open all year, Tent & RV camping: Free, Road not maintained for passenger cars, Elev: 9290ft/2832m, Tel: 307-782-6555, Nearest town: Mountain View (WY), Agency: USFS, GPS: 40.919191, -110.319507

31993 • FSR 131 Dispersed 3 - USFS

Dispersed sites, No water, No toilets, Reservations not accepted, Open all year, Tent & RV camping: Free, Several sites in this area, Elev: 7605ft/2318m, Tel: 435-738-2482, Nearest town: Altamont, Agency: USFS, GPS: 40.529299, -110.455625

31994 • FSR 131 Dispersed 4 - USFS

Dispersed sites, No water, No toilets, Reservations not accepted, Open all year, Tent & RV camping: Free, Elev: 7817ft/2383m, Tel: 435-783-4338, Nearest town: Spanish Fork, Agency: USFS, GPS: 40.093093, -111.149238

31995 • FSR 131 Dispersed 5 - USFS

Dispersed sites, No water, No toilets, Reservations not accepted, Open all year, Tent & RV camping: Free, Elev: 7867ft/2398m, Tel: 435-783-4338, Nearest town: Spanish Fork, Agency: USFS, GPS: 40.089947, -111.150161

31996 • FSR 131 Dispersed 6 - USFS

Dispersed sites, No water, No toilets, Reservations not accepted, Open all year, Tent & RV camping: Free, Elev: 7908ft/2410m, Tel: 435-783-4338, Nearest town: Spanish Fork, Agency: USFS, GPS: 40.084948, -111.151232

31997 • FSR 131 Dispersed 7 - USFS

Dispersed sites, No water, No toilets, Reservations not accepted, Open all year, Tent & RV camping: Free, Several sites in this area, Road not maintained for passenger cars, Elev: 8608ft/2624m, Tel: 307-789-3194, Nearest town: Oakley, Agency: USFS, GPS: 40.865207, -110.825246

31998 • FSR 131 Dispersed 8 - USFS

Dispersed sites, No water, No toilets, Reservations not accepted, Open all year, Tent & RV camping: Free, Elev: 8854ft/2699m, Tel: 435-783-4338, Nearest town: Spanish Fork, Agency: USFS, GPS: 40.050913, -111.158712

31999 • FSR 131 Dispersed 9 - USFS

Dispersed sites, No water, No toilets, Reservations not accepted, Open all year, Tent & RV camping: Free, Road not maintained for passenger cars, Elev: 8653ft/2637m, Tel: 435-783-4338, Nearest town: Spanish Fork, Agency: USFS, GPS: 40.003172, -111.168329

32000 • FSR 132 (Halls Fork TH) Dispersed 7 - USFS

Dispersed sites, No water, No toilets, Reservations not accepted, Open Jun-Oct, Tent & RV camping: Free, Road not maintained for passenger cars, Elev: 7559ft/2304m, Tel: 435-783-4338, Nearest town: Springville, Agency: USFS, GPS: 40.208662, -111.287439

32001 • FSR 132 Dispersed 1 - USFS

Dispersed sites, No water, No toilets, Reservations not accepted, Open Jul-Nov, Tent & RV camping: Free, Road not maintained for passenger cars, Elev: 7273ft/2217m, Tel: 801-798-3571, Nearest town: Springville, Agency: USFS, GPS: 40.265117, -111.372536

32002 • FSR 132 Dispersed 10 - USFS

Dispersed sites, No water, No toilets, Reservations not accepted, Open Jun-Oct, Tent & RV camping: Free, Road not maintained for passenger cars, Elev: 6721ft/2049m, Tel: 435-783-4338, Nearest town: Springville, Agency: USFS, GPS: 40.193269, -111.323278

32003 • FSR 132 Dispersed 11 - USFS

Dispersed sites, No water, No toilets, Reservations not accepted, Open Jun-Oct, Tent & RV camping: Free, Road not maintained for passenger cars, Elev: 6564ft/2001m, Tel: 435-783-4338, Nearest town: Springville, Agency: USFS, GPS: 40.185103, -111.328982

32004 • FSR 132 Dispersed 12- USFS

Dispersed sites, No water, No toilets, Reservations not accepted, Open Jun-Oct, Tent & RV camping: Free, Road not maintained for passenger cars, Elev: 6500ft/1981m, Tel: 435-783-4338, Nearest town: Springville, Agency: USFS, GPS: 40.179731, -111.328235

32005 • FSR 132 Dispersed 13 - USFS

Dispersed sites, No water, No toilets, Reservations not accepted, Open all year, Tent & RV camping: Free, Road not maintained for passenger cars, Elev: 6019ft/1835m, Tel: 801-625-5112, Nearest town: Woodruff, Agency: USFS, GPS: 41.421644, -111.838808

32006 • FSR 132 Dispersed 14 - USFS

Dispersed sites, No water, No toilets, Reservations not accepted, Open all year, Tent & RV camping: Free, Road not maintained for passenger cars, Elev: 5954ft/1815m, Tel: 801-625-5112, Nearest town: Woodruff, Agency: USFS, GPS: 41.425501, -111.837488

32007 • FSR 132 Dispersed 15 - USFS

Dispersed sites, No water, No toilets, Reservations not accepted, Open all year, Tent & RV camping: Free, Elev: 9698ft/2956m, Tel: 435-826-5400, Nearest town: Escalante, Agency: USFS, GPS: 37.812488, -111.883089

32008 • FSR 132 Dispersed 16 - USFS

Dispersed sites, No water, No toilets, Reservations not accepted, Open all year, Tent & RV camping: Free, Elev: 10547ft/3215m, Tel: 435-826-5400, Nearest town: Escalante, Agency: USFS, GPS: 37.766984, -111.878792

32009 • FSR 132 Dispersed 17 - USFS

Dispersed sites, No water, No toilets, Reservations not accepted, Open all year, Tent & RV camping: Free, Elev: 10525ft/3208m, Tel: 435-826-5400, Nearest town: Escalante, Agency: USFS, GPS: 37.763869, -111.872403

32010 • FSR 132 Dispersed 18 - USFS

Dispersed sites, No water, No toilets, Reservations not accepted, Open all year, Tent & RV camping: Free, Elev: 10153ft/3095m, Tel: 435-826-5400, Nearest town: Escalante, Agency: USFS, GPS: 37.743517, -111.866037

32011 • FSR 132 Dispersed 19 - USFS

Dispersed sites, No water, No toilets, Reservations not accepted, Open all year, Tent & RV camping: Free, Elev: 10165ft/3098m, Tel: 435-826-5400, Nearest town: Escalante, Agency: USFS, GPS: 37.741658, -111.868083

32012 • FSR 132 Dispersed 2 - USFS

Dispersed sites, No water, No toilets, Reservations not accepted, Open Jul-Nov, Tent & RV camping: Free, Road not maintained for passenger cars, Elev: 7976ft/2431m, Tel: 801-798-3571, Nearest town: Springville, Agency: USFS, GPS: 40.280897, -111.349906

32013 • FSR 132 Dispersed 20 - USFS

Dispersed sites, No water, No toilets, Reservations not accepted, Open all year, Tent & RV camping: Free, Elev: 10160ft/3097m, Tel: 435-826-5400, Nearest town: Escalante, Agency: USFS, GPS: 37.733623, -111.871191

32014 • FSR 132 Dispersed 3 - USFS

Dispersed sites, No water, No toilets, Reservations not accepted, Open Jul-Nov, Tent & RV camping: Free, Road not maintained for passenger cars, Elev: 8048ft/2453m, Tel: 801-798-3571, Nearest town: Springville, Agency: USFS, GPS: 40.281637, -111.345996

32015 • FSR 132 Dispersed 4 - USFS

Dispersed sites, No water, No toilets, Reservations not accepted, Open Jul-Nov, Tent & RV camping: Free, Road not maintained for passenger cars, Elev: 8375ft/2553m, Tel: 801-798-3571, Nearest town: Springville, Agency: USFS, GPS: 40.268737, -111.339234

32016 • FSR 132 Dispersed 5 - USFS

Dispersed sites, No water, No toilets, Reservations not accepted, Open Jun-Oct, Tent & RV camping: Free, Road not maintained for passenger cars, Elev: 8298ft/2529m, Tel: 435-783-4338, Nearest town: Springville, Agency: USFS, GPS: 40.239034, -111.302158

32017 • FSR 132 Dispersed 6 - USFS

Dispersed sites, No water, No toilets, Reservations not accepted, Open Jun-Oct, Tents only: Free, Road not maintained for passenger cars, Elev: 8262ft/2518m, Tel: 435-783-4338, Nearest town: Springville, Agency: USFS, GPS: 40.236125, -111.290137

32018 • FSR 132 Dispersed 8 - USFS

Dispersed sites, No water, No toilets, Reservations not accepted, Open Jun-Oct, Tent & RV camping: Free, Road not maintained for passenger cars, Elev: 7431ft/2265m, Tel: 435-783-4338, Nearest town: Springville, Agency: USFS, GPS: 40.206753, -111.292253

32019 • FSR 132 Dispersed 9 - USFS

Dispersed sites, No water, No toilets, Reservations not accepted, Open Jun-Oct, Tent & RV camping: Free, Several sites in this area, Road not maintained for passenger cars, Elev: 7046ft/2148m, Tel: 435-783-4338, Nearest town: Springville, Agency: USFS, GPS: 40.200306, -111.306244

32020 • FSR 1324 (Bluebell Knoll) Dispersed 1 - USFS

Dispersed sites, No water, No toilets, Reservations not accepted, Open all year, Tent & RV camping: Free, Road not maintained for passenger cars, Elev: 11172ft/3405m, Tel: 435-836-2800, Nearest town: Grover, Agency: USFS, GPS: 38.160608, -111.497853

32021 • FSR 1329 Dispersed 1 - USFS

Dispersed sites, No water, No toilets, Reservations not accepted, Open all year, Tent & RV camping: Free, Road not maintained for passenger cars, Elev: 8809ft/2685m, Tel: 435-836-2800, Nearest town: Grover, Agency: USFS, GPS: 38.205064, -111.406891

32022 • FSR 133 Dispersed 1 - USFS

Dispersed sites, No water, No toilets, Reservations not accepted, Open all year, Tent & RV camping: Free, Road not maintained for passenger cars, Elev: 6752ft/2058m, Tel: 435-438-2430, Nearest town: Beaver, Agency: USFS, GPS: 38.226934, -112.300315

32023 • FSR 133 Dispersed 2 - USFS

Dispersed sites, No water, No toilets, Reservations not accepted, Open all year, Tent & RV camping: Free, High-clearance vehicle required, Elev: 8093ft/2467m, Tel: 435-738-2482, Nearest town: Hanna, Agency: USFS, GPS: 40.477236, -110.522536

32024 • FSR 133 Dispersed 3 - USFS

Dispersed sites, No water, No toilets, Reservations not accepted, Open all year, Tent & RV camping: Free, Road not maintained for passenger cars, Elev: 8389ft/2557m, Tel: 435-826-5400, Nearest town: Escalante, Agency: USFS, GPS: 37.799361, -111.934103

32025 • FSR 1335 Dispersed 1 - USFS

Dispersed sites, No water, No toilets, Reservations not accepted, Open all year, Tent & RV camping: Free, Road not maintained for passenger cars, Elev: 8482ft/2585m, Tel: 435-836-2800, Nearest town: Grover, Agency: USFS, GPS: 38.190386, -111.389324

32026 • FSR 134 Dispersed 1 - USFS

Dispersed sites, No water, No toilets, Reservations not accepted, Open all year, Tent & RV camping: Free, Elev: 7355ft/2242m, Tel:

435-738-2482, Nearest town: Duchesne, Agency: USFS, GPS: 40.515362, -110.587837

32027 • FSR 134 Dispersed 10 - USFS
Dispersed sites, No water, No toilets, Reservations not accepted, Open all year, Tent & RV camping: Free, Road not maintained for passenger cars, Elev: 9516ft/2900m, Tel: 435-826-5400, Nearest town: Antimony, Agency: USFS, GPS: 38.039438, -111.877531

32028 • FSR 134 Dispersed 2 - USFS
Dispersed sites, No water, No toilets, Reservations not accepted, Open all year, Tent & RV camping: Free, Elev: 7466ft/2276m, Tel: 435-738-2482, Nearest town: Duchesne, Agency: USFS, GPS: 40.530367, -110.618052

32029 • FSR 134 Dispersed 3 - USFS
Dispersed sites, No water, No toilets, Reservations not accepted, Open all year, Tent & RV camping: Free, Road not maintained for passenger cars, Elev: 7852ft/2393m, Tel: 435-438-2430, Nearest town: Beaver, Agency: USFS, GPS: 38.243034, -112.328174

32030 • FSR 134 Dispersed 4 - USFS
Dispersed sites, No water, No toilets, Reservations not accepted, Open all year, Tent & RV camping: Free, Numerous sites in this area, Road not maintained for passenger cars, Elev: 7767ft/2367m, Tel: 435-783-4338, Nearest town: Springville, Agency: USFS, GPS: 40.227969, -111.206735

32031 • FSR 134 Dispersed 5 - USFS
Dispersed sites, No water, No toilets, Reservations not accepted, Open all year, Tent & RV camping: Free, Road not maintained for passenger cars, Elev: 7988ft/2435m, Tel: 435-783-4338, Nearest town: Springville, Agency: USFS, GPS: 40.226883, -111.227023

32032 • FSR 134 Dispersed 6 - USFS
Dispersed sites, No water, No toilets, Reservations not accepted, Open Apr-Oct, Tent & RV camping: Free, Road not maintained for passenger cars, Elev: 8178ft/2493m, Tel: 435-783-4338, Nearest town: Springville, Agency: USFS, GPS: 40.222524, -111.231195

32033 • FSR 134 Dispersed 7 - USFS
Dispersed sites, No water, No toilets, Reservations not accepted, Open Apr-Oct, Tent & RV camping: Free, Road not maintained for passenger cars, Elev: 8269ft/2520m, Tel: 435-783-4338, Nearest town: Springville, Agency: USFS, GPS: 40.222427, -111.235926

32034 • FSR 134 Dispersed 8 - USFS
Dispersed sites, No water, No toilets, Reservations not accepted, Open all year, Tent & RV camping: Free, Many sites in this area, Road not maintained for passenger cars, Elev: 8521ft/2597m, Tel: 435-783-4338, Nearest town: Springville, Agency: USFS, GPS: 40.220291, -111.247271

32035 • FSR 134 Dispersed 9 - USFS
Dispersed sites, No water, No toilets, Reservations not accepted, Open all year, Tent & RV camping: Free, Road not maintained for passenger cars, Elev: 9271ft/2826m, Tel: 435-826-5400, Nearest town: Antimony, Agency: USFS, GPS: 38.037631, -111.888786

32036 • FSR 135 Dispersed 1 - USFS
Dispersed sites, No water, No toilets, Reservations not accepted, Open all year, Tent & RV camping: Free, High-clearance vehicle required, Elev: 11152ft/3399m, Tel: 435-738-2482, Nearest town: Mountain Home, Agency: USFS, GPS: 40.528261, -110.767287

32037 • FSR 135 Dispersed 2 - USFS
Dispersed sites, No water, No toilets, Reservations not accepted, Open all year, Tent & RV camping: Free, High-clearance vehicle required, Elev: 8973ft/2735m, Tel: 435-738-2482, Nearest town: Mountain Home, Agency: USFS, GPS: 40.507597, -110.779429

32038 • FSR 135 Dispersed 3 - USFS
Dispersed sites, No water, No toilets, Reservations not accepted, Open May-Dec, Tent & RV camping: Free, Road not maintained for passenger cars, Elev: 9478ft/2889m, Tel: 307-789-3194, Nearest town: Oakley, Agency: USFS, GPS: 40.825885, -110.941425

32039 • FSR 136 (Pacer Lake) Dispersed 1 - USFS
Dispersed sites, No water, No toilets, Reservations not accepted, Open all year, Tent & RV camping: Free, Road not maintained for passenger cars, Elev: 9305ft/2836m, Tel: 435-826-5400, Nearest town: Antimony, Agency: USFS, GPS: 37.993538, -111.892963

32040 • FSR 136 Dispersed 2 - USFS
Dispersed sites, No water, No toilets, Reservations not accepted, Open all year, Tent & RV camping: Free, Road not maintained for passenger cars, Elev: 7820ft/2384m, Tel: 435-438-2430, Nearest town: Marysvale, Agency: USFS, GPS: 38.352654, -112.266704

32041 • FSR 136 Dispersed 3 - USFS
Dispersed sites, No water, No toilets, Reservations not accepted, Open Jun-Oct, Tent & RV camping: Free, Road not maintained for passenger cars, Elev: 7372ft/2247m, Tel: 435-783-4338, Nearest town: Springville, Agency: USFS, GPS: 40.191286, -111.354131

32042 • FSR 136 Dispersed 4 - USFS
Dispersed sites, No water, No toilets, Reservations not accepted, Open Jun-Oct, Tent & RV camping: Free, Road not maintained for passenger cars, Elev: 7296ft/2224m, Tel: 435-783-4338, Nearest town: Springville, Agency: USFS, GPS: 40.192514, -111.352272

32043 • FSR 137 (Maba Lake) Dispersed 11 - USFS
Dispersed sites, No water, No toilets, Reservations not accepted, Open all year, Tent & RV camping: Free, Road not maintained for passenger cars, Elev: 9942ft/3030m, Tel: 435-783-4338, Nearest town: Oakley, Agency: USFS, GPS: 40.682642, -110.869162

32044 • FSR 137 Dispersed 1 - USFS
Dispersed sites, No water, No toilets, Reservations not accepted, Open all year, Tent & RV camping: Free, Elev: 9799ft/2987m, Tel: 435-438-2430, Nearest town: Beaver, Agency: USFS, GPS: 38.222697, -112.377481

32045 • FSR 137 Dispersed 10 - USFS
Dispersed sites, No water, No toilets, Reservations not accepted, Open all year, Tent & RV camping: Free, Road not maintained for passenger cars, Elev: 9294ft/2833m, Tel: 435-783-4338, Nearest town: Oakley, Agency: USFS, GPS: 40.635597, -110.917812

32046 • FSR 137 Dispersed 2 - USFS

Dispersed sites, No water, No toilets, Reservations not accepted, Open all year, Tent & RV camping: Free, Elev: 9197ft/2803m, Tel: 435-438-2430, Nearest town: Beaver, Agency: USFS, GPS: 38.231948, -112.443035

32047 • FSR 137 Dispersed 3 - USFS

Dispersed sites, No water, No toilets, Reservations not accepted, Open all year, Tent & RV camping: Free, Elev: 9026ft/2751m, Tel: 435-438-2430, Nearest town: Beaver, Agency: USFS, GPS: 38.234274, -112.448185

32048 • FSR 137 Dispersed 4 - USFS

Dispersed sites, No water, No toilets, Reservations not accepted, Open all year, Tent & RV camping: Free, Elev: 8710ft/2655m, Tel: 435-438-2430, Nearest town: Beaver, Agency: USFS, GPS: 38.241893, -112.467492

32049 • FSR 137 Dispersed 5 - USFS

Dispersed sites, No water, No toilets, Reservations not accepted, Open all year, Tent & RV camping: Free, Road not maintained for passenger cars, Elev: 8963ft/2732m, Tel: 435-783-4338, Nearest town: Heber City, Agency: USFS, GPS: 40.336024, -111.303231

32050 • FSR 137 Dispersed 6 - USFS

Dispersed sites, No water, No toilets, Reservations not accepted, Open all year, Tent & RV camping: Free, Road not maintained for passenger cars, Elev: 9201ft/2804m, Tel: 435-783-4338, Nearest town: Heber City, Agency: USFS, GPS: 40.329763, -111.300226

32051 • FSR 137 Dispersed 7 - USFS

Dispersed sites, No water, No toilets, Reservations not accepted, Open all year, Tent & RV camping: Free, Several sites along road, Elev: 8926ft/2721m, Tel: 435-783-4338, Nearest town: Oakley, Agency: USFS, GPS: 40.631671, -110.953051

32052 • FSR 137 Dispersed 8 - USFS

Dispersed sites, No water, No toilets, Reservations not accepted, Open all year, Tent & RV camping: Free, 2 sites, Elev: 8975ft/2736m, Tel: 435-783-4338, Nearest town: Oakley, Agency: USFS, GPS: 40.633607, -110.949515

32053 • FSR 137 Dispersed 9 - USFS

Dispersed sites, No water, No toilets, Reservations not accepted, Open all year, Tent & RV camping: Free, Elev: 9302ft/2835m, Tel: 435-783-4338, Nearest town: Oakley, Agency: USFS, GPS: 40.633701, -110.935417

32054 • FSR 1378 Dispersed 1 - USFS

Dispersed sites, No water, No toilets, Reservations not accepted, Open all year, Tent & RV camping: Free, Road not maintained for passenger cars, Elev: 7952ft/2424m, Tel: 435-826-5400, Nearest town: Escalante, Agency: USFS, GPS: 37.903728, -111.792165

32055 • FSR 1378 Dispersed 2 - USFS

Dispersed sites, No water, No toilets, Reservations not accepted, Open all year, Tent & RV camping: Free, At end of road, Road not maintained for passenger cars, Elev: 8744ft/2665m, Tel: 435-826-5400, Nearest town: Escalante, Agency: USFS, GPS: 37.926432, -111.787198

32056 • FSR 137C Dispersed 1 - USFS

Dispersed sites, No water, No toilets, Reservations not accepted, Open all year, Tent & RV camping: Free, Elev: 8986ft/2739m, Tel: 435-438-2430, Nearest town: Beaver, Agency: USFS, GPS: 38.236118, -112.454448

32057 • FSR 138 Dispersed 1 - USFS

Dispersed sites, No water, No toilets, Reservations not accepted, Open all year, Tent & RV camping: Free, Both sides of road, Road not maintained for passenger cars, Elev: 6795ft/2071m, Tel: 435-826-5400, Nearest town: Antimony, Agency: USFS, GPS: 38.095508, -111.923843

32058 • FSR 138 Dispersed 10 - USFS

Dispersed sites, No water, No toilets, Reservations not accepted, Open all year, Tent & RV camping: Free, Road not maintained for passenger cars, Elev: 7023ft/2141m, Tel: 435-826-5400, Nearest town: Antimony, Agency: USFS, GPS: 38.098893, -111.893684

32059 • FSR 138 Dispersed 11 - USFS

Dispersed sites, No water, No toilets, Reservations not accepted, Open all year, Tent & RV camping: Free, Road not maintained for passenger cars, Elev: 7073ft/2156m, Tel: 435-826-5400, Nearest town: Antimony, Agency: USFS, GPS: 38.097641, -111.891957

32060 • FSR 138 Dispersed 2 - USFS

Dispersed sites, No water, No toilets, Reservations not accepted, Open all year, Tent & RV camping: Free, Both sides of road, Road not maintained for passenger cars, Elev: 6804ft/2074m, Tel: 435-826-5400, Nearest town: Antimony, Agency: USFS, GPS: 38.095337, -111.922422

32061 • FSR 138 Dispersed 3 - USFS

Dispersed sites, No water, No toilets, Reservations not accepted, Open all year, Tent & RV camping: Free, Road not maintained for passenger cars, Elev: 6832ft/2082m, Tel: 435-826-5400, Nearest town: Antimony, Agency: USFS, GPS: 38.096347, -111.919137

32062 • FSR 138 Dispersed 4 - USFS

Dispersed sites, No water, No toilets, Reservations not accepted, Open all year, Tent & RV camping: Free, Road not maintained for passenger cars, Elev: 6848ft/2087m, Tel: 435-826-5400, Nearest town: Antimony, Agency: USFS, GPS: 38.096658, -111.917206

32063 • FSR 138 Dispersed 5 - USFS

Dispersed sites, No water, No toilets, Reservations not accepted, Open all year, Tent & RV camping: Free, Road not maintained for passenger cars, Elev: 6892ft/2101m, Tel: 435-826-5400, Nearest town: Antimony, Agency: USFS, GPS: 38.096122, -111.915406

32064 • FSR 138 Dispersed 6 - USFS

Dispersed sites, No water, No toilets, Reservations not accepted, Open all year, Tent & RV camping: Free, Road not maintained for passenger cars, Elev: 6894ft/2101m, Tel: 435-826-5400, Nearest town: Antimony, Agency: USFS, GPS: 38.096883, -111.913022

32065 • FSR 138 Dispersed 7 - USFS

Dispersed sites, No water, No toilets, Reservations not accepted, Open all year, Tent & RV camping: Free, Road not maintained for passenger cars, Elev: 6891ft/2100m, Tel: 435-826-5400, Nearest town: Antimony, Agency: USFS, GPS: 38.098162, -111.910812

32066 • FSR 138 Dispersed 8 - USFS

Dispersed sites, No water, No toilets, Reservations not accepted, Open all year, Tent & RV camping: Free, Road not maintained for passenger cars, Elev: 7044ft/2147m, Tel: 435-826-5400, Nearest town: Antimony, Agency: USFS, GPS: 38.098236, -111.899496

32067 • FSR 138 Dispersed 9 - USFS

Dispersed sites, No water, No toilets, Reservations not accepted, Open all year, Tent & RV camping: Free, Road not maintained for passenger cars, Elev: 7016ft/2138m, Tel: 435-826-5400, Nearest town: Antimony, Agency: USFS, GPS: 38.098219, -111.894997

32068 • FSR 139 Dispersed 1 - USFS

Dispersed sites, No water, No toilets, Reservations not accepted, Open all year, Tent & RV camping: Free, Road not maintained for passenger cars, Elev: 7310ft/2228m, Tel: 435-438-2428, Nearest town: Beaver, Agency: USFS, GPS: 38.225524, -112.530412

32069 • FSR 139 Dispersed 2 - USFS

Dispersed sites, No water, No toilets, Reservations not accepted, Open all year, Tent & RV camping: Free, Elev: 9369ft/2856m, Tel: 435-783-4338, Nearest town: Hanna, Agency: USFS, GPS: 40.410315, -110.975303

32070 • FSR 1397 Dispersed 1 - USFS

Dispersed sites, No water, No toilets, Reservations not accepted, Open all year, Tent & RV camping: Free, Road not maintained for passenger cars, Elev: 8697ft/2651m, Tel: 435-826-5400, Nearest town: Antimony, Agency: USFS, GPS: 38.062093, -111.857072

32071 • FSR 140 Dispersed 1 - USFS

Dispersed sites, No water, No toilets, Reservations not accepted, Open all year, Tent & RV camping: Free, Elev: 10480ft/3194m, Tel: 435-826-5400, Nearest town: Escalante, Agency: USFS, GPS: 37.874446, -111.871722

32072 • FSR 140 Dispersed 2 - USFS

Dispersed sites, No water, No toilets, Reservations not accepted, Open all year, Tent & RV camping: Free, Elev: 10510ft/3203m, Tel: 435-826-5400, Nearest town: Escalante, Agency: USFS, GPS: 37.875266, -111.875879

32073 • FSR 1401 Dispersed - USFS

Dispersed sites, No water, No toilets, Reservations not accepted, Open all year, Tent & RV camping: Free, Road not maintained for passenger cars, Elev: 8294ft/2528m, Tel: 435-896-9233, Nearest town: Salina, Agency: USFS, GPS: 38.918209, -111.437039

32074 • FSR 1402 Dispersed 1 - USFS

Dispersed sites, No water, No toilets, Reservations not accepted, Open all year, Tent & RV camping: Free, Road not maintained for passenger cars, Elev: 9533ft/2906m, Tel: 435-826-5400, Nearest town: Teasdale, Agency: USFS, GPS: 38.001609, -111.529187

32075 • FSR 1407A Dispersed 1 - USFS

Dispersed sites, No water, No toilets, Reservations not accepted, Open all year, Tent & RV camping: Free, Road not maintained for passenger cars, Elev: 8291ft/2527m, Tel: 435-896-9233, Nearest town: Salina, Agency: USFS, GPS: 38.895214, -111.435151

32076 • FSR 1407B (Jolly Mill Pt) Dispersed 1 - USFS

Dispersed sites, No water, No toilets, Reservations not accepted, Open all year, Tent & RV camping: Free, Road not maintained for passenger cars, Elev: 8441ft/2573m, Tel: 435-896-9233, Nearest town: Salina, Agency: USFS, GPS: 38.899192, -111.409309

32077 • FSR 141 Dispersed 1 - USFS

Dispersed sites, No water, No toilets, Reservations not accepted, Open all year, Tent & RV camping: Free, Road not maintained for passenger cars, Elev: 8235ft/2510m, Tel: 435-836-2800, Nearest town: Salina, Agency: USFS, GPS: 38.736752, -111.504236

32078 • FSR 141 Dispersed 1 - USFS

Dispersed sites, No water, No toilets, Reservations not accepted, Open May-Dec, Tent & RV camping: Free, Several sites in this area, Road not maintained for passenger cars, Elev: 9162ft/2793m, Tel: 307-789-3194, Nearest town: Oakley, Agency: USFS, GPS: 40.855268, -110.864558

32079 • FSR 142 Dispersed 1 - USFS

Dispersed sites, No water, No toilets, Reservations not accepted, Open all year, Tent & RV camping: Free, Road not maintained for passenger cars, Elev: 5393ft/1644m, Tel: 435-755-3620, Nearest town: Logan, Agency: USFS, GPS: 41.771177, -111.754471

32080 • FSR 142 Dispersed 2 - USFS

Dispersed sites, No water, No toilets, Reservations not accepted, Open all year, Tent & RV camping: Free, Road not maintained for passenger cars, Elev: 5443ft/1659m, Tel: 435-755-3620, Nearest town: Logan, Agency: USFS, GPS: 41.772152, -111.749826

32081 • FSR 142 Dispersed 3 - USFS

Dispersed sites, No water, No toilets, Reservations not accepted, Open all year, Tent & RV camping: Free, Road not maintained for passenger cars, Elev: 5584ft/1702m, Tel: 435-755-3620, Nearest town: Logan, Agency: USFS, GPS: 41.771577, -111.743307

32082 • FSR 142 Dispersed 4 - USFS

Dispersed sites, No water, No toilets, Reservations not accepted, Open all year, Tent & RV camping: Free, Road not maintained for passenger cars, Elev: 5654ft/1723m, Tel: 435-755-3620, Nearest town: Logan, Agency: USFS, GPS: 41.772858, -111.737166

32083 • FSR 142 Dispersed 5 - USFS

Dispersed sites, No water, No toilets, Reservations not accepted, Open all year, Tent & RV camping: Free, Road not maintained for passenger cars, Elev: 5730ft/1747m, Tel: 435-755-3620, Nearest town: Logan, Agency: USFS, GPS: 41.776227, -111.731747

32084 • FSR 142 Dispersed 6 - USFS

Dispersed sites, No water, No toilets, Reservations not accepted, Open all year, Tent & RV camping: Free, Road not maintained for

passenger cars, Elev: 5826ft/1776m, Tel: 435-755-3620, Nearest town: Logan, Agency: USFS, GPS: 41.780706, -111.728798

32085 • FSR 142 Dispersed 7 - USFS

Dispersed sites, No water, No toilets, Reservations not accepted, Open all year, Tent & RV camping: Free, Road not maintained for passenger cars, Elev: 5934ft/1809m, Tel: 435-755-3620, Nearest town: Logan, Agency: USFS, GPS: 41.785541, -111.725574

32086 • FSR 143 (Powell Point Dispersed 1 - USFS

Dispersed sites, No water, No toilets, Reservations not accepted, Open all year, Tent & RV camping: Free, Road not maintained for passenger cars, Elev: 10256ft/3126m, Tel: 435-826-5400, Nearest town: Escalante, Agency: USFS, GPS: 37.693776, -111.897755

32087 • FSR 143 Dispersed 2 - USFS

Dispersed sites, No water, No toilets, Reservations not accepted, Open all year, Tent & RV camping: Free, Many sites in this area, Elev: 8099ft/2469m, Tel: 435-783-4338, Nearest town: Heber City, Agency: USFS, GPS: 40.341324, -111.229981

32088 • FSR 143 Dispersed 3 - USFS

Dispersed sites, No water, No toilets, Reservations not accepted, Open all year, Tent & RV camping: Free, Room for many rigs, Elev: 8099ft/2469m, Tel: 435-783-4338, Nearest town: Heber City, Agency: USFS, GPS: 40.338259, -111.235436

32089 • FSR 143 Dispersed 4 - USFS

Dispersed sites, No water, No toilets, Reservations not accepted, Open all year, Tent & RV camping: Free, Elev: 8115ft/2473m, Tel: 435-783-4338, Nearest town: Heber City, Agency: USFS, GPS: 40.337705, -111.238672

32090 • FSR 143 Dispersed 5 - USFS

Dispersed sites, No water, No toilets, Reservations not accepted, Open all year, Tent & RV camping: Free, Numerous sites in this area, Elev: 8230ft/2509m, Tel: 435-783-4338, Nearest town: Heber City, Agency: USFS, GPS: 40.328024, -111.250402

32091 • FSR 143 Dispersed 6 - USFS

Dispersed sites, No water, No toilets, Reservations not accepted, Open all year, Tent & RV camping: Free, Elev: 9222ft/2811m, Tel: 435-738-2482, Nearest town: Mountain Home, Agency: USFS, GPS: 40.562246, -110.753024

32092 • FSR 143 Dispersed 7 - USFS

Dispersed sites, No water, No toilets, Reservations not accepted, Open all year, Tent & RV camping: Free, Road not msaintained for passenger cars, At end of road, Elev: 10222ft/3116m, Tel: 435-738-2482, Nearest town: Mountain Home, Agency: USFS, GPS: 40.580483, -110.779381

32093 • FSR 143 Dispersed 8 - USFS

Dispersed sites, No water, No toilets, Reservations not accepted, Open May-Dec, Tent & RV camping: Free, Road not maintained for passenger cars, Elev: 9272ft/2826m, Tel: 307-789-3194, Nearest town: Oakley, Agency: USFS, GPS: 40.857991, -110.881372

32094 • FSR 1434 Dispersed 3 - USFS

Dispersed sites, No water, No toilets, Reservations not accepted, Open all year, Tent & RV camping: Free, Road not maintained for passenger cars, Elev: 9236ft/2815m, Tel: 435-826-5400, Nearest town: Boulder, Agency: USFS, GPS: 37.981813, -111.604023

32095 • FSR 144 Dispersed 1 - USFS

Dispersed sites, No water, No toilets, Reservations not accepted, Open all year, Tent & RV camping: Free, Road not maintained for passenger cars, Elev: 8389ft/2557m, Tel: 801-625-5112, Nearest town: Randolph, Agency: USFS, GPS: 41.593403, -111.443546

32096 • FSR 144 Dispersed 2 - USFS

Dispersed sites, No water, No toilets, Reservations not accepted, Open all year, Tent & RV camping: Free, Road not maintained for passenger cars, Elev: 7983ft/2433m, Tel: 801-798-3571, Nearest town: Spanish Fork, Agency: USFS, GPS: 39.966491, -111.008951

32097 • FSR 144 Dispersed 3 - USFS

Dispersed sites, No water, No toilets, Reservations not accepted, Open all year, Tent & RV camping: Free, Elev: 7521ft/2292m, Tel: 435-738-2482, Nearest town: Hanna, Agency: USFS, GPS: 40.556977, -110.888559

32098 • FSR 146 Dispersed 1- USFS

Dispersed sites, No water, No toilets, Reservations not accepted, Open Jun-Nov, Tent & RV camping: Free, Road not maintained for passenger cars, Elev: 7439ft/2267m, Tel: 435-755-3620, Nearest town: Hyrum, Agency: USFS, GPS: 41.706131, -111.554033

32099 • FSR 146 Dispersed 2- USFS

Dispersed sites, No water, No toilets, Reservations not accepted, Open Jun-Nov, Tent & RV camping: Free, Road not maintained for passenger cars, Elev: 7430ft/2265m, Tel: 435-755-3620, Nearest town: Hyrum, Agency: USFS, GPS: 41.701595, -111.555854

32100 • FSR 146 Dispersed 3- USFS

Dispersed sites, No water, No toilets, Reservations not accepted, Open Jun-Nov, Tent & RV camping: Free, Road not maintained for passenger cars, Elev: 7358ft/2243m, Tel: 435-755-3620, Nearest town: Hyrum, Agency: USFS, GPS: 41.690971, -111.555255

32101 • FSR 146 Dispersed 4 - USFS

Dispersed sites, No water, No toilets, Reservations not accepted, Open all year, Tent & RV camping: Free, Road not maintained for passenger cars, Elev: 9786ft/2983m, Tel: 435-783-4338, Nearest town: Heber City, Agency: USFS, GPS: 40.462168, -111.099954

32102 • FSR 147 Dispersed 1 - USFS

Dispersed sites, No water, No toilets, Reservations not accepted, Open Jun-Nov, Tent & RV camping: Free, Road not maintained for passenger cars, Elev: 7453ft/2272m, Tel: 435-755-3620, Nearest town: Logan, Agency: USFS, GPS: 41.724993, -111.587368

32103 • FSR 147 Dispersed 2 - USFS

Dispersed sites, No water, No toilets, Reservations not accepted, Open Jun-Nov, Tent & RV camping: Free, Road not maintained for passenger cars, Elev: 7581ft/2311m, Tel: 435-755-3620, Nearest town: Logan, Agency: USFS, GPS: 41.721586, -111.592081

32104 • FSR 147 Dispersed 3 - USFS
Dispersed sites, No water, No toilets, Reservations not accepted, Open all year, Tent & RV camping: Free, Elev: 8791ft/2679m, Tel: 307-789-3194, Nearest town: Oakley, Agency: USFS, GPS: 40.834446, -110.808139

32105 • FSR 148 Dispersed 1 - USFS
Dispersed sites, No water, No toilets, Reservations not accepted, Open Jun-Nov, Tent & RV camping: Free, Road not maintained for passenger cars, Elev: 7476ft/2279m, Tel: 435-755-3620, Nearest town: Logan, Agency: USFS, GPS: 41.749963, -111.561405

32106 • FSR 148 Dispersed 2 - USFS
Dispersed sites, No water, No toilets, Reservations not accepted, Open all year, Tent & RV camping: Free, Road not maintained for passenger cars, Elev: 7700ft/2347m, Tel: 435-783-4338, Nearest town: Spanish Fork, Agency: USFS, GPS: 40.096531, -111.191875

32107 • FSR 148 Dispersed 3 - USFS
Dispersed sites, No water, No toilets, Reservations not accepted, Open all year, Tent & RV camping: Free, High-clearance vehicle required, Elev: 8943ft/2726m, Tel: 435-738-2482, Nearest town: Spanish Fork, Agency: USFS, GPS: 39.982159, -110.974949

32108 • FSR 149 Dispersed 1 - USFS
Dispersed sites, No water, No toilets, Reservations not accepted, Open Apr-Nov, Tent & RV camping: Free, Elev: 5172ft/1576m, Tel: 435-755-3620, Nearest town: Hyrum, Agency: USFS, GPS: 41.642886, -111.708114

32109 • FSR 149 Dispersed 2 - USFS
Dispersed sites, No water, No toilets, Reservations not accepted, Open all year, Tent & RV camping: Free, Elev: 7662ft/2335m, Tel: 435-826-5400, Nearest town: Escalante, Agency: USFS, GPS: 37.887248, -111.784928

32110 • FSR 149 Dispersed 3 - USFS
Dispersed sites, No water, No toilets, Reservations not accepted, Open all year, Tent & RV camping: Free, Elev: 7655ft/2333m, Tel: 435-826-5400, Nearest town: Escalante, Agency: USFS, GPS: 37.888699, -111.785542

32111 • FSR 149 Dispersed 4 - USFS
Dispersed sites, No water, No toilets, Reservations not accepted, Open all year, Tent & RV camping: Free, Elev: 7842ft/2390m, Tel: 435-738-2482, Nearest town: Duchesne, Agency: USFS, GPS: 40.023093, -110.936779

32112 • FSR 149 Dispersed 5 - USFS
Dispersed sites, No water, No toilets, Reservations not accepted, Open all year, Tent & RV camping: Free, Elev: 7718ft/2352m, Tel: 435-738-2482, Nearest town: Duchesne, Agency: USFS, GPS: 40.035233, -110.921548

32113 • FSR 149 Dispersed 6 - USFS
Dispersed sites, No water, No toilets, Reservations not accepted, Open all year, Tent & RV camping: Free, Elev: 8820ft/2688m, Tel: 307-789-3194, Nearest town: Oakley, Agency: USFS, GPS: 40.831282, -110.804661

32114 • FSR 150 Dispersed 1 - USFS
Dispersed sites, No water, No toilets, Reservations not accepted, Open Apr-Oct, Tent & RV camping: Free, Road not maintained for passenger cars, Elev: 7894ft/2406m, Tel: 435-783-4338, Nearest town: Springville, Agency: USFS, GPS: 40.202795, -111.193583

32115 • FSR 150 Dispersed 2 - USFS
Dispersed sites, No water, No toilets, Reservations not accepted, Open Apr-Oct, Tent & RV camping: Free, Road not maintained for passenger cars, Elev: 7894ft/2406m, Tel: 435-783-4338, Nearest town: Springville, Agency: USFS, GPS: 40.205419, -111.205948

32116 • FSR 150 Dispersed 3 - USFS
Dispersed sites, No water, No toilets, Reservations not accepted, Open Apr-Oct, Tent & RV camping: Free, 2 separated sites, Road not maintained for passenger cars, Elev: 7996ft/2437m, Tel: 435-783-4338, Nearest town: Springville, Agency: USFS, GPS: 40.204083, -111.208323

32117 • FSR 150 Dispersed 4 - USFS
Dispersed sites, No water, No toilets, Reservations not accepted, Open Apr-Oct, Tent & RV camping: Free, Road not maintained for passenger cars, Elev: 8051ft/2454m, Tel: 435-783-4338, Nearest town: Springville, Agency: USFS, GPS: 40.204657, -111.211261

32118 • FSR 150 Dispersed 5 - USFS
Dispersed sites, No water, No toilets, Reservations not accepted, Open Apr-Oct, Tent & RV camping: Free, Road not maintained for passenger cars, Elev: 8151ft/2484m, Tel: 435-783-4338, Nearest town: Springville, Agency: USFS, GPS: 40.204248, -111.215683

32119 • FSR 150 Dispersed 6 - USFS
Dispersed sites, No water, No toilets, Reservations not accepted, Open Apr-Oct, Tent & RV camping: Free, Road not maintained for passenger cars, Elev: 8310ft/2533m, Tel: 435-783-4338, Nearest town: Springville, Agency: USFS, GPS: 40.205935, -111.221402

32120 • FSR 150 Dispersed 7 - USFS
Dispersed sites, No water, No toilets, Reservations not accepted, Open Apr-Oct, Tent & RV camping: Free, 3 sites, Road not maintained for passenger cars, Elev: 8515ft/2595m, Tel: 435-783-4338, Nearest town: Springville, Agency: USFS, GPS: 40.203028, -111.228192

32121 • FSR 150 Dispersed 8 - USFS
Dispersed sites, No water, No toilets, Reservations not accepted, Open Apr-Oct, Tent & RV camping: Free, Road not maintained for passenger cars, Elev: 8681ft/2646m, Tel: 435-783-4338, Nearest town: Springville, Agency: USFS, GPS: 40.200818, -111.233162

32122 • FSR 150 Dispersed 9 - USFS
Dispersed sites, No water, No toilets, Reservations not accepted, Open Apr-Oct, Tent & RV camping: Free, Road not maintained

for passenger cars, Elev: 8746ft/2666m, Tel: 435-783-4338, Nearest town: Springville, Agency: USFS, GPS: 40.199575, -111.235291

32123 • FSR 1508/1507 Dispersed 1 - USFS
Dispersed sites, No water, No toilets, Tent & RV camping: Free, Elev: 8941ft/2725m, Tel: 435-836-2800, Nearest town: Loa, Agency: USFS, GPS: 38.583559, -111.614711

32124 • FSR 151 Dispersed 1 - USFS
Dispersed sites, No water, No toilets, Reservations not accepted, Open all year, Tent & RV camping: Free, Road not maintained for passenger cars, Elev: 9648ft/2941m, Tel: 435-783-4338, Nearest town: Woodland, Agency: USFS, GPS: 40.511957, -110.958016

32125 • FSR 152 Dispersed 1 - USFS
Dispersed sites, No water, No toilets, Reservations not accepted, Open all year, Tent & RV camping: Free, Elev: 8475ft/2583m, Tel: 435-826-5400, Nearest town: Escalante, Agency: USFS, GPS: 37.893995, -111.718989

32126 • FSR 152 Dispersed 2 - USFS
Dispersed sites, No water, No toilets, Reservations not accepted, Open all year, Tent & RV camping: Free, Elev: 8554ft/2607m, Tel: 435-826-5400, Nearest town: Escalante, Agency: USFS, GPS: 37.911305, -111.705743

32127 • FSR 152 Dispersed 3 - USFS
Dispersed sites, No water, No toilets, Reservations not accepted, Open all year, Tent & RV camping: Free, High-clearance vehicle required, Elev: 7737ft/2358m, Tel: 435-738-2482, Nearest town: Duchesne, Agency: USFS, GPS: 39.921642, -110.601117

32128 • FSR 1524B Dispersed 1 - USFS
Dispersed sites, No water, No toilets, Reservations not accepted, Open all year, Tent & RV camping: Free, Road not maintained for passenger cars, Elev: 9550ft/2911m, Tel: 435-836-2800, Nearest town: Fremont, Agency: USFS, GPS: 38.645983, -111.501573

32129 • FSR 153 Dispersed 1 - USFS
Dispersed sites, No water, No toilets, Reservations not accepted, Open all year, Tent & RV camping: Free, Road not maintained for passenger cars, Elev: 6901ft/2103m, Tel: 435-755-3620, Nearest town: Logan, Agency: USFS, GPS: 41.796282, -111.579363

32130 • FSR 153 Dispersed 2 - USFS
Dispersed sites, No water, No toilets, Reservations not accepted, Open all year, Tent & RV camping: Free, Road not maintained for passenger cars, Elev: 6727ft/2050m, Tel: 435-755-3620, Nearest town: Logan, Agency: USFS, GPS: 41.801753, -111.570466

32131 • FSR 153 Dispersed 3 - USFS
Dispersed sites, No water, No toilets, Reservations not accepted, Open all year, Tent & RV camping: Free, Elev: 7952ft/2424m, Tel: 435-826-5400, Nearest town: Escalante, Agency: USFS, GPS: 37.928559, -111.668074

32132 • FSR 153 Dispersed 4 - USFS
Dispersed sites, No water, No toilets, Reservations not accepted, Open all year, Tent & RV camping: Free, Elev: 8961ft/2731m,

Tel: 435-826-5400, Nearest town: Boulder, Agency: USFS, GPS: 37.963301, -111.620308

32133 • FSR 153 Dispersed 5 - USFS
Dispersed sites, No water, No toilets, Reservations not accepted, Open all year, Tent & RV camping: Free, Elev: 8419ft/2566m, Tel: 435-826-5400, Nearest town: Boulder, Agency: USFS, GPS: 37.966286, -111.563995

32134 • FSR 153 Dispersed 6 - USFS
Dispersed sites, No water, No toilets, Reservations not accepted, Open all year, Tent & RV camping: Free, Elev: 8206ft/2501m, Tel: 435-826-5400, Nearest town: Boulder, Agency: USFS, GPS: 37.962299, -111.551287

32135 • FSR 1536 Dispersed 1 - USFS
Dispersed sites, No water, No toilets, Reservations not accepted, Open all year, Tent & RV camping: Free, Road not maintained for passenger cars, Elev: 7871ft/2399m, Tel: 435-789-1181, Nearest town: Hatch, Agency: USFS, GPS: 37.690748, -112.566957

32136 • FSR 1536 Dispersed 2 - USFS
Dispersed sites, No water, No toilets, Reservations not accepted, Open all year, Tent & RV camping: Free, Road not maintained for passenger cars, Elev: 8156ft/2486m, Tel: 435-789-1181, Nearest town: Hatch, Agency: USFS, GPS: 37.709269, -112.596357

32137 • FSR 154 (Cyclone Lake) Dispersed 2 - USFS
Dispersed sites, No water, No toilets, Reservations not accepted, Open all year, Tent & RV camping: Free, Elev: 9908ft/3020m, Tel: 435-826-5400, Nearest town: Antimony, Agency: USFS, GPS: 37.987116, -111.718718

32138 • FSR 154 Dispersed 1 - USFS
Dispersed sites, No water, No toilets, Reservations not accepted, Open all year, Tent & RV camping: Free, Elev: 8808ft/2685m, Tel: 435-826-5400, Nearest town: Escalante, Agency: USFS, GPS: 37.941314, -111.697382

32139 • FSR 154 Dispersed 3 - USFS
Dispersed sites, No water, No toilets, Reservations not accepted, Open all year, Tent & RV camping: Free, Elev: 9876ft/3010m, Tel: 435-826-5400, Nearest town: Antimony, Agency: USFS, GPS: 37.989903, -111.708679

32140 • FSR 154 Dispersed 4 - USFS
Dispersed sites, No water, No toilets, Reservations not accepted, Open all year, Tent & RV camping: Free, Elev: 9733ft/2967m, Tel: 435-826-5400, Nearest town: Antimony, Agency: USFS, GPS: 38.017108, -111.697798

32141 • FSR 154 Dispersed 5 - USFS
Dispersed sites, No water, No toilets, Reservations not accepted, Open all year, Tent & RV camping: Free, Elev: 10027ft/3056m, Tel: 435-826-5400, Nearest town: Antimony, Agency: USFS, GPS: 38.045494, -111.683823

32142 • FSR 154 Dispersed 6 - USFS

Dispersed sites, No water, No toilets, Reservations not accepted, Open all year, Tent & RV camping: Free, Elev: 10056ft/3065m, Tel: 435-826-5400, Nearest town: Antimony, Agency: USFS, GPS: 38.048351, -111.682554

32143 • FSR 154 Dispersed 7 - USFS

Dispersed sites, No water, No toilets, Reservations not accepted, Open all year, Tent & RV camping: Free, Elev: 10077ft/3071m, Tel: 435-826-5400, Nearest town: Antimony, Agency: USFS, GPS: 38.052981, -111.681517

32144 • FSR 154 Dispersed 8 - USFS

Dispersed sites, No water, No toilets, Reservations not accepted, Open all year, Tent & RV camping: Free, Elev: 6748ft/2057m, Tel: 435-738-2482, Nearest town: Duchesne, Agency: USFS, GPS: 39.955915, -110.304398

32145 • FSR 155A Dispersed 1 - USFS

Dispersed sites, No water, No toilets, Reservations not accepted, Open all year, Tents only: Free, Road not maintained for passenger cars, Elev: 8988ft/2740m, Tel: 307-782-6555, Nearest town: Mountain View (WY), Agency: USFS, GPS: 40.964232, -110.246663

32146 • FSR 156 Dispersed 1 - USFS

Dispersed sites, No water, No toilets, Reservations not accepted, Open all year, Tent & RV camping: Free, Road not maintained for passenger cars, Elev: 9067ft/2764m, Tel: 307-789-3194, Nearest town: Oakley, Agency: USFS, GPS: 40.798487, -110.881775

32147 • FSR 156 Dispersed 2 - USFS

Dispersed sites, No water, No toilets, Reservations not accepted, Open all year, Tent & RV camping: Free, Road not maintained for passenger cars, Elev: 9069ft/2764m, Tel: 307-789-3194, Nearest town: Oakley, Agency: USFS, GPS: 40.802563, -110.879732

32148 • FSR 157 (Barney Lake) Dispersed 1 - USFS

Dispersed sites, No water, No toilets, Reservations not accepted, Open all year, Tent & RV camping: Free, Road not maintained for passenger cars, Elev: 10150ft/3094m, Tel: 435-896-9233, Nearest town: Greenwich, Agency: USFS, GPS: 38.485284, -112.085421

32149 • FSR 157A Dispersed 1 - USFS

Dispersed sites, No water, No toilets, Reservations not accepted, Open all year, Tent & RV camping: Free, Road not maintained for passenger cars, Elev: 10044ft/3061m, Tel: 435-896-9233, Nearest town: Greenwich, Agency: USFS, GPS: 38.482909, -112.081524

32150 • FSR 160 (Whitney Reservoir) Dispersed 2 - USFS

Dispersed sites, No water, No toilets, Reservations not accepted, Open May-Dec, Tent & RV camping: Free, Road not maintained for passenger cars, Elev: 9304ft/2836m, Tel: 307-789-3194, Nearest town: Oakley, Agency: USFS, GPS: 40.827831, -110.928707

32151 • FSR 160 Dispersed 1 - USFS

Dispersed sites, No water, No toilets, Reservations not accepted, Open all year, Tent & RV camping: Free, Road not maintained for passenger cars, Elev: 7417ft/2261m, Tel: 435-755-3620, Nearest town: Logan, Agency: USFS, GPS: 41.718734, -111.637545

32152 • FSR 1609 Dispersed 1 - USFS

Dispersed sites, No water, No toilets, Reservations not accepted, Open all year, Tent & RV camping: Free, Road not maintained for passenger cars, Elev: 7962ft/2427m, Tel: 435-789-1181, Nearest town: Duck Creek, Agency: USFS, GPS: 37.572479, -112.595244

32153 • FSR 160A Dispersed 1 - USFS

Dispersed sites, No water, No toilets, Reservations not accepted, Open all year, Tent & RV camping: Free, Road not maintained for passenger cars, Elev: 9440ft/2877m, Tel: 435-896-9233, Nearest town: Greenwich, Agency: USFS, GPS: 38.502479, -112.008385

32154 • FSR 161 Dispersed 1 - USFS

Dispersed sites, No water, No toilets, Reservations not accepted, Open May-Dec, Tent & RV camping: Free, Road not maintained for passenger cars, Elev: 9390ft/2862m, Tel: 307-789-3194, Nearest town: Oakley, Agency: USFS, GPS: 40.823643, -110.881751

32155 • FSR 1613 Dispersed 1 - USFS

Dispersed sites, No water, No toilets, Reservations not accepted, Open all year, Tent & RV camping: Free, Elev: 8021ft/2445m, Tel: 435-789-1181, Nearest town: Duck Creek, Agency: USFS, GPS: 37.569908, -112.604473

32156 • FSR 162 Dispersed 1 - USFS

Dispersed sites, No water, No toilets, Reservations not accepted, Open all year, Tent & RV camping: Free, Road not maintained for passenger cars, Elev: 7385ft/2251m, Tel: 801-625-5112, Nearest town: Randolph, Agency: USFS, GPS: 41.582689, -111.397213

32157 • FSR 162 Dispersed 1 - USFS

Dispersed sites, No water, No toilets, Reservations not accepted, Open all year, Tent & RV camping: Free, Elev: 10419ft/3176m, Tel: 435-826-5400, Nearest town: Teasdale, Agency: USFS, GPS: 38.063648, -111.622555

32158 • FSR 162 Dispersed 2 - USFS

Dispersed sites, No water, No toilets, Reservations not accepted, Open all year, Tent & RV camping: Free, Elev: 10337ft/3151m, Tel: 435-826-5400, Nearest town: Teasdale, Agency: USFS, GPS: 38.069803, -111.608559

32159 • FSR 162 Dispersed 3 - USFS

Dispersed sites, No water, No toilets, Reservations not accepted, Open all year, Tent & RV camping: Free, Elev: 10387ft/3166m, Tel: 435-826-5400, Nearest town: Teasdale, Agency: USFS, GPS: 38.053961, -111.580627

32160 • FSR 162B Dispersed 1 - USFS

Dispersed sites, No water, No toilets, Reservations not accepted, Open all year, Tent & RV camping: Free, Road not maintained for passenger cars, Elev: 7299ft/2225m, Tel: 435-896-9233, Nearest town: Monroe, Agency: USFS, GPS: 38.613053, -112.060085

32161 • FSR 163 Dispersed - USFS
Dispersed sites, No water, No toilets, Reservations not accepted, Open all year, Tent & RV camping: Free, Elev: 7722ft/2354m, Tel: 435-755-3620, Nearest town: Garden City, Agency: USFS, GPS: 41.898467, -111.601855

32162 • FSR 163 Dispersed 1 - USFS
Dispersed sites, No water, No toilets, Reservations not accepted, Open all year, Tent & RV camping: Free, Road not maintained for passenger cars, Elev: 6674ft/2034m, Tel: 801-798-3571, Nearest town: Nephi, Agency: USFS, GPS: 39.738592, -111.740829

32163 • FSR 163 Dispersed 3 - USFS
Dispersed sites, No water, No toilets, Reservations not accepted, Open May-Dec, Tent & RV camping: Free, Road not maintained for passenger cars, Elev: 9507ft/2898m, Tel: 307-789-3194, Nearest town: Oakley, Agency: USFS, GPS: 40.819263, -110.898882

32164 • FSR 164 Dispersed 1 - USFS
Dispersed sites, No water, No toilets, Reservations not accepted, Open all year, Tent & RV camping: Free, Road not maintained for passenger cars, Elev: 8806ft/2684m, Tel: 307-782-6555, Nearest town: Mountain View (WY), Agency: USFS, GPS: 40.936902, -110.182707

32165 • FSR 164 Dispersed 2 - USFS
Dispersed sites, No water, No toilets, Reservations not accepted, Open all year, Tent & RV camping: Free, Road not maintained for passenger cars, Elev: 8909ft/2715m, Tel: 307-782-6555, Nearest town: Mountain View (WY), Agency: USFS, GPS: 40.931056, -110.182413

32166 • FSR 164 Dispersed 3 - USFS
Dispersed sites, No water, No toilets, Reservations not accepted, Open all year, Tent & RV camping: Free, Road not maintained for passenger cars, Elev: 8972ft/2735m, Tel: 307-782-6555, Nearest town: Mountain View (WY), Agency: USFS, GPS: 40.927612, -110.182744

32167 • FSR 164 Dispersed 4 - USFS
Dispersed sites, No water, No toilets, Reservations not accepted, Open all year, Tent & RV camping: Free, Road not maintained for passenger cars, Elev: 9157ft/2791m, Tel: 307-782-6555, Nearest town: Mountain View (WY), Agency: USFS, GPS: 40.922308, -110.186248

32168 • FSR 165 Dispersed 1 - USFS
Dispersed sites, No water, No toilets, Reservations not accepted, Open all year, Tent & RV camping: Free, Elev: 8258ft/2517m, Tel: 435-826-5400, Nearest town: Teasdale, Agency: USFS, GPS: 38.002013, -111.446664

32169 • FSR 165 Dispersed 2 - USFS
Dispersed sites, No water, No toilets, Reservations not accepted, Open all year, Tent & RV camping: Free, Elev: 8325ft/2537m, Tel: 435-826-5400, Nearest town: Teasdale, Agency: USFS, GPS: 38.002814, -111.452946

32170 • FSR 165 Dispersed 3 - USFS
Dispersed sites, No water, No toilets, Reservations not accepted, Open all year, Tent & RV camping: Free, Elev: 8667ft/2642m, Tel: 435-826-5400, Nearest town: Teasdale, Agency: USFS, GPS: 38.014031, -111.440036

32171 • FSR 1653A Dispersed 1 - USFS
Dispersed sites, No water, No toilets, Reservations not accepted, Open all year, Tent & RV camping: Free, Road not maintained for passenger cars, Elev: 6474ft/1973m, Tel: 435-743-5721, Nearest town: Oak City, Agency: USFS, GPS: 39.360235, -112.235167

32172 • FSR 166 Dispersed 1 - USFS
Dispersed sites, No water, No toilets, Reservations not accepted, Open all year, Tent & RV camping: Free, Road not maintained for passenger cars, Elev: 8227ft/2508m, Tel: 435-826-5400, Nearest town: Teasdale, Agency: USFS, GPS: 37.998987, -111.449205

32173 • FSR 166 Dispersed 2 - USFS
Dispersed sites, No water, No toilets, Reservations not accepted, Open all year, Tent & RV camping: Free, Road not maintained for passenger cars, Elev: 8064ft/2458m, Tel: 435-826-5400, Nearest town: Teasdale, Agency: USFS, GPS: 37.995393, -111.460991

32174 • FSR 166 Dispersed 3 - USFS
Dispersed sites, No water, No toilets, Reservations not accepted, Open all year, Tent & RV camping: Free, Road not maintained for passenger cars, Elev: 8179ft/2493m, Tel: 435-826-5400, Nearest town: Teasdale, Agency: USFS, GPS: 37.996944, -111.478298

32175 • FSR 166 Dispersed 4 - USFS
Dispersed sites, No water, No toilets, Reservations not accepted, Open all year, Tent & RV camping: Free, Road not maintained for passenger cars, Elev: 8254ft/2516m, Tel: 435-826-5400, Nearest town: Teasdale, Agency: USFS, GPS: 37.997675, -111.485447

32176 • FSR 1676 Dispersed 1 - USFS
Dispersed sites, No water, No toilets, Reservations not accepted, Open all year, Tent & RV camping: Free, Road not maintained for passenger cars, Elev: 8828ft/2691m, Tel: 435-789-1181, Nearest town: Cedar City, Agency: USFS, GPS: 37.655565, -112.684923

32177 • FSR 168 Dispersed 1 - USFS
Dispersed sites, No water, No toilets, Reservations not accepted, Open all year, Tent & RV camping: Free, Road not maintained for passenger cars, Elev: 8878ft/2706m, Tel: 435-755-3620, Nearest town: Logan, Agency: USFS, GPS: 41.728769, -111.687022

32178 • FSR 168 Dispersed 2 - USFS
Dispersed sites, No water, No toilets, Reservations not accepted, Open all year, Tent & RV camping: Free, Road not maintained for passenger cars, Elev: 7389ft/2252m, Tel: 435-755-3620, Nearest town: Millville, Agency: USFS, GPS: 41.657808, -111.745465

32179 • FSR 168 Dispersed 3 - USFS
Dispersed sites, No water, No toilets, Reservations not accepted, Open all year, Tent & RV camping: Free, High-clearance vehicle required, Elev: 7442ft/2268m, Tel: 435-738-2482, Nearest town: Duchesne, Agency: USFS, GPS: 40.054106, -110.876384

32180 • FSR 168 Dispersed 4 - USFS

Dispersed sites, No water, No toilets, Reservations not accepted, Open all year, Tent & RV camping: Free, Numerous sites in this area, Road not maintained for passenger cars, Elev: 8352ft/2546m, Tel: 435-836-2800, Nearest town: Grover, Agency: USFS, GPS: 38.097657, -111.321488

32181 • FSR 1680 Dispersed 1 - USFS

Dispersed sites, No water, No toilets, Reservations not accepted, Open all year, Tent & RV camping: Free, Elev: 7616ft/2321m, Tel: 435-743-5721, Nearest town: Joseph, Agency: USFS, GPS: 38.698534, -112.316052

32182 • FSR 1685 Dispersed 1 - USFS

Dispersed sites, No water, No toilets, Reservations not accepted, Open all year, Tent & RV camping: Free, Numerous sites in this are, Road not maintained for passenger cars, Elev: 9531ft/2905m, Tel: 435-789-1181, Nearest town: Cedar City, Agency: USFS, GPS: 37.655415, -112.737425

32183 • FSR 169 Dispersed 1 - USFS

Dispersed sites, No water, No toilets, Reservations not accepted, Open Jun-Nov, Tent & RV camping: Free, Elev: 6621ft/2018m, Tel: 435-755-3620, Nearest town: Logan, Agency: USFS, GPS: 41.799269, -111.560076

32184 • FSR 169 Dispersed 1 - USFS

Dispersed sites, No water, No toilets, Reservations not accepted, Open May-Oct, Tent & RV camping: Free, Several sites, Road not maintained for passenger cars, Elev: 8696ft/2651m, Tel: 801-798-3571, Nearest town: Nephi, Agency: USFS, GPS: 39.877834, -111.686411

32185 • FSR 169 Dispersed 3 - USFS

Dispersed sites, No water, No toilets, Reservations not accepted, Open all year, Tent & RV camping: Free, High-clearance vehicle required, Elev: 9512ft/2899m, Tel: 435-738-2482, Nearest town: Spanish Fork, Agency: USFS, GPS: 39.873524, -110.861194

32186 • FSR 169 Dispersed 4 - USFS

Dispersed sites, No water, No toilets, Reservations not accepted, Open all year, Tent & RV camping: Free, Road not maintained for passenger cars, Elev: 8671ft/2643m, Tel: 435-836-2800, Nearest town: Grover, Agency: USFS, GPS: 38.086876, -111.333035

32187 • FSR 169 Dispersed 5 - USFS

Dispersed sites, No water, No toilets, Reservations not accepted, Open all year, Tent & RV camping: Free, Road not maintained for passenger cars, Elev: 8606ft/2623m, Tel: 435-836-2800, Nearest town: Grover, Agency: USFS, GPS: 38.085923, -111.330058

32188 • FSR 169 Dispersed 6 - USFS

Dispersed sites, No water, No toilets, Reservations not accepted, Open all year, Tent & RV camping: Free, Road not maintained for passenger cars, Elev: 8538ft/2602m, Tel: 435-836-2800, Nearest town: Grover, Agency: USFS, GPS: 38.084655, -111.326548

32189 • FSR 17 Dispersed 1 - USFS

Dispersed sites, No water, No toilets, Reservations not accepted, Open all year, Tent & RV camping: Free, Elev: 8517ft/2596m, Tel: 435-826-5400, Nearest town: Escalante, Agency: USFS, GPS: 37.824113, -111.906668

32190 • FSR 170 Dispersed 1 - USFS

Dispersed sites, No water, No toilets, Reservations not accepted, Open Jun-Nov, Tent & RV camping: Free, Elev: 5942ft/1811m, Tel: 435-755-3620, Nearest town: Logan, Agency: USFS, GPS: 41.828009, -111.576595

32191 • FSR 170 Dispersed 1 - USFS

Dispersed sites, No water, No toilets, Reservations not accepted, Open Mar-Dec, Tent & RV camping: Free, Several sites, Road not maintained for passenger cars, Elev: 8072ft/2460m, Tel: 801-798-3571, Nearest town: Santaquin, Agency: USFS, GPS: 39.925709, -111.630951

32192 • FSR 1712 Dispersed 1 - USFS

Dispersed sites, No water, No toilets, Reservations not accepted, Open all year, Tent & RV camping: Free, Road not maintained for passenger cars, Elev: 7815ft/2382m, Tel: 435-789-1181, Nearest town: Alton, Agency: USFS, GPS: 37.495146, -112.557867

32193 • FSR 1712 Dispersed 2 - USFS

Dispersed sites, No water, No toilets, Reservations not accepted, Open all year, Tent & RV camping: Free, Road not maintained for passenger cars, Elev: 7793ft/2375m, Tel: 435-789-1181, Nearest town: Alton, Agency: USFS, GPS: 37.503996, -112.551647

32194 • FSR 173 Dispersed 1 - USFS

Dispersed sites, No water, No toilets, Reservations not accepted, Open all year, Tent & RV camping: Free, Road not maintained for passenger cars, Elev: 8116ft/2474m, Tel: 435-755-3620, Nearest town: Garden City, Agency: USFS, GPS: 41.892935, -111.495154

32195 • FSR 173 Dispersed 2 - USFS

Dispersed sites, No water, No toilets, Reservations not accepted, Open all year, Tent & RV camping: Free, Road not maintained for passenger cars, Elev: 8022ft/2445m, Tel: 435-755-3620, Nearest town: Garden City, Agency: USFS, GPS: 41.890047, -111.488653

32196 • FSR 173-A Dispersed 1 - USFS

Dispersed sites, No water, No toilets, Reservations not accepted, Open all year, Tent & RV camping: Free, Road not maintained for passenger cars, Elev: 8290ft/2527m, Tel: 435-755-3620, Nearest town: Garden City, Agency: USFS, GPS: 41.892975, -111.535364

32197 • FSR 1730 Dispersed 1 - USFS

Dispersed sites, No water, No toilets, Reservations not accepted, Open all year, Tent & RV camping: Free, Road not maintained for passenger cars, Elev: 8097ft/2468m, Tel: 435-789-1181, Nearest town: Duck Creek, Agency: USFS, GPS: 37.507939, -112.612299

32198 • FSR 1739 Dispersed 1 - USFS

Dispersed sites, No water, No toilets, Reservations not accepted, Open all year, Tent & RV camping: Free, Road not maintained for

passenger cars, Elev: 5483ft/1671m, Tel: 435-743-5721, Nearest town: Delta, Agency: USFS, GPS: 39.301165, -112.351412

32199 • FSR 174 Dispersed 1 - USFS
Dispersed sites, No water, No toilets, Reservations not accepted, Open Jun-Nov, Tent & RV camping: Free, Elev: 6191ft/1887m, Tel: 435-755-3620, Nearest town: Garden City, Agency: USFS, GPS: 41.876347, -111.564209

32200 • FSR 174 Dispersed 1 - USFS
Dispersed sites, No water, No toilets, Reservations not accepted, Open all year, Tent & RV camping: Free, Elev: 9656ft/2943m, Tel: 435-738-2482, Nearest town: Hanna, Agency: USFS, GPS: 40.527354, -110.924929

32201 • FSR 174 Dispersed 10 - USFS
Dispersed sites, No water, No toilets, Reservations not accepted, Open all year, Tent & RV camping: Free, Road not maintained for passenger cars, Elev: 9431ft/2875m, Tel: 435-783-4338, Nearest town: Heber City, Agency: USFS, GPS: 40.505115, -111.009262

32202 • FSR 174 Dispersed 11 - USFS
Dispersed sites, No water, No toilets, Reservations not accepted, Open all year, Tent & RV camping: Free, Road not maintained for passenger cars, Elev: 9499ft/2895m, Tel: 435-783-4338, Nearest town: Heber City, Agency: USFS, GPS: 40.501814, -111.012355

32203 • FSR 174 Dispersed 12 - USFS
Dispersed sites, No water, No toilets, Reservations not accepted, Open all year, Tent & RV camping: Free, Road not maintained for passenger cars, Elev: 9567ft/2916m, Tel: 435-783-4338, Nearest town: Heber City, Agency: USFS, GPS: 40.500042, -111.015666

32204 • FSR 174 Dispersed 13 - USFS
Dispersed sites, No water, No toilets, Reservations not accepted, Open all year, Tent & RV camping: Free, Road not maintained for passenger cars, Elev: 9601ft/2926m, Tel: 435-783-4338, Nearest town: Heber City, Agency: USFS, GPS: 40.497347, -111.016517

32205 • FSR 174 Dispersed 2 - USFS
Dispersed sites, No water, No toilets, Reservations not accepted, Open all year, Tent & RV camping: Free, Elev: 9128ft/2782m, Tel: 435-738-2482, Nearest town: Hanna, Agency: USFS, GPS: 40.507794, -110.899837

32206 • FSR 174 Dispersed 3 - USFS
Dispersed sites, No water, No toilets, Reservations not accepted, Open all year, Tent & RV camping: Free, Road not maintained for passenger cars, Elev: 9704ft/2958m, Tel: 435-783-4338, Nearest town: Heber City, Agency: USFS, GPS: 40.515777, -110.970806

32207 • FSR 174 Dispersed 4 - USFS
Dispersed sites, No water, No toilets, Reservations not accepted, Open all year, Tent & RV camping: Free, Road not maintained for passenger cars, Elev: 9799ft/2987m, Tel: 435-783-4338, Nearest town: Heber City, Agency: USFS, GPS: 40.517189, -110.975063

32208 • FSR 174 Dispersed 5 - USFS
Dispersed sites, No water, No toilets, Reservations not accepted, Open all year, Tent & RV camping: Free, Road not maintained for passenger cars, Elev: 9826ft/2995m, Tel: 435-783-4338, Nearest town: Heber City, Agency: USFS, GPS: 40.516329, -110.975874

32209 • FSR 174 Dispersed 6 - USFS
Dispersed sites, No water, No toilets, Reservations not accepted, Open all year, Tent & RV camping: Free, Road not maintained for passenger cars, Elev: 9877ft/3011m, Tel: 435-783-4338, Nearest town: Heber City, Agency: USFS, GPS: 40.512694, -110.980564

32210 • FSR 174 Dispersed 7 - USFS
Dispersed sites, No water, No toilets, Reservations not accepted, Open all year, Tent & RV camping: Free, Road not maintained for passenger cars, Elev: 9876ft/3010m, Tel: 435-783-4338, Nearest town: Heber City, Agency: USFS, GPS: 40.510965, -110.980291

32211 • FSR 174 Dispersed 8 - USFS
Dispersed sites, No water, No toilets, Reservations not accepted, Open all year, Tent & RV camping: Free, Road not maintained for passenger cars, Elev: 9843ft/3000m, Tel: 435-783-4338, Nearest town: Heber City, Agency: USFS, GPS: 40.508773, -110.983597

32212 • FSR 174 Dispersed 9 - USFS
Dispersed sites, No water, No toilets, Reservations not accepted, Open all year, Tent & RV camping: Free, Road not maintained for passenger cars, Elev: 9529ft/2904m, Tel: 435-783-4338, Nearest town: Heber City, Agency: USFS, GPS: 40.506881, -110.996371

32213 • FSR 1745 Dispersed 1 - USFS
Dispersed sites, No water, No toilets, Reservations not accepted, Open all year, Tent & RV camping: Free, Road not maintained for passenger cars, Elev: 8387ft/2556m, Tel: 435-789-1181, Nearest town: Duck Creek, Agency: USFS, GPS: 37.535361, -112.640601

32214 • FSR 174A Dispersed1 - USFS
Dispersed sites, No water, No toilets, Reservations not accepted, Tent & RV camping: Free, Elev: 6165ft/1879m, Tel: 435-755-3620, Nearest town: Garden City, Agency: USFS, GPS: 41.872117, -111.565173

32215 • FSR 175 Dispersed 1 - USFS
Dispersed sites, No water, No toilets, Reservations not accepted, Open all year, Tent & RV camping: Free, Several sites in area, Road not maintained for passenger cars, Elev: 8499ft/2590m, Tel: 435-755-3620, Nearest town: Garden City, Agency: USFS, GPS: 41.864163, -111.497422

32216 • FSR 1755 Dispersed 1 - USFS
Dispersed sites, No water, No toilets, Reservations not accepted, Open all year, Tent & RV camping: Free, Elev: 8144ft/2482m, Tel: 435-789-1181, Nearest town: Duck Creek, Agency: USFS, GPS: 37.512476, -112.619564

32217 • FSR 176 Dispersed 1 - USFS
Dispersed sites, No water, No toilets, Reservations not accepted, Open all year, Tent & RV camping: Free, Several sites in this area,

Elev: 10271ft/3131m, Tel: 435-826-5400, Nearest town: Teasdale, Agency: USFS, GPS: 38.066369, -111.585319

32218 • FSR 1767 Dispersed 1 - USFS

Dispersed sites, No water, No toilets, Reservations not accepted, Open all year, Tent & RV camping: Free, Road not maintained for passenger cars, Elev: 7901ft/2408m, Tel: 435-789-1181, Nearest town: Duck Creek, Agency: USFS, GPS: 37.533581, -112.595104

32219 • FSR 177 Dispersed 1 - USFS

Dispersed sites, No water, No toilets, Reservations not accepted, Open all year, Tent & RV camping: Free, Elev: 7029ft/2142m, Tel: 801-723-2660, Nearest town: Farmington, Agency: USFS, GPS: 40.913088, -111.828655

32220 • FSR 1771 Dispersed 1 - USFS

Dispersed sites, No water, No toilets, Reservations not accepted, Open all year, Tents only: Free, Road not maintained for passenger cars, Elev: 7763ft/2366m, Tel: 435-789-1181, Nearest town: Duck Creek, Agency: USFS, GPS: 37.547801, -112.550595

32221 • FSR 179 Dispersed 1 - USFS

Dispersed sites, No water, No toilets, Reservations not accepted, Open all year, Tent & RV camping: Free, Road not maintained for passenger cars, Elev: 8589ft/2618m, Tel: 435-836-2800, Nearest town: Grover, Agency: USFS, GPS: 38.194912, -111.391731

32222 • FSR 179 Dispersed 2 - USFS

Dispersed sites, No water, No toilets, Reservations not accepted, Open all year, Tent & RV camping: Free, Road not maintained for passenger cars, Elev: 8628ft/2630m, Tel: 435-836-2800, Nearest town: Grover, Agency: USFS, GPS: 38.193993, -111.395132

32223 • FSR 179 Dispersed 3 - USFS

Dispersed sites, No water, No toilets, Reservations not accepted, Open all year, Tent & RV camping: Free, Road not maintained for passenger cars, Elev: 8696ft/2651m, Tel: 435-836-2800, Nearest town: Grover, Agency: USFS, GPS: 38.193995, -111.400991

32224 • FSR 179 Dispersed 4 - USFS

Dispersed sites, No water, No toilets, Reservations not accepted, Open all year, Tent & RV camping: Free, Road not maintained for passenger cars, Elev: 8648ft/2636m, Tel: 435-836-2800, Nearest town: Grover, Agency: USFS, GPS: 38.195137, -111.403298

32225 • FSR 179 Dispersed 5 - USFS

Dispersed sites, No water, No toilets, Reservations not accepted, Open all year, Tent & RV camping: Free, Road not maintained for passenger cars, Elev: 9175ft/2797m, Tel: 435-836-2800, Nearest town: Grover, Agency: USFS, GPS: 38.200163, -111.414206

32226 • FSR 180 Dispersed 1 - USFS

Dispersed sites, No water, No toilets, Reservations not accepted, Open all year, Tent & RV camping: Free, Road not maintained for passenger cars, Elev: 7709ft/2350m, Tel: 801-785-3563, Nearest town: Charleston, Agency: USFS, GPS: 40.458308, -111.581748

32227 • FSR 180 Dispersed 2 - USFS

Dispersed sites, No water, No toilets, Reservations not accepted, Open all year, Tent & RV camping: Free, Road not maintained for passenger cars, Elev: 7925ft/2416m, Tel: 801-785-3563, Nearest town: Charleston, Agency: USFS, GPS: 40.464634, -111.584862

32228 • FSR 180 Dispersed 3 - USFS

Dispersed sites, No water, No toilets, Reservations not accepted, Open all year, Tent & RV camping: Free, Road not maintained for passenger cars, Elev: 7989ft/2435m, Tel: 801-785-3563, Nearest town: Charleston, Agency: USFS, GPS: 40.464461, -111.581198

32229 • FSR 180 Dispersed 4 - USFS

Dispersed sites, No water, No toilets, Reservations not accepted, Open all year, Tent & RV camping: Free, Road not maintained for passenger cars, Elev: 8070ft/2460m, Tel: 801-785-3563, Nearest town: Charleston, Agency: USFS, GPS: 40.468729, -111.582927

32230 • FSR 180 Dispersed 5 - USFS

Dispersed sites, No water, No toilets, Reservations not accepted, Open all year, Tent & RV camping: Free, Road not maintained for passenger cars, Elev: 8141ft/2481m, Tel: 801-785-3563, Nearest town: Charleston, Agency: USFS, GPS: 40.470246, -111.584386

32231 • FSR 180 Dispersed 6 - USFS

Dispersed sites, No water, No toilets, Reservations not accepted, Open all year, Tent & RV camping: Free, Road not maintained for passenger cars, Elev: 8347ft/2544m, Tel: 801-785-3563, Nearest town: Charleston, Agency: USFS, GPS: 40.474128, -111.588195

32232 • FSR 180 Dispersed 7 - USFS

Dispersed sites, No water, No toilets, Reservations not accepted, Open all year, Tent & RV camping: Free, High-clearance vehicle required, At end of road, Elev: 9021ft/2750m, Tel: 435-738-2482, Nearest town: Hanna, Agency: USFS, GPS: 40.528574, -110.900013

32233 • FSR 1800 Dispersed 1 - USFS

Dispersed sites, No water, No toilets, Reservations not accepted, Open all year, Tent & RV camping: Free, Road not maintained for passenger cars, Elev: 9146ft/2788m, Tel: 435-743-5721, Nearest town: Fillmore, Agency: USFS, GPS: 38.937096, -112.189214

32234 • FSR 1805 Dispersed 1 - USFS

Dispersed sites, No water, No toilets, Reservations not accepted, Open all year, Tent & RV camping: Free, Road not maintained for passenger cars, Elev: 7795ft/2376m, Tel: 435-438-2430, Nearest town: Beaver, Agency: USFS, GPS: 38.515884, -112.437163

32235 • FSR 1808 Dispersed 1 - USFS

Dispersed sites, No water, No toilets, Reservations not accepted, Open all year, Tents only: Free, Road not maintained for passenger cars, Elev: 6986ft/2129m, Tel: 435-438-2430, Nearest town: Beaver, Agency: USFS, GPS: 38.501221, -112.564113

32236 • FSR 181 Dispersed 1 - USFS

Dispersed sites, No water, No toilets, Reservations not accepted, Open all year, Tent & RV camping: Free, Road not maintained for

passenger cars, Elev: 7507ft/2288m, Tel: 435-755-3620, Nearest town: Logan, Agency: USFS, GPS: 41.803509, -111.459083

32237 • FSR 181 Dispersed 2 - USFS

Dispersed sites, No water, No toilets, Reservations not accepted, Open all year, Tent & RV camping: Free, Road not maintained for passenger cars, Elev: 8756ft/2669m, Tel: 435-783-4338, Nearest town: Woodland, Agency: USFS, GPS: 40.515677, -111.033827

32238 • FSR 182 Dispersed 1 - USFS

Dispersed sites, No water, No toilets, Reservations not accepted, Open Apr-Nov, Tent & RV camping: Free, Road not maintained for passenger cars, Elev: 7685ft/2342m, Tel: 801-785-3563, Nearest town: Midway, Agency: USFS, GPS: 40.530803, -111.594464

32239 • FSR 182 Dispersed 2 - USFS

Dispersed sites, No water, No toilets, Reservations not accepted, Open all year, Tents only: Free, Road not maintained for passenger cars, Elev: 6936ft/2114m, Tel: 435-789-1181, Nearest town: Manila, Agency: USFS, GPS: 40.935353, -109.673418

32240 • FSR 184 Dispersed 1 - USFS

Dispersed sites, No water, No toilets, Reservations not accepted, Open Apr-Nov, Tent & RV camping: Free, Road not maintained for passenger cars, Elev: 8937ft/2724m, Tel: 801-785-3563, Nearest town: Midway, Agency: USFS, GPS: 40.531461, -111.570454

32241 • FSR 185 Dispersed 1 - USFS

Dispersed sites, No water, No toilets, Reservations not accepted, Open all year, Tent & RV camping: Free, Road not maintained for passenger cars, Elev: 8410ft/2563m, Tel: 435-676-9316, Nearest town: Bryce, Agency: USFS, GPS: 37.604747, -112.235206

32242 • FSR 186 Dispersed 1 - USFS

Dispersed sites, No water, No toilets, Reservations not accepted, Open Apr-Nov, Tent & RV camping: Free, Road not maintained for passenger cars, Elev: 7780ft/2371m, Tel: 801-785-3563, Nearest town: Midway, Agency: USFS, GPS: 40.568915, -111.555734

32243 • FSR 186 Dispersed 2 - USFS

Dispersed sites, No water, No toilets, Reservations not accepted, Open all year, Tent & RV camping: Free, High-clearance required, Elev: 8820ft/2688m, Tel: 435-738-2482, Nearest town: Altamont, Agency: USFS, GPS: 40.529343, -110.492617

32244 • FSR 1864 Dispersed 1 - USFS

Dispersed sites, No water, No toilets, Reservations not accepted, Open all year, Tent & RV camping: Free, Road not maintained for passenger cars, Elev: 8807ft/2684m, Tel: 435-789-1181, Nearest town: Panguitch, Agency: USFS, GPS: 37.751866, -112.629958

32245 • FSR 1867 Dispersed 1 - USFS

Dispersed sites, No water, No toilets, Max length: 18ft, Reservations not accepted, Open all year, Tent & RV camping: Free, No trailers, Road not maintained for passenger cars, Elev: 8956ft/2730m, Tel: 435-789-1181, Nearest town: Duck Creek, Agency: USFS, GPS: 37.506637, -112.710034

32246 • FSR 188 Dispersed 1 - USFS

Dispersed sites, No water, No toilets, Reservations not accepted, Open all year, Tent & RV camping: Free, Road not maintained for passenger cars, Elev: 8527ft/2599m, Tel: 801-625-5112, Nearest town: Woodruff, Agency: USFS, GPS: 41.406983, -111.491501

32247 • FSR 188 Dispersed 2 - USFS

Dispersed sites, No water, No toilets, Reservations not accepted, Open all year, Tent & RV camping: Free, Elev: 9416ft/2870m, Tel: 307-782-6555, Nearest town: Mountain View (WY), Agency: USFS, GPS: 40.935507, -110.400199

32248 • FSR 191 Dispersed 1 - USFS

Dispersed sites, No water, No toilets, Reservations not accepted, Open all year, Tent & RV camping: Free, Road not maintained for passenger cars, Elev: 7744ft/2360m, Tel: 435-676-9307, Nearest town: Panguitch, Agency: USFS, GPS: 37.803989, -112.140671

32249 • FSR 191 Dispersed 2 - USFS

Dispersed sites, No water, No toilets, Reservations not accepted, Open all year, Tent & RV camping: Free, Road not maintained for passenger cars, Elev: 7760ft/2365m, Tel: 435-676-9307, Nearest town: Panguitch, Agency: USFS, GPS: 37.806315, -112.141055

32250 • FSR 192 Dispersed 1 - USFS

Dispersed sites, No water, No toilets, Reservations not accepted, Open all year, Tent & RV camping: Free, Road not maintained for passenger cars, Elev: 8619ft/2627m, Tel: 801-625-5112, Nearest town: Randolph, Agency: USFS, GPS: 41.589074, -111.431357

32251 • FSR 192 Dispersed 2 - USFS

Dispersed sites, No water, No toilets, Reservations not accepted, Open all year, Tent & RV camping: Free, Road not maintained for passenger cars, Elev: 8578ft/2615m, Tel: 801-625-5112, Nearest town: Randolph, Agency: USFS, GPS: 41.586628, -111.434377

32252 • FSR 192 Dispersed 3 - USFS

Dispersed sites, No water, No toilets, Reservations not accepted, Open all year, Tent & RV camping: Free, Road not maintained for passenger cars, Elev: 8514ft/2595m, Tel: 801-625-5112, Nearest town: Randolph, Agency: USFS, GPS: 41.581354, -111.434655

32253 • FSR 192 Dispersed 4 - USFS

Dispersed sites, No water, No toilets, Reservations not accepted, Open all year, Tent & RV camping: Free, Road not maintained for passenger cars, Elev: 9003ft/2744m, Tel: 435-896-9233, Nearest town: Greenwich, Agency: USFS, GPS: 38.481415, -112.001116

32254 • FSR 193 Dispersed 1 - USFS

Dispersed sites, No water, No toilets, Reservations not accepted, Open all year, Tent & RV camping: Free, Road not maintained for passenger cars, Elev: 7351ft/2241m, Tel: 435-789-1181, Nearest town: Hatch, Agency: USFS, GPS: 37.539416, -112.515945

32255 • FSR 194 (Forest Lake) Dispersed 2 - USFS

Dispersed sites, No water, No toilets, Reservations not accepted, Open Apr-Nov, Tent & RV camping: Free, Road not maintained for passenger cars, Elev: 8553ft/2607m, Tel: 801-785-3563, Nearest town: Midway, Agency: USFS, GPS: 40.511425, -111.589044

32256 • FSR 194 Dispersed 1 - USFS

Dispersed sites, No water, No toilets, Reservations not accepted, Open Apr-Nov, Tent & RV camping: Free, Several sites in this areas, Road not maintained for passenger cars, Elev: 7593ft/2314m, Tel: 801-785-3563, Nearest town: Midway, Agency: USFS, GPS: 40.521419, -111.608191

32257 • FSR 196 Dispersed 1 - USFS

Dispersed sites, No water, No toilets, Reservations not accepted, Open all year, Tent & RV camping: Free, Several sites on this short road, Road not maintained for passenger cars, Elev: 8444ft/2574m, Tel: 801-625-5112, Nearest town: Woodruff, Agency: USFS, GPS: 41.517047, -111.507296

32258 • FSR 196 Dispersed 2 - USFS

Dispersed sites, No water, No toilets, Reservations not accepted, Open all year, Tent & RV camping: Free, Elev: 7283ft/2220m, Tel: 435-783-4338, Nearest town: Woodland, Agency: USFS, GPS: 40.564892, -111.151127

32259 • FSR 196 Dispersed 3 - USFS

Dispersed sites, No water, No toilets, Reservations not accepted, Open all year, Tent & RV camping: Free, Elev: 8463ft/2580m, Tel: 435-738-2482, Nearest town: Altamont, Agency: USFS, GPS: 40.521942, -110.385971

32260 • FSR 196 Dispersed 4 - USFS

Dispersed sites, No water, No toilets, Reservations not accepted, Open all year, Tent & RV camping: Free, Road not maintained for passenger cars, Elev: 8150ft/2484m, Tel: 435-789-1181, Nearest town: Cedar City, Agency: USFS, GPS: 37.616666, -112.660603

32261 • FSR 196 Dispersed 5 - USFS

Dispersed sites, No water, No toilets, Reservations not accepted, Open all year, Tent & RV camping: Free, Road not maintained for passenger cars, Elev: 8280ft/2524m, Tel: 435-789-1181, Nearest town: Cedar City, Agency: USFS, GPS: 37.613149, -112.668496

32262 • FSR 197 Dispersed 1 - USFS

Dispersed sites, No water, No toilets, Reservations not accepted, Open Apr-Nov, Tent & RV camping: Free, Road not maintained for passenger cars, Elev: 8082ft/2463m, Tel: 801-785-3563, Nearest town: Midway, Agency: USFS, GPS: 40.558653, -111.548176

32263 • FSR 197 Dispersed 2 - USFS

Dispersed sites, No water, No toilets, Reservations not accepted, Open all year, Tent & RV camping: Free, High-clearance vehicle required, Elev: 8999ft/2743m, Tel: 435-738-2482, Nearest town: Hanna, Agency: USFS, GPS: 40.494655, -110.693888

32264 • FSR 198 Dispersed 1 - USFS

Dispersed sites, No water, No toilets, Reservations not accepted, Open Apr-Nov, Tent & RV camping: Free, Road not maintained for passenger cars, Elev: 7784ft/2373m, Tel: 801-785-3563, Nearest town: Midway, Agency: USFS, GPS: 40.539743, -111.591873

32265 • FSR 198 Dispersed 2 - USFS

Dispersed sites, No water, No toilets, Reservations not accepted, Open Apr-Nov, Tent & RV camping: Free, Road not maintained for passenger cars, Elev: 8277ft/2523m, Tel: 801-785-3563, Nearest town: Midway, Agency: USFS, GPS: 40.550076, -111.582844

32266 • FSR 198 Dispersed 3 - USFS

Dispersed sites, No water, No toilets, Reservations not accepted, Open Apr-Nov, Tent & RV camping: Free, Road not maintained for passenger cars, Elev: 8893ft/2711m, Tel: 801-785-3563, Nearest town: Midway, Agency: USFS, GPS: 40.563191, -111.586831

32267 • FSR 2004A Dispersed 1 - USFS

Dispersed sites, No water, No toilets, Reservations not accepted, Open all year, Tent & RV camping: Free, Large area, Road not maintained for passenger cars, Elev: 8546ft/2605m, Tel: 435-896-9233, Nearest town: Glenwood, Agency: USFS, GPS: 38.668311, -111.938967

32268 • FSR 202 Dispersed 1 - USFS

Dispersed sites, No water, No toilets, Reservations not accepted, Open all year, Tent & RV camping: Free, Road not maintained for passenger cars, Elev: 8828ft/2691m, Tel: 801-625-5112, Nearest town: Woodruff, Agency: USFS, GPS: 41.439429, -111.493021

32269 • FSR 202 Dispersed 2 - USFS

Dispersed sites, No water, No toilets, Reservations not accepted, Open all year, Tent & RV camping: Free, Elev: 7196ft/2193m, Tel: 435-783-4338, Nearest town: Woodland, Agency: USFS, GPS: 40.561129, -111.154725

32270 • FSR 202 Dispersed 3 - USFS

Dispersed sites, No water, No toilets, Reservations not accepted, Open all year, Tent & RV camping: Free, Elev: 7306ft/2227m, Tel: 435-783-4338, Nearest town: Woodland, Agency: USFS, GPS: 40.562958, -111.145491

32271 • FSR 2020 Dispersed 1 - USFS

Dispersed sites, No water, No toilets, Reservations not accepted, Open all year, Tent & RV camping: Free, Road not maintained for passenger cars, Elev: 8046ft/2452m, Tel: 435-896-9233, Nearest town: Salina, Agency: USFS, GPS: 38.879351, -111.516781

32272 • FSR 2024 Dispersed 1 - USFS

Dispersed sites, No water, No toilets, Reservations not accepted, Open all year, Tent & RV camping: Free, Several sites in this area, Elev: 8368ft/2551m, Tel: 435-789-1181, Nearest town: Duck Creek, Agency: USFS, GPS: 37.544705, -112.647694

32273 • FSR 203 Dispersed 1 - USFS

Dispersed sites, No water, No toilets, Reservations not accepted, Open all year, Tent & RV camping: Free, Road not maintained for passenger cars, Elev: 8522ft/2598m, Tel: 435-676-9316, Nearest town: Alton, Agency: USFS, GPS: 37.442448, -112.298227

32274 • FSR 203 Dispersed 2 - USFS

Dispersed sites, No water, No toilets, Reservations not accepted, Open all year, Tents only: Free, On edge of 800' bluff, Road not maintained for passenger cars, Elev: 9014ft/2747m, Tel: 435-676-9316, Nearest town: Alton, Agency: USFS, GPS: 37.440696, -112.313421

32275 • FSR 203 Dispersed 3 - USFS

Dispersed sites, No water, No toilets, Reservations not accepted, Open all year, Tent & RV camping: Free, Road not maintained for passenger cars, Elev: 9898ft/3017m, Tel: 435-836-2800, Nearest town: Lyman, Agency: USFS, GPS: 38.473176, -111.460378

32276 • FSR 205 Dispersed 1 - USFS

Dispersed sites, No water, No toilets, Reservations not accepted, Open all year, Tent & RV camping: Free, Road not maintained for passenger cars, Elev: 8743ft/2665m, Tel: 801-625-5112, Nearest town: Randolph, Agency: USFS, GPS: 41.640242, -111.417709

32277 • FSR 2059 Dispersed 1 - USFS

Dispersed sites, No water, No toilets, Reservations not accepted, Open all year, Tent & RV camping: Free, Road not maintained for passenger cars, Elev: 8048ft/2453m, Tel: 435-789-1181, Nearest town: Hatch, Agency: USFS, GPS: 37.669419, -112.513405

32278 • FSR 206 Dispersed 1 - USFS

Dispersed sites, No water, No toilets, Reservations not accepted, Open all year, Tent & RV camping: Free, Road not maintained for passenger cars, Elev: 8278ft/2523m, Tel: 801-625-5112, Nearest town: Woodruff, Agency: USFS, GPS: 41.394001, -111.467407

32279 • FSR 206 Dispersed 2 - USFS

Dispersed sites, No water, No toilets, Reservations not accepted, Open all year, Tent & RV camping: Free, Road not maintained for passenger cars, Elev: 9431ft/2875m, Tel: 435-836-2800, Nearest town: Lyman, Agency: USFS, GPS: 38.493931, -111.460711

32280 • FSR 206 Dispersed 3 - USFS

Dispersed sites, No water, No toilets, Reservations not accepted, Open all year, Tent & RV camping: Free, Road not maintained for passenger cars, Elev: 9764ft/2976m, Tel: 435-836-2800, Nearest town: Lyman, Agency: USFS, GPS: 38.478772, -111.459549

32281 • FSR 206D Dispersed 1 - USFS

Dispersed sites, No water, No toilets, Reservations not accepted, Open all year, Tent & RV camping: Free, Elev: 9410ft/2868m, Tel: 435-836-2800, Nearest town: Lyman, Agency: USFS, GPS: 38.509915, -111.476067

32282 • FSR 206F Dispersed 1 - USFS

Dispersed sites, No water, No toilets, Reservations not accepted, Open all year, Tent & RV camping: Free, Elev: 9385ft/2861m, Tel: 435-836-2800, Nearest town: Lyman, Agency: USFS, GPS: 38.509078, -111.474279

32283 • FSR 206H Dispersed 1 - USFS

Dispersed sites, No water, No toilets, Reservations not accepted, Open all year, Tent & RV camping: Free, Elev: 9416ft/2870m, Tel: 435-836-2800, Nearest town: Lyman, Agency: USFS, GPS: 38.505178, -111.469846

32284 • FSR 206J Dispersed 1 - USFS

Dispersed sites, No water, No toilets, Reservations not accepted, Open all year, Tent & RV camping: Free, Elev: 9435ft/2876m, Tel: 435-836-2800, Nearest town: Lyman, Agency: USFS, GPS: 38.505387, -111.462933

32285 • FSR 206K Dispersed 1 - USFS

Dispersed sites, No water, No toilets, Reservations not accepted, Open all year, Tent & RV camping: Free, Elev: 9426ft/2873m, Tel: 435-836-2800, Nearest town: Lyman, Agency: USFS, GPS: 38.504616, -111.467312

32286 • FSR 206M Dispersed 1 - USFS

Dispersed sites, No water, No toilets, Reservations not accepted, Open all year, Tent & RV camping: Free, Elev: 9464ft/2885m, Tel: 435-836-2800, Nearest town: Lyman, Agency: USFS, GPS: 38.500912, -111.465344

32287 • FSR 206U Dispersed 1 - USFS

Dispersed sites, No water, No toilets, Reservations not accepted, Open all year, Tent & RV camping: Free, Road not maintained for passenger cars, Elev: 9884ft/3013m, Tel: 435-836-2800, Nearest town: Lyman, Agency: USFS, GPS: 38.469166, -111.456025

32288 • FSR 207 Dispersed 1 - USFS

Dispersed sites, No water, No toilets, Reservations not accepted, Open all year, Tent & RV camping: Free, Road not maintained for passenger cars, Elev: 7165ft/2184m, Tel: 435-836-2800, Nearest town: Torrey, Agency: USFS, GPS: 38.321343, -111.450353

32289 • FSR 208 Dispersed 1 - USFS

Dispersed sites, No water, No toilets, Reservations not accepted, Open all year, Tent & RV camping: Free, Elev: 6050ft/1844m, Tel: 435-789-1181, Nearest town: Manila, Agency: USFS, GPS: 40.983395, -109.542189

32290 • FSR 208 Dispersed 2 - USFS

Dispersed sites, No water, No toilets, Reservations not accepted, Open all year, Tents only: Free, Spectacular spot on top of 1000' bluff, Road not maintained for passenger cars, Elev: 8943ft/2726m, Tel: 435-676-9316, Nearest town: Alton, Agency: USFS, GPS: 37.430908, -112.398484

32291 • FSR 208 Dispersed 3- USFS

Dispersed sites, No water, No toilets, Reservations not accepted, Open all year, Tent & RV camping: Free, At end of road, Road not maintained for passenger cars, Elev: 9758ft/2974m, Tel: 435-836-2800, Nearest town: Lyman, Agency: USFS, GPS: 38.381382, -111.503137

32292 • FSR 209 Dispersed 1 - USFS

Dispersed sites, No water, No toilets, Reservations not accepted, Open all year, Tent & RV camping: Free, Road not maintained for passenger cars, Elev: 9840ft/2999m, Tel: 435-836-2800, Nearest town: Lyman, Agency: USFS, GPS: 38.467213, -111.456463

32293 • FSR 209 Dispersed 2 - USFS

Dispersed sites, No water, No toilets, Reservations not accepted, Open all year, Tents only: Free, Road not maintained for passenger cars, Elev: 10528ft/3209m, Tel: 435-836-2800, Nearest town: Lyman, Agency: USFS, GPS: 38.438455, -111.463513

32294 • FSR 209 Dispersed 3 - USFS

Dispersed sites, No water, No toilets, Reservations not accepted, Open all year, Tent & RV camping: Free, Road not maintained for

passenger cars, Elev: 10547ft/3215m, Tel: 435-836-2800, Nearest town: Lyman, Agency: USFS, GPS: 38.408994, -111.460309

32295 • FSR 209 Dispersed 4 - USFS

Dispersed sites, No water, No toilets, Reservations not accepted, Open all year, Tent & RV camping: Free, 2nd spot just west of here, Elev: 6060ft/1847m, Tel: 435-789-1181, Nearest town: Manila, Agency: USFS, GPS: 40.989547, -109.529219

32296 • FSR 209 Dispersed 5 - USFS

Dispersed sites, No water, No toilets, Reservations not accepted, Open all year, Tent & RV camping: Free, Road not maintained for passenger cars, Elev: 8704ft/2653m, Tel: 435-676-9316, Nearest town: Alton, Agency: USFS, GPS: 37.409295, -112.361444

32297 • FSR 2092 Dispersed 1 - USFS

Dispersed sites, No water, No toilets, Reservations not accepted, Open all year, Tent & RV camping: Free, Road not maintained for passenger cars, Elev: 7412ft/2259m, Tel: 435-789-1181, Nearest town: Panguitch, Agency: USFS, GPS: 37.829934, -112.515345

32298 • FSR 209P Dispersed 1 - USFS

Dispersed sites, No water, No toilets, Reservations not accepted, Open all year, Tent & RV camping: Free, Road not maintained for passenger cars, Elev: 10562ft/3219m, Tel: 435-836-2800, Nearest town: Lyman, Agency: USFS, GPS: 38.419335, -111.460088

32299 • FSR 210 (Salamander Flat) Dispersed - USFS

Dispersed sites, No water, No toilets, Reservations not accepted, Open May-Oct, Tent & RV camping: Free, Road not maintained for passenger cars, Elev: 7585ft/2312m, Tel: 801-785-3563, Nearest town: Charleston, Agency: USFS, GPS: 40.439778, -111.626918

32300 • FSR 2108 Dispersed 1 - USFS

Dispersed sites, No water, No toilets, Reservations not accepted, Open all year, Tent & RV camping: Free, Road not maintained for passenger cars, Elev: 8863ft/2701m, Tel: 435-896-9233, Nearest town: Salina, Agency: USFS, GPS: 38.818605, -111.662442

32301 • FSR 211 Dispersed 1 - USFS

Dispersed sites, No water, No toilets, Reservations not accepted, Open all year, Tent & RV camping: Free, Road not maintained for passenger cars, Elev: 7861ft/2396m, Tel: 435-789-1181, Nearest town: Kanarraville, Agency: USFS, GPS: 37.577434, -113.311059

32302 • FSR 212 Dispersed 1 - USFS

Dispersed sites, No water, No toilets, Reservations not accepted, Open all year, Tent & RV camping: Free, Elev: 8485ft/2586m, Tel: 801-625-5112, Nearest town: Randolph, Agency: USFS, GPS: 41.615239, -111.444762

32303 • FSR 212 Dispersed 2 - USFS

Dispersed sites, No water, No toilets, Reservations not accepted, Open all year, Tent & RV camping: Free, Elev: 7402ft/2256m, Tel: 435-738-2482, Nearest town: Whiterocks, Agency: USFS, GPS: 40.599001, -110.122433

32304 • FSR 2125A Dispersed 1 - USFS

Dispersed sites, No water, No toilets, Reservations not accepted, Open all year, Tent & RV camping: Free, Elev: 8528ft/2599m, Tel: 435-896-9233, Nearest town: Glenwood, Agency: USFS, GPS: 38.668637, -111.942596

32305 • FSR 214 Dispersed 1 - USFS

Dispersed sites, No water, No toilets, Reservations not accepted, Open all year, Tent & RV camping: Free, Several sites in this area, Road not maintained for passenger cars, Elev: 6952ft/2119m, Tel: 801-785-3563, Nearest town: Charleston, Agency: USFS, GPS: 40.448488, -111.589554

32306 • FSR 215 Dispersed 1 - USFS

Dispersed sites, No water, No toilets, Reservations not accepted, Open Jun-Oct, Tent & RV camping: Free, Road not maintained for passenger cars, Elev: 8437ft/2572m, Tel: 435-783-4338, Nearest town: Springville, Agency: USFS, GPS: 40.252649, -111.296811

32307 • FSR 2154 Dispersed 1 - USFS

Dispersed sites, No water, No toilets, Reservations not accepted, Open all year, Tent & RV camping: Free, Elev: 7508ft/2288m, Tel: 435-896-9233, Nearest town: Monroe, Agency: USFS, GPS: 38.577312, -112.087329

32308 • FSR 216 Dispersed 1 - USFS

Dispersed sites, No water, No toilets, Reservations not accepted, Open all year, Tent & RV camping: Free, Road not maintained for passenger cars, Elev: 8523ft/2598m, Tel: 801-625-5112, Nearest town: Randolph, Agency: USFS, GPS: 41.580069, -111.433736

32309 • FSR 216 Dispersed 2 - USFS

Dispersed sites, No water, No toilets, Reservations not accepted, Open all year, Tent & RV camping: Free, Road not maintained for passenger cars, Elev: 8049ft/2453m, Tel: 435-836-2800, Nearest town: Fremont, Agency: USFS, GPS: 38.640319, -111.425932

32310 • FSR 2168 Dispersed 1 - USFS

Dispersed sites, No water, No toilets, Reservations not accepted, Open all year, Tent & RV camping: Free, Road not maintained for passenger cars, Elev: 9054ft/2760m, Tel: 435-896-9233, Nearest town: Koosharem, Agency: USFS, GPS: 38.526444, -111.973127

32311 • FSR 216A Dispersed 1 - USFS

Dispersed sites, No water, Vault toilets, Reservations not accepted, Open all year, Tent & RV camping: Free, Elev: 7476ft/2279m, Tel: 435-738-2482, Nearest town: Hanna, Agency: USFS, GPS: 40.552087, -110.887992

32312 • FSR 217 Dispersed 1 - USFS

Dispersed sites, No water, No toilets, Reservations not accepted, Open all year, Tent & RV camping: Free, Road not maintained for passenger cars, Elev: 7437ft/2267m, Tel: 801-785-3563, Nearest town: Charleston, Agency: USFS, GPS: 40.447055, -111.607363

32313 • FSR 2176 Dispersed 1 - USFS

Dispersed sites, No water, No toilets, Reservations not accepted, Open all year, Tent & RV camping: Free, Elev: 8055ft/2455m, Tel:

435-896-9233, Nearest town: Koosharem, Agency: USFS, GPS: 38.521969, -111.937808

32314 • FSR 218 Dispersed 1 - USFS

Dispersed sites, No water, No toilets, Reservations not accepted, Open all year, Tent & RV camping: Free, Elev: 8323ft/2537m, Tel: 435-789-1181, Nearest town: Manila, Agency: USFS, GPS: 40.881442, -109.763683

32315 • FSR 218 Dispersed 2 - USFS

Dispersed sites, No water, No toilets, Reservations not accepted, Open all year, Tent & RV camping: Free, Road not maintained for passenger cars, Elev: 9042ft/2756m, Tel: 307-782-6555, Nearest town: Mountain View (WY), Agency: USFS, GPS: 40.939283, -110.234089

32316 • FSR 219 Dispersed 1 - USFS

Dispersed sites, No water, No toilets, Reservations not accepted, Open Jun-Oct, Tent & RV camping: Free, Road not maintained for passenger cars, Elev: 7182ft/2189m, Tel: 435-783-4338, Nearest town: Springville, Agency: USFS, GPS: 40.121584, -111.294483

32317 • FSR 220 Dispersed 1 - USFS

Dispersed sites, No water, No toilets, Reservations not accepted, Open all year, Tent & RV camping: Free, Elev: 7957ft/2425m, Tel: 801-785-3563, Nearest town: Charleston, Agency: USFS, GPS: 40.430155, -111.611128

32318 • FSR 221 Dispersed 1 - USFS

Dispersed sites, No water, No toilets, Reservations not accepted, Open all year, Tent & RV camping: Free, Road not maintained for passenger cars, Elev: 8400ft/2560m, Tel: 801-625-5112, Nearest town: Randolph, Agency: USFS, GPS: 41.572479, -111.448954

32319 • FSR 221 Dispersed 2 - USFS

Dispersed sites, No water, No toilets, Reservations not accepted, Open all year, Tent & RV camping: Free, Elev: 8320ft/2536m, Tel: 435-789-1181, Nearest town: Manila, Agency: USFS, GPS: 40.877626, -109.765827

32320 • FSR 221 Dispersed 3 - USFS

Dispersed sites, No water, No toilets, Reservations not accepted, Open all year, Tent & RV camping: Free, Elev: 8667ft/2642m, Tel: 435-789-1181, Nearest town: Manila, Agency: USFS, GPS: 40.882716, -109.863823

32321 • FSR 221 Dispersed 4 - USFS

Dispersed sites, No water, No toilets, Reservations not accepted, Open all year, Tent & RV camping: Free, Elev: 8575ft/2614m, Tel: 435-789-1181, Nearest town: Manila, Agency: USFS, GPS: 40.888917, -109.884039

32322 • FSR 221 Dispersed 5 - USFS

Dispersed sites, No water, No toilets, Reservations not accepted, Open all year, Tent & RV camping: Free, Elev: 8858ft/2700m, Tel: 435-789-1181, Nearest town: Manila, Agency: USFS, GPS: 40.919304, -110.000564

32323 • FSR 221 Dispersed 6 - USFS

Dispersed sites, No water, No toilets, Reservations not accepted, Open all year, Tent & RV camping: Free, Road not maintained for passenger cars, Elev: 7798ft/2377m, Tel: 435-836-2800, Nearest town: Salina, Agency: USFS, GPS: 38.749819, -111.487942

32324 • FSR 222 Dispersed 1 - USFS

Dispersed sites, No water, No toilets, Reservations not accepted, Open all year, Tent & RV camping: Free, Road not maintained for passenger cars, Elev: 8540ft/2603m, Tel: 801-625-5112, Nearest town: Woodruff, Agency: USFS, GPS: 41.379908, -111.460121

32325 • FSR 2238 Dispersed 1 - USFS

Dispersed sites, No water, No toilets, Reservations not accepted, Open all year, Tent & RV camping: Free, Road not maintained for passenger cars, Elev: 6302ft/1921m, Tel: 435-743-5721, Nearest town: Salina, Agency: USFS, GPS: 39.023848, -112.083238

32326 • FSR 2257 Dispersed 1 - USFS

Dispersed sites, No water, No toilets, Reservations not accepted, Open all year, Tent & RV camping: Free, Road not maintained for passenger cars, Elev: 5503ft/1677m, Tel: 435-743-5721, Nearest town: Kanosh, Agency: USFS, GPS: 38.721577, -112.547011

32327 • FSR 2264 Dispersed 1 - USFS

Dispersed sites, No water, No toilets, Reservations not accepted, Open all year, Tent & RV camping: Free, Several sites both sides of road, Elev: 5677ft/1730m, Tel: 435-743-5721, Nearest town: Kanosh, Agency: USFS, GPS: 38.748023, -112.357008

32328 • FSR 227 Dispersed 1 - USFS

Dispersed sites, No water, No toilets, Reservations not accepted, Open all year, Tent & RV camping: Free, Elev: 8316ft/2535m, Tel: 435-738-2482, Nearest town: Altamont, Agency: USFS, GPS: 40.539461, -110.355122

32329 • FSR 227 Dispersed 2 - USFS

Dispersed sites, No water, No toilets, Reservations not accepted, Open all year, Tent & RV camping: Free, Elev: 8422ft/2567m, Tel: 435-738-2482, Nearest town: Altamont, Agency: USFS, GPS: 40.549366, -110.353773

32330 • FSR 227 Dispersed 3 - USFS

Dispersed sites, No water, No toilets, Reservations not accepted, Open all year, Tent & RV camping: Free, Elev: 8430ft/2569m, Tel: 435-738-2482, Nearest town: Altamont, Agency: USFS, GPS: 40.550433, -110.351784

32331 • FSR 2284 Dispersed 1 - USFS

Dispersed sites, No water, No toilets, Reservations not accepted, Open all year, Tent & RV camping: Free, Elev: 7046ft/2148m, Tel: 435-743-5721, Nearest town: Elsinore, Agency: USFS, GPS: 38.714668, -112.188621

32332 • FSR 2285 Dispersed 1 - USFS

Dispersed sites, No water, No toilets, Reservations not accepted, Open all year, Tent & RV camping: Free, Elev: 7054ft/2150m, Tel: 435-743-5721, Nearest town: Elsinore, Agency: USFS, GPS: 38.710137, -112.187805

32333 • FSR 2286 Dispersed 1 - USFS
Dispersed sites, No water, No toilets, Reservations not accepted, Open all year, Tent & RV camping: Free, Elev: 6958ft/2121m, Tel: 435-743-5721, Nearest town: Elsinore, Agency: USFS, GPS: 38.709313, -112.181252

32334 • FSR 2287 Dispersed 1 - USFS
Dispersed sites, No water, No toilets, Reservations not accepted, Open all year, Tent & RV camping: Free, Road not maintained for passenger cars, Elev: 6892ft/2101m, Tel: 435-743-5721, Nearest town: Elsinore, Agency: USFS, GPS: 38.704774, -112.182128

32335 • FSR 229 Dispersed 1 - USFS
Dispersed sites, No water, No toilets, Reservations not accepted, Open all year, Tent & RV camping: Free, Road not maintained for passenger cars, Elev: 8117ft/2474m, Tel: 435-789-1181, Nearest town: Manila, Agency: USFS, GPS: 40.844065, -109.712438

32336 • FSR 2293 Dispersed 1 - USFS
Dispersed sites, No water, No toilets, Reservations not accepted, Open all year, Tent & RV camping: Free, Road not maintained for passenger cars, Elev: 6977ft/2127m, Tel: 435-743-5721, Nearest town: Kanosh, Agency: USFS, GPS: 38.696302, -112.441773

32337 • FSR 230 Dispersed 1 - USFS
Dispersed sites, No water, No toilets, Reservations not accepted, Open all year, Tent & RV camping: Free, Road not maintained for passenger cars, Elev: 8265ft/2519m, Tel: 435-789-1181, Nearest town: Duck Creek, Agency: USFS, GPS: 37.554027, -112.628415

32338 • FSR 230 Dispersed 2 - USFS
Dispersed sites, No water, No toilets, Reservations not accepted, Open all year, Tent & RV camping: Free, Road not maintained for passenger cars, Elev: 8269ft/2520m, Tel: 435-789-1181, Nearest town: Duck Creek, Agency: USFS, GPS: 37.554224, -112.625702

32339 • FSR 231 Dispersed 1 - USFS
Dispersed sites, No water, No toilets, Reservations not accepted, Open Apr-Nov, Tent & RV camping: Free, Elev: 5605ft/1708m, Tel: 435-755-3620, Nearest town: Hyrum, Agency: USFS, GPS: 41.671378, -111.618626

32340 • FSR 231 Dispersed 2 - USFS
Dispersed sites, No water, No toilets, Reservations not accepted, Open Apr-Nov, Tents only: Free, Elev: 5684ft/1732m, Tel: 435-755-3620, Nearest town: Hyrum, Agency: USFS, GPS: 41.678335, -111.604356

32341 • FSR 231 Dispersed 3 - USFS
Dispersed sites, No water, No toilets, Reservations not accepted, Open Apr-Nov, Tent & RV camping: Free, Elev: 5881ft/1793m, Tel: 435-755-3620, Nearest town: Hyrum, Agency: USFS, GPS: 41.676517, -111.573543

32342 • FSR 2315 Dispersed 1 - USFS
Dispersed sites, No water, No toilets, Reservations not accepted, Open all year, Tent & RV camping: Free, Road not maintained for passenger cars, Elev: 6433ft/1961m, Tel: 435-438-2430, Nearest town: Sevier, Agency: USFS, GPS: 38.584673, -112.429342

32343 • FSR 232 Dispersed 1 - USFS
Dispersed sites, No water, No toilets, Reservations not accepted, Open all year, Tent & RV camping: Free, Elev: 8177ft/2492m, Tel: 435-738-2482, Nearest town: Altamont, Agency: USFS, GPS: 40.526986, -110.282641

32344 • FSR 232 Dispersed 2 - USFS
Dispersed sites, No water, No toilets, Reservations not accepted, Open all year, Tent & RV camping: Free, Elev: 8193ft/2497m, Tel: 435-738-2482, Nearest town: Altamont, Agency: USFS, GPS: 40.529198, -110.282779

32345 • FSR 232 Dispersed 3 - USFS
Dispersed sites, No water, No toilets, Reservations not accepted, Open all year, Tent & RV camping: Free, Elev: 8221ft/2506m, Tel: 435-738-2482, Nearest town: Altamont, Agency: USFS, GPS: 40.530286, -110.286515

32346 • FSR 232 Dispersed 4 - USFS
Dispersed sites, No water, No toilets, Reservations not accepted, Open all year, Tent & RV camping: Free, Elev: 8256ft/2516m, Tel: 435-738-2482, Nearest town: Altamont, Agency: USFS, GPS: 40.538619, -110.283814

32347 • FSR 232 Dispersed 5 - USFS
Dispersed sites, No water, No toilets, Reservations not accepted, Open all year, Tent & RV camping: Free, Elev: 8277ft/2523m, Tel: 435-738-2482, Nearest town: Altamont, Agency: USFS, GPS: 40.540772, -110.284263

32348 • FSR 233 Dispersed - USFS
Dispersed sites, No water, No toilets, Reservations not accepted, Open all year, Tent & RV camping: Free, Road not maintained for passenger cars, Elev: 8263ft/2519m, Tel: 435-676-9316, Nearest town: Hatch, Agency: USFS, GPS: 37.570887, -112.307836

32349 • FSR 234 Dispersed 1 - USFS
Dispersed sites, No water, No toilets, Reservations not accepted, Open all year, Tent & RV camping: Free, Road not maintained for passenger cars, Elev: 8340ft/2542m, Tel: 435-826-5400, Nearest town: Antimony, Agency: USFS, GPS: 37.896384, -111.945593

32350 • FSR 234 Dispersed 2 - USFS
Dispersed sites, No water, No toilets, Reservations not accepted, Open all year, Tent & RV camping: Free, Road not maintained for passenger cars, Elev: 8399ft/2560m, Tel: 435-826-5400, Nearest town: Antimony, Agency: USFS, GPS: 37.922466, -111.940475

32351 • FSR 234 Dispersed 3 - USFS
Dispersed sites, No water, No toilets, Reservations not accepted, Open all year, Tent & RV camping: Free, Road not maintained for passenger cars, Elev: 8833ft/2692m, Tel: 435-789-1181, Nearest town: Vernal, Agency: USFS, GPS: 40.626492, -109.738974

32352 • FSR 234 Dispersed 4 - USFS
Dispersed sites, No water, No toilets, Reservations not accepted, Open all year, Tent & RV camping: Free, Road not maintained for passenger cars, Elev: 9029ft/2752m, Tel: 435-789-1181, Nearest town: Vernal, Agency: USFS, GPS: 40.638421, -109.748159

32353 • FSR 2367 Dispersed 1 - USFS

Dispersed sites, No water, No toilets, Reservations not accepted, Open all year, Tent & RV camping: Free, Road not maintained for passenger cars, Elev: 10285ft/3135m, Tel: 435-438-2430, Nearest town: Junction, Agency: USFS, GPS: 38.269964, -112.363922

32354 • FSR 2367C Dispersed 1 - USFS

Dispersed sites, No water, No toilets, Reservations not accepted, Open all year, Tent & RV camping: Free, Road not maintained for passenger cars, Elev: 10275ft/3132m, Tel: 435-438-2430, Nearest town: Junction, Agency: USFS, GPS: 38.268016, -112.365601

32355 • FSR 237 (Old Smith Basin) Dispersed 1 - USFS

Dispersed sites, No water, No toilets, Reservations not accepted, Open all year, Tent & RV camping: Free, Road not maintained for passenger cars, Elev: 9871ft/3009m, Tel: 435-783-4338, Nearest town: Heber City, Agency: USFS, GPS: 40.381047, -111.168431

32356 • FSR 2372 Dispersed 1 - USFS

Dispersed sites, No water, No toilets, Reservations not accepted, Open all year, Tent & RV camping: Free, Road not maintained for passenger cars, Elev: 9573ft/2918m, Tel: 435-789-1181, Nearest town: Cedar City, Agency: USFS, GPS: 37.649897, -112.742188

32357 • FSR 2374 Dispersed 1 - USFS

Dispersed sites, No water, No toilets, Reservations not accepted, Open all year, Tent & RV camping: Free, Road not maintained for passenger cars, Elev: 10176ft/3102m, Tel: 435-438-2430, Nearest town: Junction, Agency: USFS, GPS: 38.271235, -112.376912

32358 • FSR 238 Dispersed 1 - USFS

Dispersed sites, No water, No toilets, Reservations not accepted, Open all year, Tent & RV camping: Free, Road not maintained for passenger cars, Elev: 8323ft/2537m, Tel: 435-755-3620, Nearest town: Garden City, Agency: USFS, GPS: 41.875945, -111.490056

32359 • FSR 238 Dispersed 2 - USFS

Dispersed sites, No water, No toilets, Reservations not accepted, Open all year, Tent & RV camping: Free, Road not maintained for passenger cars, Elev: 8343ft/2543m, Tel: 435-755-3620, Nearest town: Garden City, Agency: USFS, GPS: 41.875271, -111.491873

32360 • FSR 238 Dispersed 3 - USFS

Dispersed sites, No water, No toilets, Reservations not accepted, Open all year, Tent & RV camping: Free, Road not maintained for passenger cars, Elev: 8368ft/2551m, Tel: 435-755-3620, Nearest town: Garden City, Agency: USFS, GPS: 41.874573, -111.493615

32361 • FSR 238 Dispersed 4 - USFS

Dispersed sites, No water, No toilets, Reservations not accepted, Open all year, Tent & RV camping: Free, Road not maintained for passenger cars, Elev: 8309ft/2533m, Tel: 435-755-3620, Nearest town: Garden City, Agency: USFS, GPS: 41.873768, -111.493259

32362 • FSR 239 Dispersed 1 - USFS

Dispersed sites, No water, No toilets, Reservations not accepted, Open all year, Tent & RV camping: Free, Elev: 8334ft/2540m, Tel: 435-789-1181, Nearest town: Duck Creek, Agency: USFS, GPS: 37.480053, -112.641816

32363 • FSR 2391 Dispersed 1 - USFS

Dispersed sites, No water, No toilets, Reservations not accepted, Open all year, Tent & RV camping: Free, Road not maintained for passenger cars, Elev: 9968ft/3038m, Tel: 435-438-2430, Nearest town: Circleville, Agency: USFS, GPS: 38.227215, -112.406418

32364 • FSR 240 Dispersed 1 - USFS

Dispersed sites, No water, No toilets, Reservations not accepted, Open all year, Tent & RV camping: Free, Elev: 9541ft/2908m, Tel: 435-789-1181, Nearest town: Cedar City, Agency: USFS, GPS: 37.654445, -112.740457

32365 • FSR 240 Dispersed 10 - USFS

Dispersed sites, No water, No toilets, Reservations not accepted, Open all year, Tent & RV camping: Free, Elev: 9546ft/2910m, Tel: 435-789-1181, Nearest town: Duck Creek, Agency: USFS, GPS: 37.582778, -112.765708

32366 • FSR 240 Dispersed 11 - USFS

Dispersed sites, No water, No toilets, Max length: 18ft, Reservations not accepted, Open all year, Tent & RV camping: Free, Elev: 9709ft/2959m, Tel: 435-789-1181, Nearest town: Duck Creek, Agency: USFS, GPS: 37.579083, -112.773796

32367 • FSR 240 Dispersed 12 - USFS

Dispersed sites, No water, No toilets, Reservations not accepted, Open all year, Tent & RV camping: Free, Elev: 9668ft/2947m, Tel: 435-789-1181, Nearest town: Duck Creek, Agency: USFS, GPS: 37.576641, -112.781187

32368 • FSR 240 Dispersed 13 - USFS

Dispersed sites, No water, No toilets, Reservations not accepted, Open all year, Tent & RV camping: Free, Elev: 9664ft/2946m, Tel: 435-789-1181, Nearest town: Duck Creek, Agency: USFS, GPS: 37.576193, -112.788784

32369 • FSR 240 Dispersed 2 - USFS

Dispersed sites, No water, No toilets, Reservations not accepted, Open all year, Tent & RV camping: Free, Elev: 9514ft/2900m, Tel: 435-789-1181, Nearest town: Cedar City, Agency: USFS, GPS: 37.650958, -112.736919

32370 • FSR 240 Dispersed 3 - USFS

Dispersed sites, No water, No toilets, Reservations not accepted, Open all year, Tent & RV camping: Free, Elev: 9522ft/2902m, Tel: 435-789-1181, Nearest town: Cedar City, Agency: USFS, GPS: 37.648594, -112.730161

32371 • FSR 240 Dispersed 4 - USFS

Dispersed sites, No water, No toilets, Reservations not accepted, Open all year, Tent & RV camping: Free, Elev: 9476ft/2888m, Tel: 435-789-1181, Nearest town: Cedar City, Agency: USFS, GPS: 37.647256, -112.724436

32372 • FSR 240 Dispersed 5 - USFS

Dispersed sites, No water, No toilets, Reservations not accepted, Open all year, Tent & RV camping: Free, Elev: 9430ft/2874m, Tel: 435-789-1181, Nearest town: Cedar City, Agency: USFS, GPS: 37.643105, -112.723761

32373 • FSR 240 Dispersed 6 - USFS

Dispersed sites, No water, No toilets, Reservations not accepted, Open all year, Tent & RV camping: Free, Elev: 9393ft/2863m, Tel: 435-789-1181, Nearest town: Cedar City, Agency: USFS, GPS: 37.640964, -112.722444

32374 • FSR 240 Dispersed 7 - USFS

Dispersed sites, No water, No toilets, Reservations not accepted, Open all year, Tent & RV camping: Free, Elev: 9494ft/2894m, Tel: 435-789-1181, Nearest town: Cedar City, Agency: USFS, GPS: 37.634774, -112.727497

32375 • FSR 240 Dispersed 8 - USFS

Dispersed sites, No water, No toilets, Reservations not accepted, Open all year, Tent & RV camping: Free, Elev: 9579ft/2920m, Tel: 435-789-1181, Nearest town: Duck Creek, Agency: USFS, GPS: 37.586249, -112.743515

32376 • FSR 240 Dispersed 9 - USFS

Dispersed sites, No water, No toilets, Reservations not accepted, Open all year, Tent & RV camping: Free, Elev: 9476ft/2888m, Tel: 435-789-1181, Nearest town: Duck Creek, Agency: USFS, GPS: 37.579788, -112.744442

32377 • FSR 241 Dispersed 1 - USFS

Dispersed sites, No water, No toilets, Reservations not accepted, Open all year, Tent & RV camping: Free, Road not maintained for passenger cars, Elev: 8091ft/2466m, Tel: 435-789-1181, Nearest town: Hatch, Agency: USFS, GPS: 37.668005, -112.515795

32378 • FSR 242 Dispersed 1 - USFS

Dispersed sites, No water, No toilets, Reservations not accepted, Open all year, Tent & RV camping: Free, Road not maintained for passenger cars, Elev: 7244ft/2208m, Tel: 435-676-9316, Nearest town: Alton, Agency: USFS, GPS: 37.442274, -112.227651

32379 • FSR 242 Dispersed 2 - USFS

Dispersed sites, No water, No toilets, Reservations not accepted, Open all year, Tent & RV camping: Free, Road not maintained for passenger cars, Elev: 9324ft/2842m, Tel: 435-783-4338, Nearest town: Heber City, Agency: USFS, GPS: 40.322499, -111.130122

32380 • FSR 243 Dispersed 1 - USFS

Dispersed sites, No water, No toilets, Reservations not accepted, Open all year, Tent & RV camping: Free, Elev: 7328ft/2234m, Tel: 435-738-2482, Nearest town: Duchesne, Agency: USFS, GPS: 40.514242, -110.589827

32381 • FSR 243 Dispersed 2 - USFS

Dispersed sites, No water, No toilets, Reservations not accepted, Open all year, Tent & RV camping: Free, Road not maintained for passenger cars, Elev: 8911ft/2716m, Tel: 435-783-4338, Nearest town: Heber City, Agency: USFS, GPS: 40.353366, -111.137785

32382 • FSR 244 Dispersed 1 - USFS

Dispersed sites, No water, No toilets, Reservations not accepted, Open all year, Tent & RV camping: Free, Road not maintained for passenger cars, Elev: 8789ft/2679m, Tel: 435-783-4338, Nearest town: Woodland, Agency: USFS, GPS: 40.520256, -111.033599

32383 • FSR 245 Dispersed 1 - USFS

Dispersed sites, No water, No toilets, Reservations not accepted, Open Apr-Nov, Tent & RV camping: Free, Elev: 5138ft/1566m, Tel: 435-755-3620, Nearest town: Hyrum, Agency: USFS, GPS: 41.640523, -111.707808

32384 • FSR 245 Dispersed 10 - USFS

Dispersed sites, No water, No toilets, Reservations not accepted, Open Apr-Nov, Tent & RV camping: Free, Elev: 5463ft/1665m, Tel: 435-755-3620, Nearest town: Hyrum, Agency: USFS, GPS: 41.662724, -111.662376

32385 • FSR 245 Dispersed 11 - USFS

Dispersed sites, No water, No toilets, Reservations not accepted, Open Apr-Nov, Tents only: Free, Elev: 5461ft/1665m, Tel: 435-755-3620, Nearest town: Hyrum, Agency: USFS, GPS: 41.663067, -111.659657

32386 • FSR 245 Dispersed 12 - USFS

Dispersed sites, No water, No toilets, Reservations not accepted, Open Apr-Nov, Tent & RV camping: Free, Elev: 5532ft/1686m, Tel: 435-755-3620, Nearest town: Hyrum, Agency: USFS, GPS: 41.662167, -111.637713

32387 • FSR 245 Dispersed 13 - USFS

Dispersed sites, No water, No toilets, Reservations not accepted, Open Apr-Nov, Tent & RV camping: Free, Elev: 5543ft/1690m, Tel: 435-755-3620, Nearest town: Hyrum, Agency: USFS, GPS: 41.663119, -111.634137

32388 • FSR 245 Dispersed 14 - USFS

Dispersed sites, No water, No toilets, Reservations not accepted, Open Apr-Nov, Tent & RV camping: Free, Elev: 5568ft/1697m, Tel: 435-755-3620, Nearest town: Hyrum, Agency: USFS, GPS: 41.667043, -111.627189

32389 • FSR 245 Dispersed 2 - USFS

Dispersed sites, No water, No toilets, Reservations not accepted, Open Apr-Nov, Tent & RV camping: Free, Several sites in this area, Elev: 5160ft/1573m, Tel: 435-755-3620, Nearest town: Hyrum, Agency: USFS, GPS: 41.644163, -111.705948

32390 • FSR 245 Dispersed 3 - USFS

Dispersed sites, No water, No toilets, Reservations not accepted, Open Apr-Nov, Tent & RV camping: Free, Elev: 5215ft/1590m, Tel: 435-755-3620, Nearest town: Hyrum, Agency: USFS, GPS: 41.649277, -111.702068

32391 • FSR 245 Dispersed 4 - USFS

Dispersed sites, No water, No toilets, Reservations not accepted, Open Apr-Nov, Tent & RV camping: Free, Elev: 5232ft/1595m, Tel: 435-755-3620, Nearest town: Hyrum, Agency: USFS, GPS: 41.651534, -111.697932

32392 • FSR 245 Dispersed 5 - USFS

Dispersed sites, No water, No toilets, Reservations not accepted, Open Apr-Nov, Tent & RV camping: Free, Elev: 5340ft/1628m, Tel: 435-755-3620, Nearest town: Hyrum, Agency: USFS, GPS: 41.658071, -111.685893

32393 • FSR 245 Dispersed 6 - USFS
Dispersed sites, No water, No toilets, Reservations not accepted, Open Apr-Nov, Tent & RV camping: Free, Elev: 5360ft/1634m, Tel: 435-755-3620, Nearest town: Hyrum, Agency: USFS, GPS: 41.658748, -111.684548

32394 • FSR 245 Dispersed 7 - USFS
Dispersed sites, No water, No toilets, Reservations not accepted, Open Apr-Nov, Tent & RV camping: Free, Elev: 5372ft/1637m, Tel: 435-755-3620, Nearest town: Hyrum, Agency: USFS, GPS: 41.658907, -111.681197

32395 • FSR 245 Dispersed 8 - USFS
Dispersed sites, No water, No toilets, Reservations not accepted, Open Apr-Nov, Tent & RV camping: Free, Elev: 5376ft/1639m, Tel: 435-755-3620, Nearest town: Hyrum, Agency: USFS, GPS: 41.658334, -111.678671

32396 • FSR 245 Dispersed 9 - USFS
Dispersed sites, No water, No toilets, Reservations not accepted, Open Apr-Nov, Tent & RV camping: Free, Elev: 5414ft/1650m, Tel: 435-755-3620, Nearest town: Hyrum, Agency: USFS, GPS: 41.659761, -111.668754

32397 • FSR 246 Dispersed 1 - USFS
Dispersed sites, No water, No toilets, Reservations not accepted, Open all year, Tent & RV camping: Free, Road not maintained for passenger cars, Elev: 9500ft/2896m, Tel: 435-783-4338, Nearest town: Heber City, Agency: USFS, GPS: 40.297041, -111.115197

32398 • FSR 246 Dispersed 2 - USFS
Dispersed sites, No water, No toilets, Reservations not accepted, Open all year, Tent & RV camping: Free, Road not maintained for passenger cars, Elev: 9663ft/2945m, Tel: 435-783-4338, Nearest town: Heber City, Agency: USFS, GPS: 40.301088, -111.103832

32399 • FSR 247 Dispersed 1 - USFS
Dispersed sites, No water, No toilets, Reservations not accepted, Open all year, Tent & RV camping: Free, Road not maintained for passenger cars, Elev: 8746ft/2666m, Tel: 435-836-2800, Nearest town: Grover, Agency: USFS, GPS: 38.108932, -111.340644

32400 • FSR 247 Dispersed 2 - USFS
Dispersed sites, No water, No toilets, Reservations not accepted, Open all year, Tent & RV camping: Free, Road not maintained for passenger cars, Elev: 8854ft/2699m, Tel: 435-836-2800, Nearest town: Grover, Agency: USFS, GPS: 38.107032, -111.347016

32401 • FSR 247 Dispersed 3 - USFS
Dispersed sites, No water, No toilets, Reservations not accepted, Open all year, Tent & RV camping: Free, Road not maintained for passenger cars, Elev: 9550ft/2911m, Tel: 435-783-4338, Nearest town: Heber City, Agency: USFS, GPS: 40.297883, -111.084203

32402 • FSR 248 Dispersed 1 - USFS
Dispersed sites, No water, No toilets, Reservations not accepted, Open all year, Tent & RV camping: Free, Road not maintained for passenger cars, Elev: 10345ft/3153m, Tel: 435-836-2800, Nearest town: Lyman, Agency: USFS, GPS: 38.404777, -111.456689

32403 • FSR 2486A Dispersed 1 - USFS
Dispersed sites, No water, No toilets, Reservations not accepted, Open all year, Tent & RV camping: Free, Road not maintained for passenger cars, Elev: 8163ft/2488m, Tel: 435-896-9233, Nearest town: Salina, Agency: USFS, GPS: 38.941074, -111.464088

32404 • FSR 2487A Dispersed 1 - USFS
Dispersed sites, No water, No toilets, Reservations not accepted, Open all year, Tent & RV camping: Free, Road not maintained for passenger cars, Elev: 8263ft/2519m, Tel: 435-896-9233, Nearest town: Salina, Agency: USFS, GPS: 38.920604, -111.441042

32405 • FSR 249 Dispersed 1 - USFS
Dispersed sites, No water, No toilets, Reservations not accepted, Open all year, Tent & RV camping: Free, Road not maintained for passenger cars, Elev: 9273ft/2826m, Tel: 435-783-4338, Nearest town: Heber City, Agency: USFS, GPS: 40.276545, -111.101602

32406 • FSR 251 Dispersed 1 - USFS
Dispersed sites, No water, No toilets, Reservations not accepted, Open all year, Tent & RV camping: Free, Road not maintained for passenger cars, Elev: 8550ft/2606m, Tel: 435-755-3620, Nearest town: Garden City, Agency: USFS, GPS: 41.837886, -111.505137

32407 • FSR 251 Dispersed 2 - USFS
Dispersed sites, No water, No toilets, Reservations not accepted, Open all year, Tent & RV camping: Free, Road not maintained for passenger cars, Elev: 8558ft/2608m, Tel: 435-755-3620, Nearest town: Garden City, Agency: USFS, GPS: 41.835325, -111.506636

32408 • FSR 251 Dispersed 3 - USFS
Dispersed sites, No water, No toilets, Reservations not accepted, Open all year, Tent & RV camping: Free, Numerous sites in this area, Elev: 10051ft/3064m, Tel: 435-789-1181, Nearest town: Duck Creek, Agency: USFS, GPS: 37.577974, -112.819596

32409 • FSR 252 Dispersed 1 - USFS
Dispersed sites, No water, No toilets, Reservations not accepted, Open all year, Tent & RV camping: Free, Road not maintained for passenger cars, Elev: 8562ft/2610m, Tel: 435-755-3620, Nearest town: Garden City, Agency: USFS, GPS: 41.847419, -111.500572

32410 • FSR 252 Dispersed 2 - USFS
Dispersed sites, No water, No toilets, Reservations not accepted, Open all year, Tent & RV camping: Free, Road not maintained for passenger cars, Elev: 8606ft/2623m, Tel: 435-755-3620, Nearest town: Garden City, Agency: USFS, GPS: 41.845299, -111.502676

32411 • FSR 253 Dispersed 1 - USFS
Dispersed sites, No water, No toilets, Reservations not accepted, Open all year, Tent & RV camping: Free, Road not maintained for passenger cars, Elev: 6782ft/2067m, Tel: 435-789-1181, Nearest town: Pine Valley, Agency: USFS, GPS: 37.417257, -113.523282

32412 • FSR 253 Dispersed 2 - USFS
Dispersed sites, No water, No toilets, Reservations not accepted, Open all year, Tent & RV camping: Free, Road not maintained for passenger cars, Elev: 6855ft/2089m, Tel: 435-789-1181, Nearest town: Pine Valley, Agency: USFS, GPS: 37.421686, -113.519952

32413 • FSR 253 Dispersed 3 - USFS

Dispersed sites, No water, No toilets, Reservations not accepted, Open all year, Tent & RV camping: Free, Road not maintained for passenger cars, Several sites in this area, Elev: 8551ft/2606m, Tel: 435-789-1181, Nearest town: Dutch John, Agency: USFS, GPS: 40.757675, -109.451246

32414 • FSR 2533 Dispersed 1 - USFS

Dispersed sites, No water, No toilets, Reservations not accepted, Open all year, Tent & RV camping: Free, Several sites in this area, Road not maintained for passenger cars, Elev: 8161ft/2487m, Tel: 435-836-2800, Nearest town: Fremont, Agency: USFS, GPS: 38.653183, -111.449179

32415 • FSR 255 Dispersed 1 - USFS

Dispersed sites, No water, No toilets, Reservations not accepted, Open all year, Tent & RV camping: Free, Road not maintained for passenger cars, Elev: 7082ft/2159m, Tel: 435-789-1181, Nearest town: Pine Valley, Agency: USFS, GPS: 37.454528, -113.456619

32416 • FSR 2570A Dispersed 1 - USFS

Dispersed sites, No water, No toilets, Reservations not accepted, Open all year, Tent & RV camping: Free, Road not maintained for passenger cars, Elev: 9822ft/2994m, Tel: 435-836-2800, Nearest town: Koosharem, Agency: USFS, GPS: 38.570155, -111.777321

32417 • FSR 2592 Dispersed 1 - USFS

Dispersed sites, No water, No toilets, Reservations not accepted, Open all year, Tent & RV camping: Free, Road not maintained for passenger cars, Elev: 9981ft/3042m, Tel: 435-836-2800, Nearest town: Koosharem, Agency: USFS, GPS: 38.541891, -111.693577

32418 • FSR 260 Dispersed 1 - USFS

Dispersed sites, No water, No toilets, Reservations not accepted, Open all year, Tent & RV camping: Free, Road not maintained for passenger cars, Elev: 9292ft/2832m, Tel: 801-723-2660, Nearest town: Farmington, Agency: USFS, GPS: 41.036961, -111.833442

32419 • FSR 261 Dispersed 1 - USFS

Dispersed sites, No water, No toilets, Reservations not accepted, Open all year, Tent & RV camping: Free, 2 separated sites, Road not maintained for passenger cars, Elev: 9331ft/2844m, Tel: 435-783-4338, Nearest town: Woodland, Agency: USFS, GPS: 40.530451, -110.989096

32420 • FSR 262 (Row Lakes) Dispersed 1 - USFS

Dispersed sites, No water, No toilets, Reservations not accepted, Open all year, Tent & RV camping: Free, Road not maintained for passenger cars, Elev: 10270ft/3130m, Tel: 435-836-2800, Nearest town: Teasdale, Agency: USFS, GPS: 38.081799, -111.584192

32421 • FSR 263 Dispersed 1 - USFS

Dispersed sites, No water, Vault toilets, Reservations not accepted, Open all year, Tent & RV camping: Free, Road not maintained for passenger cars, Elev: 7827ft/2386m, Tel: 435-783-4338, Nearest town: Heber City, Agency: USFS, GPS: 40.286952, -111.241546

32422 • FSR 263 Dispersed 2 - USFS

Dispersed sites, No water, Vault toilets, Reservations not accepted, Open all year, Tent & RV camping: Free, Road not maintained for passenger cars, Elev: 8077ft/2462m, Tel: 435-783-4338, Nearest town: Heber City, Agency: USFS, GPS: 40.304164, -111.242655

32423 • FSR 263 Dispersed 3 - USFS

Dispersed sites, No water, Vault toilets, Reservations not accepted, Open all year, Tent & RV camping: Free, Parking lot, Road not maintained for passenger cars, Elev: 8081ft/2463m, Tel: 435-783-4338, Nearest town: Heber City, Agency: USFS, GPS: 40.306498, -111.247941

32424 • FSR 2663 Dispersed 1 - USFS

Dispersed sites, No water, No toilets, Reservations not accepted, Open all year, Tent & RV camping: Free, Road not maintained for passenger cars, Elev: 8232ft/2509m, Tel: 435-896-9233, Nearest town: Salina, Agency: USFS, GPS: 38.909965, -111.446186

32425 • FSR 2663 Dispersed 2 - USFS

Dispersed sites, No water, No toilets, Reservations not accepted, Open all year, Tent & RV camping: Free, Road not maintained for passenger cars, Elev: 8268ft/2520m, Tel: 435-896-9233, Nearest town: Salina, Agency: USFS, GPS: 38.911183, -111.440624

32426 • FSR 267 Dispersed 1 - USFS

Dispersed sites, No water, No toilets, Reservations not accepted, Open all year, Tent & RV camping: Free, Nothing larger than van/pickup, Road not maintained for passenger cars, Elev: 8933ft/2723m, Tel: 435-783-4338, Nearest town: Heber City, Agency: USFS, GPS: 40.386231, -111.217565

32427 • FSR 2674 Dispersed 1 - USFS

Dispersed sites, No water, No toilets, Reservations not accepted, Open all year, Tent & RV camping: Free, Road not maintained for passenger cars, Elev: 7757ft/2364m, Tel: 435-896-9233, Nearest town: Redmond, Agency: USFS, GPS: 38.990176, -111.639356

32428 • FSR 2676 Dispersed 1 - USFS

Dispersed sites, No water, No toilets, Reservations not accepted, Open all year, Tent & RV camping: Free, Road not maintained for passenger cars, Elev: 6646ft/2026m, Tel: 435-743-5721, Nearest town: Fillmore, Agency: USFS, GPS: 38.879675, -112.323728

32429 • FSR 268 (Daniels Reservoir) Dispersed 1 - USFS

Dispersed sites, No water, No toilets, Reservations not accepted, Open all year, Tent & RV camping: Free, Road not maintained for passenger cars, Elev: 9755ft/2973m, Tel: 435-783-4338, Nearest town: Heber City, Agency: USFS, GPS: 40.392447, -111.191291

32430 • FSR 269 Dispersed 1 - USFS

Dispersed sites, No water, No toilets, Reservations not accepted, Open all year, Tent & RV camping: Free, Road not maintained for passenger cars, Elev: 9732ft/2966m, Tel: 435-783-4338, Nearest town: Heber City, Agency: USFS, GPS: 40.459386, -111.140035

32431 • FSR 270 Dispersed 1 - USFS

Dispersed sites, No water, No toilets, Reservations not accepted, Open all year, Tent & RV camping: Free, Road not maintained for

passenger cars, Elev: 9038ft/2755m, Tel: 435-783-4338, Nearest town: Heber City, Agency: USFS, GPS: 40.442805, -111.148255

32432 • FSR 2702 Dispersed 1 - USFS

Dispersed sites, No water, No toilets, Reservations not accepted, Open all year, Tent & RV camping: Free, Elev: 7431ft/2265m, Tel: 435-896-9233, Nearest town: Glenwood, Agency: USFS, GPS: 38.715148, -111.950768

32433 • FSR 272 Dispersed 1 - USFS

Dispersed sites, No water, No toilets, Reservations not accepted, Open all year, Tent & RV camping: Free, Road not maintained for passenger cars, Elev: 8551ft/2606m, Tel: 435-755-3620, Nearest town: Garden City, Agency: USFS, GPS: 41.859851, -111.499139

32434 • FSR 274 (Hodges Canyon TH) Dispersed - USFS

Dispersed sites, No water, No toilets, Reservations not accepted, Open all year, Tent & RV camping: Free, Road not maintained for passenger cars, Elev: 7716ft/2352m, Tel: 435-755-3620, Nearest town: Garden City, Agency: USFS, GPS: 41.907216, -111.474549

32435 • FSR 275 Dispersed 1 - USFS

Dispersed sites, No water, No toilets, Reservations not accepted, Open all year, Tents only: Free, High-clearance vehicle required, Elev: 8320ft/2536m, Tel: 435-738-2482, Nearest town: Altamont, Agency: USFS, GPS: 40.549204, -110.283455

32436 • FSR 275 Dispersed 2 - USFS

Dispersed sites, No water, No toilets, Reservations not accepted, Open all year, Tents only: Free, Road not maintained for passenger cars, Elev: 8905ft/2714m, Tel: 435-789-1181, Nearest town: Panguitch, Agency: USFS, GPS: 37.737603, -112.669786

32437 • FSR 282 Dispersed 1 - USFS

Dispersed sites, No water, No toilets, Reservations not accepted, Open all year, Tent & RV camping: Free, Road not maintained for passenger cars, Elev: 8373ft/2552m, Tel: 435-826-5400, Nearest town: Escalante, Agency: USFS, GPS: 37.726601, -111.955119

32438 • FSR 282 Dispersed 2 - USFS

Dispersed sites, No water, No toilets, Reservations not accepted, Open all year, Tent & RV camping: Free, Road not maintained for passenger cars, Elev: 8422ft/2567m, Tel: 435-826-5400, Nearest town: Escalante, Agency: USFS, GPS: 37.725376, -111.951425

32439 • FSR 282 Dispersed 3 - USFS

Dispersed sites, No water, No toilets, Reservations not accepted, Open all year, Tent & RV camping: Free, Road not maintained for passenger cars, Elev: 8872ft/2704m, Tel: 435-826-5400, Nearest town: Escalante, Agency: USFS, GPS: 37.718971, -111.928329

32440 • FSR 285 Dispersed 1 - USFS

Dispersed sites, No water, No toilets, Reservations not accepted, Open all year, Tent & RV camping: Free, Road not maintained for passenger cars, Elev: 9122ft/2780m, Tel: 435-836-2800, Nearest town: Teasdale, Agency: USFS, GPS: 38.140017, -111.584029

32441 • FSR 285 Dispersed 2 - USFS

Dispersed sites, No water, No toilets, Reservations not accepted, Open all year, Tent & RV camping: Free, Road not maintained for passenger cars, Elev: 9260ft/2822m, Tel: 435-836-2800, Nearest town: Teasdale, Agency: USFS, GPS: 38.148631, -111.581292

32442 • FSR 288 Dispersed 1 - USFS

Dispersed sites, No water, No toilets, Reservations not accepted, Open all year, Tent & RV camping: Free, Road not maintained for passenger cars, Elev: 5787ft/1764m, Tel: 435-789-1181, Nearest town: Enterprise, Agency: USFS, GPS: 37.515603, -113.866433

32443 • FSR 288 Dispersed 2 - USFS

Dispersed sites, No water, No toilets, Reservations not accepted, Open all year, Tent & RV camping: Free, Road not maintained for passenger cars, Elev: 9724ft/2964m, Tel: 435-783-4338, Nearest town: Heber City, Agency: USFS, GPS: 40.457905, -111.141208

32444 • FSR 289 Dispersed 1 - USFS

Dispersed sites, No water, No toilets, Reservations not accepted, Open all year, Tent & RV camping: Free, Road not maintained for passenger cars, Elev: 7829ft/2386m, Tel: 435-755-3620, Nearest town: Garden City, Agency: USFS, GPS: 41.969849, -111.611501

32445 • FSR 289 Dispersed 2 - USFS

Dispersed sites, No water, No toilets, Reservations not accepted, Open all year, Tent & RV camping: Free, Road not maintained for passenger cars, Elev: 8039ft/2450m, Tel: 435-755-3620, Nearest town: Garden City, Agency: USFS, GPS: 41.970726, -111.623213

32446 • FSR 289 Dispersed 3 - USFS

Dispersed sites, No water, No toilets, Reservations not accepted, Tents only: Free, Elev: 8139ft/2481m, Tel: 435-755-3620, Nearest town: Garden City, Agency: USFS, GPS: 41.971405, -111.626659

32447 • FSR 289 Dispersed 4 - USFS

Dispersed sites, No water, No toilets, Reservations not accepted, Open all year, Tent & RV camping: Free, High-clearance vehicle required, Elev: 8287ft/2526m, Tel: 435-738-2482, Nearest town: Whiterocks, Agency: USFS, GPS: 40.607952, -110.097436

32448 • FSR 289 Dispersed 5 - USFS

Dispersed sites, No water, No toilets, Reservations not accepted, Open all year, Tent & RV camping: Free, High-clearance vehicle required, Elev: 8267ft/2520m, Tel: 435-738-2482, Nearest town: Whiterocks, Agency: USFS, GPS: 40.608975, -110.094155

32449 • FSR 290 Dispersed 1 - USFS

Dispersed sites, No water, No toilets, Reservations not accepted, Open all year, Tent & RV camping: Free, Numerous sites in this area, Elev: 8095ft/2467m, Tel: 435-789-1181, Nearest town: Duck Creek, Agency: USFS, GPS: 37.504677, -112.619773

32450 • FSR 292 Dispersed 1 - USFS

Dispersed sites, No water, No toilets, Reservations not accepted, Open all year, Tent & RV camping: Free, Elev: 7784ft/2373m, Tel: 435-789-1181, Nearest town: Duck Creek, Agency: USFS, GPS: 37.529253, -112.567608

32451 • FSR 292 Dispersed 2 - USFS

Dispersed sites, No water, No toilets, Reservations not accepted, Open all year, Tent & RV camping: Free, Elev: 7789ft/2374m, Tel: 435-789-1181, Nearest town: Duck Creek, Agency: USFS, GPS: 37.528975, -112.564547

32452 • FSR 292 Dispersed 3 - USFS

Dispersed sites, No water, No toilets, Reservations not accepted, Open Apr-Oct, Tent & RV camping: Free, Numerous sites in this area, Road not maintained for passenger cars, Elev: 7716ft/2352m, Tel: 435-783-4338, Nearest town: Springville, Agency: USFS, GPS: 40.203796, -111.199779

32453 • FSR 293 Dispersed 1 - USFS

Dispersed sites, No water, No toilets, Reservations not accepted, Open all year, Tent & RV camping: Free, Elev: 9956ft/3035m, Tel: 435-738-2482, Nearest town: Whiterocks, Agency: USFS, GPS: 40.621281, -110.035887

32454 • FSR 298 Dispersed 1- USFS

Dispersed sites, No water, No toilets, Reservations not accepted, Open all year, Tent & RV camping: Free, Road not maintained for passenger cars, Elev: 9677ft/2950m, Tel: 435-789-1181, Nearest town: Vernal, Agency: USFS, GPS: 40.613566, -109.891667

32455 • FSR 298 Dispersed 2 - USFS

Dispersed sites, No water, No toilets, Reservations not accepted, Open all year, Tents only: Free, Road not maintained for passenger cars, Elev: 9897ft/3017m, Tel: 435-789-1181, Nearest town: Vernal, Agency: USFS, GPS: 40.604988, -109.909798

32456 • FSR 3019 Dispersed 1 - USFS

Dispersed sites, No water, No toilets, Reservations not accepted, Open all year, Tent & RV camping: Free, Road not maintained for passenger cars, Elev: 7441ft/2268m, Tel: 435-789-1181, Nearest town: Paragonah, Agency: USFS, GPS: 37.876599, -112.658003

32457 • FSR 302 Dispersed 1 - USFS

Dispersed sites, No water, No toilets, Reservations not accepted, Open all year, Tent & RV camping: Free, Several sites along road, High-clearance vehicle required, Elev: 7493ft/2284m, Tel: 435-738-2482, Nearest town: Duchesne, Agency: USFS, GPS: 39.938119, -110.666235

32458 • FSR 3023 Dispersed 1 - USFS

Total sites: 6, RV sites: 6, Elec sites: 0, No water, No toilets, Tent & RV camping: Free, Elev: 8340ft/2542m, Tel: 435-865-3200, Nearest town: Parowan, Agency: USFS, GPS: 37.772495, -112.746534

32459 • FSR 3026 Dispersed 1 - USFS

Total sites: 16, RV sites: 16, Elec sites: 0, No water, No toilets, Tent & RV camping: Free, Elev: 8238ft/2511m, Tel: 435-865-3200, Nearest town: Parowan, Agency: USFS, GPS: 37.769644, -112.753658

32460 • FSR 3027 Dispersed 1 - USFS

Total sites: 8, RV sites: 8, Elec sites: 0, No water, No toilets, Tent & RV camping: Free, Elev: 8255ft/2516m, Tel: 435-865-3200, Nearest town: Parowan, Agency: USFS, GPS: 37.76979, -112.75046

32461 • FSR 304 Dispersed - USFS

Dispersed sites, No water, No toilets, Reservations not accepted, Open all year, Tent & RV camping: Free, Elev: 8127ft/2477m, Tel: 435-738-2482, Nearest town: Duchesne, Agency: USFS, GPS: 39.903488, -110.718071

32462 • FSR 304 Dispersed 1 - USFS

Dispersed sites, No water, No toilets, Reservations not accepted, Open all year, Tent & RV camping: Free, Road not maintained for passenger cars, Elev: 8654ft/2638m, Tel: 435-783-4338, Nearest town: Woodland, Agency: USFS, GPS: 40.542066, -111.020235

32463 • FSR 304 Dispersed 2 - USFS

Dispersed sites, No water, No toilets, Reservations not accepted, Open all year, Tent & RV camping: Free, Road not maintained for passenger cars, Elev: 8751ft/2667m, Tel: 435-783-4338, Nearest town: Woodland, Agency: USFS, GPS: 40.546042, -111.004866

32464 • FSR 304 Dispersed 3 - USFS

Dispersed sites, No water, No toilets, Reservations not accepted, Open all year, Tent & RV camping: Free, Road not maintained for passenger cars, Elev: 9163ft/2793m, Tel: 435-783-4338, Nearest town: Woodland, Agency: USFS, GPS: 40.548704, -110.983644

32465 • FSR 304 Dispersed 4 - USFS

Dispersed sites, No water, No toilets, Reservations not accepted, Open all year, Tent & RV camping: Free, Road not maintained for passenger cars, Elev: 9370ft/2856m, Tel: 435-783-4338, Nearest town: Woodland, Agency: USFS, GPS: 40.553739, -110.973936

32466 • FSR 305 Dispersed 1 - USFS

Dispersed sites, No water, No toilets, Reservations not accepted, Open all year, Tent & RV camping: Free, High-clearance vehicle required, Elev: 10595ft/3229m, Tel: 435-738-2482, Nearest town: Whiterocks, Agency: USFS, GPS: 40.669401, -110.091716

32467 • FSR 306 Dispersed 1 - USFS

Dispersed sites, No water, No toilets, Reservations not accepted, Open all year, Tent & RV camping: Free, Several sites in this area, Road not maintained for passenger cars, Elev: 8589ft/2618m, Tel: 307-789-3194, Nearest town: Oakley, Agency: USFS, GPS: 40.863757, -110.831239

32468 • FSR 307 Dispersed 1 - USFS

Dispersed sites, No water, No toilets, Reservations not accepted, Open all year, Tent & RV camping: Free, Elev: 7775ft/2370m, Tel: 435-783-4338, Nearest town: Springville, Agency: USFS, GPS: 40.219584, -111.195123

32469 • FSR 3073 Dispersed 1 - USFS

Dispersed sites, No water, No toilets, Reservations not accepted, Open all year, Tent & RV camping: Free, Road not maintained for passenger cars, Elev: 8239ft/2511m, Tel: 435-789-1181, Nearest town: Panguitch, Agency: USFS, GPS: 37.709272, -112.627884

32470 • FSR 3076 Dispersed 1 - USFS

Dispersed sites, No water, No toilets, Reservations not accepted, Open all year, Tent & RV camping: Free, Road not maintained for

passenger cars, Elev: 8231ft/2509m, Tel: 435-789-1181, Nearest town: Panguitch, Agency: USFS, GPS: 37.708721, -112.651537

32471 • FSR 308 Dispersed 1 - USFS
Dispersed sites, No water, No toilets, Reservations not accepted, Open all year, Tent & RV camping: Free, Road not maintained for passenger cars, Many sites long this road, Elev: 8310ft/2533m, Tel: 435-789-1181, Nearest town: Dutch John, Agency: USFS, GPS: 40.774405, -109.465014

32472 • FSR 3085 Dispersed 1 - USFS
Dispersed sites, No water, No toilets, Reservations not accepted, Open all year, Tent & RV camping: Free, Road not maintained for passenger cars, Elev: 8713ft/2656m, Tel: 435-789-1181, Nearest town: Hatch, Agency: USFS, GPS: 37.671201, -112.649628

32473 • FSR 309 (Beaver Lake) Dispersed 9 - USFS
Dispersed sites, No water, No toilets, Reservations not accepted, Open all year, Tent & RV camping: Free, Road not maintained for passenger cars, Elev: 9465ft/2885m, Tel: 307-789-3194, Nearest town: Oakley, Agency: USFS, GPS: 40.828029, -110.939971

32474 • FSR 310 Dispersed 1 - USFS
Dispersed sites, No water, No toilets, Reservations not accepted, Open all year, Tent & RV camping: Free, Road not maintained for passenger cars, Elev: 9246ft/2818m, Tel: 307-789-3194, Nearest town: Oakley, Agency: USFS, GPS: 40.852231, -110.881192

32475 • FSR 310 Dispersed 2 - USFS
Dispersed sites, No water, No toilets, Reservations not accepted, Open all year, Tent & RV camping: Free, Road not maintained for passenger cars, Elev: 9691ft/2954m, Tel: 307-789-3194, Nearest town: Oakley, Agency: USFS, GPS: 40.827223, -110.895972

32476 • FSR 312 Dispersed 1 - USFS
Dispersed sites, No water, No toilets, Reservations not accepted, Open Jun-Nov, Tent & RV camping: Free, Elev: 6883ft/2098m, Tel: 801-798-3571, Nearest town: Payson, Agency: USFS, GPS: 39.942579, -111.675983

32477 • FSR 312 Dispersed 2 - USFS
Dispersed sites, No water, No toilets, Reservations not accepted, Open Jun-Nov, Tent & RV camping: Free, Elev: 6921ft/2110m, Tel: 801-798-3571, Nearest town: Santaquin, Agency: USFS, GPS: 39.941832, -111.677633

32478 • FSR 312 Dispersed 3 - USFS
Dispersed sites, No water, No toilets, Reservations not accepted, Open Jun-Nov, Tent & RV camping: Free, Road not maintained for passenger cars, Elev: 6867ft/2093m, Tel: 801-798-3571, Nearest town: Santaquin, Agency: USFS, GPS: 39.940563, -111.677649

32479 • FSR 312 Dispersed 4 - USFS
Dispersed sites, No water, No toilets, Reservations not accepted, Open Jun-Nov, Tent & RV camping: Free, Road not maintained for passenger cars, Elev: 7124ft/2171m, Tel: 801-798-3571, Nearest town: Santaquin, Agency: USFS, GPS: 39.934987, -111.678298

32480 • FSR 312 Dispersed 5 - USFS
Dispersed sites, No water, No toilets, Reservations not accepted, Open Jun-Nov, Tent & RV camping: Free, Road not maintained for passenger cars, Elev: 7113ft/2168m, Tel: 801-798-3571, Nearest town: Santaquin, Agency: USFS, GPS: 39.937325, -111.681799

32481 • FSR 312 Dispersed 6 - USFS
Dispersed sites, No water, No toilets, Reservations not accepted, Open Jun-Nov, Tent & RV camping: Free, Road not maintained for passenger cars, Elev: 7014ft/2138m, Tel: 801-798-3571, Nearest town: Santaquin, Agency: USFS, GPS: 39.940017, -111.687365

32482 • FSR 312 Dispersed 7 - USFS
Dispersed sites, No water, No toilets, Reservations not accepted, Open Jun-Nov, Tent & RV camping: Free, Road not maintained for passenger cars, Elev: 7061ft/2152m, Tel: 801-798-3571, Nearest town: Santaquin, Agency: USFS, GPS: 39.943605, -111.690114

32483 • FSR 312 Dispersed 8 - USFS
Dispersed sites, No water, No toilets, Reservations not accepted, Open Jun-Nov, Tent & RV camping: Free, Road not maintained for passenger cars, Elev: 7079ft/2158m, Tel: 801-798-3571, Nearest town: Santaquin, Agency: USFS, GPS: 39.946194, -111.690314

32484 • FSR 313 Dispersed 1 - USFS
Dispersed sites, No water, No toilets, Reservations not accepted, Open all year, Tent & RV camping: Free, Numerous sites in this area, Elev: 8761ft/2670m, Tel: 307-789-3194, Nearest town: Oakley, Agency: USFS, GPS: 40.834952, -110.811059

32485 • FSR 3141 Dispersed 1 - USFS
Dispersed sites, No water, No toilets, Reservations not accepted, Open all year, Tent & RV camping: Free, Road not maintained for passenger cars, Elev: 7818ft/2383m, Tel: 435-789-1181, Nearest town: Alton, Agency: USFS, GPS: 37.502025, -112.554563

32486 • FSR 315 Dispersed 1 - USFS
Dispersed sites, No water, No toilets, Reservations not accepted, Open all year, Tent & RV camping: Free, Elev: 9698ft/2956m, Tel: 435-738-2482, Nearest town: Hanna, Agency: USFS, GPS: 40.566389, -110.828371

32487 • FSR 3151 Dispersed 1 - USFS
Dispersed sites, No water, No toilets, Reservations not accepted, Open all year, Tent & RV camping: Free, Road not maintained for passenger cars, Elev: 7854ft/2394m, Tel: 435-789-1181, Nearest town: Duck Creek, Agency: USFS, GPS: 37.491608, -112.586563

32488 • FSR 319 Dispersed 1 - USFS
Dispersed sites, No water, No toilets, Reservations not accepted, Open all year, Tent & RV camping: Free, Elev: 6046ft/1843m, Tel: 435-789-1181, Nearest town: Manila, Agency: USFS, GPS: 40.988622, -109.537295

32489 • FSR 320 Dispersed 1 - USFS
Dispersed sites, No water, No toilets, Reservations not accepted, Open Apr-Nov, Tent & RV camping: Free, Road not maintained for passenger cars, Elev: 7522ft/2293m, Tel: 801-785-3563, Nearest town: Midway, Agency: USFS, GPS: 40.522125, -111.614067

32490 • FSR 320 Dispersed 2 - USFS

Dispersed sites, No water, No toilets, Reservations not accepted, Open Apr-Nov, Tent & RV camping: Free, Road not maintained for passenger cars, Elev: 7517ft/2291m, Tel: 801-785-3563, Nearest town: Midway, Agency: USFS, GPS: 40.521634, -111.615474

32491 • FSR 320 Dispersed 3 - USFS

Dispersed sites, No water, No toilets, Reservations not accepted, Open all year, Tent & RV camping: Free, High-clearance vehicle required, Elev: 8392ft/2558m, Tel: 435-738-2482, Nearest town: Spanish Fork, Agency: USFS, GPS: 39.973034, -110.931004

32492 • FSR 321 (Sage Flat Overlook) Dispersed 1 - USFS

Dispersed sites, No water, No toilets, Reservations not accepted, Open May-Oct, Tent & RV camping: Free, Road not maintained for passenger cars, Elev: 8183ft/2494m, Tel: 801-785-3563, Nearest town: Pleasant Grove, Agency: USFS, GPS: 40.409288, -111.691739

32493 • FSR 322 (NG Gravel Pit) Dispersed 3 - USFS

Dispersed sites, No water, No toilets, Reservations not accepted, Open May-Nov, Tent & RV camping: Free, Road not maintained for passenger cars, Elev: 7567ft/2306m, Tel: 801-785-3563, Nearest town: Orem, Agency: USFS, GPS: 40.292374, -111.603832

32494 • FSR 322 Dispersed 1 - USFS

Dispersed sites, No water, No toilets, Reservations not accepted, Open all year, Tent & RV camping: Free, At end of road, Road not maintained for passenger cars, Elev: 6891ft/2100m, Tel: 435-789-1181, Nearest town: Pine Valley, Agency: USFS, GPS: 37.309449, -113.504635

32495 • FSR 322 Dispersed 2 - USFS

Dispersed sites, No water, No toilets, Reservations not accepted, Open all year, Tent & RV camping: Free, Road not maintained for passenger cars, Elev: 9913ft/3021m, Tel: 435-836-2800, Nearest town: Koosharem, Agency: USFS, GPS: 38.536166, -111.703031

32496 • FSR 324 Dispersed 1 - USFS

Dispersed sites, No water, No toilets, Reservations not accepted, Open all year, Tent & RV camping: Free, Road not maintained for passenger cars, Elev: 7849ft/2392m, Tel: 435-783-4338, Nearest town: Heber City, Agency: USFS, GPS: 40.283664, -111.247545

32497 • FSR 324 Dispersed 2 - USFS

Dispersed sites, No water, No toilets, Reservations not accepted, Open all year, Tent & RV camping: Free, Road not maintained for passenger cars, Elev: 7912ft/2412m, Tel: 435-783-4338, Nearest town: Heber City, Agency: USFS, GPS: 40.286108, -111.249021

32498 • FSR 324 Dispersed 3 - USFS

Dispersed sites, No water, No toilets, Reservations not accepted, Open May-Dec, Tent & RV camping: Free, Road not maintained for passenger cars, Elev: 9276ft/2827m, Tel: 307-789-3194, Nearest town: Oakley, Agency: USFS, GPS: 40.853719, -110.938183

32499 • FSR 326 Dispersed 1 - USFS

Dispersed sites, No water, No toilets, Reservations not accepted, Open all year, Tent & RV camping: Free, High-clearance vehicle

required, Elev: 9390ft/2862m, Tel: 435-738-2482, Nearest town: Spanish Fork, Agency: USFS, GPS: 39.876175, -110.853984

32500 • FSR 327 (Hunters Camp) Dispersed 1 - USFS

Dispersed sites, No water, No toilets, Reservations not accepted, Open all year, Tent & RV camping: Free, Road not maintained for passenger cars, Elev: 8277ft/2523m, Tel: 435-783-4338, Nearest town: Heber City, Agency: USFS, GPS: 40.335364, -111.244672

32501 • FSR 329 Dispersed 1 - USFS

Dispersed sites, No water, No toilets, Reservations not accepted, Open all year, Tent & RV camping: Free, Room for several igs, Elev: 8182ft/2494m, Tel: 435-783-4338, Nearest town: Heber City, Agency: USFS, GPS: 40.349321, -111.226608

32502 • FSR 330 Dispersed 1 - USFS

Dispersed sites, No water, No toilets, Reservations not accepted, Open all year, Tent & RV camping: Free, High-clearance vehicle required, Elev: 7351ft/2241m, Tel: 435-738-2482, Nearest town: Duchesne, Agency: USFS, GPS: 39.976502, -110.672157

32503 • FSR 330 Dispersed 2 - USFS

Dispersed sites, No water, No toilets, Reservations not accepted, Open all year, Tent & RV camping: Free, Elev: 8222ft/2506m, Tel: 435-783-4338, Nearest town: Heber City, Agency: USFS, GPS: 40.351576, -111.226355

32504 • FSR 3302 (Deer Creek TH) Dispersed 1 - USFS

Dispersed sites, No water, No toilets, Reservations not accepted, Open all year, Tent & RV camping: Free, Road not maintained for passenger cars, Elev: 9300ft/2835m, Tel: 435-826-5400, Nearest town: Teasdale, Agency: USFS, GPS: 38.014525, -111.376245

32505 • FSR 3313 Dispersed 1 - USFS

Dispersed sites, No water, No toilets, Reservations not accepted, Open all year, Tent & RV camping: Free, Road not maintained for passenger cars, Elev: 8382ft/2555m, Tel: 435-836-2800, Nearest town: Grover, Agency: USFS, GPS: 38.166171, -111.338565

32506 • FSR 3317 Dispersed 1 - USFS

Dispersed sites, No water, No toilets, Reservations not accepted, Open all year, Tent & RV camping: Free, Elev: 8820ft/2688m, Tel: 435-836-2800, Nearest town: Grover, Agency: USFS, GPS: 38.094912, -111.346418

32507 • FSR 333 (Rim Lake) Dispersed 1 - USFS

Dispersed sites, No water, No toilets, Reservations not accepted, Open all year, Tent & RV camping: Free, Road not maintained for passenger cars, Elev: 10901ft/3323m, Tel: 435-836-2800, Nearest town: Grover, Agency: USFS, GPS: 38.073548, -111.509637

32508 • FSR 333 Dispersed 2 - USFS

Dispersed sites, No water, No toilets, Reservations not accepted, Open all year, Tent & RV camping: Free, Elev: 8350ft/2545m, Tel: 435-738-2482, Nearest town: Duchesne, Agency: USFS, GPS: 39.941053, -110.439543

32509 • FSR 3332 Dispersed 1 - USFS

Dispersed sites, No water, No toilets, Reservations not accepted, Open all year, Tent & RV camping: Free, Road not maintained for passenger cars, Elev: 7925ft/2416m, Tel: 435-836-2800, Nearest town: Teasdale, Agency: USFS, GPS: 38.235983, -111.598871

32510 • FSR 3350 Dispersed 1 - USFS

Dispersed sites, No water, No toilets, Reservations not accepted, Open all year, Tent & RV camping: Free, Road not maintained for passenger cars, Elev: 6170ft/1881m, Tel: 435-789-1181, Nearest town: Enterprise, Agency: USFS, GPS: 37.598096, -114.040898

32511 • FSR 3352 Dispersed 1 - USFS

Dispersed sites, No water, No toilets, Reservations not accepted, Open all year, Tent & RV camping: Free, Road not maintained for passenger cars, Elev: 4552ft/1387m, Tel: 435-789-1181, Nearest town: St George, Agency: USFS, GPS: 37.235238, -113.486174

32512 • FSR 3358 Dispersed 1 - USFS

Dispersed sites, No water, No toilets, Reservations not accepted, Open all year, Tent & RV camping: Free, Elev: 4623ft/1409m, Tel: 435-789-1181, Nearest town: Leeds, Agency: USFS, GPS: 37.281507, -113.395158

32513 • FSR 337 Dispersed 1 - USFS

Dispersed sites, No water, No toilets, Reservations not accepted, Open all year, Tent & RV camping: Free, High-clearance vehicle required, Elev: 7524ft/2293m, Tel: 435-738-2482, Nearest town: Duchesne, Agency: USFS, GPS: 39.929336, -110.302416

32514 • FSR 337 Dispersed 2 - USFS

Dispersed sites, No water, No toilets, Reservations not accepted, Open all year, Tent & RV camping: Free, High-clearance vehicle required, Elev: 7435ft/2266m, Tel: 435-738-2482, Nearest town: Duchesne, Agency: USFS, GPS: 39.946962, -110.291158

32515 • FSR 338 Dispersed 1 - USFS

Dispersed sites, No water, No toilets, Reservations not accepted, Open all year, Tent & RV camping: Free, Both sides of road, Road not maintained for passenger cars, Elev: 8890ft/2710m, Tel: 307-789-3194, Nearest town: Oakley, Agency: USFS, GPS: 40.914635, -110.775879

32516 • FSR 3383 Dispersed 1 - USFS

Dispersed sites, No water, No toilets, Reservations not accepted, Open all year, Tent & RV camping: Free, Road not maintained for passenger cars, Elev: 5520ft/1682m, Tel: 435-789-1181, Nearest town: Enterprise, Agency: USFS, GPS: 37.548895, -113.708496

32517 • FSR 3390 Dispersed 1 - USFS

Dispersed sites, No water, No toilets, Reservations not accepted, Open all year, Tent & RV camping: Free, Road not maintained for passenger cars, Elev: 6340ft/1932m, Tel: 435-789-1181, Nearest town: Newcastle, Agency: USFS, GPS: 37.502707, -113.491729

32518 • FSR 3391 Dispersed 1 - USFS

Dispersed sites, No water, No toilets, Reservations not accepted, Open all year, Tent & RV camping: Free, Road not maintained for passenger cars, Elev: 7006ft/2135m, Tel: 435-789-1181, Nearest town: Pine Valley, Agency: USFS, GPS: 37.432668, -113.494933

32519 • FSR 3393 Dispersed 1 - USFS

Dispersed sites, No water, No toilets, Reservations not accepted, Open all year, Tent & RV camping: Free, Road not maintained for passenger cars, Elev: 6470ft/1972m, Tel: 435-789-1181, Nearest town: Newcastle, Agency: USFS, GPS: 37.541594, -113.403077

32520 • FSR 340 Dispersed - USFS

Dispersed sites, No water, No toilets, Reservations not accepted, Open all year, Tent & RV camping: Free, Road not maintained for passenger cars, Elev: 6708ft/2045m, Tel: 435-755-3620, Nearest town: Garden City, Agency: USFS, GPS: 41.933811, -111.570333

32521 • FSR 3404 Dispersed 1 - USFS

Dispersed sites, No water, No toilets, Reservations not accepted, Open all year, Tent & RV camping: Free, Road not maintained for passenger cars, Elev: 7090ft/2161m, Tel: 435-789-1181, Nearest town: Pine Valley, Agency: USFS, GPS: 37.441836, -113.521248

32522 • FSR 341 Dispersed 1 - USFS

Dispersed sites, No water, No toilets, Reservations not accepted, Open all year, Tent & RV camping: Free, Several sites in this area, Elev: 6058ft/1846m, Tel: 435-789-1181, Nearest town: Manila, Agency: USFS, GPS: 40.990771, -109.514552

32523 • FSR 3415 Dispersed 1 - USFS

Dispersed sites, No water, No toilets, Reservations not accepted, Open all year, Tent & RV camping: Free, Road not maintained for passenger cars, Elev: 6286ft/1916m, Tel: 435-789-1181, Nearest town: Newcastle, Agency: USFS, GPS: 37.533047, -113.543583

32524 • FSR 343 Dispersed 1 - USFS

Dispersed sites, No water, No toilets, Reservations not accepted, Open May-Dec, Tent & RV camping: Free, Numerous sites in this area, Elev: 8496ft/2590m, Tel: 307-789-3194, Nearest town: Oakley, Agency: USFS, GPS: 40.897706, -110.825263

32525 • FSR 344 Dispersed 1 - USFS

Dispersed sites, No water, No toilets, Reservations not accepted, Open all year, Tents only: Free, Road not maintained for passenger cars, Elev: 6089ft/1856m, Tel: 435-789-1181, Nearest town: Enterprise, Agency: USFS, GPS: 37.561632, -113.600032

32526 • FSR 344 Dispersed 2 - USFS

Dispersed sites, No water, No toilets, Reservations not accepted, Open all year, Tent & RV camping: Free, Elev: 10539ft/3212m, Tel: 435-789-1181, Nearest town: Whiterocks, Agency: USFS, GPS: 40.765053, -110.025782

32527 • FSR 345 Dispersed 1 - USFS

Dispersed sites, No water, No toilets, Reservations not accepted, Open all year, Tent & RV camping: Free, Road not maintained for passenger cars, Elev: 9095ft/2772m, Tel: 307-789-3194, Nearest town: Oakley, Agency: USFS, GPS: 40.930694, -110.606322

32528 • FSR 3455 Dispersed 1 - USFS

Dispersed sites, No water, No toilets, Reservations not accepted, Open all year, Tent & RV camping: Free, Elev: 9827ft/2995m, Tel: 435-789-1181, Nearest town: Duck Creek, Agency: USFS, GPS: 37.573817, -112.803055

32529 • FSR 3466 Dispersed 1 - USFS

Dispersed sites, No water, No toilets, Reservations not accepted, Open all year, Tent & RV camping: Free, Road not maintained for passenger cars, Elev: 8225ft/2507m, Tel: 435-789-1181, Nearest town: Panguitch, Agency: USFS, GPS: 37.723508, -112.630062

32530 • FSR 3468 Dispersed 1 - USFS

Dispersed sites, No water, No toilets, Reservations not accepted, Open all year, Tent & RV camping: Free, Road not maintained for passenger cars, Elev: 8250ft/2515m, Tel: 435-789-1181, Nearest town: Hatch, Agency: USFS, GPS: 37.717225, -112.607259

32531 • FSR 3469 Dispersed 1 - USFS

Dispersed sites, No water, No toilets, Reservations not accepted, Open all year, Tent & RV camping: Free, Road not maintained for passenger cars, Elev: 8235ft/2510m, Tel: 435-789-1181, Nearest town: Hatch, Agency: USFS, GPS: 37.713287, -112.602535

32532 • FSR 349 Dispersed 1 - USFS

Dispersed sites, No water, No toilets, Reservations not accepted, Open all year, Tent & RV camping: Free, Elev: 5706ft/1739m, Tel: 435-789-1181, Nearest town: Enterprise, Agency: USFS, GPS: 37.533396, -113.753876

32533 • FSR 349 Dispersed 2 - USFS

Dispersed sites, No water, No toilets, Reservations not accepted, Open all year, Tent & RV camping: Free, Elev: 5710ft/1740m, Tel: 435-789-1181, Nearest town: Enterprise, Agency: USFS, GPS: 37.531831, -113.756026

32534 • FSR 349 Dispersed 3 - USFS

Dispersed sites, No water, No toilets, Reservations not accepted, Open all year, Tent & RV camping: Free, Road not maintained for passenger cars, Elev: 7915ft/2412m, Tel: 435-896-9233, Nearest town: Salina, Agency: USFS, GPS: 38.827996, -111.632618

32535 • FSR 349 Dispersed 4 - USFS

Dispersed sites, No water, No toilets, Reservations not accepted, Open all year, Tent & RV camping: Free, High-clearance vehicle required, Elev: 9946ft/3032m, Tel: 435-738-2482, Nearest town: Whiterocks, Agency: USFS, GPS: 40.617324, -110.038765

32536 • FSR 350 Dispersed 1 - USFS

Dispersed sites, No water, No toilets, Reservations not accepted, Open all year, Tent & RV camping: Free, 3 separated sites in area, Road not maintained for passenger cars, Elev: 9799ft/2987m, Tel: 435-836-2800, Nearest town: Koosharem, Agency: USFS, GPS: 38.700973, -111.704349

32537 • FSR 3512 Dispersed 1 - USFS

Dispersed sites, No water, No toilets, Reservations not accepted, Open all year, Tent & RV camping: Free, Road not maintained for passenger cars, Elev: 7844ft/2391m, Tel: 435-789-1181, Nearest town: Paragonah, Agency: USFS, GPS: 37.874221, -112.682918

32538 • FSR 3514 Dispersed 1 - USFS

Dispersed sites, No water, No toilets, Reservations not accepted, Open all year, Tent & RV camping: Free, Road not maintained for passenger cars, Elev: 7786ft/2373m, Tel: 435-789-1181, Nearest town: Paragonah, Agency: USFS, GPS: 37.870418, -112.680849

32539 • FSR 352 Dispersed 1 - USFS

Dispersed sites, No water, No toilets, Reservations not accepted, Open all year, Tent & RV camping: Free, Road not maintained for passenger cars, Elev: 10027ft/3056m, Tel: 435-836-2800, Nearest town: Koosharem, Agency: USFS, GPS: 38.544862, -111.754741

32540 • FSR 354 Dispersed 1 - USFS

Dispersed sites, No water, No toilets, Reservations not accepted, Open all year, Tent & RV camping: Free, 2 sites, Elev: 7462ft/2274m, Tel: 435-738-2482, Nearest town: Whiterocks, Agency: USFS, GPS: 40.601299, -110.121479

32541 • FSR 356 Dispersed 1 - USFS

Dispersed sites, No water, No toilets, Reservations not accepted, Open all year, Tent & RV camping: Free, Road not maintained for passenger cars, Elev: 6396ft/1950m, Tel: 435-789-1181, Nearest town: Enterprise, Agency: USFS, GPS: 37.475819, -113.728816

32542 • FSR 356 Dispersed 2 - USFS

Dispersed sites, No water, No toilets, Reservations not accepted, Open all year, Tent & RV camping: Free, Road not maintained for passenger cars, Elev: 6369ft/1941m, Tel: 435-789-1181, Nearest town: Enterprise, Agency: USFS, GPS: 37.460427, -113.718876

32543 • FSR 356 Dispersed 3 - USFS

Dispersed sites, No water, No toilets, Reservations not accepted, Open all year, Tent & RV camping: Free, Large open area, Elev: 7634ft/2327m, Tel: 435-738-2482, Nearest town: Whiterocks, Agency: USFS, GPS: 40.611115, -110.124558

32544 • FSR 359 Dispersed 1 - USFS

Dispersed sites, No water, No toilets, Reservations not accepted, Open all year, Tent & RV camping: Free, Elev: 7591ft/2314m, Tel: 435-738-2482, Nearest town: Whiterocks, Agency: USFS, GPS: 40.613561, -110.127212

32545 • FSR 360 Dispersed 1 - USFS

Dispersed sites, No water, No toilets, Reservations not accepted, Open all year, Tent & RV camping: Free, High-clearance vehicle required, Elev: 8655ft/2638m, Tel: 435-738-2482, Nearest town: Duchesne, Agency: USFS, GPS: 40.014326, -110.973579

32546 • FSR 361 Dispersed 1 - USFS

Dispersed sites, No water, No toilets, Reservations not accepted, Open all year, Tent & RV camping: Free, Elev: 7623ft/2323m, Tel: 435-738-2482, Nearest town: Whiterocks, Agency: USFS, GPS: 40.618004, -110.133307

32547 • FSR 361 Dispersed 1 - USFS

Dispersed sites, No water, No toilets, Reservations not accepted, Open all year, Tent & RV camping: Free, Road not maintained for passenger cars, Elev: 8878ft/2706m, Tel: 435-789-1181, Nearest town: Cedar City, Agency: USFS, GPS: 37.593992, -112.895182

32548 • FSR 361 Dispersed 2 - USFS

Dispersed sites, No water, No toilets, Reservations not accepted, Open all year, Tent & RV camping: Free, Elev: 7699ft/2347m, Tel: 435-738-2482, Nearest town: Whiterocks, Agency: USFS, GPS: 40.619192, -110.131817

32549 • FSR 361 Dispersed 2 - USFS

Dispersed sites, No water, No toilets, Reservations not accepted, Open all year, Tent & RV camping: Free, Road not maintained for passenger cars, Elev: 9109ft/2776m, Tel: 435-789-1181, Nearest town: Cedar City, Agency: USFS, GPS: 37.600657, -112.895999

32550 • FSR 3632 Dispersed 1 - USFS

Dispersed sites, No water, No toilets, Reservations not accepted, Open all year, Tent & RV camping: Free, Road not maintained for passenger cars, Elev: 10603ft/3232m, Tel: 435-676-9302, Nearest town: Circleville, Agency: USFS, GPS: 38.014923, -112.206812

32551 • FSR 3638 Dispersed 1 - USFS

Dispersed sites, No water, No toilets, Reservations not accepted, Open all year, Tent & RV camping: Free, Road not maintained for passenger cars, Elev: 8744ft/2665m, Tel: 435-676-9308, Nearest town: Panguitch, Agency: USFS, GPS: 37.797595, -112.222129

32552 • FSR 3661 Dispersed 1 - USFS

Dispersed sites, No water, No toilets, Reservations not accepted, Open all year, Tent & RV camping: Free, Road not maintained for passenger cars, Elev: 8067ft/2459m, Tel: 435-676-9312, Nearest town: Hatch, Agency: USFS, GPS: 37.670611, -112.270945

32553 • FSR 367 Dispersed 1 - USFS

Dispersed sites, No water, No toilets, Reservations not accepted, Open all year, Tent & RV camping: Free, Elev: 8077ft/2462m, Tel: 435-738-2482, Nearest town: Altamont, Agency: USFS, GPS: 40.586954, -110.331096

32554 • FSR 3678 Dispersed 1 - USFS

Dispersed sites, No water, No toilets, Reservations not accepted, Open all year, Tent & RV camping: Free, Road not maintained for passenger cars, Elev: 8129ft/2478m, Tel: 435-676-9316, Nearest town: Hatch, Agency: USFS, GPS: 37.573076, -112.289989

32555 • FSR 3679 Dispersed 1 - USFS

Dispersed sites, No water, No toilets, Reservations not accepted, Open all year, Tent & RV camping: Free, Road not maintained for passenger cars, Elev: 8587ft/2617m, Tel: 435-676-9313, Nearest town: Hatch, Agency: USFS, GPS: 37.611408, -112.331557

32556 • FSR 3702 Dispersed 1 - USFS

Dispersed sites, No water, No toilets, Reservations not accepted, Open all year, Tent & RV camping: Free, Road not maintained for passenger cars, Elev: 8045ft/2452m, Tel: 435-676-9316, Nearest town: Hatch, Agency: USFS, GPS: 37.533061, -112.302757

32557 • FSR 371 Dispersed 1 - USFS

Dispersed sites, No water, No toilets, Reservations not accepted, Open all year, Tent & RV camping: Free, Elev: 7912ft/2412m, Tel: 435-789-1181, Nearest town: Duck Creek, Agency: USFS, GPS: 37.543529, -112.587399

32558 • FSR 371 Dispersed 2 - USFS

Dispersed sites, No water, No toilets, Reservations not accepted, Open all year, Tent & RV camping: Free, 2 separated sites, Elev: 7904ft/2409m, Tel: 435-789-1181, Nearest town: Duck Creek, Agency: USFS, GPS: 37.544506, -112.582693

32559 • FSR 371 Dispersed 3 - USFS

Dispersed sites, No water, No toilets, Reservations not accepted, Open all year, Tent & RV camping: Free, Elev: 7972ft/2430m, Tel: 435-789-1181, Nearest town: Duck Creek, Agency: USFS, GPS: 37.545782, -112.570018

32560 • FSR 3739 Dispersed - USFS

Dispersed sites, No water, No toilets, Reservations not accepted, Open all year, Tent & RV camping: Free, Road not maintained for passenger cars, Elev: 9627ft/2934m, Tel: 435-676-9301, Nearest town: Antimony, Agency: USFS, GPS: 38.065656, -112.149856

32561 • FSR 375 Dispersed 1 - USFS

Dispersed sites, No water, No toilets, Reservations not accepted, Open all year, Tent & RV camping: Free, 2nd spot 300' south, Road not maintained for passenger cars, Elev: 8437ft/2572m, Tel: 307-789-3194, Nearest town: Oakley, Agency: USFS, GPS: 40.910087, -110.821715

32562 • FSR 376 Dispersed 1 - USFS

Dispersed sites, No water, No toilets, Reservations not accepted, Open all year, Tent & RV camping: Free, 2nd spot 500' further down road, Road not maintained for passenger cars, Elev: 8495ft/2589m, Tel: 307-789-3194, Nearest town: Oakley, Agency: USFS, GPS: 40.909272, -110.818058

32563 • FSR 377 Dispersed 1 - USFS

Dispersed sites, No water, No toilets, Reservations not accepted, Open all year, Tent & RV camping: Free, Numerous sites in this area, Road not maintained for passenger cars, Elev: 7971ft/2430m, Tel: 435-783-4338, Nearest town: Heber City, Agency: USFS, GPS: 40.357349, -111.077997

32564 • FSR 377 Dispersed 1 - USFS

Dispersed sites, No water, No toilets, Reservations not accepted, Open all year, Tent & RV camping: Free, 2nd site 600' further along road, Road not maintained for passenger cars, Elev: 8530ft/2600m, Tel: 307-789-3194, Nearest town: Oakley, Agency: USFS, GPS: 40.905751, -110.807855

32565 • FSR 377 Dispersed 2 - USFS

Dispersed sites, No water, No toilets, Reservations not accepted, Open all year, Tent & RV camping: Free, Road not maintained for passenger cars, Elev: 8589ft/2618m, Tel: 307-789-3194, Nearest town: Oakley, Agency: USFS, GPS: 40.904774, -110.805064

32566 • FSR 378 Dispersed 1 - USFS

Dispersed sites, No water, No toilets, Reservations not accepted, Tent & RV camping: Free, Elev: 8643ft/2634m, Tel: 307-789-3194, Nearest town: Evanston, Agency: USFS, GPS: 40.896272, -110.802552

32567 • FSR 381 Dispersed 1 - USFS

Dispersed sites, No water, No toilets, Reservations not accepted, Open all year, Tent & RV camping: Free, Road not maintained for passenger cars, Elev: 6809ft/2075m, Tel: 435-438-2430, Nearest town: Beaver, Agency: USFS, GPS: 38.590212, -112.474857

32568 • FSR 381 Dispersed 2 - USFS

Dispersed sites, No water, No toilets, Reservations not accepted, Open all year, Tent & RV camping: Free, Road not maintained for passenger cars, Elev: 8546ft/2605m, Tel: 307-789-3194, Nearest town: Oakley, Agency: USFS, GPS: 40.895982, -110.822661

32569 • FSR 3825 Dispersed 1 - USFS

Dispersed sites, No water, No toilets, Reservations not accepted, Open all year, Tent & RV camping: Free, Road not maintained for passenger cars, Elev: 8669ft/2642m, Tel: 435-826-5400, Nearest town: Antimony, Agency: USFS, GPS: 38.068902, -111.856009

32570 • FSR 3839 Dispersed 1 - USFS

Dispersed sites, No water, No toilets, Reservations not accepted, Open all year, Tent & RV camping: Free, Road not maintained for passenger cars, Elev: 8345ft/2544m, Tel: 435-826-5400, Nearest town: Escalante, Agency: USFS, GPS: 37.802173, -111.957714

32571 • FSR 384 Dispersed 1 - USFS

Dispersed sites, No water, Vault toilets, Reservations not accepted, Open all year, Tent & RV camping: Free, Parking lot, Road not maintained for passenger cars, Elev: 7768ft/2368m, Tel: 435-783-4338, Nearest town: Heber City, Agency: USFS, GPS: 40.283014, -111.228166

32572 • FSR 384 Dispersed 2 - USFS

Dispersed sites, No water, No toilets, Reservations not accepted, Open all year, Tent & RV camping: Free, Numerous sites in this area, Road not maintained for passenger cars, Elev: 8504ft/2592m, Tel: 307-789-3194, Nearest town: Oakley, Agency: USFS, GPS: 40.873848, -110.833929

32573 • FSR 389 Dispersed 1 - USFS

Dispersed sites, No water, No toilets, Reservations not accepted, Open all year, Tent & RV camping: Free, Road not maintained for passenger cars, Elev: 7848ft/2392m, Tel: 435-783-4338, Nearest town: Heber City, Agency: USFS, GPS: 40.292091, -111.216164

32574 • FSR 393 Dispersed 1 - USFS

Dispersed sites, No water, No toilets, Reservations not accepted, Open all year, Tent & RV camping: Free, Elev: 8125ft/2476m, Tel: 435-783-4338, Nearest town: Heber City, Agency: USFS, GPS: 40.291073, -111.171912

32575 • FSR 394 (Lily Lake) Dispersed 1 - USFS

Dispersed sites, No water, No toilets, Reservations not accepted, Open all year, Tent & RV camping: Free, Road not maintained for passenger cars, Elev: 8905ft/2714m, Tel: 307-789-3194, Nearest town: Oakley, Agency: USFS, GPS: 40.879044, -110.812022

32576 • FSR 3950 Dispersed 1 - USFS

Dispersed sites, No water, No toilets, Reservations not accepted, Open all year, Tent & RV camping: Free, Road not maintained for passenger cars, Elev: 9001ft/2744m, Tel: 435-826-5400, Nearest town: Escalante, Agency: USFS, GPS: 37.918113, -111.806865

32577 • FSR 3956 Dispersed 1 - USFS

Dispersed sites, No water, No toilets, Reservations not accepted, Open all year, Tent & RV camping: Free, Road not maintained for passenger cars, Elev: 9236ft/2815m, Tel: 435-826-5400, Nearest town: Antimony, Agency: USFS, GPS: 38.095915, -111.829844

32578 • FSR 3963 Dispersed 1 - USFS

Dispersed sites, No water, No toilets, Reservations not accepted, Open all year, Tent & RV camping: Free, Road not maintained for passenger cars, Elev: 9938ft/3029m, Tel: 435-826-5400, Nearest town: Antimony, Agency: USFS, GPS: 37.981819, -111.806988

32579 • FSR 397 Dispersed 1 - USFS

Dispersed sites, No water, Vault toilets, Reservations not accepted, Open all year, Tent & RV camping: Free, Road not maintained for passenger cars, Elev: 8953ft/2729m, Tel: 307-782-6555, Nearest town: Mountain View (WY), Agency: USFS, GPS: 40.960688, -110.314614

32580 • FSR 3980 Dispersed 1 - USFS

Dispersed sites, No water, No toilets, Reservations not accepted, Open all year, Tent & RV camping: Free, Road not maintained for passenger cars, Elev: 9523ft/2903m, Tel: 435-836-2800, Nearest town: Grover, Agency: USFS, GPS: 38.053582, -111.321957

32581 • FSR 3985 Dispersed 1 - USFS

Dispersed sites, No water, No toilets, Reservations not accepted, Open all year, Tent & RV camping: Free, Road not maintained for passenger cars, Elev: 6426ft/1959m, Tel: 435-826-5400, Nearest town: Escalante, Agency: USFS, GPS: 37.863554, -111.637082

32582 • FSR 399 Dispersed 1 - USFS

Dispersed sites, No water, No toilets, Reservations not accepted, Open all year, Tent & RV camping: Free, Road not maintained for passenger cars, Elev: 6167ft/1880m, Tel: 435-743-5721, Nearest town: Fillmore, Agency: USFS, GPS: 38.980322, -112.249927

32583 • FSR 403 Dispersed 1 - USFS

Dispersed sites, No water, No toilets, Reservations not accepted, Open all year, Tent & RV camping: Free, Elev: 8179ft/2493m, Tel: 435-738-2482, Nearest town: Altamont, Agency: USFS, GPS: 40.597597, -110.338412

32584 • FSR 4039 Dispersed 1 - USFS

Dispersed sites, No water, No toilets, Reservations not accepted, Open May-Oct, Tent & RV camping: Free, Elev: 6299ft/1920m, Tel: 435-789-1181, Nearest town: Leeds, Agency: USFS, GPS: 37.317225, -113.443479

32585 • FSR 404 Dispersed 1 - USFS

Dispersed sites, No water, No toilets, Reservations not accepted, Open all year, Tent & RV camping: Free, Road not maintained for passenger cars, Elev: 7826ft/2385m, Tel: 435-783-4338, Nearest town: Woodland, Agency: USFS, GPS: 40.573828, -111.041547

32586 • FSR 404 Dispersed 2 - USFS

Dispersed sites, No water, No toilets, Reservations not accepted, Open all year, Tent & RV camping: Free, Road not maintained for passenger cars, Elev: 7843ft/2391m, Tel: 435-783-4338, Nearest town: Woodland, Agency: USFS, GPS: 40.574966, -111.036846

32587 • FSR 4040 Dispersed 1 - USFS

Dispersed sites, No water, No toilets, Reservations not accepted, Open May-Oct, Tent & RV camping: Free, Elev: 4800ft/1463m, Tel: 435-789-1181, Nearest town: Leeds, Agency: USFS, GPS: 37.285469, -113.402597

32588 • FSR 405 Dispersed 1 - USFS

Dispersed sites, No water, No toilets, Reservations not accepted, Open all year, Tent & RV camping: Free, Elev: 8140ft/2481m, Tel: 435-738-2482, Nearest town: Altamont, Agency: USFS, GPS: 40.598033, -110.339718

32589 • FSR 4053 Dispersed 1 - USFS

Dispersed sites, No water, No toilets, Reservations not accepted, Open all year, Tent & RV camping: Free, Road not maintained for passenger cars, Elev: 4566ft/1392m, Tel: 435-789-1181, Nearest town: St George, Agency: USFS, GPS: 37.233597, -113.485135

32590 • FSR 4056 Dispersed 1 - USFS

Dispersed sites, No water, No toilets, Reservations not accepted, Open all year, Tent & RV camping: Free, Road not maintained for passenger cars, Elev: 4353ft/1327m, Tel: 435-789-1181, Nearest town: St George, Agency: USFS, GPS: 37.235574, -113.442606

32591 • FSR 4057 Dispersed 1 - USFS

Dispersed sites, No water, No toilets, Reservations not accepted, Open all year, Tent & RV camping: Free, Road not maintained for passenger cars, Elev: 4216ft/1285m, Tel: 435-789-1181, Nearest town: St George, Agency: USFS, GPS: 37.250163, -113.430103

32592 • FSR 4059 Dispersed 1 - USFS

Dispersed sites, No water, No toilets, Reservations not accepted, Open all year, Tent & RV camping: Free, Road not maintained for passenger cars, Elev: 4189ft/1277m, Tel: 435-789-1181, Nearest town: St George, Agency: USFS, GPS: 37.254819, -113.428352

32593 • FSR 406 Dispersed 1 - USFS

Dispersed sites, No water, No toilets, Reservations not accepted, Open all year, Tent & RV camping: Free, Road not maintained for passenger cars, Elev: 8478ft/2584m, Tel: 435-789-1181, Nearest town: Cedar City, Agency: USFS, GPS: 37.646316, -112.668447

32594 • FSR 4074 Dispersed 1 - USFS

Dispersed sites, No water, No toilets, Reservations not accepted, Open all year, Tent & RV camping: Free, Road not maintained for passenger cars, Elev: 6478ft/1974m, Tel: 435-789-1181, Nearest town: Enterprise, Agency: USFS, GPS: 37.468402, -113.728257

32595 • FSR 408 Dispersed - USFS

Dispersed sites, No water, No toilets, Reservations not accepted, Open all year, Tent & RV camping: Free, Road not maintained for passenger cars, Elev: 8084ft/2464m, Tel: 435-783-4338, Nearest town: Oakley, Agency: USFS, GPS: 40.648421, -111.229925

32596 • FSR 409 Dispersed 1 - USFS

Dispersed sites, No water, No toilets, Reservations not accepted, Open all year, Tent & RV camping: Free, Road not maintained for passenger cars, Elev: 6163ft/1878m, Tel: 435-743-5721, Nearest town: Fillmore, Agency: USFS, GPS: 38.915068, -112.287687

32597 • FSR 409 Dispersed 2 - USFS

Dispersed sites, No water, No toilets, Reservations not accepted, Open all year, Tent & RV camping: Free, Road not maintained for passenger cars, Elev: 9274ft/2827m, Tel: 307-782-6555, Nearest town: Mountain View (WY), Agency: USFS, GPS: 40.903878, -110.088051

32598 • FSR 410 (Echo Lake) Dispersed - USFS

Dispersed sites, No water, No toilets, Reservations not accepted, Open all year, Tent & RV camping: Free, Several sites, Road not maintained for passenger cars, Elev: 9760ft/2975m, Tel: 435-783-4338, Nearest town: Oakley, Agency: USFS, GPS: 40.661194, -110.894464

32599 • FSR 412 (Hoop Lake) Dispersed 2 - USFS

Dispersed sites, No water, No toilets, Reservations not accepted, Open all year, Tent & RV camping: Free, Road not maintained for passenger cars, Elev: 9230ft/2813m, Tel: 307-782-6555, Nearest town: Mountain View (WY), Agency: USFS, GPS: 40.922261, -110.112124

32600 • FSR 412 Dispersed 1 - USFS

Dispersed sites, No water, No toilets, Reservations not accepted, Open all year, Tent & RV camping: Free, Road not maintained for passenger cars, Elev: 9261ft/2823m, Tel: 307-782-6555, Nearest town: Mountain View (WY), Agency: USFS, GPS: 40.923104, -110.107088

32601 • FSR 412A Dispersed 1 - USFS

Dispersed sites, No water, No toilets, Reservations not accepted, Open all year, Tent & RV camping: Free, High-clearance vehicle required, Elev: 10088ft/3075m, Tel: 435-738-2482, Nearest town: Hanna, Agency: USFS, GPS: 40.551806, -110.922123

32602 • FSR 4130 Dispersed - USFS

Dispersed sites, No water, No toilets, Reservations not accepted, Open all year, Tent & RV camping: Free, Road not maintained for passenger cars, Elev: 7812ft/2381m, Tel: 435-789-1181, Nearest town: Alton, Agency: USFS, GPS: 37.497713, -112.557348

32603 • FSR 414 (Iron Mine Lake) Dispersed 5 - USFS

Dispersed sites, No water, No toilets, Reservations not accepted, Open all year, Tent & RV camping: Free, Road not maintained for passenger cars, Elev: 9581ft/2920m, Tel: 435-783-4338, Nearest town: Woodland, Agency: USFS, GPS: 40.566449, -110.936763

32604 • FSR 414 Dispersed 1 - USFS
Dispersed sites, No water, No toilets, Reservations not accepted, Open all year, Tent & RV camping: Free, Road not maintained for passenger cars, Elev: 8701ft/2652m, Tel: 435-783-4338, Nearest town: Woodland, Agency: USFS, GPS: 40.572341, -111.023462

32605 • FSR 414 Dispersed 2 - USFS
Dispersed sites, No water, No toilets, Reservations not accepted, Open all year, Tent & RV camping: Free, Road not maintained for passenger cars, Elev: 9013ft/2747m, Tel: 435-783-4338, Nearest town: Woodland, Agency: USFS, GPS: 40.583451, -111.002202

32606 • FSR 414 Dispersed 3 - USFS
Dispersed sites, No water, No toilets, Reservations not accepted, Open all year, Tent & RV camping: Free, Road not maintained for passenger cars, Elev: 9180ft/2798m, Tel: 435-783-4338, Nearest town: Woodland, Agency: USFS, GPS: 40.585836, -110.978852

32607 • FSR 414 Dispersed 4 - USFS
Dispersed sites, No water, No toilets, Reservations not accepted, Open all year, Tent & RV camping: Free, Road not maintained for passenger cars, Elev: 9867ft/3007m, Tel: 435-783-4338, Nearest town: Woodland, Agency: USFS, GPS: 40.580131, -110.938568

32608 • FSR 414 Dispersed 6 - USFS
Dispersed sites, No water, No toilets, Reservations not accepted, Open all year, Tent & RV camping: Free, Road not maintained for passenger cars, Elev: 6802ft/2073m, Tel: 435-743-5721, Nearest town: Oak City, Agency: USFS, GPS: 39.359964, -112.221064

32609 • FSR 416 Dispersed 1 - USFS
Dispersed sites, No water, No toilets, Reservations not accepted, Open all year, Tent & RV camping: Free, Road not maintained for passenger cars, Elev: 5669ft/1728m, Tel: 435-743-5721, Nearest town: Oak City, Agency: USFS, GPS: 39.349224, -112.294702

32610 • FSR 416 Dispersed 1 - USFS
Dispersed sites, No water, No toilets, Reservations not accepted, Open May-Oct, Tent & RV camping: Free, Road not maintained for passenger cars, Elev: 7576ft/2309m, Tel: 801-785-3563, Nearest town: Pleasant Grove, Agency: USFS, GPS: 40.386382, -111.687143

32611 • FSR 416 Dispersed 1 - USFS
Dispersed sites, No water, No toilets, Reservations not accepted, Open all year, Tent & RV camping: Free, Road not maintained for passenger cars, Elev: 9216ft/2809m, Tel: 435-783-4338, Nearest town: Oakley, Agency: USFS, GPS: 40.636532, -110.941235

32612 • FSR 420 Dispersed 1 - USFS
Dispersed sites, No water, No toilets, Reservations not accepted, Open Apr-Nov, Tent & RV camping: Free, Road not maintained for passenger cars, Elev: 8303ft/2531m, Tel: 801-785-3563, Nearest town: Midway, Agency: USFS, GPS: 40.559678, -111.557935

32613 • FSR 422 Dispersed 1 - USFS
Dispersed sites, No water, No toilets, Reservations not accepted, Open Apr-Nov, Tent & RV camping: Free, Road not maintained

for passenger cars, Elev: 7772ft/2369m, Tel: 801-785-3563, Nearest town: Midway, Agency: USFS, GPS: 40.542558, -111.592722

32614 • FSR 431 Dispersed 1 - USFS
Dispersed sites, No water, No toilets, Reservations not accepted, Tent & RV camping: Free, Several sites in this area, Elev: 7045ft/2147m, Tel: 435-783-4338, Nearest town: Kamas, Agency: USFS, GPS: 40.632503, -111.190247

32615 • FSR 436 Dispersed 1 - USFS
Dispersed sites, No water, No toilets, Reservations not accepted, Open all year, Tent & RV camping: Free, Numerous sites along road, Road not maintained for passenger cars, Elev: 9055ft/2760m, Tel: 435-783-4338, Nearest town: Heber City, Agency: USFS, GPS: 40.485282, -111.118387

32616 • FSR 441 (Japanese Monument) Dispersed 1 - USFS
Dispersed sites, No water, No toilets, Reservations not accepted, Open all year, Tent & RV camping: Free, Elev: 8421ft/2567m, Tel: 435-783-4338, Nearest town: Woodland, Agency: USFS, GPS: 40.515795, -111.049264

32617 • FSR 441 (Otter Lake) Dispersed 3 - USFS
Dispersed sites, No water, No toilets, Reservations not accepted, Open all year, Tent & RV camping: Free, Road not maintained for passenger cars, Elev: 9737ft/2968m, Tel: 435-826-5400, Nearest town: Antimony, Agency: USFS, GPS: 37.944656, -111.895346

32618 • FSR 441 Dispersed 2 - USFS
Dispersed sites, No water, No toilets, Reservations not accepted, Open all year, Tent & RV camping: Free, Road not maintained for passenger cars, Elev: 8681ft/2646m, Tel: 435-826-5400, Nearest town: Antimony, Agency: USFS, GPS: 37.907174, -111.939259

32619 • FSR 443 Dispersed 1 - USFS
Dispersed sites, No water, No toilets, Reservations not accepted, Open all year, Tent & RV camping: Free, Road not maintained for passenger cars, Elev: 9302ft/2835m, Tel: 435-826-5400, Nearest town: Antimony, Agency: USFS, GPS: 37.988355, -111.893349

32620 • FSR 444 (Dee Mills Reservoir) Dispersed 1 - USFS
Dispersed sites, No water, No toilets, Reservations not accepted, Open all year, Tent & RV camping: Free, Several sites in this area, Road not maintained for passenger cars, Elev: 9200ft/2804m, Tel: 435-783-4338, Nearest town: Heber City, Agency: USFS, GPS: 40.432075, -111.200775

32621 • FSR 450 Dispersed 1 - USFS
Dispersed sites, No water, No toilets, Reservations not accepted, Open all year, Tent & RV camping: Free, Road not maintained for passenger cars, Elev: 7778ft/2371m, Tel: 435-789-1181, Nearest town: Vernal, Agency: USFS, GPS: 40.623707, -109.789286

32622 • FSR 450 Dispersed 2 - USFS
Dispersed sites, No water, No toilets, Reservations not accepted, Open all year, Tent & RV camping: Free, Road not maintained for passenger cars, Elev: 7817ft/2383m, Tel: 435-789-1181, Nearest town: Vernal, Agency: USFS, GPS: 40.623599, -109.792913

32623 • FSR 450 Dispersed 3 - USFS
Dispersed sites, No water, No toilets, Reservations not accepted, Open all year, Tent & RV camping: Free, Several spots in this area, Road not maintained for passenger cars, Elev: 7894ft/2406m, Tel: 435-789-1181, Nearest town: Vernal, Agency: USFS, GPS: 40.624223, -109.798897

32624 • FSR 455 Dispersed 1 - USFS
Dispersed sites, No water, No toilets, Reservations not accepted, Open all year, Tent & RV camping: Free, Elev: 7544ft/2299m, Tel: 435-738-2482, Nearest town: Whiterocks, Agency: USFS, GPS: 40.613442, -110.130017

32625 • FSR 456 Dispersed 1 - USFS
Dispersed sites, No water, No toilets, Reservations not accepted, Open Jun-Oct, Tent & RV camping: Free, Road not maintained for passenger cars, Elev: 6852ft/2088m, Tel: 435-783-4338, Nearest town: Spanish Fork, Agency: USFS, GPS: 40.055337, -111.296828

32626 • FSR 457 (First Water Corral) Dispersed 1 - USFS
Dispersed sites, No water, No toilets, Reservations not accepted, Open Jun-Oct, Tent & RV camping: Free, Road not maintained for passenger cars, Elev: 7249ft/2209m, Tel: 435-783-4338, Nearest town: Spanish Fork, Agency: USFS, GPS: 40.040946, -111.276252

32627 • FSR 458 Dispersed 1 - USFS
Dispersed sites, No water, No toilets, Reservations not accepted, Open all year, Tent & RV camping: Free, Road not maintained for passenger cars, Elev: 6562ft/2000m, Tel: 435-743-5721, Nearest town: Scipio, Agency: USFS, GPS: 39.247423, -112.198215

32628 • FSR 460 Dispersed 1 - USFS
Dispersed sites, No water, No toilets, Reservations not accepted, Open all year, Tent & RV camping: Free, Elev: 7134ft/2174m, Tel: 435-738-2482, Nearest town: Hanna, Agency: USFS, GPS: 40.492635, -110.844616

32629 • FSR 462 Dispersed 1 - USFS
Dispersed sites, No water, No toilets, Reservations not accepted, Open all year, Tent & RV camping: Free, Elev: 7600ft/2316m, Tel: 435-738-2482, Nearest town: Hanna, Agency: USFS, GPS: 40.535728, -110.865574

32630 • FSR 467 Dispersed 1 - USFS
Dispersed sites, No water, No toilets, Reservations not accepted, Open Jun-Nov, Tent & RV camping: Free, Elev: 9402ft/2866m, Tel: 801-798-3571, Nearest town: Nephi, Agency: USFS, GPS: 39.850387, -111.704446

32631 • FSR 469 Dispersed 1 - USFS
Dispersed sites, No water, No toilets, Reservations not accepted, Open Jun-Nov, Tent & RV camping: Free, Road not maintained for passenger cars, Elev: 7353ft/2241m, Tel: 801-798-3571, Nearest town: Nephi, Agency: USFS, GPS: 39.789142, -111.687316

32632 • FSR 469 Dispersed 2 - USFS
Dispersed sites, No water, No toilets, Reservations not accepted, Open Jun-Nov, Tent & RV camping: Free, Road not maintained for passenger cars, Elev: 7200ft/2195m, Tel: 801-798-3571, Nearest town: Nephi, Agency: USFS, GPS: 39.784588, -111.689408

32633 • FSR 470 Dispersed 1 - USFS
Dispersed sites, No water, No toilets, Reservations not accepted, Open Jun-Oct, Tent & RV camping: Free, Road not maintained for passenger cars, Elev: 7928ft/2416m, Tel: 435-783-4338, Nearest town: Springville, Agency: USFS, GPS: 40.167729, -111.356981

32634 • FSR 471 Dispersed 1 - USFS
Dispersed sites, No water, No toilets, Reservations not accepted, Open all year, Tent & RV camping: Free, Elev: 7702ft/2348m, Tel: 435-783-4338, Nearest town: Heber City, Agency: USFS, GPS: 40.343284, -111.062768

32635 • FSR 471 Dispersed 2 - USFS
Dispersed sites, No water, No toilets, Reservations not accepted, Open all year, Tent & RV camping: Free, Road not maintained for passenger cars, Elev: 10129ft/3087m, Tel: 435-826-5400, Nearest town: Teasdale, Agency: USFS, GPS: 38.058161, -111.594055

32636 • FSR 472 Dispersed 1 - USFS
Dispersed sites, No water, No toilets, Reservations not accepted, Open all year, Tent & RV camping: Free, Elev: 7797ft/2377m, Tel: 435-783-4338, Nearest town: Woodland, Agency: USFS, GPS: 40.577982, -111.048815

32637 • FSR 4725 (Mt Peale) 1 - USFS
Dispersed sites, No water, No toilets, Tents only: Free, 4x4 required, Elev: 10568ft/3221m, Tel: 435-259-7155, Nearest town: Moab, Agency: USFS, GPS: 38.432889, -109.243325

32638 • FSR 474 Dispersed 1 - USFS
Dispersed sites, No water, No toilets, Reservations not accepted, Open all year, Tent & RV camping: Free, Road not maintained for passenger cars, Elev: 8362ft/2549m, Tel: 435-438-2430, Nearest town: Marysvale, Agency: USFS, GPS: 38.472346, -112.351275

32639 • FSR 475 Dispersed 1 - USFS
Dispersed sites, No water, No toilets, Reservations not accepted, Open all year, Tent & RV camping: Free, Road not maintained for passenger cars, Elev: 5975ft/1821m, Tel: 801-785-3563, Nearest town: Charleston, Agency: USFS, GPS: 40.440082, -111.555758

32640 • FSR 475 Dispersed 2 - USFS
Dispersed sites, No water, No toilets, Reservations not accepted, Open all year, Tent & RV camping: Free, Road not maintained for passenger cars, Elev: 5964ft/1818m, Tel: 801-785-3563, Nearest town: Charleston, Agency: USFS, GPS: 40.438757, -111.555849

32641 • FSR 4759 Dispersed 1 - USFS
Dispersed sites, No water, No toilets, Reservations not accepted, Open all year, Tent & RV camping: Free, 2nd spot 500' NE, Road not maintained for passenger cars, Elev: 8033ft/2448m, Tel: 435-789-1181, Nearest town: Duck Creek, Agency: USFS, GPS: 37.574693, -112.608184

32642 • FSR 477 Dispersed 1 - USFS

Dispersed sites, No water, No toilets, Reservations not accepted, Open all year, Tent & RV camping: Free, Road not maintained for passenger cars, Elev: 9738ft/2968m, Tel: 435-438-2430, Nearest town: Beaver, Agency: USFS, GPS: 38.227491, -112.374296

32643 • FSR 480 Dispersed 1 - USFS

Dispersed sites, No water, No toilets, Reservations not accepted, Open all year, Tent & RV camping: Free, Road not maintained for passenger cars, Elev: 6911ft/2106m, Tel: 435-783-4338, Nearest town: Oakley, Agency: USFS, GPS: 40.740835, -111.224556

32644 • FSR 483 Dispersed 1 - USFS

Dispersed sites, No water, No toilets, Reservations not accepted, Open all year, Tent & RV camping: Free, Road not maintained for passenger cars, Elev: 6967ft/2124m, Tel: 435-438-2430, Nearest town: Joseph, Agency: USFS, GPS: 38.556925, -112.475982

32645 • FSR 483 Dispersed 2 - USFS

Dispersed sites, No water, No toilets, Reservations not accepted, Open all year, Tent & RV camping: Free, At end of road, Road not maintained for passenger cars, Elev: 6943ft/2116m, Tel: 435-438-2430, Nearest town: Joseph, Agency: USFS, GPS: 38.554249, -112.477405

32646 • FSR 483 Dispersed 3 - USFS

Dispersed sites, No water, No toilets, Reservations not accepted, Tent & RV camping: Free, Elev: 8870ft/2704m, Tel: 435-638-1069, Nearest town: Loa, Agency: USFS, GPS: 38.522786, -111.749232

32647 • FSR 486 (Kirk's Campsite) Dispersed 1 - USFS

Dispersed sites, No water, No toilets, Reservations not accepted, Open all year, Tent & RV camping: Free, Road not maintained for passenger cars, Elev: 9561ft/2914m, Tel: 435-783-4338, Nearest town: Heber City, Agency: USFS, GPS: 40.383617, -111.157089

32648 • FSR 488 Dispersed 1 - USFS

Dispersed sites, No water, No toilets, Reservations not accepted, Open all year, Tent & RV camping: Free, Road not maintained for passenger cars, Elev: 5467ft/1666m, Tel: 435-743-5721, Nearest town: Kanosh, Agency: USFS, GPS: 38.735555, -112.528736

32649 • FSR 488 Dispersed 2 - USFS

Dispersed sites, No water, No toilets, Reservations not accepted, Open all year, Tent & RV camping: Free, Road not maintained for passenger cars, Elev: 5717ft/1743m, Tel: 435-743-5721, Nearest town: Kanosh, Agency: USFS, GPS: 38.723776, -112.521743

32650 • FSR 488 Dispersed 3 - USFS

Dispersed sites, No water, No toilets, Reservations not accepted, Tent & RV camping: Free, Elev: 7703ft/2348m, Tel: 435-738-2482, Nearest town: Mountain Home, Agency: USFS, GPS: 40.545842, -110.656631

32651 • FSR 4883 Dispersed 1 - USFS

Dispersed sites, No water, No toilets, Reservations not accepted, Open all year, Tent & RV camping: Free, Road not maintained for passenger cars, Elev: 8738ft/2663m, Tel: 435-896-9233, Nearest town: Redmond, Agency: USFS, GPS: 38.986206, -111.582104

32652 • FSR 489 Dispersed 1 - USFS

Dispersed sites, No water, No toilets, Reservations not accepted, Open all year, Tent & RV camping: Free, Road not maintained for passenger cars, Elev: 5540ft/1689m, Tel: 435-743-5721, Nearest town: Kanosh, Agency: USFS, GPS: 38.755537, -112.488537

32653 • FSR 491 Dispersed 1 - USFS

Dispersed sites, No water, No toilets, Reservations not accepted, Open all year, Tent & RV camping: Free, Several sites, Road not maintained for passenger cars, Elev: 8673ft/2644m, Tel: 435-783-4338, Nearest town: Heber City, Agency: USFS, GPS: 40.294554, -111.287611

32654 • FSR 492 Dispersed 1 - USFS

Dispersed sites, No water, No toilets, Reservations not accepted, Open all year, Tent & RV camping: Free, Road not maintained for passenger cars, Elev: 7407ft/2258m, Tel: 435-789-1181, Nearest town: Vernal, Agency: USFS, GPS: 40.614068, -109.938303

32655 • FSR 492 Dispersed 2 - USFS

Dispersed sites, No water, No toilets, Reservations not accepted, Open all year, Tent & RV camping: Free, Road not maintained for passenger cars, Elev: 7505ft/2288m, Tel: 435-789-1181, Nearest town: Vernal, Agency: USFS, GPS: 40.622096, -109.944786

32656 • FSR 494 (McGrath Lake) Dispersed 1 - USFS

Dispersed sites, No water, No toilets, Reservations not accepted, Open all year, Tent & RV camping: Free, Road not maintained for passenger cars, Elev: 9407ft/2867m, Tel: 435-826-5400, Nearest town: Teasdale, Agency: USFS, GPS: 37.997826, -111.570491

32657 • FSR 496 Dispersed 1 - USFS

Dispersed sites, No water, No toilets, Reservations not accepted, Open Jun-Oct, Tent & RV camping: Free, Road not maintained for passenger cars, Elev: 6596ft/2010m, Tel: 435-783-4338, Nearest town: Springville, Agency: USFS, GPS: 40.187599, -111.328283

32658 • FSR 50002 Dispersed 1 - USFS

Dispersed sites, No water, No toilets, Reservations not accepted, Open all year, Tent & RV camping: Free, Road not maintained for passenger cars, Elev: 10070ft/3069m, Tel: 435-637-2817, Nearest town: Manti, Agency: USFS, GPS: 39.264876, -111.366614

32659 • FSR 50002 Dispersed 2 - USFS

Dispersed sites, No water, No toilets, Reservations not accepted, Open all year, Tent & RV camping: Free, Road not maintained for passenger cars, Elev: 10141ft/3091m, Tel: 435-637-2817, Nearest town: Manti, Agency: USFS, GPS: 39.273156, -111.392236

32660 • FSR 50002 Dispersed 3 - USFS

Dispersed sites, No water, No toilets, Reservations not accepted, Open all year, Tent & RV camping: Free, Several spots in area, Road not maintained for passenger cars, Elev: 10157ft/3096m, Tel: 435-637-2817, Nearest town: Manti, Agency: USFS, GPS: 39.280116, -111.427131

32661 • FSR 50002 Dispersed 4 - USFS

Dispersed sites, No water, No toilets, Reservations not accepted, Open all year, Tent & RV camping: Free, Several spots in area,

Road not maintained for passenger cars, Elev: 10156ft/3096m, Tel: 435-637-2817, Nearest town: Manti, Agency: USFS, GPS: 39.284716, -111.428033

32662 • FSR 50002 Dispersed 5 - USFS
Dispersed sites, No water, No toilets, Reservations not accepted, Open all year, Tent & RV camping: Free, Road not maintained for passenger cars, Elev: 10325ft/3147m, Tel: 435-637-2817, Nearest town: Manti, Agency: USFS, GPS: 39.288771, -111.441951

32663 • FSR 50002 Dispersed 6 - USFS
Dispersed sites, No water, No toilets, Reservations not accepted, Open all year, Tent & RV camping: Free, Road not maintained for passenger cars, Elev: 10386ft/3166m, Tel: 435-637-2817, Nearest town: Manti, Agency: USFS, GPS: 39.290276, -111.443002

32664 • FSR 50002 Dispersed 7 - USFS
Dispersed sites, No water, No toilets, Reservations not accepted, Open all year, Tent & RV camping: Free, Road not maintained for passenger cars, Elev: 10404ft/3171m, Tel: 435-637-2817, Nearest town: Manti, Agency: USFS, GPS: 39.292628, -111.442185

32665 • FSR 50004 Dispersed 1 - USFS3
Dispersed sites, No water, No toilets, Reservations not accepted, Open all year, Tent & RV camping: Free, Road not maintained for passenger cars, Elev: 9858ft/3005m, Tel: 435-637-2817, Nearest town: Manti, Agency: USFS, GPS: 39.223434, -111.384942

32666 • FSR 50004 Dispersed 2 - USFS
Dispersed sites, No water, No toilets, Reservations not accepted, Open all year, Tent & RV camping: Free, Road not maintained for passenger cars, Elev: 10370ft/3161m, Tel: 435-637-2817, Nearest town: Manti, Agency: USFS, GPS: 39.229994, -111.408206

32667 • FSR 50004 Dispersed 3 - USFS
Dispersed sites, No water, No toilets, Reservations not accepted, Open all year, Tent & RV camping: Free, Road not maintained for passenger cars, Elev: 10525ft/3208m, Tel: 435-637-2817, Nearest town: Manti, Agency: USFS, GPS: 39.249482, -111.440942

32668 • FSR 50008 Dispersed 1 - USFS
Dispersed sites, No water, No toilets, Reservations not accepted, Open all year, Tent & RV camping: Free, Elev: 9096ft/2772m, Tel: 435-637-2817, Nearest town: Spanish Fork, Agency: USFS, GPS: 39.835892, -111.288821

32669 • FSR 50008 Dispersed 2 - USFS
Dispersed sites, No water, No toilets, Reservations not accepted, Open all year, Tent & RV camping: Free, Elev: 9024ft/2751m, Tel: 435-637-2817, Nearest town: Spanish Fork, Agency: USFS, GPS: 39.834558, -111.282654

32670 • FSR 50008 Dispersed 3 - USFS
Dispersed sites, No water, No toilets, Reservations not accepted, Open all year, Tent & RV camping: Free, Elev: 9010ft/2746m, Tel: 435-637-2817, Nearest town: Spanish Fork, Agency: USFS, GPS: 39.832767, -111.280052

32671 • FSR 50008 Dispersed 4 - USFS
Dispersed sites, No water, No toilets, Reservations not accepted, Open all year, Tent & RV camping: Free, Elev: 9012ft/2747m, Tel: 435-637-2817, Nearest town: Spanish Fork, Agency: USFS, GPS: 39.830399, -111.276138

32672 • FSR 50008 Dispersed 5 - USFS
Dispersed sites, No water, No toilets, Reservations not accepted, Open all year, Tent & RV camping: Free, Elev: 8982ft/2738m, Tel: 435-637-2817, Nearest town: Spanish Fork, Agency: USFS, GPS: 39.829767, -111.268869

32673 • FSR 50008 Dispersed 6 - USFS
Dispersed sites, No water, No toilets, Reservations not accepted, Open all year, Tent & RV camping: Free, Elev: 9188ft/2801m, Tel: 435-637-2817, Nearest town: Spanish Fork, Agency: USFS, GPS: 39.828077, -111.241128

32674 • FSR 50013 (Blue Lake) Dispersed 1 - USFS
Dispersed sites, No water, No toilets, Reservations not accepted, Open all year, Tent & RV camping: Free, Road not maintained for passenger cars, Elev: 10310ft/3142m, Tel: 435-637-2817, Nearest town: Mayfield, Agency: USFS, GPS: 39.055655, -111.503549

32675 • FSR 50014 Dispersed 1 - USFS
Dispersed sites, No water, No toilets, Reservations not accepted, Open Jun-Dec, Tent & RV camping: Free, Elev: 7471ft/2277m, Tel: 435-637-2817, Nearest town: Huntington, Agency: USFS, GPS: 39.351439, -111.266521

32676 • FSR 50014 Dispersed 10 - USFS
Dispersed sites, No water, No toilets, Reservations not accepted, Open Jun-Dec, Tent & RV camping: Free, Elev: 8479ft/2584m, Tel: 435-637-2817, Nearest town: Mount Pleasant, Agency: USFS, GPS: 39.535143, -111.251923

32677 • FSR 50014 Dispersed 11 - USFS
Dispersed sites, No water, No toilets, Reservations not accepted, Open Jun-Dec, Tent & RV camping: Free, Road not maintained for passenger cars, Elev: 8821ft/2689m, Tel: 435-637-2817, Nearest town: Mount Pleasant, Agency: USFS, GPS: 39.572548, -111.248037

32678 • FSR 50014 Dispersed 12 - USFS
Dispersed sites, No water, No toilets, Reservations not accepted, Open Jun-Dec, Tent & RV camping: Free, Elev: 8957ft/2730m, Tel: 435-637-2817, Nearest town: Mount Pleasant, Agency: USFS, GPS: 39.581473, -111.250121

32679 • FSR 50014 Dispersed 2 - USFS
Dispersed sites, No water, No toilets, Reservations not accepted, Open Jun-Dec, Tent & RV camping: Free, Elev: 8099ft/2469m, Tel: 435-637-2817, Nearest town: Huntington, Agency: USFS, GPS: 39.368383, -111.258688

32680 • FSR 50014 Dispersed 3 - USFS
Dispersed sites, No water, No toilets, Reservations not accepted, Open Jun-Dec, Tent & RV camping: Free, 2 separated sites, Elev:

8093ft/2467m, Tel: 435-637-2817, Nearest town: Huntington, Agency: USFS, GPS: 39.371206, -111.256374

32681 • FSR 50014 Dispersed 4 - USFS

Dispersed sites, No water, No toilets, Reservations not accepted, Open Jun-Dec, Tent & RV camping: Free, Elev: 8396ft/2559m, Tel: 435-637-2817, Nearest town: Huntington, Agency: USFS, GPS: 39.390136, -111.250228

32682 • FSR 50014 Dispersed 5 - USFS

Dispersed sites, No water, No toilets, Reservations not accepted, Open Jun-Dec, Tent & RV camping: Free, Elev: 8497ft/2590m, Tel: 435-637-2817, Nearest town: Huntington, Agency: USFS, GPS: 39.398056, -111.247994

32683 • FSR 50014 Dispersed 6 - USFS

Dispersed sites, No water, No toilets, Reservations not accepted, Open Jun-Dec, Tent & RV camping: Free, 2 separated sites, Elev: 8538ft/2602m, Tel: 435-637-2817, Nearest town: Huntington, Agency: USFS, GPS: 39.405706, -111.248182

32684 • FSR 50014 Dispersed 7 - USFS

Dispersed sites, No water, No toilets, Reservations not accepted, Open Jun-Dec, Tent & RV camping: Free, Elev: 8577ft/2614m, Tel: 435-637-2817, Nearest town: Huntington, Agency: USFS, GPS: 39.410523, -111.247668

32685 • FSR 50014 Dispersed 8 - USFS

Dispersed sites, No water, No toilets, Reservations not accepted, Open Jun-Dec, Tent & RV camping: Free, Numerous locations in this area, Elev: 8638ft/2633m, Tel: 435-637-2817, Nearest town: Huntington, Agency: USFS, GPS: 39.430847, -111.248624

32686 • FSR 50014 Dispersed 9 - USFS

Dispersed sites, No water, No toilets, Reservations not accepted, Open Jun-Dec, Tent & RV camping: Free, Both sites of road, Elev: 8745ft/2665m, Tel: 435-637-2817, Nearest town: Huntington, Agency: USFS, GPS: 39.436082, -111.255128

32687 • FSR 50017 Dispersed 1 - USFS

Dispersed sites, No water, No toilets, Reservations not accepted, Open Jun-Dec, Tent & RV camping: Free, Elev: 8703ft/2653m, Tel: 435-637-2817, Nearest town: Huntington, Agency: USFS, GPS: 39.430682, -111.239369

32688 • FSR 50017 Dispersed 2 - USFS

Dispersed sites, No water, No toilets, Reservations not accepted, Open Jun-Dec, Tent & RV camping: Free, Elev: 8729ft/2661m, Tel: 435-637-2817, Nearest town: Huntington, Agency: USFS, GPS: 39.436028, -111.238875

32689 • FSR 50017 Dispersed 3 - USFS

Dispersed sites, No water, No toilets, Reservations not accepted, Open Jun-Dec, Tent & RV camping: Free, Elev: 8680ft/2646m, Tel: 435-637-2817, Nearest town: Huntington, Agency: USFS, GPS: 39.436899, -111.241021

32690 • FSR 50017 Dispersed 4 - USFS

Dispersed sites, No water, No toilets, Reservations not accepted, Open Jun-Dec, Tent & RV camping: Free, Elev: 8728ft/2660m, Tel: 435-637-2817, Nearest town: Huntington, Agency: USFS, GPS: 39.437341, -111.239416

32691 • FSR 50017 Dispersed 5 - USFS

Dispersed sites, No water, No toilets, Reservations not accepted, Open Jun-Dec, Tent & RV camping: Free, Road not maintained for passenger cars, Elev: 8897ft/2712m, Tel: 435-637-2817, Nearest town: Huntington, Agency: USFS, GPS: 39.451224, -111.235767

32692 • FSR 50017 Dispersed 6 - USFS

Dispersed sites, No water, No toilets, Reservations not accepted, Open Jun-Dec, Tent & RV camping: Free, Road not maintained for passenger cars, Elev: 8946ft/2727m, Tel: 435-637-2817, Nearest town: Huntington, Agency: USFS, GPS: 39.455509, -111.233482

32693 • FSR 50018 Dispersed 1 - USFS

Dispersed sites, No water, No toilets, Reservations not accepted, Open Jun-Dec, Tent & RV camping: Free, Elev: 9581ft/2920m, Tel: 435-637-2817, Nearest town: Fairview, Agency: USFS, GPS: 39.655468, -111.207078

32694 • FSR 50018 Dispersed 2 - USFS

Dispersed sites, No water, No toilets, Reservations not accepted, Open Jun-Dec, Tent & RV camping: Free, Elev: 9865ft/3007m, Tel: 435-637-2817, Nearest town: Fairview, Agency: USFS, GPS: 39.651788, -111.202578

32695 • FSR 50018 Dispersed 3 - USFS

Dispersed sites, No water, No toilets, Reservations not accepted, Open Jun-Dec, Tent & RV camping: Free, Elev: 9733ft/2967m, Tel: 435-637-2817, Nearest town: Fairview, Agency: USFS, GPS: 39.627102, -111.188428

32696 • FSR 50018 Dispersed 4 - USFS

Dispersed sites, No water, No toilets, Reservations not accepted, Open Jun-Dec, Tent & RV camping: Free, Elev: 10062ft/3067m, Tel: 435-637-2817, Nearest town: Fairview, Agency: USFS, GPS: 39.614181, -111.186147

32697 • FSR 50018 Dispersed 5 - USFS

Dispersed sites, No water, No toilets, Reservations not accepted, Open Jun-Dec, Tent & RV camping: Free, Elev: 9961ft/3036m, Tel: 435-637-2817, Nearest town: Huntington, Agency: USFS, GPS: 39.594184, -111.162465

32698 • FSR 50018 Dispersed 6 - USFS

Dispersed sites, No water, No toilets, Reservations not accepted, Open Jun-Dec, Tent & RV camping: Free, At end of road, Road not maintained for passenger cars, Elev: 9858ft/3005m, Tel: 435-637-2817, Nearest town: Huntington, Agency: USFS, GPS: 39.565205, -111.147049

32699 • FSR 50022 Dispersed 1 - USFS

Dispersed sites, No water, No toilets, Reservations not accepted, Open all year, Tent & RV camping: Free, Elev: 6335ft/1931m,

Tel: 435-637-2817, Nearest town: Ferron, Agency: USFS, GPS: 39.107606, -111.231871

32700 • FSR 50022 Dispersed 10 - USFS
Dispersed sites, No water, No toilets, Reservations not accepted, Open May-Dec, Tent & RV camping: Free, Elev: 9283ft/2829m, Tel: 435-637-2817, Nearest town: Ferron, Agency: USFS, GPS: 39.138256, -111.430638

32701 • FSR 50022 Dispersed 11 - USFS
Dispersed sites, No water, No toilets, Reservations not accepted, Open all year, Tent & RV camping: Free, Elev: 9563ft/2915m, Tel: 435-637-2817, Nearest town: Mayfield, Agency: USFS, GPS: 39.141016, -111.499533

32702 • FSR 50022 Dispersed 12 - USFS
Dispersed sites, No water, No toilets, Reservations not accepted, Open all year, Tent & RV camping: Free, Elev: 8902ft/2713m, Tel: 435-637-2817, Nearest town: Mayfield, Agency: USFS, GPS: 39.143152, -111.531645

32703 • FSR 50022 Dispersed 13 - USFS
Dispersed sites, No water, No toilets, Reservations not accepted, Open all year, Tent & RV camping: Free, Elev: 8806ft/2684m, Tel: 435-637-2817, Nearest town: Mayfield, Agency: USFS, GPS: 39.145266, -111.537879

32704 • FSR 50022 Dispersed 14 - USFS
Dispersed sites, No water, No toilets, Reservations not accepted, Open all year, Tent & RV camping: Free, Several nearby spots, Elev: 8863ft/2701m, Tel: 435-637-2817, Nearest town: Mayfield, Agency: USFS, GPS: 39.151446, -111.548783

32705 • FSR 50022 Dispersed 15 - USFS
Dispersed sites, No water, No toilets, Reservations not accepted, Open all year, Tent & RV camping: Free, Elev: 8950ft/2728m, Tel: 435-637-2817, Nearest town: Mayfield, Agency: USFS, GPS: 39.151176, -111.556933

32706 • FSR 50022 Dispersed 16 - USFS
Dispersed sites, No water, No toilets, Reservations not accepted, Open all year, Tent & RV camping: Free, Numerous spots in this area, Elev: 9042ft/2756m, Tel: 435-637-2817, Nearest town: Mayfield, Agency: USFS, GPS: 39.151197, -111.564879

32707 • FSR 50022 Dispersed 17 - USFS
Dispersed sites, No water, No toilets, Reservations not accepted, Open all year, Tent & RV camping: Free, Elev: 8953ft/2729m, Tel: 435-637-2817, Nearest town: Mayfield, Agency: USFS, GPS: 39.150834, -111.571765

32708 • FSR 50022 Dispersed 18 - USFS
Dispersed sites, No water, No toilets, Reservations not accepted, Open all year, Tent & RV camping: Free, Elev: 8350ft/2545m, Tel: 435-637-2817, Nearest town: Mayfield, Agency: USFS, GPS: 39.137898, -111.578776

32709 • FSR 50022 Dispersed 19 - USFS
Dispersed sites, No water, No toilets, Reservations not accepted, Open all year, Tent & RV camping: Free, Elev: 8266ft/2519m, Tel: 435-637-2817, Nearest town: Mayfield, Agency: USFS, GPS: 39.137455, -111.583499

32710 • FSR 50022 Dispersed 2 - USFS
Dispersed sites, No water, No toilets, Reservations not accepted, Open all year, Tent & RV camping: Free, Elev: 6391ft/1948m, Tel: 435-637-2817, Nearest town: Ferron, Agency: USFS, GPS: 39.111183, -111.238886

32711 • FSR 50022 Dispersed 20 - USFS
Dispersed sites, No water, Vault toilets, Reservations not accepted, Open all year, Tent & RV camping: Free, Several sites, Elev: 7850ft/2393m, Tel: 435-637-2817, Nearest town: Mayfield, Agency: USFS, GPS: 39.135884, -111.603141

32712 • FSR 50022 Dispersed 21 - USFS
Dispersed sites, No water, No toilets, Reservations not accepted, Open all year, Tent & RV camping: Free, Elev: 7375ft/2248m, Tel: 435-637-2817, Nearest town: Mayfield, Agency: USFS, GPS: 39.124534, -111.604332

32713 • FSR 50022 Dispersed 3 - USFS
Dispersed sites, No water, No toilets, Reservations not accepted, Open all year, Tent & RV camping: Free, Elev: 6535ft/1992m, Tel: 435-637-2817, Nearest town: Ferron, Agency: USFS, GPS: 39.136599, -111.268184

32714 • FSR 50022 Dispersed 4 - USFS
Dispersed sites, No water, No toilets, Reservations not accepted, Open May-Dec, Tent & RV camping: Free, Elev: 8869ft/2703m, Tel: 435-637-2817, Nearest town: Ferron, Agency: USFS, GPS: 39.118601, -111.318706

32715 • FSR 50022 Dispersed 5 - USFS
Dispersed sites, No water, No toilets, Reservations not accepted, Open May-Dec, Tent & RV camping: Free, Elev: 8819ft/2688m, Tel: 435-637-2817, Nearest town: Ferron, Agency: USFS, GPS: 39.121298, -111.321724

32716 • FSR 50022 Dispersed 6 - USFS
Dispersed sites, No water, No toilets, Reservations not accepted, Open May-Dec, Tent & RV camping: Free, Elev: 8980ft/2737m, Tel: 435-637-2817, Nearest town: Ferron, Agency: USFS, GPS: 39.136698, -111.325624

32717 • FSR 50022 Dispersed 7 - USFS
Dispersed sites, No water, No toilets, Reservations not accepted, Open May-Dec, Tent & RV camping: Free, Elev: 8995ft/2742m, Tel: 435-637-2817, Nearest town: Ferron, Agency: USFS, GPS: 39.137139, -111.346233

32718 • FSR 50022 Dispersed 8 - USFS
Dispersed sites, No water, No toilets, Reservations not accepted, Open May-Dec, Tent & RV camping: Free, Elev: 9657ft/2943m, Tel: 435-637-2817, Nearest town: Ferron, Agency: USFS, GPS: 39.136843, -111.387264

32719 • FSR 50022 Dispersed 9 - USFS

Dispersed sites, No water, No toilets, Reservations not accepted, Open May-Dec, Tent & RV camping: Free, Elev: 9630ft/2935m, Tel: 435-637-2817, Nearest town: Ferron, Agency: USFS, GPS: 39.135322, -111.390429

32720 • FSR 50028 Dispersed 1 - USFS

Dispersed sites, No water, No toilets, Reservations not accepted, Open Apr-Nov, Tent & RV camping: Free, Road not maintained for passenger cars, Elev: 8756ft/2669m, Tel: 435-637-2817, Nearest town: Mayfield, Agency: USFS, GPS: 38.976516, -111.303946

32721 • FSR 50031 Dispersed 1 - USFS

Dispersed sites, No water, No toilets, Reservations not accepted, Open all year, Tent & RV camping: Free, Road not maintained for passenger cars, Elev: 8897ft/2712m, Tel: 435-637-2817, Nearest town: Ferron, Agency: USFS, GPS: 39.182869, -111.428966

32722 • FSR 50033 Dispersed 1 - USFS

Dispersed sites, No water, No toilets, Reservations not accepted, Open all year, Tent & RV camping: Free, Road not maintained for passenger cars, Elev: 7544ft/2299m, Tel: 435-259-7155, Nearest town: Moab, Agency: USFS, GPS: 38.644328, -109.156097

32723 • FSR 50033 Dispersed 2 - USFS

Dispersed sites, No water, No toilets, Reservations not accepted, Open all year, Tent & RV camping: Free, Road not maintained for passenger cars, Elev: 8132ft/2479m, Tel: 435-259-7155, Nearest town: Moab, Agency: USFS, GPS: 38.621287, -109.172424

32724 • FSR 50033 Dispersed 3 - USFS

Dispersed sites, No water, No toilets, Reservations not accepted, Open all year, Tent & RV camping: Free, Road not maintained for passenger cars, Elev: 8411ft/2564m, Tel: 435-259-7155, Nearest town: Moab, Agency: USFS, GPS: 38.611095, -109.211616

32725 • FSR 50036 Dispersed 1 - USFS

Dispersed sites, No water, No toilets, Reservations not accepted, Open all year, Tent & RV camping: Free, Elev: 6992ft/2131m, Tel: 435-637-2817, Nearest town: Huntington, Agency: USFS, GPS: 39.455962, -111.426595

32726 • FSR 50036 Dispersed 2 - USFS

Dispersed sites, No water, No toilets, Reservations not accepted, Open all year, Tent & RV camping: Free, Elev: 7170ft/2185m, Tel: 435-637-2817, Nearest town: Huntington, Agency: USFS, GPS: 39.448884, -111.426236

32727 • FSR 50036 Dispersed 3 - USFS

Dispersed sites, No water, No toilets, Reservations not accepted, Open all year, Tent & RV camping: Free, Elev: 7880ft/2402m, Tel: 435-637-2817, Nearest town: Huntington, Agency: USFS, GPS: 39.444182, -111.412401

32728 • FSR 50036 Dispersed 4 - USFS

Dispersed sites, No water, No toilets, Reservations not accepted, Open all year, Tent & RV camping: Free, Elev: 8433ft/2570m, Tel: 435-637-2817, Nearest town: Huntington, Agency: USFS, GPS: 39.439331, -111.405997

32729 • FSR 50036 Dispersed 5 - USFS

Dispersed sites, No water, No toilets, Reservations not accepted, Open Jul-Dec, Tent & RV camping: Free, Road not maintained for passenger cars, Elev: 9111ft/2777m, Tel: 435-637-2817, Nearest town: Huntington, Agency: USFS, GPS: 39.433461, -111.379081

32730 • FSR 50037 Dispersed 1 - USFS

Dispersed sites, No water, No toilets, Reservations not accepted, Open all year, Tent & RV camping: Free, Road not maintained for passenger cars, Elev: 8802ft/2683m, Tel: 435-637-2817, Nearest town: Mount Pleasant, Agency: USFS, GPS: 39.521343, -111.324259

32731 • FSR 50037 Dispersed 2 - USFS

Dispersed sites, No water, No toilets, Reservations not accepted, Open all year, Tent & RV camping: Free, Road not maintained for passenger cars, Elev: 9624ft/2933m, Tel: 435-637-2817, Nearest town: Mount Pleasant, Agency: USFS, GPS: 39.509437, -111.313181

32732 • FSR 50038 Dispersed 1 - USFS

Dispersed sites, No water, No toilets, Reservations not accepted, Open Jun-Dec, Tent & RV camping: Free, Several sites in this area, Road not maintained for passenger cars, Elev: 8893ft/2711m, Tel: 435-637-2817, Nearest town: Huntington, Agency: USFS, GPS: 39.445816, -111.259833

32733 • FSR 50038 Dispersed 2 - USFS

Dispersed sites, No water, No toilets, Reservations not accepted, Open Jun-Dec, Tent & RV camping: Free, Road not maintained for passenger cars, Elev: 8797ft/2681m, Tel: 435-637-2817, Nearest town: Huntington, Agency: USFS, GPS: 39.442328, -111.261135

32734 • FSR 50038 Dispersed 3 - USFS

Dispersed sites, No water, No toilets, Reservations not accepted, Open Jun-Dec, Tent & RV camping: Free, Road not maintained for passenger cars, Elev: 8809ft/2685m, Tel: 435-637-2817, Nearest town: Huntington, Agency: USFS, GPS: 39.439767, -111.262753

32735 • FSR 50038 Dispersed 4 - USFS

Dispersed sites, No water, No toilets, Reservations not accepted, Open Jun-Dec, Tent & RV camping: Free, Road not maintained for passenger cars, Elev: 8082ft/2463m, Tel: 435-637-2817, Nearest town: Huntington, Agency: USFS, GPS: 39.414081, -111.272023

32736 • FSR 50038 Dispersed 5 - USFS

Dispersed sites, No water, No toilets, Reservations not accepted, Open Jun-Dec, Tent & RV camping: Free, Road not maintained for passenger cars, Elev: 7988ft/2435m, Tel: 435-637-2817, Nearest town: Huntington, Agency: USFS, GPS: 39.406804, -111.272526

32737 • FSR 50038 Dispersed 6 - USFS

Dispersed sites, No water, No toilets, Reservations not accepted, Open Jun-Dec, Tent & RV camping: Free, Several spots, Road not maintained for passenger cars, Elev: 7676ft/2340m, Tel: 435-637-2817, Nearest town: Huntington, Agency: USFS, GPS: 39.386382, -111.275243

32738 • FSR 50038 Dispersed 7 - USFS

Dispersed sites, No water, No toilets, Reservations not accepted, Open Jun-Dec, Tent & RV camping: Free, Several spots, Road not maintained for passenger cars, Elev: 7646ft/2331m, Tel: 435-637-2817, Nearest town: Huntington, Agency: USFS, GPS: 39.382209, -111.273657

32739 • FSR 50038 Dispersed 8 - USFS

Dispersed sites, No water, No toilets, Reservations not accepted, Open Jun-Dec, Tent & RV camping: Free, Road not maintained for passenger cars, Elev: 7443ft/2269m, Tel: 435-637-2817, Nearest town: Huntington, Agency: USFS, GPS: 39.365515, -111.274938

32740 • FSR 50039 Dispersed 1 - USFS

Dispersed sites, No water, No toilets, Reservations not accepted, Open all year, Tent & RV camping: Free, Elev: 8618ft/2627m, Tel: 435-637-2817, Nearest town: Ephraim, Agency: USFS, GPS: 39.364263, -111.466408

32741 • FSR 50040 Dispersed 1 - USFS

Dispersed sites, No water, No toilets, Reservations not accepted, Open all year, Tent & RV camping: Free, Elev: 7621ft/2323m, Tel: 435-637-2817, Nearest town: Huntington, Agency: USFS, GPS: 39.331499, -111.196185

32742 • FSR 50040 Dispersed 2 - USFS

Dispersed sites, No water, No toilets, Reservations not accepted, Open May-Dec, Tent & RV camping: Free, Elev: 8675ft/2644m, Tel: 435-637-2817, Nearest town: Huntington, Agency: USFS, GPS: 39.381689, -111.220432

32743 • FSR 50040 Dispersed 3 - USFS

Dispersed sites, No water, No toilets, Reservations not accepted, Open May-Dec, Tent & RV camping: Free, Elev: 8884ft/2708m, Tel: 435-637-2817, Nearest town: Huntington, Agency: USFS, GPS: 39.391635, -111.220554

32744 • FSR 50040 Dispersed 4 - USFS

Dispersed sites, No water, No toilets, Reservations not accepted, Open May-Dec, Tent & RV camping: Free, Several sites in this area, Elev: 9104ft/2775m, Tel: 435-637-2817, Nearest town: Huntington, Agency: USFS, GPS: 39.401702, -111.224946

32745 • FSR 50041 (Marys Lake) Dispersed 3 - USFS

Dispersed sites, No water, No toilets, Reservations not accepted, Open all year, Tent & RV camping: Free, Road not maintained for passenger cars, Elev: 8860ft/2701m, Tel: 435-637-2817, Nearest town: Ferron, Agency: USFS, GPS: 39.254187, -111.322207

32746 • FSR 50041 Dispersed 1 - USFS

Dispersed sites, No water, No toilets, Reservations not accepted, Open all year, Tent & RV camping: Free, Road not maintained for passenger cars, Elev: 8177ft/2492m, Tel: 435-637-2817, Nearest town: Ferron, Agency: USFS, GPS: 39.239043, -111.296348

32747 • FSR 50041 Dispersed 2 - USFS

Dispersed sites, No water, No toilets, Reservations not accepted, Open all year, Tent & RV camping: Free, Road not maintained for passenger cars, Elev: 8761ft/2670m, Tel: 435-637-2817, Nearest town: Ferron, Agency: USFS, GPS: 39.221365, -111.303197

32748 • FSR 50043 (Wrigley Springs Reservoir) Dispersed 3 - USFS

Dispersed sites, No water, No toilets, Reservations not accepted, Open all year, Tent & RV camping: Free, Elev: 8933ft/2723m, Tel: 435-637-2817, Nearest town: Ferron, Agency: USFS, GPS: 39.091656, -111.301159

32749 • FSR 50043 Dispersed 1 - USFS

Dispersed sites, No water, No toilets, Reservations not accepted, Open all year, Tent & RV camping: Free, Elev: 9522ft/2902m, Tel: 435-637-2817, Nearest town: Ferron, Agency: USFS, GPS: 39.084698, -111.317897

32750 • FSR 50043 Dispersed 2 - USFS

Dispersed sites, No water, No toilets, Reservations not accepted, Open all year, Tent & RV camping: Free, Elev: 9170ft/2795m, Tel: 435-637-2817, Nearest town: Ferron, Agency: USFS, GPS: 39.087384, -111.308575

32751 • FSR 50043 Dispersed 4 - USFS

Dispersed sites, No water, No toilets, Reservations not accepted, Open all year, Tent & RV camping: Free, Elev: 8244ft/2513m, Tel: 435-637-2817, Nearest town: Ferron, Agency: USFS, GPS: 39.116485, -111.290273

32752 • FSR 50043 Dispersed 5 - USFS

Dispersed sites, No water, No toilets, Reservations not accepted, Open May-Dec, Tent & RV camping: Free, Elev: 9510ft/2899m, Tel: 435-637-2817, Nearest town: Mayfield, Agency: USFS, GPS: 39.097461, -111.361039

32753 • FSR 50043 Dispersed 6 - USFS

Dispersed sites, No water, No toilets, Reservations not accepted, Open May-Dec, Tent & RV camping: Free, Several spots this area, Road not maintained for passenger cars, Elev: 9758ft/2974m, Tel: 435-637-2817, Nearest town: Mayfield, Agency: USFS, GPS: 39.106463, -111.477959

32754 • FSR 50044 Dispersed 1 - USFS

Dispersed sites, No water, No toilets, Reservations not accepted, Open all year, Tent & RV camping: Free, Road not maintained for passenger cars, Elev: 8257ft/2517m, Tel: 435-637-2817, Nearest town: Mayfield, Agency: USFS, GPS: 39.028106, -111.387458

32755 • FSR 50044 Dispersed 2 - USFS

Dispersed sites, No water, No toilets, Reservations not accepted, Open all year, Tent & RV camping: Free, Road not maintained for passenger cars, Elev: 9175ft/2797m, Tel: 435-637-2817, Nearest town: Mayfield, Agency: USFS, GPS: 39.033617, -111.465755

32756 • FSR 50044 Dispersed 3 - USFS

Dispersed sites, No water, No toilets, Reservations not accepted, Open all year, Tent & RV camping: Free, Road not maintained for passenger cars, Elev: 9220ft/2810m, Tel: 435-637-2817, Nearest town: Mayfield, Agency: USFS, GPS: 39.039535, -111.468186

32757 • FSR 50044 Dispersed 4 - USFS

Dispersed sites, No water, No toilets, Reservations not accepted, Open all year, Tent & RV camping: Free, Road not maintained for passenger cars, Elev: 9202ft/2805m, Tel: 435-637-2817, Nearest town: Mayfield, Agency: USFS, GPS: 39.047259, -111.467725

32758 • FSR 50044 Dispersed 5 - USFS

Dispersed sites, No water, No toilets, Reservations not accepted, Open all year, Tent & RV camping: Free, Road not maintained for passenger cars, Elev: 9751ft/2972m, Tel: 435-637-2817, Nearest town: Mayfield, Agency: USFS, GPS: 39.083957, -111.477274

32759 • FSR 50045 Dispersed 1 - USFS

Dispersed sites, No water, No toilets, Reservations not accepted, Open all year, Tent & RV camping: Free, Elev: 7207ft/2197m, Tel: 435-637-2817, Nearest town: Manti, Agency: USFS, GPS: 39.256041, -111.555638

32760 • FSR 50045 Dispersed 10 - USFS

Dispersed sites, No water, No toilets, Reservations not accepted, Open all year, Tent & RV camping: Free, Road not maintained for passenger cars, Elev: 9587ft/2922m, Tel: 435-637-2817, Nearest town: Manti, Agency: USFS, GPS: 39.225915, -111.505829

32761 • FSR 50045 Dispersed 11 - USFS

Dispersed sites, No water, No toilets, Reservations not accepted, Open all year, Tent & RV camping: Free, Road not maintained for passenger cars, Elev: 9679ft/2950m, Tel: 435-637-2817, Nearest town: Manti, Agency: USFS, GPS: 39.224519, -111.503245

32762 • FSR 50045 Dispersed 12 - USFS

Dispersed sites, No water, No toilets, Reservations not accepted, Open all year, Tent & RV camping: Free, Road not maintained for passenger cars, Elev: 9897ft/3017m, Tel: 435-637-2817, Nearest town: Manti, Agency: USFS, GPS: 39.222138, -111.505232

32763 • FSR 50045 Dispersed 2 - USFS

Dispersed sites, No water, No toilets, Reservations not accepted, Open all year, Tent & RV camping: Free, Elev: 7300ft/2225m, Tel: 435-637-2817, Nearest town: Manti, Agency: USFS, GPS: 39.255325, -111.551253

32764 • FSR 50045 Dispersed 3 - USFS

Dispersed sites, No water, No toilets, Reservations not accepted, Open all year, Tent & RV camping: Free, Elev: 7577ft/2309m, Tel: 435-637-2817, Nearest town: Manti, Agency: USFS, GPS: 39.255849, -111.539053

32765 • FSR 50045 Dispersed 4 - USFS

Dispersed sites, No water, No toilets, Reservations not accepted, Open all year, Tent & RV camping: Free, Several sites both sides of road, Elev: 7603ft/2317m, Tel: 435-637-2817, Nearest town: Manti, Agency: USFS, GPS: 39.256357, -111.537791

32766 • FSR 50045 Dispersed 5 - USFS

Dispersed sites, No water, No toilets, Reservations not accepted, Open all year, Tent & RV camping: Free, Elev: 7755ft/2364m, Tel: 435-637-2817, Nearest town: Manti, Agency: USFS, GPS: 39.257487, -111.530223

32767 • FSR 50045 Dispersed 6 - USFS

Dispersed sites, No water, No toilets, Reservations not accepted, Open all year, Tent & RV camping: Free, Elev: 7966ft/2428m, Tel: 435-637-2817, Nearest town: Manti, Agency: USFS, GPS: 39.253188, -111.527524

32768 • FSR 50045 Dispersed 7 - USFS

Dispersed sites, No water, No toilets, Reservations not accepted, Open all year, Tent & RV camping: Free, Road not maintained for passenger cars, Elev: 8349ft/2545m, Tel: 435-637-2817, Nearest town: Manti, Agency: USFS, GPS: 39.243652, -111.524189

32769 • FSR 50045 Dispersed 8 - USFS

Dispersed sites, No water, No toilets, Reservations not accepted, Open all year, Tent & RV camping: Free, Road not maintained for passenger cars, Elev: 9184ft/2799m, Tel: 435-637-2817, Nearest town: Manti, Agency: USFS, GPS: 39.233254, -111.510433

32770 • FSR 50045 Dispersed 9 - USFS

Dispersed sites, No water, No toilets, Reservations not accepted, Open all year, Tent & RV camping: Free, Road not maintained for passenger cars, Elev: 9351ft/2850m, Tel: 435-637-2817, Nearest town: Manti, Agency: USFS, GPS: 39.229571, -111.504778

32771 • FSR 50046 Dispersed 1 - USFS

Dispersed sites, No water, No toilets, Reservations not accepted, Open all year, Tent & RV camping: Free, Road not maintained for passenger cars, Elev: 10038ft/3060m, Tel: 435-637-2817, Nearest town: Manti, Agency: USFS, GPS: 39.266854, -111.463314

32772 • FSR 50046 Dispersed 2 - USFS

Dispersed sites, No water, No toilets, Reservations not accepted, Open all year, Tent & RV camping: Free, Road not maintained for passenger cars, Elev: 10053ft/3064m, Tel: 435-637-2817, Nearest town: Manti, Agency: USFS, GPS: 39.264809, -111.463339

32773 • FSR 50047 Dispersed 1 - USFS

Dispersed sites, No water, No toilets, Reservations not accepted, Open all year, Tent & RV camping: Free, Road not maintained for passenger cars, Elev: 9648ft/2941m, Tel: 435-637-2817, Nearest town: Mayfield, Agency: USFS, GPS: 39.144587, -111.508295

32774 • FSR 50047 Dispersed 2 - USFS

Dispersed sites, No water, No toilets, Reservations not accepted, Open all year, Tent & RV camping: Free, Road not maintained for passenger cars, Elev: 10070ft/3069m, Tel: 435-637-2817, Nearest town: Mayfield, Agency: USFS, GPS: 39.150033, -111.497321

32775 • FSR 50047 Dispersed 3 - USFS

Dispersed sites, No water, No toilets, Reservations not accepted, Open all year, Tent & RV camping: Free, Road not maintained for passenger cars, Elev: 9011ft/2747m, Tel: 435-637-2817, Nearest town: Mayfield, Agency: USFS, GPS: 39.187029, -111.537334

32776 • FSR 50047 Dispersed 4 - USFS

Dispersed sites, No water, No toilets, Reservations not accepted, Open all year, Tent & RV camping: Free, Road not maintained for passenger cars, Elev: 8953ft/2729m, Tel: 435-637-2817, Nearest town: Mayfield, Agency: USFS, GPS: 39.187955, -111.541314

32777 • FSR 50047 Dispersed 5 - USFS

Dispersed sites, No water, No toilets, Reservations not accepted, Open all year, Tent & RV camping: Free, Road not maintained for passenger cars, Elev: 8772ft/2674m, Tel: 435-637-2817, Nearest town: Mayfield, Agency: USFS, GPS: 39.191486, -111.553699

32778 • FSR 50049 (Duck Fort Reservoir) Dispersed 6 - USFS

Dispersed sites, No water, No toilets, Reservations not accepted, Open all year, Tent & RV camping: Free, Elev: 9239ft/2816m, Tel: 435-637-2817, Nearest town: Ferron, Agency: USFS, GPS: 39.172467, -111.447107

32779 • FSR 50049 Dispersed 1 - USFS

Dispersed sites, No water, No toilets, Reservations not accepted, Open all year, Tent & RV camping: Free, Elev: 9388ft/2861m, Tel: 435-637-2817, Nearest town: Ferron, Agency: USFS, GPS: 39.148146, -111.439705

32780 • FSR 50049 Dispersed 2 - USFS

Dispersed sites, No water, No toilets, Reservations not accepted, Open all year, Tent & RV camping: Free, Several sites in area, Elev: 9336ft/2846m, Tel: 435-637-2817, Nearest town: Ferron, Agency: USFS, GPS: 39.150008, -111.433643

32781 • FSR 50049 Dispersed 3 - USFS

Dispersed sites, No water, No toilets, Reservations not accepted, Open all year, Tent & RV camping: Free, Elev: 9520ft/2902m, Tel: 435-637-2817, Nearest town: Ferron, Agency: USFS, GPS: 39.158722, -111.427935

32782 • FSR 50049 Dispersed 4 - USFS

Dispersed sites, No water, No toilets, Reservations not accepted, Open all year, Tent & RV camping: Free, Several sites in area, Elev: 9216ft/2809m, Tel: 435-637-2817, Nearest town: Ferron, Agency: USFS, GPS: 39.175388, -111.420769

32783 • FSR 50049 Dispersed 5 - USFS

Dispersed sites, No water, No toilets, Reservations not accepted, Open all year, Tent & RV camping: Free, Elev: 9223ft/2811m, Tel: 435-637-2817, Nearest town: Ferron, Agency: USFS, GPS: 39.175822, -111.425414

32784 • FSR 50050 Dispersed 1 - USFS

Dispersed sites, No water, No toilets, Reservations not accepted, Open all year, Tent & RV camping: Free, Road not maintained for passenger cars, Elev: 10061ft/3067m, Tel: 435-637-2817, Nearest town: Ephraim, Agency: USFS, GPS: 39.322608, -111.440298

32785 • FSR 50050 Dispersed 2 - USFS

Dispersed sites, No water, No toilets, Reservations not accepted, Open all year, Tent & RV camping: Free, Road not maintained for passenger cars, Elev: 10098ft/3078m, Tel: 435-637-2817, Nearest town: Ephraim, Agency: USFS, GPS: 39.320967, -111.439267

32786 • FSR 50051 Dispersed 1 - USFS

Dispersed sites, No water, No toilets, Reservations not accepted, Open all year, Tent & RV camping: Free, Numerous spots in this area, Road not maintained for passenger cars, Elev: 7729ft/2356m, Tel: 435-637-2817, Nearest town: Ephraim, Agency: USFS, GPS: 39.329529, -111.509384

32787 • FSR 50051 Dispersed 10 - USFS

Dispersed sites, No water, No toilets, Reservations not accepted, Open all year, Tent & RV camping: Free, Road not maintained for passenger cars, Elev: 8077ft/2462m, Tel: 435-637-2817, Nearest town: Ephraim, Agency: USFS, GPS: 39.307255, -111.518762

32788 • FSR 50051 Dispersed 11 - USFS

Dispersed sites, No water, No toilets, Reservations not accepted, Open all year, Tent & RV camping: Free, Road not maintained for passenger cars, Elev: 8252ft/2515m, Tel: 435-637-2817, Nearest town: Ephraim, Agency: USFS, GPS: 39.297929, -111.519668

32789 • FSR 50051 Dispersed 2 - USFS

Dispersed sites, No water, No toilets, Reservations not accepted, Open all year, Tent & RV camping: Free, Road not maintained for passenger cars, Elev: 7748ft/2362m, Tel: 435-637-2817, Nearest town: Ephraim, Agency: USFS, GPS: 39.325572, -111.509385

32790 • FSR 50051 Dispersed 3 - USFS

Dispersed sites, No water, No toilets, Reservations not accepted, Open all year, Tent & RV camping: Free, Road not maintained for passenger cars, Elev: 7846ft/2391m, Tel: 435-637-2817, Nearest town: Ephraim, Agency: USFS, GPS: 39.323595, -111.512251

32791 • FSR 50051 Dispersed 4 - USFS

Dispersed sites, No water, No toilets, Reservations not accepted, Open all year, Tent & RV camping: Free, Road not maintained for passenger cars, Elev: 7883ft/2403m, Tel: 435-637-2817, Nearest town: Ephraim, Agency: USFS, GPS: 39.322191, -111.513051

32792 • FSR 50051 Dispersed 5 - USFS

Dispersed sites, No water, No toilets, Reservations not accepted, Open all year, Tent & RV camping: Free, Road not maintained for passenger cars, Elev: 7866ft/2398m, Tel: 435-637-2817, Nearest town: Ephraim, Agency: USFS, GPS: 39.321093, -111.515658

32793 • FSR 50051 Dispersed 6 - USFS

Dispersed sites, No water, No toilets, Reservations not accepted, Open all year, Tent & RV camping: Free, Road not maintained for passenger cars, Elev: 7894ft/2406m, Tel: 435-637-2817, Nearest town: Ephraim, Agency: USFS, GPS: 39.319313, -111.517709

32794 • FSR 50051 Dispersed 7 - USFS

Dispersed sites, No water, No toilets, Reservations not accepted, Open all year, Tent & RV camping: Free, Road not maintained for passenger cars, Elev: 7897ft/2407m, Tel: 435-637-2817, Nearest town: Ephraim, Agency: USFS, GPS: 39.318097, -111.516346

32795 • FSR 50051 Dispersed 8 - USFS

Dispersed sites, No water, No toilets, Reservations not accepted, Open all year, Tent & RV camping: Free, Road not maintained for passenger cars, Elev: 7913ft/2412m, Tel: 435-637-2817, Nearest town: Ephraim, Agency: USFS, GPS: 39.314853, -111.519236

32796 • FSR 50051 Dispersed 9 - USFS
Dispersed sites, No water, No toilets, Reservations not accepted, Open all year, Tent & RV camping: Free, Large area with room for many rigs, Road not maintained for passenger cars, Elev: 7985ft/2434m, Tel: 435-637-2817, Nearest town: Ephraim, Agency: USFS, GPS: 39.309193, -111.521056

32797 • FSR 50056 Dispersed 1 - USFS
Dispersed sites, No water, No toilets, Reservations not accepted, Open all year, Tent & RV camping: Free, Large area - many sites, Elev: 8786ft/2678m, Tel: 435-637-2817, Nearest town: Fairview, Agency: USFS, GPS: 39.644574, -111.252344

32798 • FSR 50056 Dispersed 2 - USFS
Dispersed sites, No water, No toilets, Reservations not accepted, Open all year, Tent & RV camping: Free, 3 sites, Elev: 8845ft/2696m, Tel: 435-637-2817, Nearest town: Fairview, Agency: USFS, GPS: 39.642511, -111.256407

32799 • FSR 50056 Dispersed 3 - USFS
Dispersed sites, No water, No toilets, Reservations not accepted, Open all year, Tent & RV camping: Free, Elev: 8827ft/2690m, Tel: 435-637-2817, Nearest town: Fairview, Agency: USFS, GPS: 39.639819, -111.259178

32800 • FSR 50063 Dispersed 1 - USFS
Dispersed sites, No water, No toilets, Reservations not accepted, Open May-Sep, Tent & RV camping: Free, Elev: 8613ft/2625m, Tel: 435-259-7155, Nearest town: Moab, Agency: USFS, GPS: 38.506615, -109.318873

32801 • FSR 50063 Dispersed 2 - USFS
Dispersed sites, No water, No toilets, Reservations not accepted, Open May-Sep, Tent & RV camping: Free, Elev: 9074ft/2766m, Tel: 435-259-7155, Nearest town: Moab, Agency: USFS, GPS: 38.518763, -109.292031

32802 • FSR 50067 Dispersed 1 - USFS
Dispersed sites, No water, No toilets, Reservations not accepted, Open all year, Tent & RV camping: Free, Elev: 7334ft/2235m, Tel: 435-259-7155, Nearest town: Moab, Agency: USFS, GPS: 38.560583, -109.358679

32803 • FSR 50067 Dispersed 2 - USFS
Dispersed sites, No water, No toilets, Reservations not accepted, Open all year, Tent & RV camping: Free, Elev: 7845ft/2391m, Tel: 435-259-7155, Nearest town: Moab, Agency: USFS, GPS: 38.523842, -109.341999

32804 • FSR 50068 Dispersed 1 - USFS
Dispersed sites, No water, No toilets, Reservations not accepted, Open all year, Tents only: Free, Elev: 7173ft/2186m, Tel: 435-259-7155, Nearest town: Moab, Agency: USFS, GPS: 38.474096, -109.343156

32805 • FSR 50068 Dispersed 2 - USFS
Dispersed sites, No water, No toilets, Reservations not accepted, Open all year, Tents only: Free, Elev: 8012ft/2442m, Tel: 435-259-7155, Nearest town: Moab, Agency: USFS, GPS: 38.475995, -109.304457

32806 • FSR 50068 Dispersed 3 - USFS
Dispersed sites, No water, No toilets, Reservations not accepted, Open all year, Tent & RV camping: Free, Elev: 8214ft/2504m, Tel: 435-259-7155, Nearest town: Moab, Agency: USFS, GPS: 38.477438, -109.304115

32807 • FSR 50068 Dispersed 4 - USFS
Dispersed sites, No water, No toilets, Reservations not accepted, Open all year, Tent & RV camping: Free, Elev: 8395ft/2559m, Tel: 435-259-7155, Nearest town: Moab, Agency: USFS, GPS: 38.483961, -109.303777

32808 • FSR 50070 Dispersed 1 - USFS
Dispersed sites, No water, No toilets, Reservations not accepted, Open all year, Tent & RV camping: Free, Road not maintained for passenger cars, Elev: 5466ft/1666m, Tel: 435-637-2817, Nearest town: Spanish Fork, Agency: USFS, GPS: 39.958218, -111.456153

32809 • FSR 50070 Dispersed 2 - USFS
Dispersed sites, No water, No toilets, Reservations not accepted, Open all year, Tent & RV camping: Free, Road not maintained for passenger cars, Elev: 5730ft/1747m, Tel: 435-637-2817, Nearest town: Spanish Fork, Agency: USFS, GPS: 39.953247, -111.436347

32810 • FSR 50070 Dispersed 3 - USFS
Dispersed sites, No water, No toilets, Reservations not accepted, Open all year, Tent & RV camping: Free, Road not maintained for passenger cars, Elev: 6015ft/1833m, Tel: 435-637-2817, Nearest town: Spanish Fork, Agency: USFS, GPS: 39.941784, -111.418145

32811 • FSR 50070 Dispersed 4 - USFS
Dispersed sites, No water, No toilets, Reservations not accepted, Open all year, Tent & RV camping: Free, Road not maintained for passenger cars, Elev: 6096ft/1858m, Tel: 435-637-2817, Nearest town: Spanish Fork, Agency: USFS, GPS: 39.935915, -111.413044

32812 • FSR 50070 Dispersed 5 - USFS
Dispersed sites, No water, No toilets, Reservations not accepted, Open all year, Tent & RV camping: Free, Elev: 7528ft/2295m, Tel: 435-637-2817, Nearest town: Spanish Fork, Agency: USFS, GPS: 39.854779, -111.421262

32813 • FSR 50071 Dispersed 1 - USFS
Dispersed sites, No water, No toilets, Reservations not accepted, Open all year, Tent & RV camping: Free, Elev: 8221ft/2506m, Tel: 435-259-7155, Nearest town: Moab, Agency: USFS, GPS: 38.483209, -109.312153

32814 • FSR 50071 Dispersed 2 - USFS
Dispersed sites, No water, No toilets, Reservations not accepted, Open all year, Tent & RV camping: Free, Elev: 8405ft/2562m,

Tel: 435-259-7155, Nearest town: Moab, Agency: USFS, GPS: 38.485244, -109.302505

32815 • FSR 50071 Dispersed 3 - USFS

Dispersed sites, No water, No toilets, Reservations not accepted, Open all year, Tent & RV camping: Free, Elev: 8424ft/2568m, Tel: 435-259-7155, Nearest town: Moab, Agency: USFS, GPS: 38.484017, -109.301995

32816 • FSR 50071 Dispersed 4 - USFS

Dispersed sites, No water, No toilets, Reservations not accepted, Open all year, Tent & RV camping: Free, Elev: 8672ft/2643m, Tel: 435-259-7155, Nearest town: Moab, Agency: USFS, GPS: 38.481748, -109.295071

32817 • FSR 50071 Dispersed 5 - USFS

Dispersed sites, No water, No toilets, Reservations not accepted, Open all year, Tent & RV camping: Free, Elev: 9707ft/2959m, Tel: 435-259-7155, Nearest town: Moab, Agency: USFS, GPS: 38.479659, -109.272741

32818 • FSR 50071 Dispersed 6 - USFS

Dispersed sites, No water, No toilets, Reservations not accepted, Open May-Dec, Tent & RV camping: Free, Elev: 9959ft/3036m, Tel: 435-259-7155, Nearest town: Moab, Agency: USFS, GPS: 38.481285, -109.262617

32819 • FSR 50071 Dispersed 7 - USFS

Dispersed sites, No water, No toilets, Reservations not accepted, Open May-Dec, Tent & RV camping: Free, Elev: 9953ft/3034m, Tel: 435-259-7155, Nearest town: Moab, Agency: USFS, GPS: 38.486091, -109.255663

32820 • FSR 50071 Dispersed 8 - USFS

Dispersed sites, No water, No toilets, Reservations not accepted, Open May-Dec, Tent & RV camping: Free, Elev: 10106ft/3080m, Tel: 435-259-7155, Nearest town: Moab, Agency: USFS, GPS: 38.486669, -109.245945

32821 • FSR 50072 Dispersed 1 - USFS

Dispersed sites, No water, No toilets, Reservations not accepted, Open all year, Tent & RV camping: Free, Road not maintained for passenger cars, Elev: 7424ft/2263m, Tel: 435-259-7155, Nearest town: Moab, Agency: USFS, GPS: 38.346617, -109.127553

32822 • FSR 50072 Dispersed 2 - USFS

Dispersed sites, No water, No toilets, Reservations not accepted, Open all year, Tent & RV camping: Free, Road not maintained for passenger cars, Elev: 7321ft/2231m, Tel: 435-259-7155, Nearest town: Moab, Agency: USFS, GPS: 38.351183, -109.113843

32823 • FSR 50072 Dispersed 3 - USFS

Dispersed sites, No water, No toilets, Reservations not accepted, Open all year, Tent & RV camping: Free, Road not maintained for passenger cars, Elev: 7955ft/2425m, Tel: 435-259-7155, Nearest town: Paradox, Agency: USFS, GPS: 38.398243, -109.059326

32824 • FSR 50073 Dispersed 1 - USFS

Dispersed sites, No water, No toilets, Reservations not accepted, Open all year, Tent & RV camping: Free, Elev: 7809ft/2380m, Tel: 435-259-7155, Nearest town: Moab, Agency: USFS, GPS: 38.364807, -109.186253

32825 • FSR 50073 Dispersed 10 - USFS

Dispersed sites, No water, No toilets, Reservations not accepted, Open all year, Tents only: Free, At edge of 800' bluff, Elev: 8129ft/2478m, Tel: 435-259-7155, Nearest town: Moab, Agency: USFS, GPS: 38.437309, -109.309075

32826 • FSR 50073 Dispersed 2 - USFS

Dispersed sites, No water, No toilets, Reservations not accepted, Open all year, Tent & RV camping: Free, Several sites in this area, Elev: 7909ft/2411m, Tel: 435-259-7155, Nearest town: Moab, Agency: USFS, GPS: 38.365549, -109.195153

32827 • FSR 50073 Dispersed 3 - USFS

Dispersed sites, No water, No toilets, Tent & RV camping: Free, Elev: 8005ft/2440m, Nearest town: La Sal, Agency: USFS, GPS: 38.368826, -109.197956

32828 • FSR 50073 Dispersed 4 - USFS

Dispersed sites, No water, No toilets, Reservations not accepted, Open all year, Tent & RV camping: Free, Elev: 8232ft/2509m, Tel: 435-259-7155, Nearest town: Moab, Agency: USFS, GPS: 38.377557, -109.204676

32829 • FSR 50073 Dispersed 5 - USFS

Dispersed sites, No water, No toilets, Reservations not accepted, Open all year, Tent & RV camping: Free, Elev: 8260ft/2518m, Tel: 435-259-7155, Nearest town: Moab, Agency: USFS, GPS: 38.378213, -109.205318

32830 • FSR 50073 Dispersed 6 - USFS

Dispersed sites, No water, No toilets, Reservations not accepted, Open all year, Tent & RV camping: Free, Elev: 8281ft/2524m, Tel: 435-259-7155, Nearest town: Moab, Agency: USFS, GPS: 38.384643, -109.208524

32831 • FSR 50073 Dispersed 7 - USFS

Dispersed sites, No water, No toilets, Reservations not accepted, Open all year, Tent & RV camping: Free, Elev: 8674ft/2644m, Tel: 435-259-7155, Nearest town: Moab, Agency: USFS, GPS: 38.390832, -109.206604

32832 • FSR 50073 Dispersed 8 - USFS

Dispersed sites, No water, No toilets, Reservations not accepted, Open all year, Tent & RV camping: Free, Elev: 9486ft/2891m, Tel: 435-259-7155, Nearest town: Moab, Agency: USFS, GPS: 38.414436, -109.222866

32833 • FSR 50073 Dispersed 9 - USFS

Dispersed sites, No water, No toilets, Reservations not accepted, Open all year, Tent & RV camping: Free, Elev: 10151ft/3094m, Tel: 435-259-7155, Nearest town: Moab, Agency: USFS, GPS: 38.419056, -109.252832

32834 • FSR 50076 Dispersed 1 - USFS

Dispersed sites, No water, No toilets, Reservations not accepted, Open May-Sep, Tent & RV camping: Free, Elev: 8022ft/2445m, Tel: 435-259-7155, Nearest town: Moab, Agency: USFS, GPS: 38.506812, -109.297932

32835 • FSR 50079 Dispersed 1 - USFS

Dispersed sites, No water, No toilets, Reservations not accepted, Open all year, Tent & RV camping: Free, Road not maintained for passenger cars, Elev: 7667ft/2337m, Tel: 435-587-2041, Nearest town: Blanding, Agency: USFS, GPS: 37.793302, -109.511697

32836 • FSR 50079 Dispersed 2 - USFS

Dispersed sites, No water, No toilets, Reservations not accepted, Open all year, Tent & RV camping: Free, Road not maintained for passenger cars, Elev: 7685ft/2342m, Tel: 435-587-2041, Nearest town: Blanding, Agency: USFS, GPS: 37.792617, -109.510311

32837 • FSR 50079 Dispersed 3 - USFS

Dispersed sites, No water, No toilets, Reservations not accepted, Open all year, Tent & RV camping: Free, Road not maintained for passenger cars, Elev: 7826ft/2385m, Tel: 435-587-2041, Nearest town: Blanding, Agency: USFS, GPS: 37.791126, -109.507957

32838 • FSR 50079 Dispersed 4 - USFS

Dispersed sites, No water, No toilets, Reservations not accepted, Open all year, Tent & RV camping: Free, Road not maintained for passenger cars, Elev: 8127ft/2477m, Tel: 435-587-2041, Nearest town: Blanding, Agency: USFS, GPS: 37.788818, -109.499793

32839 • FSR 50079 Dispersed 5 - USFS

Dispersed sites, No water, No toilets, Reservations not accepted, Open all year, Tent & RV camping: Free, Road not maintained for passenger cars, Elev: 8439ft/2572m, Tel: 435-587-2041, Nearest town: Monticello, Agency: USFS, GPS: 37.801334, -109.500517

32840 • FSR 50079 Dispersed 6 - USFS

Dispersed sites, No water, No toilets, Reservations not accepted, Open Jun-Sep, Tent & RV camping: Free, Road not maintained for passenger cars, Elev: 8830ft/2691m, Tel: 435-587-2041, Nearest town: Monticello, Agency: USFS, GPS: 37.816823, -109.488135

32841 • FSR 50079 Dispersed 7 - USFS

Dispersed sites, No water, No toilets, Reservations not accepted, Open Jun-Sep, Tent & RV camping: Free, Road not maintained for passenger cars, Elev: 9703ft/2957m, Tel: 435-587-2041, Nearest town: Monticello, Agency: USFS, GPS: 37.829565, -109.508016

32842 • FSR 50079 Dispersed 8 - USFS

Dispersed sites, No water, No toilets, Reservations not accepted, Open Jun-Sep, Tent & RV camping: Free, Road not maintained for passenger cars, Elev: 8884ft/2708m, Tel: 435-587-2041, Nearest town: Monticello, Agency: USFS, GPS: 37.872449, -109.448568

32843 • FSR 50083 Dispersed 1 - USFS

Dispersed sites, No water, No toilets, Reservations not accepted, Open all year, Tent & RV camping: Free, Road not maintained for passenger cars, Elev: 8251ft/2515m, Tel: 435-587-2041, Nearest town: Blanding, Agency: USFS, GPS: 37.798182, -109.501523

32844 • FSR 50083 Dispersed 2 - USFS

Dispersed sites, No water, No toilets, Reservations not accepted, Open all year, Tent & RV camping: Free, Road not maintained for passenger cars, Elev: 8212ft/2503m, Tel: 435-587-2041, Nearest town: Monticello, Agency: USFS, GPS: 37.798341, -109.503788

32845 • FSR 50087 Dispersed 1 - USFS

Dispersed sites, No water, No toilets, Reservations not accepted, Open all year, Tent & RV camping: Free, Road not maintained for passenger cars, Elev: 7565ft/2306m, Tel: 435-587-2041, Nearest town: Monticello, Agency: USFS, GPS: 37.832577, -109.381764

32846 • FSR 50087 Dispersed 2 - USFS

Dispersed sites, No water, No toilets, Reservations not accepted, Open all year, Tent & RV camping: Free, Road not maintained for passenger cars, Elev: 7613ft/2320m, Tel: 435-587-2041, Nearest town: Monticello, Agency: USFS, GPS: 37.833731, -109.385012

32847 • FSR 50087 Dispersed 3 - USFS

Dispersed sites, No water, No toilets, Reservations not accepted, Open all year, Tent & RV camping: Free, Road not maintained for passenger cars, Elev: 7636ft/2327m, Tel: 435-587-2041, Nearest town: Monticello, Agency: USFS, GPS: 37.831679, -109.386515

32848 • FSR 50087 Dispersed 4 - USFS

Dispersed sites, No water, No toilets, Reservations not accepted, Open all year, Tent & RV camping: Free, Road not maintained for passenger cars, Elev: 7895ft/2406m, Tel: 435-587-2041, Nearest town: Monticello, Agency: USFS, GPS: 37.829508, -109.401546

32849 • FSR 50087 Dispersed 5 - USFS

Dispersed sites, No water, No toilets, Reservations not accepted, Open all year, Tent & RV camping: Free, Road not maintained for passenger cars, Elev: 8184ft/2494m, Tel: 435-587-2041, Nearest town: Monticello, Agency: USFS, GPS: 37.823974, -109.413706

32850 • FSR 50088 Dispersed 1 - USFS

Dispersed sites, No water, No toilets, Reservations not accepted, Open all year, Tent & RV camping: Free, Road not maintained for passenger cars, Elev: 7536ft/2297m, Tel: 435-587-2041, Nearest town: Monticello, Agency: USFS, GPS: 37.923224, -109.756539

32851 • FSR 50088 Dispersed 10 - USFS

Dispersed sites, No water, No toilets, Reservations not accepted, Open all year, Tent & RV camping: Free, Road not maintained for passenger cars, Elev: 8520ft/2597m, Tel: 435-587-2041, Nearest town: Blanding, Agency: USFS, GPS: 37.645869, -109.853152

32852 • FSR 50088 Dispersed 11 - USFS

Dispersed sites, No water, No toilets, Reservations not accepted, Open all year, Tent & RV camping: Free, Road not maintained for passenger cars, Elev: 8129ft/2478m, Tel: 435-587-2041, Nearest town: Blanding, Agency: USFS, GPS: 37.617265, -109.868783

32853 • FSR 50088 Dispersed 2 - USFS

Dispersed sites, No water, No toilets, Reservations not accepted, Open all year, Tent & RV camping: Free, Large area, Road not maintained for passenger cars, Elev: 8551ft/2606m, Tel: 435-587-

2041, Nearest town: Monticello, Agency: USFS, GPS: 37.871936, -109.789305

32854 • FSR 50088 Dispersed 3 - USFS

Dispersed sites, No water, No toilets, Reservations not accepted, Open all year, Tent & RV camping: Free, Road not maintained for passenger cars, Elev: 8593ft/2619m, Tel: 435-587-2041, Nearest town: Monticello, Agency: USFS, GPS: 37.859068, -109.785135

32855 • FSR 50088 Dispersed 4 - USFS

Dispersed sites, No water, No toilets, Reservations not accepted, Open all year, Tent & RV camping: Free, Road not maintained for passenger cars, Elev: 8745ft/2665m, Tel: 435-587-2041, Nearest town: Monticello, Agency: USFS, GPS: 37.845931, -109.782089

32856 • FSR 50088 Dispersed 5 - USFS

Dispersed sites, No water, No toilets, Reservations not accepted, Open all year, Tent & RV camping: Free, Road not maintained for passenger cars, Elev: 8746ft/2666m, Tel: 435-587-2041, Nearest town: Monticello, Agency: USFS, GPS: 37.843606, -109.781237

32857 • FSR 50088 Dispersed 6 - USFS

Dispersed sites, No water, No toilets, Reservations not accepted, Open all year, Tent & RV camping: Free, Road not maintained for passenger cars, Elev: 8639ft/2633m, Tel: 435-587-2041, Nearest town: Monticello, Agency: USFS, GPS: 37.840029, -109.775498

32858 • FSR 50088 Dispersed 7 - USFS

Dispersed sites, No water, No toilets, Reservations not accepted, Open all year, Tent & RV camping: Free, Road not maintained for passenger cars, Elev: 8651ft/2637m, Tel: 435-587-2041, Nearest town: Monticello, Agency: USFS, GPS: 37.791861, -109.785377

32859 • FSR 50088 Dispersed 8 - USFS

Dispersed sites, No water, No toilets, Reservations not accepted, Open all year, Tents only: Free, Road not maintained for passenger cars, Elev: 8281ft/2524m, Tel: 435-587-2041, Nearest town: Blanding, Agency: USFS, GPS: 37.746425, -109.762272

32860 • FSR 50088 Dispersed 9 - USFS

Dispersed sites, No water, No toilets, Reservations not accepted, Open all year, Tent & RV camping: Free, Road not maintained for passenger cars, Elev: 8248ft/2514m, Tel: 435-587-2041, Nearest town: Blanding, Agency: USFS, GPS: 37.693929, -109.812186

32861 • FSR 50091 Dispersed 1 - USFS

Dispersed sites, No water, No toilets, Reservations not accepted, Open all year, Tent & RV camping: Free, Road not maintained for passenger cars, Elev: 8563ft/2610m, Tel: 435-587-2041, Nearest town: Monticello, Agency: USFS, GPS: 37.877512, -109.802771

32862 • FSR 50091 Dispersed 2 - USFS

Dispersed sites, No water, No toilets, Reservations not accepted, Open all year, Tent & RV camping: Free, Road not maintained for passenger cars, Elev: 8653ft/2637m, Tel: 435-587-2041, Nearest town: Monticello, Agency: USFS, GPS: 37.859935, -109.831715

32863 • FSR 50092 Dispersed 1 - USFS

Dispersed sites, No water, No toilets, Reservations not accepted, Open all year, Tent & RV camping: Free, Elev: 6200ft/1890m, Tel: 435-587-2041, Nearest town: Blanding, Agency: USFS, GPS: 37.664356, -109.680337

32864 • FSR 50092 Dispersed 2 - USFS

Dispersed sites, No water, No toilets, Reservations not accepted, Open all year, Tent & RV camping: Free, Road not maintained for passenger cars, Elev: 7229ft/2203m, Tel: 435-587-2041, Nearest town: Blanding, Agency: USFS, GPS: 37.666005, -109.721578

32865 • FSR 50092 Dispersed 3 - USFS

Dispersed sites, No water, No toilets, Reservations not accepted, Open all year, Tent & RV camping: Free, Road not maintained for passenger cars, Elev: 7774ft/2370m, Tel: 435-587-2041, Nearest town: Blanding, Agency: USFS, GPS: 37.672597, -109.749894

32866 • FSR 50092 Dispersed 4 - USFS

Dispersed sites, No water, No toilets, Reservations not accepted, Open all year, Tent & RV camping: Free, Road not maintained for passenger cars, Elev: 8320ft/2536m, Tel: 435-587-2041, Nearest town: Blanding, Agency: USFS, GPS: 37.674164, -109.813087

32867 • FSR 50092 Dispersed 5 - USFS

Dispersed sites, No water, No toilets, Reservations not accepted, Open all year, Tent & RV camping: Free, Road not maintained for passenger cars, Elev: 8505ft/2592m, Tel: 435-587-2041, Nearest town: Blanding, Agency: USFS, GPS: 37.649346, -109.853332

32868 • FSR 50095 Dispersed 1 - USFS

Dispersed sites, No water, No toilets, Reservations not accepted, Open all year, Tent & RV camping: Free, Road not maintained for passenger cars, Elev: 7698ft/2346m, Tel: 435-587-2041, Nearest town: Monticello, Agency: USFS, GPS: 37.842914, -109.733542

32869 • FSR 50095 Dispersed 2 - USFS

Dispersed sites, No water, No toilets, Reservations not accepted, Open all year, Tent & RV camping: Free, Road not maintained for passenger cars, Elev: 8514ft/2595m, Tel: 435-587-2041, Nearest town: Monticello, Agency: USFS, GPS: 37.845059, -109.771377

32870 • FSR 50096 Dispersed 1 - USFS

Dispersed sites, No water, No toilets, Reservations not accepted, Open all year, Tent & RV camping: Free, Road not maintained for passenger cars, Elev: 7794ft/2376m, Tel: 435-587-2041, Nearest town: Monticello, Agency: USFS, GPS: 37.876266, -109.694756

32871 • FSR 50097 Dispersed 1 - USFS

Dispersed sites, No water, No toilets, Reservations not accepted, Open all year, Tent & RV camping: Free, Road not maintained for passenger cars, Elev: 7094ft/2162m, Tel: 435-587-2041, Nearest town: Monticello, Agency: USFS, GPS: 37.929965, -109.707136

32872 • FSR 50098 Dispersed 1 - USFS

Dispersed sites, No water, No toilets, Reservations not accepted, Open all year, Tent & RV camping: Free, Road not maintained for passenger cars, Elev: 7909ft/2411m, Tel: 435-587-2041, Nearest town: Monticello, Agency: USFS, GPS: 37.887149, -109.757197

32873 • FSR 501 Dispersed 1 - USFS

Dispersed sites, No water, No toilets, Reservations not accepted, Open all year, Tent & RV camping: Free, Road not maintained for passenger cars, Elev: 6656ft/2029m, Tel: 435-743-5721, Nearest town: Fillmore, Agency: USFS, GPS: 38.872248, -112.297498

32874 • FSR 50106 Dispersed 1 - USFS

Dispersed sites, No water, No toilets, Reservations not accepted, Open all year, Tent & RV camping: Free, Road not maintained for passenger cars, Elev: 7469ft/2277m, Tel: 435-587-2041, Nearest town: Monticello, Agency: USFS, GPS: 37.828992, -109.737255

32875 • FSR 50108 Dispersed 1 - USFS

Dispersed sites, No water, No toilets, Reservations not accepted, Open all year, Tent & RV camping: Free, Road not maintained for passenger cars, Elev: 8425ft/2568m, Tel: 435-587-2041, Nearest town: Blanding, Agency: USFS, GPS: 37.662177, -109.884565

32876 • FSR 50108 Dispersed 2 - USFS

Dispersed sites, No water, No toilets, Reservations not accepted, Open all year, Tent & RV camping: Free, Road not maintained for passenger cars, Elev: 8421ft/2567m, Tel: 435-587-2041, Nearest town: Blanding, Agency: USFS, GPS: 37.654522, -109.873728

32877 • FSR 50111 Dispersed 1 - USFS

Dispersed sites, No water, No toilets, Reservations not accepted, Open Jun-Dec, Tent & RV camping: Free, Elev: 9903ft/3018m, Tel: 435-637-2817, Nearest town: Huntington, Agency: USFS, GPS: 39.498411, -111.081755

32878 • FSR 50111 Dispersed 2 - USFS

Dispersed sites, No water, No toilets, Reservations not accepted, Open Jun-Dec, Tent & RV camping: Free, Several sites, Elev: 9954ft/3034m, Tel: 435-637-2817, Nearest town: Huntington, Agency: USFS, GPS: 39.503162, -111.082602

32879 • FSR 50114 Dispersed 1 - USFS

Dispersed sites, No water, No toilets, Reservations not accepted, Open all year, Tent & RV camping: Free, Road not maintained for passenger cars, Elev: 8935ft/2723m, Tel: 435-637-2817, Nearest town: Ephraim, Agency: USFS, GPS: 39.325009, -111.470595

32880 • FSR 50114 Dispersed 2 - USFS

Dispersed sites, No water, No toilets, Reservations not accepted, Open all year, Tent & RV camping: Free, Road not maintained for passenger cars, Elev: 8905ft/2714m, Tel: 435-637-2817, Nearest town: Ephraim, Agency: USFS, GPS: 39.326778, -111.472253

32881 • FSR 50114 Dispersed 3 - USFS

Dispersed sites, No water, No toilets, Reservations not accepted, Open all year, Tent & RV camping: Free, Road not maintained for passenger cars, Elev: 9107ft/2776m, Tel: 435-637-2817, Nearest town: Ephraim, Agency: USFS, GPS: 39.342709, -111.468383

32882 • FSR 50122 Dispersed 1 - USFS

Dispersed sites, No water, No toilets, Reservations not accepted, Open all year, Tent & RV camping: Free, Road not maintained for passenger cars, Elev: 7777ft/2370m, Tel: 435-637-2817, Nearest town: Spanish Fork, Agency: USFS, GPS: 39.794881, -111.203877

32883 • FSR 50122 Dispersed 2 - USFS

Dispersed sites, No water, No toilets, Reservations not accepted, Open all year, Tent & RV camping: Free, Road not maintained for passenger cars, Elev: 9081ft/2768m, Tel: 435-637-2817, Nearest town: Spanish Fork, Agency: USFS, GPS: 39.836587, -111.304048

32884 • FSR 50124 Dispersed 1 - USFS

Dispersed sites, No water, No toilets, Reservations not accepted, Open Jun-Dec, Tent & RV camping: Free, Elev: 8821ft/2689m, Tel: 435-637-2817, Nearest town: Fairview, Agency: USFS, GPS: 39.689643, -111.305412

32885 • FSR 50125 Dispersed 1 - USFS

Dispersed sites, No water, No toilets, Reservations not accepted, Open all year, Tent & RV camping: Free, Road not maintained for passenger cars, Elev: 6872ft/2095m, Tel: 435-637-2817, Nearest town: Spanish Fork, Agency: USFS, GPS: 39.808507, -111.412137

32886 • FSR 50128 Dispersed 1 - USFS

Dispersed sites, No water, No toilets, Reservations not accepted, Open all year, Tent & RV camping: Free, Elev: 8148ft/2484m, Tel: 435-259-7155, Nearest town: Moab, Agency: USFS, GPS: 38.374366, -109.204243

32887 • FSR 50128 Dispersed 2 - USFS

Dispersed sites, No water, No toilets, Reservations not accepted, Open all year, Tent & RV camping: Free, Elev: 8584ft/2616m, Tel: 435-259-7155, Nearest town: Moab, Agency: USFS, GPS: 38.368148, -109.243153

32888 • FSR 50128 Dispersed 3 - USFS

Dispersed sites, No water, No toilets, Reservations not accepted, Open all year, Tent & RV camping: Free, Elev: 8612ft/2625m, Tel: 435-259-7155, Nearest town: Moab, Agency: USFS, GPS: 38.365442, -109.258267

32889 • FSR 50131 (Cove Lake) Dispersed 1 - USFS

Dispersed sites, No water, No toilets, Reservations not accepted, Open all year, Tent & RV camping: Free, Road not maintained for passenger cars, Elev: 9401ft/2865m, Tel: 435-637-2817, Nearest town: Manti, Agency: USFS, GPS: 39.212992, -111.423639

32890 • FSR 50131 Dispersed 2 - USFS

Dispersed sites, No water, No toilets, Max length: 16ft, Reservations not accepted, Open all year, Tent & RV camping: Free, Road not maintained for passenger cars, Elev: 10125ft/3086m, Tel: 435-637-2817, Nearest town: Manti, Agency: USFS, GPS: 39.240285, -111.463581

32891 • FSR 50135 Dispersed 1 - USFS

Dispersed sites, No water, No toilets, Reservations not accepted, Open all year, Tent & RV camping: Free, Road not maintained for passenger cars, Elev: 10133ft/3089m, Tel: 435-637-2817, Nearest town: Mayfield, Agency: USFS, GPS: 39.122127, -111.483626

32892 • FSR 50135 Dispersed 2 - USFS

Dispersed sites, No water, No toilets, Reservations not accepted, Open all year, Tent & RV camping: Free, Road not maintained for passenger cars, Elev: 10174ft/3101m, Tel: 435-637-2817, Nearest town: Mayfield, Agency: USFS, GPS: 39.121949, -111.481816

32893 • FSR 50138 Dispersed 1 - USFS

Dispersed sites, No water, No toilets, Reservations not accepted, Open all year, Tent & RV camping: Free, Road not maintained for passenger cars, Elev: 8982ft/2738m, Tel: 435-637-2817, Nearest town: Fairview, Agency: USFS, GPS: 39.736909, -111.353164

32894 • FSR 50140 Dispersed 1 - USFS

Dispersed sites, No water, No toilets, Reservations not accepted, Open all year, Tent & RV camping: Free, Elev: 7671ft/2338m, Tel: 435-259-7155, Nearest town: Moab, Agency: USFS, GPS: 38.339035, -109.208577

32895 • FSR 50140 Dispersed 2 - USFS

Dispersed sites, No water, No toilets, Reservations not accepted, Open all year, Tent & RV camping: Free, Elev: 7742ft/2360m, Tel: 435-259-7155, Nearest town: Moab, Agency: USFS, GPS: 38.320528, -109.171918

32896 • FSR 50140 Dispersed 3 - USFS

Dispersed sites, No water, No toilets, Reservations not accepted, Open all year, Tent & RV camping: Free, Elev: 7655ft/2333m, Tel: 435-259-7155, Nearest town: Moab, Agency: USFS, GPS: 38.312766, -109.148363

32897 • FSR 50145 Dispersed 1 - USFS

Dispersed sites, No water, No toilets, Reservations not accepted, Open May-Dec, Tent & RV camping: Free, Road not maintained for passenger cars, Elev: 10278ft/3133m, Tel: 435-637-2817, Nearest town: Huntington, Agency: USFS, GPS: 39.410324, -111.202712

32898 • FSR 50150 Dispersed 1 - USFS

Dispersed sites, No water, No toilets, Reservations not accepted, Open all year, Tent & RV camping: Free, Elev: 9578ft/2919m, Tel: 435-637-2817, Nearest town: Mayfield, Agency: USFS, GPS: 39.058705, -111.554434

32899 • FSR 50150 Dispersed 10 - USFS

Dispersed sites, No water, No toilets, Reservations not accepted, Open all year, Tent & RV camping: Free, Road not maintained for passenger cars, Elev: 10494ft/3199m, Tel: 435-637-2817, Nearest town: Ephraim, Agency: USFS, GPS: 39.282972, -111.445757

32900 • FSR 50150 Dispersed 11 - USFS

Dispersed sites, No water, No toilets, Reservations not accepted, Open all year, Tent & RV camping: Free, Road not maintained for passenger cars, Elev: 10271ft/3131m, Tel: 435-637-2817, Nearest town: Ephraim, Agency: USFS, GPS: 39.307381, -111.448339

32901 • FSR 50150 Dispersed 12 - USFS

Dispersed sites, No water, No toilets, Reservations not accepted, Open all year, Tent & RV camping: Free, Road not maintained for passenger cars, Elev: 10236ft/3120m, Tel: 435-637-2817, Nearest town: Ephraim, Agency: USFS, GPS: 39.318642, -111.440937

32902 • FSR 50150 Dispersed 13 - USFS

Dispersed sites, No water, No toilets, Reservations not accepted, Open all year, Tent & RV camping: Free, Road not maintained for passenger cars, Elev: 10195ft/3107m, Tel: 435-637-2817, Nearest town: Ephraim, Agency: USFS, GPS: 39.320462, -111.441273

32903 • FSR 50150 Dispersed 14 - USFS

Dispersed sites, No water, No toilets, Reservations not accepted, Open all year, Tent & RV camping: Free, Road not maintained for passenger cars, Elev: 10219ft/3115m, Tel: 435-637-2817, Nearest town: Ephraim, Agency: USFS, GPS: 39.328684, -111.447072

32904 • FSR 50150 Dispersed 15 - USFS

Dispersed sites, No water, No toilets, Reservations not accepted, Open Jul-Dec, Tent & RV camping: Free, Several sites in area, Road not maintained for passenger cars, Elev: 10349ft/3154m, Tel: 435-637-2817, Nearest town: Ephraim, Agency: USFS, GPS: 39.342774, -111.446158

32905 • FSR 50150 Dispersed 16 - USFS

Dispersed sites, No water, No toilets, Reservations not accepted, Open Jul-Dec, Tent & RV camping: Free, Road not maintained for passenger cars, Elev: 10302ft/3140m, Tel: 435-637-2817, Nearest town: Ephraim, Agency: USFS, GPS: 39.346215, -111.446505

32906 • FSR 50150 Dispersed 17 - USFS

Dispersed sites, No water, No toilets, Reservations not accepted, Open Jul-Dec, Tent & RV camping: Free, Road not maintained for passenger cars, Elev: 10498ft/3200m, Tel: 435-637-2817, Nearest town: Ephraim, Agency: USFS, GPS: 39.354923, -111.440929

32907 • FSR 50150 Dispersed 18 - USFS

Dispersed sites, No water, No toilets, Reservations not accepted, Open Jul-Dec, Tent & RV camping: Free, Several spots, Road not maintained for passenger cars, Elev: 10481ft/3195m, Tel: 435-637-2817, Nearest town: Huntington, Agency: USFS, GPS: 39.389215, -111.383549

32908 • FSR 50150 Dispersed 19 - USFS

Dispersed sites, No water, No toilets, Reservations not accepted, Open Jul-Dec, Tent & RV camping: Free, Road not maintained for passenger cars, Elev: 10561ft/3219m, Tel: 435-637-2817, Nearest town: Huntington, Agency: USFS, GPS: 39.401447, -111.377827

32909 • FSR 50150 Dispersed 2 - USFS

Dispersed sites, No water, No toilets, Reservations not accepted, Open all year, Tent & RV camping: Free, Several sites in area, Elev: 9853ft/3003m, Tel: 435-637-2817, Nearest town: Mayfield, Agency: USFS, GPS: 39.080021, -111.546246

32910 • FSR 50150 Dispersed 20 - USFS

Dispersed sites, No water, No toilets, Reservations not accepted, Open Jul-Dec, Tent & RV camping: Free, Road not maintained for passenger cars, Elev: 10544ft/3214m, Tel: 435-637-2817, Nearest town: Huntington, Agency: USFS, GPS: 39.420707, -111.372989

32911 • FSR 50150 Dispersed 21 - USFS

Dispersed sites, No water, No toilets, Reservations not accepted, Open Jul-Dec, Tent & RV camping: Free, Room for several rigs, Road not maintained for passenger cars, Elev: 10531ft/3210m, Tel: 435-637-2817, Nearest town: Huntington, Agency: USFS, GPS: 39.428798, -111.358507

32912 • FSR 50150 Dispersed 22 - USFS

Dispersed sites, No water, No toilets, Reservations not accepted, Open Jul-Dec, Tents only: Free, Road not maintained for passenger cars, Elev: 10504ft/3202m, Tel: 435-637-2817, Nearest town: Huntington, Agency: USFS, GPS: 39.429715, -111.350861

32913 • FSR 50150 Dispersed 23 - USFS

Dispersed sites, No water, No toilets, Reservations not accepted, Open Jul-Dec, Tent & RV camping: Free, Road not maintained for passenger cars, Elev: 10386ft/3166m, Tel: 435-637-2817, Nearest town: Huntington, Agency: USFS, GPS: 39.434622, -111.347013

32914 • FSR 50150 Dispersed 24 - USFS

Dispersed sites, No water, No toilets, Reservations not accepted, Open Jul-Dec, Tent & RV camping: Free, Road not maintained for passenger cars, Elev: 10647ft/3245m, Tel: 435-637-2817, Nearest town: Huntington, Agency: USFS, GPS: 39.468407, -111.320437

32915 • FSR 50150 Dispersed 25 - USFS

Dispersed sites, No water, No toilets, Reservations not accepted, Open Jul-Dec, Tent & RV camping: Free, Road not maintained for passenger cars, Elev: 10597ft/3230m, Tel: 435-637-2817, Nearest town: Huntington, Agency: USFS, GPS: 39.487003, -111.321156

32916 • FSR 50150 Dispersed 26 - USFS

Dispersed sites, No water, No toilets, Reservations not accepted, Open Jul-Dec, Tent & RV camping: Free, Elev: 10567ft/3221m, Tel: 435-637-2817, Nearest town: Mount Pleasant, Agency: USFS, GPS: 39.511447, -111.302072

32917 • FSR 50150 Dispersed 27 - USFS

Dispersed sites, No water, No toilets, Reservations not accepted, Open Jul-Dec, Tent & RV camping: Free, Room for several rigs, Elev: 10517ft/3206m, Tel: 435-637-2817, Nearest town: Mount Pleasant, Agency: USFS, GPS: 39.512668, -111.302457

32918 • FSR 50150 Dispersed 28 - USFS

Dispersed sites, No water, No toilets, Reservations not accepted, Open all year, Tent & RV camping: Free, Room for 8-10 rigs in cicrle, Elev: 10669ft/3252m, Tel: 435-637-2817, Nearest town: Mount Pleasant, Agency: USFS, GPS: 39.522753, -111.299875

32919 • FSR 50150 Dispersed 29 - USFS

Dispersed sites, No water, No toilets, Reservations not accepted, Open Jul-Dec, Tent & RV camping: Free, Several sites, Elev: 10465ft/3190m, Tel: 435-637-2817, Nearest town: Mount Pleasant, Agency: USFS, GPS: 39.534526, -111.298655

32920 • FSR 50150 Dispersed 3 - USFS

Dispersed sites, No water, No toilets, Reservations not accepted, Open all year, Tent & RV camping: Free, Elev: 10032ft/3058m, Tel: 435-637-2817, Nearest town: Mayfield, Agency: USFS, GPS: 39.078106, -111.537375

32921 • FSR 50150 Dispersed 30 - USFS

Dispersed sites, No water, No toilets, Reservations not accepted, Open Jul-Dec, Tent & RV camping: Free, Several sites in this area, Elev: 10172ft/3100m, Tel: 435-637-2817, Nearest town: Mount Pleasant, Agency: USFS, GPS: 39.562156, -111.308958

32922 • FSR 50150 Dispersed 31 - USFS

Dispersed sites, No water, No toilets, Reservations not accepted, Open Jul-Dec, Tent & RV camping: Free, Elev: 10110ft/3082m, Tel: 435-637-2817, Nearest town: Mount Pleasant, Agency: USFS, GPS: 39.571033, -111.309228

32923 • FSR 50150 Dispersed 32 - USFS

Dispersed sites, No water, No toilets, Reservations not accepted, Open Jul-Dec, Tent & RV camping: Free, Several sites in this area, Elev: 9809ft/2990m, Tel: 435-637-2817, Nearest town: Fairview, Agency: USFS, GPS: 39.606821, -111.313226

32924 • FSR 50150 Dispersed 33 - USFS

Dispersed sites, No water, No toilets, Reservations not accepted, Open Jul-Dec, Tent & RV camping: Free, Elev: 9567ft/2916m, Tel: 435-637-2817, Nearest town: Fairview, Agency: USFS, GPS: 39.625619, -111.320117

32925 • FSR 50150 Dispersed 34 - USFS

Dispersed sites, No water, No toilets, Reservations not accepted, Open Jul-Dec, Tent & RV camping: Free, Elev: 8899ft/2712m, Tel: 435-637-2817, Nearest town: Fairview, Agency: USFS, GPS: 39.692976, -111.318942

32926 • FSR 50150 Dispersed 35 - USFS

Dispersed sites, No water, No toilets, Reservations not accepted, Open Jul-Dec, Tent & RV camping: Free, Elev: 8934ft/2723m, Tel: 435-637-2817, Nearest town: Fairview, Agency: USFS, GPS: 39.696575, -111.324124

32927 • FSR 50150 Dispersed 36 - USFS

Dispersed sites, No water, No toilets, Reservations not accepted, Open Jul-Dec, Tent & RV camping: Free, Elev: 9163ft/2793m, Tel: 435-637-2817, Nearest town: Fairview, Agency: USFS, GPS: 39.724363, -111.334278

32928 • FSR 50150 Dispersed 37 - USFS

Dispersed sites, No water, No toilets, Reservations not accepted, Open Jul-Dec, Tent & RV camping: Free, Elev: 9139ft/2786m, Tel: 435-637-2817, Nearest town: Fairview, Agency: USFS, GPS: 39.726818, -111.335422

32929 • FSR 50150 Dispersed 38 - USFS

Dispersed sites, No water, No toilets, Reservations not accepted, Open Jul-Dec, Tent & RV camping: Free, Elev: 9124ft/2781m, Tel: 435-637-2817, Nearest town: Fairview, Agency: USFS, GPS: 39.733402, -111.335586

32930 • FSR 50150 Dispersed 39 - USFS

Dispersed sites, No water, No toilets, Reservations not accepted, Open Jul-Dec, Tent & RV camping: Free, Elev: 9132ft/2783m, Tel: 435-637-2817, Nearest town: Fairview, Agency: USFS, GPS: 39.739521, -111.334386

32931 • FSR 50150 Dispersed 4 - USFS

Dispersed sites, No water, No toilets, Reservations not accepted, Open all year, Tent & RV camping: Free, Elev: 9985ft/3043m, Tel: 435-637-2817, Nearest town: Mayfield, Agency: USFS, GPS: 39.075661, -111.536155

32932 • FSR 50150 Dispersed 40 - USFS

Dispersed sites, No water, No toilets, Reservations not accepted, Open Jul-Dec, Tent & RV camping: Free, Elev: 9218ft/2810m, Tel: 435-637-2817, Nearest town: Fairview, Agency: USFS, GPS: 39.749971, -111.320688

32933 • FSR 50150 Dispersed 41 - USFS

Dispersed sites, No water, No toilets, Reservations not accepted, Open Jul-Dec, Tent & RV camping: Free, Elev: 9179ft/2798m, Tel: 435-637-2817, Nearest town: Spanish Fork, Agency: USFS, GPS: 39.782781, -111.359272

32934 • FSR 50150 Dispersed 42 - USFS

Dispersed sites, No water, No toilets, Reservations not accepted, Open all year, Tent & RV camping: Free, Elev: 9146ft/2788m, Tel: 435-637-2817, Nearest town: Spanish Fork, Agency: USFS, GPS: 39.832351, -111.350893

32935 • FSR 50150 Dispersed 43 - USFS

Dispersed sites, No water, No toilets, Reservations not accepted, Open Jul-Dec, Tent & RV camping: Free, Elev: 9086ft/2769m, Tel: 435-637-2817, Nearest town: Spanish Fork, Agency: USFS, GPS: 39.843214, -111.335082

32936 • FSR 50150 Dispersed 44 - USFS

Dispersed sites, No water, No toilets, Reservations not accepted, Open Jul-Dec, Tent & RV camping: Free, Elev: 9014ft/2747m, Tel: 435-637-2817, Nearest town: Spanish Fork, Agency: USFS, GPS: 39.864544, -111.286931

32937 • FSR 50150 Dispersed 45 - USFS

Dispersed sites, No water, No toilets, Reservations not accepted, Open Jul-Dec, Tent & RV camping: Free, Elev: 8953ft/2729m, Tel: 435-637-2817, Nearest town: Spanish Fork, Agency: USFS, GPS: 39.867537, -111.284942

32938 • FSR 50150 Dispersed 5 - USFS

Dispersed sites, No water, No toilets, Reservations not accepted, Open all year, Tent & RV camping: Free, Elev: 10206ft/3111m, Tel: 435-637-2817, Nearest town: Mayfield, Agency: USFS, GPS: 39.098363, -111.494148

32939 • FSR 50150 Dispersed 6 - USFS

Dispersed sites, No water, No toilets, Reservations not accepted, Open all year, Tent & RV camping: Free, Several spots in area, Elev: 10171ft/3100m, Tel: 435-637-2817, Nearest town: Mayfield, Agency: USFS, GPS: 39.107877, -111.488654

32940 • FSR 50150 Dispersed 7 - USFS

Dispersed sites, No water, No toilets, Reservations not accepted, Open all year, Tent & RV camping: Free, Numerous spots in this area, Elev: 10161ft/3097m, Tel: 435-637-2817, Nearest town: Mayfield, Agency: USFS, GPS: 39.113818, -111.491541

32941 • FSR 50150 Dispersed 8 - USFS

Dispersed sites, No water, No toilets, Reservations not accepted, Open all year, Tent & RV camping: Free, Road not maintained for passenger cars, Elev: 10477ft/3193m, Tel: 435-637-2817, Nearest town: Ephraim, Agency: USFS, GPS: 39.263188, -111.448977

32942 • FSR 50150 Dispersed 9 - USFS

Dispersed sites, No water, No toilets, Reservations not accepted, Open all year, Tent & RV camping: Free, 2 separated sites, Road not maintained for passenger cars, Elev: 10441ft/3182m, Tel: 435-637-2817, Nearest town: Ephraim, Agency: USFS, GPS: 39.26931, -111.446971

32943 • FSR 50151 Dispersed 1 - USFS

Dispersed sites, No water, No toilets, Reservations not accepted, Open all year, Tent & RV camping: Free, Road not maintained for passenger cars, Elev: 10165ft/3098m, Tel: 435-637-2817, Nearest town: Mayfield, Agency: USFS, GPS: 39.075508, -111.496727

32944 • FSR 50169 Dispersed 1 - USFS

Dispersed sites, No water, No toilets, Reservations not accepted, Open all year, Tent & RV camping: Free, Road not maintained for passenger cars, Elev: 10058ft/3066m, Tel: 435-637-2817, Nearest town: Mayfield, Agency: USFS, GPS: 39.059262, -111.482181

32945 • FSR 50169 Dispersed 2 - USFS

Dispersed sites, No water, No toilets, Reservations not accepted, Open all year, Tent & RV camping: Free, Road not maintained for passenger cars, Elev: 9960ft/3036m, Tel: 435-637-2817, Nearest town: Mayfield, Agency: USFS, GPS: 39.055863, -111.480022

32946 • FSR 50173 Dispersed 1 - USFS

Dispersed sites, No water, Vault toilets, Reservations not accepted, Tent & RV camping: Free, Elev: 9646ft/2940m, Nearest town: Fairview, Agency: USFS, GPS: 39.624019, -111.303585

32947 • FSR 50175 Dispersed 1 - USFS

Dispersed sites, No water, No toilets, Reservations not accepted, Open all year, Tent & RV camping: Free, Road not maintained for passenger cars, Elev: 7165ft/2184m, Tel: 435-587-2041, Nearest town: Monticello, Agency: USFS, GPS: 37.955487, -109.380751

32948 • FSR 50175 Dispersed 2 - USFS

Dispersed sites, No water, No toilets, Reservations not accepted, Open all year, Tent & RV camping: Free, Road not maintained for passenger cars, Elev: 7173ft/2186m, Tel: 435-587-2041, Nearest town: Monticello, Agency: USFS, GPS: 37.954895, -109.393458

32949 • FSR 50175 Dispersed 3 - USFS

Dispersed sites, No water, No toilets, Reservations not accepted, Open all year, Tent & RV camping: Free, Road not maintained for passenger cars, Elev: 7127ft/2172m, Tel: 435-587-2041, Nearest town: Monticello, Agency: USFS, GPS: 37.955549, -109.396997

32950 • FSR 50175 Dispersed 4 - USFS

Dispersed sites, No water, No toilets, Reservations not accepted, Open all year, Tent & RV camping: Free, Road not maintained for passenger cars, Elev: 7244ft/2208m, Tel: 435-587-2041, Nearest town: Monticello, Agency: USFS, GPS: 37.955068, -109.402384

32951 • FSR 50175 Dispersed 5 - USFS

Dispersed sites, No water, No toilets, Reservations not accepted, Open all year, Tent & RV camping: Free, Road not maintained for passenger cars, Elev: 7470ft/2277m, Tel: 435-587-2041, Nearest town: Monticello, Agency: USFS, GPS: 37.965511, -109.425127

32952 • FSR 50180 Dispersed 1 - USFS

Dispersed sites, No water, No toilets, Reservations not accepted, Open all year, Tent & RV camping: Free, Road not maintained for passenger cars, Elev: 8493ft/2589m, Tel: 435-587-2041, Nearest town: Blanding, Agency: USFS, GPS: 37.665624, -109.830056

32953 • FSR 50180 Dispersed 2 - USFS

Dispersed sites, No water, No toilets, Reservations not accepted, Open all year, Tent & RV camping: Free, Road not maintained for passenger cars, Elev: 8447ft/2575m, Tel: 435-587-2041, Nearest town: Blanding, Agency: USFS, GPS: 37.668933, -109.833957

32954 • FSR 50180 Dispersed 3 - USFS

Dispersed sites, No water, No toilets, Reservations not accepted, Open all year, Tent & RV camping: Free, Road not maintained for passenger cars, Elev: 8537ft/2602m, Tel: 435-587-2041, Nearest town: Blanding, Agency: USFS, GPS: 37.695259, -109.837602

32955 • FSR 50181 Dispersed 1 - USFS

Dispersed sites, No water, No toilets, Reservations not accepted, Open all year, Tent & RV camping: Free, Road not maintained for passenger cars, Elev: 8401ft/2561m, Tel: 435-587-2041, Nearest town: Blanding, Agency: USFS, GPS: 37.660497, -109.884256

32956 • FSR 50192 Dispersed 1 - USFS

Dispersed sites, No water, No toilets, Reservations not accepted, Open all year, Tent & RV camping: Free, Road not maintained for passenger cars, Elev: 7707ft/2349m, Tel: 435-587-2041, Nearest town: Monticello, Agency: USFS, GPS: 37.848972, -109.727525

32957 • FSR 50193 (Patton Reservoir) Dispersed 2 - USFS

Dispersed sites, No water, No toilets, Reservations not accepted, Open all year, Tent & RV camping: Free, Road not maintained for passenger cars, Elev: 8288ft/2526m, Tel: 435-637-2817, Nearest town: Manti, Agency: USFS, GPS: 39.240119, -111.564067

32958 • FSR 50193 Dispersed 1 - USFS

Dispersed sites, No water, No toilets, Reservations not accepted, Open all year, Tent & RV camping: Free, Room for many rigs, Road not maintained for passenger cars, Elev: 8803ft/2683m, Tel: 435-637-2817, Nearest town: Manti, Agency: USFS, GPS: 39.238139, -111.519618

32959 • FSR 502 (Nephie's Camp) Dispersed 1 - USFS

Dispersed sites, No water, No toilets, Reservations not accepted, Open all year, Tent & RV camping: Free, Road not maintained for passenger cars, Elev: 9717ft/2962m, Tel: 435-783-4338, Nearest town: Heber City, Agency: USFS, GPS: 40.410216, -111.115502

32960 • FSR 50208 Dispersed 1 - USFS

Dispersed sites, No water, No toilets, Reservations not accepted, Open all year, Tent & RV camping: Free, Elev: 7742ft/2360m, Tel: 435-259-7155, Nearest town: Moab, Agency: USFS, GPS: 38.344618, -109.207283

32961 • FSR 50208 Dispersed 2 - USFS

Dispersed sites, No water, No toilets, Reservations not accepted, Open all year, Tent & RV camping: Free, Elev: 7734ft/2357m, Tel: 435-259-7155, Nearest town: Moab, Agency: USFS, GPS: 38.343039, -109.208371

32962 • FSR 50221 Dispersed 1 - USFS

Dispersed sites, No water, No toilets, Reservations not accepted, Open Jun-Dec, Tent & RV camping: Free, Elev: 9206ft/2806m, Tel: 435-637-2817, Nearest town: Fairview, Agency: USFS, GPS: 39.744441, -111.222403

32963 • FSR 50221 Dispersed 2 - USFS

Dispersed sites, No water, No toilets, Reservations not accepted, Open Jun-Dec, Tent & RV camping: Free, Elev: 9527ft/2904m, Tel: 435-637-2817, Nearest town: Fairview, Agency: USFS, GPS: 39.699327, -111.230604

32964 • FSR 50235 Dispersed 1 - USFS

Dispersed sites, No water, No toilets, Reservations not accepted, Open all year, Tent & RV camping: Free, Road not maintained for passenger cars, Elev: 8936ft/2724m, Tel: 435-637-2817, Nearest town: Fairview, Agency: USFS, GPS: 39.741909, -111.327228

32965 • FSR 50237 Dispersed1 - USFS

Dispersed sites, No water, No toilets, Reservations not accepted, Open all year, Tent & RV camping: Free, Elev: 10297ft/3139m, Tel: 435-259-7155, Nearest town: Moab, Agency: USFS, GPS: 38.416357, -109.265228

32966 • FSR 50238 Dispersed 1 - USFS

Dispersed sites, No water, Vault toilets, Reservations not accepted, Open all year, Tent & RV camping: Free, Elev: 10018ft/3053m, Tel: 435-259-7155, Nearest town: Moab, Agency: USFS, GPS: 38.416542, -109.247055

32967 • FSR 50244 Dispersed 1 - USFS

Dispersed sites, No water, No toilets, Reservations not accepted, Open May-Dec, Tent & RV camping: Free, Road not maintained for passenger cars, Elev: 10446ft/3184m, Tel: 435-637-2817, Nearest town: Huntington, Agency: USFS, GPS: 39.428206, -111.215662

32968 • FSR 50244 Dispersed 2 - USFS

Dispersed sites, No water, No toilets, Reservations not accepted, Open May-Dec, Tent & RV camping: Free, Road not maintained for passenger cars, Elev: 10395ft/3168m, Tel: 435-637-2817, Nearest town: Huntington, Agency: USFS, GPS: 39.442885, -111.213824

32969 • FSR 50244 Dispersed 3 - USFS

Dispersed sites, No water, No toilets, Reservations not accepted, Open May-Dec, Tent & RV camping: Free, Road not maintained for passenger cars, Elev: 10479ft/3194m, Tel: 435-637-2817, Nearest town: Huntington, Agency: USFS, GPS: 39.446187, -111.214573

32970 • FSR 50247 Dispersed 1 - USFS

Dispersed sites, No water, No toilets, Reservations not accepted, Open all year, Tent & RV camping: Free, Elev: 9096ft/2772m, Tel: 435-637-2817, Nearest town: Huntington, Agency: USFS, GPS: 39.619373, -111.157045

32971 • FSR 50249 Dispersed 1 - USFS

Dispersed sites, No water, No toilets, Reservations not accepted, Open all year, Tents only: Free, Road not maintained for passenger cars, Elev: 9874ft/3010m, Tel: 435-637-2817, Nearest town: Huntington, Agency: USFS, GPS: 39.533939, -111.088754

32972 • FSR 50269 Dispersed 1 - USFS

Dispersed sites, No water, No toilets, Reservations not accepted, Open Jun-Dec, Tent & RV camping: Free, Road not maintained for passenger cars, Elev: 8725ft/2659m, Tel: 435-637-2817, Nearest town: Mount Pleasant, Agency: USFS, GPS: 39.564886, -111.245769

32973 • FSR 50269 Dispersed 2 - USFS

Dispersed sites, No water, No toilets, Reservations not accepted, Open Jun-Dec, Tent & RV camping: Free, Road not maintained for passenger cars, Elev: 8864ft/2702m, Tel: 435-637-2817, Nearest town: Mount Pleasant, Agency: USFS, GPS: 39.561857, -111.252537

32974 • FSR 50270 Dispersed 1 - USFS

Dispersed sites, No water, No toilets, Reservations not accepted, Open all year, Tent & RV camping: Free, Road not maintained for passenger cars, Elev: 9032ft/2753m, Tel: 435-637-2817, Nearest town: Huntington, Agency: USFS, GPS: 39.435839, -111.382297

32975 • FSR 50271 Dispersed 1 - USFS

Dispersed sites, No water, No toilets, Reservations not accepted, Open all year, Tent & RV camping: Free, Several large sites in this area, Elev: 8848ft/2697m, Tel: 435-637-2817, Nearest town: Mount Pleasant, Agency: USFS, GPS: 39.450205, -111.262064

32976 • FSR 50271 Dispersed 2 - USFS

Dispersed sites, No water, No toilets, Reservations not accepted, Open all year, Tent & RV camping: Free, Near powerline, Elev: 9060ft/2761m, Tel: 435-637-2817, Nearest town: Huntington, Agency: USFS, GPS: 39.456245, -111.273292

32977 • FSR 50271 Dispersed 3 - USFS

Dispersed sites, No water, No toilets, Reservations not accepted, Open all year, Tent & RV camping: Free, Very near powerline, Elev: 9141ft/2786m, Tel: 435-637-2817, Nearest town: Huntington, Agency: USFS, GPS: 39.459182, -111.274815

32978 • FSR 50271 Dispersed 4 - USFS

Dispersed sites, No water, No toilets, Reservations not accepted, Open all year, Tent & RV camping: Free, Elev: 9287ft/2831m, Tel: 435-637-2817, Nearest town: Huntington, Agency: USFS, GPS: 39.465486, -111.276008

32979 • FSR 50271 Dispersed 5 - USFS

Dispersed sites, No water, No toilets, Reservations not accepted, Open all year, Tent & RV camping: Free, Road not maintained for passenger cars, Elev: 9976ft/3041m, Tel: 435-637-2817, Nearest town: Huntington, Agency: USFS, GPS: 39.477296, -111.309942

32980 • FSR 50276 Dispersed - USFS

Dispersed sites, No water, No toilets, Reservations not accepted, Open all year, Tent & RV camping: Free, Road not maintained for passenger cars, Elev: 10893ft/3320m, Tel: 435-637-2817, Nearest town: Ephraim, Agency: USFS, GPS: 39.365977, -111.388425

32981 • FSR 50279 Dispersed 1 - USFS

Dispersed sites, No water, No toilets, Reservations not accepted, Open all year, Tent & RV camping: Free, Road not maintained for passenger cars, Elev: 10522ft/3207m, Tel: 435-637-2817, Nearest town: Ephraim, Agency: USFS, GPS: 39.411484, -111.379712

32982 • FSR 50290 (Woods Lake) Dispersed 1 - USFS

Dispersed sites, No water, No toilets, Reservations not accepted, Open all year, Tent & RV camping: Free, Road not maintained for passenger cars, Elev: 9455ft/2882m, Tel: 435-637-2817, Nearest town: Mayfield, Agency: USFS, GPS: 39.068659, -111.560104

32983 • FSR 503 Dispersed 1 - USFS

Dispersed sites, No water, No toilets, Reservations not accepted, Open all year, Tent & RV camping: Free, 3 sites in this area, Road not maintained for passenger cars, Elev: 8573ft/2613m, Tel: 435-783-4338, Nearest town: Heber City, Agency: USFS, GPS: 40.297849, -111.280627

32984 • FSR 503 Dispersed 2 - USFS

Dispersed sites, No water, No toilets, Reservations not accepted, Open all year, Tent & RV camping: Free, 2 sites, Road not maintained for passenger cars, Elev: 8638ft/2633m, Tel: 435-783-4338, Nearest town: Heber City, Agency: USFS, GPS: 40.296403, -111.284287

32985 • FSR 503 Dispersed 3 - USFS

Dispersed sites, No water, No toilets, Reservations not accepted, Open all year, Tent & RV camping: Free, Both sides of road, Road not maintained for passenger cars, Elev: 8670ft/2643m, Tel: 435-783-4338, Nearest town: Heber City, Agency: USFS, GPS: 40.292965, -111.284417

32986 • FSR 503 Dispersed 4 - USFS

Dispersed sites, No water, No toilets, Reservations not accepted, Open all year, Tent & RV camping: Free, Elev: 8661ft/2640m, Tel: 435-783-4338, Nearest town: Heber City, Agency: USFS, GPS: 40.290046, -111.285695

32987 • FSR 50311 Dispersed 1 - USFS

Dispersed sites, No water, No toilets, Reservations not accepted, Open all year, Tent & RV camping: Free, Road not maintained for passenger cars, Elev: 8859ft/2700m, Tel: 435-637-2817, Nearest town: Ferron, Agency: USFS, GPS: 39.209016, -111.302177

32988 • FSR 50348 Dispersed 1 - USFS

Dispersed sites, No water, No toilets, Reservations not accepted, Open Jun-Dec, Tents only: Free, Road not maintained for passenger cars, Elev: 8863ft/2701m, Tel: 435-637-2817, Nearest town: Mount Pleasant, Agency: USFS, GPS: 39.561527, -111.254987

32989 • FSR 50349 Dispersed 1 - USFS

Dispersed sites, No water, No toilets, Reservations not accepted, Open all year, Tent & RV camping: Free, Road not maintained for passenger cars, Elev: 8266ft/2519m, Tel: 435-587-2041, Nearest town: Monticello, Agency: USFS, GPS: 37.849394, -109.622902

32990 • FSR 50349 Dispersed 2 - USFS

Dispersed sites, No water, No toilets, Reservations not accepted, Open all year, Tent & RV camping: Free, At end of road, Road not maintained for passenger cars, Elev: 8062ft/2457m, Tel: 435-587-2041, Nearest town: Monticello, Agency: USFS, GPS: 37.861801, -109.615408

32991 • FSR 50350 Dispersed 1 - USFS

Dispersed sites, No water, No toilets, Reservations not accepted, Open all year, Tent & RV camping: Free, 2 separated spots, Road not maintained for passenger cars, Elev: 9991ft/3045m, Tel: 435-637-2817, Nearest town: Ephraim, Agency: USFS, GPS: 39.299868, -111.461673

32992 • FSR 50357 Dispersed 1 - USFS

Dispersed sites, No water, No toilets, Reservations not accepted, Open all year, Tent & RV camping: Free, Road not maintained for passenger cars, Elev: 8160ft/2487m, Tel: 435-587-2041, Nearest town: Monticello, Agency: USFS, GPS: 37.827216, -109.413686

32993 • FSR 504 Dispersed 1 - USFS

Dispersed sites, No water, No toilets, Reservations not accepted, Open all year, Tent & RV camping: Free, Elev: 6086ft/1855m, Tel: 435-789-1181, Nearest town: Manila, Agency: USFS, GPS: 40.920773, -109.696269

32994 • FSR 504 Dispersed 2 - USFS

Dispersed sites, No water, No toilets, Reservations not accepted, Open all year, Tent & RV camping: Free, Elev: 6056ft/1846m, Tel: 435-789-1181, Nearest town: Manila, Agency: USFS, GPS: 40.920991, -109.687828

32995 • FSR 506 (Clegg Canyon) Dispersed 1 - USFS

Dispersed sites, No water, No toilets, Reservations not accepted, Open all year, Tent & RV camping: Free, Road not maintained for passenger cars, Elev: 6663ft/2031m, Tel: 435-783-4338, Nearest town: Heber City, Agency: USFS, GPS: 40.387285, -111.302017

32996 • FSR 508 Dispersed 1 - USFS

Dispersed sites, No water, No toilets, Reservations not accepted, Open all year, Tent & RV camping: Free, Road not maintained for passenger cars, Elev: 8490ft/2588m, Tel: 435-743-5721, Nearest town: Richfield, Agency: USFS, GPS: 38.807048, -112.235019

32997 • FSR 509 Dispersed 1 - USFS

Dispersed sites, No water, No toilets, Reservations not accepted, Open all year, Tent & RV camping: Free, Road not maintained for passenger cars, Elev: 7851ft/2393m, Tel: 435-783-4338, Nearest town: Springville, Agency: USFS, GPS: 40.161867, -111.196434

32998 • FSR 509 Dispersed 2 - USFS

Dispersed sites, No water, No toilets, Reservations not accepted, Open all year, Tent & RV camping: Free, Road not maintained for passenger cars, Elev: 9051ft/2759m, Tel: 435-789-1181, Nearest town: Vernal, Agency: USFS, GPS: 40.645364, -109.716808

32999 • FSR 510 Dispersed - USFS

Dispersed sites, No water, No toilets, Reservations not accepted, Open all year, Tent & RV camping: Free, Several sites in this area, Road not maintained for passenger cars, Elev: 8130ft/2478m, Tel: 435-783-4338, Nearest town: Heber City, Agency: USFS, GPS: 40.365365, -111.085166

33000 • FSR 5101 Dispersed 1 - USFS

Dispersed sites, No water, No toilets, Max length: 50ft, Tent & RV camping: Free, Elev: 8854ft/2699m, Nearest town: Monticello, Agency: USFS, GPS: 37.889087, -109.454956

33001 • FSR 51065 Dispersed 1 - USFS

Dispersed sites, No water, No toilets, Reservations not accepted, Open all year, Tent & RV camping: Free, Road not maintained for passenger cars, Elev: 9556ft/2913m, Tel: 435-637-2817, Nearest town: Fairview, Agency: USFS, GPS: 39.623398, -111.320031

33002 • FSR 51068 Dispersed 1 - USFS

Dispersed sites, No water, No toilets, Reservations not accepted, Open Jul-Dec, Tents only: Free, Road not maintained for passenger cars, Elev: 9690ft/2954m, Tel: 435-637-2817, Nearest town: Mount Pleasant, Agency: USFS, GPS: 39.555026, -111.322299

33003 • FSR 51115 Dispersed 1 - USFS

Dispersed sites, No water, No toilets, Reservations not accepted, Open all year, Tent & RV camping: Free, Road not maintained for passenger cars, Elev: 9744ft/2970m, Tel: 435-637-2817, Nearest town: Manti, Agency: USFS, GPS: 39.258206, -111.468788

33004 • FSR 51131 Dispersed 1 - USFS

Dispersed sites, No water, No toilets, Reservations not accepted, Open all year, Tent & RV camping: Free, Numerous spots in this area, Road not maintained for passenger cars, Elev: 8120ft/2475m, Tel: 435-637-2817, Nearest town: Manti, Agency: USFS, GPS: 39.248891, -111.525355

33005 • FSR 51143 Dispersed 1 - USFS

Dispersed sites, No water, No toilets, Reservations not accepted, Open all year, Tent & RV camping: Free, Road not maintained for

passenger cars, Elev: 9729ft/2965m, Tel: 435-637-2817, Nearest town: Mayfield, Agency: USFS, GPS: 39.175916, -111.570868

33006 • FSR 51180 Dispersed 1 - USFS

Dispersed sites, No water, No toilets, Reservations not accepted, Open all year, Tent & RV camping: Free, Road not maintained for passenger cars, Elev: 9132ft/2783m, Tel: 435-637-2817, Nearest town: Fairview, Agency: USFS, GPS: 39.728197, -111.336008

33007 • FSR 51185 Dispersed 1 - USFS

Dispersed sites, No water, No toilets, Reservations not accepted, Open all year, Tent & RV camping: Free, Numerous spots in this area, Road not maintained for passenger cars, Elev: 7447ft/2270m, Tel: 435-637-2817, Nearest town: Manti, Agency: USFS, GPS: 39.254777, -111.547259

33008 • FSR 51247 Dispersed 1 - USFS

Dispersed sites, No water, No toilets, Reservations not accepted, Open all year, Tent & RV camping: Free, Road not maintained for passenger cars, Elev: 10176ft/3102m, Tel: 435-637-2817, Nearest town: Mayfield, Agency: USFS, GPS: 39.087524, -111.501685

33009 • FSR 51256 Dispersed 1 - USFS

Dispersed sites, No water, No toilets, Reservations not accepted, Open all year, Tent & RV camping: Free, Road not maintained for passenger cars, Elev: 8182ft/2494m, Tel: 435-637-2817, Nearest town: Manti, Agency: USFS, GPS: 39.246827, -111.529549

33010 • FSR 51320 Dispersed 1 - USFS

Dispersed sites, No water, No toilets, Reservations not accepted, Open all year, Tent & RV camping: Free, Large open area - many rigs, Road not maintained for passenger cars, Elev: 10184ft/3104m, Tel: 435-637-2817, Nearest town: Manti, Agency: USFS, GPS: 39.246524, -111.459506

33011 • FSR 514 Dispersed 1 - USFS

Dispersed sites, No water, No toilets, Reservations not accepted, Open Jun-Sep, Tent & RV camping: Free, Road not maintained for passenger cars, Elev: 8946ft/2727m, Tel: 435-826-5400, Nearest town: Teasdale, Agency: USFS, GPS: 37.989719, -111.510061

33012 • FSR 517 Dispersed 1 - USFS

Dispersed sites, No water, No toilets, Reservations not accepted, Open all year, Tent & RV camping: Free, Road not maintained for passenger cars, Elev: 8822ft/2689m, Tel: 435-836-2800, Nearest town: Teasdale, Agency: USFS, GPS: 38.201135, -111.575861

33013 • FSR 517 Dispersed 2 - USFS

Dispersed sites, No water, No toilets, Reservations not accepted, Open all year, Tent & RV camping: Free, Road not maintained for passenger cars, Elev: 8720ft/2658m, Tel: 435-836-2800, Nearest town: Teasdale, Agency: USFS, GPS: 38.207002, -111.572953

33014 • FSR 517 Dispersed 3 - USFS

Dispersed sites, No water, No toilets, Reservations not accepted, Open all year, Tent & RV camping: Free, Road not maintained for passenger cars, Elev: 8672ft/2643m, Tel: 435-836-2800, Nearest town: Teasdale, Agency: USFS, GPS: 38.209336, -111.570591

33015 • FSR 518 Dispersed 1 - USFS

Dispersed sites, No water, No toilets, Reservations not accepted, Open all year, Tent & RV camping: Free, Elev: 8674ft/2644m, Tel: 435-783-4338, Nearest town: Spanish Fork, Agency: USFS, GPS: 40.072186, -111.237611

33016 • FSR 518 Dispersed 2 - USFS

Dispersed sites, No water, No toilets, Reservations not accepted, Open all year, Tent & RV camping: Free, Elev: 8557ft/2608m, Tel: 435-783-4338, Nearest town: Spanish Fork, Agency: USFS, GPS: 40.097434, -111.234994

33017 • FSR 518 Dispersed 3 - USFS

Dispersed sites, No water, No toilets, Reservations not accepted, Open all year, Tent & RV camping: Free, Road not maintained for passenger cars, Elev: 8522ft/2598m, Tel: 435-836-2800, Nearest town: Grover, Agency: USFS, GPS: 38.169426, -111.347133

33018 • FSR 52010 Dispersed 1 - USFS

Dispersed sites, No water, No toilets, Reservations not accepted, Open all year, Tent & RV camping: Free, At end of road, Road not maintained for passenger cars, Elev: 8350ft/2545m, Tel: 435-637-2817, Nearest town: Mayfield, Agency: USFS, GPS: 39.013121, -111.390012

33019 • FSR 52018 Dispersed 1 - USFS

Dispersed sites, No water, No toilets, Reservations not accepted, Open all year, Tent & RV camping: Free, Several spots this area, Road not maintained for passenger cars, Elev: 9772ft/2979m, Tel: 435-637-2817, Nearest town: Ferron, Agency: USFS, GPS: 39.075381, -111.317014

33020 • FSR 52070 Dispersed 1 - USFS

Dispersed sites, No water, No toilets, Reservations not accepted, Open May-Dec, Tent & RV camping: Free, Elev: 9448ft/2880m, Tel: 435-637-2817, Nearest town: Ferron, Agency: USFS, GPS: 39.140417, -111.436544

33021 • FSR 52078 Dispersed 1 - USFS

Dispersed sites, No water, No toilets, Reservations not accepted, Open all year, Tent & RV camping: Free, Elev: 9311ft/2838m, Tel: 435-637-2817, Nearest town: Ferron, Agency: USFS, GPS: 39.169384, -111.420326

33022 • FSR 52094 Dispersed 1 - USFS

Dispersed sites, No water, No toilets, Reservations not accepted, Open all year, Tent & RV camping: Free, Road not maintained for passenger cars, Elev: 9495ft/2894m, Tel: 435-637-2817, Nearest town: Ferron, Agency: USFS, GPS: 39.139918, -111.369021

33023 • FSR 52095 (Lizard Lake) Dispersed 1 - USFS

Dispersed sites, No water, No toilets, Reservations not accepted, Open all year, Tent & RV camping: Free, Road not maintained for passenger cars, Elev: 9466ft/2885m, Tel: 435-637-2817, Nearest town: Ferron, Agency: USFS, GPS: 39.143548, -111.365979

33024 • FSR 521 (Donkey Reservoir) Dispersed 6 - USFS

Dispersed sites, No water, No toilets, Reservations not accepted, Open all year, Tent & RV camping: Free, Road not maintained for

passenger cars, Elev: 10179ft/3103m, Tel: 435-836-2800, Nearest town: Teasdale, Agency: USFS, GPS: 38.203316, -111.487975

33025 • FSR 521 (Round Lake) Dispersed 3 - USFS
Dispersed sites, No water, No toilets, Reservations not accepted, Open all year, Tent & RV camping: Free, Road not maintained for passenger cars, Elev: 9806ft/2989m, Tel: 435-836-2800, Nearest town: Teasdale, Agency: USFS, GPS: 38.207095, -111.473139

33026 • FSR 521 (Round Lake) Dispersed 4 - USFS
Dispersed sites, No water, No toilets, Reservations not accepted, Open all year, Tent & RV camping: Free, Road not maintained for passenger cars, Elev: 9804ft/2988m, Tel: 435-836-2800, Nearest town: Teasdale, Agency: USFS, GPS: 38.205321, -111.472931

33027 • FSR 521 Dispersed 1 - USFS
Dispersed sites, No water, No toilets, Reservations not accepted, Open all year, Tent & RV camping: Free, Road not maintained for passenger cars, Elev: 8074ft/2461m, Tel: 435-836-2800, Nearest town: Teasdale, Agency: USFS, GPS: 38.261276, -111.488923

33028 • FSR 521 Dispersed 2 - USFS
Dispersed sites, No water, No toilets, Reservations not accepted, Open all year, Tent & RV camping: Free, Road not maintained for passenger cars, Elev: 9132ft/2783m, Tel: 435-836-2800, Nearest town: Teasdale, Agency: USFS, GPS: 38.228477, -111.468052

33029 • FSR 521 Dispersed 5 - USFS
Dispersed sites, No water, No toilets, Reservations not accepted, Open all year, Tent & RV camping: Free, Road not maintained for passenger cars, Elev: 10033ft/3058m, Tel: 435-836-2800, Nearest town: Teasdale, Agency: USFS, GPS: 38.201095, -111.482768

33030 • FSR 52139 Dispersed 1 - USFS
Dispersed sites, No water, No toilets, Reservations not accepted, Open Apr-Nov, Tent & RV camping: Free, Road not maintained for passenger cars, Elev: 8520ft/2597m, Tel: 435-637-2817, Nearest town: Orangeville, Agency: USFS, GPS: 39.249718, -111.173136

33031 • FSR 52146 Dispersed 1 - USFS
Dispersed sites, No water, No toilets, Reservations not accepted, Open all year, Tent & RV camping: Free, Road not maintained for passenger cars, Elev: 10132ft/3088m, Tel: 435-637-2817, Nearest town: Ephraim, Agency: USFS, GPS: 39.318011, -111.430157

33032 • FSR 52146 Dispersed 2 - USFS
Dispersed sites, No water, No toilets, Reservations not accepted, Open all year, Tent & RV camping: Free, At end of road, Road not maintained for passenger cars, Elev: 10114ft/3083m, Tel: 435-637-2817, Nearest town: Ephraim, Agency: USFS, GPS: 39.312568, -111.415322

33033 • FSR 522 (Pyramid Lake) Dispersed 1 - USFS
Dispersed sites, No water, No toilets, Reservations not accepted, Open all year, Tent & RV camping: Free, Several sites, Road not maintained for passenger cars, Elev: 9746ft/2971m, Tel: 435-783-4338, Nearest town: Oakley, Agency: USFS, GPS: 40.655749, -110.898371

33034 • FSR 52208 (Paradise Creek TH) Dispersed 1 - USFS
Dispersed sites, No water, No toilets, Reservations not accepted, Open all year, Tent & RV camping: Free, Elev: 9367ft/2855m, Tel: 435-637-2817, Nearest town: Huntington, Agency: USFS, GPS: 39.469007, -111.276289

33035 • FSR 52232 Dispersed 1 - USFS
Dispersed sites, No water, No toilets, Reservations not accepted, Open all year, Tent & RV camping: Free, Elev: 9036ft/2754m, Tel: 435-637-2817, Nearest town: Huntington, Agency: USFS, GPS: 39.454747, -111.268617

33036 • FSR 52291 Dispersed 1 - USFS
Dispersed sites, No water, No toilets, Reservations not accepted, Open all year, Tent & RV camping: Free, At end of road, Road not maintained for passenger cars, Elev: 10044ft/3061m, Tel: 435-637-2817, Nearest town: Manti, Agency: USFS, GPS: 39.283102, -111.391042

33037 • FSR 52292 Dispersed 1 - USFS
Dispersed sites, No water, No toilets, Reservations not accepted, Open all year, Tent & RV camping: Free, Several spots, Road not maintained for passenger cars, Elev: 10318ft/3145m, Tel: 435-637-2817, Nearest town: Manti, Agency: USFS, GPS: 39.299429, -111.440605

33038 • FSR 52292 Dispersed 2 - USFS
Dispersed sites, No water, No toilets, Reservations not accepted, Open all year, Tent & RV camping: Free, Road not maintained for passenger cars, Elev: 10275ft/3132m, Tel: 435-637-2817, Nearest town: Manti, Agency: USFS, GPS: 39.302111, -111.437505

33039 • FSR 52292 Dispersed 3 - USFS
Dispersed sites, No water, No toilets, Reservations not accepted, Open all year, Tent & RV camping: Free, Road not maintained for passenger cars, Elev: 10136ft/3089m, Tel: 435-637-2817, Nearest town: Manti, Agency: USFS, GPS: 39.299345, -111.428017

33040 • FSR 52292 Dispersed 4 - USFS
Dispersed sites, No water, No toilets, Reservations not accepted, Open all year, Tent & RV camping: Free, Road not maintained for passenger cars, Elev: 10132ft/3088m, Tel: 435-637-2817, Nearest town: Manti, Agency: USFS, GPS: 39.299065, -111.425611

33041 • FSR 52292 Dispersed 5 - USFS
Dispersed sites, No water, No toilets, Reservations not accepted, Open all year, Tent & RV camping: Free, At end of road, Road not maintained for passenger cars, Elev: 9915ft/3022m, Tel: 435-637-2817, Nearest town: Manti, Agency: USFS, GPS: 39.298757, -111.402948

33042 • FSR 523 Dispersed 1 - USFS
Dispersed sites, No water, No toilets, Reservations not accepted, Open all year, Tent & RV camping: Free, Elev: 6230ft/1899m, Tel: 435-789-1181, Nearest town: Manila, Agency: USFS, GPS: 40.919843, -109.679644

33043 • FSR 52320 Dispersed 1 - USFS

Dispersed sites, No water, No toilets, Reservations not accepted, Open all year, Tents only: Free, Road not maintained for passenger cars, Elev: 7813ft/2381m, Tel: 435-637-2817, Nearest town: Ferron, Agency: USFS, GPS: 39.106463, -111.276421

33044 • FSR 52332 Dispersed 1 - USFS

Dispersed sites, No water, No toilets, Reservations not accepted, Open all year, Tent & RV camping: Free, Road not maintained for passenger cars, Elev: 9643ft/2939m, Tel: 435-637-2817, Nearest town: Ferron, Agency: USFS, GPS: 39.138249, -111.373645

33045 • FSR 52333 Dispersed 1 - USFS

Dispersed sites, No water, No toilets, Reservations not accepted, Open all year, Tent & RV camping: Free, Road not maintained for passenger cars, Elev: 9297ft/2834m, Tel: 435-637-2817, Nearest town: Mayfield, Agency: USFS, GPS: 39.030286, -111.467895

33046 • FSR 52363 Dispersed 1 - USFS

Dispersed sites, No water, No toilets, Reservations not accepted, Open all year, Tent & RV camping: Free, Road not maintained for passenger cars, Elev: 9886ft/3013m, Tel: 435-637-2817, Nearest town: Mayfield, Agency: USFS, GPS: 39.077883, -111.474118

33047 • FSR 52467 Dispersed 1 - USFS

Dispersed sites, No water, No toilets, Reservations not accepted, Open all year, Tent & RV camping: Free, Road not maintained for passenger cars, Elev: 9425ft/2873m, Tel: 435-637-2817, Nearest town: Huntington, Agency: USFS, GPS: 39.413685, -111.337274

33048 • FSR 526 (Left Hand Reservoir) Dispersed 1 - USFS

Dispersed sites, No water, No toilets, Reservations not accepted, Open all year, Tent & RV camping: Free, Road not maintained for passenger cars, Elev: 9937ft/3029m, Tel: 435-836-2800, Nearest town: Teasdale, Agency: USFS, GPS: 38.201119, -111.473786

33049 • FSR 526 Dispersed 2 - USFS

Dispersed sites, No water, No toilets, Reservations not accepted, Open all year, Tent & RV camping: Free, Elev: 7280ft/2219m, Tel: 435-789-1181, Nearest town: Manila, Agency: USFS, GPS: 40.872506, -109.691805

33050 • FSR 53019 Dispersed 1 - USFS

Dispersed sites, No water, No toilets, Reservations not accepted, Open May-Dec, Tent & RV camping: Free, Road not maintained for passenger cars, Elev: 9646ft/2940m, Tel: 435-637-2817, Nearest town: Huntington, Agency: USFS, GPS: 39.365555, -111.171556

33051 • FSR 53020 Dispersed 1 - USFS

Dispersed sites, No water, No toilets, Reservations not accepted, Open Jun-Dec, Tent & RV camping: Free, Elev: 9015ft/2748m, Tel: 435-637-2817, Nearest town: Mount Pleasant, Agency: USFS, GPS: 39.481717, -111.246097

33052 • FSR 53024 Dispersed - USFS

Dispersed sites, No water, No toilets, Reservations not accepted, Open Jun-Dec, Tent & RV camping: Free, Elev: 8885ft/2708m, Tel: 435-637-2817, Nearest town: Mount Pleasant, Agency: USFS, GPS: 39.484571, -111.242485

33053 • FSR 53051 Dispersed 1 - USFS

Dispersed sites, No water, No toilets, Reservations not accepted, Open Jun-Dec, Tent & RV camping: Free, Numerous sites in this area, Elev: 8754ft/2668m, Tel: 435-637-2817, Nearest town: Mount Pleasant, Agency: USFS, GPS: 39.565747, -111.242322

33054 • FSR 53054 Dispersed 1 - USFS

Dispersed sites, No water, No toilets, Reservations not accepted, Open Jun-Dec, Tent & RV camping: Free, Several sites in this area, Elev: 8901ft/2713m, Tel: 435-637-2817, Nearest town: Mount Pleasant, Agency: USFS, GPS: 39.579232, -111.248967

33055 • FSR 531 (Buckeye Lake) Dispersed 1 - USFS

Dispersed sites, No water, No toilets, Reservations not accepted, Open all year, Tents only: Free, Road not maintained for passenger cars, Elev: 9703ft/2957m, Tel: 435-783-4338, Nearest town: Oakley, Agency: USFS, GPS: 40.638777, -110.976035

33056 • FSR 53137 Dispersed 1 - USFS

Dispersed sites, No water, No toilets, Reservations not accepted, Open Jun-Dec, Tent & RV camping: Free, Road not maintained for passenger cars, Elev: 9579ft/2920m, Tel: 435-637-2817, Nearest town: Fairview, Agency: USFS, GPS: 39.725578, -111.242081

33057 • FSR 53192 Dispersed 1 - USFS

Dispersed sites, No water, No toilets, Reservations not accepted, Open Jun-Dec, Tent & RV camping: Free, Elev: 9501ft/2896m, Tel: 435-637-2817, Nearest town: Huntington, Agency: USFS, GPS: 39.613679, -111.133884

33058 • FSR 53193 Dispersed 1 - USFS

Dispersed sites, No water, No toilets, Reservations not accepted, Open Jun-Dec, Tent & RV camping: Free, Road not maintained for passenger cars, Elev: 8858ft/2700m, Tel: 435-637-2817, Nearest town: Mount Pleasant, Agency: USFS, GPS: 39.494327, -111.256319

33059 • FSR 53199 Dispersed 1 - USFS

Dispersed sites, No water, No toilets, Reservations not accepted, Open Jun-Dec, Tent & RV camping: Free, Elev: 8860ft/2701m, Tel: 435-637-2817, Nearest town: Mount Pleasant, Agency: USFS, GPS: 39.500679, -111.250433

33060 • FSR 53224 Dispersed 1 - USFS

Dispersed sites, No water, No toilets, Reservations not accepted, Open Jun-Dec, Tent & RV camping: Free, Road not maintained for passenger cars, Elev: 8723ft/2659m, Tel: 435-637-2817, Nearest town: Mount Pleasant, Agency: USFS, GPS: 39.525228, -111.253541

33061 • FSR 53225 Dispersed 1 - USFS

Dispersed sites, No water, No toilets, Reservations not accepted, Open Jun-Dec, Tent & RV camping: Free, Road not maintained for passenger cars, Elev: 8748ft/2666m, Tel: 435-637-2817, Nearest town: Mount Pleasant, Agency: USFS, GPS: 39.524185, -111.252926

33062 • FSR 53228 (Miller Flat) Dispersed 1 - USFS

Dispersed sites, No water, Vault toilets, Reservations not accepted, Open Jun-Dec, Tent & RV camping: Free, Several sites in this area, Road not maintained for passenger cars, Elev: 8806ft/2684m, Tel: 435-637-2817, Nearest town: Mount Pleasant, Agency: USFS, GPS: 39.522823, -111.249742

33063 • FSR 53230 Dispersed 1 - USFS

Dispersed sites, No water, No toilets, Reservations not accepted, Open Jun-Dec, Tent & RV camping: Free, Elev: 8856ft/2699m, Tel: 435-637-2817, Nearest town: Mount Pleasant, Agency: USFS, GPS: 39.519639, -111.251681

33064 • FSR 53231 Dispersed 1 - USFS

Dispersed sites, No water, No toilets, Reservations not accepted, Open Jun-Dec, Tent & RV camping: Free, Elev: 8951ft/2728m, Tel: 435-637-2817, Nearest town: Mount Pleasant, Agency: USFS, GPS: 39.514005, -111.250667

33065 • FSR 53231 Dispersed 2 - USFS

Dispersed sites, No water, No toilets, Reservations not accepted, Open Jun-Dec, Tent & RV camping: Free, Several sites in this area, Elev: 8996ft/2742m, Tel: 435-637-2817, Nearest town: Mount Pleasant, Agency: USFS, GPS: 39.510734, -111.256023

33066 • FSR 53232 Dispersed 1 - USFS

Dispersed sites, No water, No toilets, Reservations not accepted, Open Jun-Dec, Tent & RV camping: Free, Elev: 8864ft/2702m, Tel: 435-637-2817, Nearest town: Mount Pleasant, Agency: USFS, GPS: 39.509184, -111.249676

33067 • FSR 53234 Dispersed 1 - USFS

Dispersed sites, No water, No toilets, Reservations not accepted, Open Jun-Dec, Tent & RV camping: Free, Room for 2-3 rigs, Road not maintained for passenger cars, Elev: 8747ft/2666m, Tel: 435-637-2817, Nearest town: Mount Pleasant, Agency: USFS, GPS: 39.523613, -111.251334

33068 • FSR 53235 Dispersed1 - USFS

Dispersed sites, No water, No toilets, Reservations not accepted, Open Jun-Dec, Tent & RV camping: Free, Several sites in this area, Road not maintained for passenger cars, Elev: 8804ft/2683m, Tel: 435-637-2817, Nearest town: Mount Pleasant, Agency: USFS, GPS: 39.522638, -111.253315

33069 • FSR 53236 Dispersed 1 - USFS

Dispersed sites, No water, No toilets, Reservations not accepted, Open Jun-Dec, Tent & RV camping: Free, Several sites, Road not maintained for passenger cars, Elev: 9963ft/3037m, Tel: 435-637-2817, Nearest town: Fairview, Agency: USFS, GPS: 39.643074, -111.203946

33070 • FSR 53238 Dispersed 1 - USFS

Dispersed sites, No water, No toilets, Reservations not accepted, Open all year, Tent & RV camping: Free, Several sites, Elev: 9007ft/2745m, Tel: 435-637-2817, Nearest town: Mount Pleasant, Agency: USFS, GPS: 39.583657, -111.251863

33071 • FSR 53308 Dispersed 1 - USFS

Dispersed sites, No water, No toilets, Reservations not accepted, Open Jul-Dec, Tent & RV camping: Free, Several sites, Road not maintained for passenger cars, Elev: 10024ft/3055m, Tel: 435-637-2817, Nearest town: Fairview, Agency: USFS, GPS: 39.594291, -111.308496

33072 • FSR 53347 Dispersed 1 - USFS

Dispersed sites, No water, No toilets, Reservations not accepted, Open all year, Tent & RV camping: Free, Road not maintained for passenger cars, Elev: 8485ft/2586m, Tel: 435-587-2041, Nearest town: Blanding, Agency: USFS, GPS: 37.645352, -109.834494

33073 • FSR 53383 Dispersed 1 - USFS

Dispersed sites, No water, No toilets, Reservations not accepted, Open all year, Tent & RV camping: Free, Road not maintained for passenger cars, Elev: 7620ft/2323m, Tel: 435-587-2041, Nearest town: Monticello, Agency: USFS, GPS: 37.942573, -109.433365

33074 • FSR 53383 Dispersed 2 - USFS

Dispersed sites, No water, No toilets, Reservations not accepted, Open all year, Tent & RV camping: Free, Road not maintained for passenger cars, Elev: 7556ft/2303m, Tel: 435-587-2041, Nearest town: Monticello, Agency: USFS, GPS: 37.946191, -109.429263

33075 • FSR 53383 Dispersed 3 - USFS

Dispersed sites, No water, No toilets, Reservations not accepted, Open all year, Tent & RV camping: Free, Road not maintained for passenger cars, Elev: 7449ft/2270m, Tel: 435-587-2041, Nearest town: Monticello, Agency: USFS, GPS: 37.948691, -109.423199

33076 • FSR 53383 Dispersed 4 - USFS

Dispersed sites, No water, No toilets, Reservations not accepted, Open all year, Tent & RV camping: Free, Road not maintained for passenger cars, Elev: 7449ft/2270m, Tel: 435-587-2041, Nearest town: Monticello, Agency: USFS, GPS: 37.949301, -109.422821

33077 • FSR 534 Dispersed 1 - USFS

Dispersed sites, No water, No toilets, Reservations not accepted, Open all year, Tent & RV camping: Free, Elev: 9205ft/2806m, Tel: 435-783-4338, Nearest town: Woodland, Agency: USFS, GPS: 40.497255, -111.035973

33078 • FSR 539 Dispersed - USFS

Dispersed sites, No water, No toilets, Reservations not accepted, Open all year, Tent & RV camping: Free, Elev: 8218ft/2505m, Tel: 435-789-1181, Nearest town: Manila, Agency: USFS, GPS: 40.873294, -109.759284

33079 • FSR 539 Dispersed 1 - USFS

Dispersed sites, No water, No toilets, Reservations not accepted, Open all year, Tent & RV camping: Free, Elev: 7771ft/2369m, Tel: 435-789-1181, Nearest town: Manila, Agency: USFS, GPS: 40.855157, -109.681083

33080 • FSR 539 Dispersed 2 - USFS

Dispersed sites, No water, No toilets, Reservations not accepted, Open all year, Tent & RV camping: Free, Several sites in this area,

Elev: 7826ft/2385m, Tel: 435-789-1181, Nearest town: Manila, Agency: USFS, GPS: 40.854069, -109.684798

33081 • FSR 539 Dispersed 3 - USFS

Dispersed sites, No water, No toilets, Reservations not accepted, Open all year, Tent & RV camping: Free, Elev: 7880ft/2402m, Tel: 435-789-1181, Nearest town: Manila, Agency: USFS, GPS: 40.851878, -109.689181

33082 • FSR 539 Dispersed 4 - USFS

Dispersed sites, No water, No toilets, Reservations not accepted, Open all year, Tent & RV camping: Free, Elev: 7955ft/2425m, Tel: 435-789-1181, Nearest town: Manila, Agency: USFS, GPS: 40.847934, -109.692931

33083 • FSR 539 Dispersed 5 - USFS

Dispersed sites, No water, No toilets, Reservations not accepted, Open all year, Tent & RV camping: Free, Elev: 8011ft/2442m, Tel: 435-789-1181, Nearest town: Manila, Agency: USFS, GPS: 40.850641, -109.701061

33084 • FSR 539 Dispersed 6 - USFS

Dispersed sites, No water, No toilets, Reservations not accepted, Open all year, Tent & RV camping: Free, Elev: 8034ft/2449m, Tel: 435-789-1181, Nearest town: Manila, Agency: USFS, GPS: 40.850648, -109.702456

33085 • FSR 539 Dispersed 7 - USFS

Dispersed sites, No water, No toilets, Reservations not accepted, Open all year, Tent & RV camping: Free, Elev: 8011ft/2442m, Tel: 435-789-1181, Nearest town: Manila, Agency: USFS, GPS: 40.854529, -109.717964

33086 • FSR 54146 Dispersed 1 - USFS

Dispersed sites, No water, No toilets, Reservations not accepted, Open all year, Tent & RV camping: Free, Elev: 7952ft/2424m, Tel: 435-259-7155, Nearest town: Moab, Agency: USFS, GPS: 38.347597, -109.226259

33087 • FSR 54361 Dispersed 1 - USFS

Dispersed sites, No water, No toilets, Reservations not accepted, Open all year, Tents only: Free, Elev: 6965ft/2123m, Tel: 435-259-7155, Nearest town: Moab, Agency: USFS, GPS: 38.566435, -109.304329

33088 • FSR 544 (Miller Lake) Dispersed 1 - USFS

Dispersed sites, No water, No toilets, Reservations not accepted, Open all year, Tent & RV camping: Free, Road not maintained for passenger cars, Elev: 10653ft/3247m, Tel: 435-836-2800, Nearest town: Teasdale, Agency: USFS, GPS: 38.159028, -111.547124

33089 • FSR 54460 Dispersed 1 - USFS

Dispersed sites, No water, No toilets, Reservations not accepted, Open all year, Tents only: Free, Road not maintained for passenger cars, Elev: 8614ft/2626m, Tel: 435-259-7155, Nearest town: Moab, Agency: USFS, GPS: 38.606048, -109.216054

33090 • FSR 54601 Dispersed 1 - USFS

Dispersed sites, No water, No toilets, Reservations not accepted, Open all year, Tent & RV camping: Free, Road not maintained for passenger cars, Elev: 8408ft/2563m, Tel: 435-259-7155, Nearest town: Moab, Agency: USFS, GPS: 38.619119, -109.229256

33091 • FSR 54601 Dispersed 2 - USFS

Dispersed sites, No water, No toilets, Reservations not accepted, Open all year, Tent & RV camping: Free, Road not maintained for passenger cars, Elev: 8365ft/2550m, Tel: 435-259-7155, Nearest town: Moab, Agency: USFS, GPS: 38.620418, -109.231234

33092 • FSR 54627 Dispersed 1 - USFS

Dispersed sites, No water, No toilets, Reservations not accepted, Open all year, Tent & RV camping: Free, Elev: 7908ft/2410m, Tel: 435-259-7155, Nearest town: Moab, Agency: USFS, GPS: 38.545942, -109.291766

33093 • FSR 54652 Dispersed 1 - USFS

Dispersed sites, No water, No toilets, Reservations not accepted, Open all year, Tent & RV camping: Free, Elev: 7574ft/2309m, Tel: 435-259-7155, Nearest town: Moab, Agency: USFS, GPS: 38.511322, -109.351891

33094 • FSR 54666 Dispersed 1 - USFS

Dispersed sites, No water, No toilets, Reservations not accepted, Open all year, Tent & RV camping: Free, Road not maintained for passenger cars, Elev: 8235ft/2510m, Tel: 435-259-7155, Nearest town: Moab, Agency: USFS, GPS: 38.616292, -109.206168

33095 • FSR 54666 Dispersed 2 - USFS

Dispersed sites, No water, No toilets, Reservations not accepted, Open all year, Tent & RV camping: Free, Road not maintained for passenger cars, Elev: 8223ft/2506m, Tel: 435-259-7155, Nearest town: Moab, Agency: USFS, GPS: 38.616967, -109.206204

33096 • FSR 54668 Dispersed 1 - USFS

Dispersed sites, No water, No toilets, Reservations not accepted, Open all year, Tents only: Free, 4x4 required, Elev: 8072ft/2460m, Tel: 435-259-7155, Nearest town: Moab, Agency: USFS, GPS: 38.603242, -109.152725

33097 • FSR 547 Dispersed 1 - USFS

Dispersed sites, No water, No toilets, Reservations not accepted, Open all year, Tent & RV camping: Free, Elev: 8848ft/2697m, Tel: 435-789-1181, Nearest town: Dutch John, Agency: USFS, GPS: 40.760664, -109.546485

33098 • FSR 547 Dispersed 2 - USFS

Dispersed sites, No water, No toilets, Reservations not accepted, Open all year, Tent & RV camping: Free, Numerous sites in this area, Elev: 8801ft/2683m, Tel: 435-789-1181, Nearest town: Dutch John, Agency: USFS, GPS: 40.758777, -109.540378

33099 • FSR 54717 Dispersed 1 - USFS

Dispersed sites, No water, No toilets, Reservations not accepted, Open all year, Tent & RV camping: Free, Elev: 8446ft/2574m, Tel: 435-259-7155, Nearest town: Moab, Agency: USFS, GPS: 38.366119, -109.263499

33100 • FSR 54728 Dispersed 1 - USFS

Dispersed sites, No water, No toilets, Tent & RV camping: Free, Elev: 8909ft/2715m, Nearest town: La Sal, Agency: USFS, GPS: 38.401667, -109.210234

33101 • FSR 54758 Dispersed 1 - USFS

Dispersed sites, No water, No toilets, Reservations not accepted, Open all year, Tent & RV camping: Free, Elev: 7185ft/2190m, Tel: 435-259-7155, Nearest town: Moab, Agency: USFS, GPS: 38.350391, -109.303027

33102 • FSR 54829 Dispersed 1 - USFS

Dispersed sites, No water, No toilets, Reservations not accepted, Open all year, Tent & RV camping: Free, Elev: 7731ft/2356m, Tel: 435-259-7155, Nearest town: Moab, Agency: USFS, GPS: 38.484748, -109.334142

33103 • FSR 55128 Dispersed 1 - USFS

Dispersed sites, No water, No toilets, Reservations not accepted, Open all year, Tent & RV camping: Free, Road not maintained for passenger cars, Elev: 8641ft/2634m, Tel: 435-587-2041, Nearest town: Monticello, Agency: USFS, GPS: 37.881836, -109.442823

33104 • FSR 55145 Dispersed 1 - USFS

Dispersed sites, No water, No toilets, Reservations not accepted, Open all year, Tent & RV camping: Free, Road not maintained for passenger cars, Elev: 8608ft/2624m, Tel: 435-587-2041, Nearest town: Monticello, Agency: USFS, GPS: 37.863242, -109.789527

33105 • FSR 55224 Dispersed 1 - USFS

Dispersed sites, No water, No toilets, Reservations not accepted, Open all year, Tent & RV camping: Free, Road not maintained for passenger cars, Elev: 7812ft/2381m, Tel: 435-587-2041, Nearest town: Blanding, Agency: USFS, GPS: 37.769135, -109.550386

33106 • FSR 55224 Dispersed 2 - USFS

Dispersed sites, No water, No toilets, Reservations not accepted, Open all year, Tent & RV camping: Free, At end of road, Road not maintained for passenger cars, Elev: 7648ft/2331m, Tel: 435-587-2041, Nearest town: Blanding, Agency: USFS, GPS: 37.760296, -109.551021

33107 • FSR 55240 Dispersed 1 - USFS

Dispersed sites, No water, No toilets, Reservations not accepted, Open all year, Tent & RV camping: Free, Road not maintained for passenger cars, Elev: 7776ft/2370m, Tel: 435-587-2041, Nearest town: Blanding, Agency: USFS, GPS: 37.787719, -109.519043

33108 • FSR 55247 Dispersed 1 - USFS

Dispersed sites, No water, No toilets, Reservations not accepted, Open all year, Tent & RV camping: Free, Road not maintained for passenger cars, Elev: 8637ft/2633m, Tel: 435-587-2041, Nearest town: Monticello, Agency: USFS, GPS: 37.813335, -109.430992

33109 • FSR 55249 Dispersed 1 - USFS

Dispersed sites, No water, No toilets, Reservations not accepted, Open all year, Tent & RV camping: Free, Road not maintained for passenger cars, Elev: 8650ft/2637m, Tel: 435-587-2041, Nearest town: Monticello, Agency: USFS, GPS: 37.822785, -109.432983

33110 • FSR 55250 Dispersed 1 - USFS

Dispersed sites, No water, No toilets, Reservations not accepted, Open all year, Tent & RV camping: Free, Road not maintained for passenger cars, Elev: 7929ft/2417m, Tel: 435-587-2041, Nearest town: Monticello, Agency: USFS, GPS: 37.810264, -109.399966

33111 • FSR 55258 Dispersed 1 - USFS

Dispersed sites, No water, No toilets, Reservations not accepted, Open all year, Tent & RV camping: Free, Road not maintained for passenger cars, Elev: 8213ft/2503m, Tel: 435-587-2041, Nearest town: Monticello, Agency: USFS, GPS: 37.815494, -109.416186

33112 • FSR 55317 Dispersed 1 - USFS

Dispersed sites, No water, No toilets, Reservations not accepted, Open all year, Tent & RV camping: Free, Road not maintained for passenger cars, Elev: 8472ft/2582m, Tel: 435-587-2041, Nearest town: Blanding, Agency: USFS, GPS: 37.723708, -109.810611

33113 • FSR 55317 Dispersed 2 - USFS

Dispersed sites, No water, No toilets, Reservations not accepted, Open all year, Tent & RV camping: Free, Road not maintained for passenger cars, Elev: 8462ft/2579m, Tel: 435-587-2041, Nearest town: Blanding, Agency: USFS, GPS: 37.724933, -109.814743

33114 • FSR 55318 Dispersed1 - USFS

Dispersed sites, No water, No toilets, Reservations not accepted, Open all year, Tent & RV camping: Free, Road not maintained for passenger cars, Elev: 8414ft/2565m, Tel: 435-587-2041, Nearest town: Blanding, Agency: USFS, GPS: 37.720306, -109.800878

33115 • FSR 55351 Dispersed 1 - USFS

Dispersed sites, No water, No toilets, Reservations not accepted, Open all year, Tent & RV camping: Free, Road not maintained for passenger cars, Elev: 8272ft/2521m, Tel: 435-587-2041, Nearest town: Blanding, Agency: USFS, GPS: 37.723359, -109.874564

33116 • FSR 55374 Dispersed 1 - USFS

Dispersed sites, No water, No toilets, Reservations not accepted, Open all year, Tents only: Free, Road not maintained for passenger cars, Elev: 8208ft/2502m, Tel: 435-587-2041, Nearest town: Blanding, Agency: USFS, GPS: 37.591572, -109.827315

33117 • FSR 55374 Dispersed 2 - USFS

Dispersed sites, No water, No toilets, Reservations not accepted, Open all year, Tents only: Free, Road not maintained for passenger cars, Elev: 8039ft/2450m, Tel: 435-587-2041, Nearest town: Blanding, Agency: USFS, GPS: 37.581918, -109.829624

33118 • FSR 55385 Dispersed 1 - USFS

Dispersed sites, No water, No toilets, Reservations not accepted, Open all year, Tent & RV camping: Free, Road not maintained for passenger cars, Elev: 7824ft/2385m, Tel: 435-587-2041, Nearest town: Blanding, Agency: USFS, GPS: 37.783968, -109.544878

33119 • FSR 554 (Long Lake) Dispersed 1 - USFS

Dispersed sites, No water, No toilets, Reservations not accepted, Open all year, Tents only: Free, Road not maintained for passenger cars, Elev: 10033ft/3058m, Tel: 435-836-2800, Nearest town: Grover, Agency: USFS, GPS: 38.058185, -111.345386

33120 • FSR 554 (Scout Lake) Dispersed 2 - USFS

Dispersed sites, No water, No toilets, Reservations not accepted, Open all year, Tents only: Free, Road not maintained for passenger cars, Elev: 10094ft/3077m, Tel: 435-836-2800, Nearest town: Grover, Agency: USFS, GPS: 38.063147, -111.355326

33121 • FSR 55425 Dispersed 1 - USFS

Dispersed sites, No water, No toilets, Reservations not accepted, Open all year, Tent & RV camping: Free, Road not maintained for passenger cars, Elev: 8448ft/2575m, Tel: 435-587-2041, Nearest town: Blanding, Agency: USFS, GPS: 37.723749, -109.802395

33122 • FSR 55439 Dispersed 1 - USFS

Dispersed sites, No water, No toilets, Reservations not accepted, Open all year, Tents only: Free, 4x4 required, Elev: 8338ft/2541m, Tel: 435-587-2041, Nearest town: Blanding, Agency: USFS, GPS: 37.614966, -109.825746

33123 • FSR 55468 Dispersed 1 - USFS

Dispersed sites, No water, No toilets, Reservations not accepted, Open all year, Tent & RV camping: Free, Road not maintained for passenger cars, Elev: 8423ft/2567m, Tel: 435-587-2041, Nearest town: Blanding, Agency: USFS, GPS: 37.658108, -109.882115

33124 • FSR 55477 Dispersed 1 - USFS

Dispersed sites, No water, No toilets, Reservations not accepted, Open all year, Tent & RV camping: Free, Road not maintained for passenger cars, Elev: 8387ft/2556m, Tel: 435-587-2041, Nearest town: Blanding, Agency: USFS, GPS: 37.650381, -109.870168

33125 • FSR 55525 Dispersed 1 - USFS

Dispersed sites, No water, No toilets, Reservations not accepted, Open all year, Tent & RV camping: Free, Road not maintained for passenger cars, Elev: 7775ft/2370m, Tel: 435-587-2041, Nearest town: Blanding, Agency: USFS, GPS: 37.773045, -109.544311

33126 • FSR 55525 Dispersed 2 - USFS

Dispersed sites, No water, No toilets, Reservations not accepted, Open all year, Tent & RV camping: Free, Road not maintained for passenger cars, Elev: 7747ft/2361m, Tel: 435-587-2041, Nearest town: Blanding, Agency: USFS, GPS: 37.770119, -109.541888

33127 • FSR 556 Dispersed 1 - USFS

Dispersed sites, No water, No toilets, Reservations not accepted, Open all year, Tent & RV camping: Free, Road not maintained for passenger cars, Elev: 6056ft/1846m, Tel: 435-789-1181, Nearest town: Manila, Agency: USFS, GPS: 40.994332, -109.651222

33128 • FSR 55615 Dispersed 1 - USFS

Dispersed sites, No water, No toilets, Reservations not accepted, Open all year, Tents only: Free, Road not maintained for passenger cars, Elev: 8589ft/2618m, Tel: 435-587-2041, Nearest town: Blanding, Agency: USFS, GPS: 37.761852, -109.775983

33129 • FSR 55621 Dispersed 1 - USFS

Dispersed sites, No water, No toilets, Reservations not accepted, Open all year, Tent & RV camping: Free, Road not maintained for passenger cars, Elev: 7768ft/2368m, Tel: 435-587-2041, Nearest town: Blanding, Agency: USFS, GPS: 37.771938, -109.544245

33130 • FSR 55630 Dispersed 1 - USFS

Dispersed sites, No water, No toilets, Reservations not accepted, Open all year, Tent & RV camping: Free, Road not maintained for passenger cars, Elev: 7858ft/2395m, Tel: 435-587-2041, Nearest town: Blanding, Agency: USFS, GPS: 37.771378, -109.547339

33131 • FSR 557 Dispersed 1 - USFS

Dispersed sites, No water, No toilets, Reservations not accepted, Open all year, Tent & RV camping: Free, Road not maintained for passenger cars, Elev: 6653ft/2028m, Tel: 801-798-3571, Nearest town: Vernon, Agency: USFS, GPS: 39.976649, -112.359122

33132 • FSR 557 Dispersed 1 - USFS

Dispersed sites, No water, No toilets, Reservations not accepted, Open all year, Tent & RV camping: Free, Road not maintained for passenger cars, Elev: 8717ft/2657m, Tel: 435-783-4338, Nearest town: Woodland, Agency: USFS, GPS: 40.554421, -111.023726

33133 • FSR 558 Dispersed 1 - USFS

Dispersed sites, No water, No toilets, Reservations not accepted, Open all year, Tent & RV camping: Free, Road not maintained for passenger cars, Elev: 6245ft/1903m, Tel: 801-798-3571, Nearest town: Vernon, Agency: USFS, GPS: 39.999408, -112.370242

33134 • FSR 558 Dispersed 2 - USFS

Dispersed sites, No water, No toilets, Reservations not accepted, Open all year, Tent & RV camping: Free, Road not maintained for passenger cars, Elev: 6276ft/1913m, Tel: 801-798-3571, Nearest town: Vernon, Agency: USFS, GPS: 39.995421, -112.366395

33135 • FSR 558 Dispersed 3 - USFS

Dispersed sites, No water, No toilets, Reservations not accepted, Open all year, Tent & RV camping: Free, Road not maintained for passenger cars, Elev: 6630ft/2021m, Tel: 801-798-3571, Nearest town: Vernon, Agency: USFS, GPS: 39.977431, -112.358305

33136 • FSR 560 Dispersed 1 - USFS

Dispersed sites, No water, No toilets, Reservations not accepted, Open all year, Tent & RV camping: Free, Road not maintained for passenger cars, Elev: 8635ft/2632m, Tel: 435-783-4338, Nearest town: Woodland, Agency: USFS, GPS: 40.489135, -110.965018

33137 • FSR 563 Dispersed 1 - USFS

Dispersed sites, No water, No toilets, Reservations not accepted, Open all year, Tent & RV camping: Free, Road not maintained for passenger cars, Elev: 5597ft/1706m, Tel: 435-789-1181, Nearest town: Enterprise, Agency: USFS, GPS: 37.538862, -113.746133

33138 • FSR 563 Dispersed 2 - USFS

Dispersed sites, No water, No toilets, Reservations not accepted, Open all year, Tent & RV camping: Free, Road not maintained for passenger cars, Elev: 5735ft/1748m, Tel: 435-789-1181, Nearest town: Enterprise, Agency: USFS, GPS: 37.545432, -113.747154

33139 • FSR 563 Dispersed 3 - USFS

Dispersed sites, No water, No toilets, Reservations not accepted, Open all year, Tent & RV camping: Free, Road not maintained for passenger cars, Elev: 9401ft/2865m, Tel: 435-783-4338, Nearest town: Woodland, Agency: USFS, GPS: 40.523572, -110.992857

33140 • FSR 565 (Frog Pond Corrals) Dispersed 1 - USFS
Dispersed sites, No water, No toilets, Reservations not accepted, Open all year, Tent & RV camping: Free, Road not maintained for passenger cars, Elev: 9352ft/2850m, Tel: 435-783-4338, Nearest town: Woodland, Agency: USFS, GPS: 40.529269, -110.994471

33141 • FSR 565 Dispersed 2 - USFS
Dispersed sites, No water, No toilets, Reservations not accepted, Open all year, Tent & RV camping: Free, Road not maintained for passenger cars, Elev: 6963ft/2122m, Tel: 435-789-1181, Nearest town: Pine Valley, Agency: USFS, GPS: 37.418501, -113.488819

33142 • FSR 566 Dispersed 1 - USFS
Dispersed sites, No water, No toilets, Reservations not accepted, Open all year, Tent & RV camping: Free, Elev: 8293ft/2528m, Tel: 435-826-5400, Nearest town: Boulder, Agency: USFS, GPS: 37.966554, -111.552907

33143 • FSR 568 Dispersed 1 - USFS
Dispersed sites, No water, No toilets, Reservations not accepted, Open all year, Tents only: Free, Road not maintained for passenger cars, Elev: 8497ft/2590m, Tel: 435-836-2800, Nearest town: Grover, Agency: USFS, GPS: 38.145136, -111.323521

33144 • FSR 569 Dispersed 1 - USFS
Dispersed sites, No water, No toilets, Reservations not accepted, Open all year, Tent & RV camping: Free, Road not maintained for passenger cars, Elev: 7370ft/2246m, Tel: 435-836-2800, Nearest town: Grover, Agency: USFS, GPS: 38.205548, -111.349142

33145 • FSR 569 Dispersed 2 - USFS
Dispersed sites, No water, No toilets, Reservations not accepted, Open all year, Tent & RV camping: Free, Elev: 8940ft/2725m, Tel: 435-783-4338, Nearest town: Heber City, Agency: USFS, GPS: 40.490441, -111.110054

33146 • FSR 582 Dispersed - USFS
Dispersed sites, No water, No toilets, Reservations not accepted, Open all year, Tent & RV camping: Free, Road not maintained for passenger cars, Elev: 10274ft/3132m, Tel: 435-438-2430, Nearest town: Junction, Agency: USFS, GPS: 38.266522, -112.366414

33147 • FSR 582C Dispersed 1 - USFS
Dispersed sites, No water, No toilets, Reservations not accepted, Open all year, Tent & RV camping: Free, Road not maintained for passenger cars, Elev: 10059ft/3066m, Tel: 435-438-2430, Nearest town: Junction, Agency: USFS, GPS: 38.260062, -112.364012

33148 • FSR 583 Dispersed 1 - USFS
Dispersed sites, No water, No toilets, Reservations not accepted, Open all year, Tent & RV camping: Free, Several sites in this area, Road not maintained for passenger cars, Elev: 6954ft/2120m, Tel: 435-438-2430, Nearest town: Joseph, Agency: USFS, GPS: 38.559782, -112.458229

33149 • FSR 585 Dispersed 1 - USFS
Dispersed sites, No water, No toilets, Reservations not accepted, Open all year, Tent & RV camping: Free, Road not maintained for passenger cars, Elev: 6896ft/2102m, Tel: 435-438-2430, Nearest town: Joseph, Agency: USFS, GPS: 38.544217, -112.409368

33150 • FSR 586 Dispersed 1 - USFS
Dispersed sites, No water, No toilets, Reservations not accepted, Open Apr-Nov, Tent & RV camping: Free, Road not maintained for passenger cars, Elev: 7826ft/2385m, Tel: 801-785-3563, Nearest town: Cedar Hills, Agency: USFS, GPS: 40.515255, -111.655885

33151 • FSR 586 Dispersed 2 - USFS
Dispersed sites, No water, No toilets, Reservations not accepted, Open Apr-Nov, Tent & RV camping: Free, Road not maintained for passenger cars, Elev: 7900ft/2408m, Tel: 801-785-3563, Nearest town: Cedar Hills, Agency: USFS, GPS: 40.517652, -111.656212

33152 • FSR 587 Dispersed 1 - USFS
Dispersed sites, No water, No toilets, Reservations not accepted, Open all year, Tents only: Free, Road not maintained for passenger cars, Elev: 8433ft/2570m, Tel: 307-782-6555, Nearest town: Mountain View (WY), Agency: USFS, GPS: 40.946446, -110.065324

33153 • FSR 588 Dispersed 1 - USFS
Dispersed sites, No water, No toilets, Reservations not accepted, Open all year, Tent & RV camping: Free, Elev: 7713ft/2351m, Tel: 435-789-1181, Nearest town: Manila, Agency: USFS, GPS: 40.857938, -109.681381

33154 • FSR 590 Dispersed 1 - USFS
Dispersed sites, No water, No toilets, Reservations not accepted, Open all year, Tent & RV camping: Free, Road not maintained for passenger cars, Elev: 7940ft/2420m, Tel: 435-789-1181, Nearest town: Manila, Agency: USFS, GPS: 40.849247, -109.633839

33155 • FSR 591 Dispersed 1 - USFS
Dispersed sites, No water, No toilets, Reservations not accepted, Open all year, Tent & RV camping: Free, Road not maintained for passenger cars, Elev: 6749ft/2057m, Tel: 435-438-2430, Nearest town: Beaver, Agency: USFS, GPS: 38.348424, -112.545427

33156 • FSR 591 Dispersed 2 - USFS
Dispersed sites, No water, No toilets, Reservations not accepted, Open all year, Tent & RV camping: Free, Must ford stream, Road not maintained for passenger cars, Elev: 7361ft/2244m, Tel: 435-438-2430, Nearest town: Beaver, Agency: USFS, GPS: 38.384169, -112.518414

33157 • FSR 593 Dispersed 1 - USFS
Dispersed sites, No water, No toilets, Reservations not accepted, Open all year, Tent & RV camping: Free, Road not maintained for passenger cars, Elev: 6379ft/1944m, Tel: 801-798-3571, Nearest town: Vernon, Agency: USFS, GPS: 39.998867, -112.604788

33158 • FSR 593 Dispersed 1 - USFS
Dispersed sites, No water, No toilets, Reservations not accepted, Open all year, Tent & RV camping: Free, Road not maintained for passenger cars, Elev: 7922ft/2415m, Tel: 435-789-1181, Nearest town: Manila, Agency: USFS, GPS: 40.840791, -109.663021

33159 • FSR 604 Dispersed 1 - USFS

Dispersed sites, No water, No toilets, Reservations not accepted, Open all year, Tent & RV camping: Free, Elev: 7556ft/2303m, Tel: 435-789-1181, Nearest town: Manila, Agency: USFS, GPS: 40.867887, -109.511188

33160 • FSR 606 Dispersed 1 - USFS

Dispersed sites, No water, No toilets, Reservations not accepted, Open all year, Tent & RV camping: Free, Right beside RR, Road not maintained for passenger cars, Elev: 5938ft/1810m, Tel: 801-798-3571, Nearest town: Vernon, Agency: USFS, GPS: 39.996107, -112.279677

33161 • FSR 607 Dispersed 1 - USFS

Dispersed sites, No water, No toilets, Reservations not accepted, Open all year, Tent & RV camping: Free, Road not maintained for passenger cars, Elev: 6001ft/1829m, Tel: 801-798-3571, Nearest town: Vernon, Agency: USFS, GPS: 39.986544, -112.275791

33162 • FSR 608 (Pink Cliff) Dispersed 1 - USFS

Dispersed sites, No water, No toilets, Reservations not accepted, Open all year, Tents only: Free, On edge of 1200' bluff, Road not maintained for passenger cars, Elev: 9402ft/2866m, Tel: 435-676-9316, Nearest town: Alton, Agency: USFS, GPS: 37.418303, -112.322881

33163 • FSR 608 Dispersed 1 - USFS

Dispersed sites, No water, No toilets, Reservations not accepted, Open all year, Tent & RV camping: Free, Road not maintained for passenger cars, Elev: 6162ft/1878m, Tel: 801-798-3571, Nearest town: Vernon, Agency: USFS, GPS: 39.989694, -112.311979

33164 • FSR 608 Dispersed 2 - USFS

Dispersed sites, No water, No toilets, Reservations not accepted, Open all year, Tent & RV camping: Free, Road not maintained for passenger cars, Elev: 6200ft/1890m, Tel: 801-798-3571, Nearest town: Vernon, Agency: USFS, GPS: 39.989097, -112.313642

33165 • FSR 609 Dispersed 1 - USFS

Dispersed sites, No water, No toilets, Reservations not accepted, Open all year, Tent & RV camping: Free, Road not maintained for passenger cars, Elev: 9646ft/2940m, Tel: 307-782-6555, Nearest town: Mountain View (WY), Agency: USFS, GPS: 40.967593, -110.358594

33166 • FSR 610 Dispersed 1 - USFS

Dispersed sites, No water, No toilets, Reservations not accepted, Open all year, Tent & RV camping: Free, Road not maintained for passenger cars, Elev: 8658ft/2639m, Tel: 435-783-4338, Nearest town: Woodland, Agency: USFS, GPS: 40.563752, -111.035472

33167 • FSR 611 Dispersed - USFS

Dispersed sites, No water, No toilets, Reservations not accepted, Open all year, Tent & RV camping: Free, Road not maintained for passenger cars, Elev: 9680ft/2950m, Tel: 307-782-6555, Nearest town: Mountain View (WY), Agency: USFS, GPS: 40.954734, -110.369723

33168 • FSR 612 Dispersed 1 - USFS

Dispersed sites, No water, No toilets, Reservations not accepted, Open all year, Tent & RV camping: Free, Elev: 8269ft/2520m, Tel: 435-789-1181, Nearest town: Duck Creek, Agency: USFS, GPS: 37.576657, -112.635847

33169 • FSR 612 Dispersed 2 - USFS

Dispersed sites, No water, No toilets, Reservations not accepted, Open all year, Tent & RV camping: Free, Elev: 8350ft/2545m, Tel: 435-789-1181, Nearest town: Duck Creek, Agency: USFS, GPS: 37.573097, -112.639377

33170 • FSR 612 Dispersed 3 - USFS

Dispersed sites, No water, No toilets, Reservations not accepted, Open all year, Tent & RV camping: Free, Elev: 8386ft/2556m, Tel: 435-789-1181, Nearest town: Duck Creek, Agency: USFS, GPS: 37.571217, -112.640513

33171 • FSR 612 Dispersed 4 - USFS

Dispersed sites, No water, No toilets, Reservations not accepted, Open all year, Tent & RV camping: Free, Numerous sites in this area, Elev: 8465ft/2580m, Tel: 435-789-1181, Nearest town: Duck Creek, Agency: USFS, GPS: 37.561046, -112.647137

33172 • FSR 613 Dispersed 1 - USFS

Dispersed sites, No water, No toilets, Reservations not accepted, Open all year, Tent & RV camping: Free, Road not maintained for passenger cars, Elev: 7828ft/2386m, Tel: 435-789-1181, Nearest town: Manila, Agency: USFS, GPS: 40.891977, -109.646419

33173 • FSR 614 Dispersed 1 - USFS

Dispersed sites, No water, No toilets, Reservations not accepted, Open all year, Tent & RV camping: Free, Road not maintained for passenger cars, Elev: 6011ft/1832m, Tel: 801-798-3571, Nearest town: Vernon, Agency: USFS, GPS: 40.049507, -112.381278

33174 • FSR 616 Dispersed 1 - USFS

Dispersed sites, No water, No toilets, Reservations not accepted, Open all year, Tent & RV camping: Free, Road not maintained for passenger cars, Elev: 8168ft/2490m, Tel: 435-789-1181, Nearest town: Manila, Agency: USFS, GPS: 40.859624, -109.761029

33175 • FSR 618 Dispersed 1 - USFS

Dispersed sites, No water, No toilets, Reservations not accepted, Open all year, Tent & RV camping: Free, Road not maintained for passenger cars, Elev: 7266ft/2215m, Tel: 435-783-4338, Nearest town: Orem, Agency: USFS, GPS: 40.302334, -111.426348

33176 • FSR 619 Dispersed 1 - USFS

Dispersed sites, No water, No toilets, Reservations not accepted, Open all year, Tent & RV camping: Free, Road not maintained for passenger cars, Elev: 8005ft/2440m, Tel: 435-783-4338, Nearest town: Springville, Agency: USFS, GPS: 40.280169, -111.359031

33177 • FSR 619 Dispersed 2 - USFS

Dispersed sites, No water, No toilets, Reservations not accepted, Open all year, Tent & RV camping: Free, Road not maintained for passenger cars, Elev: 8018ft/2444m, Tel: 435-783-4338, Nearest town: Springville, Agency: USFS, GPS: 40.275043, -111.366976

33178 • FSR 619 Dispersed 3 - USFS

Dispersed sites, No water, No toilets, Reservations not accepted, Open all year, Tent & RV camping: Free, Road not maintained for passenger cars, Elev: 6053ft/1845m, Tel: 435-789-1181, Nearest town: Manila, Agency: USFS, GPS: 40.988811, -109.560204

33179 • FSR 619 Dispersed 4 - USFS

Dispersed sites, No water, No toilets, Reservations not accepted, Open all year, Tent & RV camping: Free, Road not maintained for passenger cars, Elev: 5985ft/1824m, Tel: 801-798-3571, Nearest town: Vernon, Agency: USFS, GPS: 40.002168, -112.301597

33180 • FSR 620 Dispersed 1 - USFS

Dispersed sites, No water, No toilets, Reservations not accepted, Open all year, Tent & RV camping: Free, Road not maintained for passenger cars, Elev: 6680ft/2036m, Tel: 801-798-3571, Nearest town: Vernon, Agency: USFS, GPS: 39.999749, -112.505458

33181 • FSR 623 Dispersed 1 - USFS

Dispersed sites, No water, No toilets, Reservations not accepted, Open all year, Tent & RV camping: Free, Road not maintained for passenger cars, Elev: 5979ft/1822m, Tel: 801-798-3571, Nearest town: Vernon, Agency: USFS, GPS: 39.936597, -112.578301

33182 • FSR 626 (Gravel Pit) Dispersed 1 - USFS

Dispersed sites, No water, No toilets, Reservations not accepted, Open all year, Tent & RV camping: Free, Road not maintained for passenger cars, Elev: 5885ft/1794m, Tel: 801-798-3571, Nearest town: Vernon, Agency: USFS, GPS: 40.069253, -112.371978

33183 • FSR 627 Dispersed 1 - USFS

Dispersed sites, No water, No toilets, Reservations not accepted, Open all year, Tent & RV camping: Free, Several sites, Road not maintained for passenger cars, Elev: 8399ft/2560m, Tel: 435-789-1181, Nearest town: Manila, Agency: USFS, GPS: 40.854966, -109.815691

33184 • FSR 627 Dispersed 2 - USFS

Dispersed sites, No water, No toilets, Reservations not accepted, Open all year, Tent & RV camping: Free, Road not maintained for passenger cars, Elev: 9472ft/2887m, Tel: 435-783-4338, Nearest town: Heber City, Agency: USFS, GPS: 40.379899, -111.154031

33185 • FSR 628 Dispersed - USFS

Dispersed sites, No water, No toilets, Reservations not accepted, Open all year, Tent & RV camping: Free, Road not maintained for passenger cars, Elev: 8062ft/2457m, Tel: 435-789-1181, Nearest town: Duck Creek, Agency: USFS, GPS: 37.577593, -112.611564

33186 • FSR 630 Dispersed 1 - USFS

Dispersed sites, No water, No toilets, Reservations not accepted, Open all year, Tent & RV camping: Free, Road not maintained for passenger cars, Elev: 8239ft/2511m, Tel: 435-789-1181, Nearest town: Duck Creek, Agency: USFS, GPS: 37.573711, -112.629934

33187 • FSR 630 Dispersed 2 - USFS

Dispersed sites, No water, No toilets, Reservations not accepted, Open all year, Tent & RV camping: Free, Road not maintained for passenger cars, Elev: 8222ft/2506m, Tel: 435-789-1181, Nearest town: Duck Creek, Agency: USFS, GPS: 37.578195, -112.628377

33188 • FSR 631 Dispersed 1 - USFS

Dispersed sites, No water, No toilets, Reservations not accepted, Open all year, Tent & RV camping: Free, Road not maintained for passenger cars, Elev: 8669ft/2642m, Tel: 435-789-1181, Nearest town: Manila, Agency: USFS, GPS: 40.884524, -109.884085

33189 • FSR 631 Dispersed 2 - USFS

Dispersed sites, No water, No toilets, Reservations not accepted, Open all year, Tent & RV camping: Free, Road not maintained for passenger cars, Elev: 8682ft/2646m, Tel: 435-789-1181, Nearest town: Manila, Agency: USFS, GPS: 40.885778, -109.869595

33190 • FSR 636 Dispersed 1 - USFS

Dispersed sites, No water, No toilets, Reservations not accepted, Open all year, Tent & RV camping: Free, Elev: 8324ft/2537m, Tel: 435-789-1181, Nearest town: Manila, Agency: USFS, GPS: 40.879808, -109.760263

33191 • FSR 638 (Whitney Reservoir) Dispersed1 - USFS

Dispersed sites, No water, No toilets, Reservations not accepted, Open May-Dec, Tent & RV camping: Free, Road not maintained for passenger cars, Elev: 9317ft/2840m, Tel: 307-789-3194, Nearest town: Oakley, Agency: USFS, GPS: 40.831487, -110.933544

33192 • FSR 638 Dispersed 2 - USFS

Dispersed sites, No water, No toilets, Reservations not accepted, Open Apr-Oct, Tent & RV camping: Free, Road not maintained for passenger cars, Elev: 7741ft/2359m, Tel: 435-783-4338, Nearest town: Springville, Agency: USFS, GPS: 40.201749, -111.199549

33193 • FSR 639 (Whitney Reservoir) Dispersed 1 - USFS

Dispersed sites, No water, No toilets, Reservations not accepted, Open May-Dec, Tent & RV camping: Free, Road not maintained for passenger cars, Elev: 9364ft/2854m, Tel: 307-789-3194, Nearest town: Oakley, Agency: USFS, GPS: 40.834358, -110.935462

33194 • FSR 639 Dispersed 2 - USFS

Dispersed sites, No water, No toilets, Reservations not accepted, Open all year, Tent & RV camping: Free, Road not maintained for passenger cars, Elev: 9411ft/2868m, Tel: 435-789-1181, Nearest town: Manila, Agency: USFS, GPS: 40.911994, -109.982249

33195 • FSR 640 (Upper Mud Creek Camp) Dispersed 1 - USFS

Dispersed sites, No water, No toilets, Reservations not accepted, Open Apr-Oct, Tent & RV camping: Free, Road not maintained for passenger cars, Elev: 8905ft/2714m, Tel: 435-783-4338, Nearest town: Springville, Agency: USFS, GPS: 40.198889, -111.247859

33196 • FSR 640 Dispersed 2 - USFS

Dispersed sites, No water, No toilets, Reservations not accepted, Open all year, Tent & RV camping: Free, Elev: 8311ft/2533m, Tel: 435-789-1181, Nearest town: Manila, Agency: USFS, GPS: 40.877214, -109.762813

33197 • FSR 640 Dispersed 3 - USFS

Dispersed sites, No water, No toilets, Reservations not accepted, Open all year, Tent & RV camping: Free, Elev: 8416ft/2565m, Tel: 435-896-9233, Nearest town: Salina, Agency: USFS, GPS: 38.802592, -111.665886

33198 • FSR 640G/640H Dispersed 1 - USFS

Dispersed sites, No water, No toilets, Reservations not accepted, Open all year, Tent & RV camping: Free, Numerous sites along this stretch of road, Elev: 9230ft/2813m, Tel: 435-836-2800, Nearest town: Koosharem, Agency: USFS, GPS: 38.646099, -111.659021

33199 • FSR 641 (Whitney Reservoir) Dispersed 1 - USFS

Dispersed sites, No water, No toilets, Reservations not accepted, Open May-Dec, Tent & RV camping: Free, Road not maintained for passenger cars, Elev: 9281ft/2829m, Tel: 307-789-3194, Nearest town: Oakley, Agency: USFS, GPS: 40.839398, -110.932125

33200 • FSR 643 Dispersed 1 - USFS

Dispersed sites, No water, No toilets, Reservations not accepted, Open all year, Tent & RV camping: Free, Road not maintained for passenger cars, Elev: 8778ft/2676m, Tel: 435-789-1181, Nearest town: Manila, Agency: USFS, GPS: 40.888272, -109.900105

33201 • FSR 643 Dispersed 2 - USFS

Dispersed sites, No water, No toilets, Reservations not accepted, Open all year, Tents only: Free, Road not maintained for passenger cars, Elev: 8791ft/2679m, Tel: 435-789-1181, Nearest town: Manila, Agency: USFS, GPS: 40.887122, -109.907987

33202 • FSR 646 (Whitney Reservoir) Dispersed 1 - USFS

Dispersed sites, No water, No toilets, Reservations not accepted, Open May-Dec, Tent & RV camping: Free, Road not maintained for passenger cars, Elev: 9312ft/2838m, Tel: 307-789-3194, Nearest town: Oakley, Agency: USFS, GPS: 40.840408, -110.933054

33203 • FSR 646 Dispersed 2 - USFS

Dispersed sites, No water, No toilets, Tent & RV camping: Free, Elev: 7919ft/2414m, Tel: 435-676-9300, Nearest town: Panguitch, Agency: USFS, GPS: 37.736778, -112.244152

33204 • FSR 647 (Whitney Reservoir) Dispersed 1 - USFS

Dispersed sites, No water, No toilets, Reservations not accepted, Open May-Dec, Tent & RV camping: Free, Road not maintained for passenger cars, Elev: 9339ft/2847m, Tel: 307-789-3194, Nearest town: Oakley, Agency: USFS, GPS: 40.843409, -110.934168

33205 • FSR 647 Dispersed 2 - USFS

Dispersed sites, No water, No toilets, Reservations not accepted, Open all year, Tent & RV camping: Free, Elev: 7890ft/2405m, Tel: 435-676-9311, Nearest town: Panguitch, Agency: USFS, GPS: 37.713168, -112.266369

33206 • FSR 649 Dispersed 1 - USFS

Dispersed sites, No water, No toilets, Reservations not accepted, Open all year, Tents only: Free, High-clearance vehicle recommended, Elev: 10455ft/3187m, Tel: 435-738-2482, Nearest town: Mountain Home, Agency: USFS, GPS: 40.528474, -110.749451

33207 • FSR 652 Dispersed 1 - USFS

Dispersed sites, No water, No toilets, Reservations not accepted, Open all year, Tent & RV camping: Free, Road not maintained for passenger cars, Elev: 7808ft/2380m, Tel: 435-783-4338, Nearest town: Springville, Agency: USFS, GPS: 40.162401, -111.194205

33208 • FSR 652 Dispersed 2 - USFS

Dispersed sites, No water, No toilets, Reservations not accepted, Open all year, Tent & RV camping: Free, Road not maintained for passenger cars, Elev: 7909ft/2411m, Tel: 435-783-4338, Nearest town: Springville, Agency: USFS, GPS: 40.159522, -111.199449

33209 • FSR 652 Dispersed 3 - USFS

Dispersed sites, No water, No toilets, Reservations not accepted, Open all year, Tent & RV camping: Free, Road not maintained for passenger cars, Elev: 7967ft/2428m, Tel: 435-783-4338, Nearest town: Springville, Agency: USFS, GPS: 40.157154, -111.201961

33210 • FSR 652 Dispersed 4 - USFS

Dispersed sites, No water, No toilets, Reservations not accepted, Open all year, Tent & RV camping: Free, Road not maintained for passenger cars, Elev: 8108ft/2471m, Tel: 435-783-4338, Nearest town: Springville, Agency: USFS, GPS: 40.153781, -111.213489

33211 • FSR 652 Dispersed 5 - USFS

Dispersed sites, No water, No toilets, Reservations not accepted, Open all year, Tent & RV camping: Free, Road not maintained for passenger cars, Elev: 8089ft/2466m, Tel: 435-783-4338, Nearest town: Springville, Agency: USFS, GPS: 40.151921, -111.211889

33212 • FSR 653 Dispersed 1 - USFS

Dispersed sites, No water, No toilets, Reservations not accepted, Open May-Dec, Tent & RV camping: Free, Road not maintained for passenger cars, Elev: 9259ft/2822m, Tel: 307-789-3194, Nearest town: Oakley, Agency: USFS, GPS: 40.854449, -110.886504

33213 • FSR 654 Dispersed 1 - USFS

Dispersed sites, No water, No toilets, Reservations not accepted, Open all year, Tent & RV camping: Free, Must ford stream, Road not maintained for passenger cars, Elev: 7238ft/2206m, Tel: 435-438-2430, Nearest town: Beaver, Agency: USFS, GPS: 38.374509, -112.524221

33214 • FSR 654 Dispersed 2 - USFS

Dispersed sites, No water, No toilets, Reservations not accepted, Open all year, Tent & RV camping: Free, Road not maintained for passenger cars, Elev: 7974ft/2430m, Tel: 435-783-4338, Nearest town: Springville, Agency: USFS, GPS: 40.155117, -111.200672

33215 • FSR 654 Dispersed 3 - USFS

Dispersed sites, No water, No toilets, Reservations not accepted, Open all year, Tent & RV camping: Free, Numerous sites in this area, Road not maintained for passenger cars, Elev: 9040ft/2755m, Tel: 307-789-3194, Nearest town: Oakley, Agency: USFS, GPS: 40.805768, -110.875416

33216 • FSR 655 Dispersed 1 - USFS

Dispersed sites, No water, No toilets, Reservations not accepted, Open all year, Tent & RV camping: Free, Several sites in this area,

Road not maintained for passenger cars, Elev: 9025ft/2751m, Tel: 307-789-3194, Nearest town: Oakley, Agency: USFS, GPS: 40.813904, -110.867226

33217 • FSR 655 Dispersed 2 - USFS
Dispersed sites, No water, No toilets, Reservations not accepted, Open all year, Tent & RV camping: Free, Road not maintained for passenger cars, Elev: 9030ft/2752m, Tel: 307-789-3194, Nearest town: Oakley, Agency: USFS, GPS: 40.811239, -110.869852

33218 • FSR 655A Dispersed 1 - USFS
Dispersed sites, No water, No toilets, Reservations not accepted, Open all year, Tent & RV camping: Free, Road not maintained for passenger cars, Elev: 9067ft/2764m, Tel: 307-789-3194, Nearest town: Oakley, Agency: USFS, GPS: 40.812703, -110.871234

33219 • FSR 658 Dispersed 1 - USFS
Dispersed sites, No water, No toilets, Reservations not accepted, Open May-Dec, Tent & RV camping: Free, Elev: 9108ft/2776m, Tel: 307-789-3194, Nearest town: Oakley, Agency: USFS, GPS: 40.847668, -110.857612

33220 • FSR 660 Dispersed 1 - USFS
Dispersed sites, No water, No toilets, Reservations not accepted, Open all year, Tent & RV camping: Free, Road not maintained for passenger cars, Elev: 5791ft/1765m, Tel: 801-798-3571, Nearest town: Vernon, Agency: USFS, GPS: 40.041767, -112.341512

33221 • FSR 660 Dispersed 2 - USFS
Dispersed sites, No water, No toilets, Reservations not accepted, Open all year, Tent & RV camping: Free, Road not maintained for passenger cars, Elev: 5815ft/1772m, Tel: 801-798-3571, Nearest town: Vernon, Agency: USFS, GPS: 40.037336, -112.340038

33222 • FSR 660 Dispersed 3 - USFS
Dispersed sites, No water, No toilets, Reservations not accepted, Open all year, Tent & RV camping: Free, Road not maintained for passenger cars, Elev: 5835ft/1779m, Tel: 801-798-3571, Nearest town: Vernon, Agency: USFS, GPS: 40.033688, -112.341137

33223 • FSR 660 Dispersed 4 - USFS
Dispersed sites, No water, No toilets, Reservations not accepted, Open all year, Tent & RV camping: Free, Road not maintained for passenger cars, Elev: 6092ft/1857m, Tel: 801-798-3571, Nearest town: Vernon, Agency: USFS, GPS: 40.009254, -112.345954

33224 • FSR 661 Dispersed 1 - USFS
Dispersed sites, No water, No toilets, Reservations not accepted, Open Jun-Oct, Tent & RV camping: Free, Road not maintained for passenger cars, Elev: 7284ft/2220m, Tel: 435-783-4338, Nearest town: Springville, Agency: USFS, GPS: 40.187628, -111.355392

33225 • FSR 663 Dispersed 1 - USFS
Dispersed sites, No water, No toilets, Reservations not accepted, Open all year, Tent & RV camping: Free, Road not maintained for passenger cars, Elev: 9139ft/2786m, Tel: 435-789-1181, Nearest town: Cedar City, Agency: USFS, GPS: 37.561139, -112.911059

33226 • FSR 663 Dispersed 2 - USFS
Dispersed sites, No water, No toilets, Reservations not accepted, Open all year, Tent & RV camping: Free, Road not maintained for passenger cars, Elev: 9230ft/2813m, Tel: 435-789-1181, Nearest town: Cedar City, Agency: USFS, GPS: 37.560968, -112.918083

33227 • FSR 668 Dispersed 1 - USFS
Dispersed sites, No water, No toilets, Reservations not accepted, Open May-Dec, Tent & RV camping: Free, Road not maintained for passenger cars, Elev: 9189ft/2801m, Tel: 307-789-3194, Nearest town: Oakley, Agency: USFS, GPS: 40.853819, -110.870693

33228 • FSR 670 Dispersed 1 - USFS
Dispersed sites, No water, No toilets, Reservations not accepted, Open all year, Tent & RV camping: Free, Road not maintained for passenger cars, Elev: 6137ft/1871m, Tel: 801-798-3571, Nearest town: Vernon, Agency: USFS, GPS: 40.007489, -112.350665

33229 • FSR 674 Dispersed 1 - USFS
Dispersed sites, No water, No toilets, Reservations not accepted, Open all year, Tent & RV camping: Free, Road not maintained for passenger cars, Elev: 8043ft/2452m, Tel: 435-789-1181, Nearest town: Duck Creek, Agency: USFS, GPS: 37.578618, -112.604594

33230 • FSR 676 Dispersed 1 - USFS
Dispersed sites, No water, No toilets, Reservations not accepted, Open all year, Tent & RV camping: Free, Many sites in this area, Road not maintained for passenger cars, Elev: 7860ft/2396m, Tel: 435-783-4338, Nearest town: Spanish Fork, Agency: USFS, GPS: 40.101788, -111.195732

33231 • FSR 677 Dispersed 1 - USFS
Dispersed sites, No water, No toilets, Reservations not accepted, Open all year, Tent & RV camping: Free, High-clearance required, Elev: 7949ft/2423m, Tel: 435-738-2482, Nearest town: Altamont, Agency: USFS, GPS: 40.556613, -110.485387

33232 • FSR 678 Dispersed 1 - USFS
Dispersed sites, No water, No toilets, Reservations not accepted, Open all year, Tent & RV camping: Free, Nothing larger than van/PU, Road not maintained for passenger cars, Elev: 6736ft/2053m, Tel: 801-798-3571, Nearest town: Vernon, Agency: USFS, GPS: 39.983353, -112.349494

33233 • FSR 678 Dispersed 2 - USFS
Dispersed sites, No water, No toilets, Reservations not accepted, Open all year, Tent & RV camping: Free, Road not maintained for passenger cars, Elev: 9789ft/2984m, Tel: 435-783-4338, Nearest town: Spanish Fork, Agency: USFS, GPS: 40.052015, -111.040196

33234 • FSR 679 Dispersed 1 - USFS
Dispersed sites, No water, No toilets, Reservations not accepted, Open all year, Tent & RV camping: Free, Elev: 8740ft/2664m, Tel: 435-789-1181, Nearest town: Manila, Agency: USFS, GPS: 40.909316, -109.915601

33235 • FSR 686 Dispersed 1 - USFS

Dispersed sites, No water, No toilets, Reservations not accepted, Open all year, Tent & RV camping: Free, High-clearance required, Elev: 10333ft/3149m, Tel: 435-738-2482, Nearest town: Altamont, Agency: USFS, GPS: 40.590348, -110.445641

33236 • FSR 699 Dispersed 1 - USFS

Dispersed sites, No water, No toilets, Reservations not accepted, Open all year, Tent & RV camping: Free, Road not maintained for passenger cars, Elev: 8265ft/2519m, Tel: 435-826-5400, Nearest town: Boulder, Agency: USFS, GPS: 37.970847, -111.512366

33237 • FSR 701 Dispersed 1 - USFS

Dispersed sites, No water, No toilets, Reservations not accepted, Open all year, Tent & RV camping: Free, Road not maintained for passenger cars, Elev: 6544ft/1995m, Tel: 435-743-5721, Nearest town: Richfield, Agency: USFS, GPS: 38.786311, -112.151915

33238 • FSR 710 Dispersed 1 - USFS

Dispersed sites, No water, No toilets, Reservations not accepted, Open all year, Tent & RV camping: Free, Road not maintained for passenger cars, Elev: 5155ft/1571m, Tel: 435-743-5721, Nearest town: Leamington, Agency: USFS, GPS: 39.495168, -112.242199

33239 • FSR 713 Dispersed 1 - USFS

Dispersed sites, No water, No toilets, Reservations not accepted, Open all year, Tent & RV camping: Free, Road not maintained for passenger cars, Elev: 8977ft/2736m, Tel: 801-625-5112, Nearest town: Woodruff, Agency: USFS, GPS: 41.448064, -111.503673

33240 • FSR 714 Dispersed 1 - USFS

Dispersed sites, No water, No toilets, Reservations not accepted, Open all year, Tent & RV camping: Free, Road not maintained for passenger cars, Elev: 7982ft/2433m, Tel: 801-625-5112, Nearest town: Randolph, Agency: USFS, GPS: 41.634234, -111.477754

33241 • FSR 714 Dispersed 2 - USFS

Dispersed sites, No water, No toilets, Reservations not accepted, Open all year, Tent & RV camping: Free, Road not maintained for passenger cars, Elev: 7994ft/2437m, Tel: 801-625-5112, Nearest town: Randolph, Agency: USFS, GPS: 41.629693, -111.482144

33242 • FSR 715 (Sixth Water Divide TH) Dispersed 7 - USFS

Dispersed sites, No water, No toilets, Reservations not accepted, Open all year, Tent & RV camping: Free, Road not maintained for passenger cars, Elev: 8142ft/2482m, Tel: 435-783-4338, Nearest town: Springville, Agency: USFS, GPS: 40.150627, -111.235542

33243 • FSR 715 (West Portal TH) Dispersed 6 - USFS

Dispersed sites, No water, No toilets, Reservations not accepted, Open Dec-Apr, Tent & RV camping: Free, Road not maintained for passenger cars, Elev: 7624ft/2324m, Tel: 435-783-4338, Nearest town: Springville, Agency: USFS, GPS: 40.162677, -111.246066

33244 • FSR 715 Dispersed 1 - USFS

Dispersed sites, No water, No toilets, Reservations not accepted, Open May-Oct, Tent & RV camping: Free, Road not maintained for passenger cars, Elev: 6945ft/2117m, Tel: 801-798-3571, Nearest town: Springville, Agency: USFS, GPS: 40.148704, -111.313931

33245 • FSR 715 Dispersed 2 - USFS

Dispersed sites, No water, No toilets, Reservations not accepted, Open Dec-Apr, Tent & RV camping: Free, Road not maintained for passenger cars, Elev: 6955ft/2120m, Tel: 435-783-4338, Nearest town: Springville, Agency: USFS, GPS: 40.160091, -111.285198

33246 • FSR 715 Dispersed 3 - USFS

Dispersed sites, No water, No toilets, Reservations not accepted, Open Dec-Apr, Tent & RV camping: Free, Road not maintained for passenger cars, Elev: 7008ft/2136m, Tel: 435-783-4338, Nearest town: Springville, Agency: USFS, GPS: 40.163584, -111.275733

33247 • FSR 715 Dispersed 4 - USFS

Dispersed sites, No water, No toilets, Reservations not accepted, Open Dec-Apr, Tent & RV camping: Free, Road not maintained for passenger cars, Elev: 7428ft/2264m, Tel: 435-783-4338, Nearest town: Springville, Agency: USFS, GPS: 40.167638, -111.256442

33248 • FSR 715 Dispersed 5 - USFS

Dispersed sites, No water, No toilets, Reservations not accepted, Open Dec-Apr, Tent & RV camping: Free, Road not maintained for passenger cars, Elev: 7504ft/2287m, Tel: 435-783-4338, Nearest town: Springville, Agency: USFS, GPS: 40.169786, -111.255103

33249 • FSR 720 Dispersed 1 - USFS

Dispersed sites, No water, No toilets, Reservations not accepted, Open all year, Tent & RV camping: Free, Road not maintained for passenger cars, Elev: 7684ft/2342m, Tel: 801-785-3563, Nearest town: Charleston, Agency: USFS, GPS: 40.460597, -111.585261

33250 • FSR 724 Dispersed 1 - USFS

Dispersed sites, No water, No toilets, Reservations not accepted, Open all year, Tent & RV camping: Free, Road not maintained for passenger cars, Elev: 8462ft/2579m, Tel: 801-625-5112, Nearest town: Woodruff, Agency: USFS, GPS: 41.522581, -111.462709

33251 • FSR 724 Dispersed 2 - USFS

Dispersed sites, No water, No toilets, Reservations not accepted, Open all year, Tent & RV camping: Free, Road not maintained for passenger cars, Elev: 8520ft/2597m, Tel: 801-625-5112, Nearest town: Woodruff, Agency: USFS, GPS: 41.520225, -111.460712

33252 • FSR 724 Dispersed 3 - USFS

Dispersed sites, No water, No toilets, Reservations not accepted, Open all year, Tent & RV camping: Free, Nothing larger than van/pu, Road not maintained for passenger cars, Elev: 8457ft/2578m, Tel: 801-625-5112, Nearest town: Woodruff, Agency: USFS, GPS: 41.517788, -111.449619

33253 • FSR 731 Dispersed 1 - USFS

Dispersed sites, No water, No toilets, Reservations not accepted, Open all year, Tent & RV camping: Free, Road not maintained for passenger cars, Elev: 9287ft/2831m, Tel: 307-782-6555, Nearest town: Mountain View (WY), Agency: USFS, GPS: 40.893815, -110.536769

33254 • FSR 732 Dispersed 1 - USFS

Dispersed sites, No water, No toilets, Reservations not accepted, Open all year, Tent & RV camping: Free, Road not maintained for passenger cars, Elev: 9755ft/2973m, Tel: 435-789-1181, Nearest town: Vernal, Agency: USFS, GPS: 40.607404, -109.903141

33255 • FSR 733 Dispersed 1 - USFS

Dispersed sites, No water, No toilets, Reservations not accepted, Open all year, Tent & RV camping: Free, Several sites, Road not maintained for passenger cars, Elev: 8703ft/2653m, Tel: 801-625-5112, Nearest town: Woodruff, Agency: USFS, GPS: 41.407729, -111.498523

33256 • FSR 735 Dispersed 1 - USFS

Dispersed sites, No water, No toilets, Reservations not accepted, Open all year, Tent & RV camping: Free, Elev: 7947ft/2422m, Tel: 435-783-4338, Nearest town: Heber City, Agency: USFS, GPS: 40.303268, -111.210714

33257 • FSR 735 Dispersed 2 - USFS

Dispersed sites, No water, No toilets, Reservations not accepted, Open all year, Tent & RV camping: Free, Elev: 7927ft/2416m, Tel: 435-783-4338, Nearest town: Heber City, Agency: USFS, GPS: 40.305377, -111.210255

33258 • FSR 736 Dispersed 1 - USFS

Dispersed sites, No water, No toilets, Reservations not accepted, Open all year, Tent & RV camping: Free, Road not maintained for passenger cars, Elev: 7696ft/2346m, Tel: 435-783-4338, Nearest town: Heber City, Agency: USFS, GPS: 40.349943, -111.061609

33259 • FSR 736 Dispersed 2 - USFS

Dispersed sites, No water, No toilets, Reservations not accepted, Open all year, Tent & RV camping: Free, High-clearance vehicle required, Elev: 8750ft/2667m, Tel: 435-738-2482, Nearest town: Spanish Fork, Agency: USFS, GPS: 39.947568, -110.974353

33260 • FSR 738 Dispersed 1 - USFS

Dispersed sites, No water, No toilets, Reservations not accepted, Open all year, Tent & RV camping: Free, Road not maintained for passenger cars, Elev: 8715ft/2656m, Tel: 801-625-5112, Nearest town: Woodruff, Agency: USFS, GPS: 41.410832, -111.500212

33261 • FSR 738 Dispersed 2 - USFS

Dispersed sites, No water, Vault toilets, Reservations not accepted, Open all year, Tent & RV camping: Free, Elev: 7921ft/2414m, Tel: 435-783-4338, Nearest town: Heber City, Agency: USFS, GPS: 40.351824, -111.046692

33262 • FSR 739 Dispersed 1 - USFS

Dispersed sites, No water, No toilets, Reservations not accepted, Tent & RV camping: Free, Many sites in this area, Elev: 8507ft/2593m, Tel: 307-789-3194, Nearest town: Evanston, Agency: USFS, GPS: 40.905788, -110.812394

33263 • FSR 740 Dispersed1 - USFS

Dispersed sites, No water, No toilets, Reservations not accepted, Open all year, Tent & RV camping: Free, Road not maintained for passenger cars, Elev: 8729ft/2661m, Tel: 435-789-1181, Nearest town: Vernal, Agency: USFS, GPS: 40.613913, -109.727479

33264 • FSR 751 Dispersed 1 - USFS

Dispersed sites, No water, No toilets, Reservations not accepted, Open all year, Tent & RV camping: Free, Road not maintained for passenger cars, Elev: 9648ft/2941m, Tel: 435-789-1181, Nearest town: Vernal, Agency: USFS, GPS: 40.616171, -109.888201

33265 • FSR 752 Dispersed 1 - USFS

Dispersed sites, No water, No toilets, Reservations not accepted, Open all year, Tent & RV camping: Free, Elev: 9973ft/3040m, Tel: 435-789-1181, Nearest town: Vernal, Agency: USFS, GPS: 40.665752, -109.917787

33266 • FSR 753 Dispersed 1 - USFS

Dispersed sites, No water, No toilets, Reservations not accepted, Open all year, Tent & RV camping: Free, Road not maintained for passenger cars, Elev: 7931ft/2417m, Tel: 435-783-4338, Nearest town: Woodland, Agency: USFS, GPS: 40.473868, -110.921662

33267 • FSR 759 Dispersed 1 - USFS

Dispersed sites, No water, No toilets, Reservations not accepted, Open May-Nov, Tent & RV camping: Free, Road not maintained for passenger cars, Elev: 6754ft/2059m, Tel: 801-798-3571, Nearest town: Orem, Agency: USFS, GPS: 40.182923, -111.540659

33268 • FSR 759 Dispersed 2 - USFS

Dispersed sites, No water, No toilets, Reservations not accepted, Open May-Nov, Tent & RV camping: Free, Road not maintained for passenger cars, Elev: 7280ft/2219m, Tel: 801-798-3571, Nearest town: Orem, Agency: USFS, GPS: 40.177009, -111.537069

33269 • FSR 763 (Camp 1) Dispersed 1 - USFS

Dispersed sites, No water, No toilets, Reservations not accepted, Open Mar-Dec, Tent & RV camping: Free, Several sites, Road not maintained for passenger cars, Elev: 7503ft/2287m, Tel: 801-798-3571, Nearest town: Santaquin, Agency: USFS, GPS: 39.943028, -111.657386

33270 • FSR 764 (Camp 2) Dispersed 1 - USFS

Dispersed sites, No water, No toilets, Reservations not accepted, Open Mar-Dec, Tent & RV camping: Free, Several sites, Road not maintained for passenger cars, Elev: 7607ft/2319m, Tel: 801-798-3571, Nearest town: Santaquin, Agency: USFS, GPS: 39.940001, -111.651445

33271 • FSR 765 (Camp 3) Dispersed 1 - USFS

Dispersed sites, No water, No toilets, Reservations not accepted, Open Mar-Dec, Tent & RV camping: Free, Several sites, Road not maintained for passenger cars, Elev: 7675ft/2339m, Tel: 801-798-3571, Nearest town: Santaquin, Agency: USFS, GPS: 39.940005, -111.646814

33272 • FSR 765 Dispersed 1 - USFS

Dispersed sites, No water, No toilets, Reservations not accepted, Open all year, Tent & RV camping: Free, Road not maintained for passenger cars, Elev: 8899ft/2712m, Tel: 435-789-1181, Nearest town: Vernal, Agency: USFS, GPS: 40.633927, -109.739243

33273 • FSR 769 Dispersed 1 - USFS

Dispersed sites, No water, No toilets, Reservations not accepted, Open all year, Tent & RV camping: Free, Elev: 9614ft/2930m, Tel: 435-789-1181, Nearest town: Vernal, Agency: USFS, GPS: 40.699391, -109.751847

33274 • FSR 780 Dispersed 1 - USFS

Dispersed sites, No water, No toilets, Reservations not accepted, Open all year, Tent & RV camping: Free, Elev: 9319ft/2840m, Tel: 435-789-1181, Nearest town: Dutch John, Agency: USFS, GPS: 40.751157, -109.671919

33275 • FSR 782 Dispersed 2 - USFS

Dispersed sites, No water, No toilets, Reservations not accepted, Open all year, Tent & RV camping: Free, Elev: 9334ft/2845m, Tel: 435-789-1181, Nearest town: Vernal, Agency: USFS, GPS: 40.747761, -109.668162

33276 • FSR 786 Dispersed 1 - USFS

Dispersed sites, No water, No toilets, Reservations not accepted, Open all year, Tent & RV camping: Free, Road not maintained for passenger cars, Elev: 5436ft/1657m, Tel: 435-789-1181, Nearest town: Enterprise, Agency: USFS, GPS: 37.542673, -113.726196

33277 • FSR 787 Dispersed 1 - USFS

Dispersed sites, No water, No toilets, Reservations not accepted, Open all year, Tent & RV camping: Free, Road not maintained for passenger cars, Elcv: 5466ft/1666m, Tel: 435-789-1181, Nearest town: Enterprise, Agency: USFS, GPS: 37.539676, -113.724916

33278 • FSR 788 Dispersed 1 - USFS

Dispersed sites, No water, No toilets, Reservations not accepted, Open all year, Tent & RV camping: Free, Road not maintained for passenger cars, Elev: 5592ft/1704m, Tel: 435-789-1181, Nearest town: Enterprise, Agency: USFS, GPS: 37.538002, -113.717988

33279 • FSR 788 Dispersed 2 - USFS

Dispersed sites, No water, No toilets, Reservations not accepted, Open all year, Tent & RV camping: Free, Road not maintained for passenger cars, Elev: 5622ft/1714m, Tel: 435-789-1181, Nearest town: Enterprise, Agency: USFS, GPS: 37.534248, -113.716797

33280 • FSR 791 Dispersed 1 - USFS

Dispersed sites, No water, No toilets, Reservations not accepted, Open all year, Tent & RV camping: Free, Road not maintained for passenger cars, Elev: 6648ft/2026m, Tel: 435-789-1181, Nearest town: Enterprise, Agency: USFS, GPS: 37.494253, -113.674837

33281 • FSR 800 Dispersed 1 - USFS

Dispersed sites, No water, No toilets, Reservations not accepted, Open all year, Tent & RV camping: Free, Road not maintained for passenger cars, Elev: 9272ft/2826m, Tel: 307-782-6555, Nearest town: Mountain View (WY), Agency: USFS, GPS: 40.891721, -110.536436

33282 • FSR 802 Dispersed 1 - USFS

Dispersed sites, No water, No toilets, Reservations not accepted, Open May-Dec, Tent & RV camping: Free, Road not maintained for passenger cars, Elev: 9428ft/2874m, Tel: 307-789-3194, Nearest town: Oakley, Agency: USFS, GPS: 40.853518, -110.911181

33283 • FSR 803 Dispersed 1 - USFS

Dispersed sites, No water, No toilets, Reservations not accepted, Open all year, Tent & RV camping: Free, Road not maintained for passenger cars, Elev: 6050ft/1844m, Tel: 435-789-1181, Nearest town: Manila, Agency: USFS, GPS: 40.981992, -109.626449

33284 • FSR 807 Dispersed 1 - USFS

Dispersed sites, No water, No toilets, Reservations not accepted, Open all year, Tent & RV camping: Free, Elev: 8264ft/2519m, Tel: 801-723-2660, Nearest town: Farmington, Agency: USFS, GPS: 40.926381, -111.791306

33285 • FSR 815 Dispersed 1 - USFS

Dispersed sites, No water, No toilets, Reservations not accepted, Open all year, Tent & RV camping: Free, Elev: 8247ft/2514m, Tel: 801-723-2660, Nearest town: Farmington, Agency: USFS, GPS: 40.927278, -111.791026

33286 • FSR 815 Dispersed 2 - USFS

Dispersed sites, No water, No toilets, Reservations not accepted, Open all year, Tent & RV camping: Free, Elev: 8373ft/2552m, Tel: 801-723-2660, Nearest town: Farmington, Agency: USFS, GPS: 40.900015, -111.776862

33287 • FSR 815 Dispersed 3 - USFS

Dispersed sites, No water, No toilets, Reservations not accepted, Open all year, Tent & RV camping: Free, Elev: 8520ft/2597m, Tel: 801-723-2660, Nearest town: Farmington, Agency: USFS, GPS: 40.890429, -111.770481

33288 • FSR 815 Dispersed 4 - USFS

Dispersed sites, No water, No toilets, Reservations not accepted, Open all year, Tent & RV camping: Free, Road not maintained for passenger cars, Elev: 8705ft/2653m, Tel: 435-789-1181, Nearest town: Manila, Agency: USFS, GPS: 40.900449, -109.884627

33289 • FSR 820 Dispersed 1 - USFS

Dispersed sites, No water, No toilets, Reservations not accepted, Open all year, Tent & RV camping: Free, Elev: 9036ft/2754m, Tel: 435-783-4338, Nearest town: Woodland, Agency: USFS, GPS: 40.527451, -111.027887

33290 • FSR 836 Dispersed 1 - USFS

Dispersed sites, No water, No toilets, Reservations not accepted, Open all year, Tents only: Free, Road not maintained for passenger cars, Elev: 7194ft/2193m, Tel: 435-789-1181, Nearest town: Pine Valley, Agency: USFS, GPS: 37.454141, -113.530253

33291 • FSR 837 Dispersed 1 - USFS

Dispersed sites, No water, No toilets, Reservations not accepted, Open all year, Tent & RV camping: Free, Road not maintained for passenger cars, Elev: 7081ft/2158m, Tel: 435-789-1181, Nearest town: Pine Valley, Agency: USFS, GPS: 37.443609, -113.522978

33292 • FSR 837 Dispersed 2 - USFS

Dispersed sites, No water, No toilets, Reservations not accepted, Open all year, Tent & RV camping: Free, Road not maintained for passenger cars, Elev: 7127ft/2172m, Tel: 435-789-1181, Nearest town: Pine Valley, Agency: USFS, GPS: 37.470676, -113.515676

33293 • FSR 845 Dispersed 1 - USFS

Dispersed sites, No water, No toilets, Reservations not accepted, Open all year, Tent & RV camping: Free, Road not maintained for passenger cars, Elev: 4826ft/1471m, Tel: 435-789-1181, Nearest town: Central, Agency: USFS, GPS: 37.401834, -113.670687

33294 • FSR 853 Dispersed 1 - USFS

Dispersed sites, No water, No toilets, Reservations not accepted, Open all year, Tent & RV camping: Free, Road not maintained for passenger cars, Elev: 8277ft/2523m, Tel: 435-676-9316, Nearest town: Hatch, Agency: USFS, GPS: 37.557453, -112.316867

33295 • FSR 855 Dispersed 1 - USFS

Dispersed sites, No water, No toilets, Reservations not accepted, Open all year, Tents only: Free, Road not maintained for passenger cars, Elev: 6685ft/2038m, Tel: 435-789-1181, Nearest town: Enterprise, Agency: USFS, GPS: 37.476582, -113.703045

33296 • FSR 860 Dispersed 1 - USFS

Dispersed sites, No water, No toilets, Reservations not accepted, Open all year, Tent & RV camping: Free, Road not maintained for passenger cars, Elev: 4257ft/1298m, Tel: 435-789-1181, Nearest town: Veyo, Agency: USFS, GPS: 37.376116, -113.723227

33297 • FSR 875 Dispersed 1 - USFS

Dispersed sites, No water, No toilets, Reservations not accepted, Open all year, Tent & RV camping: Free, Road not maintained for passenger cars, Elev: 6148ft/1874m, Tel: 435-789-1181, Nearest town: Enterprise, Agency: USFS, GPS: 37.633091, -114.038891

33298 • FSR 881 Dispersed 1 - USFS

Dispersed sites, No water, No toilets, Reservations not accepted, Open all year, Tent & RV camping: Free, Road not maintained for passenger cars, Elev: 5916ft/1803m, Tel: 435-789-1181, Nearest town: Enterprise, Agency: USFS, GPS: 37.507269, -113.895531

33299 • FSR 886 Dispersed 1 - USFS

Dispersed sites, No water, No toilets, Reservations not accepted, Open all year, Tent & RV camping: Free, Road not maintained for passenger cars, Elev: 6363ft/1939m, Tel: 435-743-5721, Nearest town: Salina, Agency: USFS, GPS: 39.022501, -112.085374

33300 • FSR 892 Dispersed 1 - USFS

Dispersed sites, No water, No toilets, Tent & RV camping: Free, Several sites in this area, Elev: 8851ft/2698m, Tel: 435-836-2800, Nearest town: Loa, Agency: USFS, GPS: 38.604973, -111.616952

33301 • FSR 901 Dispersed 1 - USFS

Dispersed sites, No water, No toilets, Reservations not accepted, Open all year, Tent & RV camping: Free, Road not maintained for passenger cars, Elev: 9695ft/2955m, Tel: 435-783-4338, Nearest town: Heber City, Agency: USFS, GPS: 40.418081, -111.155945

33302 • FSR 901 Dispersed 2 - USFS

Dispersed sites, No water, No toilets, Reservations not accepted, Open all year, Tent & RV camping: Free, Road not maintained for passenger cars, Elev: 9680ft/2950m, Tel: 435-783-4338, Nearest town: Heber City, Agency: USFS, GPS: 40.418957, -111.150306

33303 • FSR 902 Dispersed 1 - USFS

Dispersed sites, No water, No toilets, Reservations not accepted, Open all year, Tent & RV camping: Free, Road not maintained for passenger cars, Elev: 8948ft/2727m, Tel: 435-783-4338, Nearest town: Oakley, Agency: USFS, GPS: 40.671122, -111.204773

33304 • FSR 905 Dispersed 1 - USFS

Dispersed sites, No water, No toilets, Reservations not accepted, Open all year, Tent & RV camping: Free, Road not maintained for passenger cars, Elev: 4319ft/1316m, Tel: 435-789-1181, Nearest town: St George, Agency: USFS, GPS: 37.241059, -113.437666

33305 • FSR 905 Dispersed 2 - USFS

Dispersed sites, No water, No toilets, Reservations not accepted, Open all year, Tent & RV camping: Free, Road not maintained for passenger cars, Elev: 4381ft/1335m, Tel: 435-789-1181, Nearest town: St George, Agency: USFS, GPS: 37.237499, -113.436534

33306 • FSR 906 Dispersed 1 - USFS

Dispersed sites, No water, No toilets, Reservations not accepted, Open all year, Tents only: Free, Road not maintained for passenger cars, Elev: 7284ft/2220m, Tel: 435-438-2430, Nearest town: Beaver, Agency: USFS, GPS: 38.615448, -112.426084

33307 • FSR 909 Dispersed 1 - USFS

Dispersed sites, No water, No toilets, Reservations not accepted, Open all year, Tent & RV camping: Free, 2 separated sites, Elev: 8312ft/2533m, Tel: 435-789-1181, Nearest town: Manila, Agency: USFS, GPS: 40.881099, -109.737112

33308 • FSR 910 Dispersed 1 - USFS

Dispersed sites, No water, No toilets, Reservations not accepted, Open all year, Tent & RV camping: Free, Road not maintained for passenger cars, Elev: 8179ft/2493m, Tel: 435-789-1181, Nearest town: Manila, Agency: USFS, GPS: 40.861824, -109.759613

33309 • FSR 913 Dispersed 1 - USFS

Dispersed sites, No water, No toilets, Reservations not accepted, Open all year, Tent & RV camping: Free, Road not maintained for passenger cars, Elev: 6102ft/1860m, Tel: 435-789-1181, Nearest town: Enterprise, Agency: USFS, GPS: 37.539533, -114.021719

33310 • FSR 918 Dispersed 1 - USFS

Dispersed sites, No water, No toilets, Reservations not accepted, Open all year, Tent & RV camping: Free, Road not maintained for passenger cars, Several sites in this area, Elev: 8287ft/2526m, Tel: 435-789-1181, Nearest town: Red Canyon, Agency: USFS, GPS: 40.783049, -109.465196

33311 • FSR 933 Dispersed 1 - USFS

Dispersed sites, No water, No toilets, Reservations not accepted, Open all year, Tent & RV camping: Free, Road not maintained for

passenger cars, Elev: 8985ft/2739m, Tel: 435-783-4338, Nearest town: Woodland, Agency: USFS, GPS: 40.584049, -111.003247

33312 • FSR 938 (Alexander Lake) Dispersed 2 - USFS
Dispersed sites, No water, No toilets, Reservations not accepted, Open all year, Tents only: Free, Road not maintained for passenger cars, Elev: 9374ft/2857m, Tel: 435-783-4338, Nearest town: Oakley, Agency: USFS, GPS: 40.609329, -110.974584

33313 • FSR 938A (Alexander Lake) Dispersed 1 - USFS
Dispersed sites, No water, No toilets, Reservations not accepted, Open all year, Tents only: Free, Several sites, Road not maintained for passenger cars, Elev: 9371ft/2856m, Tel: 435-783-4338, Nearest town: Oakley, Agency: USFS, GPS: 40.611044, -110.976558

33314 • FSR 942 Dispersed 1 - USFS
Dispersed sites, No water, No toilets, Reservations not accepted, Open all year, Tents only: Free, Road not maintained for passenger cars, Elev: 9360ft/2853m, Tel: 435-783-4338, Nearest town: Oakley, Agency: USFS, GPS: 40.608329, -110.980985

33315 • FSR 947 Dispersed 1 - USFS
Dispersed sites, No water, No toilets, Reservations not accepted, Open all year, Tent & RV camping: Free, Road not maintained for passenger cars, Elev: 8777ft/2675m, Tel: 435-783-4338, Nearest town: Oakley, Agency: USFS, GPS: 40.602886, -110.999557

33316 • FSR 948 Dispersed 1 - USFS
Dispersed sites, No water, No toilets, Reservations not accepted, Open all year, Tent & RV camping: Free, Road not maintained for passenger cars, Elev: 7475ft/2278m, Tel: 435-743-5721, Nearest town: Elsinore, Agency: USFS, GPS: 38.723793, -112.199457

33317 • FSR 952 Dispersed 1 - USFS
Dispersed sites, No water, No toilets, Reservations not accepted, Open all year, Tent & RV camping: Free, Road not maintained for passenger cars, Elev: 9701ft/2957m, Tel: 435-783-4338, Nearest town: Oakley, Agency: USFS, GPS: 40.626871, -110.977404

33318 • FSR 961 (Beth Lake) Dispersed 1 - USFS
Dispersed sites, No water, No toilets, Reservations not accepted, Open all year, Tents only: Free, Walk-to sites, Road not maintained for passenger cars, Elev: 9816ft/2992m, Tel: 435-783-4338, Nearest town: Oakley, Agency: USFS, GPS: 40.652746, -110.966765

33319 • FSR 963 Dispersed 1 - USFS
Dispersed sites, No water, No toilets, Reservations not accepted, Open all year, Tent & RV camping: Free, Road not maintained for passenger cars, Elev: 9878ft/3011m, Tel: 435-783-4338, Nearest town: Oakley, Agency: USFS, GPS: 40.652464, -110.959548

33320 • FSR 963 Dispersed 2 - USFS
Dispersed sites, No water, No toilets, Reservations not accepted, Open all year, Tent & RV camping: Free, Road not maintained for passenger cars, Elev: 9906ft/3019m, Tel: 435-783-4338, Nearest town: Oakley, Agency: USFS, GPS: 40.648503, -110.957062

33321 • FSR 964 (Trident Lake) Dispersed 1 - USFS
Dispersed sites, No water, No toilets, Reservations not accepted, Open all year, Tent & RV camping: Free, Road not maintained for passenger cars, Elev: 9761ft/2975m, Tel: 435-783-4338, Nearest town: Oakley, Agency: USFS, GPS: 40.647448, -110.962033

33322 • FSR 967 Dispersed 1 - USFS
Dispersed sites, No water, No toilets, Reservations not accepted, Open all year, Tent & RV camping: Free, Road not maintained for passenger cars, Elev: 9815ft/2992m, Tel: 435-783-4338, Nearest town: Oakley, Agency: USFS, GPS: 40.662956, -110.962899

33323 • FSR 969 Dispersed 1 - USFS
Dispersed sites, No water, No toilets, Reservations not accepted, Open all year, Tent & RV camping: Free, Several sites, Elev: 8993ft/2741m, Tel: 435-783-4338, Nearest town: Oakley, Agency: USFS, GPS: 40.634678, -110.948784

33324 • FSR 975 Dispersed 1 - USFS
Dispersed sites, No water, No toilets, Reservations not accepted, Open all year, Tents only: Free, Road not maintained for passenger cars, Elev: 7329ft/2234m, Tel: 435-438-2430, Nearest town: Beaver, Agency: USFS, GPS: 38.617651, -112.464621

33325 • FSR 975A Dispersed 1 - USFS
Dispersed sites, No water, No toilets, Reservations not accepted, Open all year, Tent & RV camping: Free, Road not maintained for passenger cars, Elev: 7253ft/2211m, Tel: 435-438-2430, Nearest town: Beaver, Agency: USFS, GPS: 38.620938, -112.458118

33326 • FSR 976 Dispersed 1 - USFS
Dispersed sites, No water, No toilets, Reservations not accepted, Open all year, Tents only: Free, Road not maintained for passenger cars, Elev: 10013ft/3052m, Tel: 435-783-4338, Nearest town: Oakley, Agency: USFS, GPS: 40.672972, -110.874323

33327 • FSR 980 Dispersed 1 - USFS
Dispersed sites, No water, No toilets, Reservations not accepted, Open all year, Tent & RV camping: Free, Road not maintained for passenger cars, Elev: 9844ft/3000m, Tel: 435-783-4338, Nearest town: Woodland, Agency: USFS, GPS: 40.583725, -110.934283

33328 • FSR 996 Dispersed 1 - USFS
Dispersed sites, No water, No toilets, Reservations not accepted, Open all year, Tent & RV camping: Free, Road not maintained for passenger cars, Elev: 8682ft/2646m, Tel: 435-789-1181, Nearest town: Cedar City, Agency: USFS, GPS: 37.645762, -112.684171

33329 • Gates Lake - USFS
Dispersed sites, No water, Tent & RV camping: Free, Elev: 9714ft/2961m, Tel: 435-896-9233, Nearest town: Salina, Agency: USFS, GPS: 38.766228, -111.685419

33330 • Gaucamole TH - BLM
Dispersed sites, No water, No toilets, Tent & RV camping: Free, Steep narrow road - bad when wet, Elev: 4467ft/1362m, Nearest town: Virgin, Agency: BLM, GPS: 37.227215, -113.114954

33331 • Glen Canyon NRA - 6 Mile Camps
Dispersed sites, No water, No toilets, Reservations not accepted, Open all year, Tents only: Free, Boat-in, Elev: 4249ft/1295m, Tel: 928-608-6200, Nearest town: Page, Agency: NP, GPS: 36.875069, -111.566068

33332 • Glen Canyon NRA - 7 1/2 Mile Camps
Dispersed sites, No water, No toilets, Reservations not accepted, Open all year, Tents only: Free, Boat-in, Elev: 3829ft/1167m, Tel: 928-608-6200, Nearest town: Page, Agency: NP, GPS: 36.878794, -111.530001

33333 • Glen Canyon NRA - 8 Mile Bar Camps
Dispersed sites, No water, No toilets, Reservations not accepted, Open all year, Tents only: Free, Boat-in, Elev: 3655ft/1114m, Tel: 928-608-6200, Nearest town: Page, Agency: NP, GPS: 36.878249, -111.524251

33334 • Glen Canyon NRA - 9 Mile Camps
Dispersed sites, No water, No toilets, Reservations not accepted, Open all year, Tents only: Free, Boat-in, Elev: 3661ft/1116m, Tel: 928-608-6200, Nearest town: Page, Agency: NP, GPS: 36.879561, -111.515117

33335 • Glen Canyon NRA - Alstrom Point
Dispersed sites, No water, No toilets, Reservations not accepted, Tent & RV camping: Free, Elev: 4690ft/1430m, Nearest town: Big Water, Agency: NP, GPS: 37.059277, -111.364684

33336 • Glen Canyon NRA - Blue Notch Canyon
Dispersed sites, No water, No toilets, Reservations not accepted, Tents only: Free, Elev: 3740ft/1140m, Tel: 928-608-6200, Nearest town: Hite, Agency: NP, GPS: 37.719151, -110.433411

33337 • Glen Canyon NRA - Bullfrog FHU
Total sites: 24, RV sites: 24, Elec sites: 24, Water at site, RV dump, Showers, Flush toilets, Max length: 50ft, Reservations accepted, No tents/RV's: $46, 24 FHU, Elev: 3760ft/1146m, Tel: 435-684-3032, Nearest town: Bullfrog, Agency: NP, GPS: 37.522563, -110.724697

33338 • Glen Canyon NRA - Bullfrog Main
Total sites: 78, RV sites: 78, Elec sites: 0, Central water, RV dump, Showers, Flush toilets, Laundry, Reservations not accepted, Tent & RV camping: $20, Elev: 3746ft/1142m, Tel: 928-608-6200, Nearest town: Bullfrog, Agency: NP, GPS: 37.520477, -110.722579

33339 • Glen Canyon NRA - Dirty Devil
Dispersed sites, No water, No toilets, Reservations not accepted, Tent & RV camping: $12, Elev: 3734ft/1138m, Tel: 928-608-6200, Nearest town: Hite, Agency: NP, GPS: 37.888577, -110.401252

33340 • Glen Canyon NRA - Dispersed
Dispersed sites, No water, No toilets, Reservations not accepted, Open all year, Tent & RV camping: $6, Elev: 3707ft/1130m, Tel: 928-608-6200, Nearest town: Hite, Agency: NP, GPS: 37.902535, -110.399694

33341 • Glen Canyon NRA - Dispersed
Dispersed sites, No water, No toilets, Reservations not accepted, Open all year, Tent & RV camping: $6, Elev: 3806ft/1160m, Tel: 928-608-6200, Nearest town: Hite, Agency: NP, GPS: 37.912164, -110.398614

33342 • Glen Canyon NRA - Farley Canyon
Dispersed sites, No water, No toilets, Reservations not accepted, Open all year, Tent & RV camping: $12, Elev: 3987ft/1215m, Tel: 928-608-6200, Nearest town: Hite, Agency: NP, GPS: 37.820306, -110.396164

33343 • Glen Canyon NRA - Ferry Swale Camps
Dispersed sites, No water, No toilets, Reservations not accepted, Open all year, Tents only: Free, Boat-in, Elev: 3944ft/1202m, Tel: 928-608-6200, Nearest town: Page, Agency: NP, GPS: 36.898668, -111.522903

33344 • Glen Canyon NRA - Halls Crossing FHU
Total sites: 65, RV sites: 24, Elec sites: 24, Water at site, RV dump, Showers, Flush toilets, Laundry, Max length: 60ft, Reservations accepted, Tents: $26/RV's: $45, 24 FHU, Elev: 3750ft/1143m, Tel: 435-684-7000, Nearest town: Halls Crossing, Agency: NP, GPS: 37.472263, -110.712501

33345 • Glen Canyon NRA - Hite
Dispersed sites, No water, No toilets, Reservations not accepted, Tents only: $12, FHU sites, Elev: 3776ft/1151m, Tel: 435-684-3103, Nearest town: Hite, Agency: NP, GPS: 37.875881, -110.380731

33346 • Glen Canyon NRA - Lone Rock Beach
Dispersed sites, Central water, RV dump, No showers, Flush toilets, Generator hours: 0600-2200, Reservations not accepted, Open all year, Tent & RV camping: $14, Cold outdoor showers, Elev: 3681ft/1122m, Tel: 928-608-6200, Nearest town: Kanab, Agency: NP, GPS: 37.018887, -111.538106

33347 • Glen Canyon NRA - Ropes Trail Camps
Dispersed sites, No water, No toilets, Reservations not accepted, Open all year, Tents only: Free, Boat-in, Elev: 3884ft/1184m, Tel: 928-608-6200, Nearest town: Page, Agency: NP, GPS: 36.916287, -111.501183

33348 • Glen Canyon NRA - Stanton Creek
Dispersed sites, No water, No toilets, Reservations not accepted, Open all year, Tent & RV camping: $12, Elev: 3705ft/1129m, Tel: 928-608-6200, Nearest town: Bullfrog, Agency: NP, GPS: 37.499053, -110.699281

33349 • Glen Canyon NRA - White Canyon
Dispersed sites, No water, No toilets, Reservations not accepted, Open all year, Tents only: Free, Elev: 3730ft/1137m, Tel: 928-608-6200, Nearest town: Hite, Agency: NP, GPS: 37.787897, -110.380381

33350 • Goblin Valley SP
Total sites: 24, RV sites: 15, Elec sites: 0, Central water, RV dump, Showers, Flush toilets, Max length: 59ft, Reservations accepted, Open all year, Tent & RV camping: $30, Elev: 4997ft/1523m,

Tel: 435-275-4584, Nearest town: Hanksville, Agency: ST, GPS: 38.57287, -110.71331

33351 • Gold Bar - BLM

Total sites: 9, RV sites: 9, Elec sites: 0, No water, Vault toilets, Max length: 40ft, Reservations accepted, Open all year, Tent & RV camping: $20, 4 group sites: $75, Stay limit: 14 days, Elev: 4029ft/1228m, Tel: 435-259-2102, Nearest town: Moab, Agency: BLM, GPS: 38.575335, -109.633553

33352 • Goose Island - BLM

Total sites: 19, RV sites: 19, Elec sites: 0, No water, Vault toilets, Max length: 40ft, Reservations not accepted, Open all year, Tent & RV camping: $20, 2 reservable group sites: $75, Stay limit: 14 days, Elev: 3986ft/1215m, Tel: 435-259-2100, Nearest town: Moab, Agency: BLM, GPS: 38.610936, -109.558037

33353 • Gooseberry (Fishlake) - USFS

Total sites: 13, RV sites: 13, Elec sites: 0, Central water, No RV dump, No showers, Vault toilets, Reservations not accepted, Open Apr-Nov, Tent & RV camping: $10, Group site $20, Elev: 7894ft/2406m, Nearest town: Salina, Agency: USFS, GPS: 38.802843, -111.685251

33354 • Gooseberry Group - USFS

Total sites: 2, RV sites: 0, Elec sites: 0, Central water, No RV dump, No showers, Vault toilets, Open Jun-Sep, Group site: $40, Elev: 8639ft/2633m, Tel: 435-384-2372, Nearest town: Fairview, Agency: USFS, GPS: 39.687457, -111.298612

33355 • Gooseberry I-70 TH - USFS

Total sites: 6, RV sites: 4, Elec sites: 0, No water, Vault toilets, Tent & RV camping: Free, Elev: 5766ft/1757m, Tel: 435-896-9233, Nearest town: Salina, Agency: USFS, GPS: 38.915284, -111.732219

33356 • Gooseberry Mesa Dispersed - BLM

Dispersed sites, No water, No toilets, Tent & RV camping: Free, Rough access road, Elev: 5113ft/1558m, Tel: 435-688-3200, Nearest town: Apple Valley, Agency: BLM, GPS: 37.140161, -113.156763

33357 • Gooseberry Reservoir - USFS

Total sites: 16, RV sites: 16, Elec sites: 0, No water, Vault toilets, Open Jun-Sep, Tent & RV camping: $10, Elev: 8435ft/2571m, Tel: 435-384-2372, Nearest town: Fairview, Agency: USFS, GPS: 39.711624, -111.293841

33358 • Goosenecks SP

Total sites: 8, RV sites: 8, Elec sites: 0, No water, Vault toilets, Max length: 40ft, Reservations not accepted, Open all year, Tent & RV camping: $10, Elev: 4977ft/1517m, Tel: 435-678-2238, Nearest town: Blanding, Agency: ST, GPS: 37.17467, -109.92703

33359 • Grand Gulch - BLM

Dispersed sites, No water, No toilets, Tents only: Free, 4x4 required, Elev: 6811ft/2076m, Tel: 435-688-3200, Nearest town: Blanding, Agency: BLM, GPS: 37.582891, -109.893581

33360 • Grand Staircase Escalante NM - Calf Creek - BLM

Total sites: 13, RV sites: 13, Elec sites: 0, Potable water, No RV dump, No showers, Flush toilets, Reservations not accepted, Tent & RV camping: $15, Elev: 5410ft/1649m, Tel: 435-644-1200, Nearest town: Escalante, Agency: BLM, GPS: 37.794563, -111.413507

33361 • Grand Staircase Escalante NM - Dance Hall Rock - BLM

Dispersed sites, No water, No toilets, Tent & RV camping: Free, Free permit required, Elev: 4618ft/1408m, Tel: 435-644-1200, Nearest town: Escalante, Agency: BLM, GPS: 37.356413, -111.101489

33362 • Grand Staircase Escalante NM - Deer Creek - BLM

Total sites: 7, RV sites: 7, Elec sites: 0, No water, No RV dump, No showers, Vault toilets, Max length: 20ft, Reservations not accepted, Tent & RV camping: $10, No trailers - may have to back out, Elev: 5735ft/1748m, Tel: 435-644-1200, Nearest town: Boulder, Agency: BLM, GPS: 37.855989, -111.355417

33363 • Grand Staircase Escalante NM - Durffey Mesa

Dispersed sites, No water, No toilets, Tent & RV camping: Free, Free permit required, Elev: 5928ft/1807m, Tel: 435-644-1200, Nearest town: Boulder, Agency: BLM, GPS: 37.862834, -111.342453

33364 • Grand Staircase Escalante NM - Forty Mile Spring

Dispersed sites, No water, Vault toilets, Tent & RV camping: Free, Free permit required, Elev: 4793ft/1461m, Tel: 435-644-1200, Nearest town: Escalante, Agency: BLM, GPS: 37.392523, -111.048634

33365 • Grand Staircase Escalante NM - Harris Wash

Dispersed sites, No water, No toilets, Tent & RV camping: Free, Free permit required, Elev: 5436ft/1657m, Tel: 435-644-1200, Nearest town: Henrieville, Agency: BLM, GPS: 37.605248, -111.422393

33366 • Grand Staircase Escalante NM - Henrieville Creek

Dispersed sites, No water, No toilets, Tent & RV camping: Free, Free permit required, Elev: 6665ft/2031m, Tel: 435-644-1200, Nearest town: Henrieville, Agency: BLM, GPS: 37.617086, -111.896804

33367 • Grand Staircase Escalante NM - Hole in the Rock

Dispersed sites, No water, No toilets, Tent & RV camping: Free, Free permit required, Elev: 5738ft/1749m, Tel: 435-644-1200, Nearest town: Henrieville, Agency: BLM, GPS: 37.722533, -111.527442

33368 • Grand Staircase Escalante NM - Horse Canyon

Dispersed sites, No water, No toilets, Tent & RV camping: Free, Free permit required, Elev: 5968ft/1819m, Tel: 435-644-1200, Nearest town: Escalante, Agency: BLM, GPS: 37.922027, -111.204368

33369 • Grand Staircase Escalante NM - Kitchen Corral

Wash

Dispersed sites, No water, No toilets, Tent & RV camping: Free, Free permit required, Elev: 5371ft/1637m, Tel: 435-644-1200, Nearest town: Kanab, Agency: BLM, GPS: 37.140117, -112.091662

33370 • Grand Staircase Escalante NM - North New Home Bench - BLM

Dispersed sites, No water, No toilets, Tent & RV camping: Free, Free permit required, Elev: 6809ft/2075m, Tel: 435-644-1200, Nearest town: Boulder, Agency: BLM, GPS: 37.889317, -111.460758

33371 • Grand Staircase Escalante NM - Pump Canyon Springs - BLM

Dispersed sites, No water, No toilets, Tent & RV camping: Free, Free permit required, Elev: 5241ft/1597m, Tel: 435-644-1200, Nearest town: Kanab, Agency: BLM, GPS: 37.343314, -111.870779

33372 • Grand Staircase Escalante NM - Rock Springs Bench

Dispersed sites, No water, No toilets, Tent & RV camping: Free, Free permit required, Elev: 5809ft/1771m, Tel: 435-644-1200, Nearest town: Henrieville, Agency: BLM, GPS: 37.494131, -111.981379

33373 • Grand Staircase Escalante NM - Skutumpah Terrace - BLM

Dispersed sites, No water, No toilets, Tent & RV camping: Free, Free permit required, Elev: 6018ft/1834m, Tel: 435-644-1200, Nearest town: Kanab, Agency: BLM, GPS: 37.268283, -112.374518

33374 • Grand Staircase Escalante NM - Sooner Rocks

Dispersed sites, No water, No toilets, Tent & RV camping: Free, Free permit required, Elev: 4356ft/1328m, Tel: 435-644-1200, Nearest town: Escalante, Agency: BLM, GPS: 37.32793, -111.058817

33375 • Grand Staircase Escalante NM - Spencer Flat - BLM

Dispersed sites, No water, No toilets, Tent & RV camping: Free, Free permit required, Elev: 5958ft/1816m, Tel: 435-644-1200, Nearest town: Escalante, Agency: BLM, GPS: 37.726621, -111.443822

33376 • Grand Staircase Escalante NM - Steep Creek Bench

Dispersed sites, No water, No toilets, Tent & RV camping: Free, Free permit required, Elev: 5961ft/1817m, Tel: 435-644-1200, Nearest town: Boulder, Agency: BLM, GPS: 37.869709, -111.336259

33377 • Grand Staircase Escalante NM - Stud Horse Peaks - BLM

Dispersed sites, No water, No toilets, Tent & RV camping: Free, Free permit required, Elev: 6782ft/2067m, Tel: 435-644-1200, Nearest town: Boulder, Agency: BLM, GPS: 37.868192, -111.111702

33378 • Grand Staircase Escalante NM - Tin Can Flat - BLM

Dispersed sites, No water, No toilets, Tent & RV camping: Free, Free permit required, Elev: 5683ft/1732m, Tel: 435-644-1200, Nearest town: Escalante, Agency: BLM, GPS: 37.714589, -111.514899

33379 • Grand Staircase Escalante NM - White House

Total sites: 12, RV sites: 7, Elec sites: 0, No water, Vault toilets, Reservations not accepted, Open all year, Tent & RV camping: $5, Also walk-to sites, Elev: 4426ft/1349m, Tel: 435-644-1200, Nearest town: Page, AZ, Agency: BLM, GPS: 37.079755, -111.889953

33380 • Grandstaff - BLM

Total sites: 16, RV sites: 0, Elec sites: 0, No water, Vault toilets, Generators prohibited, Reservations not accepted, Tents only: $20, Stay limit: 14 days, Elev: 3981ft/1213m, Tel: 435-259-2100, Nearest town: Moab, Agency: BLM, GPS: 38.611726, -109.532977

33381 • Granite Flat - USFS

Total sites: 52, RV sites: 52, Elec sites: 0, Central water, No RV dump, No showers, Vault toilets, Reservations accepted, Open May-Sep, Tent & RV camping: $24, 3 group sites: $$255-$290, No water-tank filling allowed, Stay limit: 7 days, Elev: 6745ft/2056m, Tel: 801-785-3563, Nearest town: Cedar Hills, Agency: USFS, GPS: 40.488505, -111.653123

33382 • Grantsville Reservoir

Total sites: 24, RV sites: 24, Elec sites: 0, No water, Vault toilets, Tent & RV camping: $10, Elev: 5051ft/1540m, Nearest town: Grantsville, Agency: CP, GPS: 40.543898, -112.511953

33383 • Great Salt Lake Marina

Total sites: 4, RV sites: 4, Elec sites: 4, Water at site, RV dump, Showers, Flush toilets, Max length: 40ft, Reservations accepted, Open all year, No tents/RV's: $20, Elev: 4219ft/1286m, Tel: 801-250-1898, Nearest town: Salt Lake City, Agency: ST, GPS: 40.733672, -112.210086

33384 • Green River - 53-0 Jones Hole Camps 1-3 - USFS

Dispersed sites, No water, No toilets, Tents only: Free, Boat-in, Elev: 5038ft/1536m, Tel: 435-781-7700, Nearest town: Dinosaur CO, Agency: USFS, GPS: 40.541024, -109.059153

33385 • Green River - 72-0 Split Mtn Ramp (199-5) - USFS

Dispersed sites, No water, No toilets, Tents only: Free, Boat-in, Elev: 4793ft/1461m, Tel: 435-781-7700, Nearest town: Naples, Agency: USFS, GPS: 40.445778, -109.253011

33386 • Green River - Anderson Bottom - BLM

Dispersed sites, No water, No toilets, Tents only: Fee unk, Boat-in, River permit required, Elev: 3938ft/1200m, Tel: 435-636-3600, Nearest town: Moab, Agency: BLM, GPS: 38.363763, -110.014655

33387 • Green River - Backwater Camp - USFS

Dispersed sites, No water, No toilets, Open Apr-Dec, Tents only: $13, Boat-in, Elev: 5827ft/1776m, Tel: 435-784-3445, Nearest town: Dutch John, Agency: USFS, GPS: 40.906392, -109.257424

33388 • Green River - Big Island - NPS

Dispersed sites, No water, No toilets, Tents only: Fee unk, Boat-in, River permit required, Elev: 4964ft/1513m, Tel: 435-636-

3600, Nearest town: Jensen, **Agency:** BLM, GPS: 40.512737, -109.131806

33389 • Green River - Big Pine - USFS
Dispersed sites, No water, **No toilets,** Open Apr-Dec, Tents only: $13, Boat-in, Elev: 5633ft/1717m, Tel: 435-784-3445, Nearest town: Dutch John, Agency: USFS, GPS: 40.911584, -109.267025

33390 • Green River - Big Tree - BLM
Dispersed sites, No water, **No toilets,** Tents only: Fee unk, Boat-in, River permit required, Elev: 4564ft/1391m, Tel: 435-636-3600, Nearest town: Sunnyside, Agency: BLM, GPS: 39.643873, -110.011463

33391 • Green River - Bootleg Camp - USFS
Dispersed sites, No water, No toilets, Open Apr-Dec, Tents only: $13, Boat-in, Elev: 5564ft/1696m, Tel: 435-784-3445, Nearest town: Dutch John, Agency: USFS, GPS: 40.90855, -109.299755

33392 • Green River - Bull Canyon - BLM
Dispersed sites, No water, No toilets, Tents only: Fee unk, Boat-in, River permit required, Elev: 4353ft/1327m, Tel: 435-636-3600, Nearest town: East Carbon, Agency: BLM, GPS: 39.442692, -110.024064

33393 • Green River - Butler - BLM
Dispersed sites, No water, No toilets, Tents only: Fee unk, Boat-in, River permit required, Elev: 4129ft/1259m, Tel: 435-636-3600, Nearest town: Green River, Agency: BLM, GPS: 39.154178, -110.116866

33394 • Green River - Camp 13.7 - BLM
Dispersed sites, No water, No toilets, Tents only: Fee unk, Boat-in, River permit required, Elev: 4621ft/1408m, Tel: 435-636-3600, Nearest town: Sunnyside, Agency: BLM, GPS: 39.753713, -109.93002

33395 • Green River - Camp 18.6 - BLM
Dispersed sites, No water, No toilets, Tents only: Fee unk, Boat-in, River permit required, Elev: 4612ft/1406m, Tel: 435-636-3600, Nearest town: Sunnyside, Agency: BLM, GPS: 39.722281, -109.956767

33396 • Green River - Camp 19.1 - BLM
Dispersed sites, No water, No toilets, Tents only: Fee unk, Boat-in, River permit required, Elev: 4612ft/1406m, Tel: 435-636-3600, Nearest town: Sunnyside, Agency: BLM, GPS: 39.728034, -109.960865

33397 • Green River - Camp 19.4 - BLM
Dispersed sites, No water, No toilets, Tents only: Fee unk, Boat-in, River permit required, Elev: 4612ft/1406m, Tel: 435-636-3600, Nearest town: Sunnyside, Agency: BLM, GPS: 39.732293, -109.962163

33398 • Green River - Camp 19.6 - BLM
Dispersed sites, No water, **No toilets,** Tents only: Fee unk, Boat-in, River permit required, Elev: 4612ft/1406m, Tel: 435-636-

3600, Nearest town: Sunnyside, Agency: BLM, GPS: 39.735674, -109.959561

33399 • Green River - Camp 35.0 - BLM
Dispersed sites, No water, No toilets, Tents only: Fee unk, Boat-in, River permit required, Elev: 4546ft/1386m, Tel: 435-636-3600, Nearest town: Sunnyside, Agency: BLM, GPS: 39.621381, -110.012889

33400 • Green River - Camp 36.5 - BLM
Dispersed sites, No water, No toilets, Tents only: Fee unk, Boat-in, River permit required, Elev: 4528ft/1380m, Tel: 435-636-3600, Nearest town: Sunnyside, Agency: BLM, GPS: 39.602742, -110.026899

33401 • Green River - Camp 40.3 - BLM
Dispersed sites, No water, No toilets, Tents only: Fee unk, Boat-in, River permit required, Elev: 4483ft/1366m, Tel: 435-636-3600, Nearest town: Sunnyside, Agency: BLM, GPS: 39.561121, -110.038031

33402 • Green River - Camp 53.4 - BLM
Dispersed sites, No water, No toilets, Tents only: Fee unk, Boat-in, River permit required, Elev: 4321ft/1317m, Tel: 435-636-3600, Nearest town: East Carbon, Agency: BLM, GPS: 39.416089, -110.011194

33403 • Green River - Camp 61.7 - BLM
Dispersed sites, No water, No toilets, Tents only: Fee unk, Boat-in, River permit required, Elev: 4254ft/1297m, Tel: 435-636-3600, Nearest town: Green River, Agency: BLM, GPS: 39.325763, -110.049938

33404 • Green River - Cats Paw Camp - USFS
Dispersed sites, No water, No toilets, Open Apr-Dec, Tents only: $13, Boat-in, Elev: 5558ft/1694m, Tel: 435-784-3445, Nearest town: Dutch John, Agency: USFS, GPS: 40.909888, -109.297686

33405 • Green River - Chandler - BLM
Dispersed sites, No water, No toilets, Tents only: Fee unk, Boat-in, River permit required, Elev: 4382ft/1336m, Tel: 435-636-3600, Nearest town: East Carbon, Agency: BLM, GPS: 39.47223, -110.022037

33406 • Green River - Chandler Canyon - BLM
Dispersed sites, No water, No toilets, Tents only: Fee unk, Boat-in, River permit required, Elev: 4379ft/1335m, Tel: 435-636-3600, Nearest town: East Carbon, Agency: BLM, GPS: 39.468872, -110.024098

33407 • Green River - Cicada Camp - USFS
Dispersed sites, No water, No toilets, Open Apr-Dec, Tents only: $13, Boat-in, Elev: 5558ft/1694m, Tel: 435-784-3445, Nearest town: Dutch John, Agency: USFS, GPS: 40.911733, -109.274418

33408 • Green River - Coal Creek - BLM
Dispersed sites, No water, No toilets, Tents only: Fee unk, Boat-in, River permit required, Elev: 4193ft/1278m, Tel: 435-636-3600,

Nearest town: Green River, Agency: BLM, GPS: 39.248125, -110.061926

33409 • Green River - Compromise - NPS
Dispersed sites, No water, No toilets, Tents only: Fee unk, Boat-in, River permit required, Elev: 5018ft/1529m, Tel: 435-636-3600, Nearest town: Dinosaur CO, Agency: BLM, GPS: 40.538557, -109.076038

33410 • Green River - Cottonwoods River Camp - USFS
Dispersed sites, No water, No toilets, Tents only: $13, Hike-in/boat-in, Elev: 5564ft/1696m, Tel: 435-789-1181, Nearest town: Dutch John, Agency: USFS, GPS: 40.911321, -109.295892

33411 • Green River - Dripping Springs - BLM
Dispersed sites, No water, No toilets, Tents only: Fee unk, Boat-in, River permit required, Elev: 4550ft/1387m, Tel: 435-636-3600, Nearest town: Sunnyside, Agency: BLM, GPS: 39.625292, -110.003328

33412 • Green River - Duches Hole - BLM
Dispersed sites, No water, No toilets, Tents only: Fee unk, Boat-in, River permit required, Elev: 4628ft/1411m, Tel: 435-636-3600, Nearest town: Sunnyside, Agency: BLM, GPS: 39.797987, -109.889631

33413 • Green River - Firewater - BLM
Dispersed sites, No water, No toilets, Tents only: Fee unk, Boat-in, River permit required, Elev: 4576ft/1395m, Tel: 435-636-3600, Nearest town: Sunnyside, Agency: BLM, GPS: 39.658768, -109.986359

33414 • Green River - Flat Canyon - BLM
Dispersed sites, No water, No toilets, Tents only: Fee unk, Boat-in, River permit required, Elev: 4559ft/1390m, Tel: 435-636-3600, Nearest town: Sunnyside, Agency: BLM, GPS: 39.634016, -110.006098

33415 • Green River - Fort Bottom - BLM
Dispersed sites, No water, No toilets, Tents only: Fee unk, Boat-in, River permit required, Elev: 3948ft/1203m, Tel: 435-636-3600, Nearest town: Moab, Agency: BLM, GPS: 38.455074, -110.032137

33416 • Green River - Grasshopper - USFS
Dispersed sites, No water, No toilets, Open Apr-Dec, Tents only: $13, Boat-in, Elev: 5528ft/1685m, Tel: 435-784-3445, Nearest town: Dutch John, Agency: USFS, GPS: 40.91054, -109.283048

33417 • Green River - Island Park - NPS
Dispersed sites, No water, No toilets, Tents only: Fee unk, Boat-in, River permit required, Elev: 4956ft/1511m, Tel: 435-636-3600, Nearest town: Jensen, Agency: BLM, GPS: 40.521701, -109.152434

33418 • Green River - Jack Creek - BLM
Dispersed sites, No water, No toilets, Tents only: Fee unk, Boat-in, River permit required, Elev: 4598ft/1401m, Tel: 435-636-

3600, Nearest town: Sunnyside, Agency: BLM, GPS: 39.699384, -109.99436

33419 • Green River - Jackson Creek - USFS
Dispersed sites, No water, No toilets, Open Apr-Dec, Tents only: $13, Boat-in, Elev: 5558ft/1694m, Tel: 435-784-3445, Nearest town: Dutch John, Agency: USFS, GPS: 40.911468, -109.276788

33420 • Green River - Joe Hutch Canyon - BLM
Dispersed sites, No water, No toilets, Tents only: Fee unk, Boat-in, River permit required, Elev: 4304ft/1312m, Tel: 435-636-3600, Nearest town: East Carbon, Agency: BLM, GPS: 39.393216, -110.01929

33421 • Green River - Lion Hollow - BLM
Dispersed sites, No water, No toilets, Tents only: Fee unk, Boat-in, River permit required, Elev: 4391ft/1338m, Tel: 435-636-3600, Nearest town: East Carbon, Agency: BLM, GPS: 39.481568, -110.021375

33422 • Green River - Little Horse Bottom - BLM
Dispersed sites, No water, No toilets, Tents only: Fee unk, Boat-in, River permit required, Elev: 4622ft/1409m, Tel: 435-636-3600, Nearest town: Sunnyside, Agency: BLM, GPS: 39.791967, -109.918687

33423 • Green River - Log Cabin - BLM
Dispersed sites, No water, No toilets, Tents only: Fee unk, Boat-in, River permit required, Elev: 4469ft/1362m, Tel: 435-636-3600, Nearest town: Sunnyside, Agency: BLM, GPS: 39.549059, -110.027488

33424 • Green River - Lower Cedar Ridge - BLM
Dispersed sites, No water, No toilets, Tents only: Fee unk, Boat-in, River permit required, Elev: 4575ft/1394m, Tel: 435-636-3600, Nearest town: Sunnyside, Agency: BLM, GPS: 39.657166, -109.987574

33425 • Green River - Lower Gold Hole - BLM
Dispersed sites, No water, No toilets, Tents only: Fee unk, Boat-in, River permit required, Elev: 4621ft/1408m, Tel: 435-636-3600, Nearest town: Sunnyside, Agency: BLM, GPS: 39.748375, -109.93218

33426 • Green River - Lower Three Canyon - BLM
Dispersed sites, No water, No toilets, Tents only: Fee unk, Boat-in, River permit required, Elev: 4408ft/1344m, Tel: 435-636-3600, Nearest town: East Carbon, Agency: BLM, GPS: 39.504158, -110.023744

33427 • Green River - Lower Wire Fence - BLM
Dispersed sites, No water, No toilets, Tents only: Fee unk, Boat-in, River permit required, Elev: 4271ft/1302m, Tel: 435-636-3600, Nearest town: East Carbon, Agency: BLM, GPS: 39.351975, -110.023048

33428 • Green River - McPherson - BLM
Dispersed sites, No water, No toilets, Tents only: Fee unk, Boat-in, River permit required, Elev: 4290ft/1308m, Tel: 435-636-3600,

Nearest town: East Carbon, Agency: BLM, GPS: 39.381472, -110.018414

33429 • Green River - Moonwater - BLM
Dispersed sites, No water, No toilets, Tents only: Fee unk, Boat-in, River permit required, Elev: 4336ft/1322m, Tel: 435-636-3600, Nearest town: East Carbon, Agency: BLM, GPS: 39.421689, -110.019823

33430 • Green River - Mushroom - BLM
Dispersed sites, No water, No toilets, Tents only: Fee unk, Boat-in, River permit required, Elev: 4597ft/1401m, Tel: 435-636-3600, Nearest town: Sunnyside, Agency: BLM, GPS: 39.689331, -110.003976

33431 • Green River - Opposite Stampede Flat - BLM
Dispersed sites, No water, No toilets, Tents only: Fee unk, Boat-in, River permit required, Elev: 4612ft/1406m, Tel: 435-636-3600, Nearest town: Sunnyside, Agency: BLM, GPS: 39.723496, -109.949358

33432 • Green River - Poverty - BLM
Dispersed sites, No water, No toilets, Tents only: Fee unk, Boat-in, River permit required, Elev: 4185ft/1276m, Tel: 435-636-3600, Nearest town: Green River, Agency: BLM, GPS: 39.241088, -110.05823

33433 • Green River - Pugmire Pocket - USFS
Dispersed sites, No water, No toilets, Open Apr-Dec, Tents only: $13, Boat-in, Elev: 5551ft/1692m, Tel: 435-784-3445, Nearest town: Dutch John, Agency: USFS, GPS: 40.908517, -109.264092

33434 • Green River - Range Creek - BLM
Dispersed sites, No water, No toilets, Tents only: Fee unk, Boat-in, River permit required, Elev: 4233ft/1290m, Tel: 435-636-3600, Nearest town: Green River, Agency: BLM, GPS: 39.306081, -110.051728

33435 • Green River - Rattlesnake - BLM
Dispersed sites, No water, No toilets, Tents only: Fee unk, Boat-in, River permit required, Elev: 4168ft/1270m, Tel: 435-636-3600, Nearest town: Green River, Agency: BLM, GPS: 39.216946, -110.076592

33436 • Green River - Red Creek - USFS
Dispersed sites, No water, No toilets, Open Apr-Dec, Tents only: $13, Boat-in, Elev: 5735ft/1748m, Tel: 435-784-3445, Nearest town: Dutch John, Agency: USFS, GPS: 40.904662, -109.251934

33437 • Green River - Red Point - BLM
Dispersed sites, No water, No toilets, Tents only: Fee unk, Boat-in, River permit required, Elev: 4329ft/1319m, Tel: 435-636-3600, Nearest town: East Carbon, Agency: BLM, GPS: 39.418883, -110.013493

33438 • Green River - Rock House - BLM
Dispersed sites, No water, No toilets, Tents only: Fee unk, Boat-in, River permit required, Elev: 4615ft/1407m, Tel: 435-636-

3600, Nearest town: Sunnyside, Agency: BLM, GPS: 39.748671, -109.946205

33439 • Green River - Sand Camp - USFS
Dispersed sites, No water, No toilets, Open Apr-Dec, Tents only: $13, Boat-in, Elev: 5610ft/1710m, Tel: 435-784-3445, Nearest town: Dutch John, Agency: USFS, GPS: 40.908016, -109.300976

33440 • Green River - Sand Knoll - BLM
Dispersed sites, No water, No toilets, Tents only: Fee unk, Boat-in, River permit required, Elev: 4125ft/1257m, Tel: 435-636-3600, Nearest town: Green River, Agency: BLM, GPS: 39.149816, -110.113082

33441 • Green River - School Section - BLM
Dispersed sites, No water, No toilets, Tents only: Fee unk, Boat-in, River permit required, Elev: 4170ft/1271m, Tel: 435-636-3600, Nearest town: Green River, Agency: BLM, GPS: 39.222841, -110.07775

33442 • Green River - Small Camp - BLM
Dispersed sites, No water, No toilets, Tents only: Fee unk, Boat-in, River permit required, Elev: 4623ft/1409m, Tel: 435-636-3600, Nearest town: Sunnyside, Agency: BLM, GPS: 39.783966, -109.880778

33443 • Green River - Snap Canyon - BLM
Dispersed sites, No water, No toilets, Tents only: Fee unk, Boat-in, River permit required, Elev: 4429ft/1350m, Tel: 435-636-3600, Nearest town: East Carbon, Agency: BLM, GPS: 39.523848, -110.02828

33444 • Green River - Spanish Bottom - BLM
Dispersed sites, No water, No toilets, Tents only: Fee unk, Boat-in, River permit required, Elev: 3852ft/1174m, Tel: 435-636-3600, Nearest town: Hite, Agency: BLM, GPS: 38.134913, -109.946221

33445 • Green River - Steer Ridge - BLM
Dispersed sites, No water, No toilets, Tents only: Fee unk, Boat-in, River permit required, Elev: 4499ft/1371m, Tel: 435-636-3600, Nearest town: Sunnyside, Agency: BLM, GPS: 39.574112, -110.035711

33446 • Green River - Stonefly - USFS
Dispersed sites, No water, No toilets, Open Apr-Dec, Tents only: $13, Boat-in, Elev: 5607ft/1709m, Tel: 435-784-3445, Nearest town: Dutch John, Agency: USFS, GPS: 40.907449, -109.302436

33447 • Green River - The Cove - NPS
Dispersed sites, No water, No toilets, Tents only: Fee unk, Boat-in, River permit required, Elev: 4965ft/1513m, Tel: 435-636-3600, Nearest town: Jensen, Agency: BLM, GPS: 40.510012, -109.121041

33448 • Green River - Three Canyon - BLM
Dispersed sites, No water, No toilets, Tents only: Fee unk, Boat-in, River permit required, Elev: 4408ft/1344m, Tel: 435-636-3600, Nearest town: East Carbon, Agency: BLM, GPS: 39.505399, -110.022786

33449 • Green River - Thunderhole - BLM

Dispersed sites, No water, No toilets, Tents only: Fee unk, Boat-in, River permit required, Elev: 4222ft/1287m, Tel: 435-636-3600, Nearest town: Green River, Agency: BLM, GPS: 39.282247, -110.075133

33450 • Green River - Trail Canyon - BLM

Dispersed sites, No water, No toilets, Tents only: Fee unk, Boat-in, River permit required, Elev: 4370ft/1332m, Tel: 435-636-3600, Nearest town: East Carbon, Agency: BLM, GPS: 39.458195, -110.020475

33451 • Green River - Trails End Camp - USFS

Dispersed sites, No water, No toilets, Open Apr-Dec, Tents only: $13, Boat-in, Elev: 5663ft/1726m, Tel: 435-784-3445, Nearest town: Dutch John, Agency: USFS, GPS: 40.911553, -109.271451

33452 • Green River - Treetop - USFS

Dispersed sites, No water, No toilets, Open Apr-Dec, Tents only: $13, Boat-in, Elev: 5574ft/1699m, Tel: 435-784-3445, Nearest town: Dutch John, Agency: USFS, GPS: 40.89395, -109.250076

33453 • Green River - Trin-Alcove Bend - BLM

Dispersed sites, No water, No toilets, Tents only: Fee unk, Boat-in, River permit required, Elev: 3992ft/1217m, Tel: 435-636-3600, Nearest town: Green River, Agency: BLM, GPS: 38.705975, -110.122479

33454 • Green River - Upper Cedar Ridge - BLM

Dispersed sites, No water, No toilets, Tents only: Fee unk, Boat-in, River permit required, Elev: 4577ft/1395m, Tel: 435-636-3600, Nearest town: Sunnyside, Agency: BLM, GPS: 39.659583, -109.988482

33455 • Green River - Upper Wire Fence - BLM

Dispersed sites, No water, No toilets, Tents only: Fee unk, Boat-in, River permit required, Elev: 4274ft/1303m, Tel: 435-636-3600, Nearest town: East Carbon, Agency: BLM, GPS: 39.353736, -110.021822

33456 • Green River Bridge - BLM

Dispersed sites, No water, No toilets, Tent & RV camping: Free, Elev: 4721ft/1439m, Tel: 435-636-3600, Nearest town: Vernal, Agency: BLM, GPS: 40.313971, -109.482154

33457 • Green River SP

Total sites: 29, RV sites: 29, Elec sites: 21, Water at site, RV dump, Showers, Flush toilets, Max length: 47ft, Reservations accepted, Open all year, Tent & RV camping: $35, 4 FHU, Elev: 4075ft/1242m, Tel: 435-564-3633, Nearest town: Green River, Agency: ST, GPS: 38.988682, -110.152012

33458 • Greendale East Group - USFS

Total sites: 8, RV sites: 8, Elec sites: 0, Central water, No RV dump, No showers, Vault toilets, Reservations accepted, Open May-Sep, Group site: $105, Elev: 6992ft/2131m, Tel: 435-889-3000, Nearest town: Dutch John, Agency: USFS, GPS: 40.881348, -109.456097

33459 • Greendale West - USFS

Total sites: 8, RV sites: 8, Elec sites: 0, Central water, No RV dump, No showers, Vault toilets, Max length: 45ft, Reservations accepted, Open May-Sep, Tent & RV camping: $20, Elev: 7014ft/2138m, Tel: 435-889-3000, Nearest town: Dutch John, Agency: USFS, GPS: 40.882615, -109.460911

33460 • Greens Lake - USFS

Total sites: 20, RV sites: 20, Elec sites: 0, Potable water, No RV dump, No showers, Vault toilets, Max length: 45ft, Reservations accepted, Open May-Sep, Tent & RV camping: $20, 1 group site $70, Elev: 7474ft/2278m, Tel: 435-784-3445, Nearest town: Dutch John, Agency: USFS, GPS: 40.873291, -109.537354

33461 • Grizzly Ridge Meadow Dispersed - USFS

Dispersed sites, No water, No toilets, Reservations not accepted, Tent & RV camping: Free, Elev: 8468ft/2581m, Tel: 435-784-3445, Nearest town: Dutch John, Agency: USFS, GPS: 40.752319, -109.486625

33462 • Grouse Creek Community Park and Campground

Total sites: 9, RV sites: 9, Elec sites: 0, Central water, No RV dump, No showers, Vault toilets, Tent & RV camping: Fee unk, Camping available but under development, Camping also available at store, Elev: 5321ft/1622m, Tel: 801-678-6574, Nearest town: Grouse Creek, Agency: MU, GPS: 41.708497, -113.884224

33463 • Guinavah-Malibu - USFS

Total sites: 39, RV sites: 39, Elec sites: 0, Central water, No RV dump, No showers, Flush toilets, Reservations accepted, Open May-Oct, Tent & RV camping: $22, 2 group sites: $145-$170, Stay limit: 7 days, Elev: 5085ft/1550m, Tel: 801-435-3620, Nearest town: Logan, Agency: USFS, GPS: 41.761963, -111.699463

33464 • Gunlock SP

Total sites: 5, RV sites: 5, Elec sites: 0, No water, Vault toilets, Reservations not accepted, Open Mar-Oct, Tent & RV camping: $20, Beach camping allowed, Elev: 3609ft/1100m, Tel: 435-680-0715, Nearest town: St. George, Agency: ST, GPS: 37.25641, -113.77276

33465 • Hacking Lake Dispersed - USFS

Dispersed sites, No water, No toilets, Reservations not accepted, Open all year, Tent & RV camping: Free, Elev: 10626ft/3239m, Tel: 435-789-1181, Nearest town: Vernal, Agency: USFS, GPS: 40.775393, -109.808331

33466 • Hades - USFS

Total sites: 14, RV sites: 14, Elec sites: 0, No water, Vault toilets, Reservations accepted, Open May-Sep, Tent & RV camping: $10, Elev: 7434ft/2266m, Tel: 435-738-2482, Nearest town: Hanna, Agency: USFS, GPS: 40.53418, -110.873535

33467 • Hal Canyon - BLM

Total sites: 11, RV sites: 9, Elec sites: 0, No water, Vault toilets, Max length: 24ft, Reservations not accepted, Open all year, Tent & RV camping: $20, Stay limit: 14 days, Elev: 4019ft/1225m, Tel: 435-259-2100, Nearest town: Moab, Agency: BLM, GPS: 38.641179, -109.477566

33468 • Halls Creek - BLM

Dispersed sites, No water, No toilets, Tents only: Free, Very rough gravel road to overlook, but plenty of camping available on the graded roads nearby, Elev: 5276ft/1608m, Nearest town: Ticaboo, Agency: BLM, GPS: 37.717794, -110.930149

33469 • Hamburger Rock - BLM

Total sites: 10, RV sites: 10, Elec sites: 0, No water, Vault toilets, Max length: 25ft, Reservations not accepted, Open all year, Tent & RV camping: $15, Elev: 4887ft/1490m, Tel: 435-259-2102, Nearest town: Moab, Agency: BLM, GPS: 38.192048, -109.669626

33470 • Hart Point Dispersed - BLM

Dispersed sites, No water, No toilets, Tent & RV camping: Free, No large RV's, Elev: 6392ft/1948m, Nearest town: Monticello, Agency: BLM, GPS: 38.162275, -109.574864

33471 • Hart Point Road Dispersed - BLM

Dispersed sites, No water, No toilets, Tent & RV camping: Free, Elev: 6631ft/2021m, Nearest town: Monticello, Agency: BLM, GPS: 38.069763, -109.514162

33472 • Hart Point Road Dispersed - BLM

Dispersed sites, No water, No toilets, Tent & RV camping: Free, Elev: 6637ft/2023m, Nearest town: Monticello, Agency: BLM, GPS: 38.064989, -109.516922

33473 • Hart Point Road Dispersed - BLM

Dispersed sites, No water, No toilets, Tent & RV camping: Free, Elev: 6652ft/2028m, Nearest town: Monticello, Agency: BLM, GPS: 38.018738, -109.495227

33474 • Hart Point Road Dispersed - BLM

Dispersed sites, No water, No toilets, Tent & RV camping: Free, Elev: 6701ft/2042m, Nearest town: Monticello, Agency: BLM, GPS: 38.034225, -109.499171

33475 • Hart Point Road Dispersed - BLM

Dispersed sites, No water, No toilets, Tent & RV camping: Free, Elev: 6738ft/2054m, Nearest town: Monticello, Agency: BLM, GPS: 38.048863, -109.504119

33476 • Hart Point Road Dispersed - BLM

Dispersed sites, No water, No toilets, Tent & RV camping: Free, Elev: 6765ft/2062m, Nearest town: Monticello, Agency: BLM, GPS: 38.011034, -109.490983

33477 • Harves - USFS

Dispersed sites, No water, Vault toilets, Reservations not accepted, Tent & RV camping: Free, Elev: 9511ft/2899m, Tel: 435-896-9233, Nearest town: Salina, Agency: USFS, GPS: 38.768987, -111.655816

33478 • Hastings Road Dispersed - BLM

Dispersed sites, No water, No toilets, Tent & RV camping: Free, Elev: 4128ft/1258m, Nearest town: Green River, Agency: BLM, GPS: 39.122974, -110.113897

33479 • Hatch Point - BLM

Total sites: 10, RV sites: 10, Elec sites: 0, No water, Vault toilets, Max length: 24ft, Reservations not accepted, Open all year, Tent & RV camping: $20, Elev: 5830ft/1777m, Tel: 435-259-2100, Nearest town: Moab, Agency: BLM, GPS: 38.380395, -109.616857

33480 • Haycock Creek TH Dispersed - USFS

Dispersed sites, No water, No toilets, Reservations not accepted, Open all year, Tents only: Free, Road not maintained for passenger cars, Elev: 8834ft/2693m, Tel: 435-789-1181, Nearest town: Panguitch, Agency: USFS, GPS: 37.807264, -112.640984

33481 • Hayden Fork - USFS

Total sites: 9, RV sites: 9, Elec sites: 0, Central water, No RV dump, No showers, Vault toilets, Reservations not accepted, Tent & RV camping: $18, Stay limit: 14 days, Elev: 8871ft/2704m, Tel: 307-789-3194, Nearest town: Evanston, Agency: USFS, GPS: 40.829633, -110.853542

33482 • Henrys Fork Horse Camp - USFS

Total sites: 3, RV sites: 3, Elec: Unk, No water, Vault toilets, Reservations not accepted, Open all year, Tent & RV camping: Free, Elev: 9389ft/2862m, Tel: 307-782-6555, Nearest town: Mountain View (WY), Agency: USFS, GPS: 40.912636, -110.327841

33483 • Henrys Fork TH - USFS

Total sites: 4, RV sites: 4, Elec: Unk, No water, Vault toilets, Max length: 20ft, Reservations not accepted, Open all year, Tent & RV camping: Free, Elev: 9422ft/2872m, Tel: 307-782-6555, Nearest town: Mountain View (WY), Agency: USFS, GPS: 40.909777, -110.330552

33484 • Hideout Canyon Boat-In - USFS

Total sites: 18, RV sites: 0, Central water, Flush toilets, Reservations accepted, Open May-Sep, Tents only: $22, Hike-in/boat-in, Elev: 6069ft/1850m, Tel: 801-226-3564, Nearest town: Manila, Agency: USFS, GPS: 40.914304, -109.647612

33485 • High Creek - USFS

Total sites: 2, RV sites: 2, Elec sites: 0, No water, Vault toilets, Reservations not accepted, Open May-Oct, Tent & RV camping: Free, Stay limit: 7 days, Elev: 5600ft/1707m, Tel: 435-755-3620, Nearest town: Logan, Agency: USFS, GPS: 41.976, -111.735

33486 • Hittle Bottom - BLM

Total sites: 15, RV sites: 15, Elec sites: 0, No water, Vault toilets, Max length: 34ft, Reservations not accepted, Open all year, Tent & RV camping: $20, Also group site, Stay limit: 14 days, Elev: 4104ft/1251m, Tel: 435-259-2102, Nearest town: Moab, Agency: BLM, GPS: 38.760552, -109.323556

33487 • Hobble - USFS

Dispersed sites, No water, No toilets, Open all year, Tents only: Free, Elev: 5261ft/1604m, Nearest town: Huntsville, Agency: USFS, GPS: 41.275645, -111.658973

33488 • Honeycomb Rocks - USFS

Total sites: 21, RV sites: 21, Elec sites: 0, Central water, No RV dump, No showers, Vault toilets, Reservations not accepted, Open

May-Sep, Tent & RV camping: $13, Elev: 5735ft/1748m, Nearest town: Enterprise, Agency: USFS, GPS: 37.51709, -113.856445

33489 • Hoop Lake - USFS
Total sites: 44, RV sites: 44, Elec sites: 0, Central water, No RV dump, No showers, Vault toilets, Reservations not accepted, Open Jun-Nov, Tent & RV camping: $18, Stay limit: 14 days, Elev: 9218ft/2810m, Tel: 307-789-3194, Nearest town: Mountain View, WY, Agency: USFS, GPS: 40.924449, -110.124936

33490 • Hope - USFS
Total sites: 26, RV sites: 26, Elec sites: 0, No water, Vault toilets, Reservations accepted, Open May-Oct, Tent & RV camping: $24, Stay limit: 7 days, Elev: 6631ft/2021m, Tel: 801-785-3563, Nearest town: Orem, Agency: USFS, GPS: 40.301854, -111.615214

33491 • Horseman Park Rd Dispersed - BLM
Dispersed sites, No water, No toilets, Reservations not accepted, Tent & RV camping: Free, Elev: 4754ft/1449m, Nearest town: Dammeron Valley, Agency: BLM, GPS: 37.294358, -113.650176

33492 • Horseman Park Rd Dispersed - BLM
Dispersed sites, No water, No toilets, Reservations not accepted, Tent & RV camping: Free, Elev: 4792ft/1461m, Nearest town: Dammeron Valley, Agency: BLM, GPS: 37.295666, -113.647955

33493 • Horseman Park Rd Dispersed - BLM
Dispersed sites, No water, No toilets, Reservations not accepted, Tent & RV camping: Free, Elev: 4800ft/1463m, Nearest town: Dammeron Valley, Agency: BLM, GPS: 37.299309, -113.649016

33494 • Horseman Park Rd Dispersed - BLM
Dispersed sites, No water, No toilets, Reservations not accepted, Tent & RV camping: Free, Elev: 4818ft/1469m, Nearest town: Dammeron Valley, Agency: BLM, GPS: 37.300549, -113.647938

33495 • Horseman Park Rd Dispersed - BLM
Dispersed sites, No water, No toilets, Reservations not accepted, Tent & RV camping: Free, Elev: 4883ft/1488m, Nearest town: Dammeron Valley, Agency: BLM, GPS: 37.305408, -113.642457

33496 • Horseshoe Canyon - BLM
Dispersed sites, No water, Vault toilets, Tents only: Free, 4x4 recommended, Elev: 5343ft/1629m, Tel: 435-259-2652, Nearest town: Hanksville, Agency: BLM, GPS: 38.474033, -110.200291

33497 • Horsethief - BLM
Total sites: 60, RV sites: 60, Elec sites: 0, No water, Vault toilets, Max length: 40ft, Reservations not accepted, Open all year, Tent & RV camping: $20, Stay limit: 14 days, Elev: 5845ft/1782m, Tel: 435-259-2100, Nearest town: Moab, Agency: BLM, GPS: 38.584079, -109.814005

33498 • Hovenweep NM
Total sites: 31, RV sites: 7, Elec sites: 0, Central water, No RV dump, No showers, No toilets, Max length: 30ft, Generator hours: 0800-1000/1600-2000, Reservations not accepted, Open all year, Tent & RV camping: $10, Small RV's may fit on some tent sites, Elev:

5223ft/1592m, Tel: 970-562-4282 x10, Nearest town: Blanding, Agency: NP, GPS: 37.383203, -109.071292

33499 • Hunter Canyon - BLM
Total sites: 10, RV sites: 10, Elec sites: 0, No water, Vault toilets, Max length: 18ft, Reservations not accepted, Open all year, Tent & RV camping: $20, Stay limit: 14 days, Elev: 4295ft/1309m, Tel: 435-259-2100, Nearest town: Moab, Agency: BLM, GPS: 38.510154, -109.597016

33500 • Huntington Reservoir Dispersed - USFS
Dispersed sites, No water, Vault toilets, Reservations not accepted, Tent & RV camping: Free, Elev: 9098ft/2773m, Nearest town: Fairview, Agency: USFS, GPS: 39.595993, -111.270606

33501 • Huntington Reservoir Ramp - USFS
Dispersed sites, No water, Vault toilets, Reservations not accepted, Tent & RV camping: Free, Elev: 9064ft/2763m, Tel: 435-384-2372, Nearest town: Fairview, Agency: USFS, GPS: 39.585782, -111.259722

33502 • Huntington SP
Total sites: 22, RV sites: 22, Elec sites: 22, Central water, RV dump, Showers, Flush toilets, Max length: 45ft, Open Apr-Oct, Tents: $16/RV's: $20-25, 3 FHU, Dry camping in parking lot allowed in winter, Elev: 5850ft/1783m, Tel: 435-687-2491, Nearest town: Huntington, Agency: ST, GPS: 39.346253, -110.942346

33503 • Hurricane Cliffs RA -BLM
Total sites: 7, RV sites: 0, Elec: Unk, No water, No toilets, Reservations not accepted, Tents only: Free, Camp only in designated spots, Elev: 3848ft/1173m, Tel: 435-688-3200, Nearest town: Hurricane, Agency: BLM, GPS: 37.176539, -113.248409

33504 • Hurricane Cliffs RA -BLM
Total sites: 10, RV sites: 2, Elec: Unk, No water, No toilets, Reservations not accepted, Tent & RV camping: Free, Camp only in designated spots, Elev: 3756ft/1145m, Tel: 435-688-3200, Nearest town: Hurricane, Agency: BLM, GPS: 37.187725, -113.242263

33505 • Hurricane Cliffs RA -BLM
Total sites: 6, RV sites: 1, Elec: Unk, No water, No toilets, Reservations not accepted, Tent & RV camping: Free, Camp only in designated spots, Elev: 3787ft/1154m, Tel: 435-688-3200, Nearest town: Hurricane, Agency: BLM, GPS: 37.182825, -113.245121

33506 • Hurricane Cliffs RA -BLM
Total sites: 12, RV sites: 2, Elec: Unk, No water, No toilets, Reservations not accepted, Tent & RV camping: Free, Camp only in designated spots, Elev: 3882ft/1183m, Tel: 435-688-3200, Nearest town: Hurricane, Agency: BLM, GPS: 37.165868, -113.253745

33507 • Hurricane Cliffs RA -BLM
Total sites: 12, RV sites: 3, Elec: Unk, No water, No toilets, Reservations not accepted, Tent & RV camping: Free, Camp only in designated spots, 1 group site, Rough access road, Elev: 3647ft/

1112m, Tel: 435-688-3200, Nearest town: Hurricane, Agency: BLM, GPS: 37.187337, -113.223551

33508 • Hwy 24 Dispersed - BLM
Dispersed sites, No water, No toilets, Open all year, Tent & RV camping: Free, Elev: 6503ft/1982m, Nearest town: Torrey, Agency: BLM, GPS: 38.326759, -111.364144

33509 • Hwy 31 Dispersed - USFS
Dispersed sites, No water, Vault toilets, Reservations not accepted, Tent & RV camping: Free, Elev: 9148ft/2788m, Nearest town: Fairview, Agency: USFS, GPS: 39.599001, -111.272287

33510 • Hwy 31 Dispersed - USFS
Dispersed sites, No water, Vault toilets, Reservations not accepted, Tent & RV camping: Free, Several sites, Elev: 9222ft/2811m, Nearest town: Fairview, Agency: USFS, GPS: 39.600796, -111.271634

33511 • Hyrum SP
Total sites: 33, RV sites: 33, Elec sites: 10, Central water, RV dump, Showers, Flush toilets, Reservations accepted, Open all year, Tents: $30/RV's: $30-35, Elev: 4675ft/1425m, Tel: 435-245-6866, Nearest town: Hyrum, Agency: ST, GPS: 41.627434, -111.867428

33512 • Indian Creek - USFS
Dispersed sites, No water, Vault toilets, Reservations not accepted, Tent & RV camping: Free, Elev: 8025ft/2446m, Tel: 435-896-9233, Nearest town: Manderfield, Agency: USFS, GPS: 38.426169, -112.481251

33513 • Indian Creek Falls Group - BLM
Total sites: 1, RV sites: 1, Elec sites: 0, No water, Vault toilets, Reservations accepted, Open all year, Group site: $65, Elev: 4708ft/1435m, Tel: 435-719-2100, Nearest town: Monticello, Agency: BLM, GPS: 38.211797, -109.673414

33514 • Indian Creek Group - USFS
Total sites: 7, RV sites: 7, Elec sites: 0, Central water, No RV dump, No showers, Vault toilets, Reservations accepted, Open Jun-Oct, Tent & RV camping: $3, 7 reservable group sites: $30-$50, Individual sites available if not in use, Elev: 8780ft/2676m, Tel: 801-756-8616, Nearest town: Huntington, Agency: USFS, GPS: 39.442543, -111.238806

33515 • Indian Crossing - BLM
Total sites: 22, RV sites: 22, Elec sites: 0, RV dump, Vault toilets, Open May-Oct, Tent & RV camping: $5, Elev: 5495ft/1675m, Tel: 435-781-4400, Nearest town: Vernal, Agency: BLM, GPS: 40.898, -109.183

33516 • Ingham Pass Dispersed - BLM
Dispersed sites, No water, No toilets, Tents only: Free, High-clearance vehicle recommended, Elev: 7571ft/2308m, Tel: 801-977-4300, Nearest town: Grouse Creek, Agency: BLM, GPS: 41.661937, -113.741883

33517 • Intake - USFS
Total sites: 5, RV sites: 5, Elec sites: 0, No water, No toilets, Reservations not accepted, Tent & RV camping: $14, Stay limit: 7 days, Elev: 6378ft/1944m, Tel: 801-733-2660, Nearest town: Salt Lake City, Agency: USFS, GPS: 40.497694, -112.571421

33518 • Iron Mine - USFS
Total sites: 26, RV sites: 26, Elec sites: 0, Central water, No RV dump, No showers, Vault toilets, Reservations accepted, Open May-Sep, Tent & RV camping: $10, 1 group site $25, Elev: 7552ft/2302m, Tel: 435-738-2482, Nearest town: Hanna, Agency: USFS, GPS: 40.553575, -110.886683

33519 • Jackson Dispersed - USFS
Dispersed sites, No water, Vault toilets, Tent & RV camping: Free, Elev: 8465ft/2580m, Nearest town: Fruitland, Agency: USFS, GPS: 40.014071, -110.960603

33520 • Jacob's Chair - BLM
Dispersed sites, No water, No toilets, No tents/RV's: Free, Elev: 4810ft/1466m, Nearest town: Fry Canyon, Agency: BLM, GPS: 37.706932, -110.239412

33521 • Jarvies Canyon River Camp - USFS
Dispersed sites, No water, Reservations accepted, Tents only: $22, Boat-in, Fee: $105,, Elev: 5609ft/1710m, Nearest town: Dutch John, Agency: USFS, GPS: 40.902982, -109.383777

33522 • Jaycee Park - BLM
Total sites: 7, RV sites: 0, Elec sites: 0, No water, Vault toilets, Max length: 18ft, Reservations not accepted, Open all year, Tents only: $20, Walk-to sites, Stay limit: 14 days, Elev: 3976ft/1212m, Tel: 435-259-2100+AF23720, Nearest town: Moab, Agency: BLM, GPS: 38.556971, -109.590204

33523 • Jct 95-261 - BLM
Dispersed sites, No water, No toilets, Tent & RV camping: Free, Elev: 6791ft/2070m, Nearest town: Blanding, Agency: BLM, GPS: 37.570625, -109.882595

33524 • Joe's Valley - USFS
Total sites: 46, RV sites: 46, Elec sites: 0, No water, Vault toilets, Max length: 22ft, Reservations accepted, Open May-Oct, Tent & RV camping: $10-18, Elev: 7123ft/2171m, Tel: 435-384-2372, Nearest town: Orangeville, Agency: USFS, GPS: 39.295356, -111.292157

33525 • Jordan Pines Group - USFS
Total sites: 4, RV sites: 3, Elec sites: 0, Central water, No RV dump, No showers, Vault toilets, Reservations accepted, Open May-Sep, Group site: $255-$305, No pets, Elev: 7313ft/2229m, Tel: 801-733-2660, Nearest town: Wasatch, Agency: USFS, GPS: 40.645504, -111.647079

33526 • Jordanelle SP - Hailstone
Total sites: 100, RV sites: 100, Elec sites: 100, Water at site, RV dump, Showers, Flush toilets, Max length: 80ft, Reservations accepted, Open all year, Tent & RV camping: $35, Cabin(s), 14

FHU, Elev: 6247ft/1904m, Tel: 435-649-9540, Nearest town: Heber City, Agency: ST, GPS: 40.620366, -111.423675

33527 • Jordanelle SP - Keetley Walk-to
Total sites: 41, RV sites: 0, Elec sites: 0, No water, No toilets, Reservations accepted, Open all year, Tents only: $25, Walk-to sites, Elev: 6245ft/1903m, Tel: 435-782-3030, Nearest town: Heber City, Agency: ST, GPS: 40.623782, -111.424338

33528 • Jordanelle SP - McHenry
Total sites: 40, RV sites: 0, Elec sites: 0, Central water, Vault toilets, Reservations accepted, Open all year, Tents only: $30, Elev: 6245ft/1903m, Tel: 435-782-3030, Nearest town: Heber City, Agency: ST, GPS: 40.618136, -111.432579

33529 • Jordanelle SP - Rock Cliff
Total sites: 28, RV sites: 0, Elec sites: 0, No toilets, Open all year, Tents only: $25, Walk-to sites, Elev: 6207ft/1892m, Tel: 435-782-3030, Nearest town: Heber City, Agency: ST, GPS: 40.601966, -111.339897

33530 • Julius Park Reservoir Dispersed - USFS
Dispersed sites, No water, No toilets, Reservations not accepted, Open all year, Tent & RV camping: Free, Road not maintained for passenger cars, Elev: 9788ft/2983m, Tel: 435-789-1181, Nearest town: Vernal, Agency: USFS, GPS: 40.636101, -109.895498

33531 • Justesen Flats ATV - BLM
Dispersed sites, No water, No toilets, Tent & RV camping: Free, Elev: 7116ft/2169m, Nearest town: Green River, Agency: BLM, GPS: 38.842505, -110.884172

33532 • Kaler Hollow - USFS
Total sites: 4, RV sites: 0, Elec sites: 0, No water, Vault toilets, Reservations not accepted, Open May-Sep, Tents only: Free, Elev: 9022ft/2750m, Tel: 435-789-1181, Nearest town: Vernal, Agency: USFS, GPS: 40.702112, -109.614724

33533 • Kane Creek Dispersed - BLM
Dispersed sites, No water, Vault toilets, Reservations not accepted, Open all year, Tent & RV camping: $15, Elev: 4165ft/1269m, Nearest town: Moab, Agency: BLM, GPS: 38.497764, -109.618488

33534 • Kane Hollow Dispersed - USFS
Dispersed sites, No water, Vault toilets, Tents only: Free, Numerous sites in this area, Elev: 8596ft/2620m, Tel: 435-789-1181, Nearest town: Vernal, Agency: USFS, GPS: 40.712092, -109.532345

33535 • Kens Lake - BLM
Total sites: 31, RV sites: 31, Elec sites: 0, No water, Vault toilets, Max length: 40ft, Reservations not accepted, Open all year, Tent & RV camping: $20, Stay limit: 14 days, Elev: 5085ft/1550m, Tel: 435-259-2102, Nearest town: Moab, Agency: BLM, GPS: 38.477904, -109.422975

33536 • Kents Lake - USFS
Total sites: 30, RV sites: 30, Elec sites: 0, Central water, No RV dump, No showers, Vault toilets, Max length: 60ft, Reservations accepted, Open Jun-Sep, Tent & RV camping: $14, Elev: 8894ft/2711m, Tel: 435-438-2436, Nearest town: Beaver, Agency: USFS, GPS: 38.236572, -112.459961

33537 • King Creek - USFS
Total sites: 37, RV sites: 37, Elec sites: 0, Central water, RV dump, No showers, Flush toilets, Max length: 45ft, Generator hours: 0600-2200, Reservations not accepted, Open May-Sep, Tent & RV camping: $15, Elev: 7982ft/2433m, Tel: 435-676-2676, Nearest town: Panguitch, Agency: USFS, GPS: 37.609131, -112.260498

33538 • Kingfisher Island - USFS
Total sites: 8, RV sites: 0, No water, Vault toilets, Reservations not accepted, Tents only: $15, Boat-in, Elev: 6069ft/1850m, Tel: 435-789-1181, Nearest town: Manila, Agency: USFS, GPS: 40.940471, -109.640218

33539 • Kings Bottom - BLM
Total sites: 25, RV sites: 25, Elec sites: 0, No water, Vault toilets, Max length: 24ft, Reservations not accepted, Open all year, Tent & RV camping: $20, Stay limit: 14 days, Elev: 4003ft/1220m, Tel: 435-259-2100, Nearest town: Moab, Agency: BLM, GPS: 38.557407, -109.584527

33540 • Klondike Bluffs Dispersed - BLM
Dispersed sites, No water, No toilets, Open all year, Tent & RV camping: Free, 4x4 recommended, Elev: 4648ft/1417m, Nearest town: Moab, Agency: BLM, GPS: 38.758029, -109.725517

33541 • Knolls Recreation Area - BLM
Dispersed sites, No water, Vault toilets, Reservations not accepted, Open all year, Tent & RV camping: $6, Elev: 4265ft/1300m, Tel: 801-977-4300, Nearest town: Wendover, Agency: BLM, GPS: 40.710347, -113.284765

33542 • Kodachrome Basin SP - Arch Group
Total sites: 1, Elec sites: 0, Central water, No RV dump, No showers, Vault toilets, Open all year, Group site: $80, Elev: 5818ft/1773m, Tel: 435-679-8562, Nearest town: Cannonville, Agency: ST, GPS: 37.517402, -111.983487

33543 • Kodachrome Basin SP - Basin
Total sites: 34, RV sites: 34, Elec sites: 13, Central water, RV dump, Showers, Flush toilets, Generator hours: 1200-1600, Open Apr-Nov, Tents: $20/RV's: $20-30, 15 FHU, Elev: 5886ft/1794m, Tel: 435-679-8562, Nearest town: Cannonville, Agency: ST, GPS: 37.530891, -111.992017

33544 • Kodachrome Basin SP - Bryce View
Total sites: 11, RV sites: 11, Elec sites: 0, Central water, No RV dump, No showers, Vault toilets, Max length: 20ft, Open all year, Tent & RV camping: $20, Elev: 5863ft/1787m, Tel: 435-679-8562, Nearest town: Cannonville, Agency: ST, GPS: 37.515915, -111.979467

33545 • Kokopelli's Trail - Bitter Creek Overlook - BLM
Total sites: 5, RV sites: 0, Elec sites: 0, No water, No toilets, Reservations not accepted, Tents only: $20, Elev: 5060ft/1542m,

Tel: 435-259-2100, Nearest town: Mack CO, Agency: BLM, GPS: 39.157014, -109.108319

33546 • Kokopelli's Trail - Cowskin - BLM
Total sites: 10, RV sites: 10, Elec sites: 0, No water, No RV dump, No showers, No toilets, Reservations not accepted, Tent & RV camping: $20, Elev: 4733ft/1443m, Tel: 435-259-2100, Nearest town: Moab, Agency: BLM, GPS: 38.785115, -109.263282

33547 • Kokopelli's Trail - Fish Ford - BLM
Total sites: 10, RV sites: 10, Elec sites: 0, No water, No RV dump, No showers, No toilets, Reservations not accepted, Tent & RV camping: $20, Elev: 4157ft/1267m, Tel: 435-259-2100, Nearest town: Moab, Agency: BLM, GPS: 38.923652, -109.247883

33548 • Kokopelli's Trail - Hideout Canyon - BLM
Dispersed sites, No water, No toilets, Reservations not accepted, Tents only: $20, 4x4 required, Elev: 5566ft/1697m, Tel: 435-259-2100, Nearest town: Moab, Agency: BLM, GPS: 38.691031, -109.190672

33549 • Kokopelli's Trail - Porcupine Rim - USFS
Total sites: 8, RV sites: 0, Elec sites: 0, No water, No toilets, Reservations not accepted, Tents only: Free, High-clearance vehicle recommended, Elev: 7418ft/2261m, Tel: 435-259-2100, Nearest town: Castle Valley, Agency: USFS, GPS: 38.575059, -109.347123

33550 • Kokopelli's Trail - Rock Castle - BLM
Total sites: 7, RV sites: 7, Elec sites: 0, No water, No toilets, Reservations not accepted, Tent & RV camping: $20, Elev: 6411ft/1954m, Tel: 435-259-2100, Nearest town: Moab, Agency: BLM, GPS: 38.598765, -109.289473

33551 • Kokopelli's Trail - Westwater - BLM
Total sites: 15, RV sites: 0, Elec sites: 0, No water, No RV dump, No showers, Vault toilets, Reservations not accepted, Tents only: $20, Also boat-in sites, Elev: 4335ft/1321m, Tel: 435-259-2100, Nearest town: Fruita, CO, Agency: BLM, GPS: 39.087471, -109.101798

33552 • Kolob Creekside - BLM
Dispersed sites, No water, No toilets, Tent & RV camping: Free, Elev: 3610ft/1100m, Nearest town: Virgin, Agency: BLM, GPS: 37.220358, -113.161699

33553 • Kolob Reservoir Northwest - County
Dispersed sites, No water, Vault toilets, Tent & RV camping: Free, Elev: 8140ft/2481m, Tel: 435-673-3617, Nearest town: Cedar City, Agency: CP, GPS: 37.443101, -113.052127

33554 • Kolob Reservoir Southeast - County
Dispersed sites, No water, Vault toilets, Tent & RV camping: Free, Elev: 8154ft/2485m, Tel: 435-673-3617, Nearest town: Cedar City, Agency: CP, GPS: 37.433086, -113.045295

33555 • Kolob Reservoir West - County
Dispersed sites, No water, Vault toilets, Tent & RV camping: Free, Elev: 8136ft/2480m, Tel: 435-673-3617, Nearest town: Cedar City, Agency: CP, GPS: 37.438649, -113.052481

33556 • Koosharem Canyon/Paiute ATV - USFS
Dispersed sites, No water, Vault toilets, Tent & RV camping: Free, Elev: 7365ft/2245m, Tel: 435-896-9233, Nearest town: Koosharem, Agency: USFS, GPS: 38.528507, -111.914146

33557 • Koosharem Reservoir - BLM
Dispersed sites, No toilets, Reservations not accepted, Tent & RV camping: Free, Elev: 7014ft/2138m, Tel: 435-896-1500, Nearest town: Koosharem, Agency: BLM, GPS: 38.60006, -111.847175

33558 • Lake Canyon - USFS
Total sites: 9, RV sites: 9, Elec sites: 0, No water, Vault toilets, Reservations accepted, Open Jun-Oct, Tent & RV camping: $20-30, 5 group sites: $40-$60, Elev: 8963ft/2732m, Tel: 435-384-2372, Nearest town: Fairview, Agency: USFS, GPS: 39.575664, -111.258165

33559 • Lake Canyon Lake - DWR
Dispersed sites, No water, No toilets, Reservations not accepted, Tents only: Free, Elev: 6711ft/2046m, Tel: 801-538-4700, Nearest town: Duchesne, Agency: ST, GPS: 40.060673, -110.622815

33560 • Lake Hill - USFS
Total sites: 10, RV sites: 10, Elec sites: 0, Central water, No RV dump, No showers, Vault toilets, Reservations accepted, Open Jun-Sep, Tent & RV camping: $10, 2 group sites: $30-$40, Elev: 8428ft/2569m, Tel: 435-283-4151, Nearest town: Ephraim, Agency: USFS, GPS: 39.327416, -111.499333

33561 • Lake Stream TH Dispersed - USFS
Dispersed sites, No water, No toilets, Reservations not accepted, Open all year, Tent & RV camping: Free, Road not maintained for passenger cars, Elev: 10497ft/3199m, Tel: 435-438-2430, Nearest town: Junction, Agency: USFS, GPS: 38.337287, -112.341814

33562 • Lava Flat Dispersed - USFS
Dispersed sites, No water, No toilets, Reservations not accepted, Tent & RV camping: Free, Elev: 8350ft/2545m, Tel: 435-865-3200, Nearest town: Duck Creek, Agency: USFS, GPS: 37.541425, -112.644634

33563 • LeBaron Lake - USFS
Total sites: 13, RV sites: 13, Elec sites: 0, No water, Vault toilets, Reservations accepted, Open Jul-Sep, Tent & RV camping: $10, Elev: 9963ft/3037m, Tel: 435-438-2436, Nearest town: Beaver, Agency: USFS, GPS: 38.224352, -112.402527

33564 • Ledge A - BLM
Total sites: 33, RV sites: 26, Elec sites: 0, No water, Reservations not accepted, Open all year, Tent & RV camping: $20, Stay limit: 14 days, Elev: 4136ft/1261m, Tel: 435-259-2100, Nearest town: Moab, Agency: BLM, GPS: 38.492832, -109.607175

33565 • Ledge B - BLM
Total sites: 41, RV sites: 33, Elec sites: 0, No water, Vault toilets, Reservations not accepted, Open all year, Tent & RV camping: $20, Stay limit: 14 days, Elev: 4144ft/1263m, Tel: 435-259-

2100, Nearest town: Moab, Agency: BLM, GPS: 38.484609, -109.605737

33566 • Ledge C - BLM

Dispersed sites, No water, Vault toilets, Reservations not accepted, Open all year, Tent & RV camping: $20, Stay limit: 14 days, Elev: 4187ft/1276m, Tel: 435-259-2100, Nearest town: Moab, Agency: BLM, GPS: 38.472531, -109.602053

33567 • Ledge D - BLM

Total sites: 6, RV sites: 6, Elec sites: 0, No water, Vault toilets, Reservations not accepted, Open all year, Tent & RV camping: $20, Stay limit: 14 days, Elev: 4209ft/1283m, Tel: 435-259-2102, Nearest town: Moab, Agency: BLM, GPS: 38.468329, -109.600745

33568 • Ledge E Group - BLM

Total sites: 1, Elec: Unk, No water, Vault toilets, Reservations accepted, Open all year, Group site: $75-$100, Stay limit: 14 days, Elev: 4206ft/1282m, Tel: 435-259-2100, Nearest town: Moab, Agency: BLM, GPS: 38.467059, -109.601651

33569 • Ledgefork - USFS

Total sites: 73, RV sites: 73, Elec sites: 0, Central water, No RV dump, No showers, Vault toilets, Max length: 75ft, Reservations accepted, Open Jun-Oct, Tent & RV camping: $24, Stay limit: 7 days, Elev: 7740ft/2359m, Tel: 801-226-3564, Nearest town: Oakley, Agency: USFS, GPS: 40.742491, -111.098815

33570 • Levan Town Park

Total sites: 6, RV sites: 6, Elec sites: 0, Central water, No RV dump, No showers, Vault toilets, Generator hours: 0700-2200, Reservations not accepted, No tents/RV's: Donation, Elev: 5322ft/1622m, Tel: 435-623-1959, Nearest town: Levan, Agency: MU, GPS: 39.563446, -111.862072

33571 • Lewis M Turner - USFS

Total sites: 10, RV sites: 10, Elec sites: 0, Central water, No RV dump, No showers, Vault toilets, Reservations not accepted, Open Jun-Sep, Tent & RV camping: $20, Stay limit: 7 days, Elev: 6414ft/1955m, Tel: 435-755-3620, Nearest town: Garden City, Agency: USFS, GPS: 41.88501, -111.572754

33572 • Lilly Lake - USFS

Total sites: 14, RV sites: 14, Elec sites: 0, Central water, No RV dump, No showers, Vault toilets, Reservations not accepted, Tent & RV camping: $23, Stay limit: 7 days, Elev: 9948ft/3032m, Tel: 435-783-4338, Nearest town: Kamas, Agency: USFS, GPS: 40.681168, -110.939883

33573 • Lions Club RV Park

Total sites: 6, RV sites: 6, Elec sites: 0, Central water, RV dump, No showers, No toilets, Tent & RV camping: Donation, Elev: 5010ft/1527m, Nearest town: Milford, Agency: MU, GPS: 38.40117, -113.014436

33574 • Little Bear Group - USFS

Total sites: 2, RV sites: 2, Elec sites: 0, No water, Vault toilets, Reservations accepted, Open May-Oct, Group site: $30-$50, Elev:

7359ft/2243m, Tel: 435-384-2372, Nearest town: Huntington, Agency: USFS, GPS: 39.446899, -111.138486

33575 • Little Cottonwood - USFS

Total sites: 14, RV sites: 14, Elec sites: 0, Central water, No RV dump, No showers, Flush toilets, Max length: 40ft, Reservations accepted, Open May-Sep, Tent & RV camping: $16, Elev: 6463ft/1970m, Tel: 435-438-2436, Nearest town: Beaver, Agency: USFS, GPS: 38.256899, -112.543814

33576 • Little Creek - BLM

Total sites: 10, RV sites: 10, Elec sites: 0, Central water, Vault toilets, Reservations not accepted, Open Apr-Oct, Tent & RV camping: $12, Reservable group site $65, Elev: 6398ft/1950m, Tel: 801-977-4300, Nearest town: Randolph, Agency: BLM, GPS: 41.677759, -111.226079

33577 • Little Lyman Lake - USFS

Total sites: 10, RV sites: 10, Elec sites: 0, Central water, No RV dump, No showers, Reservations not accepted, Tent & RV camping: $16, Stay limit: 14 days, Elev: 9314ft/2839m, Tel: 307-789-3194, Nearest town: Mountain View, WY, Agency: USFS, GPS: 40.934409, -110.613921

33578 • Little Mill - USFS

Total sites: 36, RV sites: 36, Elec sites: 0, No water, Vault toilets, Max length: 30ft, Reservations accepted, Open May-Oct, Tent & RV camping: $24, Group site: $185, Stay limit: 7 days, Elev: 6214ft/1894m, Tel: 801-785-3563, Nearest town: American Forks, Agency: USFS, GPS: 40.450195, -111.670898

33579 • Little Reservoir - USFS

Total sites: 8, RV sites: 8, Elec sites: 0, Central water, No RV dump, No showers, Vault toilets, Max length: 40ft, Reservations not accepted, Open May-Sep, Tent & RV camping: $12, Elev: 7346ft/2239m, Tel: 435-896-9233, Nearest town: Beaver, Agency: USFS, GPS: 38.260984, -112.489468

33580 • Little Rock - USFS

Total sites: 1, RV sites: 1, Elec sites: 0, No water, No toilets, Reservations not accepted, Open May-Sep, Tent & RV camping: $5, Elev: 8100ft/2469m, Tel: 435-637-2817, Nearest town: Huntington, Agency: USFS, GPS: 39.547358, -111.168333

33581 • Little Sahara RA - Jericho - BLM

Total sites: 40, RV sites: 40, Elec sites: 0, No toilets, Reservations not accepted, Open all year, Tent & RV camping: Free, Elev: 5030ft/1533m, Tel: 435-743-3100, Nearest town: Nephi, Agency: BLM, GPS: 39.686812, -112.367833

33582 • Little Sahara RA - Oasis - BLM

Total sites: 115, RV sites: 115, Elec sites: 0, Central water, RV dump, No showers, No toilets, Reservations not accepted, Open all year, Tent & RV camping: Free, Elev: 5019ft/1530m, Tel: 435-743-3100, Nearest town: Nephi, Agency: BLM, GPS: 39.689381, -112.353918

33583 • Little Sahara RA - Sand Mt - BLM

Dispersed sites, Central water, No toilets, Reservations not accepted, Open all year, Tent & RV camping: Free, Elev: 4928ft/1502m, Tel: 435-743-3100, Nearest town: Nephi, Agency: BLM, GPS: 39.639164, -112.389114

33584 • Little Sahara RA - White Sands - BLM

Total sites: 100, Elec sites: 0, Central water, No RV dump, No showers, Vault toilets, Reservations not accepted, Open all year, Tent & RV camping: Free, No water in winter, Elev: 5338ft/1627m, Tel: 435-743-3100, Nearest town: Nephi, Agency: BLM, GPS: 39.740705, -112.314718

33585 • Little Valley Road Dispersed - BLM

Dispersed sites, No water, No toilets, Tent & RV camping: Free, Elev: 4311ft/1314m, Nearest town: Green River, Agency: BLM, GPS: 38.948153, -110.095078

33586 • Lloyd Lake - BLM

Dispersed sites, No water, Vault toilets, Tent & RV camping: Free, Elev: 7225ft/2202m, Nearest town: Monticello, Agency: BLM, GPS: 37.855068, -109.365275

33587 • Lockhart Rd South - BLM

Dispersed sites, No water, No toilets, Tent & RV camping: Free, Elev: 4914ft/1498m, Nearest town: Moab, Agency: BLM, GPS: 38.182475, -109.668137

33588 • Lodge - USFS

Total sites: 10, RV sites: 10, Elec sites: 0, Central water, No RV dump, No showers, Vault toilets, Reservations not accepted, Tent & RV camping: $20, Stay limit: 7 days, Elev: 5538ft/1688m, Tel: 435-755-3620, Nearest town: Logan, Agency: USFS, GPS: 41.778564, -111.621826

33589 • Lodgepole (Central) - USFS

Total sites: 55, RV sites: 49, Elec sites: 0, Central water, RV dump, No showers, Flush toilets, Reservations accepted, Open May-Oct, Tent & RV camping: $23, 2 group sites: $175-$335, Stay limit: 7 days, Elev: 7710ft/2350m, Tel: 801-226-3564, Nearest town: Heber City, Agency: USFS, GPS: 40.312087, -111.259508

33590 • Lodgepole at Flaming Gorge - USFS

Total sites: 35, RV sites: 35, Elec sites: 0, Central water, RV dump, No showers, Flush toilets, Max length: 22ft, Reservations accepted, Open May-Sep, Tent & RV camping: $18, Elev: 8117ft/2474m, Tel: 435-889-3000, Nearest town: Dutch John, Agency: USFS, GPS: 40.811634, -109.466297

33591 • Lone Mesa Group - BLM

Total sites: 5, RV sites: 5, Elec sites: 0, No water, Vault toilets, Max length: 50ft, Generator hours: 0800-2000, Reservations accepted, Open all year, Group site: $130-$150, Stay limit: 14 days, Elev: 5420ft/1652m, Tel: 435-259-2102, Nearest town: Moab, Agency: BLM, GPS: 38.635573, -109.805141

33592 • Lone Warrior Dispersed - BLM

Dispersed sites, No water, No toilets, Tents only: Free, Elev: 7047ft/2148m, Nearest town: Green River, Agency: BLM, GPS: 38.851844, -110.799542

33593 • Lonesome Beaver - BLM

Total sites: 5, RV sites: 0, Elec sites: 0, No water, Vault toilets, Open May-Oct, Tents only: Donation, Rough road - high clearance vehicles with 4x4 recommended, Elev: 5489ft/1673m, Tel: 435-542-3461, Nearest town: Hanksville, Agency: BLM, GPS: 38.197021, -110.747314

33594 • Long Canyon Dispersed - BLM

Dispersed sites, No water, No toilets, Tent & RV camping: Free, Elev: 5870ft/1789m, Nearest town: Moab, Agency: BLM, GPS: 38.541811, -109.707506

33595 • Long Park Reservoir - USFS

Dispersed sites, No water, Vault toilets, Tent & RV camping: Free, Elev: 9983ft/3043m, Nearest town: Vernal, Agency: USFS, GPS: 40.774065, -109.764931

33596 • Long Park Reservoir Dispersed - USFS

Dispersed sites, No water, No toilets, Reservations not accepted, Open all year, Tent & RV camping: Free, Elev: 8684ft/2647m, Tel: 435-789-1181, Nearest town: Manila, Agency: USFS, GPS: 40.904801, -109.880743

33597 • Long Valley Recreation Area - BLM

Dispersed sites, No water, No toilets, Reservations not accepted, Tent & RV camping: Free, High clearance vehicle recommended - RV-accessible when dry, Elev: 2707ft/825m, Nearest town: St. George, Agency: BLM, GPS: 37.111014, -113.439026

33598 • Loop - USFS

Total sites: 13, RV sites: 13, Elec sites: 0, No water, Reservations not accepted, Tent & RV camping: $14, Stay limit: 7 days, Elev: 7342ft/2238m, Tel: 801-733-2660, Nearest town: Salt Lake City, Agency: USFS, GPS: 40.484071, -112.606085

33599 • Losee Canyon Dispersed - USFS

Dispersed sites, No water, No toilets, Reservations not accepted, Tent & RV camping: Free, Elev: 7015ft/2138m, Tel: 435-623-1959, Nearest town: Panguitch, Agency: USFS, GPS: 37.770418, -112.346685

33600 • Losee Canyon Dispersed - USFS

Dispersed sites, No water, No toilets, Reservations not accepted, Tent & RV camping: Free, Elev: 7094ft/2162m, Tel: 435-623-1959, Nearest town: Panguitch, Agency: USFS, GPS: 37.768522, -112.338074

33601 • Lost Creek - USFS

Total sites: 35, RV sites: 35, Elec sites: 0, Central water, No RV dump, No showers, Vault toilets, Reservations accepted, Open Jun-Sep, Tent & RV camping: $23, Stay limit: 7 days, Elev: 9987ft/3044m, Tel: 801-226-3564, Nearest town: Kamas, Agency: USFS, GPS: 40.680914, -110.933045

33602 • Lower Bowns - USFS
Total sites: 2, RV sites: 2, Elec sites: 0, No water, No RV dump, No showers, Vault toilets, Reservation required, Tent & RV camping: $12, 1 Group site $45, Elev: 7434ft/2266m, Tel: 435-836-2811, Nearest town: Torrey, Agency: USFS, GPS: 38.106131, -111.276529

33603 • Lower Box Creek TH - USFS
Dispersed sites, No water, Vault toilets, Tent & RV camping: Free, Elev: 7190ft/2192m, Tel: 435-896-9233, Nearest town: Greenwich, Agency: USFS, GPS: 38.447013, -111.962615

33604 • Lower Canyon - USFS
Total sites: 6, RV sites: 6, Elec sites: 0, No water, No toilets, Tent & RV camping: Free, Elev: 7128ft/2173m, Tel: 435-783-4338, Nearest town: Kamas, Agency: USFS, GPS: 40.628795, -111.177702

33605 • Lower Farnsworth - USFS
Dispersed sites, No water, Vault toilets, Tent & RV camping: Free, Elev: 9393ft/2863m, Tel: 435-896-9233, Nearest town: Salina, Agency: USFS, GPS: 38.774004, -111.649085

33606 • Lower Little Bear - USFS
Total sites: 2, RV sites: 2, Elec sites: 0, Central water, Vault toilets, Reservations not accepted, Open May-Sep, Group site: $30-$50, Elev: 7234ft/2205m, Tel: 435-636-3500, Nearest town: Huntington, Agency: USFS, GPS: 39.443489, -111.136542

33607 • Lower Meadows - USFS
Total sites: 25, RV sites: 25, Elec sites: 0, Central water, No RV dump, No showers, Vault toilets, Generator hours: 0800-2200, Reservations accepted, Open May-Sep, Tent & RV camping: $23, Elev: 5325ft/1623m, Tel: 801-999-2103, Nearest town: Ogden, Agency: USFS, GPS: 41.286621, -111.645264

33608 • Lower Narrows - USFS
Total sites: 3, RV sites: 3, Elec sites: 0, No water, No toilets, Reservations not accepted, Tent & RV camping: $14, Stay limit: 7 days, Elev: 6890ft/2100m, Tel: 801-733-2660, Nearest town: Stockton, Agency: USFS, GPS: 40.491621, -112.591882

33609 • Lower Onion Creek - BLM
Total sites: 21, RV sites: 21, Elec sites: 0, No water, Vault toilets, Max length: 24ft, Reservations not accepted, Open all year, Tent & RV camping: $20, Group site $60, Stay limit: 14 days, Elev: 4093ft/1248m, Tel: 435-259-2100, Nearest town: Moab, Agency: BLM, GPS: 38.737172, -109.358436

33610 • Lower Provo River - USFS
Total sites: 10, RV sites: 10, Elec sites: 0, Central water, No RV dump, No showers, Vault toilets, Reservations not accepted, Open May-Oct, Tent & RV camping: $18, Stay limit: 7 days, Elev: 7418ft/2261m, Tel: 435-783-4338, Nearest town: Kamas, Agency: USFS, GPS: 40.593111, -111.116683

33611 • Lucerne Valley - USFS
Total sites: 143, RV sites: 143, Elec sites: 75, Central water, RV dump, Showers, Flush toilets, Max length: 45ft, Reservations accepted, Open Apr-Sep, Tent & RV camping: $20, Group site: $140, Elev: 6066ft/1849m, Tel: 435-784-3445, Nearest town: Manila, Agency: USFS, GPS: 40.983541, -109.591715

33612 • Lucky Strike Mine Dispersed - BLM
Dispersed sites, No water, No toilets, Tents only: Free, Elev: 5650ft/1722m, Nearest town: Green River, Agency: BLM, GPS: 38.736217, -110.965392

33613 • Lyman Lake - USFS
Dispersed sites, No water, No toilets, Tent & RV camping: Free, Elev: 9323ft/2842m, Nearest town: Mountain View, Agency: USFS, GPS: 40.937761, -110.610365

33614 • Mackinaw - USFS
Total sites: 44, RV sites: 44, Elec sites: 0, Central water, No RV dump, Showers, Flush toilets, Generator hours: 0600-2200, Reservations accepted, Open May-Sep, Tent & RV camping: $15, 4 group sites: $30, Stay limit: 10 days, Elev: 8914ft/2717m, Tel: 435-638-1069, Nearest town: Loa, Agency: USFS, GPS: 38.55542, -111.716797

33615 • Magpie - USFS
Total sites: 16, RV sites: 16, Elec sites: 0, Central water, No RV dump, No showers, Vault toilets, Generator hours: 0800-2200, Reservations not accepted, Open May-Dec, Tent & RV camping: $20, Elev: 5256ft/1602m, Tel: 801-625-5112, Nearest town: Ogden, Agency: USFS, GPS: 41.270437, -111.666087

33616 • Mahogany Cove - USFS
Total sites: 7, RV sites: 7, Elec sites: 0, Potable water, No RV dump, No showers, Vault toilets, Reservations not accepted, Open May-Sep, Tent & RV camping: $12, Group site $70, Individual sites available if no group use, Elev: 7526ft/2294m, Tel: 435-438-2436, Nearest town: Beaver, Agency: USFS, GPS: 38.269364, -112.485762

33617 • Mallard Bay Overflow - USFS
Dispersed sites, No water, Vault toilets, Reservations not accepted, Open May-Sep, Tent & RV camping: $15, Open only when all the campgrounds at Fish Lake are full, Elev: 8863ft/2701m, Tel: 435-638-1069, Nearest town: Richfield, Agency: USFS, GPS: 38.528468, -111.735836

33618 • Mammoth Springs Dispersed - USFS
Dispersed sites, No water, No toilets, Reservations not accepted, Tent & RV camping: Free, Elev: 8251ft/2515m, Tel: 435-865-3200, Nearest town: Duck Creek, Agency: USFS, GPS: 37.637845, -112.671877

33619 • Manganese Wash Dispersed - BLM
Dispersed sites, No water, No toilets, Reservations not accepted, Tent & RV camping: Free, High clearance vehicle required for river sites, Elev: 3495ft/1065m, Nearest town: Dammeron, Agency: BLM, GPS: 37.233899, -113.778946

33620 • Manning Meadow - USFS
Dispersed sites, No water, No toilets, Tent & RV camping: Free, Elev: 9786ft/2983m, Tel: 435-896-9233, Nearest town: Greenwich, Agency: USFS, GPS: 38.484985, -112.073891

33621 • Manning Meadow Reservoir - DWR Trap Station

Dispersed sites, No water, No toilets, Reservations not accepted, Tents only: Free, Elev: 9780ft/2981m, Tel: 801-538-4700, Nearest town: Greenwich, Agency: ST, GPS: 38.488836, -112.073683

33622 • Manning Meadow Reservoir - Primitive Ramp - DWR

Dispersed sites, No water, No toilets, Reservations not accepted, Tents only: Free, Elev: 8766ft/2672m, Tel: 801-538-4700, Nearest town: Greenwich, Agency: ST, GPS: 38.491628, -112.071443

33623 • Manns - USFS

Total sites: 8, RV sites: 8, Elec sites: 0, No water, Vault toilets, Reservations not accepted, Open Apr-Sep, Tent & RV camping: $12, Elev: 6158ft/1877m, Tel: 435-784-3445, Nearest town: Manila, Agency: USFS, GPS: 40.924857, -109.709071

33624 • Manti Community - USFS

Total sites: 8, RV sites: 8, Elec sites: 0, No water, No RV dump, No showers, Vault toilets, Reservations accepted, Open May-Oct, Tent & RV camping: $10, 1 group site $40, Elev: 7512ft/2290m, Tel: 435-283-4151, Nearest town: Manti, Agency: USFS, GPS: 39.253668, -111.541328

33625 • Maple Bench - USFS

Total sites: 10, RV sites: 10, Elec sites: 0, Central water, No RV dump, No showers, Vault toilets, Reservations not accepted, Open May-Oct, Tent & RV camping: $21, Stay limit: 16 days, Elev: 5899ft/1798m, Tel: 801-798-3571, Nearest town: Payson, Agency: USFS, GPS: 39.962981, -111.691831

33626 • Maple Canyon - USFS

Total sites: 12, RV sites: 12, Elec sites: 0, No water, Vault toilets, Reservations accepted, Open May-Sep, Tent & RV camping: $10, Group site: $40, Elev: 7041ft/2146m, Tel: 435-637-2817, Nearest town: Moroni, Agency: USFS, GPS: 39.556338, -111.686537

33627 • Maple Grove - USFS

Total sites: 16, RV sites: 16, Elec sites: 0, Central water, No RV dump, No showers, Vault toilets, Reservations not accepted, Open May-Sep, Tent & RV camping: $15, Reservable group site: $50-$90, Elev: 6499ft/1981m, Tel: 435-743-5721, Nearest town: Scipio, Agency: USFS, GPS: 39.016557, -112.089458

33628 • Maple Hollow - USFS

Total sites: 6, RV sites: 4, Elec sites: 0, Central water, No RV dump, No showers, Vault toilets, Reservations not accepted, Open May-Sep, Tent & RV camping: Free, Elev: 7031ft/2143m, Tel: 435-743-5721, Nearest town: Holden, Agency: USFS, GPS: 39.061151, -112.170831

33629 • Maple Lake - USFS

Total sites: 7, RV sites: 7, Elec sites: 0, No water, Vault toilets, Reservations not accepted, Open May-Oct, Tent & RV camping: $21, Stay limit: 16 days, Elev: 6447ft/1965m, Tel: 801-798-3571, Nearest town: Payson, Agency: USFS, GPS: 39.957, -111.693

33630 • Maples - USFS

Dispersed sites, No water, No toilets, Reservations not accepted, Tents only: Free, Walk-to sites, All picnic tables/firerings/restrooms have been removed, May still camp in the area but must camp away from the trail that goes through the site. All access is walk-ins/bicycles/horses only - no motor vehicles, Approximately 1/2 mile from the gate., Elev: 6332ft/1930m, Nearest town: Ogden, Agency: USFS, GPS: 41.227295, -111.86499

33631 • Marsh Lake - USFS

Total sites: 28, RV sites: 28, Elec sites: 0, Central water, Vault toilets, Reservations accepted, Open May-Sep, Tent & RV camping: $21, Group site: $60, Dump station 1.5 mile at Stateline Reservoir, Stay limit: 14 days, Elev: 9383ft/2860m, Tel: 307-782-6555, Nearest town: Mountain View, Agency: USFS, GPS: 40.952145, -110.395835

33632 • Mason Draw - USFS

Total sites: 5, RV sites: 5, Elec sites: 0, No water, Vault toilets, Reservations not accepted, Open May-Sep, Tent & RV camping: $5, Elev: 8268ft/2520m, Tel: 435-637-2817, Nearest town: Moab, Agency: USFS, GPS: 38.543, -109.303

33633 • Massey Meadow Dispersed - USFS

Dispersed sites, No water, Vault toilets, Reservations not accepted, Tent & RV camping: Free, Elev: 7782ft/2372m, Tel: 435-789-1181, Nearest town: Vernal, Agency: USFS, GPS: 40.625246, -109.786558

33634 • McCook Ridge 1 - BLM

Dispersed sites, No water, No toilets, Tent & RV camping: Free, Elev: 7101ft/2164m, Nearest town: Thompson, Agency: BLM, GPS: 39.622204, -109.230632

33635 • McCook Ridge 2 - BLM

Dispersed sites, No water, No toilets, Tent & RV camping: Free, Elev: 7306ft/2227m, Nearest town: Thompson, Agency: BLM, GPS: 39.601343, -109.204659

33636 • McMillan Spring - BLM

Total sites: 10, RV sites: 10, Elec sites: 0, Central water, No RV dump, No showers, Vault toilets, Reservations not accepted, Tent & RV camping: Donation, Elev: 8412ft/2564m, Tel: 435-542-3461, Nearest town: Hanksville, Agency: BLM, GPS: 38.072626, -110.848074

33637 • Meeks Cabin - USFS

Total sites: 24, RV sites: 24, Elec sites: 0, Potable water, No RV dump, No showers, Vault toilets, Reservations not accepted, Tent & RV camping: $24, Stay limit: 14 days, Elev: 8714ft/2656m, Tel: 307-789-3194, Nearest town: Mountain View, Agency: USFS, GPS: 41.006266, -110.584071

33638 • Mexican Hat Dispersed - BLM

Dispersed sites, No water, No toilets, Reservations not accepted, Tent & RV camping: Free, Numerous sites in area, Elev: 4234ft/1291m, Nearest town: Mexican Hat, Agency: BLM, GPS: 37.171099, -109.849266

33639 • Middle Canyon 1
Dispersed sites, No water, No toilets, Reservations accepted, Tent & RV camping: $10, Elev: 6181ft/1884m, Tel: 435-882-9041, Nearest town: Tooele, Agency: CP, GPS: 40.502952, -112.226856

33640 • Middle Canyon 2
Dispersed sites, No water, No toilets, Reservations accepted, Tent & RV camping: $10, Elev: 6240ft/1902m, Tel: 435-882-9041, Nearest town: Tooele, Agency: CP, GPS: 40.501192, -112.221205

33641 • Middle Canyon 3
Dispersed sites, No water, No toilets, Reservations accepted, Tent & RV camping: $10, Elev: 6425ft/1958m, Tel: 435-882-9041, Nearest town: Tooele, Agency: CP, GPS: 40.495925, -112.216879

33642 • Middle Canyon 4
Dispersed sites, No water, No toilets, Reservations accepted, Tent & RV camping: $10, Elev: 6499ft/1981m, Tel: 435-882-9041, Nearest town: Tooele, Agency: CP, GPS: 40.493478, -112.210995

33643 • Middle Canyon 5
Dispersed sites, No water, No toilets, Reservations accepted, Tent & RV camping: $10, Elev: 6661ft/2030m, Tel: 435-882-9041, Nearest town: Tooele, Agency: CP, GPS: 40.490537, -112.201228

33644 • Middle Canyon 6
Dispersed sites, No water, No toilets, Reservations accepted, Tent & RV camping: $10, Elev: 6822ft/2079m, Tel: 435-882-9041, Nearest town: Tooele, Agency: CP, GPS: 40.487321, -112.193858

33645 • Mill Canyon - BLM
Dispersed sites, No water, No toilets, Reservations not accepted, Tent & RV camping: Free, Elev: 4555ft/1388m, Tel: 435-259-2100, Nearest town: Moab, Agency: BLM, GPS: 38.712414, -109.739554

33646 • Mill Flat Dispersed - USFS
Dispersed sites, No water, Vault toilets, Reservations not accepted, Tent & RV camping: Free, Elev: 7549ft/2301m, Tel: 435-738-2482, Nearest town: Hanna, Agency: USFS, GPS: 40.559061, -110.887916

33647 • Mill Hollow - USFS
Total sites: 26, RV sites: 15, Elec sites: 0, Central water, No RV dump, No showers, Vault toilets, Max length: 16ft, Reservations accepted, Open Jun-Oct, Tent & RV camping: $21, Stay limit: 7 days, Elev: 8842ft/2695m, Tel: 801-226-3564, Nearest town: Woodland, Agency: USFS, GPS: 40.490514, -111.103721

33648 • Millsite SP
Total sites: 20, RV sites: 20, Elec sites: 10, Water at site, RV dump, Showers, Flush toilets, Max length: 46ft, Reservations accepted, Open all year, Tents: $20/RV's: $20-25, Elev: 6211ft/1893m, Tel: 435-384-2552, Nearest town: Ferron, Agency: ST, GPS: 39.092146, -111.194186

33649 • Milo's Kitchen TH - USFS
Dispersed sites, No water, Vault toilets, Tent & RV camping: Free, Elev: 8728ft/2660m, Tel: 435-896-9233, Nearest town: Greenwich, Agency: USFS, GPS: 38.533328, -111.953108

33650 • Mineral Point Road - BLM
Total sites: 7, RV sites: 2, Elec sites: 0, No water, No toilets, Open all year, Tent & RV camping: Free, Elev: 5775ft/1760m, Nearest town: Moab, Agency: BLM, GPS: 38.585247, -109.826302

33651 • Miners Gulch Group - USFS
Total sites: 1, RV sites: 1, Elec sites: 0, No water, Vault toilets, Open May-Sep, Group site: $25, Elev: 7523ft/2293m, Tel: 435-738-2482, Nearest town: Duchesne, Agency: USFS, GPS: 40.534601, -110.622703

33652 • Minersville Reservoir - Eastside Access - DWR
Dispersed sites, No water, No toilets, Reservations not accepted, Tents only: Free, High-clearance vehicle recommended, Elev: 5544ft/1690m, Tel: 801-538-4700, Nearest town: Minersville, Agency: ST, GPS: 38.227331, -112.814007

33653 • Minersville Reservoir CP
Total sites: 56, RV sites: 30, Elec sites: 30, Central water, RV dump, Showers, Flush toilets, Max length: 30ft, Reservations accepted, Open all year, Tents: $10/RV's: $20, 1/2 price Nov-Mar - restrooms closed, Elev: 5522ft/1683m, Tel: 435-438-5472, Nearest town: Minersville, Agency: CP, GPS: 38.218963, -112.828197

33654 • Mirror Lake - USFS
Total sites: 78, RV sites: 78, Elec sites: 0, No water, Vault toilets, Reservations accepted, Open Jul-Sep, Tent & RV camping: $23, Stay limit: 7 days, Elev: 10016ft/3053m, Tel: 435-783-4338, Nearest town: Kamas, Agency: USFS, GPS: 40.700684, -110.884277

33655 • Monte Cristo - USFS
Total sites: 45, RV sites: 45, Elec sites: 0, Central water, No RV dump, No showers, Flush toilets, Max length: 39ft, Reservations not accepted, Open Jun-Sep, Tent & RV camping: $23, 2 reservable group sites: $210, Stay limit: 7 days, Elev: 8909ft/2715m, Tel: 801-625-5112, Nearest town: Woodruff, Agency: USFS, GPS: 41.462959, -111.497642

33656 • Monticello Lake - USFS
Dispersed sites, No water, Vault toilets, Max length: 25ft, Tent & RV camping: Free, Elev: 8625ft/2629m, Nearest town: Monticello, Agency: USFS, GPS: 37.894702, -109.469101

33657 • Moon Lake - USFS
Total sites: 54, RV sites: 54, Elec sites: 0, Central water, No RV dump, No showers, Flush toilets, Max length: 22ft, Reservations accepted, Open May-Sep, Tent & RV camping: $20, Elev: 8150ft/2484m, Tel: 435-738-2482, Nearest town: Duchesne, Agency: USFS, GPS: 40.569092, -110.510254

33658 • Moon Lake Group- USFS
Total sites: 2, Elec sites: 0, Central water, No RV dump, No showers, Flush toilets, Reservations accepted, Open May-Sep,

Group site: $100, Elev: 8169ft/2490m, Tel: 435-738-2482, Nearest town: Duchesne, Agency: USFS, GPS: 40.567416, -110.503834

33659 • Moonflower Canyon - BLM
Total sites: 1, RV sites: 0, Elec sites: 0, No water, Vault toilets, Reservations not accepted, Group site: $75-$100, Stay limit: 14 days, Elev: 3974ft/1211m, Tel: 435-259-2100, Nearest town: Moab, Agency: BLM, GPS: 38.554167, -109.586954

33660 • Moosehorn - USFS
Total sites: 33, RV sites: 33, Elec sites: 0, No water, No RV dump, No showers, Vault toilets, Reservations accepted, Open Jul-Sep, Tent & RV camping: $23, Stay limit: 7 days, Elev: 10312ft/3143m, Tel: 435-783-4338, Nearest town: Kamas, Agency: USFS, GPS: 40.697266, -110.891846

33661 • Morrell Pond Eastside - USFS
Dispersed sites, No water, Vault toilets, Reservations not accepted, Tent & RV camping: Free, Road not maintained for passenger cars, Elev: 7992ft/2436m, Tel: 435-896-9233, Nearest town: Lyman, Agency: USFS, GPS: 38.547732, -111.436641

33662 • Morrell Pond Westside - USFS
Dispersed sites, No water, Vault toilets, Reservations not accepted, Tent & RV camping: Free, Road not maintained for passenger cars, Elev: 7996ft/2437m, Tel: 435-896-9233, Nearest town: Lyman, Agency: USFS, GPS: 38.547916, -111.438354

33663 • Mount Timpanogos - USFS
Total sites: 27, RV sites: 27, Elec sites: 0, Central water, No RV dump, No showers, Flush toilets, Max length: 20ft, Reservations accepted, Open Jun-Oct, Tent & RV camping: $24, Stay limit: 7 days, Elev: 6920ft/2109m, Tel: 801-885-7391, Nearest town: Orem, Agency: USFS, GPS: 40.406083, -111.606289

33664 • Mouth of Blacksmith Fork Canyon FA - DWR
Dispersed sites, No water, No toilets, Reservations not accepted, Tents only: Free, Elev: 4754ft/1449m, Tel: 801-538-4700, Nearest town: Hyrum, Agency: ST, GPS: 41.627245, -111.800687

33665 • Mt Carmel - BLM
Dispersed sites, No water, No toilets, Tent & RV camping: Free, Elev: 5500ft/1676m, Nearest town: Kanab, Agency: BLM, GPS: 37.207169, -112.675418

33666 • Mt Carmel Jct ATV - BLM
Dispersed sites, No water, No toilets, Tent & RV camping: Free, Elev: 5177ft/1578m, Nearest town: Mt Carmel, Agency: BLM, GPS: 37.215127, -112.684982

33667 • Mud Springs Plateau - BLM
Dispersed sites, No water, No toilets, Tent & RV camping: Free, Elev: 5699ft/1737m, Nearest town: Wellington, Agency: BLM, GPS: 39.513338, -110.518894

33668 • Muley Point - BLM
Dispersed sites, No water, No toilets, Reservations not accepted, Tent & RV camping: Free, 5-mile dirt road, Elev: 6194ft/1888m,

Nearest town: Mexican Hat, Agency: BLM, GPS: 37.235377, -109.992191

33669 • Murdock Basin - USFS
Dispersed sites, No water, No toilets, Tents only: Free, Elev: 8202ft/2500m, Nearest town: Kamas, Agency: USFS, GPS: 40.624602, -110.891116

33670 • Murdock Basin ATV TH Dispersed - USFS
Dispersed sites, No water, No toilets, Reservations not accepted, Open all year, Tent & RV camping: Free, Elev: 9316ft/2840m, Tel: 435-783-4338, Nearest town: Oakley, Agency: USFS, GPS: 40.633222, -110.933205

33671 • Mustang Ridge - USFS
Total sites: 70, RV sites: 70, Elec sites: 0, Central water, No RV dump, Showers, Flush toilets, Max length: 45ft, Reservations accepted, Open May-Sep, Tent & RV camping: $25, Group site: $140, Elev: 6109ft/1862m, Tel: 435-889-3000, Nearest town: Dutch John, Agency: USFS, GPS: 40.927246, -109.439941

33672 • Natural Bridges NM
Total sites: 13, RV sites: 13, Elec sites: 0, No water, Vault toilets, Max length: 26ft, Reservations not accepted, Open all year, Tent & RV camping: $15, Water available 1/2 mile at Visitor Center - 5 gal/person/day limit, Elev: 6476ft/1974m, Tel: 435-692-1234, Nearest town: Blanding, Agency: NP, GPS: 37.60956, -109.98434

33673 • Navajo Lake - USFS
Total sites: 27, RV sites: 16, Elec sites: 0, Central water, No RV dump, No showers, Flush toilets, Max length: 22ft, Reservations not accepted, Open May-Oct, Tent & RV camping: $17, Elev: 9094ft/2772m, Tel: 435-865-3200, Nearest town: Cedar City, Agency: USFS, GPS: 37.520709, -112.789445

33674 • Nebo Loop Rd - USFS
Dispersed sites, No water, No toilets, Tent & RV camping: Fee unk, Elev: 6176ft/1882m, Tel: 801-798-3571, Nearest town: Nephi, Agency: USFS, GPS: 39.736591, -111.757789

33675 • Nefertiti Rapids - BLM
Dispersed sites, No water, Vault toilets, Tent & RV camping: Free, Elev: 4163ft/1269m, Nearest town: Green River, Agency: BLM, GPS: 39.195279, -110.077249

33676 • Newcastle Reservoir - DWR
Dispersed sites, No water, No toilets, Reservations not accepted, Tent & RV camping: Free, Elev: 5485ft/1672m, Nearest town: Newcastle, Agency: ST, GPS: 37.648156, -113.527074

33677 • Newton Reservoir - BOR
Dispersed sites, No toilets, Open May-Oct, Tent & RV camping: Free, Stay limit: 14 days, Elev: 4780ft/1457m, Tel: 801-379-1000, Nearest town: Newton, Agency: BR, GPS: 41.89686, -111.97806

33678 • Niotche Creek TH - USFS
Dispersed sites, No water, Vault toilets, Tent & RV camping: Free, Elev: 8954ft/2729m, Tel: 435-896-9233, Nearest town: Salina, Agency: USFS, GPS: 38.784966, -111.634846

33679 • Nizhoni - USFS

Total sites: 25, RV sites: 25, Elec sites: 0, Central water, No RV dump, No showers, Vault toilets, Reservations accepted, Open May-Oct, Tent & RV camping: $10, 2 group sites: $50, Elev: 7812ft/2381m, Tel: 435-587-2041, Nearest town: Blanding, Agency: USFS, GPS: 37.781, -109.539

33680 • North End Rd Dispersed - USFS

Dispersed sites, No water, No toilets, Reservations not accepted, Open all year, Tent & RV camping: Free, Elev: 7780ft/2371m, Nearest town: Moab, Agency: USFS, GPS: 38.602671, -109.254612

33681 • North End Rd Dispersed - USFS

Dispersed sites, No water, No toilets, Reservations not accepted, Open all year, Tent & RV camping: Free, Elev: 8065ft/2458m, Nearest town: Moab, Agency: USFS, GPS: 38.610586, -109.242991

33682 • North Fork CP - Cold Water Canyon

Total sites: 18, RV sites: 18, Elec sites: 0, Central water, RV dump, Flush toilets, Reservations not accepted, Open May-Oct, Tent & RV camping: $20, Elev: 5831ft/1777m, Tel: 801-399-8230, Nearest town: Eden, Agency: CP, GPS: 41.371407, -111.916345

33683 • North Fork CP - Corral

Total sites: 16, RV sites: 16, Elec sites: 0, Central water, RV dump, No showers, Flush toilets, Reservations not accepted, Open May-Oct, Tent & RV camping: $20, 1 group site: $60, Elev: 5766ft/1757m, Tel: 801-399-8230, Nearest town: Eden, Agency: CP, GPS: 41.370469, -111.910451

33684 • North Fork CP - Cutler Flats

Total sites: 12, RV sites: 12, Elec sites: 0, Central water, RV dump, No showers, Flush toilets, Reservations not accepted, Open May-Oct, Tent & RV camping: $20, 2 group sites: $110, Elev: 5899ft/1798m, Tel: 801-399-8230, Nearest town: Eden, Agency: CP, GPS: 41.385477, -111.919158

33685 • North Fork CP - Loop A

Total sites: 42, RV sites: 42, Elec sites: 0, Central water, RV dump, No showers, Flush toilets, Reservations not accepted, Open May-Oct, Tent & RV camping: $20, 1 group site: $110, Elev: 5652ft/1723m, Tel: 801-399-8230, Nearest town: Eden, Agency: CP, GPS: 41.368738, -111.904562

33686 • North Fork CP - Loop B

Total sites: 26, RV sites: 26, Elec sites: 0, Central water, RV dump, No showers, Flush toilets, Reservations not accepted, Open May-Oct, Tent & RV camping: $20, Elev: 5697ft/1736m, Tel: 801-399-8230, Nearest town: Eden, Agency: CP, GPS: 41.369094, -111.907698

33687 • North Fork CP - Middle Gate

Total sites: 15, RV sites: 15, Elec sites: 0, Central water, RV dump, No showers, Flush toilets, Reservations not accepted, Open May-Oct, Tent & RV camping: $20, Elev: 5444ft/1659m, Tel: 801-399-8230, Nearest town: Eden, Agency: CP, GPS: 41.373576, -111.896391

33688 • North Fork CP - Mustang Flats

Total sites: 13, RV sites: 13, Elec sites: 0, Central water, RV dump, No showers, Flush toilets, Reservations not accepted, Open May-Oct, Tent & RV camping: $20, Elev: 5632ft/1717m, Tel: 801-399-8230, Nearest town: Eden, Agency: CP, GPS: 41.372166, -111.904152

33689 • North Fork Dispersed - USFS

Dispersed sites, No water, Vault toilets, Reservations not accepted, Open all year, Tent & RV camping: Free, Both sides of road, Elev: 9308ft/2837m, Tel: 435-789-1181, Nearest town: Vernal, Agency: USFS, GPS: 40.743396, -109.681979

33690 • North Iron Springs Dispersed Group - USFS

Dispersed sites, No water, Vault toilets, Max length: 25ft, Group site, Elev: 8740ft/2664m, Tel: 435-789-1181, Nearest town: Vernal, Agency: USFS, GPS: 40.703563, -109.556212

33691 • North Skyline Winter Staging Snowpark - USFS

Dispersed sites, No water, No toilets, Reservations not accepted, Open all year, Tent & RV camping: Free, Elev: 8859ft/2700m, Tel: 435-637-2817, Nearest town: Fairview, Agency: USFS, GPS: 39.678818, -111.313046

33692 • Notom Rd - BLM

Dispersed sites, No water, No toilets, Tent & RV camping: Free, Steep road, Elev: 5178ft/1578m, Nearest town: Hanksville, Agency: BLM, GPS: 38.278062, -111.130572

33693 • Nunns County Park

Total sites: 19, RV sites: 19, Reservations not accepted, Tent & RV camping: $20, 2-night limit for tenters, Stay limit: 7 days, Elev: 5020ft/1530m, Tel: 801-851-8600, Nearest town: Orem, Agency: CP, GPS: 40.328871, -111.620593

33694 • Oak Creek - USFS

Total sites: 9, RV sites: 9, Elec sites: 0, Central water, No RV dump, No showers, Vault toilets, Max length: 25ft, Generator hours: 0600-2200, Reservations not accepted, Open May-Sep, Tent & RV camping: $12, Elev: 8888ft/2709m, Tel: 435-896-9233, Nearest town: Teasdale, Agency: USFS, GPS: 38.088834, -111.342031

33695 • Oak Creek - USFS

Total sites: 10, RV sites: 7, Elec sites: 0, Central water, No RV dump, No showers, Vault toilets, Generator hours: 0600-2200, Reservations accepted, Open May-Sep, Tent & RV camping: $12, 4 group sites: $30-$60, Stay limit: 14 days, Elev: 6061ft/1847m, Tel: 435-743-5721, Nearest town: Oak City, Agency: USFS, GPS: 39.352459, -112.260743

33696 • Oak Grove - BLM

Total sites: 7, RV sites: 3, Elec sites: 0, No water, Vault toilets, Max length: 18ft, Reservations not accepted, Open all year, Tent & RV camping: $20, Also walk-to sites, 4 walk-to sites, Stay limit: 14 days, Elev: 4029ft/1228m, Tel: 435-259-2100, Nearest town: Moab, Agency: BLM, GPS: 38.643624, -109.476348

33697 • Oak Grove - USFS

Total sites: 7, RV sites: 5, Elec sites: 0, No water, Vault toilets, Reservations not accepted, Open May-Oct, Tent & RV camping: $2-4, Elev: 6528ft/1990m, Tel: 435-652-3100, Nearest town: Leeds, Agency: USFS, GPS: 37.316862, -113.452991

33698 • Oak Ridge TH - USFS

Dispersed sites, No water, Vault toilets, Reservations not accepted, Tent & RV camping: Free, Elev: 8692ft/2649m, Tel: 435-896-9233, Nearest town: Salina, Agency: USFS, GPS: 38.833606, -111.665573

33699 • Oaks Park - USFS

Total sites: 11, RV sites: 11, Elec sites: 0, Central water, Vault toilets, Max length: 20ft, Reservations not accepted, Open Jun-Sep, Tent & RV camping: Free, Elev: 9262ft/2823m, Tel: 435-789-1181, Nearest town: Vernal, Agency: USFS, GPS: 40.742089, -109.623605

33700 • Ogden River Middle Fork - County

Dispersed sites, No water, Vault toilets, Open Apr-Dec, Tent & RV camping: Free, Elev: 5072ft/1546m, Nearest town: Eden, Agency: CP, GPS: 41.295605, -111.754967

33701 • Old Folks Flat - USFS

Total sites: 8, RV sites: 8, Elec sites: 0, Central water, No RV dump, No showers, Flush toilets, Reservations accepted, Open May-Oct, Tent & RV camping: $10, 5 reservable group sites: $30-$75, Elev: 8123ft/2476m, Tel: 801-756-8616, Nearest town: Huntington, Agency: USFS, GPS: 39.539, -111.159

33702 • Old Quarry - USFS

Dispersed sites, No water, No toilets, Tent & RV camping: Free, Elev: 7207ft/2197m, Tel: 435-889-3000, Nearest town: Vernal, Agency: USFS, GPS: 40.875573, -109.463932

33703 • Oowah - USFS

Total sites: 11, RV sites: 0, Elec sites: 0, No water, No RV dump, No showers, Vault toilets, Reservations not accepted, Open Jun-Sep, Tents only: $5, Elev: 8842ft/2695m, Nearest town: Moab, Agency: USFS, GPS: 38.502671, -109.272236

33704 • Ophir Canyon

Total sites: 10, RV sites: 10, Elec sites: 0, No water, No RV dump, No showers, Vault toilets, Reservations accepted, Tent & RV camping: $10, Elev: 6588ft/2008m, Tel: 435-882-9041, Nearest town: Tooele, Agency: CP, GPS: 40.373555, -112.244614

33705 • Otter Creek Reservoir - Fisherman's Bench - BLM

Dispersed sites, No water, No toilets, Tent & RV camping: Free, Elev: 6417ft/1956m, Tel: 435-896-1500, Nearest town: Antimony, Agency: BLM, GPS: 38.180109, -112.012049

33706 • Otter Creek SP - Beach

Total sites: 7, RV sites: 7, Central water, RV dump, Showers, Flush toilets, Max length: 45ft, Reservations accepted, Open all year, Tent & RV camping: $30, Elev: 6388ft/1947m, Tel: 435-624-3268, Nearest town: Antimony, Agency: ST, GPS: 38.167351, -112.019029

33707 • Otter Creek SP - Main CG

Total sites: 53, RV sites: 53, Elec sites: 0, Central water, RV dump, Showers, Flush toilets, Max length: 45ft, Reservations accepted, Open all year, Tent & RV camping: $20, Elev: 6365ft/1940m, Tel: 435-624-3268, Nearest town: Antimony, Agency: ST, GPS: 38.166294, -112.016709

33708 • Pack Creek Dispersed - USFS

Dispersed sites, No water, Vault toilets, Tent & RV camping: Free, Elev: 6464ft/1970m, Nearest town: Spanish Valley, Agency: USFS, GPS: 38.433554, -109.335957

33709 • Palisade SP - Arapeen

Total sites: 22, RV sites: 22, Elec sites: 1, Central water, RV dump, Showers, Flush toilets, Max length: 55ft, Reservations accepted, Open all year, Tents: $25/RV's: $25-30, Elev: 5896ft/1797m, Tel: 435-835-7275, Nearest town: Sterling, Agency: ST, GPS: 39.208496, -111.667195

33710 • Palisade SP - Pioneer

Total sites: 8, RV sites: 8, Elec sites: 0, RV dump, Showers, Flush toilets, Reservations accepted, Open all year, Tent & RV camping: $25, Elev: 5912ft/1802m, Tel: 435-835-7275, Nearest town: Sterling, Agency: ST, GPS: 39.205657, -111.665768

33711 • Palisade SP - Sanpitch

Total sites: 21, RV sites: 21, Elec sites: 7, Water at site, RV dump, Showers, Flush toilets, Max length: 35ft, Reservations accepted, Open all year, Tents: $25/RV's: $25-30, 7 FHU, Elev: 5886ft/1794m, Tel: 435-835-7275, Nearest town: Sterling, Agency: ST, GPS: 39.202161, -111.667014

33712 • Palisade SP - Wakara

Total sites: 20, RV sites: 20, Elec sites: 20, Water at site, RV dump, No showers, No toilets, Max length: 75ft, Reservations accepted, Open all year, Tent & RV camping: $25-30, 20 FHU, Elev: 5945ft/1812m, Tel: 435-835-7275, Nearest town: Sterling, Agency: ST, GPS: 39.207782, -111.665228

33713 • Panguitch Lake North - USFS

Total sites: 47, RV sites: 47, Elec sites: 0, Central water, RV dump, No showers, Flush toilets, Max length: 22ft, Reservations not accepted, Open May-Sep, Tent & RV camping: $17, Group site: $55, Elev: 8389ft/2557m, Tel: 435-865-3200, Nearest town: Panguitch, Agency: USFS, GPS: 37.702351, -112.656904

33714 • Panguitch Lake South - USFS

Total sites: 18, RV sites: 0, Elec sites: 0, Potable water, RV dump, No showers, Flush toilets, Reservations not accepted, Open May-Sep, Tents only: $14, Elev: 8409ft/2563m, Tel: 435-865-3200, Nearest town: Panguitch, Agency: USFS, GPS: 37.700151, -112.655196

33715 • Paradise Park - USFS

Total sites: 15, RV sites: 15, Elec sites: 0, No water, Vault toilets, Max length: 25ft, Reservations not accepted, Open Jun-Sep, Tent & RV camping: $5, Elev: 9993ft/3046m, Tel: 435-789-1181, Nearest town: Lapoint, Agency: USFS, GPS: 40.666323, -109.913874

33716 • Paragonah(Red Creek) Reservoir WMA disbursed

Dispersed sites, No toilets, Tent & RV camping: Free, Elev: 7829ft/2386m, Nearest town: Paragonah, Agency: ST, GPS: 37.863395, -112.676645

33717 • Paria Contact Station - BLM

Dispersed sites, No water, No toilets, Reservations not accepted, No tents/RV's: Free, Water at Contact Station, Elev: 4387ft/1337m, Tel: 435-644-1200, Nearest town: Kanab, Agency: BLM, GPS: 37.106029, -111.903276

33718 • Paria Contact Station - BLM

Dispersed sites, No water, No toilets, Reservations not accepted, No tents/RV's: Free, Water at Contact Station, Elev: 4488ft/1368m, Tel: 435-644-1200, Nearest town: Kanab, Agency: BLM, GPS: 37.101332, -111.902334

33719 • Parowan Gap - BLM

Dispersed sites, No water, No toilets, Reservations not accepted, Open all year, Tent & RV camping: Free, Near Parowan Gap Petroglyph Site, Elev: 5710ft/1740m, Nearest town: Parowan, Agency: BLM, GPS: 37.916884, -112.978666

33720 • Payson Lakes - USFS

Total sites: 108, RV sites: 108, Elec sites: 0, Central water, No RV dump, No showers, Flush toilets, Reservations accepted, Open May-Oct, Tent & RV camping: $23, 2 group sites: $155-$220, Stay limit: 16 days, Elev: 7995ft/2437m, Tel: 801-226-3564, Nearest town: Payson, Agency: USFS, GPS: 39.930322, -111.642672

33721 • Peek-A-Boo ATV Area - BLM

Dispersed sites, No water, No toilets, Open all year, Tent & RV camping: Free, Elev: 5702ft/1738m, Nearest town: Kanab, Agency: BLM, GPS: 37.154736, -112.573671

33722 • Pelican Lake - BLM

Total sites: 13, RV sites: 13, Elec sites: 0, No water, Vault toilets, Reservations not accepted, Open May-Oct, Tent & RV camping: Free, 6 defined sites, several dispersed sites, Elev: 4817ft/1468m, Tel: 435-781-4400, Nearest town: Vernal, Agency: BLM, GPS: 40.181905, -109.692984

33723 • Perception Park - USFS

Total sites: 14, RV sites: 14, Elec sites: 0, Central water, No RV dump, No showers, Vault toilets, Generator hours: 0800-2200, Reservations not accepted, Open May-Sep, Tent & RV camping: $23, Reservable group sites $235, Designed for physically challenged, Stay limit: 7 days, Elev: 5344ft/1629m, Tel: 801-625-5112, Nearest town: Ogden, Agency: USFS, GPS: 41.288764, -111.641201

33724 • Picture Frame Arch - BLM

Total sites: 4, Elec sites: 0, No water, No toilets, Reservations not accepted, Tents only: Free, High-clearance vehicle recommended, Elev: 5544ft/1690m, Tel: 435-259-2100, Nearest town: Moab, Agency: BLM, GPS: 38.435885, -109.502916

33725 • Pine Lake - USFS

Total sites: 33, RV sites: 33, Elec sites: 0, Central water, No RV dump, No showers, Vault toilets, Max length: 22ft, Reservations accepted, Open May-Sep, Tent & RV camping: $15, 4 group sites: $45-$90, Elev: 8255ft/2516m, Tel: 435-826-5499, Nearest town: Bryce Canyon, Agency: USFS, GPS: 37.744229, -111.950891

33726 • Pine Park - USFS

Dispersed sites, No water, No toilets, Tents only: Free, Elev: 5535ft/1687m, Nearest town: Enterprise, Agency: USFS, GPS: 37.521658, -114.022944

33727 • Pine Valley Dispersed - USFS

Dispersed sites, No water, No toilets, Reservations not accepted, Tent & RV camping: Free, Several sites, Elev: 7510ft/2289m, Tel: 435-783-4338, Nearest town: Kamas, Agency: USFS, GPS: 40.600422, -111.117225

33728 • Pine Valley North Group - USFS

Total sites: 3, RV sites: 3, Elec sites: 0, No water, No RV dump, No showers, Vault toilets, Reservation required, Open May-Sep, Group sites: $170-$290, Stay limit: 7 days, Elev: 7503ft/2287m, Tel: 801-226-3564, Nearest town: Kamas, Agency: USFS, GPS: 40.598129, -111.114922

33729 • Pine Valley Rec Area - Crackfoot - USFS

Total sites: 22, RV sites: 17, Elec sites: 0, Central water, No RV dump, No showers, Vault toilets, Max length: 50ft, Generator hours: 0600-2200, Reservations not accepted, Open May-Sep, Tent & RV camping: $17, Elev: 6890ft/2100m, Tel: 435-652-3100, Nearest town: Pine Valley, Agency: USFS, GPS: 37.374185, -113.466044

33730 • Pine Valley Rec Area - Dean Gardner - USFS

Total sites: 24, RV sites: 24, Elec sites: 0, Central water, No RV dump, No showers, Vault toilets, Max length: 30ft, Generator hours: 0600-2200, Reservations not accepted, Open May-Sep, Tent & RV camping: $17, Elev: 6775ft/2065m, Tel: 435-652-3100, Nearest town: Pine Valley, Agency: USFS, GPS: 37.377722, -113.476009

33731 • Pine Valley Rec Area - Ebenezer Bryce - USFS

Total sites: 19, RV sites: 19, Elec sites: 0, Central water, No RV dump, No showers, Vault toilets, Max length: 45ft, Generator hours: 0600-2200, Reservations not accepted, Open May-Sep, Tent & RV camping: $17, Large, Elev: 6900ft/2103m, Tel: 435-652-3100, Nearest town: Pine Valley, Agency: USFS, GPS: 37.373783, -113.461586

33732 • Pine Valley Rec Area - Effie Beckstrom Group - USFS

Total sites: 17, RV sites: 17, Elec sites: 0, Central water, No RV dump, No showers, Vault toilets, Generator hours: 0600-2200, Reservations not accepted, Open May-Sep, Group site: $130-$145, Elev: 6844ft/2086m, Tel: 435-652-3100, Nearest town: Central, Agency: USFS, GPS: 37.375289, -113.466004

33733 • Pine Valley Rec Area - Equestrian - USFS
Total sites: 18, RV sites: 15, Elec sites: 0, Central water, No RV dump, No showers, Vault toilets, Generator hours: 0600-2200, Reservations accepted, Open May-Sep, Tent & RV camping: $17, Elev: 6736ft/2053m, Tel: 435-652-3100, Nearest town: Pine Valley, Agency: USFS, GPS: 37.379311, -113.483132

33734 • Pine Valley Rec Area - Mitt Moody - USFS
Total sites: 8, RV sites: 0, Elec sites: 0, Reservations not accepted, Tents only: $17, Walk-to sites, Elev: 7008ft/2136m, Tel: 435-652-3100, Nearest town: Pine Valley, Agency: USFS, GPS: 37.375365, -113.455545

33735 • Pine Valley Rec Area - Yellow Pine - USFS
Total sites: 6, RV sites: 6, Elec sites: 0, Central water, No RV dump, No showers, Vault toilets, Max length: 25ft, Generator hours: 0600-2200, Reservations not accepted, Open May-Sep, Tent & RV camping: $17, Elev: 6722ft/2049m, Tel: 435-652-3100, Nearest town: Pine Valley, Agency: USFS, GPS: 37.380242, -113.479862

33736 • Pioneer - USFS
Total sites: 18, RV sites: 18, Elec sites: 0, Central water, No RV dump, No showers, Vault toilets, Reservations not accepted, Tent & RV camping: $20, Stay limit: 7 days, Elev: 5230ft/1594m, Tel: 435-755-3620, Nearest town: Hyrum, Agency: USFS, GPS: 41.628174, -111.693359

33737 • Piute - USFS
Total sites: 47, RV sites: 47, Elec sites: 0, Central water, RV dump, No showers, Vault toilets, Reservations not accepted, Open May-Sep, Tent & RV camping: $10, Elev: 8855ft/2699m, Tel: 435-638-1069, Nearest town: Loa, Agency: USFS, GPS: 38.617854, -111.652737

33738 • Piute SP
Dispersed sites, Central water, No RV dump, No showers, No toilets, Reservations not accepted, Open all year, Tents only: $8, Elev: 5981ft/1823m, Tel: 435-624-3268, Nearest town: Antimony, Agency: ST, GPS: 38.319675, -112.198535

33739 • Plantation Flats TH - USFS
Dispersed sites, No water, Vault toilets, Reservations not accepted, Tent & RV camping: Free, Elev: 6622ft/2018m, Tel: 435-896-9233, Nearest town: Oak City, Agency: USFS, GPS: 39.355877, -112.225377

33740 • Pleasant Creek - USFS
Total sites: 16, RV sites: 16, Elec sites: 0, Central water, No RV dump, No showers, Vault toilets, Reservations not accepted, Open May-Sep, Tent & RV camping: $12, Elev: 8625ft/2629m, Tel: 435-896-9233, Nearest town: Torrey, Agency: USFS, GPS: 38.102405, -111.336141

33741 • Pole Creek Dispersed - USFS
Dispersed sites, No water, No toilets, Reservations not accepted, Open all year, Tent & RV camping: Free, Not maintained for passenger cars, Elev: 10231ft/3118m, Tel: 435-738-2482, Nearest town: Whiterocks, Agency: USFS, GPS: 40.681849, -110.055979

33742 • Pole Creek Lake - USFS
Total sites: 19, RV sites: 19, Elec sites: 0, No water, Vault toilets, Reservations not accepted, Open May-Sep, Tent & RV camping: $5, Elev: 10272ft/3131m, Tel: 435-722-5018, Nearest town: Whiterocks, Agency: USFS, GPS: 40.678467, -110.059814

33743 • Ponderosa (Uinta) - USFS
Total sites: 23, RV sites: 23, Elec sites: 0, Central water, No RV dump, No showers, Vault toilets, Reservations accepted, Open May-Sep, Tent & RV camping: $23, Stay limit: 16 days, Elev: 6293ft/1918m, Tel: 801-798-3571, Nearest town: Nephi, Agency: USFS, GPS: 39.766073, -111.713801

33744 • Ponderosa Group - USFS
Dispersed sites, No water, Vault toilets, Reservations not accepted, Open May-Oct, Group site: $105, Elev: 7072ft/2156m, Tel: 801-226-3564, Nearest town: Kamas, Agency: USFS, GPS: 40.630315, -111.198183

33745 • Posey Lake - USFS
Total sites: 21, RV sites: 21, Elec sites: 0, Central water, No RV dump, No showers, Vault toilets, Max length: 24ft, Reservations accepted, Open all year, Tent & RV camping: $11, Group site $45, Elev: 8688ft/2648m, Tel: 435-826-5499, Nearest town: Escalante, Agency: USFS, GPS: 37.935394, -111.694205

33746 • Potters Pond - USFS
Total sites: 19, RV sites: 19, Elec sites: 0, No water, Vault toilets, Reservations accepted, Open Jun-Sep, Tent & RV camping: $10, 2 group sites $30-$40, Elev: 9005ft/2745m, Tel: 435-384-2372, Nearest town: Huntington, Agency: USFS, GPS: 39.450753, -111.268867

33747 • Potters Pond Equestrian - USFS
Total sites: 4, RV sites: 4, Elec sites: 0, No water, Vault toilets, Reservations accepted, Open Jun-Sep, Tent & RV camping: $15-25, Elev: 9008ft/2746m, Tel: 435-384-2372, Nearest town: Huntington, Agency: USFS, GPS: 39.451594, -111.273141

33748 • Preston Valley - USFS
Total sites: 9, RV sites: 9, Elec sites: 0, Central water, No RV dump, No showers, Vault toilets, Reservations not accepted, Open May-Oct, Tent & RV camping: $20, Elev: 5220ft/1591m, Tel: 435-755-3620, Nearest town: Logan, Agency: USFS, GPS: 41.773425, -111.654283

33749 • Price Canyon - BLM
Total sites: 12, RV sites: 7, Elec sites: 0, No water, Vault toilets, Reservations not accepted, Open May-Oct, Tent & RV camping: $8, Narrow steep access with switchbacks, Elev: 7818ft/2383m, Tel: 435-636-3600, Nearest town: Price, Agency: BLM, GPS: 39.76001, -110.91748

33750 • Pucker Pass Dispersed - BLM
Dispersed sites, No water, No toilets, Tents only: Free, 4x4 required, Elev: 6012ft/1832m, Nearest town: Moab, Agency: BLM, GPS: 38.540114, -109.715405

33751 • Quail Creek SP

Total sites: 23, RV sites: 23, Elec sites: 0, Central water, No RV dump, No showers, Vault toilets, Reservations accepted, Open all year, Tent & RV camping: $25, Elev: 3015ft/919m, Tel: 435-879-2378, Nearest town: Hurricane, Agency: ST, GPS: 37.186582, -113.395528

33752 • Range Study Area Dispersed - USFS

Dispersed sites, No water, Vault toilets, Tent & RV camping: Free, Numerous sites in this area, Elev: 8455ft/2577m, Tel: 435-789-1181, Nearest town: Vernal, Agency: USFS, GPS: 40.715012, -109.475619

33753 • Recapture Reservoir East Side - BLM

Dispersed sites, No water, No toilets, Tent & RV camping: Free, Elev: 6062ft/1848m, Nearest town: Blanding, Agency: BLM, GPS: 37.667694, -109.437298

33754 • Recapture Reservoir West Side - BLM

Dispersed sites, No water, No toilets, Tent & RV camping: Free, Elev: 6076ft/1852m, Nearest town: Blanding, Agency: BLM, GPS: 37.667068, -109.443783

33755 • Red Banks - USFS

Total sites: 12, RV sites: 12, Elec sites: 0, Central water, No RV dump, No showers, Vault toilets, Reservations not accepted, Open Jun-Oct, Tent & RV camping: $20, Stay limit: 7 days, Elev: 6358ft/1938m, Tel: 435-755-3620, Nearest town: Garden City, Agency: USFS, GPS: 41.898926, -111.564941

33756 • Red Canyon - USFS

Total sites: 37, RV sites: 37, Elec sites: 0, Central water, RV dump, Showers, Flush toilets, Max length: 32ft, Generator hours: 0600-2200, Reservations not accepted, Open May-Oct, Tent & RV camping: $18, Group site: $50-$100, Elev: 7290ft/2222m, Tel: 435-676-2676, Nearest town: Panguitch, Agency: USFS, GPS: 37.742676, -112.309082

33757 • Red Canyon (Ashley) - USFS

Total sites: 8, RV sites: 8, Elec sites: 0, Central water, No RV dump, No showers, Vault toilets, Reservations accepted, Open May-Sep, Tent & RV camping: $20, Elev: 7395ft/2254m, Tel: 435-784-3445, Nearest town: Dutch John, Agency: USFS, GPS: 40.889343, -109.559029

33758 • Red Cliffs - BLM

Total sites: 10, RV sites: 10, Elec sites: 0, No water, Vault toilets, Reservations not accepted, Open all year, Tent & RV camping: $8, 12' height restriction, Elev: 3281ft/1000m, Tel: 435-688-3200, Nearest town: Leeds, Agency: BLM, GPS: 37.224789, -113.405613

33759 • Red Cliffs Desert Reserve Dispersed - BLM

Dispersed sites, No water, No toilets, Reservations not accepted, Tent & RV camping: Free, Elev: 3190ft/972m, Nearest town: Hurricane, Agency: BLM, GPS: 37.206654, -113.330796

33760 • Red Fleet SP

Total sites: 35, RV sites: 28, Elec sites: 5, Central water, RV dump, No showers, No toilets, Reservations accepted, Open all year, Tents: $15/RV's: $25, 5 FHU, Elev: 5696ft/1736m, Tel: 435-789-4432, Nearest town: Vernal, Agency: ST, GPS: 40.585194, -109.443112

33761 • Redman - USFS

Total sites: 39, RV sites: 39, Elec sites: 0, Central water, No RV dump, No showers, Flush toilets, Max length: 30ft, Reservations accepted, Open Jul-Sep, Tent & RV camping: $26, 2 group sites - $130-$175, Stay limit: 7 days, Elev: 8317ft/2535m, Tel: 801-733-2660, Nearest town: Murray, Agency: USFS, GPS: 40.615273, -111.588783

33762 • Renegade - USFS

Total sites: 62, RV sites: 62, Elec sites: 0, Central water, No RV dump, No showers, Flush toilets, Reservations accepted, Open May-Oct, Tent & RV camping: $23, Long-term rentals available, Concessionaire, Stay limit: 7 days, Elev: 7658ft/2334m, Tel: 801-226-3564, Nearest town: Heber City, Agency: USFS, GPS: 40.119491, -111.159597

33763 • Reservoir - USFS

Total sites: 5, RV sites: 5, Elec sites: 0, Central water, No RV dump, No showers, Vault toilets, Max length: 15ft, Reservations not accepted, Open May-Sep, Tent & RV camping: $5, Elev: 7950ft/2423m, Tel: 435-722-5018, Nearest town: Roosevelt, Agency: USFS, GPS: 40.575384, -110.325523

33764 • Rex Reservoir - USFS

Dispersed sites, No water, Reservations not accepted, Tent & RV camping: Free, Elev: 7280ft/2219m, Tel: 435-896-9233, Nearest town: Salina, Agency: USFS, GPS: 38.789645, -111.775864

33765 • River Bend - USFS

Total sites: 1, RV sites: 1, Elec sites: 0, No water, No toilets, Reservations not accepted, Open May-Sep, Tent & RV camping: $3, Elev: 7126ft/2172m, Tel: 435-636-3500, Nearest town: Huntington, Agency: USFS, GPS: 39.437756, -111.133604

33766 • Riverview - USFS

Total sites: 19, RV sites: 19, Elec sites: 0, Central water, No RV dump, No showers, Vault toilets, Max length: 20ft, Reservations not accepted, Open May-Sep, Tent & RV camping: $10, Elev: 8028ft/2447m, Tel: 435-722-5018, Nearest town: Altonah, Agency: USFS, GPS: 40.590332, -110.336182

33767 • Road 033 Dispersed - BLM

Dispersed sites, No water, No toilets, Reservations not accepted, Tent & RV camping: Free, Large area, Elev: 4816ft/1468m, Nearest town: Diamond Valley, Agency: BLM, GPS: 37.273811, -113.610736

33768 • Rock Canyon Group - USFS

Total sites: 4, RV sites: 4, Elec sites: 0, No water, Vault toilets, Reservations accepted, Open May-Sep, Group sites: $81-$150, Stay limit: 7 days, Elev: 6975ft/2126m, Tel: 801-785-3563, Nearest town: Heber City, Agency: USFS, GPS: 40.269077, -111.586095

33769 • Rock Corral - BLM

Dispersed sites, No water, Vault toilets, Open May-Nov, Tent & RV camping: Free, Elev: 7093ft/2162m, Tel: 435-586-2401, Nearest town: Milford, Agency: BLM, GPS: 38.372466, -112.834018

33770 • Rock Creek Group - USFS

Total sites: 1, RV sites: 1, Elec sites: 0, No water, Vault toilets, Reservations accepted, Open May-, Group site: $50, Elev: 7464ft/2275m, Tel: 435-738-2482, Nearest town: Duchesne, Agency: USFS, GPS: 40.529196, -110.613514

33771 • Rockport SP - Cedar Point

Total sites: 6, RV sites: 0, Elec sites: 0, No water, No toilets, Reservations accepted, Open all year, Tents only: $20, Elev: 6129ft/1868m, Tel: 435-336-2241, Nearest town: Peoa, Agency: ST, GPS: 40.785231, -111.395268

33772 • Rockport SP - Cottonwood

Total sites: 20, RV sites: 20, Elec sites: 0, Central water, No RV dump, No showers, No toilets, Reservations accepted, Open all year, Tent & RV camping: $20, Elev: 6096ft/1858m, Tel: 435-336-2241, Nearest town: Peoa, Agency: ST, GPS: 40.753358, -111.371981

33773 • Rockport SP - Crandall Cove

Total sites: 10, RV sites: 9, Elec sites: 0, Central water, No RV dump, No showers, Vault toilets, Reservations accepted, Open all year, Tent & RV camping: $20, Elev: 6083ft/1854m, Tel: 435-336-2241, Nearest town: Peoa, Agency: ST, GPS: 40.765222, -111.381777

33774 • Rockport SP - Juniper

Total sites: 34, RV sites: 34, Elec sites: 34, Water at site, RV dump, Showers, Flush toilets, Reservations accepted, Open all year, Tent & RV camping: $30, Elev: 6116ft/1864m, Tel: 435-336-2241, Nearest town: Peoa, Agency: ST, GPS: 40.782599, -111.393629

33775 • Rockport SP - Pinery

Total sites: 4, RV sites: 0, Elec sites: 0, No water, No RV dump, No showers, Vault toilets, Reservations accepted, Open all year, Tents only: $20, Elev: 6053ft/1845m, Tel: 435-336-2241, Nearest town: Peoa, Agency: ST, GPS: 40.754206, -111.371862

33776 • Rockport SP - Riverside

Total sites: 17, RV sites: 17, Elec sites: 0, Central water, No RV dump, No showers, No toilets, Reservations accepted, Open all year, Tent & RV camping: $15, Elev: 5922ft/1805m, Tel: 435-336-2241, Nearest town: Peoa, Agency: ST, GPS: 40.791814, -111.405373

33777 • Rockport SP - Twin Coves

Total sites: 18, RV sites: 18, Elec sites: 0, No toilets, Reservations accepted, Open all year, Tent & RV camping: $20, Elev: 6096ft/1858m, Tel: 435-336-2241, Nearest town: Peoa, Agency: ST, GPS: 40.767232, -111.386771

33778 • Rosebud ATV - USFS

Total sites: 4, RV sites: 4, Elec sites: 0, No water, Vault toilets, Reservations accepted, Open Jun-Sep, Tent & RV camping: $20, 4 double sites, water 1 mile away, Elev: 8534ft/2601m, Nearest town: Grover, Agency: USFS, GPS: 38.100596, -111.326053

33779 • Round Lake North Dispersed - USFS

Dispersed sites, No water, No toilets, Reservations not accepted, Open all year, Tent & RV camping: Free, Road not maintained for passenger cars, Elev: 8810ft/2685m, Tel: 435-836-2800, Nearest town: Lyman, Agency: USFS, GPS: 38.495651, -111.443805

33780 • Round Lake South Dispersed - USFS

Dispersed sites, No water, Vault toilets, Reservations not accepted, Open all year, Tent & RV camping: Free, Road not maintained for passenger cars, Elev: 8805ft/2684m, Tel: 435-836-2800, Nearest town: Lyman, Agency: USFS, GPS: 38.493645, -111.442923

33781 • Salina Creek Second Crossing - USFS

Total sites: 28, RV sites: 22, Elec sites: 0, No water, No RV dump, No showers, Vault toilets, Reservations not accepted, Open Mar-Oct, Tent & RV camping: Free, Elev: 7275ft/2217m, Tel: 435-896-9233, Nearest town: Salina, Agency: USFS, GPS: 38.937869, -111.543251

33782 • Salina Reservoir - USFS

Dispersed sites, No water, Reservations not accepted, Tent & RV camping: Free, Elev: 9690ft/2954m, Tel: 435-896-9233, Nearest town: Salina, Agency: USFS, GPS: 38.760339, -111.652902

33783 • San Juan River - -0.5 Camp - BLM

Dispersed sites, No water, No toilets, Tents only: Free, Boat-in, Elev: 4291ft/1308m, Nearest town: Bluff, Agency: BLM, GPS: 37.260354, -109.603857

33784 • San Juan River - -1.3 Camp - BLM

Dispersed sites, No water, No toilets, Tents only: Free, Boat-in, Elev: 4299ft/1310m, Nearest town: Bluff, Agency: BLM, GPS: 37.262824, -109.595096

33785 • San Juan River - -1.5 Camp - BLM

Dispersed sites, No water, No toilets, Tents only: Free, Boat-in, Elev: 4299ft/1310m, Nearest town: Bluff, Agency: BLM, GPS: 37.261385, -109.592165

33786 • San Juan River - -13.3 Camp - BLM

Dispersed sites, No water, No toilets, Tents only: Free, Boat-in, Elev: 4382ft/1336m, Nearest town: Bluff, Agency: BLM, GPS: 37.274069, -109.407504

33787 • San Juan River - -15.3 Camp - BLM

Dispersed sites, No water, No toilets, Tents only: Free, Boat-in, Elev: 4390ft/1338m, Nearest town: Bluff, Agency: BLM, GPS: 37.267067, -109.372878

33788 • San Juan River - -16.6 Camp - BLM

Dispersed sites, No water, No toilets, Tents only: Free, Boat-in, Elev: 4396ft/1340m, Nearest town: Bluff, Agency: BLM, GPS: 37.265678, -109.352747

33789 • San Juan River - -4.4 Camp - BLM

Dispersed sites, No water, No toilets, Tents only: Free, Boat-in, Elev: 4313ft/1315m, Nearest town: Bluff, Agency: BLM, GPS: 37.273175, -109.544172

33790 • San Juan River - -4.7 Camp - BLM

Dispersed sites, No water, No toilets, Tents only: Free, Boat-in, Elev: 4315ft/1315m, Nearest town: Bluff, Agency: BLM, GPS: 37.276811, -109.541312

33791 • San Juan River - -5.5 Camp - BLM

Dispersed sites, No water, No toilets, Tents only: Free, Boat-in, Elev: 4324ft/1318m, Nearest town: Bluff, Agency: BLM, GPS: 37.275073, -109.527246

33792 • San Juan River - -6.0 Camp - BLM

Dispersed sites, No water, No toilets, Tents only: Free, Boat-in, Elev: 4327ft/1319m, Nearest town: Bluff, Agency: BLM, GPS: 37.276364, -109.518898

33793 • San Juan River - 1.7 Camp - BLM

Dispersed sites, No water, No toilets, Tents only: Free, Boat-in, Elev: 4284ft/1306m, Nearest town: Bluff, Agency: BLM, GPS: 37.241546, -109.620534

33794 • San Juan River - 10.3 Camp - BLM

Dispersed sites, No water, No toilets, Tents only: Free, Boat-in, Elev: 4232ft/1290m, Nearest town: Mexican Hat, Agency: BLM, GPS: 37.196529, -109.73299

33795 • San Juan River - 10.4 Camp - BLM

Dispersed sites, No water, No toilets, Tents only: Free, Boat-in, Elev: 4232ft/1290m, Nearest town: Mexican Hat, Agency: BLM, GPS: 37.198266, -109.733552

33796 • San Juan River - 14.9 Camp - BLM

Dispersed sites, No water, No toilets, Tents only: Free, Boat-in, Elev: 4169ft/1271m, Nearest town: Mexican Hat, Agency: BLM, GPS: 37.193778, -109.769503

33797 • San Juan River - 15.5 Camp - BLM

Dispersed sites, No water, No toilets, Tents only: Free, Boat-in, Elev: 4166ft/1270m, Nearest town: Mexican Hat, Agency: BLM, GPS: 37.187297, -109.766144

33798 • San Juan River - 2.2 Camp - BLM

Dispersed sites, No water, No toilets, Tents only: Free, Boat-in, Elev: 4274ft/1303m, Nearest town: Bluff, Agency: BLM, GPS: 37.241825, -109.629475

33799 • San Juan River - 25.0 Camp - BLM

Dispersed sites, No water, No toilets, Tents only: Free, Boat-in, Elev: 4079ft/1243m, Nearest town: Mexican Hat, Agency: BLM, GPS: 37.164129, -109.831541

33800 • San Juan River - 28.5 Camp - BLM

Dispersed sites, No water, No toilets, Tents only: Free, Boat-in, Elev: 4070ft/1241m, Nearest town: Mexican Hat, Agency: BLM, GPS: 37.154628, -109.875717

33801 • San Juan River - 28.7 Camp - BLM

Dispersed sites, No water, No toilets, Tents only: Free, Boat-in, Elev: 4070ft/1241m, Nearest town: Mexican Hat, Agency: BLM, GPS: 37.152956, -109.877734

33802 • San Juan River - 29.7 Camp - BLM

Dispersed sites, No water, No toilets, Tents only: Free, Boat-in, Elev: 4036ft/1230m, Nearest town: Mexican Hat, Agency: BLM, GPS: 37.155455, -109.884463

33803 • San Juan River - 3.0 Camp - BLM

Dispersed sites, No water, No toilets, Tents only: Free, Boat-in, Elev: 4271ft/1302m, Nearest town: Bluff, Agency: BLM, GPS: 37.241004, -109.644413

33804 • San Juan River - 35.0 Camp - BLM

Dispersed sites, No water, No toilets, Tents only: Free, Boat-in, Elev: 3995ft/1218m, Nearest town: Mexican Hat, Agency: BLM, GPS: 37.173894, -109.906449

33805 • San Juan River - 35.4 Camp - BLM

Dispersed sites, No water, No toilets, Tents only: Free, Boat-in, Elev: 3990ft/1216m, Nearest town: Mexican Hat, Agency: BLM, GPS: 37.180397, -109.908539

33806 • San Juan River - 37.0 Camp - BLM

Dispersed sites, No water, No toilets, Tents only: Free, Boat-in, Elev: 3989ft/1216m, Nearest town: Mexican Hat, Agency: BLM, GPS: 37.160756, -109.918222

33807 • San Juan River - 37.7 Camp - BLM

Dispersed sites, No water, No toilets, Tents only: Free, Boat-in, Elev: 3989ft/1216m, Nearest town: Mexican Hat, Agency: BLM, GPS: 37.163075, -109.925716

33808 • San Juan River - 39.7 Camp - BLM

Dispersed sites, No water, No toilets, Tents only: Free, Boat-in, Elev: 3985ft/1215m, Nearest town: Mexican Hat, Agency: BLM, GPS: 37.154609, -109.938643

33809 • San Juan River - 41.2 Camp - BLM

Dispersed sites, No water, No toilets, Tents only: Free, Boat-in, Elev: 3955ft/1205m, Nearest town: Mexican Hat, Agency: BLM, GPS: 37.168468, -109.936134

33810 • San Juan River - 42.3 Camp - BLM

Dispersed sites, No water, No toilets, Tents only: Free, Boat-in, Elev: 3955ft/1205m, Nearest town: Mexican Hat, Agency: BLM, GPS: 37.173037, -109.942155

33811 • San Juan River - 42.9 Camp - BLM

Dispersed sites, No water, No toilets, Tents only: Free, Boat-in, Elev: 3954ft/1205m, Nearest town: Mexican Hat, Agency: BLM, GPS: 37.166831, -109.948912

33812 • San Juan River - 46.6 Camp - BLM

Dispersed sites, No water, No toilets, Tents only: Free, Boat-in, Elev: 3917ft/1194m, Nearest town: Mexican Hat, Agency: BLM, GPS: 37.197187, -109.978611

33813 • San Juan River - 49.5 Camp - BLM

Dispersed sites, No water, No toilets, Tents only: Free, Boat-in, Elev: 3911ft/1192m, Nearest town: Mexican Hat, Agency: BLM, GPS: 37.204244, -109.994532

33814 • San Juan River - 49.7 Camp - BLM

Dispersed sites, No water, No toilets, Tents only: Free, Boat-in, Elev: 3911ft/1192m, Nearest town: Mexican Hat, Agency: BLM, GPS: 37.201673, -109.996529

33815 • San Juan River - 50.7 Camp - BLM

Dispersed sites, No water, No toilets, Tents only: Free, Boat-in, Elev: 3909ft/1191m, Nearest town: Mexican Hat, Agency: BLM, GPS: 37.206884, -110.00677

33816 • San Juan River - 50.9 Camp - BLM

Dispersed sites, No water, No toilets, Tents only: Free, Boat-in, Elev: 3908ft/1191m, Nearest town: Mexican Hat, Agency: BLM, GPS: 37.209365, -110.003927

33817 • San Juan River - 53.6 Camp - BLM

Dispersed sites, No water, No toilets, Tents only: Free, Boat-in, Elev: 3875ft/1181m, Nearest town: Mexican Hat, Agency: BLM, GPS: 37.221656, -110.024043

33818 • San Juan River - 53.7 Camp - BLM

Dispersed sites, No water, No toilets, Tents only: Free, Boat-in, Elev: 3875ft/1181m, Nearest town: Mexican Hat, Agency: BLM, GPS: 37.219507, -110.023709

33819 • San Juan River - 54.0 Camp - BLM

Dispersed sites, No water, No toilets, Tents only: Free, Boat-in, Elev: 3870ft/1180m, Nearest town: Mexican Hat, Agency: BLM, GPS: 37.215915, -110.026835

33820 • San Juan River - 54.2 Camp - BLM

Dispersed sites, No water, No toilets, Tents only: Free, Boat-in, Elev: 3870ft/1180m, Nearest town: Mexican Hat, Agency: BLM, GPS: 37.215637, -110.030225

33821 • San Juan River - 54.8 Camp - BLM

Dispersed sites, No water, No toilets, Tents only: Free, Boat-in, Elev: 3866ft/1178m, Nearest town: Mexican Hat, Agency: BLM, GPS: 37.221634, -110.036234

33822 • San Juan River - 56.3 Camp - BLM

Dispersed sites, No water, No toilets, Tents only: Free, Boat-in, Elev: 3832ft/1168m, Nearest town: Mexican Hat, Agency: BLM, GPS: 37.238925, -110.039726

33823 • San Juan River - 58.0 Left - BLM

Dispersed sites, No water, No toilets, Tents only: Free, Boat-in, Elev: 3831ft/1168m, Nearest town: Mexican Hat, Agency: BLM, GPS: 37.239619, -110.064085

33824 • San Juan River - 58.0 Right - BLM

Dispersed sites, No water, No toilets, Tents only: Free, Boat-in, Elev: 3831ft/1168m, Nearest town: Mexican Hat, Agency: BLM, GPS: 37.240157, -110.064095

33825 • San Juan River - 58.6 Camp - BLM

Dispersed sites, No water, No toilets, Tents only: Free, Boat-in, Elev: 3831ft/1168m, Nearest town: Mexican Hat, Agency: BLM, GPS: 37.240205, -110.07339

33826 • San Juan River - 59.3 Camp - BLM

Dispersed sites, No water, No toilets, Tents only: Free, Boat-in, Elev: 3820ft/1164m, Nearest town: Mexican Hat, Agency: BLM, GPS: 37.249737, -110.075475

33827 • San Juan River - 60.0 Camp - BLM

Dispersed sites, No water, No toilets, Tents only: Free, Boat-in, Elev: 3818ft/1164m, Nearest town: Mexican Hat, Agency: BLM, GPS: 37.256086, -110.081417

33828 • San Juan River - 61.5 Camp - BLM

Dispersed sites, No water, No toilets, Tents only: Free, Boat-in, Elev: 3778ft/1152m, Nearest town: Mexican Hat, Agency: BLM, GPS: 37.270948, -110.098824

33829 • San Juan River - 62.0 Camp - BLM

Dispersed sites, No water, No toilets, Tents only: Free, Boat-in, Elev: 3778ft/1152m, Nearest town: Mexican Hat, Agency: BLM, GPS: 37.276589, -110.102805

33830 • San Juan River - 9.5 Camp - BLM

Dispersed sites, No water, No toilets, Tents only: Free, Boat-in, Elev: 4232ft/1290m, Nearest town: Mexican Hat, Agency: BLM, GPS: 37.191505, -109.727421

33831 • San Juan River - Art Gallery - BLM

Dispersed sites, No water, No toilets, Tents only: Free, Boat-in, Elev: 3779ft/1152m, Nearest town: Mexican Hat, Agency: BLM, GPS: 37.269508, -110.098401

33832 • San Juan River - Big Stick - BLM

Dispersed sites, No water, No toilets, Tents only: Free, Boat-in, Elev: 4232ft/1290m, Nearest town: Mexican Hat, Agency: BLM, GPS: 37.202563, -109.716594

33833 • San Juan River - Bump Camp - BLM

Dispersed sites, No water, No toilets, Tents only: Free, Boat-in, Elev: 3960ft/1207m, Nearest town: Mexican Hat, Agency: BLM, GPS: 37.167642, -109.939488

33834 • San Juan River - Butler Wash - BLM

Dispersed sites, No water, No toilets, Tents only: Free, Boat-in, Elev: 4270ft/1301m, Nearest town: Bluff, Agency: BLM, GPS: 37.237894, -109.65635

33835 • San Juan River - Chinle Camp - BLM

Dispersed sites, No water, No toilets, Tents only: Free, Boat-in, Elev: 4232ft/1290m, Nearest town: Mexican Hat, Agency: BLM, GPS: 37.205016, -109.713879

33836 • San Juan River - Comb Ridge - BLM

Dispersed sites, No water, No toilets, Tents only: Free, Boat-in, Elev: 4247ft/1294m, Nearest town: Bluff, Agency: BLM, GPS: 37.21834, -109.698898

33837 • San Juan River - Cottonwood Camp - BLM

Dispersed sites, No water, No toilets, Tents only: Free, Boat-in, Elev: 4248ft/1295m, Nearest town: Bluff, Agency: BLM, GPS: 37.218386, -109.692093

33838 • San Juan River - Desecration Camp - BLM

Dispersed sites, No water, No toilets, Tents only: Free, Boat-in, Elev: 4262ft/1299m, Nearest town: Bluff, Agency: BLM, GPS: 37.228887, -109.671381

33839 • San Juan River - Desert Creek - BLM

Dispersed sites, No water, No toilets, Tents only: Free, Boat-in, Elev: 4395ft/1340m, Nearest town: Bluff, Agency: BLM, GPS: 37.265862, -109.363595

33840 • San Juan River - False Honaker - BLM

Dispersed sites, No water, No toilets, Tents only: Free, Boat-in, Elev: 3953ft/1205m, Nearest town: Mexican Hat, Agency: BLM, GPS: 37.180324, -109.958829

33841 • San Juan River - False Johns Camp - BLM

Dispersed sites, No water, No toilets, Tents only: Free, Boat-in, Elev: 3831ft/1168m, Nearest town: Mexican Hat, Agency: BLM, GPS: 37.243928, -110.042897

33842 • San Juan River - Fossil Stop - BLM

Dispersed sites, No water, No toilets, Tents only: Free, Boat-in, Elev: 4120ft/1256m, Nearest town: Mexican Hat, Agency: BLM, GPS: 37.180372, -109.826739

33843 • San Juan River - Furnace Flats - BLM

Dispersed sites, No water, No toilets, Tents only: Free, Boat-in, Elev: 3774ft/1150m, Nearest town: Mexican Hat, Agency: BLM, GPS: 37.291401, -110.117068

33844 • San Juan River - Goldmine - BLM

Dispersed sites, No water, No toilets, Tents only: Free, Boat-in, Elev: 4284ft/1306m, Nearest town: Bluff, Agency: BLM, GPS: 37.242228, -109.624711

33845 • San Juan River - Government Camp - BLM

Dispersed sites, No water, No toilets, Tents only: Free, Boat-in, Elev: 3764ft/1147m, Nearest town: Mexican Hat, Agency: BLM, GPS: 37.293771, -110.125714

33846 • San Juan River - Grand Gulch - BLM

Dispersed sites, No water, No toilets, Tents only: Free, Boat-in, Elev: 3729ft/1137m, Nearest town: Irish Green, Agency: BLM, GPS: 37.31548, -110.21172

33847 • San Juan River - GSP Camp - BLM

Dispersed sites, No water, No toilets, Tents only: Free, Boat-in, Elev: 3989ft/1216m, Nearest town: Mexican Hat, Agency: BLM, GPS: 37.170648, -109.926772

33848 • San Juan River - Honaker - BLM

Dispersed sites, No water, No toilets, Tents only: Free, Boat-in, Elev: 3952ft/1205m, Nearest town: Mexican Hat, Agency: BLM, GPS: 37.185546, -109.962359

33849 • San Juan River - Johns Canyon - BLM

Dispersed sites, No water, No toilets, Tents only: Free, Boat-in, Elev: 3824ft/1166m, Nearest town: Mexican Hat, Agency: BLM, GPS: 37.244012, -110.075752

33850 • San Juan River - Juniper - BLM

Dispersed sites, No water, No toilets, Tents only: Free, Boat-in, Elev: 3952ft/1205m, Nearest town: Mexican Hat, Agency: BLM, GPS: 37.18792, -109.959504

33851 • San Juan River - Ledge Camp - BLM

Dispersed sites, No water, No toilets, Tents only: Free, Boat-in, Elev: 4127ft/1258m, Nearest town: Mexican Hat, Agency: BLM, GPS: 37.182488, -109.812717

33852 • San Juan River - Lime Creek - BLM

Dispersed sites, No water, No toilets, Tents only: Free, Boat-in, Elev: 4114ft/1254m, Nearest town: Mexican Hat, Agency: BLM, GPS: 37.183723, -109.838792

33853 • San Juan River - Lime Ridge - BLM

Dispersed sites, No water, No toilets, Tents only: Free, Boat-in, Elev: 4232ft/1290m, Nearest town: Mexican Hat, Agency: BLM, GPS: 37.212221, -109.714405

33854 • San Juan River - Lower Chinle - BLM

Dispersed sites, No water, No toilets, Tents only: Free, Boat-in, Elev: 4232ft/1290m, Nearest town: Mexican Hat, Agency: BLM, GPS: 37.196386, -109.721372

33855 • San Juan River - Lower Eight Foot - BLM

Dispersed sites, No water, No toilets, Tents only: Free, Boat-in, Elev: 4165ft/1269m, Nearest town: Mexican Hat, Agency: BLM, GPS: 37.186966, -109.785421

33856 • San Juan River - Lower Johns Canyon - BLM

Dispersed sites, No water, No toilets, Tents only: Free, Boat-in, Elev: 3823ft/1165m, Nearest town: Mexican Hat, Agency: BLM, GPS: 37.246184, -110.075612

33857 • San Juan River - Lower Ledge - BLM

Dispersed sites, No water, No toilets, Tents only: Free, Boat-in, Elev: 4126ft/1258m, Nearest town: Mexican Hat, Agency: BLM, GPS: 37.180357, -109.814522

33858 • San Juan River - Mendenhall - BLM

Dispersed sites, No water, No toilets, Tents only: Free, Boat-in, Elev: 4034ft/1230m, Nearest town: Mexican Hat, Agency: BLM, GPS: 37.159621, -109.892337

33859 • San Juan River - Mexican Hat - BLM

Dispersed sites, No water, No toilets, Tents only: Free, Boat-in, Elev: 4098ft/1249m, Nearest town: Mexican Hat, Agency: BLM, GPS: 37.18214, -109.851969

33860 • San Juan River - Midway - BLM

Dispersed sites, No water, No toilets, Tents only: Free, Boat-in, Elev: 4200ft/1280m, Nearest town: Mexican Hat, Agency: BLM, GPS: 37.210496, -109.751626

33861 • San Juan River - Mini-Sazi Camp - BLM
Dispersed sites, No water, No toilets, Tents only: Free, Boat-in, Elev: 3990ft/1216m, Nearest town: Mexican Hat, Agency: BLM, GPS: 37.180666, -109.910158

33862 • San Juan River - Mule Ear - BLM
Dispersed sites, No water, No toilets, Tents only: Free, Boat-in, Elev: 4232ft/1290m, Nearest town: Mexican Hat, Agency: BLM, GPS: 37.191442, -109.725157

33863 • San Juan River - Oljeto Wash - BLM
Dispersed sites, No water, No toilets, Tents only: Free, Boat-in, Elev: 3709ft/1131m, Nearest town: Irish Green, Agency: BLM, GPS: 37.284277, -110.294409

33864 • San Juan River - Pontiac Wash - BLM
Dispersed sites, No water, No toilets, Tents only: Free, Boat-in, Elev: 4070ft/1241m, Nearest town: Mexican Hat, Agency: BLM, GPS: 37.148006, -109.881716

33865 • San Juan River - Pouroff - BLM
Dispersed sites, No water, No toilets, Tents only: Free, Boat-in, Elev: 4104ft/1251m, Nearest town: Mexican Hat, Agency: BLM, GPS: 37.19354, -109.853262

33866 • San Juan River - Prospector Loop - BLM
Dispersed sites, No water, No toilets, Tents only: Free, Boat-in, Elev: 4200ft/1280m, Nearest town: Mexican Hat, Agency: BLM, GPS: 37.199319, -109.741907

33867 • San Juan River - Recapture Creek - BLM
Dispersed sites, No water, No toilets, Tents only: Free, Boat-in, Elev: 4350ft/1326m, Nearest town: Bluff, Agency: BLM, GPS: 37.284624, -109.463046

33868 • San Juan River - Rock Cabin - BLM
Dispersed sites, No water, No toilets, Tents only: Free, Boat-in, Elev: 4034ft/1230m, Nearest town: Mexican Hat, Agency: BLM, GPS: 37.157144, -109.892494

33869 • San Juan River - Ross Camp - BLM
Dispersed sites, No water, No toilets, Tents only: Free, Boat-in, Elev: 3886ft/1184m, Nearest town: Mexican Hat, Agency: BLM, GPS: 37.228196, -110.011367

33870 • San Juan River - Sand Island - BLM
Total sites: 24, RV sites: 24, Elec sites: 0, Central water, No RV dump, No showers, Vault toilets, Max length: 50ft, Reservations not accepted, Open all year, Tent & RV camping: $15, Group fee: $65-$85, Elev: 4287ft/1307m, Tel: 435-259-2102, Nearest town: Bluff, Agency: BLM, GPS: 37.261056, -109.617842

33871 • San Juan River - Slickhorn A - BLM
Dispersed sites, No water, No toilets, Tents only: Free, Boat-in, Elev: 3752ft/1144m, Nearest town: Irish Green, Agency: BLM, GPS: 37.311364, -110.151765

33872 • San Juan River - Slickhorn B, C, D - BLM
Dispersed sites, No water, No toilets, Tents only: Free, Boat-in, Elev: 3749ft/1143m, Nearest town: Irish Green, Agency: BLM, GPS: 37.316878, -110.148617

33873 • San Juan River - Slickhorn E - BLM
Dispersed sites, No water, No toilets, Tents only: Free, Boat-in, Elev: 3745ft/1141m, Nearest town: Irish Green, Agency: BLM, GPS: 37.319936, -110.150502

33874 • San Juan River - Steer Gulch - BLM
Dispersed sites, No water, No toilets, Tents only: Free, Boat-in, Elev: 3708ft/1130m, Nearest town: Irish Green, Agency: BLM, GPS: 37.304751, -110.311081

33875 • San Juan River - Sunset Camp - BLM
Dispersed sites, No water, No toilets, Tents only: Free, Boat-in, Elev: 4398ft/1341m, Nearest town: Bluff, Agency: BLM, GPS: 37.267216, -109.348357

33876 • San Juan River - Swinging Bridge - BLM
Dispersed sites, No water, No toilets, Tents only: Free, Also boat-in sites, Elev: 4339ft/1323m, Nearest town: Bluff, Agency: BLM, GPS: 37.279537, -109.492814

33877 • San Juan River - Tabernacle - BLM
Dispersed sites, No water, No toilets, Tents only: Free, Boat-in, Elev: 4033ft/1229m, Nearest town: Mexican Hat, Agency: BLM, GPS: 37.178833, -109.894369

33878 • San Juan River - Trimble Camp - BLM
Dispersed sites, No water, No toilets, Tents only: Free, Boat-in, Elev: 3724ft/1135m, Nearest town: Irish Green, Agency: BLM, GPS: 37.297013, -110.227722

33879 • San Juan River - Twin Canyons - BLM
Dispersed sites, No water, No toilets, Tents only: Free, Boat-in, Elev: 3917ft/1194m, Nearest town: Mexican Hat, Agency: BLM, GPS: 37.215017, -109.985671

33880 • San Juan River - Upper Chinle - BLM
Dispersed sites, No water, No toilets, Tents only: Free, Boat-in, Elev: 4232ft/1290m, Nearest town: Mexican Hat, Agency: BLM, GPS: 37.208123, -109.71334

33881 • San Juan River - Upper Honaker - BLM
Dispersed sites, No water, No toilets, Tents only: Free, Boat-in, Elev: 3953ft/1205m, Nearest town: Mexican Hat, Agency: BLM, GPS: 37.183727, -109.963905

33882 • San Rafael Bridge - BLM
Total sites: 11, RV sites: 11, Elec sites: 0, No water, Vault toilets, Tent & RV camping: $6, Elev: 5118ft/1560m, Tel: 435-636-3600, Nearest town: Cleveland, Agency: BLM, GPS: 39.079382, -110.665914

33883 • San Rafael River Dispersed - BLM
Dispersed sites, No water, No toilets, Tent & RV camping: Free, Elev: 5118ft/1560m, Nearest town: Green River, Agency: BLM, GPS: 39.058956, -110.631925

33884 • San Rafael Swell Dispersed - BLM
Dispersed sites, No water, No toilets, Tent & RV camping: Free, Elev: 5600ft/1707m, Nearest town: Green River, Agency: BLM, GPS: 38.656072, -110.710213

33885 • Sand Flat Rec Area - Juniper - BLM
Total sites: 15, RV sites: 15, Elec sites: 0, No water, Vault toilets, Reservations not accepted, Tents: $15/RV's: $15-20, Elev: 5732ft/1747m, Nearest town: Moab, Agency: BLM, GPS: 38.579956, -109.429027

33886 • Sand Flats - Area A - BLM
Total sites: 19, RV sites: 13, Elec sites: 0, No water, Vault toilets, Max length: 34ft, Reservations not accepted, Open all year, Tents: $15/RV's: $15-20, Stay limit: 14 days, Elev: 4663ft/1421m, Tel: 435-259-2100, Nearest town: Moab, Agency: BLM, GPS: 38.576479, -109.520135

33887 • Sand Flats - Area B - BLM
Total sites: 16, RV sites: 12, Elec sites: 0, No water, Vault toilets, Max length: 34ft, Reservations not accepted, Open all year, Tents: $15/RV's: $15-20, Stay limit: 14 days, Elev: 4633ft/1412m, Tel: 435-259-2100, Nearest town: Moab, Agency: BLM, GPS: 38.580921, -109.518597

33888 • Sand Flats - Area C/D - BLM
Total sites: 26, RV sites: 0, Elec sites: 0, No water, Vault toilets, Max length: 34ft, Reservations not accepted, Open all year, Tents only: $15, Stay limit: 14 days, Elev: 4707ft/1435m, Tel: 435-259-2100, Nearest town: Moab, Agency: BLM, GPS: 38.581751, -109.514182

33889 • Sand Flats - Area E - BLM
Total sites: 9, RV sites: 7, Elec sites: 0, No water, Vault toilets, Max length: 34ft, Reservations not accepted, Open all year, Tents: $15/RV's: $15-20, Group site: $50, Stay limit: 14 days, Elev: 4754ft/1449m, Tel: 435-259-2100, Nearest town: Moab, Agency: BLM, GPS: 38.580582, -109.499392

33890 • Sand Flats - Area F/G/H - BLM
Total sites: 28, RV sites: 0, Elec sites: 0, No water, Vault toilets, Max length: 34ft, Reservations not accepted, Open all year, Tents only: $15, Stay limit: 14 days, Elev: 4769ft/1454m, Tel: 435-259-2100, Nearest town: Moab, Agency: BLM, GPS: 38.582922, -109.485045

33891 • Sand Hollow SP - Sand Pit
Total sites: 29, RV sites: 29, Elec sites: 6, Water at site, No RV dump, Showers, Flush toilets, Reservations accepted, Open all year, Tents: $28/RV's: $28-35, Elev: 3061ft/933m, Tel: 435-680-0715, Nearest town: Hurricane, Agency: ST, GPS: 37.100533, -113.369596

33892 • Sand Hollow SP - Westside
Total sites: 50, RV sites: 50, Elec sites: 50, Water at site, RV dump, Showers, Flush toilets, Reservations accepted, Open all year, Tent & RV camping: $38, 50 FHU, Elev: 3071ft/936m, Tel: 435-680-0715, Nearest town: Hurricane, Agency: ST, GPS: 37.122614, -113.384971

33893 • Sandthrax Dispersed - BLM
Total sites: 17, RV sites: 7, Elec: Unk, No water, No toilets, Tent & RV camping: Free, Beware of deep sand, Elev: 4450ft/1356m, Tel: 435-542-3461, Nearest town: Hanksville, Agency: BLM, GPS: 38.016308, -110.532063

33894 • Sawmill Hollow - USFS
Total sites: 6, RV sites: 4, Elec sites: 0, No water, No RV dump, No showers, Vault toilets, Max length: 30ft, Tent & RV camping: Free, Elev: 6207ft/1892m, Tel: 801-798-3571, Nearest town: Mapleton, Agency: USFS, GPS: 40.141, -111.341

33895 • Scofield SP - Madsen Bay
Total sites: 36, RV sites: 36, Elec sites: 36, Water at site, RV dump, No showers, No toilets, Open all year, Tent & RV camping: $25, Elev: 7667ft/2337m, Tel: 435-448-9449, Nearest town: Huntington, Agency: ST, GPS: 39.813975, -111.136551

33896 • Scofield SP - Mountain View
Total sites: 33, RV sites: 33, Elec sites: 0, No toilets, Open all year, Tent & RV camping: $20, Elev: 7677ft/2340m, Tel: 435-448-9449, Nearest town: Huntington, Agency: ST, GPS: 39.790347, -111.130098

33897 • Seep Ridge - BLM
Dispersed sites, No water, No toilets, Tent & RV camping: Free, Numerous dispersed sites along road, Elev: 8043ft/2452m, Nearest town: Mack CO, Agency: BLM, GPS: 39.462642, -109.283744

33898 • Settlement Canyon - Main
Total sites: 12, RV sites: 12, Elec sites: 12, Central water, Vault toilets, Reservations accepted, Open Apr-Oct, Tents: $15/RV's: $25, Elev: 5440ft/1658m, Tel: 435-882-9041, Nearest town: Tooele, Agency: CP, GPS: 40.500917, -112.288611

33899 • Shady Dell - USFS
Total sites: 20, RV sites: 20, Elec sites: 0, Central water, No RV dump, No showers, Vault toilets, Reservations not accepted, Open Jun-Oct, Tent & RV camping: $21, Stay limit: 7 days, Elev: 8074ft/2461m, Tel: 435-654-0470, Nearest town: Kamas, Agency: USFS, GPS: 40.591797, -111.011963

33900 • Sheep Creek - USFS
Dispersed sites, No toilets, Tent & RV camping: Free, Elev: 5937ft/1810m, Nearest town: Thistle, Agency: USFS, GPS: 39.983956, -111.332665

33901 • Sheep Creek Bay - USFS
Dispersed sites, No water, Vault toilets, Max length: 45ft, Reservations not accepted, Open Apr-Sep, No tents/RV's: $10, Elev: 6084ft/1854m, Tel: 435-789-1181, Nearest town: Manila, Agency: USFS, GPS: 40.920835, -109.674975

33902 • Sheep Creek Lake - USFS
Dispersed sites, Vault toilets, Tent & RV camping: Free, Elev: 8606ft/2623m, Nearest town: Flaming Gorge, Agency: USFS, GPS: 40.887156, -109.849263

33903 • Shingle Creek ATV - USFS

Total sites: 21, RV sites: 21, Elec sites: 0, Potable water, No RV dump, No showers, Vault toilets, Reservations not accepted, Open May-Oct, Tent & RV camping: $18, Stay limit: 7 days, Elev: 7497ft/2285m, Tel: 435-783-4338, Nearest town: Kamas, Agency: USFS, GPS: 40.615715, -111.132215

33904 • Shingle Creek Rec Area - USFS

Dispersed sites, No water, No toilets, Reservations not accepted, Tent & RV camping: Free, Use extreme caution when rainy - road becomes very slick and travel is not recommended, Stay limit: 16 days, Elev: 6663ft/2031m, Nearest town: Cove Fort, Agency: USFS, GPS: 38.570851, -112.463326

33905 • Simpson Springs - BLM

Total sites: 20, RV sites: 20, Elec sites: 0, Central water, Vault toilets, Reservations not accepted, Open all year, Tent & RV camping: $15, Elev: 5115ft/1559m, Tel: 801-977-4300, Nearest town: Lehi, Agency: BLM, GPS: 40.034791, -112.782234

33906 • Singletree - USFS

Total sites: 31, RV sites: 31, Elec sites: 0, Central water, RV dump, No showers, Flush toilets, Max length: 32ft, Reservations accepted, Open May-Oct, Tent & RV camping: $12, 2 group sites: $50, Elev: 8255ft/2516m, Tel: 435-896-9233, Nearest town: Torrey, Agency: USFS, GPS: 38.162434, -111.331178

33907 • Skull Creek - USFS

Total sites: 17, RV sites: 17, Elec sites: 0, No water, No RV dump, No showers, Vault toilets, Max length: 30ft, Reservations accepted, Open May-Sep, Tent & RV camping: $12, Elev: 7434ft/2266m, Tel: 435-784-3445, Nearest town: Dutch John, Agency: USFS, GPS: 40.864905, -109.526508

33908 • Smith-Morehouse - USFS

Total sites: 34, RV sites: 34, Elec sites: 0, Central water, No RV dump, No showers, Vault toilets, Reservations accepted, Open May-Sep, Tent & RV camping: $24, Stay limit: 7 days, Elev: 7644ft/2330m, Tel: 435-783-4338, Nearest town: Oakley, Agency: USFS, GPS: 40.768031, -111.107141

33909 • Smithfield - USFS

Total sites: 6, RV sites: 6, Elec sites: 0, Central water, No RV dump, No showers, Vault toilets, Reservations not accepted, Open May-Sep, Tent & RV camping: $20, Stay limit: 7 days, Elev: 5482ft/1671m, Tel: 435-755-3620, Nearest town: Heber City, Agency: USFS, GPS: 41.870399, -111.753995

33910 • Smithsonian Butte Dispersed - BLM

Dispersed sites, No water, No toilets, Tent & RV camping: Free, 4x4 required, Must camp > .5 mile from main road, Elev: 3764ft/1147m, Nearest town: Rockville, Agency: BLM, GPS: 37.150993, -113.058648

33911 • Snow Canyon SP

Total sites: 29, RV sites: 29, Elec sites: 16, Water at site, RV dump, Showers, Flush toilets, Max length: 40ft, Reservations accepted, Open all year, Tents: $20/RV's: $25, 2 group sites: $75-$100 minimuim, Elev: 3491ft/1064m, Tel: 435-628-2255, Nearest town: Ivins, Agency: ST, GPS: 37.203096, -113.640261

33912 • Snow Lake Dispersed - USFS

Dispersed sites, No water, No toilets, Reservations not accepted, Open all year, Tent & RV camping: Free, Road not maintained for passenger cars, Elev: 10539ft/3212m, Tel: 435-836-2800, Nearest town: Lyman, Agency: USFS, GPS: 38.426143, -111.458597

33913 • Soapstone - USFS

Total sites: 32, RV sites: 32, Elec sites: 0, Central water, No RV dump, No showers, Vault toilets, Reservations accepted, Open May-Oct, Tent & RV camping: $23, Stay limit: 7 days, Elev: 7920ft/2414m, Tel: 435-783-4338, Nearest town: Kamas, Agency: USFS, GPS: 40.578369, -111.026611

33914 • Soldier Creek - USFS

Total sites: 160, RV sites: 160, Elec sites: 0, Central water, RV dump, No showers, Flush toilets, Reservations accepted, Open May-Oct, Tent & RV camping: $15-23, Long-term rentals available, Concessionaire, Elev: 7674ft/2339m, Tel: 435-654-0470, Nearest town: Heber City, Agency: USFS, GPS: 40.152733, -111.051206

33915 • South Cascade Springs Dispersed - USFS

Dispersed sites, No water, No toilets, Tents only: Free, Elev: 6171ft/1881m, Nearest town: Charleston, Agency: USFS, GPS: 40.450143, -111.551682

33916 • South Creek (Lower) TH - USFS

Dispersed sites, No water, Reservations not accepted, Tent & RV camping: Free, Elev: 7422ft/2262m, Tel: 435-438-2436, Nearest town: Beaver, Agency: USFS, GPS: 38.175917, -112.505288

33917 • South Fork - USFS

Total sites: 43, RV sites: 43, Elec sites: 0, Central water, No RV dump, No showers, Vault toilets, Max length: 22ft, Generator hours: 0800-2200, Reservations accepted, Open May-Sep, Tent & RV camping: $23, Stay limit: 7 days, Elev: 5295ft/1614m, Tel: 801-625-5112, Nearest town: Huntsville, Agency: USFS, GPS: 41.281696, -111.654018

33918 • South Fork - USFS

Total sites: 6, RV sites: 6, Elec sites: 0, No water, Vault toilets, Reservations not accepted, Tent & RV camping: Free, Elev: 9688ft/2953m, Nearest town: Mountain Home, Agency: USFS, GPS: 40.734967, -109.739576

33919 • South Logging Road Dispersed - USFS

Dispersed sites, No water, No toilets, Max length: 20ft, Reservations not accepted, Tent & RV camping: Free, Elev: 7922ft/2415m, Nearest town: Monticello, Agency: USFS, GPS: 37.868088, -109.402557

33920 • South Stuart - USFS

Dispersed sites, No water, No toilets, Tents only: Free, Elev: 7989ft/2435m, Nearest town: Standardville, Agency: USFS, GPS: 39.527736, -111.153811

33921 • South Temple Wash - BLM
Dispersed sites, No water, Vault toilets, Tent & RV camping: Free, Jeep and ATV area, Elev: 5318ft/1621m, Nearest town: Hanksville, Agency: BLM, GPS: 38.656662, -110.661364

33922 • Spanish Fork River Park
Total sites: 9, RV sites: 9, Elec sites: 0, Central water, No RV dump, No showers, No toilets, Tent & RV camping: $20, Elev: 5003ft/1525m, Tel: 801-851-8600, Nearest town: Spanish Fork, Agency: CP, GPS: 40.023591, -111.502142

33923 • Spanish Oaks City CG
Total sites: 24, RV sites: 12, Elec sites: 0, Central water, Vault toilets, Reservations accepted, Open Apr-Oct, Tent & RV camping: $20, Stay limit: 7 days, Elev: 5181ft/1579m, Tel: 801-804-4600, Nearest town: Spanish Fork, Agency: MU, GPS: 40.070373, -111.599191

33924 • Spirit Lake - USFS
Total sites: 24, RV sites: 24, Elec sites: 0, No water, Vault toilets, Max length: 30ft, Reservations not accepted, Open May-Sep, Tent & RV camping: $14, Elev: 10207ft/3111m, Tel: 435-789-1181, Nearest town: Manila, Agency: USFS, GPS: 40.837438, -110.000379

33925 • Splash Dam Dispersed - USFS
Dispersed sites, No water, Vault toilets, Reservations not accepted, Tent & RV camping: Free, Elev: 9185ft/2800m, Nearest town: Hanna, Agency: USFS, GPS: 40.560721, -110.838496

33926 • Spring - USFS
Total sites: 3, RV sites: 3, Elec sites: 0, Central water, No RV dump, No showers, Vault toilets, Reservations not accepted, Tent & RV camping: $12, Stay limit: 7 days, Elev: 5584ft/1702m, Tel: 435-755-3620, Nearest town: Logan, Agency: USFS, GPS: 41.661984, -111.653988

33927 • Spring Canyon Road - Site 1 - BLM
Dispersed sites, No water, No toilets, Tent & RV camping: Free, Elev: 5111ft/1558m, Nearest town: Moab, Agency: BLM, GPS: 38.633541, -109.871174

33928 • Spring Canyon Road - Site 2 - BLM
Dispersed sites, No water, No toilets, Tent & RV camping: Free, Elev: 5054ft/1540m, Nearest town: Moab, Agency: BLM, GPS: 38.634518, -109.897116

33929 • Spring Canyon Road - Site 3 - BLM
Dispersed sites, No water, No toilets, Tent & RV camping: Free, Elev: 5297ft/1615m, Nearest town: Moab, Agency: BLM, GPS: 38.622306, -109.931642

33930 • Spring Canyon Road - Site 4 - BLM
Dispersed sites, No water, No toilets, Tent & RV camping: Free, Elev: 5162ft/1573m, Nearest town: Moab, Agency: BLM, GPS: 38.630445, -109.953867

33931 • Spring Canyon Road - Site 5 - BLM
Dispersed sites, No water, No toilets, Tent & RV camping: Free, Elev: 4830ft/1472m, Nearest town: Moab, Agency: BLM, GPS: 38.639143, -109.976254

33932 • Spring Hollow - USFS
Total sites: 12, RV sites: 12, Elec sites: 0, Central water, No RV dump, No showers, Vault toilets, Reservations accepted, Open May-Oct, Tent & RV camping: $22, 2 group sites: $70-$140, Stay limit: 7 days, Elev: 5033ft/1534m, Tel: 801-226-3564, Nearest town: Logan, Agency: USFS, GPS: 41.752735, -111.716653

33933 • Spring Site - BLM
Total sites: 4, RV sites: 0, Elec sites: 0, No water, Vault toilets, Tents only: $5, Elev: 4321ft/1317m, Nearest town: Moab, Agency: BLM, GPS: 38.518216, -109.594747

33934 • Spruces - USFS
Total sites: 92, RV sites: 92, Elec sites: 0, Central water, No RV dump, No showers, Flush toilets, Reservations accepted, Open May-Sep, Tent & RV camping: $26, Group sites: $180, No pets, Stay limit: 7 days, Elev: 7438ft/2267m, Tel: 435-649-7534, Nearest town: Salt Lake City, Agency: USFS, GPS: 40.642179, -111.637703

33935 • Spruces (Navajo Lake) - USFS
Total sites: 28, RV sites: 25, Elec sites: 0, Central water, No RV dump, No showers, Flush toilets, Generator hours: 0600-2200, Reservations not accepted, Open May-Sep, Tent & RV camping: $17, Also walk-to sites, 3 walk-to sites, Elev: 9075ft/2766m, Tel: 435-865-3200, Nearest town: Cedar City, Agency: USFS, GPS: 37.518715, -112.774349

33936 • Starr Springs - BLM
Total sites: 12, RV sites: 12, Elec sites: 0, No water, Vault toilets, Open Apr-Nov, Tent & RV camping: Fee unk, Elev: 6220ft/1896m, Tel: 435-542-3461, Nearest town: Hanksville, Agency: BLM, GPS: 37.849886, -110.662685

33937 • Stateline - BLM
Total sites: 4, RV sites: 3, Elec sites: 0, No water, Vault toilets, Open all year, Tent & RV camping: Free, Elev: 4977ft/1517m, Tel: 435-688-3200, Nearest town: Kanab, Agency: BLM, GPS: 37.001113, -112.035385

33938 • Stateline Reservoir - USFS
Total sites: 41, RV sites: 41, Elec sites: 0, Central water, RV dump, No showers, Vault toilets, Reservations accepted, Open May-Sep, Tent & RV camping: $21, Elev: 9252ft/2820m, Tel: 307-782-6555, Nearest town: Mountain View, Agency: USFS, GPS: 40.981884, -110.384703

33939 • Steinaker SP
Total sites: 31, RV sites: 31, Elec sites: 16, Water at site, RV dump, No showers, No toilets, Max length: 45ft, Reservations accepted, Open all year, Tents: $15/RV's: $23-28, 8 FHU, 1 group site $125, Elev: 5532ft/1686m, Tel: 435-789-4432, Nearest town: Vernal, Agency: ST, GPS: 40.517969, -109.541379

33940 • Stillwater - USFS

Total sites: 17, RV sites: 17, Elec sites: 0, Central water, No RV dump, No showers, Vault toilets, Reservations accepted, Open Jun-Oct, Tent & RV camping: $21, 4 group sites: $70-$80, Stay limit: 14 days, Elev: 8510ft/2594m, Tel: 307-789-3194, Nearest town: Evanston, Agency: USFS, GPS: 40.868896, -110.835449

33941 • Strawberry Bay - Loop F - USFS

Total sites: 47, RV sites: 47, Elec sites: 0, Central water, No showers, Flush toilets, Reservations accepted, Open May-Oct, Tent & RV camping: $23, Elev: 7618ft/2322m, Tel: 801-226-3564, Nearest town: Provo, Agency: USFS, GPS: 40.185091, -111.158096

33942 • Strawberry Bay - Loop G - USFS

Total sites: 59, RV sites: 59, Elec sites: 0, Central water, No showers, Flush toilets, Reservations accepted, Open May-Oct, Tent & RV camping: $23, Elev: 7634ft/2327m, Tel: 801-226-3564, Nearest town: Provo, Agency: USFS, GPS: 40.181986, -111.156582

33943 • Strawberry Bay - Loops A-E - USFS

Total sites: 175, RV sites: 175, Elec sites: 26, Water at site, No showers, Flush toilets, Reservations accepted, Open May-Oct, Tents: $23/RV's: $23-36, $10 Elec fee, 1 group site $200, Elev: 7628ft/2325m, Tel: 801-226-3564, Nearest town: Provo, Agency: USFS, GPS: 40.175939, -111.171908

33944 • Strawberry Bay - Overflow - USFS

Total sites: 72, RV sites: 72, Elec sites: 0, Central water, No showers, Flush toilets, Reservations not accepted, Open May-Oct, Tent & RV camping: $23, Elev: 7697ft/2346m, Tel: 801-226-3564, Nearest town: Provo, Agency: USFS, GPS: 40.179788, -111.178281

33945 • Strawberry Ridge Rd - USFS

Dispersed sites, No water, No toilets, Tent & RV camping: Free, Elev: 8200ft/2499m, Nearest town: Duck Creek, Agency: USFS, GPS: 37.492996, -112.625329

33946 • Sulphur - USFS

Total sites: 21, RV sites: 21, Elec sites: 0, Central water, No RV dump, No showers, Vault toilets, Reservations accepted, Open May-Oct, Tent & RV camping: $21, Group site: $60, Stay limit: 14 days, Elev: 9104ft/2775m, Tel: 307-789-3194, Nearest town: Evanston, WY, Agency: USFS, GPS: 40.788873, -110.884809

33947 • Sundance - BLM

Dispersed sites, No water, No toilets, Tents only: Free, Elev: 5623ft/1714m, Nearest town: Hite, Agency: BLM, GPS: 37.847602, -110.190984

33948 • Sunglow - USFS

Total sites: 6, RV sites: 6, Elec sites: 0, Central water, No RV dump, No showers, Flush toilets, Generator hours: 0600-2200, Reservations accepted, Open all year, Tent & RV camping: $12, Group site $30, No water in winter, Elev: 7287ft/2221m, Tel: 435-836-2811, Nearest town: Bicknell, Agency: USFS, GPS: 38.342035, -111.519529

33949 • Sunrise - USFS

Total sites: 26, RV sites: 26, Elec sites: 0, Central water, No RV dump, No showers, Vault toilets, Max length: 22ft, Reservations accepted, Open Jun-Oct, Tent & RV camping: $20, Stay limit: 7 days, Elev: 7615ft/2321m, Tel: 435-755-3620, Nearest town: Garden City, Agency: USFS, GPS: 41.919605, -111.461689

33950 • Superbowl - BLM

Total sites: 16, RV sites: 16, Elec sites: 0, No water, Vault toilets, Reservations not accepted, Open all year, Tent & RV camping: $15, Elev: 4957ft/1511m, Tel: 435-587-1500, Nearest town: Monticello, Agency: BLM, GPS: 38.148005, -109.621295

33951 • Swasey's Beach - BLM

Total sites: 12, RV sites: 7, Elec sites: 0, No water, Vault toilets, Reservations not accepted, Tent & RV camping: $15, Group site: $75-$100, Elev: 4137ft/1261m, Nearest town: Green River, Agency: BLM, GPS: 39.112121, -110.108914

33952 • Swift Creek - USFS

Total sites: 13, RV sites: 13, Elec sites: 0, Central water, No RV dump, No showers, Vault toilets, Reservations not accepted, Tent & RV camping: $8, Elev: 8153ft/2485m, Tel: 435-722-5018, Nearest town: Altamont, Agency: USFS, GPS: 40.601074, -110.3479

33953 • Tanners Flat - USFS

Total sites: 34, RV sites: 34, Elec sites: 0, Central water, No RV dump, No showers, Flush toilets, Max length: 35ft, Reservations accepted, Open Jun-Oct, Tent & RV camping: $26, 4 group sites: $105-$175, Stay limit: 7 days, Elev: 7293ft/2223m, Tel: 435-649-7402, Nearest town: Sandy, Agency: USFS, GPS: 40.572394, -111.699051

33954 • Tasha Equestrian - USFS

Total sites: 10, RV sites: 10, Elec sites: 0, Central water, No RV dump, No showers, Flush toilets, Reservations accepted, Open May-Sep, Tent & RV camping: $10, Group site: $35, Must have horse, Elev: 9111ft/2777m, Tel: 435-638-1069, Nearest town: Loa, Agency: USFS, GPS: 38.621591, -111.659449

33955 • Taylor Flat Dispersed - BLM

Dispersed sites, No water, No toilets, Tent & RV camping: Free, Elev: 6709ft/2045m, Nearest town: Green River, Agency: BLM, GPS: 38.753533, -110.763605

33956 • Taylors Fork ATV - USFS

Total sites: 11, RV sites: 11, Elec sites: 0, Central water, No RV dump, No showers, Vault toilets, Reservations not accepted, Open May-Oct, Tent & RV camping: $14, Stay limit: 7 days, Elev: 7418ft/2261m, Tel: 435-783-4338, Nearest town: Kamas, Agency: USFS, GPS: 40.620014, -111.137581

33957 • Te-ah - USFS

Total sites: 42, RV sites: 42, Elec sites: 0, Central water, RV dump, No showers, Flush toilets, Max length: 32ft, Reservations accepted, Open May-Sep, Tent & RV camping: $17, 1 group site $40, Elev: 9203ft/2805m, Tel: 435-865-3200, Nearest town: Cedar City, Agency: USFS, GPS: 37.533676, -112.818909

33958 • Temple Mt Dispersed - BLM

Dispersed sites, No water, Vault toilets, Tent & RV camping: Free, Elev: 5453ft/1662m, Nearest town: Green River, Agency: BLM, GPS: 38.667704, -110.684824

33959 • The Arch site 1 - BLM

Dispersed sites, No water, No toilets, Reservations not accepted, Tent & RV camping: Free, Elev: 5657ft/1724m, Nearest town: Kanab, Agency: BLM, GPS: 37.142956, -112.584759

33960 • The Arch site 2 - BLM

Dispersed sites, No water, No toilets, Reservations not accepted, Tent & RV camping: Free, Elev: 5584ft/1702m, Nearest town: Kanab, Agency: BLM, GPS: 37.146552, -112.582172

33961 • The Arch site 3 - BLM

Dispersed sites, No water, No toilets, Reservations not accepted, Tent & RV camping: Free, Elev: 5611ft/1710m, Nearest town: Kanab, Agency: BLM, GPS: 37.147408, -112.585359

33962 • The Chute Group - USFS

Dispersed sites, No water, Vault toilets, Reservations accepted, Open May-Oct, Group site: $50, Elev: 8186ft/2495m, Tel: 435-637-2817, Nearest town: Huntington, Agency: USFS, GPS: 39.570068, -111.182633

33963 • The Mix Pad - BLM

Dispersed sites, No water, No toilets, Tent & RV camping: Free, Dispersed camping along road, Subject to flooding, Elev: 4665ft/1422m, Nearest town: Hanksville, Agency: BLM, GPS: 38.339493, -111.030876

33964 • The Wedge Overlook - BLM

Total sites: 6, RV sites: 6, Elec sites: 0, No water, Vault toilets, Open all year, Tent & RV camping: Free, Elev: 6291ft/1917m, Nearest town: Green River, Agency: BLM, GPS: 39.093267, -110.758928

33965 • The Wickiup Dispersed - BLM

Dispersed sites, No water, No toilets, Tent & RV camping: Free, Elev: 6700ft/2042m, Nearest town: Green River, Agency: BLM, GPS: 38.893472, -110.652176

33966 • Theater in the Pines Group - USFS

Total sites: 1, RV sites: 1, Elec sites: 0, Central water, No RV dump, No showers, Vault toilets, Reservations accepted, Open May-Sep, Group site: $295, Stay limit: 7 days, Elev: 6965ft/2123m, Tel: 801-885-7391, Nearest town: Orem, Agency: USFS, GPS: 40.405089, -111.607308

33967 • Timid Springs Dispersed - USFS

Dispersed sites, No water, Vault toilets, Reservations not accepted, Tent & RV camping: Free, Elev: 10302ft/3140m, Nearest town: Junction, Agency: USFS, GPS: 38.301737, -112.358314

33968 • Timpooneke - USFS

Total sites: 27, RV sites: 27, Elec sites: 0, Central water, No RV dump, No showers, Vault toilets, Max length: 16ft, Reservations accepted, Open Jun-Oct, Tent & RV camping: $24, 1 group site $115, 9 equestrian sites, Stay limit: 7 days, Elev: 7576ft/2309m, Tel: 801-885-7391, Nearest town: American Forks, Agency: USFS, GPS: 40.431947, -111.645916

33969 • Tinney Flat - USFS

Total sites: 13, RV sites: 13, Elec sites: 0, Central water, No RV dump, No showers, Vault toilets, Reservations accepted, Open May-Sep, Tent & RV camping: $23, 3 group sites: $115, Stay limit: 16 days, Elev: 7192ft/2192m, Tel: 801-798-3571, Nearest town: Santaquin, Agency: USFS, GPS: 39.900527, -111.727811

33970 • Tony Grove - USFS

Total sites: 33, RV sites: 33, Elec sites: 0, No water, No RV dump, No showers, Vault toilets, Max length: 35ft, Reservations accepted, Open Jul-Sep, Tent & RV camping: $22, Stay limit: 7 days, Elev: 8081ft/2463m, Tel: 435-755-3620, Nearest town: Logan, Agency: USFS, GPS: 41.891186, -111.640694

33971 • Toquerville Falls - BLM

Dispersed sites, No water, No toilets, Tent & RV camping: Free, Elev: 3764ft/1147m, Nearest town: Toquerville, Agency: BLM, GPS: 37.299361, -113.246888

33972 • Trial Lake - USFS

Total sites: 60, RV sites: 60, Elec sites: 0, Central water, No RV dump, No showers, Vault toilets, Reservations accepted, Open Jul-Sep, Tent & RV camping: $23, Stay limit: 7 days, Elev: 9879ft/3011m, Tel: 435-783-4338, Nearest town: Kamas, Agency: USFS, GPS: 40.681624, -110.950247

33973 • Tushar - USFS

Total sites: 24, RV sites: 24, Elec sites: 0, Central water, No RV dump, No showers, Flush toilets, Reservations accepted, Open Jun-Sep, Tent & RV camping: $12, Group fee: $50-$160, Elev: 8691ft/2649m, Tel: 435-438-2436, Nearest town: Beaver, Agency: USFS, GPS: 38.238026, -112.469397

33974 • Twelve Mile Flat - USFS

Total sites: 14, RV sites: 14, Elec sites: 0, No water, No RV dump, No showers, Vault toilets, Reservations accepted, Open Jun-Sep, Tent & RV camping: $7-12, Group site $40, Elev: 10118ft/3084m, Tel: 435-283-4151, Nearest town: Mayfield, Agency: USFS, GPS: 39.123032, -111.487814

33975 • Twin Hollows Canyon Dispersed - BLM

Dispersed sites, No water, No toilets, Tent & RV camping: Free, Elev: 5139ft/1566m, Nearest town: Mt Carmel Jct, Agency: BLM, GPS: 37.207192, -112.689751

33976 • Twin Knolls Dispersed - BLM

Dispersed sites, No water, No toilets, Tent & RV camping: Free, Elev: 6696ft/2041m, Nearest town: Green River, Agency: BLM, GPS: 38.788848, -110.709829

33977 • Twin Lake - USFS

Total sites: 21, RV sites: 21, Elec sites: 0, No water, Vault toilets, Reservations accepted, Open May-Oct, Tent & RV camping: $10, Group site $30, Elev: 7211ft/2198m, Tel: 435-283-4151, Nearest town: Mayfield, Agency: USFS, GPS: 39.118654, -111.604125

33978 • Twin Ponds - USFS
Total sites: 13, RV sites: 13, Elec sites: 0, No water, No RV dump, No showers, Vault toilets, Reservations not accepted, Tent & RV camping: Free, Elev: 9098ft/2773m, Tel: 435-896-9233, Nearest town: Salina, Agency: USFS, GPS: 38.786458, -111.640573

33979 • Uinta Canyon - USFS
Total sites: 24, RV sites: 24, Elec sites: 0, No water, Vault toilets, Max length: 22ft, Reservations not accepted, Tent & RV camping: $5, Elev: 7634ft/2327m, Nearest town: Roosevelt, Agency: USFS, GPS: 40.623291, -110.143799

33980 • Uinta Flat Dispersed - USFS
Dispersed sites, No water, No toilets, Reservations not accepted, Tent & RV camping: Free, Elev: 8123ft/2476m, Tel: 435-865-3200, Nearest town: Duck Creek, Agency: USFS, GPS: 37.513264, -112.614155

33981 • Uinta River Group - USFS
Total sites: 1, RV sites: 1, Elec: Unk, No water, Vault toilets, Reservations accepted, Open May-Sep, Group site: $50, Elev: 7680ft/2341m, Tel: 435-722-5018, Nearest town: Roosevelt, Agency: USFS, GPS: 40.628108, -110.149948

33982 • Unicorn Ridge - USFS
Total sites: 5, RV sites: 5, Elec sites: 0, No water, Vault toilets, Reservations not accepted, Open May-Oct, Tent & RV camping: Free, Elev: 7591ft/2314m, Nearest town: Thistle, Agency: USFS, GPS: 40.029454, -111.281752

33983 • Upper Big Bend - BLM
Total sites: 8, RV sites: 8, Elec sites: 0, No water, Vault toilets, Max length: 18ft, Reservations not accepted, Open all year, Tent & RV camping: $20, Rough entrance road, Stay limit: 14 days, Elev: 4042ft/1232m, Tel: 435-259-2100, Nearest town: Moab, Agency: BLM, GPS: 38.649104, -109.488694

33984 • Upper Box Creek Reservoir - USFS
Dispersed sites, No water, Vault toilets, Reservations not accepted, Tent & RV camping: Free, Elev: 8889ft/2709m, Tel: 435-896-9233, Nearest town: Greenwich, Agency: USFS, GPS: 38.478137, -112.002965

33985 • Upper Joes Valley - USFS
Dispersed sites, No water, No toilets, Reservations not accepted, Open Jun-Dec, Tent & RV camping: Free, Elev: 7374ft/2248m, Tel: 435-637-2817, Nearest town: Huntington, Agency: USFS, GPS: 39.347172, -111.269908

33986 • Upper Meadows - USFS
Total sites: 9, RV sites: 9, Elec sites: 0, Central water, No RV dump, No showers, Vault toilets, Reservations not accepted, Open May-Sep, Tent & RV camping: $20, Stay limit: 7 days, Elev: 5361ft/1634m, Tel: 801-625-5112, Nearest town: Ogden, Agency: USFS, GPS: 41.291, -111.636

33987 • Upper Narrows - USFS
Total sites: 6, RV sites: 6, Elec sites: 0, No water, Vault toilets, Reservations not accepted, Open Jun-Oct, Tent & RV camping: $14, Group site $45-$80, Stay limit: 7 days, Elev: 6965ft/2123m, Tel: 801-733-2660, Nearest town: Salt Lake City, Agency: USFS, GPS: 40.491541, -112.594503

33988 • Upper Onion Creek - BLM
Total sites: 14, RV sites: 14, Elec sites: 0, No water, Vault toilets, Reservations not accepted, Open all year, Tent & RV camping: $20, 2 group sites, Stay limit: 14 days, Elev: 4222ft/1287m, Tel: 435-259-2100, Nearest town: Moab, Agency: BLM, GPS: 38.721737, -109.343328

33989 • Upper Provo River - USFS
Dispersed sites, No water, Vault toilets, Reservations not accepted, Tent & RV camping: Free, Elev: 9222ft/2811m, Nearest town: Defas Park, Agency: USFS, GPS: 40.648859, -110.945511

33990 • Upper Six Mile Ponds - USFS
Total sites: 5, RV sites: 5, Elec sites: 0, No water, Vault toilets, Reservations not accepted, Open Jun-Oct, Tent & RV camping: Free, Rough road, 4x4 recommended, Elev: 8986ft/2739m, Nearest town: Sterling, Agency: USFS, GPS: 39.188436, -111.540601

33991 • Upper Stillwater - USFS
Total sites: 11, RV sites: 11, Elec sites: 0, Central water, No RV dump, No showers, Flush toilets, Reservations accepted, Open May-Sep, Tent & RV camping: $10, Group site: $30, Elev: 8061ft/2457m, Tel: 435-789-1181, Nearest town: Mountain Home, Agency: USFS, GPS: 40.555894, -110.700582

33992 • UT 153 Dispersed - USFS
Dispersed sites, No water, No toilets, Reservations not accepted, Open all year, Tent & RV camping: Free, Elev: 6299ft/1920m, Tel: 435-438-2429, Nearest town: Beaver, Agency: USFS, GPS: 38.277997, -112.560225

33993 • UT 153 Dispersed - USFS
Dispersed sites, No water, No toilets, Reservations not accepted, Open all year, Tent & RV camping: Free, Elev: 6312ft/1924m, Tel: 435-438-2429, Nearest town: Beaver, Agency: USFS, GPS: 38.273974, -112.553425

33994 • UT 153 Dispersed - USFS
Dispersed sites, No water, No toilets, Reservations not accepted, Open all year, Tent & RV camping: Free, Elev: 6348ft/1935m, Tel: 435-438-2429, Nearest town: Beaver, Agency: USFS, GPS: 38.269555, -112.550338

33995 • UT 153 Dispersed - USFS
Dispersed sites, No water, No toilets, Reservations not accepted, Open all year, Tent & RV camping: Free, Elev: 6358ft/1938m, Tel: 435-438-2429, Nearest town: Beaver, Agency: USFS, GPS: 38.267693, -112.549429

33996 • UT 153 Dispersed - USFS
Dispersed sites, No water, No toilets, Reservations not accepted, Open all year, Tent & RV camping: Free, Elev: 6759ft/2060m, Tel: 435-438-2429, Nearest town: Beaver, Agency: USFS, GPS: 38.259393, -112.521222

33997 • UT 153 Dispersed - USFS

Dispersed sites, No water, No toilets, Reservations not accepted, Open all year, Tent & RV camping: Free, Elev: 6870ft/2094m, Tel: 435-438-2429, Nearest town: Beaver, Agency: USFS, GPS: 38.261045, -112.514444

33998 • UT 44 Dispersed - USFS

Dispersed sites, No water, No toilets, Reservations not accepted, Open all year, Tent & RV camping: Free, Elev: 7533ft/2296m, Tel: 435-789-1181, Nearest town: Manila, Agency: USFS, GPS: 40.865521, -109.516829

33999 • UT 44 Dispersed - USFS

Dispersed sites, No water, No toilets, Reservations not accepted, Open all year, Tent & RV camping: Free, Elev: 7606ft/2318m, Tel: 435-789-1181, Nearest town: Manila, Agency: USFS, GPS: 40.859962, -109.539708

34000 • UT 44 Dispersed - USFS

Dispersed sites, No water, No toilets, Reservations not accepted, Open all year, Tent & RV camping: Free, Both sides of road, Elev: 7823ft/2384m, Tel: 435-789-1181, Nearest town: Manila, Agency: USFS, GPS: 40.851608, -109.625741

34001 • UT 44 Dispersed - USFS

Dispersed sites, No water, No toilets, Reservations not accepted, Open all year, Tent & RV camping: Free, Elev: 7945ft/2422m, Tel: 435-789-1181, Nearest town: Manila, Agency: USFS, GPS: 40.849089, -109.637235

34002 • UT 54 Dispersed 1 - USFS

Dispersed sites, No water, No toilets, Reservations not accepted, Open all year, Tent & RV camping: Free, Elev: 6887ft/2099m, Tel: 435-755-3620, Nearest town: Hyrum, Agency: USFS, GPS: 41.678381, -111.521877

34003 • UT 54 Dispersed 2 - USFS

Dispersed sites, No water, No toilets, Reservations not accepted, Open all year, Tent & RV camping: Free, Elev: 6941ft/2116m, Tel: 435-755-3620, Nearest town: Hyrum, Agency: USFS, GPS: 41.675096, -111.523501

34004 • UT 54 Dispersed 3 - USFS

Dispersed sites, No water, No toilets, Reservations not accepted, Open all year, Tent & RV camping: Free, Elev: 6857ft/2090m, Tel: 435-755-3620, Nearest town: Hyrum, Agency: USFS, GPS: 41.673439, -111.526824

34005 • UT 54 Dispersed 4 - USFS

Dispersed sites, No water, No toilets, Reservations not accepted, Open all year, Tent & RV camping: Free, Elev: 6715ft/2047m, Tel: 435-755-3620, Nearest town: Hyrum, Agency: USFS, GPS: 41.668148, -111.531312

34006 • UT 54 Dispersed 5 - USFS

Dispersed sites, No water, No toilets, Reservations not accepted, Open all year, Tent & RV camping: Free, Room for many rigs, Elev: 6521ft/1988m, Tel: 435-755-3620, Nearest town: Hyrum, Agency: USFS, GPS: 41.659791, -111.534564

34007 • Utah Lake SP

Total sites: 55, RV sites: 55, Elec sites: 55, Water at site, RV dump, Showers, Flush toilets, Reservations accepted, Open all year, Tent & RV camping: $30, Elev: 4498ft/1371m, Tel: 801-375-0731, Nearest town: Provo, Agency: ST, GPS: 40.239831, -111.735349

34008 • Valley of the Gods - BLM

Dispersed sites, No water, No toilets, Reservations not accepted, Tent & RV camping: Free, No campfires, Elev: 4997ft/1523m, Tel: 435-587-1500, Nearest town: Bluff, Agency: BLM, GPS: 37.316424, -109.850376

34009 • Vernon Reservoir - USFS

Total sites: 10, RV sites: 10, Elec sites: 0, No water, Vault toilets, Reservations not accepted, Open Apr-Dec, Tent & RV camping: Free, Stay limit: 16 days, Elev: 6191ft/1887m, Tel: 801-798-3571, Nearest town: Vernon, Agency: USFS, GPS: 39.991743, -112.385556

34010 • Virgin Dam Dispersed - BLM

Total sites: 1, RV sites: 0, Elec: Unk, No water, No toilets, Reservations not accepted, Tents only: Free, Beware of private property boundaries, Elev: 3613ft/1101m, Nearest town: La Verkin, Agency: BLM, GPS: 37.206212, -113.237516

34011 • Virgin Dam Dispersed - BLM

Total sites: 1, RV sites: 1, Elec: Unk, No water, No toilets, Reservations not accepted, Tent & RV camping: Free, Beware of private property boundaries, Elev: 3584ft/1092m, Nearest town: La Verkin, Agency: BLM, GPS: 37.204937, -113.231983

34012 • Virgin Dam Dispersed - BLM

Total sites: 1, RV sites: 1, Elec: Unk, No water, No toilets, Reservations not accepted, Tent & RV camping: Free, Beware of private property boundaries, Camp only in designated spots, Elev: 3587ft/1093m, Nearest town: La Verkin, Agency: BLM, GPS: 37.202553, -113.231866

34013 • Virgin Dam Dispersed - BLM

Total sites: 5, RV sites: 4, Elec: Unk, No water, No toilets, Reservations not accepted, Tent & RV camping: Free, Beware of private property boundaries, Elev: 3620ft/1103m, Nearest town: La Verkin, Agency: BLM, GPS: 37.206323, -113.240447

34014 • Wandin - USFS

Total sites: 4, RV sites: 4, Elec sites: 0, No water, Vault toilets, Max length: 15ft, Reservations not accepted, Tent & RV camping: $5, Elev: 7795ft/2376m, Nearest town: Roosevelt, Agency: USFS, GPS: 40.630702, -110.153772

34015 • Wapiti FA - DWR

Dispersed sites, No water, Vault toilets, Reservations not accepted, Tent & RV camping: Free, Elev: 5474ft/1668m, Tel: 801-538-4700, Nearest town: Hyrum, Agency: ST, GPS: 41.605033, -111.589521

34016 • Warner Lake - USFS

Total sites: 20, RV sites: 20, Elec sites: 0, No water, No RV dump, No showers, Vault toilets, Reservations accepted, Open Jun-Sep, Tent & RV camping: $10, Group site $50, Elev: 9436ft/2876m,

Tel: 435-636-3360, Nearest town: Moab, Agency: USFS, GPS: 38.519524, -109.277145

34017 • Wasatch Mountain SP - Cottonwood

Total sites: 46, RV sites: 46, Elec sites: 46, Water at site, RV dump, Showers, Flush toilets, Max length: 45ft, Reservations accepted, Open all year, Tent & RV camping: $25-30, 25 FHU, Elev: 5879ft/1792m, Tel: 435-654-1791, Nearest town: Midway, Agency: ST, GPS: 40.542288, -111.487133

34018 • Wasatch Mountain SP - Little Deer Creek

Total sites: 17, RV sites: 17, Elec sites: 0, Central water, No RV dump, No showers, No toilets, Reservations not accepted, Open all year, Tent & RV camping: $14, 1 group site $50, Elev: 7201ft/2195m, Tel: 435-654-1791, Nearest town: Midway, Agency: ST, GPS: 40.503066, -111.536425

34019 • Wasatch Mountain SP - Mahogany

Total sites: 30, RV sites: 30, Elec sites: 30, Water at site, RV dump, Showers, Flush toilets, Max length: 50ft, Reservations accepted, Open all year, Tent & RV camping: $30, 30 FHU, Elev: 6007ft/1831m, Tel: 435-654-1791, Nearest town: Midway, Agency: ST, GPS: 40.546314, -111.489362

34020 • Wasatch Mountain SP - Oak Hollow

Total sites: 37, RV sites: 37, Elec sites: 37, Water at site, RV dump, Showers, Flush toilets, Max length: 35ft, Reservations accepted, Open all year, Tent & RV camping: $25, Elev: 6060ft/1847m, Tel: 435-654-1791, Nearest town: Midway, Agency: ST, GPS: 40.548605, -111.489429

34021 • Washington Lake - USFS

Total sites: 45, RV sites: 45, Elec sites: 0, No water, No RV dump, No showers, Vault toilets, Reservations accepted, Open Jul-Sep, Tent & RV camping: $23, 5 group sites $130-$190, Stay limit: 7 days, Elev: 10007ft/3050m, Tel: 435-654-0470, Nearest town: Kamas, Agency: USFS, GPS: 40.679014, -110.961644

34022 • Washington Lake Group - USFS

Total sites: 5, Elec: Unk, Reservations accepted, Group sites: $130-$190, Elev: 9963ft/3037m, Tel: 435-783-4338, Nearest town: Oakley, Agency: USFS, GPS: 40.672989, -110.961362

34023 • Weber Memorial Park

Total sites: 58, RV sites: 58, Elec sites: 0, Central water, No showers, Flush toilets, Reservations not accepted, Open May-Oct, Tent & RV camping: $20, 3 group sites: $110-$140, Elev: 5500ft/1676m, Tel: 801-399-8230, Nearest town: Huntsville, Agency: CP, GPS: 41.297165, -111.596189

34024 • West Marsh Lake - USFS

Total sites: 17, RV sites: 17, Elec sites: 0, Central water, Vault toilets, Reservations accepted, Open Jun-Sep, Tent & RV camping: $21, Group site: $60, Dump station 1.5 mi at Stateline, Stay limit: 14 days, Elev: 9354ft/2851m, Tel: 307-782-6555, Nearest town: Mountain View, Agency: USFS, GPS: 40.955502, -110.396994

34025 • White Bridge - USFS

Total sites: 29, RV sites: 29, Elec sites: 0, Central water, RV dump, No showers, Flush toilets, Max length: 32ft, Reservations accepted, Open May-Sep, Tent & RV camping: $17, Elev: 7881ft/2402m, Tel: 435-865-3200, Nearest town: Panguitch, Agency: USFS, GPS: 37.745827, -112.587909

34026 • White Rock Dispersed - BLM

Dispersed sites, No water, No toilets, Reservations not accepted, Tent & RV camping: Free, Elev: 5346ft/1629m, Nearest town: Tooele, Agency: BLM, GPS: 40.322602, -112.905177

34027 • White Wash Sand Dunes - BLM

Dispersed sites, No water, No toilets, Tent & RV camping: Free, Portable toilets required if not self-contained, Elev: 4147ft/1264m, Tel: 435-259-2100, Nearest town: Moab, Agency: BLM, GPS: 38.800522, -110.033257

34028 • Whiterocks - USFS

Total sites: 21, RV sites: 21, Elec sites: 0, Central water, No RV dump, No showers, Vault toilets, Max length: 25ft, Reservations not accepted, Open May-Sep, Tent & RV camping: $8, Elev: 7510ft/2289m, Tel: 435-789-1181, Nearest town: Whiterocks, Agency: USFS, GPS: 40.619388, -109.941458

34029 • Whiting - USFS

Total sites: 26, RV sites: 26, Elec sites: 0, Central water, No RV dump, No showers, Flush toilets, Reservations accepted, Open May-Sep, Tent & RV camping: $23, 2 group sites: $220-$440, 3 sites equipped for horses, RV's may NOT fill water tanks, Stay limit: 16 days, Elev: 5532ft/1686m, Tel: 801-798-3571, Nearest town: Mapleton, Agency: USFS, GPS: 40.131495, -111.527386

34030 • Wild Horse Dispersed - BLM

Dispersed sites, No water, No toilets, Tent & RV camping: Free, Nothing larger than van/TC, Elev: 5101ft/1555m, Nearest town: Green River, Agency: BLM, GPS: 38.575297, -110.797697

34031 • Willard Basin Dispersed - USFS

Total sites: 5, RV sites: 5, Elec sites: 0, Elec sites: 0, No water, No RV dump, No showers, No toilets, Reservations not accepted, Open Jul-Nov, Tent & RV camping: Free, Road not maintained for passenger cars, Elev: 8681ft/2646m, Tel: 801-625-5112, Nearest town: Woodruff, Agency: USFS, GPS: 41.391842, -111.977999

34032 • Willard Bay SP - Cottonwood

Total sites: 39, RV sites: 39, Elec sites: 39, Water at site, No RV dump, Showers, Flush toilets, Max length: 48ft, Reservations accepted, Open all year, Tent & RV camping: $30, 39 FHU, Elev: 4245ft/1294m, Tel: 435-734-9494, Nearest town: Willard, Agency: ST, GPS: 41.416724, -112.052835

34033 • Willard Bay SP - South Marina

Total sites: 29, RV sites: 23, Elec sites: 23, Central water, Reservations accepted, Open all year, Tent & RV camping: $20-25, 23 FHU, Elev: 4216ft/1285m, Tel: 435-734-9494, Nearest town: Willard, Agency: ST, GPS: 41.352753, -112.077749

34034 • Willard Bay SP - Willow Creek
Total sites: 39, RV sites: 39, Elec sites: 0, Central water, RV dump, Showers, Flush toilets, Max length: 45ft, Reservations accepted, Open all year, Tent & RV camping: $20, Elev: 4239ft/1292m, Tel: 435-734-9494, Nearest town: Willard, Agency: ST, GPS: 41.418951, -112.056185

34035 • Williams Bottom - BLM
Total sites: 17, RV sites: 17, Elec sites: 0, No water, Vault toilets, Max length: 24ft, Reservations not accepted, Open all year, Tent & RV camping: $20, Stay limit: 14 days, Elev: 3995ft/1218m, Tel: 435-259-2100, Nearest town: Moab, Agency: BLM, GPS: 38.538594, -109.603818

34036 • Willow Lake - USFS
Total sites: 10, RV sites: 10, Elec sites: 0, No water, Vault toilets, Reservations accepted, Open Jun-Sep, Tent & RV camping: $7, Elev: 9649ft/2941m, Tel: 435-384-2372, Nearest town: Ferron, Agency: USFS, GPS: 39.134811, -111.381332

34037 • Willow Park
Total sites: 40, RV sites: 40, Elec sites: 0, Central water, Tent & RV camping: $20, Several large group areas: $175, Elev: 4505ft/1373m, Tel: 801-851-8640, Nearest town: Lehi, Agency: CP, GPS: 40.391426, -111.901311

34038 • Willow Springs Trail Dispersed 1 - BLM
Dispersed sites, No water, No toilets, Open all year, Tent & RV camping: Free, Elev: 4443ft/1354m, Nearest town: Moab, Agency: BLM, GPS: 38.697618, -109.692145

34039 • Willow Springs Trail Dispersed 2 - BLM
Dispersed sites, No water, No toilets, Open all year, Tent & RV camping: Free, Elev: 4360ft/1329m, Nearest town: Moab, Agency: BLM, GPS: 38.696216, -109.673125

34040 • Willows - USFS
Total sites: 17, RV sites: 17, Elec sites: 0, Central water, No RV dump, No showers, Vault toilets, Max length: 40ft, Generator hours: 0800-2200, Reservations not accepted, Open May-Sep, Tent & RV camping: $20, Stay limit: 7 days, Elev: 5371ft/1637m, Tel: 801-625-5112, Nearest town: Ogden, Agency: USFS, GPS: 41.291695, -111.633153

34041 • Willows - USFS
Total sites: 8, RV sites: 8, Elec sites: 0, No water, Vault toilets, Reservations not accepted, Open Apr-Sep, Tent & RV camping: $12, Elev: 6165ft/1879m, Tel: 435-784-3445, Nearest town: Manila, Agency: USFS, GPS: 40.925959, -109.714713

34042 • Windwhistle - BLM
Total sites: 15, RV sites: 15, Elec sites: 0, Central water, Vault toilets, Max length: 30ft, Reservations not accepted, Open all year, Tent & RV camping: $20, Reservable group site: $75, Elev: 6037ft/1840m, Tel: 435-259-2102, Nearest town: Moab, Agency: BLM, GPS: 38.176227, -109.462162

34043 • Windy Park Dispersed - USFS
Dispersed sites, No water, Vault toilets, Reservations not accepted, Tent & RV camping: Free, Elev: 9419ft/2871m, Tel: 435-789-1181, Nearest town: Vernal, Agency: USFS, GPS: 40.760758, -109.640047

34044 • Winter Ridge - BLM
Dispersed sites, No water, No toilets, Tent & RV camping: Free, Nothing larger than van/TC, Elev: 7544ft/2299m, Nearest town: Mack CO, Agency: BLM, GPS: 39.460987, -109.460495

34045 • Wire Pass TH - BLM
Dispersed sites, No water, Vault toilets, Tent & RV camping: Fee unk, Permit required - available only online, Elev: 4885ft/1489m, Tel: 435-644-1300, Nearest town: Glen Canyon, Agency: BLM, GPS: 37.019177, -112.025125

34046 • Wld Horse Road Dispersed - BLM
Dispersed sites, No water, No toilets, Tent & RV camping: Free, Numerous spots, Elev: 4879ft/1487m, Nearest town: Hanksville, Agency: BLM, GPS: 38.577351, -110.772861

34047 • Wolf Creek - USFS
Total sites: 3, RV sites: 3, Elec sites: 0, Central water, No RV dump, No showers, Vault toilets, Reservations not accepted, Open Jun-Sep, Tent & RV camping: $18, 2 reservable group sites $115-$200, Stay limit: 7 days, Elev: 9471ft/2887m, Tel: 435-783-4338, Nearest town: Heber City, Agency: USFS, GPS: 40.482476, -111.033555

34048 • Wolverine ATV - USFS
Total sites: 7, RV sites: 6, Elec sites: 0, No water, No RV dump, No showers, Vault toilets, Reservations not accepted, Tent & RV camping: $16, Elev: 9101ft/2774m, Tel: 801-466-6411, Nearest town: Peoa, Agency: USFS, GPS: 40.845957, -110.814671

34049 • Wolverine ATV Dispersed - USFS
Dispersed sites, No water, No toilets, Reservations not accepted, Tent & RV camping: Free, Elev: 8389ft/2557m, Tel: 307-789-3194, Nearest town: Evanston, Agency: USFS, GPS: 40.912953, -110.826877

34050 • Wood Camp - USFS
Total sites: 6, RV sites: 6, Elec sites: 0, No water, No RV dump, No showers, Vault toilets, Reservations not accepted, Open May-Oct, Tent & RV camping: $20, Stay limit: 7 days, Elev: 5377ft/1639m, Tel: 435-755-3620, Nearest town: Logan, Agency: USFS, GPS: 41.797363, -111.64502

34051 • Yankee Meadow - USFS
Total sites: 29, RV sites: 29, Elec sites: 0, Central water, No RV dump, No showers, Vault toilets, Reservations not accepted, Open May-Sep, Tent & RV camping: $15, Elev: 8520ft/2597m, Tel: 435-865-3200, Nearest town: Cedar City, Agency: USFS, GPS: 37.760232, -112.760014

34052 • Yellow Pine (Ashley) - USFS
Total sites: 11, RV sites: 11, Elec sites: 0, Central water, RV dump, No showers, Flush toilets, Max length: 36ft, Reservations accepted, Open May-Sep, Tent & RV camping: $10, 1 group site $30, Elev:

7555ft/2303m, Tel: 435-738-2482, Nearest town: Mountain Home, Agency: USFS, GPS: 40.536416, -110.639975

34053 • Yellow Pine (Wasatch)- USFS
Total sites: 33, RV sites: 33, Elec sites: 0, Central water, No RV dump, No showers, Vault toilets, Max length: 25ft, Reservations not accepted, Open May-Oct, Tent & RV camping: $18, Stay limit: 7 days, Elev: 7293ft/2223m, Tel: 435-783-4338, Nearest town: Kamas, Agency: USFS, GPS: 40.630859, -111.173828

34054 • Yellowjacket Canyon Dispersed - BLM
Dispersed sites, No water, No toilets, Tent & RV camping: Free, Elev: 5667ft/1727m, Nearest town: Kanab, Agency: BLM, GPS: 37.144836, -112.672894

34055 • Yellowjacket Spring Dispersed - BLM
Dispersed sites, No water, No toilets, Tent & RV camping: Free, Elev: 6145ft/1873m, Nearest town: Kanab, Agency: BLM, GPS: 37.089272, -112.696388

34056 • Yellowstone - USFS
Total sites: 4, RV sites: 4, Elec sites: 0, Central water, No RV dump, No showers, Vault toilets, Reservations not accepted, Open May-Sep, Tent & RV camping: $10, Reservable group site: $30, Elev: 7661ft/2335m, Tel: 435-722-5018, Nearest town: Mountain Home, Agency: USFS, GPS: 40.542425, -110.336645

34057 • Yuba SP - Eagle View
Total sites: 20, RV sites: 14, Elec sites: 0, No water, Vault toilets, Open all year, Tent & RV camping: $25, Elev: 5076ft/1547m, Tel: 435-758-2611, Nearest town: Levan, Agency: ST, GPS: 39.367474, -111.971072

34058 • Yuba SP - North and West Beaches (BLM)
Dispersed sites, No water, Vault toilets, Open all year, Tent & RV camping: $25, 4x4 recommended, Elev: 5033ft/1534m, Tel: 435-758-2611, Nearest town: Levan, Agency: ST, GPS: 39.402149, -112.029063

34059 • Yuba SP - Oasis
Total sites: 28, RV sites: 28, Elec sites: 13, Water at site, RV dump, Showers, Flush toilets, Max length: 45ft, Open all year, Tents: $30/RV's: $30-35, Elev: 5049ft/1539m, Tel: 435-758-2611, Nearest town: Levan, Agency: ST, GPS: 39.378739, -112.027104

34060 • Yuba SP - Painted Rocks
Total sites: 41, RV sites: 38, Elec sites: 38, Central water, RV dump, No showers, Vault toilets, Max length: 90ft, Open all year, Tents: $20/RV's: $30, Elev: 5095ft/1553m, Tel: 435-758-2611, Nearest town: Levan, Agency: ST, GPS: 39.352992, -111.942378

34061 • Zion NP - Bear Camp
Dispersed sites, Reservations not accepted, Tents only: Fee unk, Hike-in, Permit required - $15-$2, La Verkin Trail, Elev: 5755ft/1754m, Tel: 435-772-0170, Nearest town: Rockville, Agency: NP, GPS: 37.431474, -113.126581

34062 • Zion NP - Big Spring
Dispersed sites, Reservations accepted, Tents only: Fee unk, Hike-in, Permit required - $15-$25, The Narrows, Elev: 4731ft/1442m, Tel: 435-772-0170, Nearest town: Rockville, Agency: NP, GPS: 37.331159, -112.956794

34063 • Zion NP - Bird Camp
Dispersed sites, Reservations not accepted, Tents only: Fee unk, Hike-in, Permit required - $15-$25, La Verkin Trail, Elev: 5257ft/1602m, Tel: 435-772-0170, Nearest town: Rockville, Agency: NP, GPS: 37.415866, -113.150148

34064 • Zion NP - Camp 1
Dispersed sites, Reservations not accepted, Tents only: Fee unk, Hike-in, Permit required - $15-$25, West Rim Trail , Affected by 2007 fire, Elev: 6782ft/2067m, Tel: 435-772-0170, Nearest town: Rockville, Agency: NP, GPS: 37.288185, -112.969153

34065 • Zion NP - Camp 2
Dispersed sites, Reservations accepted, Tents only: Fee unk, Hike-in, Permit required - $15-$25, West Rim Trail , Affected by 2007 fire, Elev: 6713ft/2046m, Tel: 435-772-0170, Nearest town: Rockville, Agency: NP, GPS: 37.285482, -112.968867

34066 • Zion NP - Camp 3
Dispersed sites, Reservations not accepted, Tents only: Fee unk, Hike-in, Permit required - $15-$25, West Rim Trail , Affected by 2007 fire, Elev: 7018ft/2139m, Tel: 435-772-0170, Nearest town: Rockville, Agency: NP, GPS: 37.285429, -112.971137

34067 • Zion NP - Camp 4
Dispersed sites, Reservations accepted, Tents only: Fee unk, Hike-in, Permit required - $15-$25, West Rim Trail , Affected by 2007 fire, Elev: 7290ft/2222m, Tel: 435-772-0170, Nearest town: Rockville, Agency: NP, GPS: 37.284534, -112.982731

34068 • Zion NP - Camp 5
Dispersed sites, Reservations not accepted, Tents only: Fee unk, Hike-in, Permit required - $15-$25, West Rim Trail , Affected by 2007 fire, Elev: 7362ft/2244m, Tel: 435-772-0170, Nearest town: Rockville, Agency: NP, GPS: 37.292318, -112.987722

34069 • Zion NP - Camp 6
Dispersed sites, Reservations accepted, Tents only: Fee unk, Hike-in, Permit required - $15-$25, West Rim Trail , Affected by 2007 fire, Elev: 7305ft/2227m, Tel: 435-772-0170, Nearest town: Rockville, Agency: NP, GPS: 37.304376, -112.987751

34070 • Zion NP - Camp 7
Dispersed sites, Reservations not accepted, Tents only: Fee unk, Hike-in, Permit required - $15-$25, West Rim Trail , Seasonal water, Elev: 4869ft/1484m, Tel: 435-772-0170, Nearest town: Rockville, Agency: NP, GPS: 37.344765, -112.950781

34071 • Zion NP - Camp 7
Dispersed sites, Reservations not accepted, Tents only: Fee unk, Hike-in, Permit required - $15-$25, The Narrows, Elev: 6844ft/2086m, Tel: 435-772-0170, Nearest town: Rockville, Agency: NP, GPS: 37.320261, -112.990145

34072 • Zion NP - Camp 9

Dispersed sites, Reservations not accepted, Tents only: Fee unk, Hike-in, Permit required - $15-$25, The Narrows, Elev: 4772ft/1455m, Tel: 435-772-0170, Nearest town: Rockville, Agency: NP, GPS: 37.339418, -112.955709

34073 • Zion NP - Coal Pit Wash

Dispersed sites, Tents only: Fee unk, Hike-in, Permit required - $15-$25,, Elev: 4106ft/1252m, Tel: 435-772-0170, Nearest town: Rockville, Agency: NP, GPS: 37.215841, -113.077799

34074 • Zion NP - Coal Pits Ridge

Dispersed sites, Tents only: Fee unk, Hike-in, Permit required - $15-$25,, Elev: 4127ft/1258m, Tel: 435-772-0170, Nearest town: Rockville, Agency: NP, GPS: 37.212164, -113.078243

34075 • Zion NP - Cottonwood Camp

Dispersed sites, Reservations not accepted, Tents only: Fee unk, Hike-in, Permit required - $15-$25, La Verkin Trail, Elev: 5360ft/1634m, Tel: 435-772-0170, Nearest town: Rockville, Agency: NP, GPS: 37.421443, -113.139605

34076 • Zion NP - Cougar Camp

Dispersed sites, Reservations accepted, Tents only: Fee unk, Hike-in, Permit required - $15-$25, La Verkin Trail, Elev: 5298ft/1615m, Tel: 435-772-0170, Nearest town: Rockville, Agency: NP, GPS: 37.417141, -113.143179

34077 • Zion NP - Cross Creek West Camp

Dispersed sites, Reservations not accepted, Tents only: Fee unk, Hike-in, Permit required - $15-$25, La Verkin Trail, Elev: 5226ft/1593m, Tel: 435-772-0170, Nearest town: Rockville, Agency: NP, GPS: 37.415106, -113.151404

34078 • Zion NP - Deep Creek

Dispersed sites, Reservations accepted, Tents only: Fee unk, Hike-in, Permit required - $15-$25, The Narrows, Elev: 4972ft/1515m, Tel: 435-772-0170, Nearest town: Rockville, Agency: NP, GPS: 37.359395, -112.951557

34079 • Zion NP - Deer Camp

Dispersed sites, Reservations not accepted, Tents only: Fee unk, Hike-in, Permit required - $15-$25, La Verkin Trail, Elev: 5419ft/1652m, Tel: 435-772-0170, Nearest town: Rockville, Agency: NP, GPS: 37.422731, -113.195859

34080 • Zion NP - Dipper Camp

Dispersed sites, Reservations not accepted, Tents only: Fee unk, Hike-in, Permit required - $15-$25, La Verkin Trail, Elev: 5107ft/1557m, Tel: 435-772-0170, Nearest town: Rockville, Agency: NP, GPS: 37.410847, -113.167479

34081 • Zion NP - Dry Camp

Dispersed sites, Reservations not accepted, Tents only: Fee unk, Hike-in, Permit required - $15-$25, La Verkin Trail, Elev: 5456ft/1663m, Tel: 435-772-0170, Nearest town: Rockville, Agency: NP, GPS: 37.407192, -113.196793

34082 • Zion NP - Flat Rock

Dispersed sites, Reservations not accepted, Tents only: Fee unk, Hike-in, Permit required - $15-$25, The Narrows, Elev: 4908ft/1496m, Tel: 435-772-0170, Nearest town: Rockville, Agency: NP, GPS: 37.350216, -112.949708

34083 • Zion NP - Flat Rock Camp

Dispersed sites, Reservations accepted, Tents only: Fee unk, Hike-in, Permit required - $15-$25, La Verkin Trail, Elev: 5223ft/1592m, Tel: 435-772-0170, Nearest town: Rockville, Agency: NP, GPS: 37.415427, -113.152172

34084 • Zion NP - Goose Creek

Dispersed sites, Reservations accepted, Tents only: Fee unk, Hike-in, Permit required - $15-$25, The Narrows, Elev: 4763ft/1452m, Tel: 435-772-0170, Nearest town: Rockville, Agency: NP, GPS: 37.338335, -112.957145

34085 • Zion NP - Hop Valley

Dispersed sites, Reservations not accepted, Tents only: Fee unk, Hike-in, Permit required - $15-$25, Hop Valley Trail, Elev: 5730ft/1747m, Tel: 435-772-0170, Nearest town: Rockville, Agency: NP, GPS: 37.401512, -113.137898

34086 • Zion NP - Hop Valley Horse Camp

Dispersed sites, Reservations not accepted, Tents only: Fee unk, Hike-in, Permit required - $15-$25, Hop Valley Trail, Elev: 5720ft/1743m, Tel: 435-772-0170, Nearest town: Rockville, Agency: NP, GPS: 37.403614, -113.139292

34087 • Zion NP - Junction

Dispersed sites, Tents only: Fee unk, Hike-in, Permit required - $15-$25,, Elev: 3805ft/1160m, Tel: 435-772-0170, Nearest town: Rockville, Agency: NP, GPS: 37.194164, -113.076181

34088 • Zion NP - Juniper Camp

Dispersed sites, Reservations accepted, Tents only: Fee unk, Hike-in, Permit required - $15-$25, La Verkin Trail, Elev: 5082ft/1549m, Tel: 435-772-0170, Nearest town: Rockville, Agency: NP, GPS: 37.407301, -113.175558

34089 • Zion NP - Kolob Creek

Dispersed sites, Reservations not accepted, Tents only: Fee unk, Hike-in, Permit required - $15-$25, The Narrows, Elev: 4895ft/1492m, Tel: 435-772-0170, Nearest town: Rockville, Agency: NP, GPS: 37.349505, -112.950747

34090 • Zion NP - Lava Point

Total sites: 6, RV sites: 6, Elec sites: 0, No water, Vault toilets, Max length: 19ft, Reservations not accepted, Open Jun-Oct, Tent & RV camping: Free, Elev: 7917ft/2413m, Tel: 435-772-3256, Nearest town: Springdale, Agency: NP, GPS: 37.383707, -113.032797

34091 • Zion NP - Neagle Camp

Dispersed sites, Reservations accepted, Tents only: Fee unk, Hike-in, Permit required - $15-$25, La Verkin Trail, Elev: 5097ft/1554m, Tel: 435-772-0170, Nearest town: Rockville, Agency: NP, GPS: 37.410329, -113.170002

34092 • Zion NP - Oak Point Camp

Dispersed sites, Reservations accepted, Tents only: Fee unk, Hike-in, Permit required - $15-$25, La Verkin Trail, Elev: 5189ft/1582m, Tel: 435-772-0170, Nearest town: Rockville, Agency: NP, GPS: 37.414199, -113.155817

34093 • Zion NP - Potato Hollow

Dispersed sites, Reservations accepted, Tents only: Fee unk, Hike-in, Permit required - $15-$25, West Rim Trail , Seasonal water, Elev: 6777ft/2066m, Tel: 435-772-0170, Nearest town: Rockville, Agency: NP, GPS: 37.321642, -112.985398

34094 • Zion NP - Right Bench

Dispersed sites, Reservations accepted, Tents only: Fee unk, Hike-in, Permit required - $15-$25, The Narrows, Elev: 4923ft/1501m, Tel: 435-772-0170, Nearest town: Rockville, Agency: NP, GPS: 37.35327, -112.95133

34095 • Zion NP - Ringtail Camp

Dispersed sites, Reservations accepted, Tents only: Fee unk, Hike-in, Permit required - $15-$25, La Verkin Trail, Elev: 5344ft/1629m, Tel: 435-772-0170, Nearest town: Rockville, Agency: NP, GPS: 37.413319, -113.194773

34096 • Zion NP - River Bend

Dispersed sites, Reservations not accepted, Tents only: Fee unk, Hike-in, Permit required - $15-$25, The Narrows, Elev: 4941ft/1506m, Tel: 435-772-0170, Nearest town: Rockville, Agency: NP, GPS: 37.356292, -112.950974

34097 • Zion NP - Sawmill Springs

Dispersed sites, Reservations not accepted, Tents only: Fee unk, Hike-in, Permit required - $15-$25, West Rim Trail, Elev: 7218ft/2200m, Tel: 435-772-0170, Nearest town: Rockville, Agency: NP, GPS: 37.370098, -113.016924

34098 • Zion NP - Scoggins Wash

Dispersed sites, Tents only: Fee unk, Hike-in, Permit required - $15-$25,, Elev: 4205ft/1282m, Tel: 435-772-0170, Nearest town: Rockville, Agency: NP, GPS: 37.210687, -113.050846

34099 • Zion NP - Simon Gulch`

Dispersed sites, Reservations not accepted, Tents only: Fee unk, Hike-in, Permit required - $15-$25, The Narrows, Elev: 5290ft/1612m, Tel: 435-772-0170, Nearest town: Rockville, Agency: NP, GPS: 37.371467, -112.912438

34100 • Zion NP - South CG

Total sites: 127, RV sites: 127, Elec sites: 0, Central water, RV dump, No showers, Vault toilets, Generator hours: 0800-1000/1800-2000, Reservations accepted, Open Mar-Nov, Tent & RV camping: $20, Group site: $50, Max height 13ft, Elev: 3970ft/1210m, Tel: 435-772-3256, Nearest town: Springdale, Agency: NP, GPS: 37.203613, -112.981689

34101 • Zion NP - Spotted Owl

Dispersed sites, Reservations not accepted, Tents only: Fee unk, Hike-in, Permit required - $15-$25, The Narrows, Elev: 4761ft/1451m, Tel: 435-772-0170, Nearest town: Rockville, Agency: NP, GPS: 37.333899, -112.955681

34102 • Zion NP - Temple View

Dispersed sites, Tents only: Fee unk, Hike-in, Permit required - $15-$25,, Elev: 4420ft/1347m, Tel: 435-772-0170, Nearest town: Rockville, Agency: NP, GPS: 37.205979, -113.054834

34103 • Zion NP - The Grotto

Dispersed sites, Reservations not accepted, Tents only: Fee unk, Hike-in, Permit required - $15-$25, The Narrows, Elev: 4860ft/1481m, Tel: 435-772-0170, Nearest town: Rockville, Agency: NP, GPS: 37.342982, -112.954176

34104 • Zion NP - Watchman CG

Total sites: 164, RV sites: 95, Elec sites: 95, Central water, RV dump, No showers, Vault toilets, Generators prohibited, Reservations accepted, Open all year, Tents: $20/RV's: $30, 6 group sites, Elev: 3960ft/1207m, Tel: 435-772-3256, Nearest town: Springdale, Agency: NP, GPS: 37.195801, -112.987061

34105 • Zion NP - Yucca

Dispersed sites, Tents only: Fee unk, Hike-in, Permit required - $15-$25,, Elev: 4200ft/1280m, Tel: 435-772-0170, Nearest town: Rockville, Agency: NP, GPS: 37.203386, -113.067906

34106 • Zion View - BLM

Dispersed sites, No water, No toilets, Tent & RV camping: Free, Elev: 5594ft/1705m, Nearest town: Virgin, Agency: BLM, GPS: 37.266967, -113.176154

Made in United States
Troutdale, OR
01/30/2024

17291681R00120